DOWNFALL

DOWNFALL

The End of the
Imperial
Japanese Empire

RICHARD B. FRANK

RANDOM HOUSE

NEW YORK

Grateful acknowledgment is made to the following
for permission to use both published and unpublished material:
Clemson University: Quotes from the James F. Byrnes papers
housed in Special Collections, Clemson University Libraries.
Used by permission.
William Morrow & Company: Excerpts from *Prisoners of the Japanese,*
by Gavan Daws. Copyright © 1994 by Gavan Daws.
Reprinted by permission of William Morrow & Company.
Princeton University: Excerpts from the James V. Forrestal Diaries
covering the period of March through August 1945,
housed at the Seeley G. Mudd Manuscript Library, Princeton University Library.
Published with the permission of the Princeton University Library.
Yale University: Diary entries dated 1 May 1944 through 21 September 1944
by Henry Lewis Stimson, housed in the Henry Lewis Stimson Papers,
Manuscripts and Archives, Yale University Library.
Used by permission.

Library of Congress Cataloging-in-Publication Data
Frank, Richard B.
Downfall : the end of the Imperial Japanese Empire / Richard B. Frank.
p.   cm.
Includes bibliographical references and index.
ISBN 0-679-41424-X (hc)
1. World War, 1939–1945—Campaigns—Japan.   2. World War, 1939–1945—
Aerial operations, American.   3. Japan—History—Bombardment, 1945.
4. Japan—History—1926–1945.   5. B-29 bomber.   I. Title.
D767.2.F73 1999
940.54′25—dc21   99-11838

Random House website address: www.atrandom.com
Printed in the United States of America on acid-free paper
2 4 6 8 9 7 5 3
First Edition
Book design by Victoria Wong

*To the memory of
my brother
Lawrence Victor Frank
1957–1994*

*We didn't know beans about the military situation
in Japan.*

J. Robert Oppenheimer,
Scientific Director, Los Alamos Laboratory
Manhattan Project

*The Supreme War Council . . . was making every
possible preparation to meet [an American] landing.
They proceeded with that plan until the Atomic Bomb
was dropped, after which they believed the United States
would no longer attempt to land when it had such a
superior weapon—that the United States need not land
when it had such a weapon; so at that point they decided
that it would be best to sue for peace.*

Kantaro Suzuki,
Prime Minister of Japan
April–August 1945

Acknowledgments

My deep thanks must commence with my agent, Robert Gottlieb, and my editor, Robert Loomis, who wisely counseled me that this subject offered the most promise of any I was considering in 1991. How right they were.

The core of this work comes from the various archives that house collections of American military and naval records. Cheerful and skilled assistance was tendered by a huge number of staff members at these facilities, but I wish to particularly single out the following. At the National Archives, it was my privilege to again receive the attention and wise advice of one of America's great living treasures, John Taylor. Will Mahoney, Larry MacDonald, and Sandy Smith also provided invaluable assistance on record safaris. I send a salute to Dr. Richard J. Sommers at the United States Army Military History Institute at Carlisle, Dennis Bilger at the Harry S. Truman Library, Lynn Gama at the Air Force Center at Maxwell, and Brigadier General Edwin Simmons (USMC Ret.), who was the director at the Marine Corps History Center when I did my research there. At the MacArthur Archive, I was both precisely guided and provided an exceptional welcome by Colonel William Davis (USMC Ret.), the director, and James Zobel, Beth Carter, and Jeff Acosta of his staff. Very special thanks are also due to the Naval Historical Center, the place where I feel most at home. There, at one time or another over this long gestation period, I was aided by the former director, Dr. Dean Allard, as well as the current director, Dr. William Dudley, and his wonderful staff, including particularly Bernard Cavalcante, Kathy Lloyd, Mike Walker, and Edwin Finney. A special acknowledgment is due to Robert Cressman and Charles Haberlein, who are both members of the staff of the Naval Historical Center and old friends.

Barton Bernstein, Edward J. Drea, and Sadao Asada brought their deep knowledge of this area to bear in reviewing and critiquing earlier versions of this manuscript, to my enormous profit. A further word is also due Barton Bernstein, who provided assistance in research and served over a long period as a most stimulating sounding board. His command of sources and rigor is unexcelled in this area. In important respects, this narrative is built upon the pioneering work of Edward J. Drea and John Ray Skates, who brought to the fore important issues and made vital discoveries. With one penetrating question at a McCormick Foundation and Naval Institute Seminar, Gerhard Weinberg shaped the analysis presented here to a significant degree. Greg Embree, Dennis Fontana, Mary Gallagher, John Lundstrom, James Sawruk, and Robert Sullivan reviewed the manuscript and made shrewd contributions to its narrative pace and emphasis, as well as saving me from many grammatical crimes. All of them are good friends who also offered strong moral support over these many years. Likewise, Jerome Gough professed that he was never bored with the story of my travails on this project.

I cannot repay the debt I owe to Bunichi Ohtsuka, my translator and friend. His contribution was indispensable to presenting a more complete and accurate picture of the Japanese side of the story.

At Random House, Robert Loomis patiently nurtured this project as it metamorphosed radically from the initial concept. He provided both sound advice and sustained moral support. My debt to him is beyond calculation. My gratitude also is extended to Benjamin Dreyer for his patient oversight of the publication process, Timothy Mennel for his highly skilled copyediting, and the always cheerful Barbé Hammer for her multiple contributions.

Last, but by no means least, my unbounded thanks are due to my wife, Janet, and children, Rachel and Mitchell, for their unfailing love, understanding, and support over these many years.

Contents

16. Hiroshima   252

17. Manchuria and Nagasaki   273

18. The Decisive Day   288

19. Surrender   308

20. Assessing Realities   331

21. Alternatives and Conclusions   349

     Appendix A   361

     Appendix B   363

     Notes   365

     Bibliographic Note   445

     Index   461

Maps

Introduction

How World War II ended in the Pacific remains one of the great controversies in American—and Japanese—history. At the center of this controversy is the atomic bomb. Indeed, almost all accounts of this period position atomic weaponry as the hub around which all other considerations orbit. This approach, however, profoundly fails to re-create history as it originally unfolded. For Americans and Japanese of all stations, the events of that time involved a great deal more than the advent of atomic weapons.

This narrative is a work of restoration that strives to permit us to see that period through contemporary American and Japanese eyes. It starts from the fundamental premise that military and naval realities, and how they were perceived on both sides, dominated the relationship between the United States and Japan between January and August 1945. These critical realities encompass strategic plans and operations directed at the preservation or extinction of Imperial Japan. They include air and sea operations aimed at the Japanese Homeland, plans to invade Japan, preparations to resist such an invasion, and the operations arising from Soviet entry into this theater of the war. It does not include a detailed examination of American or Allied campaigns in the Philippines, at Iwo Jima or Okinawa, or elsewhere in Asia or the Pacific.

Neither side neglected diplomacy during these months. Both, however, viewed it as subordinate to military calculations, and that relationship is maintained here. Diplomatic questions, however, were vitally connected with Allied, mainly American, success at code breaking, and this account illuminates the importance of the decryption of not only Japanese diplomatic messages but also military messages on American strategy and diplomacy. Likewise, the space allocated here to the use of atomic weapons reflects how much their employment fit into a broader military and political strategy.

This narrative also differs in method from most prior treatments of the period. To the maximum extent possible, events are presented here as they were perceived and recorded by American and Japanese participants in 1945—not years or decades thereafter. Where it proved impossible to avoid resorting to recollections, as is particularly the case with Japanese political developments, their reliability has been approached from a critical stance and tested as much as possible against contemporary evidence. This approach reveals a very new story about a dramatic transformation of American calculations in the last two months of hostilities. These changes go to the very heart of the contentious issues concerning invasion plans and the program of air bombardment. Among the other vital issues thus set in fresh light are the stance of senior American naval leaders on the prospective invasion of Japan, casualty estimates for an invasion, and the procurement, interpretation, and dissemination of Ultra and Magic intelligence information.

Particular effort also has been made to maintain a balanced perspective, with extensive coverage of developments in Japan. This is intended expressly to prevent the distortions that inevitably stem from a failure to respect the autonomy that Japanese decision makers exercised in choosing military and diplomatic strategies. The exploration of the Japanese viewpoint also breaks new ground in using more comprehensive and authoritative Japanese sources, particularly the volumes in the massive official Japanese War History Series that have been prepared over the last three decades. These cover planning and operations for the defense of the Homeland and, of paramount importance, the development of strategic policy within Imperial General Headquarters. Of special note is that the account of Imperial General Headquarters branches into the political arena and sheds new light on core Japanese positions on invasion and blockade as well as on reaction to the use of atomic bombs, Soviet intervention, and the struggle to end the war.

In the center of these events in Japan stood Emperor Hirohito. After his passing in 1989, new and important evidence about his role in the war came to light. The most significant piece of this fresh evidence was a lengthy statement he dictated in early 1946. Reading this document critically with other evidence is essential to assessing correctly his views and role. And this, in turn, goes to the heart of understanding how near or far Japan stood from peace before Hiroshima and Nagasaki.

Finally, much attention has been given—quite properly—to the indiscriminate effects of the atomic bombs that seared, blasted, and irradiated tens of thousands of noncombatants. But central to understanding this period is the basic fact that atomic bombs were not the sole agents of mass death. Thus, this account begins with the graphic reality of conventional air bombardment as practiced in the final six months of the war.

DOWNFALL

1

Tokyo Burns:
Raid of March 9–10

"A silver curtain falling"

With the night came north winds, blowing bitter and cold across the uneasy city. By 8:00 P.M., great shuddering gusts, at 45 to 67 miles per hour, "violent as a spring typhoon," shoved against the wooden walls and pried at the doors and windows of the dwellings of Tokyo's 4.3 million citizens. Elsewhere, the winds toppled or jammed radar antennas and made mischief with communications. On the pitching seas to the south, picketboats raised frantic alerts of many approaching bombers, but faulty radio reception—and faulty organization—muffled the alarms.

On radios throughout the capital, the voice of Hidetoshi Matsumura, the spokesman for Imperial General Headquarters, hailed the coming day, March 10, as Army Day. His oration ended in the weary cliché: "The darkest hour is just before dawn." His words had barely faded when, at 10:30 P.M., sirens sounded the long, steady wail warning of distant but potentially threatening aircraft. In contrast to the pervasive disorder that had invaded and overwhelmed all aspects of daily life in the capital, the air-raid alert system that roused many from mid-slumber was still respected for its efficiency. With electric lights forbidden after nightfall and cooking gas nonexistent, most families now habitually prepared and ate meals at twilight and then retired early. But even in repose, Tokyo's denizens remained partly dressed, usually in shapeless, loose *monpe* trousers.

Near midnight, coast watchers reported droning noises that were likely from B-29s. The listeners could speak with authority, for the dreaded

Superfortresses—known to the Tokyoites as *"bikko,"* "B-san," "Lord B.," *"okyakusama"* (visitors), and "regular mail"—had come many times to the capital, though only once at night, and never in such numbers or so low. Surprised and confused, civil-defense authorities hesitated, and the sirens did not exclaim the sharp, broken notes of the air-raid alarm, signifying an imminent attack, until 12:15 A.M. By then, bombs had been falling for seven minutes, and rusty red-yellow roses of flame already flowered across eastern Tokyo.

A Danish diplomat, Lars Tillitse, dutifully ventured outside to make sure that his property betrayed no light. A "terrific noise" assailed him as the four-motored bombers thundered by overhead. Another Western observer, Robert Guillain, was more exact: A B-29 passed with "an odd, rhythmic buzzing that filled the night with deep, powerful pulsation and made my whole house vibrate." Tillitse observed his neighbors erupting from their homes, animating the dark narrow streets, the men in helmets, everyone else in padded air-raid hoods. "Radios were going full blast and doors and windows were open, so that people in the street could keep informed," recalled Tillitse. "Already we could see fires."

Radios proclaimed the approach of another wave of bombers, and Tillitse stayed outside to watch. Energetic searchlight crews fanned the slender, probing white columns of their beams from horizon to zenith. As the diplomat gazed upward, six or seven times a bomber punctured a column of illumination, whereupon five or six other lights converged to hold it. Centered in an aura, the silvery body became the target for gunners, who sent shells skyward. But in each case, the shiny cross glided on unhurt. Then Tillitse heard the crowd cheer and swiveled his head to behold one B-29 alight. The whole body glowed red, but the plane continued its flight until, like lightning, white flames burst from the sides. Enveloped in fire, the Superfortress plummeted to the ground.

Everywhere across Tokyo, the night teemed with citizens scurrying from their houses clutching sleeping mats and carefully culled possessions—pots and pans and, above all, treasured hoards of rice and soya paste—seeking refuge. The entire city had only eighteen satisfactory concrete shelters, with a total capacity of five thousand, little more than one space for every thousand persons. The next-best shelters comprised the basements of the relatively few Western-style buildings, constructed to resist earthquakes, and some equally sparse cave shelters. But the mass of citizens lacked any adequate haven. Some families gathered in clothes cupboards within their homes, as the government recommended. Most citizens, however, headed for their *bokugo,* little holes that had been bored beside their houses or in the little ribbon of earth between street and sidewalk. These were typically crude, two to five meters long, one meter across, and one and one-half to two meters deep, covered with a roof made with a few poles, bamboo rafters, and a thin crust of earth. The citizens provided these rudimentary protections themselves, chanting "oh, one, two, oh, one, two" as they dug, around which many then planted flowers, and into which many a man or woman tripped, breaking bones.

The absence of any comprehensive public shelter system partially reflected the fact that Tokyo rested upon unstable soil that precluded extensive excavation; more conspicuously, it betrayed the utter inadequacy of both resources and foresight. The issue had first been raised after World War I, when images of bombers raining explosives, poison gas, or both on cities had found expression. Contemplation of these lurid prospects led Tokyo's undertakers to make discreet inquiries to military authorities as to the number of fatalities that could be expected in one year. The answer they got was thirty thousand. The first recorded air-raid drill in Japan occurred in June 1928. By 1932, an air-raid exercise, actually no more than a practice blackout, had become an annual Tokyo ritual. Air-defense preparations were initially vested in local governments, but in 1937 the National Civilian Air Defense Law transferred responsibilities to national and prefectural (state) authorities. This new ukase, however, ignited bureaucratic warfare and spawned rival and conflicting rules and concepts, frittering away time and effort.

It was the bedrock conviction that Tokyo would not be bombed, however, that hobbled all efforts, and the nearly unbroken string of triumphs in China and in the first months of the war with the United States served to make such a threat seem unthinkable. On the evening of April 17, 1942, the German-born wife of Japanese Foreign Minister Shigenori Togo informed the spouse of a neutral diplomat at a dinner that she need not "worry about sending her furs and jewels and wines out of Tokyo or go to the expense of building an air-raid shelter, since the Americans could never bomb Tokyo." The next day, Lieutenant Colonel James Doolittle hit targets in Japan, including Tokyo, with sixteen B-25s. The raid generated shock, but, perversely, its small amount of damage and few casualties enhanced complacency.

There was also the question of public morale and the prestige of the government and the military. Official preoccupation with air raids and drills would transmit the message that such events might come to pass. This in turn would mean that Japan's leaders believed their warriors would be unable to keep the enemy at bay. It was only with the fall of Saipan in July 1944, observed Danish diplomat Tillitse, that "Japanese with insight knew that Japan had to prepare for the worst." But the government decided that extensive preparations would likely disrupt the war effort just as the struggle had reached a critical phase, and elected to give priority to production over civilian protection.

Before 1944, serious evacuation preparations had been sporadic and erratic. The cabinet decided on October 15, 1943, to remove persons not involved in war production from urban areas, but as the home minister confessed to the Diet in March 1944, "I haven't come across much public sentiment for picking up and leaving." By July 1944, movie theaters featured a short entitled *Evacuation,* which aimed to instill compliance in citizens with images of blazing neighborhoods; it, too, met with scant success.

At the end of June 1944, the cabinet published an "Outline for Encouraging the Evacuation of Schoolchildren." The government earmarked 350,000 third- through sixth-graders in a dozen major cities for evacuation to rural areas. They joined the almost 300,000 schoolchildren parents had voluntarily shipped from the cities. Another 100,000 first- and second-graders followed in March 1945. The separations, almost as traumatic as the air raids themselves, spread an epidemic of homesickness as illustrated in one child's letter: "Mother, please listen to Mitsuko's one great request. Mother, as soon as this letter arrives, please come to see me that very day. . . . Mother, every day Mitsuko goes on crying."

Prime Minister Kuniaki Koiso summoned the Japanese people on January 1, 1945, to "strengthen the national structure to prosecute the war" by perfecting air-raid defenses and warned, "With the progress of the war, difficulties in people's daily life will increase, and there is also the danger of air raids becoming more intensive." These exhortations and formal programs, upon the heels of early B-29 raids, ultimately caused over 1.7 million citizens to leave Tokyo by March 1945. This number included thousands who lost their homes in the massive effort to lay a grid of firebreaks over the city's contours in order to constrict damage to the closely packed wooden houses in the poorer districts. American photographic reconnaissance identified 31 miles of these firebreaks, ranging from 45 to 110 yards wide. Japanese sources report the destruction of 207,370 homes to clear these gaps, as well as to create open spaces around vital buildings and installations. But these numbers belie the fact that fundamentally both resources and resolve were lacking; in far too many cases, even when structures had been demolished, the boards were left where they fell, providing even more ideal kindling.

But on the night of March 9–10, the forfeit for lost time and opportunity was paid by Tokyo's remaining civilian population. From an overlook at the Jesuit Sophia University, Father Gustav Bruno Maria Bitter gazed out to see the first "circle of fire," which reminded him of "a silver curtain falling, like the *lametta,* the silver tinsel that we hung from Christmas trees in Germany. . . . And where these silver streamers would touch the earth, red fires would spring up." To Lars Tillitse, the incendiaries "did not fall; they descended rather slowly, like a cascade of silvery water. One single bomb covered quite a big area, and what they covered they devoured."

Bitter and Tillitse surveyed the attack from western and northern Tokyo, the hilly *yamanote* where the middle and upper classes made their communities. But the American targets were the packed wards of the lower, flat plain called the *shitamachi,* especially Honjo, Fukagawa, Joto, Edogawa, and Mukojima. "It was called the 'plain side' as distinguished from the 'mountain side,'" as it was once described, "the hills to the west and south dotted with residential districts." The plain contained a vast overgrown tangle of wooden homes ("massed like piles of dry wood at a building site") and factories, finely veined with winding alleys, rather than streets, and stagnant canals. Apart from a few avenues and electric train lines, the only substantial feature was the Sumida River. On its left bank rested the Fukagawa docks facing Tokyo Bay, as well as the Honjo and Mukojima factory districts; along its right bank stretched Asakusa, Shitaya, and the outskirts of Kanda and Nihombashi. These communities, among the most densely populated in the world, had suffered heavily in the great 1923 earthquake. Lots in Tokyo typically measured twenty-five feet across at the street front but often were packed up to three houses deep. About 98 percent of the buildings were of wood and paper construction.

"Inflammability was probably the chief qualification these quarters had as targets for fire bombing," noted a leading scholar of the raid, Gordon Daniels, "but one cannot deny that these areas played at least some role in Japanese war production." The demarcation between residential and industrial was "often non-existent." The intermixture of modest and medium-sized enterprises with private dwellings played an important role in armament production. The output of a major factory, and there were a great many in Tokyo, depended typically upon a flow of component parts from feeder firms across the city. Each factory was like a tree radiating a web of roots throughout the surrounding living areas from which it drew both workers and parts. "The destruction of any thickly peopled *shitamachi* area," observed Daniels, "would destroy some of the tap-roots of military output, besides leading to the permanent or temporary absenteeism of workers living in the locality."

As 8,519 clusters of incendiary bombs burst apart, they released over 496,000 individual 6.2-pound cylinders, each with a strip of cloth—the "silver streamers" Father Bitter described—flapping from the rear. When a cylinder struck anything solid, it spewed a column of "flaming dew" that skittered across rooftops, setting its immediate environment afire. The wind fanned the flames to adjacent structures. Initially, it often seemed a home was unaffected, until the windows began to shine from within and then glowed "like a paper lantern" from a ball of fire that sprouted tentacles that danced out from beneath the eaves to envelop the house until it crumbled inward upon itself.

Only six cities in Japan boasted regular, professional fire-fighting services. All the rest used volunteers. The Tokyo Fire Department, descended from a feudal organization of knights, reached a peak strength of 8,100 in November 1944 (2,500 of these were junior firemen between the ages of seventeen and twenty). Its 287 stations were by far the best accoutred in Japan, with 1,117 pieces of equipment, including much apparatus drafted from nearby rural regions. But their inventory included just three aerial extension ladders (only one of which worked), because a web of wires and obstructions littered the air above Tokyo's neighborhoods.

The conflagration this night, with potent incendiaries falling "like rain drops," was more than any city fire department in the world could have handled. There were far too many fires—each Superfortress bomb load covered an area 1,500 to 2,000 feet long and 300 feet wide—and the heat and fleeing crowds made it impossible to get to some places. Once the fires gained hold, the scorching winds projected "great clots of flame" on short trajectories but also launched live sparks on vaulting arcs up into the sky. Then, as they gathered strength, the fires propelled upward burning bits of wood or paper that tumbled across neighborhoods and then whole wards in fiery showers. Distant observers could see "torch clusters" explode and then sink back in "wavy lines across the city," with individual blasts that looked like "flaming hair."

After only an hour, the fire department conceded total defeat. During the night, the flames consumed 96 fire engines and 128 firemen died or were missing, as were some 500 civil guards who had assisted them. At one station, a fire left only a tangle of corpses around a melted fire engine.

It fell to Tokyo's citizens to face a conflagration with spiritual, not material, resources. Officially, 2.75 million people had been organized formally into the air-raid defense network. Over 140,000 neighborhood associations of ten to twenty families each formed the basic units. They had taken the "air defense oath of certain victory," rendering pledges with their neighbors that they would "follow orders," "refrain from selfish conduct," and "cooperate with one another in air defense." This energetic and courageous communal effort, the government had promised, would protect and save them. "No matter what sort of air raid comes, this neighborhood association will be safe," was a typical attitude. "Fight, don't run" was the policy. And thus the onslaught was faced primarily by citizens armed with wet mats, sandbags, and buckets. The "stand your ground" policy enormously swelled the death toll in circumstances for which communal effort offered no antidote.

American reports show that the B-29s released 1,665 tons of incendiaries into a designated target area measuring ten square miles. This patch of Tokyo included the Asakusa ward, which featured an extremely high roof density of 65 percent—the most built-up factory area did not exceed 40 percent. Moreover, while the overall population density in the targeted districts nudged 103,000 per square mile, in Asakusa it reached 135,000. Official Japanese reports said the first incendiaries fell in Kiba, along the Tokyo waterfront, and stoked large fires, spread by the wind. Two minutes later, fires unfurled in two more spots, and within fourteen minutes "the hellfire began."

The individual fires became blazes that the great winds roused up in towering whirlwinds of jagged flames of yellow, red, and white. The center of the conflagration acted like a bellows, inhaling swift currents of superheated air and spouting up a giant rising column of incandescent gases that spewed out a whistling blizzard of sparks and firebrands, "like a huge borealis," until it became a firestorm that turned the night into a "black and pink day." Robert Guillain reported: "We could hear a crackling like the sound of bonfires—the noise, it seemed, of houses collapsing." "Now and then," recalled Lars Tillitse, "I heard the thud of falling roofs and walls."

The planes came, shining golden against the dark roof of heaven or glittering blue, like meteors, in the searchlight beams tracing the vault of night sky from horizon to horizon. Robert Guillain described them: "Their long glinting wings, sharp as blades, could be seen through the opaque columns of smoke rising from the city, suddenly reflecting the fire from the furnace below." Father Bitter watched the "red and yellow flames reflecting from below on the silvery undersides so that they were like giant dragon flies with jeweled wings against the upper darkness."

Driven by the winds, the fire marched northwest with extreme rapidity. It took only an hour for a huge swath of eastern Tokyo to be consumed. Those who stood their ground, defending their homes, perished quickly— in the clothes cupboard, in the *bokugo,* or in the rubble—often whole families at once. The key to survival was to grasp quickly that the situation was hopeless and flee. One survivor fixed the interval between when she first realized incendiary bombs were starting fires and the moment when she fled to be about ten minutes. A great many citizens—no one knows the proportions—ultimately took flight before the flames, through smoke that hung so thickly in places that they could not see more than ten feet, all "panting 'huh, huh, huh' as they ran."

The paths open to them were few and constricted: the handful of relatively broad streets, the firebreaks themselves, or the electric train lines. Salvation appeared to beckon from large solid structures, such as schools or theaters, open spaces, or bodies of water. Based upon the experience of the fires that accompanied the 1923 earthquake, rebuilding plans had incorporated three large and thirty smaller parks. "But the flames followed them," said a Japanese author, "raging in those sixty-, seventy-, and eighty-mile-per-hour winds, and swept over whole wide spaces, carrying the fiery death."

As the fires bore down on her home, Funato Kazuyo fled with her family to a nearby school yard, where she knew there were trenches. A bright red glow from Fukagawa to the west heralded the approaching fire. Then incendiaries began to fall near the school:

> People panicked, Running screaming, "We're all going to die! The Fire is coming!" The sound of incendiary bombs falling, "Whizzz," the deafening reverberations of the planes, and the great roar of the fire and wind overwhelmed us. "If we stay here we'll die! Let's run!" . . . "Women and children follow us, Why are you hesitating?"

They began to run but had to backtrack. "Even two or three minutes was a terrible loss of time," she recalled. "Sparks flew everywhere. Electric wires sparked and toppled." Her sister Hiroko's turban caught fire. It had been cinched tight to keep it from being blown off in the wind, and now it would not come loose. Her sister tried to pull it off and burned her hands; the fire then burned her hair. Finally, they managed to tear it off and smother it with their legs.

Masuko Harino was in a hostel in Nihombashi ward. When incendiaries commenced tumbling all around the hostel, the manager, reacting as his government instructed him, declared, "We will fight the fires to the last." He did; he died. Harino chose flight. She sprinted toward the electric machinery factory where she worked:

> People's clothes were on fire. . . . Some people were writhing about in torment and no one had time to help them. . . . Intense heat was coming from the fire storm. My eyes seemed about to pop out. Yoshikawa-san cut her way through the mob and I followed along the road, seeking some respite from the flowing heat of the terrible fire. We ran. We saw fleeing shapes, but little else.

A telephone pole collapsed and twisted electric wires snaked out along the ground. The road on both sides was full of people's possessions, burning up.
My eyes hurt. Breathing was difficult and I felt that life was escaping me. I found a broken hydrant and soaked my *zukin* [air-raid turban] and put it on my head, almost unconsciously. Finally, I fled as far as Kiyosu bridge.

Nineteen-year-old Kimie Ono looked out to see fires igniting all around his home, lighting the neighborhood up like noon. He chose an electric train line as his route of escape. Many other people chose the same path. They began laden with packs, sleeping mats, babies, clothing, and household goods in their arms or on makeshift carts, and they shouted, shoved, and jostled one another. But the flames, mounted on the winds, galloped in easy strides, outpaced the churning feet and spinning wheels, and soon framed the route. The people desperately discarded possessions to flee the faster, and the road became paved with clothes and goods. "No one stopped to loot; to stop was to die." The heated wind felled victim after victim, who staggered and then collapsed to the ground. Intermixed with the howls of wind were voices shouting, yelling, and weeping as the mass of humanity trampled over the fallen. Just ahead of him, Ono saw a mother and child running. "Suddenly the fire storm swept out a finger to lick them, and in a second, before his eyes, the mother and child burst into flames. . . . Their clothes afire, they staggered and fell to the ground. No one stopped to help them."

Even in flight, however, some neighbors tried to maintain a communal effort. One typical neighborhood association fled in groups of ten to twenty, holding on to long ropes so as not to become separated. But as the running, bobbing knots of humanity threaded the narrow alleys and streets, again and again they found their path blocked by a "barricade of fire." After trying to gauge the wind, they recoiled and darted off in another direction, often only to find it, too, was now blocked by the fires spread by the shifting winds or newly fallen bombs.

One boy running down a street, gripping his younger brother's hand, reached an intersection where crowds collided from four directions. There was a moment of milling confusion until one group broke away in one direction and the rest followed. Too often, however, individuals, families, or groups eventually came to realize they were trapped in a labyrinth walled off by flames. Then they would succumb to the spirit of *shikada ga nai* ("It is hopeless to try to do more") and kneel in the streets, facing toward the palace of the Emperor, and die there as the fire swept over them.

One of the few to survive the passage of the fire was Masatake Obata. He owned precisely the type of enterprise targeted by the Americans: a small manufacturing concern networking together household workshops that supplied component parts for aircraft. On this night, there were eight persons in his household: Obata, his wife, his four children, and his two sisters, who had come to share the sweet-potato bounty they had reaped, like so many other city dwellers at this time, from bargains with farmers. About midnight, Obata, an air-raid warden, immediately recognized the danger and hustled his family and sisters into their clothes and directed them to Fuji Park. The neighborhood association forged a quick consensus that everyone should go to Sumida Park, a large open space deemed safe. Obata dispatched his own household there but stayed behind to assure that all his neighbors followed.

When Obata finally satisfied himself that he had fulfilled his responsibilities, he turned to join his family. He was slapping at his air-raid hood to put out a fire when, not ten feet away, a cluster of incendiary bombs struck the ground and exploded. One bomb caught him in the face, knocking him unconscious. How long he lay, he never knew, but when he woke up, his shoes had been burned off, as had his toes, his arms were nearly black, and his clothes still burned. He put the fires out by rolling on the ground. He got up and staggered to a trench harboring seven badly burned people. Obata soon had them yelling at each other to stay awake and alive and chanting Buddhist prayers together.

In Asakusa, a crowd sought succor around an old and lovely Buddhist temple, dedicated to Kannon, goddess of mercy, which drew up to sixty thousand visitors per day. It was deemed absolutely safe since the seventeenth-century building had survived all the fires and the great 1923 earthquake. This time, firebrands ignited the vast wooden structure. "The great ginkgo trees in the park went up in flames, along with the gardens—and the people."

Some of the worst killing grounds were the schools. Hidezo Tsuchikura hustled his two children to the Futaba school, famous for its large swimming pool. They were among the first to arrive, but swarms of neighbors followed and gradually Tsuchikura moved his family from the basement air-raid shelter first to the gym and ultimately to the roof. It was "like hell," as the leaping flames surrounded the school compound and pelted sparks and flaming wood over the exposed area. Still, the heat on the roof was more bearable than the impending sultry suffocation Tsuchikura had sensed inside the building. His daughter shrieked as her clothes caught fire. Tsuchikura found a water tank and used it to put out the flames. Then his son's and his own clothes ignited. For the next ninety minutes, first one then another of them doused fires in the tank of water, though as soon as they came out their clothes began steaming under the intense heat. When the fires finally receded after consuming the entire surrounding neighbor-hood, Tsuchikura discovered that only his little family and twelve other people who had also sought refuge on the roof survived at the school. Ac-cording to him:

> The entire building had become a huge oven three stories high. Every human being inside the school was literally baked or boiled alive in heat. Dead bod-ies were everywhere in grisly heaps. None of them appeared to be badly charred. They looked like mannequins, some of them with a pinkish com-plexion. . . .
>
> But the swimming pool was the most horrible sight of all. It was hideous. More than a thousand people, we estimated, had jammed into the pool. The pool had been filled to its brim when we first arrived. Now there wasn't a drop of water, only the bodies of the adults and children who had died.

Many thousands sought salvation in other bodies of water, such as the stagnant canals and rivers that had once given the city so much of its com-mercial vitality. A witness to these efforts was Kinosuke Wakabayashi, a senior official in the Sumida district. Heeding suggestions from superiors, he had dispatched all of his family, save one teenage daughter, to the coun-tryside. When the bombers struck, he first made sure his neighbors evacu-ated. Then it was time to save himself and his daughter. They made for the Asashi Brewery warehouse along the Sumida River. There they sheltered in the lee of the concrete walls, mute spectators to the horror about them. They saw the figures of people running to the river, leaping through walls of flame and then diving into the water or onto the riverbanks. Soon the banks on both sides were clogged. But here as so many places elsewhere, people leaped in layer upon layer, crushing the early arrivals, and then the tidal wave of flames closed in so that to hold one's head above water was to risk being choked by smoke or seared by flame. The fire sucked the oxy-gen away, leaving thousands dead, "like so many fish left gasping on the bottom of a lake that has been drained."

In their extremity, people took any shelter they could find. Miwa Koshiba, a housewife, fled with her young children and husband from a hole in their garden to the Sumida River, a half mile away. They found the river almost completely ablaze. With people dropping all around, she guided her family to a large sewer pipe that drained into the river. She re-mained all night in the sewer pipe, bathing the children in the waste to ward off the heat, until they were caked with filth.

By the time the all clear sounded at 2:37 A.M., March 10, the raid had lasted approximately two hours and forty minutes. Across nearly sixteen square miles of Tokyo there was a "burned empty prairie," filled with "a sort of underbrush of roasted sheet-metal and reddish-blackish iron and heavy shards of gray tile." But it was empty only in the sense that virtually no human structure remained upright and recognizable. The vista greeting a reporter "was nothing but heaps of ashes, bits of corrugated iron, bricks, concrete blocks, a few twisted girders, and here and there the shell of a burned-out concrete building. Skeletons of motor vehicles, including fire engines, dotted the landscape."

"The people who came back were like ghosts, uttering no words. They simply staggered back," said Funato Kazuyo, who led her badly burned sister back to their home. Her sister succumbed several days later to typhus. By dawn, Masuko Harino, who had fled from the hostel, rose from the roadside where she had lain and found some water to wash her face and restore her vision. The faces of everyone she saw were black from the grime baked on by the heat. Many survivors later manifested a darkening of the skin that lasted "days, weeks, months, and sometimes forever because of the intensity of the heat." Harino made her way gingerly barefoot over broken glass, nails, and jagged spikes of wood that lay thick upon the ground, taking particular care to avoid fallen power lines. All around, she gazed at swollen, contorted, blackened bodies that resembled "enormous ginseng roots." Whether they had been men or women she could not tell. When she reached the hostel, she waited until the other survivors gathered: There were only two others.

Everywhere, the survivors stirred to be assaulted by yet more horrors. People staggered or lay writhing in pain, with skin charred or hanging in strips, issuing screams that received no succor. Masatake Obata faced the dawn with his seven companions in their makeshift shelter. He finally left them, seeking help for his serious burns, but at the hospital a doctor said of him, "It's not necessary to take him to any ward. Take him downstairs to the morgue in the basement. Let him join the other dead. There is no hope." He was taken to a straw mat and left to die without food or water. Three days later, his mother found him, still alive. His wife, four children, and two sisters had all perished trying to reach Sumida Park.

The horizon of almost all of these survivors extended no further than his or her particular refuge and the path back home. Captain Shigenori Kubota, however, obtained a far more comprehensive vista of the devastation. His regular assignment was that of a teacher at the Imperial Japanese Army Medical School, but his alternate assignment was as commander of the school's Number One Rescue Unit. Kubota's detachment ostensibly incorporated nine subunits for the general public and five for the Imperial

Palace. But this night, Kubota mustered only twenty-four men in a half-dozen vehicles when he set off at 3:50 A.M. His orders directed him to the Honjo district to treat the injured, who numbered perhaps one hundred thousand spread over a twenty-five-square-mile area. He was told to cooperate with private doctors, but he knew that virtually all of them were in the armed services. (Later accounting showed that of 250 "medical services" operated by the government or the Red Cross, over 100 had been destroyed.)

Kubota's convoy penetrated the devastated areas, where a low roof of smoke hung over still-smoldering fires and bright embers that marked where thousands of homes had once been. He passed the Miya mansion of Kaya, a "once-resplendent building, with its tall columns and ornate wood work, [which] now looked like a charcoal drawing, blackened pillars with smoking ruins collapsed around them, standing lonely in a sea of burning rubble." Likewise, he observed "charcoal" trolley cars, the sides of which collapsed at the touch.

The scene at Ryogoku Bridge stunned Captain Kubota: a "forest of corpses" packed so closely that they must have been touching as they died. They now had returned to humanity's carbon essence, crumbling at the touch. An even more horrifying vision assaulted him at the Sumida River.

The entire river surface was black as far as the eye could see, black with burned corpses, logs, and who knew what else, but uniformly black from the immense heat that had seared its way through the area as the fire dragon passed. It was impossible to tell the bodies from the logs at a distance. The bodies were all nude, the clothes had been burned away, and there was a dreadful sameness about them, no telling men from women or even children. All that remained were pieces of charred meat. Bodies and parts of bodies were carbonized and absolutely black.

As Kubota watched, angry waves receded from the riverbanks to reveal

stacked in neat precision, as though by some machine . . . row upon row of corpses. The instrument was the tide, which had come and gone since the fire storm passed by, leaving rows of bodies like so much cordwood cast up on the beach. . . . How many bodies had washed out to sea was impossible to tell, but they must have been in the thousands, for there were tens of thousands in the river.

Kubota ended his tour of horrors and set up his unit in Honjo ward. A stream of injured flooded in, many with searing, painful burns. Virtually without exception, they had conjunctivitis from the heated, smoky winds. But Kubota worried most about the victims of smoke inhalation. One man told him, "It hurts so much I'd like to cut open my chest and let some clear air in." Many thousands died over the next several days, including those with shock and infections for which there was little medicine. Even such fundamental essentials as bandages were in short supply, and doctors were compelled to reuse them as minimum hygiene standards collapsed.

As the hours of March 10 passed, Kubota was joined by a legion of civil-defense workers who now converged upon the scene, described by a reporter:

> On some broad streets, as far as one could see, there was an even row of bodies where men, women and children, trapped by the flames, had futilely tried to escape them by lying down in the center of the paving. There were heaps of bodies in school yards, in parks, in public shelters, in vacant lots, and huddled under railroad viaducts.

For several days, bodies were pulled from the Sumida River and canals, but "often it was impossible to distinguish even the sex of the bodies because they had been so mutilated by the flames," said a Japanese journalist, reiterating a common observation. "We were instructed to report on actual conditions," one Japanese police official later acknowledged, "[but] most of us were unable to do this because of the horrifying conditions beyond imagination."

It was clear that this was Tokyo's greatest disaster, even surpassing the 1923 earthquake. Of the thirty-five wards of the city, the Home Ministry officially counted "most parts" of five as destroyed: Shitaya, Asakusa, Fukagawa, Honjo, and Joto. Another seven districts were approximately half destroyed: Ashidate, Kanda, Kojima, Nihombashi, Hongo, Shiba, and Arakawa. The destruction gouged out parts of another fourteen wards, for a total of at least twenty-six. American photographic reconnaissance revealed that flames had consumed 15.8 square miles of the city. By American calculation, this included 18 percent of the industrial area and 63 percent of the commercial area. In the explicit ten-square-mile target area, damage totaled 82 percent, with twenty-two industries previously assigned target numbers (meaning they had been identified as having military significance) "and many other unidentified industries . . . destroyed or damaged." The American figures did not exaggerate. The Tokyo fire chief listed forty-three factories as damaged. Asakusa ward, "the amusement center of Tokyo" with its restaurants, geisha, and prostitution houses, was virtually leveled, with 99 percent of its rooms (even of the houses still standing) gutted. Japanese calculation ultimately totaled the destruction at 261,000 houses, leaving 1.15 million homeless.

Knots of survivors and staggering files of the homeless, with "muddied, cinder smeared padding bulged from their quilts, making them look like soiled bandages," floundered through the devastated area looking for aid. The pervasive sense of emergency suspended the customary punctilious insistence on certificates of entitlement for emergency food and shelter. Citizens of Tokyo and surrounding communities freely opened temples, schools, and theaters to house and feed the refugees. Perhaps above all, no documents were demanded of those seeking to evacuate Tokyo by train. Over the course of the next few weeks, more than a million people migrated from the metropolis with speed and determination never roused by official exhortation. More than 90 percent of the refugees found shelter with relatives in nearby prefectures.

The government organized twenty-nine special trains devoted solely to evacuation, but they could haul only a small percentage of the total. Others took to the roads by bicycle, tricycle, oxcart, and horsecart—any kind of vehicle that did not depend on scarce gasoline—stacked and stuffed with heirlooms, clothes, bedding, kitchen utensils, the assorted accumulations of a million lifetimes, pale babies and tired children sprawled at the tops of the heaps. In an abortive burst of creative thinking, some bureaucrats conceived of transporting the evacuees to the northernmost Home Island, Hokkaido, to toil at farms to ease the food crisis. This scheme foundered from lack of will and energy.

Whereas after earlier raids the streets had been cleared and utilities and telephones had been restored with reasonable dispatch, now a lethargy of despair retarded or halted such efforts. So great was the blow to morale that even the highest civil-defense authorities abandoned training programs. Instead, they applied what energy they had to evacuation and the further closing of schools in order to free students to labor in factories and on farms.

The dead also needed tending. Prior to March 10, there had been only 1,292 deaths from all the air raids on Tokyo, and the remains were handled in a planned, orderly system of identification and internment. But in this one night, by actual—and minimum—count, at least 79,466 perished: 64 claimed by families, 1,805 handled by private crematories, 2,495 cremated on the spot, 6,002 identified and buried in temporary individual graves, and 69,100 buried in common pits of groups of up to twenty or more. The very precision of these figures betrays their inadequacy: They account for only identified and counted bodies. The director of health submitted a figure of 83,600, and the later authoritative United States Strategic Bombing

Survey report acknowledges that many dead were not counted. A contemporary intercepted coded message from a German attaché, citing Imperial Navy sources, placed the dead at "about 100,000."

One reason the count could not be stated with absolute certainty was that the recent massive population shifts had left officials without a firm base from which to calculate. Moreover, the raid disrupted the administrative apparatus of the city, and in the devastated wards the dead citizens could not report to the dead civil authorities. Then there was the macabre mechanics of the disaster: Many remains must have been reduced to ash in the intense flames, and the tidal rivers washed many bodies out to sea. Later, a figure of 90,000 to 100,000 came to be accepted, but even these immense totals are sometimes challenged as too low. Whatever the number, it took at least twenty days to clear all the remains.

On March 10, no newspapers were published in Tokyo, and the city was in disarray save for the incongruous spectacle of a parade of marching soldiers marking Army Day side by side with a stream of refugees. The next day, the Diet was in session, but there was no comment about the raid, and efforts were made to conceal the information within Japan. Within a few hours, however, word began to spread throughout the country.

Far away, behind the moat of the Imperial Palace at Chiyoda in the center of Tokyo, the Emperor soon heard of the horror. Explorations by his retainers convinced them that the Emperor must be prevented from seeing such sights as the two- or three-foot-high "rice plant mounds" that on close inspection proved to be stacks of melted and fused bodies. But the Emperor would not be denied, and on March 18 he set forth in a general's uniform and riding boots. He had been told the worst tragedy of the raid lay concentrated by the Sumida River, and he directed his caravan to that area. With the red and gold chrysanthemum pennon snapping over a fender, his maroon car rolled past his surprised subjects. Those who quickly recognized His Majesty and bowed in time were repaid with a gracious salute, but mostly his gaze fell over acres of destruction. A military aide later recalled that

> the victims, who had been digging through the rubble with empty expressions on their faces, watched the imperial motorcade pass by with reproachful expressions. . . . Were they grudgeful to the emperor because they had lost their relatives, their houses and belongings? Or were they in a state of utter exhaustion and bewilderment?

At a ramshackle camp of tents and shacks, the Emperor paused for a moment to talk to rag-clad refugees. After being driven a little farther, he halted to talk to survivors. Then he remounted his car and headed back to the Imperial Palace without revealing his inner thoughts.

Before the calendar ran out on this year, fiery devastation was to come to more than sixty other Japanese cities. Those Japanese not killed in air raids would stand on the precipice of extinction through starvation. A great invasion would be planned but not executed. The Soviet Union would unleash a mechanized assault in Manchuria and plan to seize a Home island. Millions were to die, only a minority of them Japanese, and the Imperial Empire was to vanish in two atomic flashes. The Emperor would play a pivotal role in stanching—but not halting—the bloodshed, and when he did so he was to write a poem:

> Thinking of the people dying endlessly in the air raids
> I ended the war
> Having no thought of my own fate

There might seem to be some solace from the million aggregated horrors of this night in Tokyo to believe that it played some significant role in persuading the Emperor that the war was not only lost but must be halted soon. The story of the events to follow, however, admits of no such ready consolation.

2

Strategies Old, Strategies New

"There is no alternative to annihilation"

War Plan Orange and the Advent of War

The American strategy to defeat Japan in 1945 represented a fusion of two concepts: a long-established Navy scheme of blockade and bombardment and a far more recent Army vision of invasion. The Navy had labored persistently and rigorously on plans for war with Japan—eventually including massive use of airpower—from 1906 to 1941. In these plans, Japan was code-named Orange and the United States Blue; hence the series passed under the title of War Plan Orange. As the plan evolved, its details were reordered many times, but a framework of a three-phase war endured. During Phase 1, Japan was expected to strike south and west, seizing the lightly defended American outposts in the Far East and securing access to vital raw materials. During Phase 2, superior American air and sea forces would forge westward across the Central Pacific, fighting small-scale but intense attrition battles with Japanese forces and establishing advance bases. After two or three years, the deciding moment would come when, in the words of Edward S. Miller, the leading American student of War Plan Orange, "at a time and place of Japan's choosing, the two battle fleets would meet in a cataclysmic gunnery engagement which the American dreadnoughts would win." Phase 3 would then witness American forces progressing northward from the Philippines across the islands paralleling the Asian coast, installing bases from which to strangle Japan's imports and to ravage her urban areas by air bombardment. Japan would then sue for peace, noted Miller, "even though [her] proud army stood intact in the home islands and China."

Phase 2 received by far the most extensive study by the Navy of any aspect of War Plan Orange. By contrast, Phase 3 secured the least attention from the strategic planners, and very little at all after 1928. A 1923 draft of the plan emphasized that the Phase 3 campaign would be:

> directed towards the isolation of Japan through control of all waters surrounding Japan, through the equivalent of blockade operations, and through the capture and occupation of all outlying Japanese islands, intensified by an air war over Japanese territory.

Most American strategists believed that war with Japan would be a "long drawn out operation" with Japan's fanatical resistance extracting mounting casualties the closer American forces drew to the Home Islands. Blockade, even if it took years to gain effect, looked attractive in this context.

By the date this statement was drafted, the term *blockade* carried weighty implications. The use of blockades stretched back thousands of years, but within legal and moral conventions that sanctioned only selective application to particular harbors or such legitimate "contraband" as arms and equipment. In World War I, however, the British fundamentally altered the reach of a blockade to encompass entire enemy countries and defined as contraband all items, assuming everything had military utility, including food. This produced vast privation and death among not only combatants but more so among noncombatants, notably the young, the old, and the ill. As a result of the British blockade of Germany, by 1918 the diet of German civilians included dogs and cats (the latter dubbed "roof rabbits"). The blockade killed perhaps a half-million German civilians by starvation and its side effects; it was also a decisive factor in Germany's defeat.

"It was an article of faith among all [Navy] planners," observed Miller, "that the United States need never invade Japan." But during the 1920s, staff officers nevertheless delved deeply into an invasion scenario. One study in 1922 found that an invasion offered "almost no prospect of success." In this, the U.S. Army found common ground with their blue-suited colleagues. In 1927, Army planners held that the prospects for an invasion were "extremely doubtful . . . regardless of our greater potential man power and munitions, because the enemy can always concentrate forces greatly superior to the successive expeditions into which our land forces must be organized for overseas transportation." Moreover, the Army War College held Japan was "almost invulnerable" due to the legendary ferocity of the Imperial Army and the notorious topography, alternatingly steep and soaked, which was certain to negate the United States's superiority in heavy equipment.

From the earliest days, moreover, American officers harbored doubts much more profound than those concerning material factors. Beginning with the great prophet of maritime strategy himself, Admiral Alfred Thayer Mahan, many naval officers were convinced that American society would not countenance a long and bloody war. They therefore propounded strategies of rapid, even reckless, advance that seemed to offer prospects of an abbreviated conflict. Other voices challenged Mahan and his party, but a leading strategist noted that in a war with Japan, "the patience and temper of the American people would be severely tried." Conversely, advances in aeronautics tempted planners with vastly more abundant prospects of victory through a more rigorous blockade and direct bombing attacks on Japan's war-making capacity. Airpower figured prominently in plans for Phase 3 from the 1920s.

War Plan Orange remained the template for a Pacific war for virtually all senior American sea officers, but it became subordinate to strategies fashioned for a global struggle. Following Japan's aggression into China in July 1937, the American government, accurately reflecting public opinion, took the side of China with progressively more strident diplomatic, but not military, measures. While the danger of war with Japan remained real, Japan posed no serious menace to the Western Hemisphere. A real and terrifying direct threat to the United States rose from another quarter: Adolf Hitler's Germany. In American eyes, Hitler's conquest of Western Europe in 1940 confirmed his march for world domination, a march that in 1940 and 1941 appeared unstoppable. American military and naval strategists feverishly prepared plans to defend the citadel of the continental United States in hopes that a better day would eventually arrive. This moment remained a fresh and searing memory for American policy makers for the rest of the conflict, reminding them of how near the Axis had verged on triumph. This memory argued for a greater war aim than driving the aggressors back behind their original borders.

The survival of the United Kingdom by a slender thread in the Battle of Britain brightened the strategic horizon. The president and senior American military and naval leaders forged a new consensus: To save itself, America must ultimately enter the war on the side of Britain. They concluded that in such a conflict, America would either evade war with Japan or at least conduct a defensive struggle in the Pacific while focusing on Europe. This decision flowed from well-founded concern about German technological capabilities and from the awesome repute that the German Army and Air Force won early in the war.

The primacy of the European phase of the war remained the bedrock principle of all subsequent American strategy. The U.S. Army's capabilities and its institutional interests in the employment of massive ground and air units best fitted the nature of the war in Europe. Also coloring Army thinking was the view that the Japanese were markedly inferior to the Germans as practitioners of modern war. As one distinguished historian phrased it, generals in Europe "dismiss[ed] the Pacific as the bush leagues." Nor was this attitude confined to career soldiers. Secretary of War Henry L. Stimson confessed in his diary as late as February 1945 that he had never studied concepts for a final campaign against Japan as he had for Germany. From at least as early as November 1940, the U.S. Navy acknowledged that the overall top priority must be given to Europe, but throughout the war the Navy regarded the Pacific as its preeminent theater and held the Imperial Navy (if not the Imperial Army) as a worthy, if hated, foe.

A critical turning point came in June 1941, when Hitler turned eastward with an attack on his erstwhile ally, the Soviet Union. To the surprise of American and British military leaders, the Red Army, despite fearful losses, failed to collapse under the German onslaught. Keeping the Soviet Union in the war thus became a key component of British and American strategy in Europe.

But embrace of the "Russian dictatorship" (President Franklin D. Roosevelt's term) came at tremendous moral cost. "To welcome Russia as an associate in the defense of democracy would invite misunderstanding of our own position," noted American diplomat George Kennan, "and would lend to the German war effort a gratuitous and sorely needed aura of morality." In the same statement in which he pledged British alliance with the Soviets, Prime Minister Winston Churchill declared that "the Nazi regime is indistinguishable from the worst features of communism." Yet both Churchill, Roosevelt, and their governments toiled endlessly to maintain that the war was a clear-cut case of good against evil. As a noted scholar of Roosevelt's foreign policy has explained:

> Convinced that only a stark contrast between freedom and totalitarianism would provide the emotional wherewithal for Americans to fight, Roosevelt wished to identify the Russians, regardless of Soviet realities, with Anglo-American ideals as fully as he could.

Those "Soviet realities" encompassed the slaughter of millions before the war during drives to collectivize agriculture and industrialize as well as in a great reign of terror, and this system of repression continued to produce hundreds of thousands of victims during the war. In any ranking of the most morally troubling aspects of the conduct of the war by Britain and the United States, the manner in which the Soviets were presented overshadows all other controversies but remains the least confronted.

The significance of "Soviet realities" for the Pacific war remained latent for many months, for when Japan attacked in December 1941, she added the United States and Great Britain, but not the Soviet Union, to her adversaries. The Imperial Army and Navy staked out Japan's new territorial claims with a speed and skill and to a depth that exceeded any prewar expectation. This expansion, plus the political decision by Roosevelt and Churchill that Australia and New Zealand must be held (the U.S. Army was prepared to at least contemplate their abandonment), provided the ingredients for unanticipated campaigns in the South Pacific that began in April 1942.

This season of Japanese expansion necessitated the division of the Pacific in March 1942 between two great commands. General Douglas MacArthur, ordered back by Roosevelt from his doomed command in the Philippines, was appointed to control the Southwest Pacific theater, which encompassed Australia and New Guinea, as well as the Philippines. The remainder of the North, Central, and South Pacific became the province of Admiral Chester W. Nimitz, who wielded his authority from Hawaii. The summer of 1942 found MacArthur's forces locked in desperate combat with the Japanese on New Guinea, while Nimitz embarked on a tumultuous campaign commencing at Guadalcanal.

Although the British defended imperial interests in Malaya, Burma, and India, scarce resources compelled Churchill's government to relegate the Pacific to a priority far below the European and Mediterranean theaters. Likewise, China, while carrying on a struggle that tied down many Japanese forces, remained weak in capabilities, internally divided, and on the defensive. The main burden of fighting in the Pacific was to be borne throughout the war by the United States; with this burden came the privilege of selecting strategy.

Between 1942 and late 1944, American planners grappled with two challenges: how to bring about the ultimate defeat of Japan and how to deploy resources to secure positions from which that defeat might be obtained. MacArthur was allowed sufficient men, ships, and planes to finish a campaign in the Solomons and, by mid-1944, to drive along the coast of New Guinea. But priority in the Pacific went to Nimitz, who executed the

Japan and Operation Downfall:
The Invasion of Japan, November 1, 1945–March 1, 1946

SAKHALIN

KURIL ISLANDS

MANCHUKUO

SOVIET UNION

HOKKAIDO

Sea of Japan

KOREA

HONSHU

JAPAN

Yokohama

Tokyo

Nagoya

Kobe

Osaka

Hiroshima

Tsushima Strait

Tsushima

SHIKOKU

Nagasaki

KYUSHU

OPERATION CORONET
March 1, 1946

First Army	Eighth Army	Tenth Army

OPERATION OLYMPIC
November 1, 1945

Sixth Army

Tanegashima

Amami

Okinawa

HONSHU

Shimonoseki Strait

Shimonoseki

Moji

Kokura

Inland Sea

Fukuoka

Iwo Jima

KYUSHU

0		100 miles
0		150 km

basic design of War Plan Orange. From late 1943 to August 1944, Nimitz struck across the Central Pacific via the Gilbert, Marshall, and Mariana Islands.

From these positions, the overwhelming air and sea forces of MacArthur and Nimitz converged to seize the Philippines, beginning at Leyte in October 1944. In January 1945, MacArthur's troops landed on the main Philippine island of Luzon, but Japanese forces, aiming to delay and pin down American forces, evaded a decisive battle. The one exception was Manila, where a Japanese admiral defied orders and conducted a house-by-house struggle that devastated the city. In concert with the savage fighting, Japanese soldiers and sailors unleashed a frenzy of murder and rapine upon the Filipino populace that, together with losses in the liberation effort, killed about 100,000 civilians—more than the loss in the soon-to-come Tokyo fire raid. Thereafter, MacArthur, with no legal warrant, liberated the rest of the Philippines. Meanwhile, Nimitz's forces targeted Iwo Jima in February 1945 and Okinawa in April.

Concurrent with these advances close to Japan, a series of decisions shaped the environment in which strategy for the ultimate defeat of Japan was being formed. In January 1943, American and British leaders assembled for the Casablanca Conference. There, Admiral Ernest J. King, the commander in chief of the United States Navy, stated that "the key to our successful attack on the Japanese homeland is the geographical position and manpower of China." During the first half of the Pacific war, considerable American effort went to bolstering China to fit this role, which, it should be noted, was motivated directly by the desire to keep American casualties down.

But it was a political decision, not a military one, at Casablanca that was to reverberate profoundly down to the very last minutes of the conflict. As early as May 1942, President Roosevelt had privately touted the concept of demanding the unconditional surrender of all the Axis powers, primarily because of the manner in which Hitler had brandished the "stab in the back" theory during his rise to power—that German soldiers in World War I were not beaten on the battlefield but were betrayed on the home front by leftists and Jews. Unconditional surrender was a simple and powerful slogan to mobilize public opinion, but it also contained (or became inextricably linked to) another message: never again. Americans of all stations were overwhelmingly convinced that the failure to reorder German society after World War I was the seed of the second world war in a generation, and they resolved not to make the mistake again. As the American historian Herbert Bix correctly notes: "[Unconditional surrender] never aimed at just smashing the fascist states. Its true objective was the military occupation and postwar reform—always the two together—of those states so that the philosophies of fascism and militarism could be uprooted and their societies democratized."

Before about fifty reporters at Casablanca, Roosevelt commented:

> I think we have all had it in our hearts and heads before, but I don't think that it has ever been put down on paper by the Prime Minister and myself, and that is the determination that peace can come to the world only by the total elimination of German and Japanese war power. . . . The elimination of German, Japanese and Italian war power means the unconditional surrender of Germany, Italy and Japan.

Roosevelt's later claim that this idea just "popped" into his mind at a press conference is clearly refuted by a trail of documents. These papers reflect negotiations by Churchill with his cabinet over whether the demand should explicitly exclude Italy, the better to secure her capitulation. No one appears to have contemplated the impact of this policy on Japan.

American and British leaders set the ultimate goal at Casablanca, but they fixed a timetable at Quebec in August 1943. During the one year since the launching in 1942 of a Pacific counteroffensive at Guadalcanal and on New Guinea, the total westward advance had totaled less than two hundred miles. "At [this] rate, one journalist snidely observed," notes Miller, "we would get to Tokyo in 1960." Admiral King's chief planner, Rear Admiral Charles M. ("Savvy") Cooke, proposed setting an objective of defeating Japan within one year of the end of the war with Germany. Harkening to the primordial anxieties of American strategists, Cooke argued that the resources to achieve this aim would be available; more important, it was fundamental for political purposes to maintain public support. Otherwise, the public would weary of war and demand a negotiated peace, which Cooke equated with defeat. His army colleagues agreed, and General George C. Marshall seconded, "forcing the issue." These arguments twanged a responsive chord in Churchill, who overruled his chiefs and committed his government likewise to Cooke's objective.

Concepts for the Ultimate Defeat of Japan

In the year after the Casablanca conference, American strategic planning had fundamentally veered from a final approach to Japan via China to one mounted from the Pacific. The timetable adopted at Quebec impelled planners to thresh out the character of the final, decisive operations. As early as April 1944, the Strategy Section of the Operations Division of the War Department pronounced a view that the Army maintained thereafter: Only invasion, not blockade and bombardment, could assure Japan's collapse.

As the time for decisions on these issues neared in mid-1944, the logic of dry staff papers confronted raw experience. In the European-Mediterranean theater and the Pacific, total American combat fatalities had doubled in seven months, from 62,092 between December 1941 and the end of 1943, to 63,182 between January and July 1944. But it was the character of the Pacific enemy, not just its capacity to inflict casualties, that was most sobering. Understanding the Imperial Army, remarked an American Army officer, was like "attempting to describe the other side of the moon." A later generation of Americans might gaze back at these events and see race as the pervasive motif, but while race was certainly present, it was something beyond race that distinguished the Imperial Army and Navy: their collective valor on a scale never surpassed. The Japanese "are the bravest people I have ever met," wrote John Masters, a British officer who fought them in Burma.

> In our armies, any of them, nearly every Japanese would have had a Congressional Medal [of Honor] or a Victoria Cross. It is the fashion to dismiss their courage as fanaticism, but this only begs the question. They believed in something, and they were willing to die for it, for any smallest detail that would help to achieve it. What else is bravery?

The first intimations that the Japanese would literally choose death over surrender—and not merely an elite warrior caste but the rank and file—came in August 1942 at Guadalcanal. After two small Imperial Navy island garrisons fought to virtual extinction, the Marines trapped and nearly annihilated a fresh Imperial Army contingent of about eight hundred men. A few Japanese escaped; only fifteen survived as prisoners, and twelve of them were wounded before capture. Major General Alexander Archer Vandegrift, the Marine commander, wrote:

> I have never heard or read of this kind of fighting. These people refuse to surrender. The wounded wait until men come up to examine them . . . and blow themselves and the other fellow to pieces with a hand grenade.

During 1943, the Japanese availed themselves of the opportunity of withdrawing units or survivors as the circumstances permitted at Guadalcanal, New Georgia, New Guinea, and Kiska. But in May 1943, at Attu in the Aleutians, with no evacuation feasible, the Japanese garrison of about 2,350 fought to the end; just 29 became prisoners of war, a fatality rate of

98.8 percent. In the Gilbert Islands during November 1943, the combatant Japanese forces at Tarawa, the Sasebo Seventh Special Naval Landing Force, counted 2,571 men on its rolls before the Marine landing. The only survivors were eight men captured alive, making a casualty rate of 99.7 percent. On adjacent Makin, of about three hundred Japanese combat troops, exactly one was taken alive. At the Marshalls in February 1944, on Roi-Namur the Japanese lost 3,472 and only 51 were captured, a fatality rate of 98.5 percent. At Kwajalein, the Japanese garrison lost 4,938, with only 79 taken prisoner, a fatality rate of 98.4 percent.

But the seizure of Saipan in the Marianas, which began on June 15 and ended on July 9, administered a still more powerful shock. As was by now the norm, the garrison of nearly 30,000 Japanese soldiers and sailors fought to the death; only 921 (3 percent) were taken prisoner. Of the 71,034 officers and men of the American landing force, 14,111 became casualties (including 3,426 killed), nearly 20 percent. But on Saipan the Americans also encountered for the first time a significant population of Japanese civilians, numbering at least 20,000. By August 5, the total of these who surrendered to internment numbered only 10,258. Then, and for decades thereafter, it was believed that upward of another 10,000 chose death to surrender, with the peak of frenzied extinction at Marpi Point on July 11, two days after the fighting officially ended. There, hundreds of civilians spurned invitations to surrender from Marines and even pleas from fellow Japanese, who described the good treatment they experienced by surrendering. In a carnival of death that shocked even battle-hardened Marines, whole families waded into the sea to drown together or huddled to blow themselves up with grenades; parents tossed their children off cliffs before leaping to join them in death. An officer on a minesweeper reported:

> Part of the area is so congested with floating bodies we simply can't avoid running them down. I remember one woman in khaki trousers and a white polka dot blouse, with her black hair streaming in the water. I'm afraid every time I see that kind of blouse, I'll think of that girl. There was another one, nude, who had drowned herself while giving birth to a baby. The baby's head had entered this world, but that was all of him. A small boy of four or five had drowned with his arm firmly clenched around the neck of a Jap soldier; the two bodies rocked crazily in the waves.

Why this mass suicide of civilians? Because, noted the American historian John Dower, Japanese political and military authorities inoculated them with the terror that "the Americans would rape, torture and murder them, and that it was more honorable to take their own lives."

Recent scholarship has demonstrated that the actual number of suicides probably did not much exceed one thousand. But the image of mass civilian suicides proved potent, and only a few days after the slaughter on Marpi Point there was a key shift in Allied policy. At a meeting on July 14 of the Combined Chiefs of Staff (the most senior commanders of the U.S. and British armed forces), General Marshall explained that

> as a result of recent operations in the Pacific it was now clear to the United States Chiefs of Staff that, in order to finish the war with the Japanese quickly, it will be necessary to invade the industrial heart of Japan.

Following Marshall's motion, the new directive adopted by the Combined Chiefs of Staff redefined the ultimate aims as:

> To force the unconditional surrender of Japan by: (1) Lowering Japanese ability and will to resist by establishing sea and air blockades, conducting intensive air bombardment, and destroying Japanese air and naval strength. (2) Invading and seizing objectives in the industrial heart of Japan.

This statement was formally approved by Roosevelt and Churchill at their second meeting in Quebec in September 1944.

At this same time, sobering thoughts about the prospects for the final defeat of Japan emerged in a paper generated by the Joint Strategic Survey Committee of the Joint Chiefs of Staff:

> Our great superiority over the Japanese rests in our capacity to produce and to employ more effectively and in overwhelming strength machines of war—primarily naval vessels and aircraft. Enemy strength rests in his land forces, some 3,500,000 strong. In our Saipan operation it cost approximately one American killed and several wounded to exterminate seven Japanese soldiers. On this basis it might cost us a half million American lives and many times that number in wounded to exterminate the Japanese ground forces that conceivably could be employed against us in the home islands.*

---

* D. M. Giangreco argues that "this 'Saipan ratio' set the standard for strategic level casualty projections in the Pacific," but this argument is deeply flawed. While Marshall may have referred to the "Saipan ratio" subsequently in 1944, nowhere in the later, complete versions of the planning considerations within the 924 series (i.e., 924/5, 924/8, 924/15, etc.) does the "Saipan ratio" appear. When the JCS did adopt 924/15, setting out the strategic considerations for a combined blockade and invasion strategy in April 1945, it addressed invasion casualty projections not with reference to the "Saipan ratio" but in terms of rates of U.S. casualties per thousand men per day developed by the Surgeon General of the Army, as will be discussed in chapter 9. D. M. Giangreco, "Casualty Projections for the U.S. Invasions of Japan, 1945–46: Planning and Policy Implications," *The Journal of Military History* 61 (spring 1997): 535.

Contemplation of the increasingly daunting prospects for the final assault led inevitably to consideration of the roles other nations would play. In mid-1944, the British proposed supplying six divisions and two British-trained Dutch divisions for the final assault on Japan. The British also offered a force of forty squadrons of Lancaster heavy bombers to be operational by October 1945. Half the squadrons were to comprise tankers to refuel the other half, so that the Lancasters could achieve a radius of 1,500 miles. Ultimately, the question of the location of bases relegated the project to efforts to install ten squadrons on Okinawa as the war ended, at which time there existed an agreement "in principle" for participation of a British Commonwealth land force of three to five divisions, accompanied "if possible" by a small tactical air force. These elements, however, could not be available before the spring of 1946.

During this same period, American planners abandoned any remaining illusions about the will or ability of China to participate in operations against the Home Islands. The bubbling dissatisfaction with Chiang Kai-shek's regime came to a head in the summer of 1944 as the Imperial Army plunged deeper into the interior of the nation, inflicting a new calamity on the Chinese people and ruthlessly exposing what appeared to be the paltry results of the American investment in the Chinese armies. By early 1945, all the blooms had fallen from Admiral King's original vision of China having a pivotal role in bringing the war to an end. As one blunt Navy paper observed: "The Central Government [of China] seems to have adopted the attitude since the turn of the tide of the war that the U.S. will win the war anyway, so why worry?"

As the value of China declined, the importance of Soviet participation rose. The American burden would be much relieved if the Red Army could tie down and defeat the vast Japanese Kwantung Army in Manchuria, keeping its formidable legions away from invasion beaches. As a September 1943 paper of the Joint War Plans Committee of the Joint Chiefs of Staff noted, Soviet entry was "essential to the prompt and crushing defeat of Japan at far less cost to the United States and Great Britain." The committee also envisioned the use of Soviet bases for American and Soviet air attacks, but none of the American planners appears to have contemplated a Soviet assault on the Japanese Home Islands.

Josef Stalin promised Soviet entry into the war at the Tehran Conference with Roosevelt and Churchill in November 1943, but major questions persisted about whether and under what circumstances he would redeem this pledge. During discussions in Moscow in October 1944, Stalin declared that the Soviet Union would enter the Pacific war three months after Germany's defeat, and he agreed to permit the establishment of American strategic air-force bases in the Soviet Maritime Territories and Kamchatka, as well as a naval base at an indeterminate time. As the purchase price for these grants, Stalin presented a huge tabulation of supply demands, which were met.

While few doubted that Stalin would honor his pledge, Allied officers obtained extremely little coordinating information from their Soviet counterparts. More disturbing still was the fact that the Soviets had reneged on earlier promises to grant their allies air or naval bases in the Maritime Territories. With a second great conference with Stalin set for Yalta in February 1945, planners at the Joint Chiefs of Staff, on their own initiative, prepared a paper that concluded that while Japan could be defeated without Soviet participation, the Soviet Union's own interests in the Far East would compel its entry. This paper culminated in a statement of principles that held that the United States desired early Soviet entry for two purposes: containing Japanese forces in northern China and Manchuria to prevent their participation in defense of the Homeland; and conducting air operations against the Japanese Homeland and lines of communication. The Joint Chiefs of Staff formally adopted this paper, thereby putting them on record as urging Soviet entry into the war, and made these views known to the President.

At Yalta, Stalin raised the "political conditions" of Soviet entry into the war. These consisted primarily of a list of spoils the Soviets expected, which he represented as necessary to "explain" to the Soviet people why there must be war with Japan. Basically, Stalin sought to reestablish the Russian position as it had existed prior to the Russo-Japanese War of 1904–1905. The lower half of Sakhalin Island was to return to Soviet control, as were the Kuril Islands. The Soviets were to secure leases for the ports of Dairen and Port Arthur and for the railways built by Russia, specifically the line from Vladivostok to Dairen. Stalin pledged not to interfere with Chinese sovereignty over Manchuria and requested a recognition of the status quo in Outer Mongolia. Roosevelt declined to submit these proposals to Chiang Kai-shek, but did insert a proviso that the generalissimo's concurrence was necessary as concerned the ports, railways, and status of Outer Mongolia. Otherwise, with very minor changes and little discussion, these terms were ratified by Roosevelt, Churchill, and Stalin on February 11.

Despite the fact that the ink was well dried on a commitment to invade Japan and that Soviet entry into the Pacific war was seemingly secured, the Joint Chiefs of Staff continued an intense review of strategy deep into the spring. Their attention fell upon the substantial gap in scheduled operations between Okinawa in March and the draft plan for a two-phase invasion of Japan commencing with Kyushu in November, followed by Honshu in March 1946. For weeks, planners assessed and reassessed both "intermediate" operations (those before the invasion of Honshu) and potential "contributory" operations (envisioned as efforts to secure additional positions to enhance the blockade and bombardment operations prior to the outright invasion).

Korea, China, Hokkaido, and Kyushu became the focus of discussions for intermediate operations. Geography and the potential for "major, costly and protracted land campaigns against large enemy ground forces" ruled out Korea and China. Hokkaido, either in lieu of Kyushu as an intermediate operation or as a contributory one, earned the advocacy of the Army Air Force. The Navy countered that such an operation would likely preclude an attack on Kyushu, which offered a much superior strategic position, and would throw away the advantages of the bases already secured from the Philippines to Okinawa.

While this renewed analysis served to confirm the choice of Kyushu as the intermediate operation, no contributory operation was authorized, despite Admiral King's vigorous advocacy for a landing on the China coast. "The most significant single factor which will restrict our capability to conduct contributory operations . . . ," noted one study, "is the lack of sufficient forces available in the Pacific prior to redeployment following the defeat of Germany." Quite simply, unless Germany capitulated by early 1945, there would be insufficient resources for any additional major operation between Okinawa and Kyushu. After the German Ardennes offensive in December 1944 thoroughly subdued American expectations for an early end to hostilities in Europe, nothing in the following months could move the tide in King's favor.

The Joint Chiefs of Staff also wrestled with the thorny question of Pacific commands for the final campaigns. With the prospect for the first time of really large-scale land battles, the Army pressed for a single ground-forces commander not under Navy control. This, of course, would be MacArthur, who, coincidentally with the capture of most of Luzon, had simultaneously secured virtually all of the territory originally delegated to his command in early 1942. General Marshall forced this issue at the end of February, and, although the bickering lingered into April, the final agreement reflected the Army plan. There would be a Commander in Chief, U.S. Army Forces, Pacific to parallel the longstanding role filled by Nimitz as Commander in Chief, Pacific Fleet.

Even before the command arrangements were settled, Washington turned to the two Pacific theater commanders for their judgments on final operations. On the day before President Roosevelt's death, April 11, 1945,

King formally solicited Nimitz's views on a strategy for the ultimate defeat of Japan. King posited three basic alternatives: (1) encirclement, meaning blockade and bombardment; (2) invasion; and (3) both, pursuing encirclement while preparing fully for invasion. Nimitz, who had pushed strongly at the beginning of the year for an encirclement strategy in order to avoid "enormous casualties" in an invasion, replied on April 28. "Until we are able to invade Japan with assurance of success," he advised, "we should continue to encircle and isolate" Japan by landings on the China coast. The China incursion, argued Nimitz, would ensure Russian entry into the war. "However," he indicated, "I am in agreement with the invasion of Kyushu at the earliest date as the way to achieve decisive victory."

Running in parallel with this exchange were messages between Marshall and MacArthur. On April 12, Marshall alerted MacArthur to the forthcoming strategy discussions but suggested the choice would be one of only two options. While blockade and bombardment might avoid the high casualties of an invasion, particularly in light of the "Japanese reaction to a landing on the sacred soil of Japan," noted Marshall, the "other school" of thought favored invasion, contingent on Russian entry into the war. This second opinion was based on experience in the Philippines and "even Okinawa" that with deployment of full American combat power and maneuver, casualties could be kept to "acceptable losses."

MacArthur's response on April 20 broadened the choices to three. The first was to encircle Japan, apply maximum airpower, and then attack Kyushu followed by Honshu, or perhaps make a direct thrust to Honshu. The second option was to blockade and bombard, and the third was to attack Kyushu, install an air garrison, and then go to Honshu. MacArthur favored the third option. He believed it permitted full application of superior American combat power on land, at sea, and in the air; he estimated that Kyushu would be lightly defended in 1945; and he maintained that this sequence would place American forces in a position for a decisive operation in 1946. He identified logistics as the most critical impediment but believed that by pooling all resources in the Pacific, the support could be found in all categories save one: hospital beds, of which there would remain a shortage of thirty-six thousand. Thus, both Nimitz and MacArthur had endorsed Kyushu, but Nimitz had not cast a vote for Honshu.

On April 25, the Joint Staff Planners submitted to the Joint Chiefs of Staff a comprehensive study of Pacific strategy that represented the culmination of the thinking of senior officers concerning the end of the war. The planners did not neglect fundamentals and observed that it "appear[ed]" that Allied war aims encompassed the restoration of territories seized by Japan, the "creation of conditions which will insure that Japan will not again become a menace to the peace and security of the world," and the "eventual emergence" of a Japanese government that would "respect the rights of other states and Japan's international obligations." "The agreed strategy and national policy," they noted, "is that the accomplishment of these aims is to be brought about by unconditional surrender."

The planners frankly questioned, however, whether unconditional surrender "can be brought about by any means." "What can be accomplished," they emphasized,

> is decisive military defeat and the results equivalent to unconditional surrender, similar to the present situation in Germany. In no case to date in this war have organized Japanese units surrendered. The concept of "unconditional surrender" is foreign to the Japanese nature. Therefore, "unconditional surrender" should be defined in terms understandable to the Japanese, who must be convinced that destruction or national suicide is not implied. This could be done by an announcement on a governmental level of a "declaration of intentions" which would tell the Japanese what their future holds. Once convinced of the inevitability of defeat, it is possible that *a government could be formed in Japan that would sign and could enforce a surrender instrument.*
>
> Unless a definition of unconditional surrender can be given which is acceptable to the Japanese, there is no alternative to annihilation and no prospect that the threat of absolute defeat will bring about capitulation [emphasis added].

Given their doubts about Japanese surrender, the planners believed a campaign of only blockade and bombardment would likely produce nothing better than a negotiated peace, if that, and if the blockade failed, an invasion might still be called for. On the other hand, an invasion could be carried through to absolute defeat, if necessary. "Therefore, the invasion of Japan is considered the most suitable strategy to accomplish unconditional surrender or ultimate defeat."

The planners extracted from intelligence estimates more evidence favoring invasion. By December 1945, Japanese air and naval forces would lack the capacity for anything other than an all-out suicide defense, Japan's resources would be ebbing drastically, and ground forces would total two million men in thirty field and fourteen depot (training) divisions. The planners fixed the potential of the Japanese to reinforce the Home Islands from Asia at a rate of only one division per month. Calculations by a separate committee demonstrated that an air campaign would achieve a "situation necessary for invasion" by December 1, but that air attacks would thereafter achieve "little significance."

In either a campaign of blockade and bombardment or one of invasion, the planners found that China was no longer a factor, which permitted the United States to evade "becoming embroiled in Chinese internal political problems." This conclusion led to another significant one:

> Because of our estimated ability to interdict Japanese movement between the Asiatic mainland and Japan proper, early Russian entry into the war against Japan and attendant containing of the Kwantung army is no longer necessary to make invasion feasible. . . .
>
> If Russia enters the war her forces will probably be the first into Manchuria. This will raise the question of introducing at least token U.S. forces into China.

Further, they estimated that a campaign of blockade and bombardment would demand the commitment of twenty-eight divisions, whereas the Homeland invasion would require thirty-six divisions. While the former was projected to end the war by the fall of 1946, invasion might conclude it by June 1946.

Finally, the planners recommended the following "Optimum Strategy":

(a) application of full and unremitting pressure against Japan by strategic bombing and carrier raids to reduce war-making potential and morale in preparation for invasion;
(b) use air and naval forces to tighten the blockade, to include severing communication with Korea;
(c) limit contributory operations to only those essential as prerequisites to invasion;
(d) invade Japan at the earliest practicable date;
(e) occupy such industrial areas as required to bring about unconditional surrender and to establish absolute military control.

The Joint Chiefs of Staff adopted this paper as the basis for planning the final campaigns, and it provided the foundation for the formal directive issued on May 25 to MacArthur and Nimitz to invade Kyushu with a target date of November 1, 1945.

The Joint Chiefs of Staff paper and the May 25 order can be interpreted two ways. On the one hand, the fact that the Army checked King's preference for a contributory operation on the China coast and installed an invasion as the capstone of the strategy, in contravention of the fundamental premises of War Plan Orange, can be viewed as a triumph of argument and leadership by the Army, particularly by Marshall's chief planner, Brigadier

General George Lincoln. On the other hand, there is strong evidence that the Army secured a far less favorable bargain. It was certain that the blockade and bombardment strategy would run at least a half-year course, but there was no absolute guarantee of a landing on Japanese shores. Admiral King gave blunt notice of his real thinking in a memorandum at the end of April to his colleagues on the Joint Chiefs of Staff:

> It is clear that, if the invasion of Kyushu is to be undertaken on 1 November, a directive to that effect must be issued now in order that the necessary preparations can go forward. It is my belief that, if such a directive is issued and the operation is given top priority, the necessary resources can be assembled. . . . If at a later date, such as August or September, 1945, the Chiefs of Staff should decide against the Kyushu operation, they will then be in a position to exercise the choice.

King's highly contingent agreement to prepare for but not necessarily execute an invasion challenged the whole strategic design. But King's actual stance on the invasion forms only part of the pervasive misunderstanding of American strategy. The April 25 staff paper identified the most sobering specter not as an invasion but as the prospect of no organized surrender of the Japanese armed forces. The invasion, in fact, was justified not simply because it offered the chance to obtain a general capitulation but because it, unlike the program of blockade and bombardment, would position the United States to enforce unconditional surrender against unyielding Japanese legions scattered across the Homeland—and perhaps across Asia and the Pacific. The cost of an invasion paled in light of this. Army aviators, however, like King believed that blockade and bombardment could secure general surrender and were striving mightily to make their vision a reality.

3

From Zeppelins to B-29s

"An absolutely devastating, exterminating attack
by very heavy bombers"

Dreams and Nightmares of Air Warfare

In August 1917, a British committee reported on defense against the rudimentary air attacks mounted with zeppelin airships and Gotha bombers on England. Its chairman, Jan Christian Smuts, acknowledged that

> the day may not be far off when aerial operations, with their devastation of enemy lands and destruction of industrial and populous centers on a vast scale, may become the principal operations of war, to which the older forms of military and naval operations may become secondary and subordinate.

After the Great War, aviators around the world were stimulated, in some cases to intoxication, by the vision of independent airpower supplanting ground and naval forces as the decisive arm. The leading visionaries included Air Marshal H. M. Trenchard in Britain, Count Caproni di Taliedo and General Giulio Douhet in Italy, and General William "Billy" Mitchell in the United States. In a typical example of the exuberant declarations of these proponents, Mitchell observed in 1926 that "there has never been anything that has come which has changed war the way the advent of air power has."

While one vision enticed aviators, another equally repelled them: the nightmare slaughter in the trench stalemate of the Western Front from 1914 to 1918. Why, asked the aviators, should war be a protracted series of indecisive ground battles with the bloodshed vastly disproportionate to the results obtained? Mitchell asserted flatly that bombing "vital centers" (he meant cities) to quickly end a war was "more humane than the present methods of blowing up people to bits by cannon projectiles or butchering them with bayonets."

The aviators imagined the new warfare from the cockpits of bombers soaring through pristine skies, unleashing bombs on strategic "targets" deep in the enemy heartland. As to what those targets should be, the theorists divided—broadly and by no means cleanly—between those who would drop bombs on armament industries and military facilities and those, like Douhet, who would drop bombs, filled with high explosives or poison gas, on the population to shatter enemy "morale." Civilians and their political leaders imagined the new warfare from the earth, a nightmare of huddled fear beneath the shriek and blast of the bombs, and perhaps the curling whorls of poison gas.

The 1930s disabused many of the hope that revulsion about the puny air attacks of the Great War would preclude repetition on a broad scale in a renewed conflict. In 1935, Italian forces deployed aerial firepower, including poison gas, against Ethiopian forces. But it was a raid on the Basque town of Guernica during the Spanish Civil War by German airmen on behalf of Francisco Franco's Nationalists that became emblematic of "what modern war means," in the words of a *New York Times* writer. Luridly exaggerated newspaper accounts, and perhaps above all Pablo Picasso's most famous painting, conveyed the image of the annihilating power of aerial bombardment: ruthlessly aimed at the symbolic cradle of the Basque people and indiscriminately striking down half the town's population of 5,000 ("officially" calculated as 1,654 dead and 889 wounded).

The facts were far more prosaic. Only forty-three German aircraft dumped a paltry fifty tons of high explosive, incendiary, and shrapnel bombs into Guernica on April 26, 1937. The German commanders were oblivious to Guernica's symbolism, and although they did not purposefully set out to spread terror, they were indifferent to the inevitable significant civilian casualties (actually about three hundred killed) when bombs fell in a built-up area.

Nevertheless, in the short run, the potent imagery of these events worked to the advantage of Hitler. The prospect that Germany possessed the will and capability to obliterate whole cities intimidated many Europeans. Nor were the Germans alone. When Japan entered its seemingly endless war with China in 1937, bombers wearing Rising Sun insignia attacked Chungking, Chiang Kai-shek's second capital, as well as other population centers, producing international outcry at the subsequent indelible visual depictions of slaughtered civilians. But in the long run, the Germans and the Japanese were to pay dearly for changing the norms of warfare.

With the outbreak of European hostilities in September 1939, a series of events further endorsed the impression that German airmen struck routinely at "morale" targets, as the Germans themselves dabbled in terror attacks. Warsaw received a severe bombardment prior to Polish capitulation, though what fraction of the estimated forty thousand civilian deaths in the city can be attributed to air attack is unknown. When the onslaught in the West began in May 1940, German forces rapidly overwhelmed the Dutch, but while surrender negotiations were in progress, a single German bomber wing attacked Rotterdam, killing eight hundred and making eighty thousand homeless. The Dutch commander surrendered the following day, explicitly citing a fear of other cities sharing Rotterdam's fate. One historian noted that the Germans "were not hesitant to note the connection."

American airmen followed all these developments with intense interest. The United States Army Air Corps Tactical School had examined alternative targets and strategies in the interwar period and settled upon an established doctrine of daylight precision attacks on armament and essential industries. This doctrine rested upon what proved to be wildly optimistic expectations about bombing accuracy and destructiveness under operational conditions. Air Force officers grasped that even precision attacks would result in death or wounds to thousands of civilians, but they rejected an explicit strategy of attacks on enemy urban populations. With the outbreak of World War II, Army Air Forces officers drafted plans that called for sequential attacks on 154 specific targets to first neutralize German air defenses and then progressively destroy a series of primary targets involving electric power, petroleum supply, and transportation (railroads and canals). A blunt effort to topple the German state by attacking cities appeared only as an option "as German morale begins to crack."

Between August 1942, when the new strategic-bombing force, christened the Eighth Air Force, commenced operations over continental Europe, and the autumn of 1943, American bombing theory intersected with rigorous reality. It required far longer to establish a numerically strong and technically proficient strategic-bombardment force in Europe than Army Air Forces officers expected, and for months losses were many and results few. Moreover, they discovered the two great forces arrayed against the bombers: weather and fierce air defenses. Northern Europe afforded only a scant number of days with even marginal weather conditions over both bases and targets, often four to six hundred miles away. Worse yet, Germany's technically advanced and resourceful defenses exacted a toll on nearly every mission into the skies of the Third Reich. By the fall of 1943, the faith of Army Air Forces officers in daylight precision bombardment was shaken, and they became receptive to alternative strategies.

The Royal Air Force had commenced the war operating under much the same precepts as the Army Air Forces. Within a few months, however, the attrition inflicted by German defenses demanded that the RAF choose between abandoning strategic attack or shifting to night operations. The instinctive election by airmen to continue operations at night received emphatic endorsement from other officers and political leaders, particularly Churchill, for two reasons. Public sentiment supplied the justification of reprisals for German attacks; grand strategy supplied the rationale. When "I look around," wrote Churchill on July 8, 1940, "to see how we can win the war I see that there is only one sure path . . . and that is an absolutely devastating, exterminating attack by very heavy bombers from this country upon the Nazi homeland."

But the idea of night precision attack on a target as small as an individual factory proved a chimera. A chilling report in August 1941 documented that only about one bomb in five landed within even a five-mile radius of the designated target. If Bomber Command could not hit what it would, it would hit what it could. That meant an "exterminating" rain of high explosives and incendiaries on urban centers to destroy civilian "morale"—"a cosmetic word for massacre," observed John Terraine. This path, it must always be remembered, had been literally and figuratively blazed by the Axis on Chungking, Rotterdam, London, Coventry, and elsewhere. The leader of Bomber Command, Air Marshal Arthur Harris, pursued this strategy with ruthless zeal. He also fully exploited new technological developments in radar and radio aids that permitted concentrated nocturnal blows at urban targets. Bomber Command displayed its new, spectacular capabilities in July and August 1943, when a series of raids on Hamburg started the first firestorm in recorded history, which killed nearly 45,000 human beings, all but about eight hundred of them civilians. RAF losses were 100 aircraft and 552 airmen.

Eighth Air Force bombers joined the Battle of Hamburg with two strikes at the city's shipyards by day. These raids killed fewer than 1 percent of all the Hamburg residents who died in the battle. But they inflicted little damage on war production at a relatively steep cost: 16 aircraft and 150 crew. Then in August and October 1943, successive American raids attacking a classic precision target—the Schweinfurt ball-bearing factory—produced totally unacceptable losses: 60 of 376 B-17s in August and 60 of 320 in October.

These events brought the American effort to a crossroads. The nation, with the enthusiastic endorsement of President Roosevelt, had made a fundamental commitment in 1940–1942 to a grand strategy that deliberately constrained the size of the ground army in favor of heavy emphasis on vast air and naval forces and the production of armaments for the Allies. By October 1943, those basic decisions could not be reversed without a tremendous and wholly unacceptable lengthening of the duration of the war. The momentum generated by this investment is exemplified in the enormous growth of the striking power of the Eighth Air Force in Europe: Where 320 bombers represented its maximum effort in October 1943, by March 1944 it could loft 730 and by May over 1,000. Army Air Forces leaders chose not to abandon the daylight bomber offensive but to scrap sole reliance on visually aimed bombing. Radar aids permitted operations on many days where weather barred visual bombing. It also led to many more noncombatant casualties. The Army Air Forces officially sanctioned radar bombing in November 1943 and "without ever publicly or privately admitting it," recorded one historian, "abandoned its unquestioning faith in prewar bombing doctrines." By the end of the war, Eighth Air Force bombers had aimed 343,185 tons of bombs visually and 343,966 tons by radar.

Lessons

While practical experience defined realistic capabilities, it also appeared to teach "lessons" that further leached away the American doctrine of selective attack. Intense bombing of the island of Pantelleria in the Mediterranean in 1943 led to the surrender of its Italian garrison without an invasion. "The human mind cannot adjust itself to bombardment on an ascending scale," announced Lieutenant General Carl A. Spaatz, commander of the American air units. Aviators, with the backing of their military and civilian superiors, decided to try this technique on a wide scale for large stakes: the surrender of the Italian state. After attacks on Naples, American bombers went to Rome on July 19. The attack was a "textbook example of precision bombing" that inflicted severe damage on its intended targets, railway yards. But some bombs still fell outside the targets and killed 700 and wounded 1,600 civilians in the Eternal City. Six days later, Benito Mussolini was deposed; a little over six weeks later, Italy surrendered. The obvious "lesson" was that "morale" bombing could work.

The next step was to apply the Rome lesson to Germany's Balkan allies. Between November 1943 and late 1944, the Army Air Forces dispatched a series of sporadic, though explicit, attacks on civilians in Bulgaria and Romania. These raids unleashed only a minuscule amount of bomb tonnage in the total scheme of things and, while they killed a good many civilians, this vacillating and feeble effort did not knock the Axis allies out of the war.

The prelude to the Normandy invasion produced a far more momentous turn in the evolution of Army Air Forces doctrine. Like the RAF, the Army Air Forces sought from 1942 to the spring of 1944 to minimize civilian casualties from bombing in German-occupied Allied countries. Despite earnest efforts, however, inevitable errors led to thousands of civilian deaths that antagonized the very people for whom the Allies were fighting and provided grist for German propaganda. One particularly egregious incident occurred on April 5, 1943, in an Eighth Air Force raid on an aircraft-engine plant in Antwerp. The mission left the factory untouched, but 936 civilians—209 of them children—were killed.

The fundamental policy of minimizing risk to Allied citizens under occupation was challenged when a British scientist, Solly Zuckerman, convinced General Eisenhower and his British deputy, Air Marshal Arthur Tedder, to adopt the Transportation Plan to knock out railway facilities prior to the invasion of France in order to impede or prevent German reinforcements from moving to the battle area. This proposal provoked strong opposition. Some critics argued that it would kill twenty to forty thousand French and Belgian civilians. With the backing of Roosevelt and over Churchill's protests, Eisenhower ordered his air commanders to carry out the plan. Fortunately, actual Allied civilian losses were far fewer than the dire forecasts. By one accounting, they totaled approximately 4,750; almost certainly they numbered no more than 12,000.

One of the major arguments that had been arrayed against the Transportation Plan was that it would divert American strategic bombers from a campaign air leaders believed would force German surrender without invasion: the Oil Plan. The Americans commenced the Oil Plan on May 12, 1944, which German Armaments Minister Albert Speer later described as "the day the technological war was decided." Despite Speer's hyperbole, the Oil Plan, which marked synthetic-oil plants for destruction, produced great but not decisive military success.

The plan, however, was not the only method U.S. and British air leaders pursued to compel a German capitulation by aerial assault. Evidence found by Zuckerman in Paris confirming the startling effects of the Transportation Plan on the French railway system led to a similar attack on the German railway system, the Reichsbahn. These missions, beginning in September 1944, aimed particularly at marshaling yards, the critical nodes in the system. The campaign absolutely devastated the German war economy as a whole by early 1945. But these attacks took longer than expected to succeed, and at first the evidence of their effects was weak, disputable, or, as for example when the Germans launched the Battle of the Bulge, apparently indicative of failure.

From approximately mid-1944 to the end of the war, the Oil and Transportation Plans competed for top priority in a series of targeting directives governing efforts of the British and American strategic air forces. During this interval, increasingly refined target-locating and -marking techniques permitted British Bomber Command to achieve—at times—astounding precision in night attacks. By contrast, equipment limitations and bad weather channeled American bombers into a pattern that significantly increased noncombatant casualties. Technical and logistical considerations constrained Germany to situate synthetic-oil-generation plants far from urban areas. Marshaling yards, however, invariably abutted major metropolitan clusters. The available radar-bombing aids could not locate even the relatively sprawling metallic mass of an oil plant but could identify a city. With only a handful of days per month that permitted visual-bombing conditions, General Spaatz realized that every one must be dedicated to oil targets. By necessity, transportation targets then became the routine objective for radar efforts on the far more numerous poor-weather days each month.

Before either the oil or the transportation attacks reached their strides, the Germans initiated attacks with pilotless, jet-propelled robot bombs—the V-1s—in an indiscriminate barrage against London that loosened any remaining British restraints concerning the use of air weapons. (Churchill seriously insisted on considering the use of poison gas for retaliation against the various "V" weapons.) Some British air leaders reverted to concepts of terminating the war by even more comprehensive terror raids against civilians. One such plan secured the code name Thunderclap: a plan to "saturat[e] the core of the Nazi capital with so many bombs that no one could imagine escaping death."

Under this British plan, attacks would be made around the clock and involve bombers of both nations, with the avowed purpose of changing the mental state of the German high command and securing surrender before Germany disintegrated and guerrilla warfare commenced. But some Americans believed a disproportionate share of the saturating would be done by their bombers, and that Thunderclap would succeed only after causing stupendous loss to ordinary civilians. One reviewer branded Thunderclap's real aim as "retaliation and intimidation for the future." Thus, American planners objected explicitly to pure "terror" bombing but acquiesced in operational techniques that guaranteed large losses among noncombatants. Spaatz's biographer observed: "Apparently, it was acceptable to attack German civilians if they lived in cities with military targets, but not acceptable to make German civilians targets in and of themselves." Ultimately, Thunderclap was postponed not on moral grounds but because of the inability to assemble a huge fighter force to cover the bombers.

With Thunderclap in abeyance, General Henry H. Arnold ordered the Army Air Forces to develop a near cousin, code-named Clarion. This, too, involved a strike at civilian morale, but not quite so crudely as Thunderclap. It envisioned roving flights of bombers and fighters saturating all of Germany with strikes at military targets, "giving every citizen a chance to witness the strength of Allied air power." Initially, weather ruled out Clarion and several concurrent schemes, permitting time for further reflection on both political and military objectives. Some officers were concerned that Clarion and Thunderclap would so embitter the German populace as to lay seeds of future strife. Secretary of War Stimson objected as well, but when President Roosevelt signed an authorization for what became the United States Strategic Bombing Survey to analyze comprehensively the effects of airpower, the charter carried within it implicit sanction for attacks to terrorize civilians.

In December 1944, the shocking surprise German attack that resulted in the Battle of the Bulge alarmed Allied policy makers and generated efforts to seek out yet another abrupt end to the war through airpower. A late January 1945 joint Anglo-American list of targets continued to give priority to oil on days of adequate visual weather, but second on the list now were Berlin, Leipzig, Dresden, and "associated cities," for days of bad weather. Transportation attacks slipped to third place. Proponents advertised the attacks on Berlin and cities in eastern Germany as support for Soviet ground armies, although it was acknowledged that in addition to showing Allied willingness to assist, they could caution the Soviets with their might. One senior Army Air Forces general protested that this new list effectively moved "unequivocally into the business of area bombardment of congested civil populations."

On February 3, 1945, 937 B-17s hit Berlin with 2,266 tons of bombs. Since the attack was not systematically followed up, it was not pure Thunderclap, and American commanders insisted that actual military objectives were designated as targets, not just the city center. Later that month, the new policy gave birth to the most controversial air operation of the European war. In an attack on the night of February 13–14, Bomber Command ignited a firestorm in Dresden with a raid by 805 aircraft that dropped 1,478 tons of high explosives and 1,182 tons of incendiaries. In these flames it is believed that as many as sixty thousand people died, almost all civilians. Two successive American attacks on Dresden's railway yards followed in which a total of 521 bombers released 1,232 tons of explosives. Their fighter escorts swooped down to strafe roads, packed with civilian refugees, so as to "add to the chaos." The U.S. raids swelled the toll, but unquestionably the firestorm inflicted by far the greatest slaughter.

Plans for Clarion were now activated, with adjustments, and on February 22 and 23 thousands of Army Air Forces and Royal Air Force bombers and fighters executed massive low-level bombing and strafing attacks against transportation and targets of opportunity. The Eighth Air Force alone on February 22 struck forty-one road and rail targets in 1,372 bomber and 817 fighter sorties that unleashed 3,895 tons of bombs. On the night after the official end of Clarion, February 23–24, Bomber Command mounted its sole raid of the war on Pforzheim. Coming in low at eight thousand feet, 380 aircraft released 1,825 tons in 22 minutes, leveling 83 percent of the city, a single-raid proportion exceeded only by the Japanese city of Toyama. In the fire and explosions, at least seventeen thousand Germans perished, the third-highest single-raid total for the war in Europe.

Allied bombing killed at least 300,000, and perhaps as many as 593,000, German civilians. Thus, wrote historian Richard Overy, "the most striking moral paradox of the war years was the willingness of ostensibly liberal states to engage in the deliberate killing of hundreds of thousands of enemy civilians from the air." From 1942 onward, British Bomber Command practiced ever more sophisticated fire-raising techniques that produced the majority of this toll. Hamburg, Dresden, and Pforzheim represented peak achievements, not aberrations. And while official U.S. Army Air Forces policy in the European theater remained selective precision attack, from late 1943 the precision was honored primarily only by the designation of an aiming point, virtually always a legitimate military target. Defenders of American bombing policy point correctly to where the bombs were aimed to distinguish this policy from the British and Axis ones, but critics speak with reason about where too many of the bombs landed. It is fair to say that blind bombing by radar aids, a method employed for about half the tonnage dropped, lurched close to simple "area," "morale," or flat "terror" bombing; operations such as the small series of attacks aimed at civilians in Bulgaria and Romania, and Clarion, though a very slim fraction of the total bomb tonnage, crossed the line.

The reasons for this massive application of aerial firepower were multiple and cumulative. The whole train of events was initiated by the wanton bombing of civilians by Axis nations, which first defied the attempt between the wars to proscribe indiscriminate bombing. But the Axis reaped the whirlwind in another way now too easily overlooked. Ever more distant generations casually assume the inevitability of Allied triumph. From this it is but a short step to a presumption that contemporary leaders foresaw the outcome and thus felt free to calibrate the amount and type of destruction required to defeat the Axis. The reality is that Allied leaders keenly sensed the contingency of these events. Secretary of War Stimson, an exemplar of unflappable determination, found the Battle of the Bulge, which began in December 1944, a thoroughly sobering shock to Allied confidence on a par with the attack on Pearl Harbor. Allied leaders were further seared by the knowledge of how near the Axis had come to triumph. As Max Hastings, a student of Bomber Command, wrote, "At no time after the fall of France did the Allied warlords consider restricting the bomber offensive for moral reasons." That American civilian leaders—as well as Arnold, Marshall, and Eisenhower—supported or certainly did not intervene to halt the movement to less discriminate attacks is clear, but they did so because of a shared perspective that ultimate Allied security rested not simply on driving the aggressors back behind their borders but on reordering their societies. The completeness of a victory of unconditional surrender comported with the application of unlimited power.

Western leaders also made a deliberate choice to exploit advanced technology to preserve the lives of their servicemen. By this decision they did not simply honor ideas, they also aimed to maintain morale to see the war to a decisive finish. The creation of vast air fleets generated tremendous inertial forces mandating that the investment pay off. Decisions made between 1940 and 1942 produced the bombers that dropped at least 75 percent of all aerial munitions after January 1944 and about 50 percent after June 1944. This plenitude of resources also tempted American airmen into experiments such as Clarion to shock Germany into surrender by blunt terror attacks. Technology also inserted a vast distance between those who planned and executed the raids and the noncombatants caught beneath the bombs. It made easy the use of euphemistic language, such as "de-housing," which suggested that only inanimate buildings, not their largely civilian inhabitants, would suffer.

It is indisputable that U.S. airmen abandoned precision bombing as it was understood prior to the war, but later charges that a sort of evil madness—"the triumphs of technological fanaticism," in the words of one writer—explains policy and practice fail to fit the evolution of American air doctrine into its full context. Richard Davis captured the achievements and the costs of strategic bombing in Europe when he noted:

The decision to bomb transportation . . . would eventually result in the complete disruption of German economic life. It would also firmly affix to the concept of daylight strategic bombing the stigma of the wanton destruction of German cities and the callous slaughter of thousands of German noncombatants.

Strategic Attack on Japan

In light of all the events that were to follow during the summer of 1945, including the use of atomic bombs, the most fundamental point about the history of bombing in Europe is that it had trampled down every moral barrier to the use of massive aerial firepower (though not poison gas) against legitimate targets, even when it was clear that the destruction of the target would entail death for large numbers of noncombatants. Army Air Forces officers used European lessons as a catechism for planning raids on Japan, but Japan's peculiar vulnerability to fire had long been a topic of discussion. General William Mitchell commented publicly in the 1920s that Japan's teeming cities erected of "paper and wood and other inflammable structures" comprised "the greatest aerial targets the world has ever seen. . . . Incendiary projectiles would burn the cities to the ground in short order."

Visions became plans in the fall of 1941. As Boeing Flying Fortresses rushed to the Philippines to deter Japanese aggression, General Marshall, in a secret press briefing on November 15, pronounced forthrightly that if war came, "we'll fight mercilessly. Flying Fortresses will be dispatched immediately to set the paper cities of Japan on fire." The power and speed of the Japanese onslaught aborted any attempt to execute these plans and deprived the United States of bases for launching direct attacks on Japan.

Preliminary work commenced on selecting bombing targets in Japan well before the practical means came to hand. Army Air Forces intelligence officers identified 199 vital targets in nine groups. Arnold handed over the task of determining the order in which these groups should be attacked to the Committee of Operations Analysts (COA). Although headed by an officer, the COA was dominated by civilians—economists, corporation directors, and attorneys—some wearing very recent direct commissions, who enjoyed "extensive experience in dealing with complex business and industrial problems." After laboring from spring to November 1943, the COA presented Arnold with a recommendation list of the most critical target systems: (1) merchant shipping; (2) iron and steel production; (3) urban industrial areas; (4) aircraft plants; (5) the antifriction ball-bearing industry; (6) the electronics industry; and (7) the petroleum industry.

The COA, like Army Air Forces officers who studied targeting in Japan before and after, found there was extremely little information to guide them. Unlike in Europe, where the American airmen could draw upon excellent work by the British or even upon data derived from commercial transactions, rigorous Japanese secrecy and limited trade and immigration effectively shielded from American eyes knowledge of the location or organization of Japan's war-making potential. What American planners did know was that Japan's industries were markedly concentrated in a few cities and that those cities were vulnerable to fire.

Matterhorn

The prospect of major air operations from China elicited barely tepid interest from senior officers in Washington, but its proponents more than made up for this deficit by securing the enthusiastic support of the commander in chief. The air officers focused on the logistical nightmare of sustaining huge and complex air units in any area lacking ready sea or land communications, but President Roosevelt's complex attitudes about China left him malleable to spells cast by the senior local American air commander, Major General Claire L. Chennault, who seriously argued at one time that he could defeat Japan with 105 fighters and 30 medium and 12 heavy bombers, supported by merely 67 transport planes, a total of 214 (not 213 or 215) planes. Chennault later doubled or trebled this figure, and with the full backing of Chiang Kai-shek he won a bureaucratic victory over his rival, General Joseph Stilwell, in the spring of 1943. "Politically [I] must support Chiang Kai-shek and that given the state of Chinese morale the air program was therefore of great importance," wrote President Roosevelt, explaining his directives that disregarded the advice of his military advisers.

Coincidentally, General Arnold was looking to employ the new B-29 very long range bomber against the Japanese Homeland as soon as possible. Pending capture of the Marianas, however, only China provided suitable base sites for the planes. Accordingly, staff officers drafted plans to dispatch a B-29 wing to China, a project code-named Matterhorn. No one doubted that extraordinary difficulty would attend the effort or that the quantity of bombs the Superfortresses could deliver from China would be relatively small. But the COA identified a target system that appeared to justify the enterprise. All of Japan's steel making required coke, which was manufactured in highly vulnerable plants that would require years to replace. Just six of these plants, three on Kyushu, two near Mukden in Manchuria, and one in Korea, produced 66 percent of Japan's coke. All six plants lay within the long reach of B-29s based around Chengtu in China.

Arnold's vision of Superfortress employment also incorporated a very special command arrangement. He and his staff won approval for the creation of a strategic air force directly under the Joint Chiefs of Staff, rather than subordinate to any theater commander. Arnold himself would act as the commander of this air force and as the executive agent of the Joint Chiefs of Staff. On April 12, 1944, the Twentieth Air Force was created. Although Arnold was the nominal commander, his chief of staff, Brigadier General Haywood Hansell, Jr., exercised effective command. Initial plans envisioned about 1,000 to 1,500 operational B-29s, divided among three or four subordinate units: the XX Bomber Command in China-India-Burma; the XXI Bomber Command in the Marianas; the XXII Bomber Command in the Philippines, Formosa, or Okinawa; and perhaps a XXIII Bomber Command in Alaska.

The initial leader of the XX Bomber Command, Brigadier General Kenneth B. Wolfe, took its major operational unit, the 58th Bomb Wing, to the China-India-Burma theater beginning in April 1944 to stage attacks through China. By early May, there were 130 B-29s in India. Before they could conduct any bombing, however, they had to shuttle both themselves and their own supplies, particularly fuel, over the Himalayas, whose peaks thrust up almost to 30,000 feet. It took seven trips over "the Hump," as it was styled, to amass the material for one sortie against the Japanese. Transport aircraft supplemented and eventually supplanted the B-29s in this role, but not before twelve were lost on supply missions.

On the night of June 15–16, sixty-eight B-29s lifted from Chengtu bases to raid the coke and steel plant at Yawata on Kyushu. A single bomb hit the plant. Japanese defenses accounted for one of the raiders, but defects and bad weather downed six more. The mechanical immaturity of the Superfortress, plus the difficult logistics of operations in China, hobbled all efforts of the XX Bomber Command. Wolfe, a masterly engineer bereft of operational experience, was sent home to work on the airframe and power plant. He was replaced in August 1944 by an entirely different character, Major General Curtis E. LeMay. A highly controversial figure in the Cold War era, LeMay came from humble beginnings. He saw a future in flying, and unlike many of his peers, developed a passion for navigation and instrument flying. He also won a reputation for bluntness that earned him the ironic nickname "The Diplomat." He admitted that he gleaned little from a brief stint in the Air Corps Tactical School, his only exposure to formal doctrine. As late as January 1, 1940, he was still a lieutenant with a dozen years of service who had not even commanded a squadron.

Service with the Eighth Air Force in Europe ignited his rocketlike as-cent. His availability rather than any particular glimmer of promise gained him command of one of the first fledgling B-17 groups dispatched to England. LeMay swiftly made his mark as a practical genius at innovating tactics and procedure. His reputation spread as a yelling, snarling, cigar-chewing "iron ass." In fact, a biographer noted, LeMay "was too miserly with words to spend them on sermons or harangues," and his most common and effective signal of displeasure was a glare or cold stare. He also cultivated a remarkably free exchange of ideas with all ranks in his command, and when he formulated doctrine and policy, "I never said 'I,' " he noted, "I always said 'we.' "

Spectacular command performance in the deadly skies over Germany made LeMay the youngest major general in the Army Air Forces by March 1944. He came to the XX Bomber Command with a reputation as an "operator," someone who made things happen. His stamp was soon evident in retraining and in new procedures on the ground and in the air. He vastly increased operational efficiency, but strategic results still eluded the command. Of forty-nine missions flown from China, only nine were to Japan proper, and only 12,407 tons of bombs and mines were dropped. These missions cost eighty-two B-29s, plus those lost on supply and training flights, for very little effect.

During his operations in China, LeMay came to several important judgments. Based on his personal experience on a mission to Anshan and analysis of other missions, he graded Japanese fighter tactics and effectiveness as far inferior to those of the Luftwaffe. He also became intimately familiar with the many bugs in the B-29 and knew how to eliminate or ameliorate them. Finally, he filed away a lesson in the effectiveness of incendiary attacks. General Chennault had urged repeatedly for an incendiary attack on the main Japanese supply base at Hankow. LeMay objected strenuously that this was a mission for Chennault's airmen, but eventually the Joint Chiefs of Staff supported the new theater commander, General Albert C. Wedemeyer, who had replaced Stilwell, and adopted Chennault's concept. On December 18, LeMay sent ninety-four Superfortresses to Hankow, where they dropped 511 tons of incendiaries, which ignited spectacular fires and, said Chennault, "destroyed Hankow as a major base."

While LeMay and Wedemeyer had differed over Hankow, they concurred on the overall utility of operations by B-29s from China. LeMay called the whole setup "basically unsound"; Wedemeyer informed his superiors that there simply was not enough gasoline flowing over the Hump to sustain B-29s, Chennault's Fourteenth Air Force, and Nationalist China. Something had to go, and that, said Wedemeyer, should be LeMay's com-

mand. It was January 15, 1945, when the Joint Chiefs of Staff granted
Wedemeyer's request, but by then LeMay was in another job.

From the Marianas

The daunting operational handicaps faced by the XX Bomber Command
in China served to subdue expectations for it from the beginning. In stark
contrast, an absence of such handicaps inflated expectations, perhaps unreasonably, for the XXI Bomber Command in the Marianas from the outset. Senior Army Air Forces officers, and above all General Arnold, hoped
the B-29 would prove the case for an independent air service by defeating
Japan, thus fulfilling a dream that had been incubating in their minds for
decades.

Unlike the restricted menu of targets available to B-29s from China,
bases in the Marianas allowed access to all but the northernmost reaches of
the Home Islands, including the critical core of Japanese war industry.
American target planners saw that core as remarkably concentrated and
vulnerable, and for good reason. A line connecting the industrialized centers of Japan in 1944 and 1945 would inscribe an elongated S, with the
upper tip at Niigata, the sinuous bends encircling the great centers of
Tokyo, Yokohama, Nagoya, and Kobe, and the lower tip running through
Hiroshima-Kure and Yawata. The six largest cities housed slightly more
than one half of all industry; 64 percent of national output flowed from
twenty-four cities. Since these percentages reflect end products, the total
amount of manufacturing was even higher, ranging to about 75 percent in
the half-dozen largest cities.

Several other measures indicate the concentration of industry. Tokyo,
Nagoya, and Kobe-Osaka standing alone mustered 35 percent of the total
industrial labor force and more than 40 percent of the electric-power stations. The six largest Japanese cities held a fifth of the nation's citizens; the
sixty-six Japanese cities ultimately raided by B-29s held 28 percent of the
national population and 75 percent of the urban population.

The opportunities before the Twentieth Air Force as a whole, particularly the XXI Bomber Command, also engendered an

> extreme pressure to perform. One major slip and the critics would have their
> way—[the] Twentieth Air Force would have been dismembered and
> parceled out to the various theaters. . . . We had given a pledge to launch an
> air offensive against Japan in November 1944. This proposed offensive was
> tied into the carefully prepared plans for the Pacific campaigns of Admiral
> Nimitz and General MacArthur. The target date had to be met, and the suc-

cess of a highly controversial operation had to be demonstrated, if strategic air power was to reach fruition in the Pacific.

These words were written by Brigadier General Hansell. Arnold informed him in late spring 1944 that he would lead the XXI Bomber Command, but it was August before Hansell effectively took charge. Hansell arrived with the conviction, transfused from experience in Europe and carrying the imprimatur of the Joint Chiefs of Staff, that their primary target must be the Japanese aircraft industry. American intelligence recognized thirteen aircraft and engine plants in Japan, though in many instances only the city in which they were located. Hansell believed that only daylight precision bombing could destroy these targets, and he insisted on this operational technique for his first wing, the 73rd, under Brigadier General Emmett "Rosey" O'Donnell.

In November 1944, teletypes at the XXI Bomber Command clattered off a new Japanese target list from Washington: (1) the aircraft industry; (2) urban industrial areas; and (3) shipping. Behind these came a list of secondary targets: coke, steel, and oil. Hansell later commented: "It is surprising that these three vital selective target systems should have been assigned a priority below 'Japanese urban industrial areas.' "

In his postwar writings, Hansell espoused the view that a momentous change came over Washington in its "strategic interest" after he left the air staff to assume his command. During his tenure, he adhered to and deeply believed in a policy of selective attack. It was doctrine he had taught at the Air Corps Tactical School and had applied in Europe, but it was no longer the exclusive doctrine endorsed by the chief of staff of the Army Air Forces. Unknown to Hansell, as early as April 1944 Arnold wrote to General Spaatz about the proposed Strategic Bombing Survey and commented: "Of particular interest to me would be some idea as to the most effective mixture of high explosives and incendiaries against heavily built up areas."

On November 17, Hansell's crews were briefed for the first raid on Japan: the Nakajima Musashino aircraft-engine plant in northwest Tokyo, officially designated as Target 357. But bad weather blanketed the air bases on Saipan for a full week, so it was not until November 24 that 111 Superfortresses lifted off. The mission served as a primer on the obstacles the command was to face. Along the route, various mechanical maladies compelled seventeen B-29s to abort the mission. Over the target, pilots and bombardiers discovered what is now called the jet stream: 130-mile-per-hour winds that virtually foreclosed the possibility of accurate bombing. Moreover, clouds obscured the target such that only twenty-four of the raiders secured any chance to hit the plant.

But the Japanese also came away from the day with reason to be discouraged. The Superfortresses easily weathered all the antiaircraft fire the defenders put up, and with their swift speed, high altitude, and heavy firepower they readily foiled the estimated 125 fighters that rose in defense of the capital. The only combat loss to the attackers came when a Japanese fighter deliberately rammed into a B-29. Both aircraft fell with no survivors. One other aspect of this mission is remarkable. During early operations in Europe, Eighth Air Force bomber crews persistently made grossly inflated claims about their destruction of German fighters. The XXI Bomber Command invoked much more rigorous standards. Returning crews claimed destruction of seven Japanese fighters, probable destruction of eighteen more, and damage to nine. Japanese returns precisely matched the claims for certain destruction: seven.

The eighty-one crews dispatched on the second mission, on November 27, discovered Tokyo again roofed by cloud. American bombs were thus poorly aimed—at best by radar. Two days later, the last mission of the month was a modest radar-guided night-bombing effort by twenty-nine aircraft. During December, the bomber command remained hostage to the elements. On December 3 and 27, missions were again aimed at the Musashino plant in Tokyo. The raiders achieved little damage but lost eight aircraft. Hansell's fliers headed for the Mitsubishi aircraft-engine plant in Nagoya on three occasions during the month. Two raids inflicted the first damage on a target, but the missions cost eleven planes. Nevertheless, the raid of December 18 represented, in Hansell's mind, "our first reasonably successful attack on the aircraft facilities."

Hansell realized that he occupied the job on which General Arnold believed the dream of an independent air force rested. In a letter on December 19, Arnold began, "Your units have been doing a wonderful job," but followed with paragraphs of criticism. The same day, Hansell received a directive on targeting that marked an important turning point in his tenure. In light of the success of the previous day's precision attack, he was shocked that the new directive specified a full-scale incendiary attack on Nagoya. He reflected later:

We were just beginning to show some improvement in bombing accuracy, both visual and radar. Now we were directed to reverse our painfully achieved progress in accuracy and turn to area bombing. It was no good trying to achieve real accuracy with incendiaries. Their imprecise ballistic characteristics precluded any accuracy in delivery even if sighting performance should be perfect.

Hansell fired off a protest to Washington, noting that he had "with great difficulty implanted the principle that our mission is the destruction of primary targets by sustained attacks using precision bombing methods both visual and radar." While conceding that no "acceptable measure of success" had so far been achieved, he did believe he was being diverted from an effort that was just showing promise. Back came the reply signed by a staff officer for Arnold stating that, while the aircraft industry still had priority, a fire raid was "simply a special requirement resulting from the necessity for future planning." Hansell ordered the mission but made the aiming point the factory, not the urban area.

Behind this new directive lay a revised blueprint drafted and issued by the COA in October 1944. The genesis of this report, in turn, was in the work of a subcommittee on incendiaries, commissioned in June, that plumbed the exceedingly complex problem of the forces required to burn down six major Japanese urban areas on Honshu (Tokyo, Yokohama, Kawasaki, Nagoya, Osaka, and Kobe), as well as the probable military, economic, and psychological results of such an effort. Despite the obvious vulnerability to fire of Japanese cities, figuring the density of incendiaries required to induce a holocaust was not easy. Calculation of how a fire would spread, for example, demanded consideration of variables such as building characteristics, weather, and the skill and will of firefighters.

The subcommittee also examined the results of an exceedingly meticulous effort to test various types of incendiaries on precision replicas of Axis cities. During 1943, structures re-creating those found in Berlin and Tokyo were assembled at Dugway Proving Grounds in Utah. The intense research about these buildings included interrogation of architects who had worked in those cities. A large San Francisco buyer of imported furniture provided information, as did the RKO Studios photographic archives, which had thousands of pictures of items ranging from a living-room chair in Berlin to a tatami mat in Osaka. Tatami mats proved hard to find or manufacture, but the requisite number were collected from Japanese-American homes and offices in Hawaii. The Dugway tests conclusively established the M-69 as almost three times as effective as its rivals in creating the most intense and uncontrollable blazes. The potency of the M-69 came from its newly invented incendiary gel filler, which, when mixed with gasoline, made a thick jelly that came to be known as napalm (from *nap*hthenic and *palm*itic acids). Individual 6.2-pound M-69s were gathered in clusters. On release from an aircraft, each bundle dispersed and out of each M-69 popped a small three-foot streamer that stabilized the bomb and controlled its descent. Contact with a roof triggered a fuse that three to five seconds later detonated a charge that first ejected the filler from the tail—up to one hundred feet—and then ignited it. By some accounts the M-69 was "the most destructive munition of the war."

In Washington, the urge to unleash massive incendiary attacks on Japanese urban areas was at full tide. The weapons—the B-29s and the M-69s—were ready. The orders had been given. Only Hansell's refusal to resort to these tactics now held back the flood of fire.

4

LeMay Takes Command

"Being a little unorthodox was all right with Hap Arnold"

Further Frustration

On January 7, 1945, General Lauris Norstad reached Guam to deliver in person orders from General Arnold: Hansell was to be relieved as leader of the XXI Bomber Command and replaced by Curtis LeMay. As Norstad noted later:

> General Arnold—and all of us, including, I think [Hansell]—now know that this LeMay is the best man in the Air Force right now for this particular job. . . . LeMay is an operator, the rest of us are planners.

There can be no doubt that LeMay's performance in China far outshone Hansell's in the Marianas or, for that matter, that of any other Army Air Forces officer. About this time, an operations analyst submitted a report that documents LeMay's accomplishments. Whereas the highest figure for heavy-bomber operations overseas in any month (save one exceptional month in the Mediterranean theater) rested at eighty-one hours per airplane, LeMay had achieved ninety-two hours per Superfortress in China, with immature aircraft at the end of an appalling logistical pipeline. Even more startling was the fact that the stateside training command, which enjoyed a maintenance force three times the size of LeMay's, attained only 102 hours per month per Superfortress. The author of this report was Lieutenant Colonel Robert S. McNamara, who later became Secretary of Defense under President John F. Kennedy and found himself violently at odds with LeMay.*

LeMay reached Guam on January 8 with no inkling about the orders that awaited him. Hansell, ever a gentleman, deported himself with dignity and tried his best to put LeMay—his onetime subordinate—and Norstad at ease. Meanwhile, operations under Hansell continued. On January 9, B-29s attempted for the fifth time to hit the Musashino plant in Tokyo. Six of seventy-two Superfortresses failed to return in exchange for destruction of merely one warehouse. On January 14, seventy-three planes headed for the Mitsubishi plant in Nagoya. They inflicted little damage at the cost of four Superfortresses.

Hansell's valedictory mission came on January 19. The target for eighty Superfortresses was the Kawasaki aircraft plant at Akashi, in southern Honshu. Finding for once clear weather, the sixty-two B-29s that reached the target dropped 152.5 tons of bombs with devastating accuracy. The plant sustained such damage that production ceased, never to resume at that location, although postwar investigation showed that the machine tools mostly survived and permitted production to continue in another location. All the B-29s came home.

Akashi aside, Hansell left a legacy of minuscule accomplishment in terms of target destruction coupled with serious losses. According to another memorandum by McNamara on January 23, losses in the XX and XXI Bomber Commands ran 100 percent above those experienced by the Eighth Air Force in Europe during the second half of 1944. The lack of achievements and painful losses strained morale, and first impressions of LeMay did not augur well. The first mission under LeMay's aegis targeted the aircraft-engine plant in Nagoya on January 23. Of the seventy-three aircraft dispatched, however, only twenty-three managed to bomb the primary target through heavy clouds. Another twenty-seven dropped on the secondary target: the Nagoya urban area. One Superfortress crashed on takeoff, and another fell to Japanese interceptors. Poststrike photographs demonstrated that no more than four bombs and a few incendiaries hit the primary target, causing slight damage. The change of leadership had brought no instant success and accurately reflected the three great problems the B-29s faced: weather, poor bombing results, and mechanical gremlins.

Japanese fighter opposition over Nagoya had been fierce, but it peaked in the next raid. For the all-too-familiar target of the Musashino aircraft-

---

* McNamara's report included the opinion that the commander of the training unit should be obtaining up to twice as many hours per Superfortress each month as he currently was, thus plainly implying that he should be relieved.

engine works, seventy-six 73rd Wing planes set forth on January 27. An even dozen returned early, but the others forged on to Tokyo, where they ran into an estimated 190 interceptors. Bomber crews counted a total of 984 attacks, no fewer than 554 directed at the leading, seventeen-plane formation of the 497th Bomb Group. One 497th Superfortress, "Irish Lassie," was rammed not once but twice: One plane sliced off eight feet of the port wing and a second crashed into the tail. Miraculously, "Irish Lassie" still brought her crew home, but the mission cost nine Superfortresses with seventy-eight crewmen. The Japanese classed damage on the ground as "considerable."

By the time LeMay mounted his next mission, his unit's strength had increased. Brigadier General John H. Davies's 313th Wing, composed of the 6th, 9th, 504th, and 505th Bomb Groups, had arrived at North Field, Tinian. Two groups from the 313th dispatched thirty-eight aircraft to join seventy-two from the veteran 73rd Wing on a February 4 mission to Kobe, Japan's greatest port and shipbuilding center. LeMay selected Kobe in part to spread out Japanese defenses, but the mission summary acknowledged that a September 1, 1944, report, "Incendiary Attacks on Japanese Cities," also influenced planning. Bomb loads followed the report's prescription: predominantly incendiaries with some fragmentation bombs to discourage firefighting. Clouds and navigation problems limited the number of planes over the target to sixty-nine, which dispensed 159.2 tons of incendiaries and 13.6 tons of fragmentation bombs. Photographic reconnaissance showed that 2.6 million square feet of target area were damaged. Losses numbered two planes in combat and one operational.

Six days later, on February 10, LeMay sent 118 aircraft to attack the Nakajima aircraft-engine plant at Ota, near Tokyo. About ninety-seven bombs hit the target area, but nearly half were duds. A variety of causes produced the appalling loss of twelve aircraft, including nine of the thirty-five lofted by the novice 313th Wing. LeMay insisted on postmission critiques with his wing commanders. When General Davies volunteered that the bombing was good, LeMay snorted: "My general comment on the bombing is that it was poor." Davies then ventured that frosted windows probably figured in the midair collision that destroyed two Superfortresses. Displaying his utter mastery of all technical aspects of air operations, LeMay rattled off methods to prevent frosting. The windows, he said, must be thoroughly clean before takeoff and the aircraft dried out by opening all windows before starting the climb to altitude. If frost appeared at altitude, "depressurize the aircraft and open the windows. . . . You can fly along at 40 degrees below zero with the windows open and the crew will be fairly comfortable."

On February 15, weather effectively spoiled an attack by 117 Super-fortresses on the Mitsubishi plant at Nagoya. The mission cost one 313th Wing aircraft that ditched, but Japanese records show no fewer than seventeen fighters lost that day. On February 16 and 17, carrier planes raided Japan for the first time. Despite bad weather, the Navy fliers returned with claims of downing 341 Japanese aircraft in the air and destroying another 190 on the ground. American losses came to sixty aircraft in combat, twenty-eight operationally. The dark blue planes attacked a number of aircraft plants around Tokyo and inflicted severe damage on the Musashino plant, the XXI Bomber Command's elusive grail.

General Arnold was recuperating from his fourth heart attack when he read about the Navy raids along with an announcement that the one thousandth B-29 had been produced. He drafted an "eyes only" letter to his deputy, General Barney Giles, venting his mounting dissatisfaction with the bomber command:

> I know that there are one thousand other reasons for not getting two, three or four hundred B-29s over Japan on every possible occasion. This cannot be done if we accept excuses and do not face the issue. . . . From my viewpoint, . . . I would not be surprised any day to see the control of the 20th Air Force pass either to Nimitz or MacArthur.

It is likely that LeMay learned of the general import of Arnold's views.

The XXI Bomber Command launched the first full two-wing effort on February 19. One hundred and fifty Superfortresses headed for the Musashino engine plant with a twofold purpose: support the invasion of Iwo Jima and destroy a very high priority target. Yet again, the weather, this time clouds, effectively defended this supreme target. Not one plane dropped bombs on the plant; 119 used radar to pummel the secondary target, the Tokyo urban area, with 457.7 tons of bombs and incendiaries. All six losses came from the 73rd Wing.

Iwo Jima rests almost exactly midway between Saipan and Tokyo: 625 miles north of the former and 660 miles south of the latter. In September 1944, Admiral Nimitz won approval for its seizure to serve both as an emergency-landing facility for B-29s and as a base for escort fighters. But the Japanese could read a map, too, and packed Iwo Jima with almost 21,000 men. Their commander, Lieutenant General Tadamichi Kuribayashi, invigorated the garrison to create a labyrinth of tunnels and caves in the island's volcanic ash to further his concept of defense in depth.

Despite heavy prelanding bombing and bombardment, the Marine V Amphibious Corps, 75,144 strong, encountered savage and protracted resistance. In the five weeks after the landing on February 19, the Marines sustained 22,099 casualties, including 5,931 dead. Navy losses came to 982 killed and 1,652 wounded, for a grand total of 24,733 casualties including 6,913 killed. Of the Japanese garrison, only 1,083 had been captured through May. By the end of the war, 3,092 B-29s had landed on Iwo Jima, most with battle damage or short of fuel, and several thousand crewmen owed their lives to this haven.

A second effort by the XXI Bomber Command to render indirect support to the Iwo Jima invasion came on February 25. Originally, LeMay intended to go back after the Musashino plant, but bad weather dictated a radar bombing effort, with the aiming point set as a feature 3.5 miles up the Sumida River in Tokyo, where the land-water contrast would show up well on radar. Bomb loads per plane comprised only one 500-pound bomb and bundles of M-69s. By now, the bomber command included the first two groups of the new 314th Wing under the dynamic but autocratic Brigadier General Thomas S. Power. With twenty-two planes from the 314th, the XXI Bomber Command put on its largest raid yet with 229 Superfortresses airborne. No fewer than twenty-eight planes—over a tenth of the force—aborted, but the rest pressed on through appalling weather that had grounded Japanese interceptors. Radar guided 453.7 tons of bombs from 172 aircraft. Two 73rd Wing aircraft embraced in a midair collision, with fatal results for all aboard; a 313th Wing plane was surveyed as a loss after return. Despite all these negative augurs, poststrike photographs amazed: Fires leveled about one square mile and consumed 27,970 buildings.

Earlier that same day, American carrier planes raided Tokyo. They were known as "the little ones" by Japanese people, who did not fear these "loud and angry-sounding" visitors as deeply as they did the "B-san." When the hands of the clock pointed to ten sharp, the cold eased, and large soft flakes of snow "whispering thickly down" began to cover Tokyo. Near midday, radios again warned, "Enemy planes approaching." From his overlook, Father Gustav Bitter, rector of the Jesuit Sophia University, watched a circle of light stripe the murky sky from west to south. The "early radiance" caught the imagination of the citizens but was soon blanketed by smoke that the hovering sky pressed down over the rooftops, where it dyed the tumbling flakes black. To Tokyo's citizens, this day became known as the Day of the Black Snow.

Seven days later, on March 4, the Musashino plant again became the goal of 192 aircraft. One hundred fifty-nine aircraft released 479.8 tons of bombs by radar through solid clouds over the secondary target: the Tokyo urban area. No fighters rose to contest the sky, and flak damaged only seven planes, one of which ditched on the path back to the Marianas with two crewmen lost. There was no damage assessment because no strike photographs could be taken.

The Decision

Curtis LeMay's tenure now totaled nearly seven weeks. In eight missions to Japan, his command had dispatched 1,065 sorties, but only 386 aircraft (36.2 percent) had bombed their primary targets. Losses numbered 36 planes with 37 airmen killed, 238 missing, and 49 wounded or injured, for a total of 324. None of the targets had been destroyed. As LeMay later admitted, "I hadn't gotten anything much done any better than Possum Hansell had." The brutal reality he faced was that the weather might (or might not) grant seven days a month for visual bombing, assuming he received accurate forecasts. "We were still going in too high," recalled LeMay, "still running into those big jet streams upstairs. And the weather was almost always bad."

LeMay's forte was his ability to take a dauntingly complex problem and reduce it to its basic elements. He identified the ills of the XXI Bomber Command as extremely fundamental: selecting a target system, finding the individual aiming points, and hitting them. By March 1945, the target system appeared both obvious and inevitable: Japanese cities, not individual facilities. This idea was not original with LeMay. Billy Mitchell's words still echoed, while civilian advisers championed this mode and developed the M-69 expressly for use against the "paper cities of Japan." Washington had been gradually elevating the priority of attacks on urban industrial areas on target lists, and on February 19 LeMay received the latest target directive. While the aircraft industry in the Nagoya-Tokyo-Shizuoka area remained the priority, the emphasis on urban-area incendiary attacks had again been increased.

According to the record, LeMay was hesitant to adapt his operations to urban-area attacks. It took direct orders during his tenure with the XX Bomber Command to compel him to attack Hankow with incendiaries. In eight missions from the Marianas, only Kobe on February 4 and Tokyo on February 25 were planned as incendiary attacks on urban industrial areas (and Tokyo solely because of the necessity to attack on that date to support the Iwo Jima invasion). But the results on February 25 had exceeded all expectations. This mission set Thomas Power, the 314th Wing commander, to thinking: What if more B-29s attacked at lower altitudes, permitting much greater bomb loads per aircraft, and what if those increased bomb loads were mostly incendiaries? LeMay took the thread and began to spin it: not only a single fire raid, but a campaign against a series of Japanese cities.

Radar promised to provide electronic eyes to find and hit an aiming point day or night, but the XXI Bomber Command's radar accomplishments so far had been disappointing. In Europe, only selected pathfinder bombers sported radar. As the Cadillac of American bombers, each B-29 came already equipped with one radar set, but a classic bureaucratic blunder nearly undermined this capability. LeMay found that gunners had been drafted as radar operators, but, he observed, "the idea about a gunner was that he couldn't absorb enough training to become a radio operator or an engineer." LeMay turned to a special technical consultant, Dr. King Gould from the Massachusetts Institute of Technology, and asked him to see if the operators could identify a simple land-water contrast that would show up well on the radar set as a navigation checkpoint. Gould reported they could.

The outstanding feature in the plan incubating in LeMay's mind was the attack altitude. One writer later commented that LeMay's "command genius lay in his decision to avoid introducing these methods piecemeal, to take the parts and throw them together at once, producing a whole dwarfing the sum of its parts." LeMay did more than simply link up several lines of thought originating with others, for by far the most radical part of the plan enjoyed no antecedent—or at least none that recommended itself. Over Europe, low-level operations by heavy bombers had been few and far between, on account of venomous German flak.

Did the Japanese have comparable defenses? LeMay understood that, compared with the Germans, Japanese night fighters were both very few and of low efficiency. He also knew that Japan had a fair quantity of guns of 75 mm or greater caliber that could strike bombers above twenty thousand feet. Photographic reconnaissance and radio intelligence failed to confirm that significant numbers of light-flak weapons protected Japanese urban areas. But as LeMay recalled: "How the hell were we going to prove one hundred percent that the light flak *wasn't* there?" He summoned his flak experts; "almost to a man" they predicted losses at 70 percent in a low-altitude attack.

But LeMay knew that flying low promised a good deal more than improved accuracy. The strain on the planes' engines would also be markedly reduced, thereby enhancing their reliability. There would also be tremendous savings in fuel, the weight of which could be converted directly into bomb loads. LeMay reached another startling conclusion as well: In a night mission with many aircraft flying independently where there were few, if any, night fighters to be expected, it was far more likely that bomber gunners would fire at friendly planes than at enemy ones. Therefore, LeMay decided to remove all guns and gunners from the attack force, once again with gains in bomb loads.

LeMay sought out Norstad: "You know General Arnold, I don't know him. Does he ever go for a gamble?" Norstad was noncommittal, but LeMay gained the impression that "being a little unorthodox was all right with Hap Arnold." He also discussed his thoughts with a "very few" of his officers. Some saw in the plan a revolutionary breakthrough; others saw in it a prescription for a bloodbath. Norstad carried another message LeMay understood very well and later described as: "You go ahead and get results with the B-29. If you don't get results, you'll be fired. If you don't get results, also, there'll never be any Strategic Air Forces of the Pacific. . . . If you don't get results it will mean eventually a mass amphibious invasion of Japan."

LeMay selected Tokyo as the first target of the radically changed bombing offensive. He technically informed Arnold of his plan but did so less than twenty-four hours before takeoff of the first aircraft, almost certainly precluding intervention from Washington. As LeMay stated later: "[Arnold's] on the hook, in order to get some results out of the B-29's. But if I set up *this* deal, and Arnold O.K.'s it beforehand, then he would have to assume some of the responsibility. And if I don't tell him, and it's all a failure, and I don't produce any results, then he can fire me. And he can put another commander in here, and still have a chance to make something out of the 29's."

Gnawing at LeMay was the fact that he personally could not go on this, the most daring mission he had devised. This violated one of the hallmarks of his leadership in Europe: literally leading missions. But shortly after taking charge of the XXI Bomber Command, LeMay was visited by a colonel with impressive credentials who briefed him on development of the atomic bomb. Once privy to this secret, LeMay knew it was pointless to ask if he could fly any mission over Japan where he might be shot down and captured.

For initiation of this dramatically transformed strategy, the XXI Bomber Command mounted a maximum effort. The 73rd Wing provided 169 aircraft, or 93 percent of its total. Similarly, the 313th readied 121 aircraft, and the two available groups of the 314th provided 56, making a total of 346. Target planners sought to achieve a distribution of incendiaries of sixty tons per square mile for the entire target zone, in order to ensure that Tokyo's firefighters would be overwhelmed. Anticipating a westerly wind, they sequenced the bombing from east to west to keep smoke from obscuring the four selected aiming points.

Calculations of the ratio between necessary fuel loads and bomb loads revealed that each aircraft of the 73rd and 313th Wings could lug seven tons of bombs, while the 314th, which had a greater distance to fly, could carry five tons. Accordingly, the 346 B-29s scheduled for the mission carried more bomb tonnage than a mass raid by over one thousand B-17s in the European theater.

Each wing was assigned a bombing altitude in bands varying from 5,000 to 7,800 feet. The capabilities of Japanese antiaircraft defenses and considerations of bombing accuracy dictated this range. By flying in this channel, the B-29s would be above the effective range of the estimated 307 automatic weapons and below the effective range of the estimated 331 heavy guns in the Tokyo defenses. Likewise, the routes specified from landfall to bomb runs placed aircraft within the heavily defended areas for the shortest possible periods of time.

The first aircraft lifted off one minute behind schedule at 4:36 P.M., March 9, from the 314th Wing base on Guam. The wheels of the last of the 325 aircraft to get airborne parted from the soil at 7:10 P.M. Early aircraft had no difficulty locating the aiming points, and their bombs kindled fires that following aircraft employed as markers, even in heavy smoke. Later aircraft found visibility reduced to zero because of smoke, and some bombed fires outside the target area in the belief that they were aiming points. "The primary difficulties encountered on this mission resulted from the severe turbulence encountered by the later aircraft over the target," dryly noted the poststrike report. In the 313th Wing, for example, one man was seriously injured and another slightly injured by severe buffeting over the target.

LeMay later recalled: "I walked the floor because I couldn't go on it. . . . I'll admit I was nervous about it. I made the decision. I weighed the odds. I knew the odds were in my favor. But still, it was something new. I could have lost a lot of people, appeared to be an idiot." In fact, he passed a major portion of the night in the company of St. Clair McKelway, his public-information officer. During the afternoon, McKelway organized a press conference in which Norstad and LeMay described the daring new tactics. After watching the takeoffs, the correspondents prepared stories for release as soon as the strike reports were received.

It was 2:00 A.M., March 10 (Guam time), when McKelway entered the operations center to await the first "bombs away" messages. There he found, besides the small number of men on duty, LeMay, seated on a wooden bench beneath the mission-control boards. At LeMay's direction, his principal staff officers were in bed. Despite the now habitual cigar in his mouth, LeMay managed a smile and acknowledged: "I'm sweating this one out myself. A lot could go wrong. I can't sleep. I usually can, but not tonight."

McKelway sat down beside the young commander and proceeded on the premise that LeMay might like to talk for once. He was correct. LeMay poured out his thoughts and some fears in unadorned prose, concluding, "I never think anything is going to work until I've seen the pictures after the raid, but if this one works, we will shorten this damned war out here."

After a quick glance at his watch, LeMay observed: "We won't get a bombs away for another half hour. Would you like a Coca-Cola? I can sneak in my quarters without waking up the other guys and get two Coca-Colas and we can drink them in my car. That'll kill most of the half hour." Seated in the car, they talked about India. "The way all those people are in India gets you down. It makes you feel rotten," sighed LeMay. The irony of this compared with what the people in Tokyo were experiencing did not seem to occur to him.

They returned to the operations room in time for the first strike reports. LeMay read, "Bombing the primary target visually. Large fires observed. Flak moderate. Fighter opposition nil." Then came a cascade of messages from other groups. All reported "conflagration" and moderate flak with little if any sighting of night fighters. When staff officers appeared, LeMay told them, "It looks pretty good. But we can't really tell a damn thing about results until we get pictures tomorrow night. Anyway, there doesn't seem to have been much flak. We don't seem to have lost more than a few airplanes." He shifted the cigar and broke into a smile for the first time.

The first aircraft to return touched down at 6:10 A.M., March 10, and all of the 313 to return were in by 11:27 A.M. Debriefing showed that 279 aircraft bombed Tokyo with 1,665 tons of bombs at altitudes ranging from 4,900 to 9,200 feet. Nineteen other aircraft dropped 100.2 tons on targets of opportunity or targets of last resort.

As LeMay anticipated, enemy air opposition was very weak. Crews sighted only seventy-four fighters that managed only forty attacks. "The enemy pilots intercepting appeared to have little or no knowledge of night fighting," recorded the mission report. Intense and accurate antiaircraft fire over Tokyo and from ships in the bay greeted the initial aircraft but diminished in volume and accuracy "as each succeeding plane came over the target." Twelve aircraft failed to return. Of these losses, one was ascribed to antiaircraft fire over the target, four to ditching (including one damaged by antiaircraft fire), and seven to unknown causes, although crew reports strongly suggest that four were to flak. Forty-two returning aircraft displayed damage from antiaircraft fire.

The losses were not spread evenly. The 73rd Wing, which put up the most aircraft, lost only one. The 313th lost only three of 121, but the novice 314th Wing lost no fewer than eight out of only fifty-four aircraft dispatched. Two other aircraft were damaged so badly that they were "surveyed," or written off, bringing total aircraft losses to fourteen. Of the 3,307 airmen who flew the mission, forty survived the four ditchings. Killed or missing numbered ninety-six, and six others were wounded or injured.

The aircraft LeMay was most anxious about landed at North Field, Guam, at 9:00 A.M. A window cracked open and out peered the head of Thomas Power, his face drawn in fatigue, with circles under his eyes. "It was a hell of a good mission," he shouted down to LeMay. Then Power dismounted to show his commander a map of the city of Tokyo on which he had marked the fires. All the other crew reports were similar, but the clinching evidence came near midnight with development of the reconnaissance photos.

From Arnold first came a terse message: "Congratulations. This mission shows your crews have the guts for anything." Ten days later, Arnold elaborated:

As one of my first acts in returning to Washington after an absence of several weeks, I want to commend you and your Command on the superb operations you have conducted during the last month. . . . A study of the Tokyo attack of March 10 and the knowledge of the fact that by July 1 you will have nearly a thousand B-29s under your control, leads one to conclusions which are impressive even to old hands at bombardment operations. Under reasonably favorable conditions you should then have the ability to destroy whole industrial cities should that be required.

LeMay understood very well that he now possessed such an ability. He believed it was required, and he later professed that he was untroubled by the prospect. As he said in his memoirs:

We were going after military targets. No point in slaughtering civilians for the mere sake of slaughter. Of course there is a pretty thin veneer in Japan, but the veneer was there. It was their system of dispersal of industry. . . . I'll never forget Yokohama. That was what impressed me: drill presses. There they were, like a forest of scorched trees and stumps, growing up throughout that residential area. Flimsy construction all gone . . . everything burned down, or up, and drill presses standing like skeletons.

LeMay saved his regrets for losses among his crews. "Seemed to me that if I had done a better job we might have saved a few more crews."

5

Fire and Mud

"Like the fall of a castle in the days of old"

The Blitz

Photographs of a 15.8-square-mile burned-out scar in Tokyo verified crew reports of stupendous damage. LeMay perceived that a portion of the large fuel reserves carried by returning aircraft could be exchanged for greater bomb loads, while the much-reduced demands of low-altitude flight markedly improved engine reliability and promised much greater aircraft availability. But crew observations misled planners into surmising that still greater destruction was attainable by spreading the bomb load of each aircraft over a wider area. This proved to be a major mistake.

With 1.5 million people, Nagoya was Japan's third-largest city in population. American planners believed that about 25 percent of the workers there toiled in the aircraft industry, making it the nation's capital in that respect. On March 11, the XXI Bomber Command dispatched 310 aircraft for Nagoya. One aircraft crashed after takeoff, the sole loss of the mission. But photographic reconnaissance demonstrated that the less concentrated bombing produced only a small fraction of the devastation in Tokyo. This raid consumed just 2.05 square miles of the city.

LeMay designated Osaka as the third target in the fire blitz. With a prewar citizenry of 3.2 million, Osaka ranked second in population, third among ports, and high as a railway hub. Target planners applied two lessons from the Nagoya attack: compress the duration of the attack and contract the expanse covered by individual bomb loads. Out of 274 aircraft dispatched on the night of March 13–14, one crashed on takeoff, but the crew survived; another Superfortress disappeared. Poststrike reconnaissance depicted an 8.1-square-mile charred hole in urban Osaka.

Kobe, Japan's premier port and ship-construction center, became the target for the fourth fire raid, on March 16–17. LeMay's staff "selected for attack" the "highly congested core of the city," with population densities of 100,000 per square mile. The three wings lofted 331 aircraft, which found half the sky over Kobe roofed with clouds. The raid cost three B-29s but leveled three of the fourteen square miles classified as part of the city.

LeMay's original scheme envisioned a blitz targeting five different cities on alternate days, but the relative failure of the second mission mandated a return to Nagoya on March 18–19. To the population of the city, still reeling from the attack only a week before, this second fire raid was a profound shock. The mission was remarkable for the fact that not one American died. Antiaircraft fire forced one aircraft to ditch, but its crew was plucked from the sea. This attack burned out 2.95 square miles of Nagoya.

The chalkboards listed Nagoya yet again for the attack slated for the night of March 23–24. This time, however, LeMay attempted a night precision attack with 251 Superfortresses on the Mitsubishi aircraft-engine plant, using techniques copied from the British Bomber Command over Europe: pathfinders to mark and illuminate the target and an airborne commander over the city (the "Master of Ceremonies") to direct bombing. But clouds and smoke frustrated the American airmen, who inflicted little or no damage to the primary target. This near fiasco also exacted an exorbitant price: five aircraft with fifty-two crewmen lost.

During all the missions prior to March 9, the XXI Bomber Command had ineffectively dropped about seven thousand tons of bombs and lost one hundred aircraft. During the blitz of March 9–25, the command inflicted immense damage with nine thousand tons of munitions at a cost of only twenty-four Superfortresses. LeMay terminated the incendiary raids because he literally ran out of bombs. Furthermore, he faced the demand for his bombers to fly support for the seizure of Okinawa, an island only 340 miles from the shores of Japan.

Okinawa and Invasion Support, March 27–May 11

At the end of March, the Japanese Thirty-second Army on Okinawa under Lieutenant General Mitsuru Ushijima awaited an American assault. Orders from Tokyo, however, had stripped him of the best division in the garrison in order to reinforce Formosa. Morale was sorely depressed and for good reason. Ushijima's staff officers expected the Americans to attack with six to ten divisions, each of which would project five to six times the firepower of his two and one-half divisions. Indeed, while the Thirty-second Army rosters totaled 100,000 men, only about 76,000 actually rated as trained combatants; the remainder comprised recently impressed Okinawan militias.

There seemed little doubt that the Thirty-second Army would be annihilated to no purpose. But the operations officer, Colonel Hiromichi Yahara, circulated a pamphlet titled "The Road to Certain Victory" that proposed "sleeping tactics," whereby the use of cave fortifications would negate the enemy's numerical and firepower advantages. Infused with new faith, the two divisions, the 24th and 62nd, had dug vigorously for one hundred days (totally without mechanized equipment) to prepare their positions; the 44th Independent Mixed Brigade (IMB) matched them in only fifty days.

Yahara concentrated all units in southern Okinawa and effectively abandoned the airfields in the center of the island, where the main American landing occurred on April 1. Although its population is ethnically distinct, Okinawa was an actual prefecture of the Home Islands and looked to be a preview of an invasion of Japan. Thus, the eerie quiet of the landings mystified the attackers, the Tenth Army with four army and two Marine divisions, as did the ease with which they secured the airfields and the northern half of the island. The American 7th and 96th Infantry Divisions discovered the Japanese abruptly on April 8 as they pushed south. Between April 9 and 28, the two army units, joined by the 27th Infantry Division, shoved against the stubborn Japanese resistance.

The deeply excavated caves and underground positions of the Japanese proved impervious even to unprecedented heavy-caliber bombardment from afloat and ashore, totaling over 2.3 million shells. The battle degenerated into a series of desperate rushes against prepared defenses—the results of which very closely resembled the horrors of the worst of trench warfare in World War I. One by one, all the American units were bled down, including the 77th Infantry Division and the 1st and 6th Marine Divisions. Rain fell freely over hillsides fouled with shallow graves or unburied dead of both sides, amid excrement and the refuse of battle. Eugene Sledge, a member of the hardened 1st Marine Division, reported:

> The situation was bad enough, but when enemy artillery shells exploded in the area, the eruptions of soil and mud uncovered previously buried Japanese dead and scattered chunks of corpses. Like the area around our gunpits, the ridge was a stinking compost pile.
>
> If a Marine slipped and slid down the back slope of the muddy ridge, he was apt to reach the bottom vomiting. I saw more than one man lose his foot-

ing and slip and slide all the way to the bottom only to stand horror stricken as he watched in disbelief while fat maggots tumbled out of his muddy dungaree pockets, cartridge belt, legging lacings, and the like. Then he and a buddy would shake or scrape them away with a piece of ammo box or a knife blade.

We didn't talk about such things. They were too horrible and obscene even for hardened veterans. The conditions taxed the toughest I knew almost to the point of screaming.

The fighting ashore—described in *Time* magazine as "one foot at a time against the kind of savage, rat-in-a-hole defense that only the Japanese can offer"—appeared protracted and seemingly pointless to many, rousing a storm of criticism in the American press and across the nation. Meanwhile, the Japanese unleashed massive attacks with kamikazes on the U.S. fleet.

At the end of the campaign in late June, for the first time in the Pacific conflict, a substantial number of prisoners of war were captured (7,401), of whom perhaps as many as two thirds were ethnic Japanese. Even so, more than 80 percent of the prisoners were taken only after the organized defense collapsed. The rest of the Japanese and Okinawan defenders, over 92,000 of them, died. According to the official U.S. Army account, total American battle casualties numbered 12,520 killed or missing (4,675 army, 2,938 Marine, and 4,907 navy) and 36,613 wounded. To put these totals in perspective, the navy and Marine loses at Okinawa constituted about 17 percent of all the casualties sustained by those services for the whole war. By another accounting, however, total American casualties on Okinawa proper (that is, not including casualties aboard ships offshore) included 6,319 killed, 32,943 wounded, and 33,096 "nonbattle" casualties (including psychiatric cases, injuries, illnesses, and deaths). Thus, total American losses reached 72,358, approximately the total of 76,000 trained defenders, an extremely ominous indicator amid preparations for an invasion of Japan.*

The fighting for Okinawa devastated the southern part of the island, but the evidence concerning civilian deaths is conflicting. By Japanese ac-

* Was the Japanese "fight to the death" spirit as invincible as it was perceived during the war? The Office of War Information, Foreign Morale Analysis Division, in Washington concluded that Japanese morale was cracking in 1944 and 1945 and that a psychological warfare campaign could both hasten surrender and increase battlefield surrenders (Dower, *War Without Mercy,* pp. 136–38). More recently, Allison B. Gilmore assembled an excellent study of the sophisticated and large-scale psychological warfare campaign directed by Brigadier General Bonner Fellers for MacArthur in the Southwest Pacific (*You Can't Fight Tanks with Bayonets: Psychological Warfare Against the Japanese Army in the Southwest Pacific* [Lincoln & London: University of Nebraska Press, 1998]). She argues persuasively that the morale of Japanese servicemen, once Japan's military situation clearly began to collapse in a way visible to the average soldier or sailor, proved more vulnerable to psychological warfare

counts, about 80,000 of the Okinawan population of 463,000 had been evacuated to Kyushu before the battle, and another 60,000 were herded forcibly into the northern portion of the island. In a preview of the blue-print for the final battle in the Homeland, the Thirty-second Army drafted a total of 39,000 males, ages eighteen to forty-five, of whom 24,000 formed a home guard that suffered fearful losses. About 1,500 male and 600 female youths were inducted into Iron and Blood Volunteer Units or nursing detachments, respectively.

A report to the White House on August 2 indicated 320,762 civilians were under American control; adding this to the 80,000 evacuated to Kyushu would place deaths at about 62,000. Okinawa historians, however, insist on far larger tolls, at least 100,000 and possibly as many as 150,000 deaths. These numbers are credible if the original census figures or the number of evacuees to Kyushu are in error.

Against this backdrop, on March 27, the XXI Bomber Command began bombing Kyushu to destroy airfield installations and to entice Japanese fighters away from sorties to Okinawa in order to protect their own bases. In total, between the first effort on March 27 and the last on May 10, they flew 2,235 sorties and lost twenty-two B-29s. By the airmen's count, the cratering of airfields did little to impede the kamikaze attacks, and the bombs destroyed pathetically few Japanese aircraft.

Return to the Cities

Given the vast devastation spread by night area-incendiary attacks and their apparent success, other commanders might have ceased experimen-tation in operational techniques, but not LeMay. He ordered a set of mis-sions between March 30 and April 3 to test various methods of night

---

than is usually acknowledged. Translating depressed morale into a greater rate of battlefield surren-ders, much less a national surrender, however, is another matter. She reports that 7,297 Japanese were captured on Luzon. But since the total size of the garrison was 287,000 (Edward J. Drea, *MacArthur's Ultra: Codebreaking and the War Against Japan, 1942–1945* [Lawrence: University Press of Kansas, 1992], p. 184), this makes the rate of battlefield surrenders just 2.5 percent, which is virtually indis-tinguishable from the 1 to 3 percent rates in the ferocious battles elsewhere. Gilmore goes on to cal-culate that at least 19,000 Japanese soldiers were captured in the Southwest Pacific, which she states "alone defies the stereotype of the Japanese soldier as invulnerable to psychological warfare" (p. 155). A very rough estimate is that more than 600,000 Japanese faced MacArthur in the Southwest Pacific (over 440,000 in the Philippines and 170,000 on New Guinea and the Bismarcks). (M. Hamlin Can-non, *Leyte: Return to the Philippines* [Washington, D.C.: Government Printing Office, 1954], p. 368; Robert Ross Smith, *The Approach to the Philippines* [Washington, D.C.: Government Printing Office, 1979], p. 93.) Thus, only about 3.1 percent of this total became POWs.

precision bombing. Owing to equipment limitations, none of them produced worthwhile results. In the course of 363 sorties, seven aircraft were lost. LeMay assessed the raids as failures, but after the war it was learned that one strike had halted production of the engine used in Japanese jet fighters.

When weather precluded attacks in support of the Okinawa operations, LeMay seized the opportunity to aim daylight missions at the Japanese aircraft industry. For the first of these, LeMay exploited the opportunity afforded by the installation on Iwo Jima of the 15th and 21st Fighter Groups, equipped with the superb P-51D Mustang fighter. He assigned the 116 aircraft readied by the two fighter units solely to the 73rd Wing, which lofted 107 Superfortresses toward the Nakajima Musashino aircraft-engine plant in Tokyo on April 7. A second mission comprised 194 B-29s from the 313th and 314th Wings, which headed for the Mitsubishi aircraft-engine plant in Nagoya. Postwar analysis revealed that the Nagoya raiders delivered the most devastating single blow of the war against a Japanese aircraft plant. At the Mitsubishi No. 2 and No. 4 engine works, bombs destroyed no fewer than 860 of 2,200 critical machine tools. Total American losses for the day were five B-29s and two P-51s. LeMay dispatched six more daylight missions between April 12 and May 19 aimed at aircraft-industry targets. These raids cost fifteen B-29s and five P-51s, with mixed results.

The main business of the XXI Bomber Command, however, remained the destruction by fire of major Japanese cities. The second maximum-effort incendiary strike on Tokyo occurred on the night of April 13–14. The objective was the Tokyo arsenal, the largest in the empire. The 348 B-29s released munitions that gutted 10.7 square miles. The last aircraft encountered smoke at ten thousand feet with turbulence so violent that it required two pilots to maintain flight control. Losses numbered seven B-29s. Only two B-29s actually hit the arsenal, but after the raid only about one half of the employees returned to work, causing a marked loss of production. "The people of Tokyo were fully cognizant of the great loss of life in the fire of 10 March," noted a postwar American report, "and consequently were reluctant to stay in the target area to perform fire fighting duties." As a result, civilian casualties were relatively low. For April 15, LeMay sent the 73rd Wing back to Tokyo and the other two wings to the immediately adjacent city of Kawasaki. At a cost of thirteen aircraft, 303 Superfortresses burned out a total of 9.6 square miles.

On May 5, the 58th Bomb Wing, transferring from China to Tinian, joined the XXI Bomber Command. The XX Bomber Command thus ended. On May 14, freed from Okinawa support duties, LeMay hurled

542 B-29s from four wings at Nagoya in a high-altitude daylight raid. At a price of eleven Superfortresses, they torched an additional 3.15 square miles of the city. On May 17, they returned to Nagoya with 516 B-29s, but this time for a low-level night attack. The tonnage cascading down on the city illustrated again the marked increase in carrying capacity of B-29s in low-level attacks: The 457 aircraft dropped 3,609.2 tons; the 472 aircraft that had bombed in daylight had released only 2,515.1 tons, a 44 percent increase in tonnage despite fifteen fewer aircraft over the target. Losses numbered three, all to mechanical causes.

The raid destroyed 3.87 square miles, bringing the total for the two successive raids to 7.02 square miles, or 13.7 percent of the city, with heavy damage to war industries. This marked the last of four major incendiary attacks on Nagoya since March 11. In the words of an American assessment, Nagoya proved to be "one of the most difficult cities in Japan to burn because of the difficulties of approach, the shape and size of the city, the relatively small fire divisions in the urban sections, the numerous fire breaks and the high percentage of fire resistant structures."

LeMay decided to return to Tokyo for two maximum-effort raids intended to reduce the value of the war industries remaining in the capital. For the night of May 23–24, the four wings put up 558 B-29s, seventeen of which were lost. A firestorm raged in the financial, commercial, and government districts, reducing 5.3 square miles to ashes. The flames also closed in on the Tokyo military prison, which housed four hundred Japanese servicemen inmates but also sixty-two American aviators, many of them B-29 crewmen who had been shot down on prior raids. The blaze consumed the entire prison and all the Americans. The prison commandant was later convicted of war crimes when it was revealed that all four hundred Japanese inmates survived.

Despite the sharp rise in losses, LeMay struck again at Tokyo on the night of May 25–26. The target area this time was a patch of the city measuring roughly three miles by five miles, west of the waterfront and directly south of the Imperial Palace. This area housed industrial, commercial, residential, and governmental buildings, including the largest railway marshaling yard in Japan. The XXI Bomber Command's 498 strike aircraft met heavy night-fighter and antiaircraft opposition. A total of 464 aircraft dropped 3,262 tons on Tokyo, nearly double the amount that created the March 9–10 holocaust. Losses this night for the XXI Bomber Command were the greatest for any single mission of the war: twenty-six. Photographic coverage showed the mission burned out twenty square miles of Tokyo (more than the night of March 9–10).

In Tokyo, it was "a fine night with a strong southerly wind" and 50 percent humidity. The incendiaries ignited fires that charred the symbols of the government: the War Ministry, the Navy Ministry, the Army General Staff Headquarters, the official residence of the war minister, the Transportation Ministry, and the Greater East Asia Ministry. They fell on the Yasukuni Shrine to war dead, the central markets, the Kabuki theater, Keio University, the Yomiuri Press, the old American embassy, and the historic Imperial Hotel, designed by Frank Lloyd Wright, which had survived the 1923 earthquake.

After the all clear sounded, the Emperor and Empress emerged from their underground shelter, the *Obunko*. Only five minutes later, flames erupted from cypress-wood latticework above the ceiling of the main palace as though propelled by a flamethrower. The flames darted down the glass-paned, wooden hallways, ignoring frenzied efforts by firemen to play feeble streams of water upon them. Then a shift of wind commanded the flames to march from the front palace to the rear palace, where the Imperial family had lived before taking to the *Obunko*. Swarming soldiers wielding mallets and crowbars frantically sought to rip down the pillars and beams of the hallways connecting the buildings. Elsewhere, other soldiers stripped out twenty truckloads of furniture, straw mats, gilt doors, books, paintings, clothing, and the crown prince's toys. After four hours, of twenty-seven buildings, only a reception chamber remained.

The impact of this event, noted American historian Alvin D. Coox, was profound:

> There had been something like a religious faith, held even among those at the top of the government, that the Imperial Palace was immune from the foe; few had believed that its survival until 25th May was attributable to sheer luck. The actuality was an immense shock, "like the fall of a castle in the days of old."

The marked increase in aircraft losses in the last two night-incendiary attacks on Tokyo, however, compelled a change in American tactics. A four-wing raid on the Yokohama urban industrial area was scheduled for May 29, but as a daylight, high-altitude mission with fighter escort. By the 1940 census, Yokohama stood as the fifth-largest city in Japan with a population of 968,091. It was the second-largest port and counted among its most important industrial activities shipbuilding and automotive manufacturing. The four wings put up 510 B-29s; seven of the Superfortresses and three of 101 Mustangs did not return. This raid burned out 6.9 square miles, or approximately 34 percent of the city.

LeMay's planners eyed Osaka for another daylight visit on June 1, striking the untouched swaths outside the fire-blackened area. The four wings lofted a total of 509 B-29s. Their loads torched another 3.15 square miles of that metropolis, plus 0.11 square miles of the adjacent city of Amagasaki. The cost of this mission was high: ten B-29s. But it was the escorting fighters that sustained the most devastating losses. One hundred forty-eight Mustangs from the 15th, 21st, and the fresh 506th Fighter Groups encountered a phalanx of foul weather extending from the wave tops to 23,000 feet with "zero visibility, intense turbulence, heavy rain, snow and icing," which scattered the flights. Twenty-seven planes failed to return, and only three of their pilots were rescued. This was by far the biggest disaster for Pacific escort fighters of the war.

Next, it was Kobe's turn to be revisited. Of the 523 B-29s airborne with bomb loads on June 5, 474 struck Kobe, at the cost of eleven Superfortresses. Photographs demonstrated that this raid destroyed 4.35 square miles, or 28 percent of the built-up area. On June 7, bombers returned to Osaka to follow up the June 1 mission, but clouds forced the 409 aircraft to employ radar aiming. Losses came to two B-29s and one of 152 Mustangs.

For June 10, the command mounted an adventurous, simultaneous daylight visual strike against six targets, using a total of 312 aircraft. Weather, however, disposed of this mission. Clouds covered the primary visual targets for three missions, forcing radar bombing of secondary targets. Amazingly, the 73rd Wing lined up radar scopes on the Hitachi Engineering Company's Kaigan plant and destroyed it. This whole effort cost only one Mustang and one 314th Wing machine, from which a submarine rescued two crewmen.

All four wings participated in a daylight incendiary attack on the Osaka and Amagasaki area on June 15. Both losses on this mission occurred on takeoff. Virtually all of the 444 B-29s of the 511 airborne that bombed the primary targets did so by radar.

With the June 15 mission, the campaign against six of the seven largest Japanese cities ended. (The fourth largest, Kyoto, the ancient Imperial capital, was deliberately spared from attack.) According to a postwar Japanese tabulation of casualties and damage and American figures for square miles of destruction, the losses in these six cities from air raids during the war—far and away the largest part due to the incendiary missions of the XXI Bomber Command—reached the following totals:

Losses to Aerial Attack in Major Japanese Cities

City	Casualties		Dwellings Totally Destroyed	Square Miles Destroyed
	Total	*Dead*		
Tokyo	216,988	97,031	713,366	56.30 (50.8%)
Osaka	35,467	9,246	328,237	15.59 (26.0%)
Nagoya	18,759	8,079	136,556	12.37 (31.2%)
Yokohama	18,830	4,616	93,793	8.94 (44.0%)
Kobe	23,353	6,789	131,528	8.73 (51.0%)
Kawasaki	2,525	1,001	35,635	3.37 (68.0%)
Total	315,922	126,762	1,439,115	105.30

As destructive as these raids had been, they were not the only onslaught on the Japanese war economy and the fabric of Japanese society during these months. The B-29s had begun to wield another weapon that indirectly threatened mass destruction: the mine.

Mines

It is doubtful that any effort in World War II returned such a dramatic strategic effect for such a relatively trivial investment of resources as did the aerial minelaying campaign against Japan. A handful of visionary naval officers first contrived both the hardware and the concepts and then convinced their senior leaders to pursue the program. It found an unexpected champion in Curtis LeMay, who controlled the vital means, the B-29. Perhaps most important, however, it came close upon the climax of the devastating campaign against Japanese commerce conducted primarily by American submarines.

Once inventions and events solved the practical problems of means and bases, Admiral Nimitz proposed a concerted aerial mining campaign against what the Americans termed the Inner Zone of the Japanese Empire, roughly the area north of Shanghai. The Joint Chiefs of Staff awarded it high priority as a task for Marianas-based B-29s. Planners identified three ambitious objectives for the campaign. Mines would: (1) halt Japan's importing of raw materials and food; (2) interrupt deployment and supply of its armed forces; and (3) disrupt its marine traffic within the Inland Sea, the body of water between Honshu, Kyushu, and Shikoku. The cutoff of food imports would starve the Japanese population, and this, coupled with the incendiary raids, would undermine their will to continue the war. The title assigned to this task advertised its intent bluntly: Operation Starvation.

The plan drew deadly aim upon Japan's greatest vulnerability. Among

many gambles that marked Japan's initiation of war, the most crucial was
this: Japan needed about ten million tons of shipping to maintain her economy, and only about six million tons wore the Rising Sun flag in 1941. The
rest had been supplied in peacetime mainly by those who became enemies.
Japan's initial wartime surge captured about 700,000 tons, but this still left
a very large deficit.

The following table briefly tells the story of Japan's plummeting merchant-shipping position to January 1, 1945, and the role of American submarines:

Japanese Merchant-Shipping Status, 1941–1944

| | Losses | | | Construction | |
| | Combat | | Noncombat | or other | |
Date	Submarine	Other		gains	Available
12/7/1941	—	—	—	—	6,384,000
1942	612,039	272,889	92,999	661,800	5,942,600
1943	1,312,353	355,733	99,538	1,067,100	4,944,000
1944	2,388,709	1,305,317	129,459	1,735,100	2,564,000

A decoded message at the beginning of April 1945 confirmed that
American air- and sea power had effectively severed communications between Japan and the southern resource areas, leaving much of its shipping
stranded in far waters and about 627,100 tons of oil tankers without useful
purpose. Two basic tasks occupied the remaining merchant fleet: hauling
imports from the Asian continent and transporting raw materials, food, and
finished products within the Home Islands. China and Korea delivered to
Japan 88 percent of its needed iron ore (essential for steelmaking), 24 percent of all its coal, and roughly 20 percent of its food. American analysts
estimated these imports totaled about 1 to 1.5 million tons per month, and
these vital supplies sustained war industries and the civilian population.
These sea-lanes were also used to transfer troops from garrisons on the
Asian mainland in order to buttress resistance to an expected invasion.
Further, given Japan's underdeveloped railway system and rudimentary
roads, shipping accounted for two thirds to three quarters of transportation
within the Home Islands.

The great bulk of Japan's overseas commerce traversed the Sea of Japan
to reach the great ports and industrial centers along the Inland Sea. Both the
Sea of Japan and the Inland Sea have only a few narrow entrances, which
were protected by mines and defenses affording sanctuary from submarines. The mine campaign aimed to deny Japan these final havens,
among which American planners identified the Shimonoseki Strait as the

key. This aperture between Honshu and Kyushu is flanked by the port cities of Shimonoseki and Moji. Through the straits flowed raw materials for Tokyo, Nagoya, and Kobe-Osaka. The final design of the campaign called for sealing the Shimonoseki Strait, then the Inland Sea shipping routes, and ultimately Korean ports.

The two kinds of aerial mines deployed for this campaign weighed either one thousand or two thousand pounds each and were brutish cylinders—ugly, stolid, and, once in place, utterly impartial. A parachute served to break their fall from an aircraft. They then rested on the bottom of the sea, which restricted their use to relatively shallow water. The real devilry resided in the five varieties of firing mechanisms. There were two magnetic firing mechanisms (M-9 and M-11) that responded to the magnetic field radiated by a steel hull, two acoustic firing mechanisms (A-3, triggered by propeller noises, and A-5, activated by subsonic hull vibrations), and one pressure firing mechanism (A-6, sensitized to the reduced water pressure generated by ship motion). While the A-5 and A-6 mechanisms were expected to be unsweepable, neither was initially on hand.

Despite the enthusiasm of the Navy and the sanction of the Joint Chiefs of Staff, the opposition of many aviators, including General Arnold, threatened to leave the minelaying plan stillborn. But LeMay recognized the plan's potential, and action followed swiftly, for he commanded the critical means. After delay due to the first series of incendiary raids, the 313th Wing mounted the first mission on March 27. Thereafter, the campaign passed through five phases:

Summary of the Minelaying Campaign against Japan

	Missions	*Dates*	*Sorties*	*Losses*	*Mines*
Phase 1:	Okinawa support				
	7	March 27– April 12	246	5	2,231
Phase 2:	Industrial-center (Inland Sea) blockade				
	2	May 3–5	195	0	1,549
Phase 3:	Northwest Honshu-Kyushu blockade				
	8	May 8–27	209	3	1,425
Phase 4:	Intensified northwest Honshu-Kyushu blockade				
	14	June 7– July 3	404	1	3,848
Phase 5:	Total blockade				
	15	July 9– August 14	474	6	4,049
Totals	46		1,528	15	13,102

Once the mining began, another weapon came into play: code breaking. While Allied cryptanalysts lacked absolute mastery over every maritime communication sent over the airwaves by the Japanese, what they could read proved ample. If a ship hit a mine and sent a report or distress signal, the message was usually intercepted and read. Notices of blocked channels or the scheduled opening of a previously blocked channel (to the hour) or, more deadly yet, of a new channel were intercepted and read. Japanese intelligence exchanges on the secrets of the mines and their firing devices were intercepted and read. If the Japanese broadcast information about the characteristics and limitations of a new sweeping device, that, too, was intercepted and read.

The postwar United States Strategic Bombing Survey damned Japanese countermeasures to the minelaying campaign as "neither extensive, efficient, nor adequate for the purpose." Several reasons lay behind the failure. Institutionally, the Imperial Navy stressed the offensive spirit, leaving no place of distinction for defensive measures such as antisubmarine warfare or mine countermeasures. The Imperial Navy ignored early warnings of the dangers posed by mines and failed to marshal the resources and the scientific and technical talent to counter them. Moreover, by mixing the types of mines in each field, the Americans geometrically increased the difficulty of clearance. An American counter device added a further complication by only arming the mine after several ships had passed—particularly minesweepers—so that waters thought safe became the grave of the next unwary ship. By war's end, the Japanese operated 350 minesweepers of all types, manned by 20,283 crewmen. Overall, however, limitations of equipment and numbers assured that no more than about one out of six mines dropped in Japanese waters was swept.

The impact of mines extended far beyond simply sinking ships. By the end of May, the near closure of the Shimonoseki Strait meant that most damaged ships could not even reach eighteen of the twenty-one repair yards located along the Inland Sea. Moreover, blockade of the Shimonoseki Strait compelled the Japanese to use ill-equipped ports along the Sea of Japan, which in turn inflicted tremendous delays as idled ships waited for the unloading of their cargoes, which then had to be transferred for rail shipment to the major urban industrial centers.

By late summer, the Japanese could clearly foresee the end of the empire's overseas waterborne transportation. Neither food nor reinforcements could be moved from the continent to Japan. Moreover, the ability of Japan to move raw materials, food, or military resources within the Home Islands was being curbed severely. Mines were restricting and ultimately nearly precluded use of the dwindling number of large vessels.

Tremendous pressure was being thrust upon Japan's rail system to move bulk materials, foremost among them food.

The Collapsing Japanese War Economy

"Although the Americans overrated Japan's economic potential," wrote Thomas Havens, "the wonder is that production held up as long and as well as it did." This represents a judicious assessment, but it would have afforded no succor to Japanese leaders in 1945. A frenzied effort swelled Japanese production of war goods to a crest in the last half of 1944, with the all-time production peak for war industries in October 1944. But this effort drew down dwindling stocks of raw materials and used up the last slack in the male labor force. Moreover, ten years of war and deprivation, particularly of food, had sapped the efficiency of Japanese workers. The blockade and bombing campaigns struck this tottering system with devastating results.

A great mass of data assembled after the war for the United States Strategic Bombing Survey charted the collapse of the Japanese war economy in the spring and summer of 1945. The principal reason for this disintegration was the destruction of Japanese merchant shipping and the resulting raw-material famine. The following table succinctly illustrates this point:

Selected Japanese Imports
(by fiscal year, April 1 to March 30, in tons)

	Coal	*Iron Ore*	*Rubber*	*Fertilizer*
1941	24,144,617	4,874,674	31,818	1,136,942
1942	19,595,929	4,663,776	44,085	1,031,039
1943	14,030,076	3,292,956	41,276	581,141
1944	8,294,748	1,073,065	19,595	405,841
1945	1,780,565	129,955	0	137,470

Oil demands special attention. Japan needed between six and seven million tons of petroleum per year for war, but domestic production totaled only 250,000 tons. The oil reserves of the Dutch East Indies and British Borneo became the grail for which Japan launched the war. Once under heel, these fields gushed seven million tons of oil per year, ample supplies to power Japan's war machine—provided that the crude products could be moved to Japan's refineries and then back to the war fronts. Thus, the central petroleum problem for Japan was not supply but transportation. And here Japan failed dramatically. Despite a vigorous Japanese program of construction and conversion, Allied submariners and airmen ravaged Japan's tanker fleet. Then the recapture of the Philippines cut off the resource areas from Japan. No tanker reached Japan after March 1945.

The United States Strategic Bombing Survey later concluded that the lack of raw materials alone would have gradually reduced the output of Japanese industries to insignificance or forced them to total closure even without the strategic bombing campaign. But other factors contributed to the collapse of Japan's war machine. On the labor front, the Japanese worker—who toiled on average eleven hours a day—was as patriotic and dedicated as any. But he found himself buffeted by inflation that eroded his wages by a third by 1944 (and worse in 1945), while a shortage of foodstuffs sapped his productivity and drove him on many days to abandon the workplace in quest for food. Meanwhile, a government dispersal program aimed at alleviating the hazard of Japan's inordinate industrial concentration proved to be a stupendous disaster that did more to stifle production than American bombing.

With the advent of air attacks, armament production tumbled with astonishing speed. It fell by 11 percent between March and April, followed by another decline of 14 percent between May and June. By July, production was down to 50 percent of its peak. The following numbers for selected critical elements compare the output level of July 1945 as a percent of the wartime peaks achieved in 1944:

Electrical output	50	Army ordnance	44
Coal consumption	50	Navy ordnance	57
Aluminum	9	Explosives	45

The urban area attacks—and the absenteeism produced by them—contributed importantly to this reduction.

By the summer of 1945, probably the most important indicator of Japan's capacity to offer effective, sustained resistance was aircraft manufacturing. From a total of only 445 planes in 1930, Japanese aircraft production reached 5,088 in 1941. Thereafter, it continued to make impressive strides to 8,861 in 1942, 16,693 in 1943, and 28,180 in 1944, when it peaked. In September 1944, Japanese factories rolled out 2,572 planes, the all-time high. But even then Japanese production faced a dim future due to the crippling effects of the blockade and shipping losses. Then came the bombing campaign and the dispersal fiasco. In July 1945, airframe production totaled only 1,131, and aircraft-engine production dropped to 1,257 from about 5,090 in June 1944.

It might appear obvious in hindsight that Japan's leaders should have recognized the impossibility of continuing a modern war of attrition and that the clear course was to surrender. The reality, however, is that they chose a different path.

6

The "Fundamental Policy"

"The one ray of hope I thought was to strike a blow against the Americans and British at Yunnan"

Military Prospects

The conventional retrospective portrayal presents Japan's military situation on New Year's Day 1945 as a vista of gloom. Its once-mighty navy had been smashed in the Philippines in October 1944. There, too, its soldiers, already vanquished on Leyte, braced for an invasion of Luzon. Its once-potent air strength could harry but not halt the still modest assaults of B-29s on the Homeland. American submarines had sent most of its merchant fleet to the bottom, choking off imports and threatening to idle its war industries.

But at Imperial General Headquarters in Tokyo, a different outlook reigned in 1945. True, Japan had lost its navy and with it control of the Western Pacific right up to its shores. But the Imperial realm still included huge territories with vast resources and hundreds of millions of vassals on the continent and to the south. These territories also represented potential bargaining chips—some to keep to show a profit from the gamble on war and others to trade away to secure those gains or, in the final accounting, to at least maintain the old order in the Homeland. Though airpower was much diminished, there remained thousands of planes and a bountiful supply of young men prepared to crash them into enemy ships. Above all, there was still a formidable army, backed by a stalwart civilian population, and the priceless asset of Japan's home soil—arranged by providence to negate all the advantages of an attacker dependent upon machines rather than men.

Officers at Imperial Headquarters coupled a reassuring assessment of the current strategic picture with an acute appreciation of future U.S. intentions. Americans lacked the patience for a protracted blockade and bombardment; they therefore surely would seek to end the war quickly by an invasion of the Homeland. If the initial assault could be repulsed, or if its cost could be made prohibitive, Japan could yet extricate herself from the war with honor. It was with this goal in mind that the Emperor sanctioned a new strategic directive published on January 20 that candidly declared the Homeland itself would be the arena for the "final decisive battle" of the war. Japan's armed forces were to gird for this Armageddon by completing construction in February or March of bristling positions along the perimeter of the "national defense sphere" delineated by the Bonin Islands (Iwo Jima), Formosa, the coastal sector of east China, and southern Korea. Soldiers and sailors along this perimeter, supported strongly by air units, would diminish the enemy's preponderance on the ground, in the air, and at sea, deny him advanced bases, sap his morale, and delay an invasion of the Homeland.

Preparations for the defense of the Homeland itself demanded new commands, plans, and forces. The most acrimonious command issue involved air units. For the desperate Imperial Navy, now with few ships remaining, control of its aviation units represented the last vestige of autonomy. The Joint Army-Navy Air Agreement of February 6 provided that all Homeland air units (except training and air-defense components) were to be concentrated to protect the national defense sphere from an invasion force, primarily with suicide attacks. But the agreement eschewed unity of command under a single army or navy officer in favor of a cooperative arrangement. A subsequent series of orders streamlined the Imperial Army's aviation components into an Air General Army commanded by General Masakazu Kawabe. The Imperial Navy consolidated aviation units into the Fifth Air Fleet, responsible for the Kyushu-Ryukyu area, and the Third Air Fleet, responsible for the rest of the Homeland.

With sole jurisdiction over major ground units, the Imperial Army executed its own new Homeland defense scheme. This plan basically created two theater commands. The First General Army (roughly equivalent to an American army group), with headquarters in Tokyo, was responsible for most of central and northern Honshu. The Second General Army, with headquarters at Hiroshima, had jurisdiction over forces on western Honshu, Shikoku, and Kyushu. Under each general army were several area armies (effectively the equivalent of an American army). Imperial Headquarters separately entrusted the defense of Hokkaido, the northernmost Home Island, to the Fifth Area Army.

There were only twelve field divisions in all of Japan on New Year's Day 1945. With so few units available, Imperial Headquarters embarked on a huge program of Homeland reinforcement. From Manchuria came four divisions (two armored and two infantry). But by far the largest increase in strength came as the result of a February 26 order for a gigantic, three-phase mobilization program to create new legions as follows:

	General Army Headquarters	Army Headquarters	Coastal Division	Counter-attack Division	Independent Mixed Brigade	Tank Brigade
Phase 1	—	—	13	—	1	—
Phase 2	2	8	—	8	—	6
Phase 3	—	—	9	7	14	—
Total	2	8	22	15	15	6

The mobilization spawned two distinctive creations. The first was the static coastal-combat division, designed to grapple in close-quarter fighting with a landing force a short distance inland from the water's edge. The second was the mobile counterattack division, effectively a reduced-strength field division organized to march rapidly from inland positions and deliver punishing blows against a beachhead. At the end of the mobilization, the forces available to defend the Homeland were to number sixty divisions (thirty-six field and counterattack, twenty-two coastal combat, and two armored divisions) and thirty-four brigades (twenty-seven infantry and seven tank). Counting the necessary logistic and administrative infrastructure, the mobilization was to add 1.5 million men to the home-defense commands. The aggregate strength of the Homeland armies would then total 2,903,000 men, 292,000 horses, and 27,500 motor vehicles.

On April 8, frenzied staff officers in Tokyo completed a sprawling master defense plan for the impending struggle for the Homeland and contiguous areas, crowned as *Ketsu-Go* ("Decisive" Operation). This plan envisioned that American invaders would be confronted and crushed in one of seven key areas, with emphasis on the Kanto-Tokyo area and Kyushu. Preparations were to extend in three phases from April to October, but forces on Kyushu were to be ready by early June.

Three features marked the Ketsu-Go plan. First, operations were not aimed at destroying the enemy either at the water's edge (the tactics prior to mid-1944) or far inland (the tactics from mid-1944 to Ketsu-Go). The Japanese realized the folly of immediate beach defense in the face of massive American prelanding bombardments, but they also grasped that their adversary never could be dislodged if permitted to consolidate their positions after a landing. Therefore, Ketsu-Go aimed to destroy the beachhead, the perimeter established by the invader a few days after the landing, anchored on the coast, but stretching only a few miles inland.

The second distinctive feature of Ketsu-Go was the comprehensive devotion to *tokko* (special attack or suicide) tactics, not only the now-routine air and sea efforts but also ashore. The incorporation of the civilian population into the defense scheme represented the third singular feature of Ketsu-Go. Under the National Resistance Program, commanders would summon all able-bodied civilians, regardless of gender, to combat. Should the Americans overrun any portion of the Homeland, swarms of guerrillas would beset them.

The first and second phases of the massive mobilization were completed successfully. During this same interval and extending for some time thereafter, a series of orders and publications, such as the *National Resistance Manual,* elaborated a comprehensive scheme for the final defense of the Homeland. The inexorable progress of American forces on Okinawa in May, however, triggered a series of urgent measures that shuffled more (and better) units to Kyushu. This supreme effort utterly exhausted equipment resources for units not so deployed; Imperial Headquarters could only hope production would catch up by October.

Political Prospects

The adoption of a strategy that reached first for military triumph before even contemplating diplomatic parleys has been argued as evidence that militarists gripped the reins of power tightly. But it was not just Japan's uniformed leaders who staked their faith in Ketsu-Go, nor was the fight-to-the-finish strategy embraced over the passive resistance of key civilians, including the Emperor.

The power of the militarists in Japan during the war was very real, and they exercised their domination through means both legal and extralegal. A regulation introduced in 1900 decreed that the army minister in the cabinet must be a serving general. The regulation moored the minister's loyalties to the service and its objectives, not to civilians and their factions. Even more significant, the regulation vested the Army with the right to nominate—or refuse to nominate—its own minister. The Army thus exercised veto power over the formation of every cabinet, and no cabinet could survive the resignation of the army minister. This empowered the Imperial Army (the Imperial Navy gained parallel authority) to abort the creation of "unsuitable" governments or bring down any that strayed.

Japan's armed forces also wielded two potent extralegal methods of political mastery. The first was terror. The murder of Prime Minister Tsuyoshi Inukai by Imperial Navy officers in 1932—just one of sixty-four incidents of right-wing political violence between 1921 and 1944—halted Japan's hesitant steps toward democracy. Further assassinations in the 1930s, as well as five coup attempts, served to maintain the military's intimidation of the ruling class. The control of information constituted a more subtle second but still effective tool. By the adroit orchestration of propaganda for the masses, coupled with denial of accurate information to the small circle of men franchised to participate in steering Japan's future in any meaningful sense, the militarists forestalled criticism or dissent.

An extraordinarily select circle of men maintained a stranglehold over Japan's political structure in 1945. In the final accounting, those who exercised any say whatsoever numbered no more than a few score; those who wielded actual power of decision numbered no more than eight: the six members of an inner cabinet titled the Supreme Council for the Direction of the War, the Emperor, and his principal adviser, Lord Keeper of the Privy Seal Marquis Koichi Kido.

Even within this tiny elite, in the end Japan's fate ultimately was chosen by one man, Emperor Hirohito. His mysterious path to what became known as the *Seidan* (Sacred Decision) to halt the war was fraught then and until his death in 1989 with transcendent political importance both within Japan and for her adversaries. His intervention in August 1945 posed an obvious question: If the Emperor could stop the war then, why did he not do so earlier, and, indeed, why did he not prevent the war altogether? The answer, insisted one camp, was that the Sacred Decision merely proved that the Emperor had always commanded from behind the scenes. A second camp cast the Emperor in the pose of a constitutional, or "symbol," monarch who reigned but did not rule. His feat of successfully terminating the conflict was the unique product of an unprecedented impasse in internal Japanese politics. This view not only spared the Emperor from being tried as a war criminal but also resonated within Japan to separate the Emperor himself from the war and to preserve the entire imperial system. This interpretation also did unanticipated service as the linchpin for much postwar argument that different military or political moves by the United States could have obtained Japan's surrender without the use of atomic weapons.

Neither of these polar positions is accurate, but determining the Emperor's actual responsibility and role requires understanding both how the Emperor viewed the situation in 1945 and what his actual power was. This is not a simple task. During the interval between the surrender and the occupation, Japanese officials destroyed massive amounts of documents to prevent their use in war-crimes trials. It is unlikely that anything placing the Emperor in a favorable light was destroyed. Surviving contemporary evidence on the Emperor's stance is sparse, but it does include a record of undisputed authenticity: Koichi Kido's daily diary, which provides priceless insight into the Emperor's thinking.

Postwar investigations produced a body of statements from Japanese officials about the Emperor and his role, but these must be approached with care. Some Japanese officials may have said what they thought American officials wanted to hear. Others, with the complicity of American occupation authorities, mounted what appears to be a concerted effort to protect the Emperor by misrepresenting events in a fashion that endorsed the sympathetic portrait of the monarchy.

The decades following the war brought to light additional evidence, but new revelations followed the Emperor's death in 1989. These included a vital document: *Showa Tenno Dokuhakuroku—Terasaki Hidenari, Goyogakkari Nikki* (The Showa Emperor's Monologue and the Diary of Hidenari Terasaki). The Emperor's motives for dictating this lengthy statement in March and April 1946 remain uncertain. It might have been prepared as the Emperor's testimony, were he summoned to face war-crimes trials, as a friend of the court brief to help the prosecution, as a valedictory to his reign in anticipation of his abdication, or just as a way to set down his views for posterity. Whatever prompted its creation, it represents Hirohito's personal recollections of his role in the conflict, and it undoubtedly aimed to defend the Imperial institution and himself. Thus, its key revelations about his thinking carry enormous credibility.

At a minimum, this body of evidence proves that the Emperor was no mere ceremonial symbol. He was first of all extremely knowledgeable about the progress of military operations. He received daily updates and frequent comprehensive briefings from senior officers. Not only did these sessions keep him well versed on Japan's situation, they also permitted him to challenge Japan's uniformed leaders with penetrating questions. But there is a vast gap between knowledge and actual influence. The array of sources affords far too many examples of Imperial Headquarters ignoring or subverting the Emperor's expressed views in order to sustain a portrait of the Emperor as the "fighting generalissimo" or the functional commander in chief with Imperial Headquarters as merely his dutiful secretariat.

By controlling the flow of information, Imperial Headquarters assured that the Emperor saw events through the eyes of his military chiefs. This

enormously facilitated their ability to obtain his support for their strategies. The view of events at Imperial Headquarters, however, was far from
accurate. Senior Japanese officers failed to stringently examine and verify
the claims flowing in from field commanders, and in the latter half of the
war the degree of exaggeration in these battle reports verged into the fantastic. The mass of misinformation led both Imperial Headquarters and the
Emperor to believe that American morale was being seriously strained by
the high prices of each campaign.

The Emperor and his military chiefs all assimilated information within
a framework that took the Russo-Japanese War of 1904–1905 as its historic template. In that conflict, the Imperial Navy victory at Tsushima
proved the "decisive battle" that determined the outcome of the war. Japanese leaders assumed, as a matter of course, that the war with the United
States would be decided ultimately in a similarly great "decisive battle."

The Imperial Navy thus confused its carefully developed plan for a
great decisive battle in the Western Pacific with an overall strategy. The
Imperial Army, by contrast, settled on a vague general theory that Japan
would subdue China while Germany and Italy brought England to its
knees, thereby causing "America's loss of will to continue the war." As historian Edward Drea aptly phrased it, undergirding all Japanese strategy
was a dismissive view that "Americans [were] products of liberalism and
individualism and incapable of fighting a protracted war." During 1942
and 1943, Japan pursued a decisive victory successively at Midway and in
the South Pacific. When the effort to make the defense of the Marianas the
decisive battle failed by July 1944, the War Journal of Imperial Headquarters concluded:

> We can no longer direct the war with any hope of success. The only course
> left is for Japan's one hundred million people to sacrifice their lives by
> charging the enemy to make them lose the will to fight.
>
> In judging the situation . . . there is unanimous agreement that henceforth
> we will slowly fall into a state of ruin. So it is necessary to plan for a quick
> end to the war.*

While Imperial Headquarters withheld this judgment from the Japanese
populace, the fall of the Marianas marked a turning point that no artful
public pronouncements could disguise. On July 18, 1944, the *jushin,* composed of all the living former premiers, met to discuss the replacement of

---

* Japanese propaganda persistently referred to the nation's population as 100 million, whereas the actual count in the 1944 census was about 72 million.

the government of General Hideki Tojo, who had led the nation into war. The *jushin* recommended three generals, and the Emperor selected Kuni-aki Koiso.

Koiso was unequal to his role, but he did manage to take one key step. Although he failed to gain the right to participate in supreme command, he replaced the jury-rigged administrative apparatus that coordinated the civilian government and Imperial Headquarters with a new Supreme Council for the Direction of the War (*Saiko Senso Shido Kaigi*). The council had six members: the premier, the foreign minister, the army and navy ministers, and the chiefs of staff of the Imperial Army and Navy. The Big Six, as it was commonly styled, ruled by unanimity, not majority vote, and its recommendations remained subject to the formality of cabinet approval.

Koiso's military and diplomatic strategies proved his undoing. Under Koiso's leadership, the Supreme Council for the Direction of the War, in the presence of the Emperor, declared the Philippines the scene of the decisive battle. On November 8, 1944, Koiso publicly committed his government to victory at Leyte. He compounded his peril by likening it to the Battle of Tennozan in 1582, a great turning point in Japanese history. Thus, Koiso effectively proclaimed to the nation that the victor at Leyte would win the war. After a costly effusion of material resources and blood, Imperial General Headquarters decided on December 20 to abandon Leyte.

Following defeat on Leyte and the early raids of B-29s, the Emperor instructed his confidant Kido that it was time to consult the senior statesmen about the war situation. To avoid arousing army concerns, the Emperor met individually with the *jushin* between February 7 and 26, ostensibly to receive New Year greetings. This provided an opportunity for frank exchanges, but the records disclose little that could be construed as an urge for prompt peace. The exception to the general reticence was Prince Fumimaro Konoe. In a "Memorial to the Throne" of February 1945, he reiterated themes he had expressed before: In defeat, the throne could be preserved, but in a communist revolution it might perish. The Emperor's response to Konoe's importuning was long suppressed because it is so revealing: It is premature, said Hirohito, to seek peace "unless we make one more military gain."*

Nor is this the only evidence of the Emperor's pugnacious instincts. When MacArthur's forces landed on the main Philippine island of Luzon

---

* The Emperor stuck to his commitment to one last battle even in light of disturbing news from another quarter. An intelligence report by Imperial Headquarters on February 15 concluded that the Soviets were likely to abrogate their neutrality pact with Japan and pounce anytime thereafter that suited their purposes.

in January 1945, the Emperor pressed for a "vigorous" fight. The local Japanese commander, General Tomoyuki Yamashita, chose to conduct a protracted attrition campaign, however, and Army Chief of Staff General Yoshijiro Umezu refused to intervene, despite the Emperor's direct pleas. The Emperor was not alone within the palace in his belief that Japan could still obtain a decisive victory. Both Kido and his chief secretary, Marquis Yasumasa Matsudaira, concurred in mid-March that if the Army could secure one triumph, the Emperor could then overtly support ending the war.

Just as Koiso's military strategy fell to ruins, his maladroit diplomatic approaches to Nationalist China and tentative probes of the Soviets came to naught. On April 4, 1945, Koiso advised Kido of his intent to resign. At the same time, Koiso laid a proposal before the war and navy ministers as well as the chiefs of the army and navy general staffs that the next government should be formed as an Imperial Headquarters cabinet to mesh together for the first time the government and the home fronts with the supreme command and the war fronts. The militarists summarily rebuffed this potential erosion of their power. This same day, General Tojo, participating for the first time in a meeting of the *jushin*, explicitly warned of the military's power to make or break any cabinet. Tojo also thrust forward the proposition that the senior statesmen should grasp the nettle and decide whether Japan should battle on or seek peace. His peers demurred, pleading that they lacked the authority for such a decision. In reality, some might also have been evading a ploy by Tojo to ferret out anyone harboring thoughts of peace so as to mark them for a rendezvous with an assassin's bullet.

After much muddled discussion, the *jushin* selected as the new premier Admiral Kantaro Suzuki, president of the privy council. As a young officer, he had commanded extraordinarily heroic torpedo attacks in wars with China and Russia. These exploits had lifted his name into a prominent orbit. Suzuki embodied the virtues of exemplary personal courage, absolute integrity, and pure fidelity to the throne that were the epitome of the revered samurai tradition.

After the war, Suzuki's supporters, spearheaded by his cabinet secretary, Hisatsune Sakomizu, argued that from the outset the new premier had pursued a secret peace agenda. They depicted Suzuki as playing *haragei* (the stomach game), which supposedly reconciled his private views with a clear record of espousing the fight-to-the-finish strategy.

Though Suzuki might indeed have seen peace as a distant goal, he had no design to achieve it within any immediate time span or on any terms acceptable to the Allies. His own comments at the conference of senior statesmen gave no hint that he favored an early cessation of the war.

Suzuki promptly signed a pledge presented by a delegation of generals from Imperial Headquarters committing himself to prosecute the war to the bitter end, to "properly" settle the question of Army-Navy unification (a move certain to increase the power of the Army and its commitment to fight to the finish), and to exert every possible effort to totally mobilize the nation. One state minister pressing for peace, Vice Admiral Sakonji, later conceded that Suzuki took up his appointment with no vision of ending the war in the near term and very much convinced that he must bide his time until some "splendid success" of Japanese arms made peace palatable to the Imperial Army.

Suzuki's selections for the most critical cabinet posts were, with one exception, not advocates of an early peace either. Suzuki incorporated incumbent Navy Minister Mitsumasa Yonai into his cabinet. The selection of Yonai, a known opponent of the war, was later represented as evidence of Suzuki's secret peace agenda. But Yonai's own actions and comments in 1945 establish that while he consistently advocated a negotiated peace, he lacked a sense of urgency about ending the conflict.

Suzuki secured the service of General Korechika Anami for the crucial portfolio of army minister because they had worked together before and shared great trust. Suzuki believed that Anami could control the Army, which would be essential if the war was to be terminated successfully at some future point. But Anami advocated no peace terms the Allies were likely to accept. This left those seeking to end the war with the problem of controlling Anami.

Anami was not a man easily controlled. The vice chief of the Imperial Army General Staff, Lieutenant General Torashiro Kawabe, a shrewd observer, characterized Anami as a quintessential "man of will power rather than of resourcefulness." The army minister had flunked the examination for entry into the military academy four times before succeeding. He then steadfastly remained outside the orbit of any of the jostling factions within the Imperial Army in his climb to eminence. Anami spoke easily with subordinates, often with his trademark adages such as "simplicity represents strength" and "morality is a fighting strength." In his personification of willpower over cleverness, he perfectly represented the ethos of the Imperial Army.

Anami's "pure and transparent character" was in almost complete contrast with that of Chief of Staff Umezu, a man five years his senior, who shared with Anami the ability to forcibly alter Japan's fate. According to Kawabe, Umezu was "complex" and a "very politically minded" character, who kept his personal views concealed even from his closest staff (his nickname was "the Ivory Mask"). Despite these sharp differences, the army minister and the chief of staff were bonded by respect and friendship, linked in part from the fact that both hailed from the same small village on Kyushu.

Suzuki knew Shigenori Togo only by reputation as the foreign minister at the time of Pearl Harbor who could neither abide Tojo's judgment to seek war nor truckle to Tojo's autocratic manner. Togo was by now a clear disciple of peace, but an interview convinced him that Suzuki was not. In fact, Togo recalled later that Suzuki spoke in terms of continuing the war for two or three years. Togo reluctantly agreed to join the cabinet only on the condition that Suzuki commission a detailed study of Japan's situation, for the purpose of opening the admiral's eyes to reality.

The public notice of the formation of Suzuki's new government coincided with a bombshell. On April 5, the Soviet Union announced that its neutrality pact with Japan would not be renewed. This, however, did not equal a declaration of hostilities and, despite the ominous overtones, many Japanese officials clutched to the language in the pact that provided that it would remain in effect for one year from the date of renunciation.

Just over one month later, the end of the war in Europe on May 8 provided an excellent opening for Japan to barter for the termination of the Pacific conflict on better terms than unconditional surrender and without Soviet intervention. The Suzuki government mounted no effort to seize this opportunity, but the German surrender did lead to one positive step. In a series of meetings from May 11 to 14, Foreign Minister Togo succeeded in persuading the Big Six to meet in closed session without their staffs for substantive talks. This stanched the baleful influence of at least the army members of the fanatical secretariat staff who faithfully reflected the do-or-die spirit of the typical field-grade officers in the Imperial Army. The Big Six were thus freed from the all-too-real threat of assassination for any sign of less than stalwart devotion to "victory."

In the Suzuki cabinet, the Big Six comprised Prime Minister Suzuki, Foreign Minister Togo, Navy Minister Yonai, Army Minister Anami, Chief of the Naval General Staff Koshiro Oikawa, and Chief of the Army General Staff Umezu. In the later part of May, Yonai contrived the replacement of Oikawa with Admiral Soemu Toyoda. Yonai told American inquisitors after the war that he engineered this switch to add a persuasive voice for peace to the Big Six, exploiting the fact that Toyoda hailed from the same clan as Anami and Umezu. The record belies this claim, for Toyoda proved a fervent and articulate exponent of Ketsu-Go to the end.

The May meetings produced the very first formal and concrete discussion of terminating the war and demonstrated that Anami, Umezu, and Oikawa (and later Toyoda) were not among those officers who preferred the extinction of Japan to any taint of compromise. Togo effectively entrusted his life to their discretion, and they did not betray him. But the actual exchanges in these sessions revealed vastly divergent agendas. The Army sought primarily to keep the Soviets out of the war, to permit withdrawal of forces from Manchuria in order to bolster Ketsu-Go. The Navy's vision did not pause there but roamed on to hallucinate an exchange of some cruisers and resources for oil and aircraft, with a distant goal of forming an alliance with the Soviets. Foreign Minister Togo stomped on these fantasies by noting acidly that diplomacy depended on the military situation and warning that the Soviets might well have already reached an agreement with the United States and the United Kingdom.

The upshot of these conversations was only a warrant for Togo to preserve Soviet neutrality and perhaps secure Soviet friendship. The discussion pigeonholed authorization for Togo to enlist the Soviets in mediating an end to the war. The military vetoed any objective beyond rapprochement with the Soviet Union that would enable Japan to continue the Pacific War. Insofar as peace was concerned, Army Minister Anami thundered that they must remember "above all" that Japan had not lost the war and still occupied vast swaths of territories.

Even a modest Japanese effort to solicit Soviet aid, either passive or active, appears strange given the strong history of their enmity in the twentieth century. Two basic (and negative) reasons, however, drove the initiative. A direct attempt to parley with the United States and the United Kingdom would presumably extract only a reiteration of the unconditional-surrender terms and place Japan in a supplicant role that was anathema to the military diehards. Second, probes or circumstances ruled out all other potential intermediaries. As Togo and Kido quaintly phrased it, the Japanese rejected the Vatican due to the "Pope's negative attitude toward the war." The Chinese had rebuffed early explorations and then subsequently endorsed unconditional surrender. As for Sweden or Switzerland, the Japanese doubted that either of them would mount a "serious effort," and it seemed maladroit to turn to them when there was an ostensibly neutral major power available.

In addition, a démarche through the Soviets offered several positive incentives. First, the ostensible pursuit of Soviet neutrality, or even aid, would conceal the ultimate peace negotiations from zealots who would destroy any government embarked toward surrender. Then there was the expectation, observed scholar Leon Sigal, that "only an active mediation by a power willing to throw its weight behind Japan could possibly obtain the terms the Japanese leaders considered the minimum necessary for a settlement." Finally, as Army Minister Anami argued, the Soviets might extend aid to Japan to avoid her becoming an ally of the United States in a post-war world dominated by U.S.-Soviet rivalry.

The reasoning of Suzuki's cabinet in this matter was profoundly flawed. Only Togo apprehended the possibility that the Soviets might have already pocketed a hefty payment at the Yalta Conference in February 1945 to enter the war on the other side. Japan's rulers also operated under the sorely mistaken belief that they had nearly a year left on their Soviet neutrality pact. This might account for the halting steps to implement the initiative. Foreign Minister Togo selected former premier and onetime ambassador to Moscow Koki Hirota to approach Soviet Ambassador Jacob A. Malik. It took over two weeks to prepare Hirota for his mission, but Malik provided a frigid response and left only with the comment that he must await the reply of the Soviet government.

Although Togo successfully excluded second- and third-echelon staff from meetings of the Big Six, he lacked the authority to switch off the whirling gears of the bureaucracy that continued to assemble agendas and plans. Now, according to the customary practice for each new government to declare its purposes, the bureaucracy rolled from its workshops a document entitled "The Fundamental Policy to Be Followed Henceforth in the Conduct of the War." This proclaimed that Japan must fight to the finish and choose extinction before surrender. The new national policy was to be ratified at a meeting in the presence of the Emperor, which, according to Cabinet Secretary Sakomizu, would give it "indisputable dignity" and make it impregnable.

This ambitious project hosted two malignant cells. As in any bureaucracy, the staff generated papers to support the ultimate policy document. The Army submitted one titled "Estimate of the World Situation," but a second document, "The Present State of National Power," also appeared. This was the fruit of Suzuki's promise to Togo for a study of Japan's situation, and its principal author was Sakomizu. The dogged factual depiction of Japan's plight in both papers undermined rather than buttressed the "Fundamental Policy" document. This was particularly marked with respect to "The Present State." This assessment commenced with the observation that the war had taken an ominous turn; both the material resources of the country and national morale required immediate attention. While acknowledging both the people's loyalty to the throne and their will to resist invasion, the paper also identified a longing for a turnaround in the situation and the growth of criticism of the government and the military.

Moving on to the objective measures of power, "The Present State" detailed shortcomings in manpower mobilization, shipping, and steel and chemical production, as well as a critical shortage of petroleum. The report emphasized the alarming shortage of food. The period before the next harvest was forecast to be potentially the gravest time since the beginning of the war. Even assuming that the planned import levels of provisions, cereals, and table salt from the continent were met, the rations would be very meager and salt intake would be at a level of minimum survival. A combination of import reductions and communication interruptions due to enemy action and bad weather could generate local famines that would fracture civil order.

A crowded formal meeting convened on June 6 reviewed the "Fundamental Policy." The Army launched a psychological blitzkrieg, expertly aimed to rout the facts and foreclose any dissent. Prime Minister Suzuki uncorked as much fervor for the fight to the finish as anyone present. Foreign Minister Togo alone sought without avail to lead his comrades to a rational examination of reality.

The meeting terminated with Japan effectively locked on course for a fight to the last man, woman, and child. After perfunctory approval by the cabinet, thirteen officials assembled in the presence of the Emperor on June 8. Most speakers recited an edited version of the discussions of the past two days. Only Togo voiced a warning that the prospects for diplomacy could be no brighter than those of the bleak war situation. The Emperor listened in silence, but Admiral Toyoda, for one, noted that "discontent was written all over him." Then the assembled ministers rose and bowed. The Emperor withdrew. The meeting had conferred Imperial sanction upon the decision to fight to the death.

There is no doubt the Emperor and Lord Keeper of the Privy Seal Kido bestirred themselves after this meeting for the first time to take concrete steps at least to energize a diplomatic strategy to end the war. There is conflict concerning their exact thinking at this juncture. After the war, Kido asserted that the contents of the "Fundamental Policy" staggered him, and Suzuki's apparent acquiescence stunned him. This account not only advanced Kido's bona fides as an advocate of peace but, given their extraordinarily close relationship, implied the Emperor had long shared such convictions.

Examination of the contemporary evidence and subsequent revelations, however, provide a far more convincing alternative explanation. In this interpretation, prior to about mid-May, Kido and the Emperor had sensed no urgency to open negotiations, much less secure peace, because they still viewed a military victory as a prerequisite to any peace move. The obvious disconnection between Japan's situation and the government's goals at the Imperial Conference marked merely one link, but perhaps the last one, in a chain of events that finally swayed the Emperor and Kido to adjust their perceptions of Japan's realistic courses of action. Moreover, it is now known that a group of seven professors from Tokyo University, who had been in communication with Kido since March, had pressed a blueprint for termination of the war that incorporated a decision by the Emperor memorialized in an Imperial edict. Thus, Kido concurrently came into both an understanding of the need for action and a plan.

It is undisputed that the next day, June 9, Kido wrote out a paper titled "Draft Plan for Controlling the Crisis Situation" (*Jikyoku Shushu No Taisaku Shian*). This assessment recounted the salient points about the military situation: Okinawa was about to be lost; by the end of the year, the nation's ability to prosecute a modern war would be extinguished; overwhelming enemy airpower would intensify the destruction of small towns and villages; and the losses and suffering intensified by the coming winter would spark civil unrest that the government would be unable to contain. Kido emphasized that the Allies' main object was to overthrow the "so-called militarist clique." While, Kido noted, it was customary to initiate negotiations with a peace proposal from the military,

> this would be almost impossible at present, considering the current condition of our country. Also, we are most likely to lose a good chance should we wait until the opportunity matures. As a result, we cannot be sure we will not share the fate of Germany and be reduced to adverse circumstances under which we will not attain even our supreme object of safeguarding the Imperial Household and preserving the national polity.

The situation, he declared, called for unprecedented measures—namely, the direct intervention of the Emperor with a personal message to initiate negotiations with a mediating country, just as advocated by the Tokyo University professors. The message, noted Kido, would

> make it known that the Throne, who had always been interested in peace— citing the imperial rescript on the declaration of war—has decided, in view of the impossibly heavy war damages we have sustained, to bring the war to a close on "very generous terms."

But the terms Kido envisioned definitely had limits. Japan would give up her occupation of European colonies only as they were granted independence. Japanese armed forces overseas would withdraw on their own accord. The nation would face "strong demands" for disarmament and must be prepared to be "content with minimum defense."

Several salient facets of this analysis bear emphasis. In his brief of the overall situation, Kido acknowledged explicitly that military defeat could extinguish the Imperial institution, but he also alluded to peril to the Imperial system from uncontrolled civil unrest. The recognition of deadly threats from within is a key to understanding the motivations of some of the tiny handful of men controlling Japan's destiny. The attraction of negotiations thus is not solely to foreclose the end of the Imperial institution by defeat but to assure as well that its internal bulwarks remained intact.

It is also significant that Kido's minimum peace terms by no means approached unconditional surrender. His proviso that occupied territories would have to gain independence would permit Japan's rulers to claim moral triumph over European colonialism and justification for the sacrifices of the war. While Kido contemplated a period of enforced disarmament, there would be no occupation of Japan. This is altogether evocative of the Treaty of Versailles that ended World War I—and which was followed by a militarily resurgent Germany within less than twenty years. Finally, Kido mentioned no demand for a guarantee of the Emperor's status because this was a moot point.

By Kido's postwar account, the Emperor was "greatly satisfied" by the paper and readily authorized the Lord Privy Seal to explore the plan with the prime minister and other leaders. Yet on this same day, June 9, an Imperial Rescript was published coincident with the special session of the Diet. In this Imperial Rescript, the Emperor summoned the nation to "smash the inordinate ambitions of the enemy nations" to "achieve the goals of the war." The rescript gave no hint of any policy beyond a fight to the finish, and thus in no way enlisted public understanding, much less support, of the covert and halting moves for peace. Owing to delay caused by the busy Diet schedule, it was June 13 before Kido briefly outlined the plan to Prime Minister Suzuki, who promised further talks once the Diet was adjourned. Kido then spoke to Navy Minister Yonai, the only one of the four military chiefs he was certain would not betray the plan. Yonai replied cautiously, "Of course, very good idea, but I wonder how the Prime Minister really feels about the war?"

When Suzuki returned from the Diet session to deliver the traditional report to the Emperor, he tarried first with Kido. There, he read Kido's paper and, according to Kido, promised to steer by its course. He appeared to retain some reservations and inquired of Kido, "I wonder what Admiral Yonai thinks about all this?" When Kido replied, "Yonai said the same thing about you," Suzuki found this humorous. Kido reported this left him unsettled, for it demonstrated that neither the Prime Minister nor the Navy Minister comprehended what the other "had in his stomach."

Kido approached one other member of the Big Six. As he anticipated, Foreign Minister Togo eagerly enlisted. Kido initially did not dare approach the remaining three military members of the Big Six, but soon, when closeted with General Anami, he took a bold gamble, perhaps because he and Anami had once worked intimately when Anami was military aide to the Emperor and Kido was the chief secretary to the Privy Seal. Kido laid out his plan, including the role of the throne, and Anami supposedly "agreed in principle," according to Kido's postwar account. Kido's contemporary diary at best documents Anami's ambivalence, for the Army Minister insisted that diplomacy would be much more likely to succeed if it was stayed until "after the United States has sustained heavy losses in [Ketsu-Go]." Kido now believed the time was ripe to air his plan before the Big Six.

The contemporary and postwar evidence demonstrates that the Emperor's entire view of the situation underwent a sea change during this period. Having already confided to Prince Konoe in February 1945 that he was wedded to one more military victory, as late as early May the Emperor still confirmed to Kido that he believed there remained a chance for a military success on Okinawa. But the Emperor also provided a startling confession in *Showa Tenno Dokuhakuroku*. When he finally recognized the approach of defeat at Okinawa, the Emperor explained that

the one ray of hope I thought was to strike a blow against the Americans and British at Yunnan [China] together with Burma operations. I spoke to [Army Chief of Staff] Umezu about it, but he was opposed saying the logistics could not be sustained. When I spoke to Prince Kaya, Commandant of the Army War College, about it, he said something probably could be done as a temporary measure and he would try to research it. However, it came to nothing in the end.

It is probably a mark of his desperation that the Emperor seriously entertained the odd strategic concept that a meaningful blow could be struck in a peripheral theater. Nonetheless, this admission makes it clear beyond dispute that even when he began to examine alternatives to Ketsu-Go, his instinct remained that a military triumph must precede any diplomatic maneuver. The significance of this is that there would be no need for the bargaining leverage of a recent victory if the Emperor was prepared to accept terms approximating unconditional surrender.

Even as the Emperor's aggressive plans met rebuff, however, he obtained several sobering critical reports on Japan's material means. One of the most important of these came when Umezu returned from an inspection trip that had kept him from the June Imperial Conference. The chief of staff disclosed to the Emperor that the combined strength of all Japanese troops in China equaled the combat power of only about eight American divisions. Further, their ammunition stocks were sufficient for only one battle. This was the first time Umezu had exhibited such pessimism before the Emperor, and it followed closely upon his inability to provide a definite reply to the Emperor's explicit request for an assessment of the Army's capacity to defend Tokyo. Also at about this time, the Emperor discussed plans for the final decisive battle in the Homeland but expressed his doubts about the ability of the population to withstand the air bombardment until then.

While Kido circulated his "Draft Plan," the Emperor received another revelation about Japan's actual military capabilities. In February, he had commissioned Admiral Kiyoshi Hasegawa to investigate both the morale and the material strength of the Imperial Navy. The admiral's thorough efforts consumed March, April, and May, and on June 12 he stood before the Emperor to read his formal report. Navy morale presented no problem, asserted Hasegawa, but material matters told another story altogether. The admiral detailed gross deficiencies in both the quantity and quality of navy munitions that invited "grave reflection."

Concurrent with Hasegawa's presentation, another report reached the Emperor. He described it in *Showa Tenno Dokuhakuroku:*

Prince [Moriatsu] Higashikuni arrived and reported specifically on numerous affairs. I had been informed until then that the coastal defenses were in bad shape, but according to his report it was not just the coastal defense; the divisions reserved to engage in the decisive battle also did not have sufficient numbers of weapons. I was told that the iron from bomb fragments dropped by the enemy was being used to make shovels. This confirmed my opinion that we were no longer in a position to continue the war.

The Emperor did not fail to notice that the reports on Japan's actual situation presented at the Imperial Conference on the "Fundamental Policy" showed that "taking all information into account, it was impossible to continue with the war," in flagrant contradiction to the arguments of the military and naval leaders that "the war be continued because there was no question that victory could be achieved." As he described his attitude later, he "decided that [as] there was no longer any hope of success for the Yunnan war plan, I decided that there was no other way out but to call for a negotiated peace." In *Showa Tenno Dokuhakuroku,* however, the Emperor stated clearly that negotiations would not be conducted through the smaller neutral nations because they would be forced to present only unconditional surrender. The Soviets alone had the power to "stand between" the British, the Americans, and the Japanese.

The Emperor's concern over the reaction of the Army to an attempt to end the war before Ketsu-Go no doubt also contributed to his choice of a circuitous diplomacy. On the day following Hasegawa's report, he learned the details of Imperial Army plans to move both Imperial Headquarters and the palace to alternative sites secretly under construction in the mountains of Matsushiro, northwest of Tokyo. The Emperor tersely rejected this scheme that was ostensibly for his protection with the words "I'm not going." But he also recognized the more sinister implications harbored in the proposed move. As Edward Drea has highlighted, with the Emperor a captive in an isolated mountain fortress, Imperial Army leaders "could carry on the war to suicidal extremes to preserve *kokutai* [usually rendered in English as "the national polity"] in his name." Nor was the Emperor ignorant of rumors about plots to have his brother Prince Takamatsu either replace him or become regent after he abdicated in favor of his young son. Thus, he realized that the prestige and influence of both himself and the throne, as well as any hope for efforts by his court to end the war, were linked to his remaining in Tokyo.

On June 18, Suzuki summoned the Big Six to a meeting. Given that only ten days earlier they had adopted the Fundamental Policy, it is perhaps surprising that the army minister and the chiefs of staff of the Army and Navy assented essentially to approaching the Soviet Union as a negotiator. They still maintained, however, that no direct efforts should begin until after the first invasion battle, which they were convinced would go in Japan's favor and thus enormously enhance their bargaining position.

The next day, June 19, Togo paid a visit to Koki Hirota at his home to urge the former premier to press his talks with Malik in accordance with the new guidance from the Supreme Council. On June 20, the Emperor granted Togo an audience at which the Foreign Minister explained Hirota's mission and the checkered course of his contacts with Malik to date. This was the initial word the Emperor received not only of Hirota's exertions but also of the plan adopted by the Big Six in May, which Suzuki had neglected to mention. The Emperor chose to reveal to Togo the import of the special reports he had obtained from Hasegawa and Umezu, which had convinced him that Japan's military posture was so thoroughly deficient that the war must be ended. Togo cautioned that it would be extremely hard to obtain favorable terms but pledged his "heart and soul" to fulfilling the Emperor's wish.

With the stage now set, at Kido's urging the Emperor summoned the Big

Six on the evening of June 22. The Emperor, breaking ritual, spoke first to open the meeting "with what might have been a bombshell had the wording been more positive," commented historian Robert Butow.

The Emperor acknowledged that the meeting of June 8 had set a course for a fight to the end, but now "I desire that concrete plans to end the war, unhampered by existing policy, be speedily studied and that efforts be made to implement them." Suzuki explained that indeed negotiations had been considered, and Togo described the initial approaches to Soviet Ambassador Malik. "When will an envoy be sent to the Soviet Union? Is there any chance of success?" asked the Emperor. Togo projected that an envoy would not be installed in Moscow before mid-July. He warned that the Soviets would demand huge concessions and that they must make peace while Japan still retained the ability to fight, or any negotiations would surely fail.

The Emperor next invited comment from the other members of the Big Six. Army Minister Anami confined his remarks to an admonishment about appearing too anxious to stop the war and thus displaying weakness before the enemy. Army Chief of Staff Umezu likewise raised the banner of caution, which prompted the Emperor to ask if timidity might cause Japan to miss the moment entirely. Whether or not this was a rebuke, it served to bring Umezu immediately into agreement that negotiations should begin at once.

When this meeting adjourned, the eight principal decision makers in Japan agreed on only one point: pursuit of peace negotiations through the Soviets. There was no consensus about what peace terms Japan might offer, much less accept. The only explicit framework appeared in Kido's plan, which resembled the Treaty of Versailles, not unconditional surrender. Nor was there any agreed time frame for securing peace. Togo, and perhaps the Emperor and Kido, might have conceived this process as being of relatively short duration. For the military participants, such as Anami, however, the opening of the conduit integrated easily into an underlying strategy of negotiated peace after Ketsu-Go had exacted its blood price, a point still in the relatively distant future. At this juncture, then, Japan had neared only negotiation, not peace.

7

Magic Insights

"Are they sincere or are they intoxicated?"

Other Gentlemen's Mail

In a remarkable, repeating pattern, American success at penetrating Japanese diplomatic codes has lurched from triumph to controversy three times in the twentieth century. In 1920, Herbert O. Yardley's team deciphered Japanese diplomatic traffic at the Washington Naval Conference, to the profit of U.S. envoys. When Secretary of State Henry Stimson subsequently learned of this, he decided in a famous phrase that "gentlemen do not read each other's mail" and closed the operation. This prompted a disgruntled Yardley to publish a book trumpeting his accomplishment, much to the embarrassment of the American government.

In 1940–1941, American code breakers mastered the purportedly invulnerable machine encryption of Japanese diplomatic exchanges. This achievement now is best remembered not for its stunning intellectual brilliance but as one ring of the circuslike controversy over the attack on Pearl Harbor. A prong of a postwar congressional investigation delved into alleged forewarning of the disaster and compelled public disclosure of both the code-breaking apparatus and specific decrypted Japanese diplomatic messages. The congressional subpoena did not demand, and code breakers did not voluntarily surrender, evidence that Japanese diplomatic traffic continued to be read down to the final days of the war. This reticence preserved one of the great secrets of the war: The decoded dispatches of the Japanese ambassador to Berlin, General Hiroshi Oshima, constituted one of the critical sources of Allied information on Hitler's war plans and preparations. But the concealment of code-breaking feats in 1945 ultimately engendered serious consequences in the historical debate over the end of the war.

By roughly the end of the second decade after the war, critics of the use of atomic weapons routinely propounded a thesis that Japan was actively seeking to surrender in 1945, that American policy makers knew this primarily from code breaking, and that thus the use of atomic weapons was unnecessary. Understanding how this thesis was assembled and then measuring its validity requires a sketch of the overall organization of code-breaking activities during the war and then a brief examination of how the tardy release of classified information both skewed and nurtured the post-war debate.

By New Year's Day 1945, an elite group of analysts culled the significant dispatches from the pervasive Allied penetration of Japanese diplomatic encryption systems and prepared a mimeographed document running from six to thirty-two pages titled "Magic Diplomatic Summary." The messages themselves or key passages, in verbatim translations, appeared under capsule headlines. The editors usually supplemented each text with commentary, background information, and cross-references to earlier dispatches. The Magic Diplomatic Summary was delivered seven days a week to a select band of senior American policy makers, with the White House at the top of the list. Thus, the now-declassified daily editions of this summary not only provide evidence of which Japanese diplomatic messages were decrypted but also constitute hard evidence of what American policy makers learned or could learn from them.

But the Magic Diplomatic Summary was far from the only compendium of decoded Japanese messages. Nor was it the only code-breaking source that shed light on Japanese political developments. The daily radio communications among Japanese diplomats were a relative trickle compared with the cataract of Imperial Army and Imperial Navy traffic that was intercepted and decrypted under the code name "Ultra" in Washington and centers in the Pacific. Summaries of intercepted Ultra messages also existed and circulated side by side with the Magic Diplomatic Summary. Given the political dominance of the Japanese armed forces, particularly the Imperial Army, intentions and policies unmasked by Ultra likewise illuminated Japanese diplomatic strategy. Policy makers could thus measure Japanese aims from two streams of decoded messages.

Proponents of the thesis that Imperial Japan was actively seeking peace on terms acceptable to the Allies—and that American policy makers knew this—have found their arguments primarily in selected Magic messages, both to establish "real" Japanese intentions and to "prove" American

knowledge of those intentions. The Magic evidence is sometimes embel-
lished with an assortment of reports from the Office of Strategic Services
(OSS) that were forwarded to President Harry S. Truman (whether he read
them and, if so, what he thought of them is another matter) and a few messages that reached the State Department from American diplomats. Magic,
however, always remains the touchstone.

In retrospect, the declassification process has signally aided the cause of
these proponents. The first disclosures in the early 1950s of code breaking
from this period made no reference to the massive Ultra stream of military
and naval traffic but consisted only of references to, or the text of, a smat-
tering of Japanese diplomatic messages that appeared in Magic. Even this
handful of dispatches was only a fraction of those relating to a Japanese effort to open negotiations through the Soviet Union beginning in mid-July
1945. It thus proved relatively easy to assemble an illusory image of a
flurry of Japanese peace feelers and initiatives.

These early revelations were followed by the publication of translations
of complete Japanese diplomatic messages in the volumes of the *Foreign
Relations of the United States* series on the Potsdam Conference. These
translations lacked both the vital commentary and the editing provided by
the editors of the Magic Diplomatic Summary, or any reference to Ultra. It
was only after arguments about how Magic messages established that the
Japanese were trying to surrender gained currency that a relatively complete
set of the Magic Diplomatic Summary appeared in 1978. This set contained
a significant number of censored (literally whited-out) sections, which left
some questions open. Finally, a complete set of the Magic Diplomatic Summary was released in 1995. A comparison of the two sets reveals that an obvious reason for the reluctance to declassify the Magic summaries is that
they proved that code breakers were reading not merely Japanese diplomatic
messages but also messages from at least thirty other governments, including formal American allies and prominent neutrals: Argentina, Belgium, Bo-
livia, Bulgaria, Chile, China (Chiang Kai-shek), China (Japanese client
regime), Colombia, Cuba, France (both the government of Charles de
Gaulle and the residual Vichy government ensconced in Indochina), Greece,
Iran, Italy, Lebanon, Liberia, Luxembourg, Mexico, Mongolia (Japanese
client state), the Netherlands, Nicaragua, Peru, Portugal, Saudi Arabia,
Spain, Switzerland, Syria, Turkey, Uruguay, and Venezuela.*

---

* In addition to the Magic Diplomatic Summary, also released to the National Archives was a separate
set of summary and analysis papers concerning Japanese diplomacy from June to August 1945, prepared for the chief of naval operations. These are Special Research Histories (SRH) 078, 079, 084,
085, 086, and 088 (Record Group 457). These papers, which contain little or no omitted text, confirm
the completeness of the 1995 release of the Magic Diplomatic Summary.

With the release of the Magic Diplomatic Summary and other material pertaining to decryption and interpretation, the plausibility of a picture of a peace-seeking Japan can be tested. Moreover, the accuracy of that picture can also now be validated by revelations from Japanese source material. In any assessment of evidence actually available to American policy makers in 1945, the most fundamental points to bear in mind are that only Magic could verify the bona fides of Japanese diplomats and that only code breaking (both Magic and Ultra) could authenticate the actual intentions of Japan's rulers. Thus, analysis from the OSS (which generally was not privy to Magic or Ultra) or its agent reports, as well as reports from American diplomats were in no way comparable in weight to Magic or Ultra intercepts.

The body of evidence available to American policy makers concerning Japanese diplomacy in 1945 partitions logically into two intervals, with the dividing line on July 13, when evidence appeared that the Emperor had intervened directly into the process. While the Emperor's initiative recast the picture in significant ways, there were important benchmarks before July 13, both in code-breaking evidence and in approaches from Japanese diplomats in Europe. The most prominent of the bare handful of messages in early 1945 that provided any evidence that Japan was contemplating peace emerged in a dispatch from the German naval attaché in Tokyo to his government on May 5, three days before the German surrender, in which he stated:

> An influential member of the [Imperial Navy] Staff has given me to understand that, since the situation is clearly recognized to be hopeless, large sections of the Japanese armed forces would not regard with disfavor an American request for capitulation even if the terms were hard, provided they were halfway honorable.

The Magic editors emended this excerpt with background information that previous traffic had "commented on signs of war weariness in official Japanese Navy circles, but have not mentioned such an attitude in Army quarters." This observation clearly discounted the import of the message, since it was the Imperial Army, not the Imperial Navy, that exercised by far the greatest weight in Japanese political decisions. Apart from this message, three others (one each from Portuguese, Spanish, and Swedish diplomats) identified unconditional surrender or a general lack of expressed Allied terms as serious impediments to bringing Japan to surrender.

In contrast to this scanty list of cables, a great many more messages portrayed Japanese determination to fight to the bitter end. Moreover, diplomatic traffic reaffirmed the exact point made by the Magic editors: The Imperial Army, the dominant political force in Japan, remained committed to a struggle to the finish, no matter how objectively bleak the outlook was. A message transmitted on January 20, 1945, by French Ambassador to Japan Cosme is typical. He reported that "thinking people at the Court and in the Navy . . . appear inclined to believe that an end must be put to this war." Cosme's omission of Imperial Army officers from the category of "thinking people" suggested the meager prospects for actual peace, a point he confirmed only two days later when he wired that while the loss of the Philippines might "logically" result in an opening for diplomacy,

> when one questions the military, one hears a different tune. Are they sincere or are they intoxicated? The only thing certain is that they refuse to see the possibility of defeat. As for the people, they have no definite attitude; they are resigned to all physical suffering and . . . [are] confident in their leaders.

Soon after Magic disclosed these insights, it featured a circular from the vice chief of the Imperial Army general staff to his European attachés. The commentary appended to his message by the Magic Diplomatic Summary observed that the circular "displays an unrelieved pessimism on all aspects of the war which is entirely without precedent in available traffic out of Tokyo." But while the circular projected with rigorous objectivity a constriction of Japan's defenses followed by a landing in the Homeland itself at midyear, the vice chief of staff proclaimed that Japan "preserves unaltered her conviction of inevitable victory."

The February 1 Magic Diplomatic Summary contained a mid-January wire from German Ambassador Stahmer to Berlin, warning of the shaky position of the Koiso government. Stahmer expressed concern over the attitude of the Imperial Navy and advised that a

> new Cabinet would probably be formed of liberal personalities whose past would facilitate a settlement with the Americans. Such a Cabinet would then be overthrown, however, by nationalist groups who demand total war until final victory and would oppose with their full strength—and probably with violence—a compromise Cabinet. If these nationalist groups obtain control—which is possible—it will mean a substantial increase in Japan's total war effort.

On March 12, an intercepted message from Swiss Minister Camille Gorge observed that the Japanese government "is being criticized more and more." But far from linking the criticism with a move to peace, he reported pressures to convene the Diet to remedy the situation. Further, there was even talk of transferring the greater part of Japan's war industry to Manchuria in order to carry the war "as far as possible to Chinese soil." Ironically, at this same time, a 1944 year-end summary from the German military attaché in Tokyo was decoded that provided a gauge of how little the outlook of the Japanese government had changed. The attaché reported recent increases in preparations to defend the Homeland and noted that "total mobilization is progressing." He affirmed the determination of the "Japanese Army and the circles it influences to go through with the war without compromise on the side of Germany."

On May 6, Portuguese Minister Fernandes advised his government that "the fortification of coasts and mountains continues, giving the impression that this country, like Germany, is disposed to prosecute the war to its very end without the least probability of victory."

On June 22, Gorge reported that "Japan does not expect to win, but is still hoping to escape [defeat] by prolonging the war long enough to exhaust [her] enemies."

A total of at least thirteen diplomatic messages affirmed that, no matter how desperate the situation, Japan intended to fight to the bitter end. The Magic Diplomatic Summary also published indirect evidence of Japan's resolve in its revelation of a scheme to produce synthetic aircraft fuels that would take two years to mature; plans for regional government authorities designed for continued resistance from a fragmented Japan; and preparations to induct boys ages fourteen and up among Japanese colonists in China.

The Magic Diplomatic Summary provided yet another gauge for measuring Japanese resolve: enumerations of the horrifying toll of homes consumed and human beings killed in LeMay's firebombing campaign— shoulder to shoulder with declarations of the negligible impact of such blows on Japanese morale. The first stingy acknowledgment of the disasters peeked from the March 11 issue of the weekly intelligence circular to Japan's military attachés from the vice chief of the Imperial Army general staff. This summary informed its readers that the great fire raid on Tokyo of March 9–10 marked the first attack by large numbers of planes at night and that "the greater part" of five city wards "were destroyed by fire. However, damage to important installations was light." The dispatch asserted that "contrary to what might be expected," the attack stiffened civil morale and did not perturb domestic order. Two days later, Foreign Minister Mamoru Shigemitsu dispatched a "confidential war report" to Ambassador Oshima in Berlin. Shigemitsu acknowledged that the raid had destroyed 240,000 dwellings and left about 1,050,000 persons homeless. He, too, felt compelled to comment, "There are no particular signs of disturbance among the populace."

On April 4, Portuguese Minister Fernandes informed his government that the raid had killed 70,000 people, destroyed 120,000 homes, and rendered over one million persons homeless. The Magic editors noted that on March 14 the Japanese Greater East Asia Ministry (the cabinet department dedicated to managing Japan's vast colonial empire) estimated that deaths totaled 14,000, while the following day the German naval attaché in Tokyo reported that the Imperial Navy Headquarters placed the toll at "about 100,000." Messages on other raids in the fire blitz described much less damage and infinitely smaller loss of life.

After the fall of the Koiso government on April 5, Magic experts sifted the diplomatic traffic for signs of the new government's intentions and found some early glimmers of hope. The German ambassador provided the first assessment:

> To judge by its inner make-up, the new Cabinet is devoting itself to continuing the war with the utmost exertion of energy. It is seeking to reach an agreement with Russia, even if this involves the greatest sacrifices. By this means, in addition to protection in the rear, a more favorable basis for later negotiations with America is expected.

Swiss Minister Gorge's initial optimism that the Suzuki government might seek peace soon evaporated. On May 5 he wired his government that he saw "no perceptible difference between the present government and its predecessor." The Portuguese minister predicted the Suzuki cabinet would be short-lived, "since the military and the nation in general are not yet prepared to make peace." Echoing this theme was an April message from the Spanish minister, who reported that Prince Konoe, "a well-known pacifist, refused to form part of the Government."

Interspersed among these messages depicting the suffering of the Japanese people and the obstinacy of Japan's warlords were graphic vignettes revealing the dark underside of Japanese domination of subject peoples. A plaintive dispatch from the Greater East Asia Ministry in Tokyo acknowledged the "astonishing" death rate among Chinese workers drafted for labor in Japan and noted that "the consignees are extremely irritated at the trouble, time and expense involved in disposing of their bodies." In one episode involving 591 mine workers, 95 died and 36 were seriously ill, while in another group of only 300, the death toll was 108 and the seriously ill numbered 62.

Further, Magic periodically showed the declining faith in Japan's fortunes among its subject peoples. This was particularly notable in Manchuria, whence an official of the Greater East Asia Ministry signaled Tokyo on March 6 that "it is now quite apparent that there are those who have lost faith in us and some even assume an unfriendly attitude. However, there is still no evidence of any general disturbance." By April, the situation had deteriorated sharply. A revolt of armed peasants broke out east of Harbin, and similar events were occurring "all over the country." By June, a report from Manchuria acknowledged that, without exception, the various ethnic groups believed Japan's defeat was inevitable and "the number of individuals who are studying English and Russian is increasing."

Another intercepted report indicated that "since the turn in the tide of war at Guadalcanal, general public sentiment in Korea has followed a course toward deliberate unrest." Now even those with "marked pro-Japanese leanings" foresaw "the inevitable defeat of the Empire." Protest, even violent protest, already had occurred and more was expected. But it was not the puny threat from the subjugated peoples within Japan's empire that occasioned reflection in Tokyo.

The End of Germany and New Beginnings
with the Soviet Union

The advent of the Suzuki government in April triggered special vigilance by Magic analysts, but so did the collapse of Hitler's Third Reich in May. From Bern, in April, Japanese Minister Shunichi Kase provided an intriguing account of his "rather concrete knowledge" of German preparations for Hitler or party leaders to fly to Japan. At the same time, he expressed alarm over the swelling bitterness in Allied countries as stories of German atrocities spread. The aircraft report was not without foundation. On April 12, the Japanese military and naval attachés in Germany jointly asked Tokyo for permission for a very long range aircraft to fly from Norway to Japanese territory. Reportedly, the plane was to bear German Assistant Air Attaché Wild and "one other passenger." In the event, the plane did not get away before the German surrender on May 8.

The spectacle of Germany's death throes prompted a request on April 28 that the Japanese military attaché in Lisbon report "as fully as possible" on the last stage of resistance "in order to furnish reference material for the decisive battle" in the Homeland. His attention was directed to matters such as the training of civilian militias, as well as whether the direct participation of the German High Command in combat and the death of Hitler in Berlin would brace German morale and "determination to defend the Capital to the bitter end." This message conveyed obvious implications about the path Imperial Headquarters was contemplating.

Yet another topic of singular interest to Magic analysts was Japan's evolving relations with the Soviets. The prospect that the Soviets would cancel the neutrality pact as a prelude to entering the war naturally induced considerable anxiety in Tokyo. Code breaking permitted American officials to follow the Japanese efforts to forecast Soviet attitudes and, if possible, avoid a breach.

One of the very first messages in this series contained an explosion from Naotake Sato, a former foreign minister, now entrusted with the critical task of representing Japan in Moscow. On February 12, Sato blasted his nominal superiors for asking him to sound out the Soviets on the status of their neutrality pact without first equipping him with any knowledge of his government's intentions on so "important and delicate a question." Ignoring the outburst, Foreign Minister Shigemitsu supplied "detailed" instructions in February and then in March sent further messages intended to arm Sato with arguments for the renewal of the pact, or at least for avoiding its abrogation.

From February to April, Sato dutifully reported his exertions and attempted to divine Soviet policies not merely from formal exchanges but also from the atmosphere in his encounters with wily and famously glacial Soviet Foreign Minister Vyacheslav Molotov. To the amusement of Magic analysts, Sato reported of a meeting on February 22 that "Molotov as usual was amiable and smiling and I was conscious of the warmth of his personality throughout the entire interview."

When the Soviets did announce the abrogation on April 5, Magic confirmed that this event, though it came only two hours after the announcement of the collapse of the Koiso cabinet, was not related to Koiso's fate. The message from Ambassador Sato describing the session in which Molotov notified him of the abrogation revealed that Molotov implied initially that the pact was no longer in effect at all but later admitted that the pact remained valid for one year and that Soviet attitudes would be "set accordingly."

Messages from the vice chief of the Imperial Army general staff disclosed no illusions, however, about ultimate Soviet actions. On April 12, he advised the attaché in Berlin: "Russia will carefully gauge the decline in Japan's military strength and . . . seize some pretext or other to enter the war against our country." But he also held out hope that such an action would "complicate" the already fragile relationship between the Soviets and the Americans. By early May, the vice chief acknowledged that the anti-Japan attitude in the Soviet Union was becoming "more vigorous," noting that "we must view with alarm the possibility of future military activity against Japan." A Japanese intelligence officer predicted (accurately, as it developed) that it would take only three months for the Soviets to transfer troops from Europe to the Far East and begin hostilities.

Following the capitulation of Germany, Ambassador Sato sent Tokyo his detailed strategic survey. The situation, he said, obviously provided the Soviets with a golden opportunity to strike against Japan. On the other hand, the Soviets might seek to mediate a peace that would be "very close to unconditional surrender" and entail the "dissolution of our Army and Navy," coupled with substantial territorial concessions. Sato urged that Japan increase its military strength to avoid being forced to "dance to whatever tune strikes the Russian fancy" and that the war against the Anglo-Americans continue.

On May 21, the new Japanese foreign minister, Togo, dispatched two important messages. In the first, a circular to all diplomats, he flatly denied that "Japan has ever made peace proposals to America and England." In a second message to Moscow, Togo directed that Sato see Molotov "as soon as possible . . . and sound him out on Russia's intentions towards Japan." At the same time, Sato should try to pick up any information on the United Nations' San Francisco Conference.* Sato finally secured the interview with Molotov on May 28. A United States Navy intelligence officer reconstructed the event:

> Sato's account of the interview with Molotov leaves a mental picture of a spaniel in the presence of a mastiff who also knows where the bone is hidden. With the obsequiousness which he himself had foreseen and feared, Sato saw as "a matter for congratulation" Russia's "great victory in the war against Germany"; while, with Japan, who "no longer had any of her former allies, the situation was somewhat delicate." He earnestly hoped that "no important change would take place in Russo-Japanese relations." While Japan, following Russia's example, desired "to end hostilities as quickly as possible," the Pacific war was a "matter of life and death." "As a result of America's attitude," Japan had "no choice but to continue the fight."

Sato emphasized to Tokyo that "we are facing future trouble with Russia" and that it was imperative that "the Cabinet or the Supreme Council for the Direction of the War decide how far they are willing to go in making concessions to Russia."

* It had been announced publicly that the now huge coalition of nations against the Axis powers planned to meet in San Francisco in April to work on a postwar international order.

On June 1, following the recent flurry of raids on Tokyo that burned down the Foreign Ministry, Togo instructed Sato:

> In view of our situation both at home and abroad, it is quite clear that we will find it extremely difficult to reach any settlement with Russia. We must realize, however, that it is a matter of the utmost urgency that we should not only prevent Russia from entering the war, but should also induce them to adopt a favorable attitude toward Japan. I would therefore like you to miss no opportunity to talk to the Soviet leaders.

He added that he was directing former premier Koki Hirota to talk to Soviet Ambassador Jacob Malik in Tokyo.

As early June arrived, message traffic disclosed Japanese efforts to prevent Soviet entry into the war and to tender her attitude to Japan. While the messages showed a realistic appraisal of how difficult these tasks were, they did not betray any overtures for peace with the Western Allies. This period concluded with a gloomy message from Sato. He analyzed all the public statements he had perused on Germany since her capitulation. These, he concluded, pointed to the "absolute completeness of unconditional surrender."

Japanese Diplomatic Peace Entrepreneurs in Europe

While those in Tokyo disposed to end the war moved very cautiously, if at all, some Japanese diplomats in Europe vied to become the midwives of peace, now uninhibited by the intimidating edifice of Nazi Germany and beyond reach of the weapons of Japanese military fanatics. Code breaking revealed their conflicting initiatives, but above all Magic mercilessly disclosed their complete want of official sanction.

In Stockholm, Magic unmasked tangled intrigue at the Japanese embassy. Minister Suemasa Okamoto advised Tokyo in colorful language ("The unreasonable way in which things have been done already reveals a glimpse of the cloven hoof") that the military attaché, General Onodera, had embarked on unsanctioned peace negotiations. This prompted a thunderously officious message from the vice chief of the Imperial Army general staff, dated June 24, that could scarcely fail to reinforce American perceptions of Japan's resolve to struggle to the end:

> As we have said before, Japan is firmly determined to prosecute the Greater East Asia war to the very end. There is a report, however, to the effect that some Japanese official stationed in Sweden is making peace overtures to

America. That is demagoguery pure and simple, and if you have any idea as to the source of those reports please inform us.

The Vatican also entered into efforts to bring peace. In an exchange of messages beginning in early June, the Japanese envoy at the Vatican, Ken Harada, reported an indirect effort to establish contact via Monsignor Vagnozzi, a former counselor of the apostolic delegation in the United States, who claimed to enjoy important American contacts. What the detailed exchange ultimately demonstrated, however, was that even Japan's representatives overseas were by no means braced to accept unconditional surrender or a near kin. In a like example, a May 8 message from the former Japanese ambassador to France, now in Switzerland, urged peace but rejected out of hand unconditional surrender.

The most serious peace efforts by Japanese representatives abroad transpired in Switzerland but took divergent tracks. One involved the persistent efforts of Commander Yoshiro Fujimura in Bern. In May 1945 Fujimura initiated a series of attempts to convince his superiors in Japan that peace could and should be negotiated through OSS officials in Switzerland. Fujimura enlisted Captain Nishihara, also stationed in Bern, but burdened himself with a dubious German associate and attempted to conceal from his American contacts the utter indifference of his superiors. His proposals, however, fell well short of anything like unconditional surrender. On June 20, the Imperial Navy Ministry formally terminated any vestige of authority for Fujimura or Nishihara to act on behalf of Japan.

Concurrent with Fujimura's exertions, Japan's military attaché in Zurich and Basel, Lieutenant General Seigo Okamoto, launched his own independent effort to bring peace. From the start, Okamoto presented his views and intentions to Imperial Army Chief of Staff Umezu, seeking to secure official sanction. Okamoto counted upon the fact that he and Umezu were old comrades and friends. Nevertheless, Okamoto, too, failed to secure any official endorsement.

The failure of these initiatives must be ascribed basically to the inability of any peace entrepreneur to gain official authorization for his actions. This reflects the conscious choice in Tokyo to refuse direct negotiations with the Western Allies in favor of an attempt to conduct mediation through the Soviet Union. In a late June Magic Diplomatic Summary, American analysts demonstrated that they clearly grasped the dubious significance of the Japanese diplomats' efforts. The occasion was a newly decrypted message, dated April 28, from a Tokyo official of the Formosan Government General to a high official in the Formosan Police Affairs Bureau, reporting that "sources connected with the [Suzuki] Cabinet and from a certain person well posted on news from official quarters" indicated that the Japanese would be seeking a negotiated peace, not unconditional surrender. As the editors of the Magic Diplomatic Summary quickly pointed out, this

> constitutes the first Japanese message emanating from Japan to acknowledge the existence of peace sentiment there. While neutral observers in Japan have mentioned a desire for peace in unofficial and some official circles, and a number of Japanese representatives abroad have urged a negotiated peace (as distinguished from unconditional surrender), until now the Japanese traffic out of Tokyo has contained only reiterations of Japan's determination to "fight to the bitter end."

The editors admitted that they could not evaluate the credibility of this source, or as a naval intelligence officer bluntly observed, "Little can be said of the reliability of the Formosan dopester [informer]." The glimmer of peace in this message was snuffed out almost immediately. A decryption of a May 18 message from the same source revealed that Premier Suzuki "has determined to continue the war to [the] bitter end although the thought of Russia's possible entry into the war is causing him many sleepless nights."

That the Allies recognized the lack of official backing of the Swiss and other approaches is reflected in a long statement to the press issued on July 10, 1945, in which Assistant Secretary of State Joseph C. Grew declared:

> We have received no peace offer from the Japanese Government, either through official or unofficial channels. Conversations relating to peace have been reported to the Department from various parts of the world, but in no case has an approach been made to this Government, directly or indirectly, by a person who could establish his authority to speak for the Japanese Government, and in no case has an offer to surrender been made. In no case has this Government been presented with a statement purporting to define the basis upon which the Japanese Government would be prepared to conclude peace. . . .
>
> The nature of the purported "peace feelers" must be clear to everyone. They are the usual moves in the conduct of psychological warfare by a defeated enemy. No thinking American, recalling Pearl Harbor, Wake, Manila, Japanese ruthless aggression elsewhere, will give them credence.
>
> Japanese militarism must and will be crushed. . . . The policy of this Government has been, is, and will be unconditional surrender.

Every point Grew made summarizing events through July 10, 1945, is true: There was no official contact by the Japanese government or its authorized agent, and, of course, thus neither an offer to surrender nor an offer of terms from the Japanese government. On the contrary, the Magic diplomatic traffic contained many telling indicators of Japan's determination to fight to the bitter end.

8

Downfall and Olympic Plans

"We are approaching one of the most difficult periods of the war"

The Plans

The Joint Chiefs of Staff order of May 25, 1945, provided only the general outline of a plan to invade Japan. Subordinate commanders filled in all the details, starting with the two theater commanders, General Douglas MacArthur and Admiral Chester W. Nimitz. MacArthur issued his strategic plan for an amphibious assault on Japan on May 28, code-named Downfall. His general concept was "the attainment of assigned objectives by two (2) successive operations." In the first (Operation Olympic), after "extensive air preparation," an amphibious assault on "X-Day" would seize southern Kyushu. The fourteen to seventeen divisions already available in the Pacific would establish bases to support the second (Operation Coronet), "a knock-out blow to the enemy's heart in the TOKYO area" on "Y-Day," with a force of twenty-five divisions, drawn from both units already in the Pacific and those redeployed from Europe. Thereafter, operations would continue as necessary to terminate "organized resistance" of the Imperial Army and Navy forces in the central and northern Japanese archipelago and on the "Asian Mainland as necessary." Thus, MacArthur, like the Joint Chiefs of Staff, by no means assumed that the two-phase invasion would mark the end of fighting.

The plan set forth vital assumptions:

1. The enemy "will continue the war to the utmost extent of their capabil-

ities," and the invaders would confront not only Japan's armed forces but also "a fanatically hostile population."

2. The attackers in Olympic would encounter only three Japanese divisions in southern Kyushu and three in northern Kyushu.
3. The Japanese could reinforce Kyushu to a total of no more than ten divisions.
4. No more than 2,500 Japanese aircraft would operate against Olympic.

Olympic's tentative X-Day was November 1, 1945. The Third and Fifth Fleets, operating jointly for the first time, would support Olympic. The Third Fleet would provide strategic support while the Fifth Fleet would both directly support and conduct the amphibious operations. Carriers would be the principal striking weapon, and Nimitz projected the use of sixteen fleet and six light carriers of the United States Navy and six fleet and four light carriers of the British Pacific Fleet, altogether embarking approximately 1,914 aircraft.

The ground element of Olympic would be the Sixth Army, with the mission of seizing and defending roughly the southern third of Kyushu. Forces earmarked for the Sixth Army assault were four corps, each controlling three divisions. The follow-up would deliver two more divisions, while MacArthur held three divisions in his strategic reserve. Olympic's total projected commitment numbered 766,700 men, 134,000 vehicles, and 1,470,930 tons of material. To lift the twelve divisions in the assault, CINCPAC projected the use of an armada of 1,315 major amphibious vessels. Southern Kyushu would become a huge air and naval base, and the air garrison would number forty air groups with approximately 2,794 aircraft.

Following Olympic, Coronet had a tentative Y-Day of March 1, 1946. Coronet aimed to land at and seize the Tokyo-Yokohama area to establish air, naval, and logistic facilities to support subsequent operations. MacArthur intended to personally lead the assault ground forces of the Eighth and Tenth Armies with fourteen divisions (three of which would be Marines). The First Army with ten divisions would be the follow-up. MacArthur held one division in his own strategic reserve and one three-division corps of troops to be redeployed from Europe. The air garrison would ultimately total fifty air groups with approximately 3,328 planes. CINCPAC would provide amphibious lift for fourteen divisions. Coronet's projected commitments numbered 1,026,000 personnel, 190,000 vehicles, and 2,640,000 tons of material.

The Olympic plan remained subject to progressive modification, particularly regarding the strength of the committed forces. On June 20, MacArthur issued Operational Instruction No. 1, with the tentative Sixth

Army troop list for the invasion of Kyushu. (A troop list itemizes all units to be committed with strength figures based on the authorized rather than actual personnel assigned to each unit.) The list provided for eleven U.S. Army divisions, one infantry regimental combat team, one cavalry regimental combat team, twenty-four nondivisional artillery battalions, twenty-four antiaircraft battalions, nine tank battalions, three tank-destroyer battalions, one amphibian-tank battalion, and eight amphibian-tractor battalions among the projected 252,150 combat troops. Supporting the combat components were 40,377 service troops reflecting a vast miscellany of units. The Marine V Amphibious Corps would add three more divisions and support elements totaling 87,643 men, while Army Service Command "O" would contribute 177,983 additional men. Navy forces, mostly Seabee construction battalions, numbered 15,772. The order of battle of the Far Eastern Air Forces (FEAF) would include ten fighter groups plus an "air commando" (a hybrid unit with two fighter, one troop-carrier, and three liaison-plane squadrons), six heavy bomb groups, four medium bomb groups, four light bomb groups, three reconnaissance groups, and three night-fighter squadrons. FEAF troop strength was projected at 119,370, making the grand total of committed forces 693,295. (The difference between this figure and the 766,700 in the original Downfall plan is not explained but may be partly accounted for in the three uncommitted divisions, 14,000 men each, of MacArthur's strategic reserve and their support units.)

The commander of the Sixth Army was General Walter Krueger, "a typical dogmatic German soldier," said one of his artillery commanders, James F. Collins. Krueger earned his rank the hard way. Having enlisted as a private for the Spanish-American War, he won a direct commission in 1901. His acknowledged keen mental equipment and zest for hard work (although, one officer noted, "he didn't have much of a personality") gained him a general's star before Pearl Harbor. By 1945, he had commanded everything from a squad to a field army. A deep concern for the welfare of his soldiers was a Krueger trademark.

Krueger's Sixth Army issued its Field Order No. 74 on July 28, 1945. The plan provided for preliminary operations to secure air-warning facilities and advanced naval and seaplane bases, as well as the sea routes to southern Kyushu. On X-minus five and four (five and four days, respectively, before X-Day), the 40th Infantry Division (under Brigadier General Donald Myers), reinforced to a strength of 21,897 men, would under Sixth Army control seize the clusters of small islands off southeastern and southern Kyushu. The 158th Regimental Combat Team (under Brigadier General Hanford MacNider), also under Sixth Army control, on X-minus

Plan for Operation Olympic
and Estimated Japanese Dispositions as of May 1945

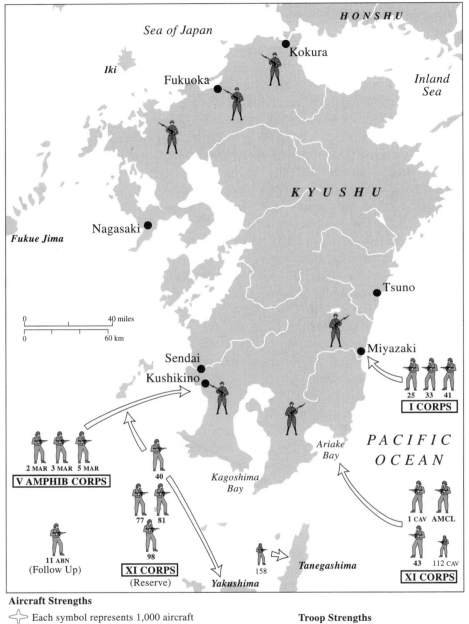

HONSHU

Sea of Japan

Iki

Kokura

Fukuoka

Inland Sea

K Y U S H U

Nagasaki

Fukue Jima

Tsuno

0 ___ 40 miles
0 ___ 60 km

Miyazaki

Sendai
Kushikino

25 33 41
I CORPS

PACIFIC OCEAN

Ariake Bay

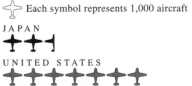

2 MAR 3 MAR 5 MAR
V AMPHIB CORPS

40

Kagoshima Bay

77 81

11 ABN
(Follow Up)

98
XI CORPS
(Reserve)

158

Tanegashima

Yakushima

1 CAV   AMCL

43   112 CAV
XI CORPS

Aircraft Strengths

Each symbol represents 1,000 aircraft

JAPAN

UNITED STATES

Troop Strengths

Japanese Division

U.S. Division

Japanese Brigade

U.S. Regiment

five would seize Tanegashima, a large island south of Kyushu. This team would be reinforced to a strength of 7,566 men.

Following these preliminaries, on X-Day the Sixth Army would land three corps at Miyazaki, Ariake Wan (Bay) at the southeastern end of Kyushu, and Kushikino in southwestern Kyushu. The three corps would consolidate beachheads and move to block reinforcements from the north along the east and west coasts. In subsequent operations, the Japanese would be expelled from southern Kyushu to the general line from Tsuno on the southeast coast to Sendai on the southwest coast. Behind the assault troops, airfields and bases, including in the port of Kagoshima, would be erected or refurbished.

The I Corps under Major General Innis P. Swift drew the Miyazaki assault. It would hit beaches between Yamazaki and Matsusaki in southern Kyushu, capture Miyazaki and its airfield, and then protect the northeast flank of the army by blocking the thrust of hostile forces along the east coast of Kyushu. The corps comprised 94,546 men of the veteran 25th, 33rd, and 41st Infantry Divisions, reinforced by two tank, one tank-destroyer, one amphibian-tank, and two amphibian-tractor battalions, plus other combat and support units.

The XI Corps, altogether 112,648 men strong, under Major General Charles P. Hall would secure beaches in the Shibushi-Kashiwaba area of Ariake Bay and capture Shibushi and its airfield. Hall's corps incorporated among its combat elements the First Cavalry, Americal, and the 43rd Infantry Divisions, the separate 112th Cavalry Regiment, as well as two tank, one amphibian-tank, one tank-destroyer, and two amphibian-tractor battalions.

The V Amphibious Corps comprised the 2nd, 3rd, and 5th Marine Divisions under Major General Harry Schmidt. The corps included only 87,340 leathernecks, but Army reinforcements brought total strength to 98,933. Reflecting the thorough Marine adherence to combined arms tactics, each division possessed its own tank battalion, and other reinforcements included four amphibian-tractor and one armored amphibian-tractor battalions. The troop list of this corps left no doubt about the severity of the anticipated struggle on Japan's home shores: Each division was authorized nine infantry battalions, but the Marines loaded six "replacement drafts," each of 1,250 men—the equivalent of over two infantry battalions for each division. V Amphibious Corps would storm ashore in the Kaminokawa-Kushikino area of southwestern Kyushu, secure Sendai, and protect the northwest flank of the Sixth Army to block the threat of any hostile force pressing down along the west coast of Kyushu.

The orders for the Sixth Army reserve, the IX Corps of three divisions of 79,155 men under Major General Charles W. Ryder, presented a series of options. From X-plus three, Ryder was to be prepared to dispatch all or part of the 98th Division to any area or to land his corps, with or without the 98th Division, on the south coast of Kyushu west of Kaimon-Dake and then conduct operations to clear the southwestern coast of Kagoshima Bay. Meanwhile, Ryder was also to be prepared to land all or parts of the 77th Division to reinforce other assaults from X-plus five. The IX Corps was reinforced with two tank, one tank-destroyer, and two amphibian-tractor battalions.

The 11th Airborne Division (under Major General Joseph M. Swing), reinforced to a strength of 14,641 men, including one tank battalion, was in Sixth Army reserve and would be afloat off Kyushu from X-plus twenty-two. It would reinforce other elements of the army as directed. Sixth Army service troops totaled another 125,364 men with 21,539 vehicles.

All these divisions except the 98th Division had combat experience and the casualty lists to show for it. This table illustrates the degree to which these units had already been blooded:

Battle Casualties for Divisions Committed to Olympic

Corps	Division	Total Battle Casualties	Killed/ Died	Wounded	Other
I	25th	5,432	1,500	3,928	4
	33rd	2,426	524	1,896	6
	41st	4,260	962	3,287	11
XI	1st Cavalry	4,055	971	3,075	9
	American	4,050	1,168	2,876	6
	43rd	6,026	1,414	4,609	3
IX	77th	7,461	1,857	5,534	70
	81st	2,314	517	1,793	4
—	11th Airborne	2,431	620	1,806	5
	40th	3,025	748	2,273	4
V Amphib.	2nd Marine	12,770	2,795	9,975	0
	3rd Marine	10,416	2,371	8,045	0
	5th Marine	9,573	2,414	7,159	0
Total		74,239	17,861	56,256	122

Redeployment and Morale

Following the German capitulation on May 8, 1945, the U.S. Army faced two intimidating challenges: massive redeployment of forces from Europe to the Pacific as an indispensable prelude to an invasion of Japan and simultaneous partial demobilization. The sheer scale of the redeployment was breathtaking. Of approximately 5.4 million army personnel en route to or already overseas, the Pacific count totaled only 1.2 million (22 percent). All eighty-nine active Army divisions were overseas, with no fewer than sixty-eight in the European-Mediterranean theaters. According to the plans in effect on the date of Germany's surrender, fifteen of the divisions in Europe were to augment the twenty-one Army and six Marine divisions already in the Pacific to fulfill the requirements of Downfall. No fewer than sixty-three air groups likewise were to migrate to the Pacific. The War Department also planned to recall another twenty-one divisions from Europe to the United States as a strategic reserve, while retaining 400,000 men in Europe for occupation duty. Another two million men would be demobilized.

When the Joint Chiefs of Staff secured sanction for the goal of ending the war in the Pacific within twelve months of the termination of hostilities in Europe, they explicitly laid down a time frame for planning redeployment and implicitly moved to forestall anticipated war weariness. Redeployment was a complex equation full of unknowns, including not least the date of the end of the war in Europe, progress of the campaigns in the Pacific, the nature of plans to terminate the war against Japan, and a medley of interrelated logistical factors involving shipping and bases. No wonder V-E Day found redeployment planners still grappling with endless chains of variables.

At the heart of this process was an explosive political factor. Military planners recognized that a one-front war against an opponent clearly not as strong as Germany could not justify a force structure of the magnitude dictated by the original two-front war. The American public would expect— indeed, demand—a partial demobilization. A crucial impetus behind public pressure for demobilization as well as a deep wellspring of the desire of individual servicemen for the earliest possible discharge was a pervasive fear that once the torrent of public expenditure on the war ceased, the nation would promptly plunge back into an economic depression. Those home first presumably would have, by far, better chances to secure jobs.

Such a demobilization was fraught with contentious issues of how many and which servicemen were to be discharged and which were to be redeployed. To defuse the issue, as early as September 1944 the War Department issued a public plan that contained a bedrock principle: Demobilization would be by individuals, not units. This action reversed the World War I practice in order to proscribe an inherent inequity. Those units with the longest and most arduous overseas service typically contained a minority of battle-worn veterans amid a mass of relatively fresh replacements. Discharging the latter with the former discriminated against individuals with longer and more demanding service careers. Therefore, to equitably select individuals for demobilization, a point system was devised. Individuals received points for length of service (one point for each month), overseas service (one point for each month), battle participation (five points for each campaign), decorations (five points each), and dependents (twelve points per child for up to three children). Those with the highest scores would be discharged—subject to involuntary retention under a "military necessity clause"—and those with the lowest scores would find themselves on occupation duty or bound for the Pacific. While in the European-Mediterranean theaters whole units might be redeployed to the Pacific or the United States, no such unit reclassification was slated for the Pacific or China-Burma-India theaters, but to the extent "consistent with the build-up and projected operations" high-point individuals were shipped home for discharge as their replacements arrived.

Once Germany surrendered, the worst fears of military planners were realized. A poll showed 72 percent of Americans expected a partial demobilization—the rest wanted even more. Under a growing deluge of mail, Congress insisted that the Army "reduce its size immediately by 1 million men." Fred Vinson, the director of the Office of War Mobilization and Reconversion, spoke of overwhelming public outcry for an increase in availability of consumer goods and warned the Joint Chiefs of Staff that he had never seen "the people in their present frame of mind." He was fearful of "unrest in the country."

For most individual servicemen, the importance of V-E Day was immediately overshadowed by May 12, 1945, for on this date they totaled their points to set their Adjusted Service Rating (ASR)—the score that would determine their role in the final phase of the Pacific war. The magic number was eighty-five: Those with this score or higher automatically accrued a right to discharge; those with lower scores were subject to redeployment to the Pacific. Then came the whirlwind. Thirty days were authorized for each major command to accomplish "personnel readjustment" before divisions moved for embarkation. Units scheduled for redeployment transferred out their high-point veterans while other units swapped low-point men to units destined for the Pacific. Some individuals in critical specialties discovered that they were ineligible regardless of their points. Further, credits continued to be recalculated, which dramatically changed the status of some servicemen. The 2nd Infantry Division, for example, had stabilized its roster just days before its scheduled sailing date when the award of two additional campaign credits immediately qualified 2,700 men for discharge, about one of every five men it had.

When the war ended, the fifteen divisions (now filled with low-point servicemen) identified for redeployment included two armored (13th and 20th) and thirteen infantry divisions (2nd, 4th, 5th, 8th, 28th, 35th, 45th, 86th, 87th, 91st, 95th, 97th, and 104th). Of these, the first to arrive in the United States were the 86th and 97th on June 17 and 24, respectively. Behind them in Europe, readjustment worked like a potent acid, eating away at all orderly plans. The 28th Division in one week experienced a 20 percent turnover of enlisted men; within forty days, 46 percent of its officers turned over. Some smaller units fared worse. The 804th Tank Destroyer Battalion rotated out 50 percent of its strength; by August, the 330th Ordnance Depot Company reported 73 percent of its personnel had been present for less than one month. Conversely, the 122nd Signal Radio Intelligence Company acknowledged that 95 percent of its personnel possessed an ASR score that qualified them for early separation. The most egregious case was the 45th Infantry Division. This veteran and respected National Guard division, having battled since the Sicily landings in July 1943, reported in July that eleven thousand of its enlisted men and six hundred of its officers qualified for separation—83 percent of the division. In the division artillery staff, only one officer would be left: the commander himself.

Readjustment completely fractured the accumulations of well-honed skills, teamwork, cohesion, and esprit that made units effective. The experienced and decorated infantrymen that Marshall called "the first team" departed, as did the seasoned sergeants and corporals that "made a unit dependable in battle." In short order, the formidable combat efficiency of veteran units, earned at such blood cost, evaporated. General Dwight D. Eisenhower estimated it would take at least six months of further training to restore the redeployed European units to combat readiness.

The profoundly different character of fighting in the Pacific also mandated retraining of redeployed units. American soldiers viscerally recognized a difference in their opponents. As one publication, "Battle Experience Against the Japanese," noted, if the German was the

professional heavy weight prizefighter—fighting was his business and he WAS good at it . . . the Jap is definitely a lightweight—not a professional but an alley fighter who is not above a thumb in the eye, a knee in the crotch or a brickbat when you're not looking. Furthermore, he's a left hander so to speak, with a style that's hard to solve until you get on to it.

Army Ground Forces had crafted a training program that was a minimum of eight weeks long and emphasized features that would be peculiar to fighting the Japanese in their Homeland, not least attacks against positions fortified with earth and logs, using flamethrowers and bulldozers and fighting in Japanese villages.

The Army Air Forces leaders initially and perhaps fatuously supposed that they could exempt their units from the program of individual demobilization. Apart from a few units left for occupation duties, the rest of the massive air component in Europe would be shifted to the Pacific directly and without opportunity for leave in the United States. Most units, moreover, would face the challenge of exchanging their old equipment, such as B-17s or B-24s, for newer but different models such as B-29s. Reality roughly kicked over these plans, and the Army Air Forces found itself spinning in the whirlwinds of demobilization, readjustment, and redeployment—through the United States—just like the Army Ground Forces. "Utter confusion, pervading all echelons of command," reigned, according to one unit historian.

The Navy and the Marine Corps initially planned for but refused to embark on demobilization. Moreover, on July 20 Nimitz expressly recommended to King that all discharges and rotations should be deferred until after Olympic. By July 31, however, the Navy issued a "computed age" formula for discharge, though by the end of the war it had yet to yield any discharges. Whether the Navy Department would have been able to breast public opinion through Olympic is very much in doubt.

Meanwhile, the entire Army retraining program, already severely pressured, began to collapse under the acceleration of the operational schedule. Orders on August 7 assigned new readiness dates for units embarking to the Pacific that precluded any retraining in the United States. The plan under consideration at the end of the war would have left the 20th Armored Division with only twenty days for redeployment training and the 13th Armored Division with only nine. In light of this, a key officer in the G-3 Section of Army Ground Forces Headquarters pronounced: "The capitulation of Hirohito on 14 August saved our necks. . . . It would have been absolutely impossible for us to have sent well-trained teams to the Pacific for participation in the scheduled invasion of Japan."

Potential casualties and redeployment were the two major threats to morale, a topic deeply worrisome to Marshall and Stimson. The Office of War Information (OWI) advised the Joint Chiefs of Staff in late February that the steep losses on Iwo Jima had unsettled the American public. The OWI recommended efforts to gird the nation "for the heavy losses which undoubtedly would occur." In a speech to the Academy of Political Science in April, Marshall declared, "We are approaching one of the most difficult periods of the war." Once victory was achieved in Europe, Marshall foresaw that a "great impatience" of many Americans to restore normalcy would collide with the "stern necessity of maintaining the momentum of the war in the Pacific in order to shorten it by every possible day." He feared both "the possibility of a general let down in this country" with its effect on "the morale of the Army during this period of redeployment." By May, Marshall cautioned his Joint Chiefs of Staff colleagues that "war weariness in the United States may demand the return home of those who have fought long and well in the European war regardless of the effect of such a return on the prosecution of the Japanese war." Stimson observed army units from Europe redeploying for the final battles with Japan and later wrote, "These men were weary in a way that no one merely reading reports could readily understand."

A tangible manifestation of the profound concern for troop morale emerged in a radical plan in train at war's end. The Army Ground Forces had come to admire and envy the Army Air Forces' "tour of missions" criteria for combat exposure. Once an aviator accumulated the fixed "tour," which was calculated to give the individual flier a 50 percent chance of survival, he was eligible to return home. This proved a key prop to morale. The horrendous attrition in the European and Italian campaigns had precluded granting riflemen anything like this, and morale had slumped—and the rate of psychoneurotic casualties had soared—in the face of severe losses. With the end of the war in Europe, the Army Ground Forces labored to secure for riflemen in the Pacific the same 50 percent survival chance, with two startling innovations. First, additional infantry regiments would be provided so that every division in the final campaign would have four regiments and thus would be able—indeed, would be required—to have one of its rifle regiments out of the line at all times, resting, refitting, and recuperating. Second, a pool of individual replacements would permit the rotation of a portion of the theater's infantrymen back to the United States each month for domestic duty or discharge. This would be over and above the general policy of rotation for all arms and services. These policies presaged the use of tours in Korea and Vietnam, where it had decidedly mixed effects on unit cohesion and effectiveness.

Both expected attrition and the scheme for providing individual replacements meant that the Army required an influx of trained manpower. By 1945, the Army drew virtually all of its recruits from the draft managed by the Selective Service system. These men had to be provided instruction for their expected roles. Thus, the levels of induction and the capacity of the Army's training establishment provide direct evidence of the anticipated costs of defeating Japan.

The pattern of Selective Service inductions during 1945 is revealing when placed in context of the full war. During the great buildup of the armed services in 1942 and 1943, over three million men were inducted each year within the continental United States. This number fell dramatically to 1,612,492 in 1944 because in April the Army exceeded its authorized strength of over seven million, a number set to maintain a balance between soldiers in the field and workers producing war goods. Inductions fell significantly in the last five months of the year, with the monthly totals of men accepted for service ranging between only 72,270 and 83,446.

The Battle of the Bulge both resulted in heavy loss and made leaders far more cautious about the duration and cost of finishing the war. Induction calls again surged in 1945 and remained high for the seven complete months of hostilities from January to July.* Total inductions were 94,827 in January and 95,168 in July; for the span from February to June, total inductions ran above 108,000 per month. The January induction call into the Army alone within the continental United States was 60,000, and this rose to 80,000 in February and then to 100,000 from March to June before falling to 70,000 in July. Raw numbers of men actually accepted for service were between 62,493 in January and 92,632 in June. The total number of men accepted for Army service was 562,868 for January to July, an average of 80,410 per month.

Secretary of War Stimson had been deeply concerned about the capacity of the Army to provide sufficient manpower for the final phase of the war against Japan. He directed a study by Dr. Edmund P. Learned and Dr. Dan T. Smith that became known as the Learned-Smith Report. Their analysis endorsed plans for the War Department to maintain a high rate of induction and replacement training even after Germany's defeat. This would allow the service to replace losses or to increase the rate of discharges if the rate of losses fell below planning estimates. From June 1945, the replacement training system provided for a capacity of 291,177 men in the Army Ground Forces, of whom no fewer than 254,690 were for infantry. Since the infantry training cycle after May 1945 was fifteen weeks long, this provided a monthly output of about a quarter of the total, or about 63,700. It is very striking that this was the highest rate of production of infantry replacements during the entire war. But experience had

---

* Men were ordered to report for induction (called), but only after being found physically and mentally fit were they accepted for induction into the armed forces.

demonstrated that the infantry would sustain 78 percent of losses among the Army Ground Forces personnel, and finding replacement riflemen had been an ongoing crisis since mid-1944.

Absent the end of the war, and assuming that the structure of inductions and training set in the summer of 1945 would have remained in place, inductions for the Army alone would have continued to average about 80,000 per month. The yearly output of infantry replacements would have numbered around 764,000. By similar extrapolation, the Navy would have inducted 258,240 men, for a combined total of over 1.2 million men to maintain the reduced strength of the armed forces.

Supplies and Shipping

By the end of June, the War Production Board (WPB), the central management of the arsenal of democracy, had completed drafting its Program for a One-Front War. Within a total budget of $42 billion over a twelve-month period, the WPB looked to recalibrate the war economy to spew out necessary items, most importantly ammunition and bombs, while drastically reducing other products, such as guns, fire-control equipment, and—to a lesser extent—ships. Assembly lines would cease or drastically reduce production of many familiar aircraft, while new or retooled plants geared up to produce new models either suited to the long ranges of the Pacific, such as the B-29 and C-54, or with enhanced performance, such as an array of new fighters: the P-51H, the P-47N, and the jet-propelled P-80 Shooting Star. The Navy looked to replace the FM-2 Wildcat with the FR-1 Fireball, the F8F Bearcat, and the F7F Tigercat, which could fly one hundred miles per hour faster. Factories would roll out no fewer than 1,200 jet fighters and bombers in the first quarter of 1946.

By contrast, shipbuilding in the first half of 1946 would not far exceed that in a single month in late 1943. Furthermore, production of the venerable M4 Sherman tank, the mainstay of all the campaigns to date, would cease after June, though the heavy tank program, the M26 Pershing, would continue, albeit at reduced volume. Ominously for Japan, the WPB noted that "almost as much steel, explosives and incendiaries will be fired at or dropped on the Japanese as we were producing for use against both our major enemies at the high point of the two-front war."

General Brehon B. Somervell, the commander of the Army Service Forces, observed to his staff that for the ultimate phases of the Pacific war, those delivering supplies were to ensure that "we have enough but not too much." In a series of meetings, logistical planners distilled a projection that "enough" to pursue a war in the Pacific for one year totaled

53,880,000 tons of supplies. The procurement of the raw supplies occasioned no significant doubt; the means to ship, store, and receive the material in the Pacific did. To begin with, West Coast ports could not handle this material alone, and an intricate plan evolved to ship supplies from ports on the East Coast and in the Gulf of Mexico.

Planners also faced a major decision as to whether the supply pipeline should flow to an intermediate base, in much the role England had served in the European theater, or straight to the objective area. In the summer of 1945, furious construction began to erect intermediate Base X, which was Manila. By July 1945, when Lieutenant General Arthur G. Trudeau took command of the port of Manila, he supervised a labor force of 300,000, including 150,000 Filipinos. In August, the port handled 434,481 tons of supplies, rising to 479,660 tons in October. During September alone, 274 vessels arrived and 254 departed. By the end of the war, Manila housed over five million tons of supplies and had set up 37,500 hospital beds for casualties expected in an invasion of Japan.

Ultimately, planners decided against complete reliance on intermediate bases. For Downfall, after the assault phase, most supplies would move directly from the United States to Japan. Under this design, block-loaded cargo vessels, 482 for Olympic and 700 for Coronet, would sail on a schedule to a regulating station at Ulithi. From Ulithi, they would be summoned to the target area. This scheme sent a-glimmering the dream of the Army Service Forces to make the Philippines "the England of the Orient."

Thus, as the summer of 1945 arrived, American remobilization plans became deranged, morale declined, and the logistical plans showed signs of serious strain.

9

The Invasion
and the President

"My hardest decision to date"

The President Orders a Meeting

Franklin D. Roosevelt died on April 12, 1945, thus thrusting Harry S. Truman of Independence, Missouri, into the presidency. The new president, said Alonzo Hamby, a sympathetic biographer, "clearly felt small, overwhelmed, and in something of a state of shock." Well he might, for with the possible exceptions of Abraham Lincoln in 1861 and Roosevelt himself in 1933, no American had ever faced such daunting challenges immediately upon assuming the office of chief executive. No wonder Truman told a friend, "I feel like I have been struck by a bolt of lightning."

The novice president confronted not only a myriad of tangible challenges but also pervasive initial doubts about his fitness. Roosevelt's patrician background and manner, coupled with his manifold accomplishments, had made him a towering figure. Truman, by contrast, rose from humble beginnings marked by many failures until he settled into a career clouded by the sponsorship of a tainted Missouri political machine. Moreover, he was an uninspiring public speaker due to his nasal twang and lack of cadence. "To many," wrote biographer David McCullough, "it was not just that the greatest of men had fallen, but that the least of men—or at any rate the least likely of men—had assumed his place."

The initial private assessments in Washington were decidedly mixed. David E. Lilienthal, chairman of the Tennessee Valley Authority, wrote in his diary that he had a "sick, hapless feeling" when he realized who would replace Roosevelt. In his diary, Secretary of the Interior Harold Ickes observed that Truman was sincere, conscientious, and vigorous, but "he doesn't have great depth mentally." Significantly, Truman's standing was far better among those who knew him well, such as former Vice President John N. Garner, Republican Senator Arthur H. Vandenberg, and Speaker of the House Sam Rayburn. In private to Stimson, however, General Marshall articulated the question on everyone's mind: "We shall not know what he is really like until the pressure begins to be felt."

Truman announced to the cabinet and then to the nation that his mission was to discharge the legacy of his illustrious predecessor. His ordered and decisive conduct of cabinet meetings created an immediate favorable impression on Stimson. But if the new president promised continuity and projected solid executive skills, he profoundly lacked knowledge of the host of challenges rising with the end of the war in Europe and the last stage of the war in the Pacific—and of Roosevelt's policies toward them. Truman, observed Stimson, was "laboring with the terrific handicap of coming into such an office where the threads of information were so multitudinous that only long previous familiarity could allow him to control them." It was not until April 17, for example, that Truman first learned of Ultra and Magic, and Stimson briefed him on the atomic bomb program on April 25. As each unresolved issue left by Roosevelt emerged, Truman sought the counsel of those who held official responsibility or whose judgment he trusted.

It is in this context that on June 17, 1945, Truman approached his "hardest decision to date." In his diary he wrote, "I have to decide Japanese strategy, shall we invade Japan proper or shall we bomb and blockade." It speaks volumes of Truman's predicament that this initial formal review occurred some two months after he assumed office and more than three weeks after the Joint Chiefs of Staff had, on May 25, ordered preparations for an invasion of Japan. In the memorandum issued through his chief of staff, Admiral William Leahy, Truman demanded from his key advisers

an estimate of the time required and an estimate of the losses in killed and wounded that will result from an invasion of Japan proper. . . . It is [Truman's] intention to make his decision on the campaign with the purpose of economizing to the maximum extent possible in the loss of American lives. Economy in the use of time and in money cost is comparatively unimportant.

Truman's directive mirrored the widespread public concern over casualties. Anyone outfitted only with public knowledge of the size of the Japanese Homeland, a very rough estimate of Japanese armed forces, and the record of Japanese warriors throughout the Pacific war could not fail to recognize the potential for staggering American losses. Newspaper and radio commentary dwelled on the likelihood of a protracted struggle exacting immense costs in life. A widely quoted correspondent fresh from the Pacific in mid-May 1945 estimated that between five hundred thousand and a million Americans would die by the end of the war. For many, Iwo Jima and especially Okinawa looked to be foreshadowings of what the struggle in the Homeland would be like.

But there also appears to be a direct relationship between Truman's order and two recent memorandums that Truman and Stimson received from former President Herbert Hoover. Hoover urged the abandonment of the unconditional-surrender formula, not least because it would avoid an invasion that would cost "500,000 to 1,000,000" American fatalities. The staff officers assigned to respond to Hoover noted that Truman was "very much perturbed" over losses on Okinawa, but the chief of the Army Operations Division, Lieutenant General Thomas T. Handy, labeled Hoover's numbers as "entirely too high" under "our present plan of campaign."*

Nevertheless, Hoover's figures gave pause, and similar concerns about the costs of an invasion of Japan floated freely among Allied leaders. During disputes over bombing policies occasioned by the Dresden attack in February 1945, Sir Arthur Harris defended his Bomber Command in his usual acerbic tones and demanded to know if Allied leaders were prepared to abide targeting restrictions not only in Europe but also against Japan and "subsequently invade [Japan] at the cost of 3 to 6 million casualties."

All projections of casualty numbers require context. To start with, not only are total American battle casualties for the war relevant, but their very

---

* Hoover's numbers have usually been dismissed as those of a lay party, but there is evidence to the contrary. While the former president held no government position, he was receiving intelligence briefings. In an interview with Truman on May 28, 1945, Hoover gave remarkably accurate order-of-battle numbers for Soviet and Japanese troops in Manchuria. It is extremely difficult to believe he pulled these out of open sources. This suggests either that Hoover's figures came from a military source or that his assessment was based on more than public information. Unfortunately, Hoover kept no written record of his briefings, so it is impossible to establish the source of his estimates. Hoover Notes of Meeting with Truman, May 28, 1945, in Timothy Walch and Dwight M. Miller, *Herbert Hoover and Harry Truman: A Documentary History* (Worland, Wyo.: High Plains Publishing, 1992), pp. 37–43. For general background, see the Oral History interviews of John J. McCloy and General Albert C. Wedemeyer, Hoover Institution.

uneven distribution across three and one half years of war is telling, as this table shows:

Battle Deaths in All Theaters of War: U.S. Army, Army Air Force, Navy, and Marine Corps

	1941	1942	1943	1944	1945
January	—	651	1,682	4,656	16,631
February	—	1,023	1,942	5,733	16,467
March	—	1,868	1,514	4,173	20,325
April	—	3,038	1,558	4,673	18,751
May	—	14,268	1,747	6,452	8,945
June	—	639	1,040	17,784	3,565
July	—	258	4,233	19,711	1,992
August	—	2,021	2,603	13,091	626
September	—	793	2,498	14,197	29
October	—	1,107	2,707	14,539	11
November	—	3,249	6,428	16,876	15
December	2,534	1,337	3,204	19,548	19
Total	2,534	30,252	31,156	141,433	87,376
Total for war	292,751				

Comments:
1. Figures for May 1942 include all deaths among prisoners of war of the Japanese. This is the month that the last U.S. outposts in the Philippines capitulated, and apparently represents an administrative convention to avoid the extremely difficult, if not impossible, task of assigning a specific month for each prisoner-of-war death. It is extremely unlikely that even a third of them died in May 1942.
2. Figures do not include the small number of deaths prior to December 1941 (i.e., those killed on the USS *Kearney* and USS *Reuben James* in October 1941) or in 1946. Presumably, deaths after August 1945 were due predominantly to wounds received during the wartime period. Also not included are about 7,000 deaths among members of the Merchant Marine or the approximately 100,000 nonbattle deaths during the war.

These figures both prove and imply much. No fewer than 64 percent of all battle fatalities occurred in the one-year span from June 1944 to May 1945, with the heaviest loss of the war in March 1945. This reflected how American losses surged markedly when the Army and the Marine Corps became embroiled in protracted ground combat. Therefore, the tapering off of losses after the German capitulation marked not a trend but a predictable lull prior to the expected massive ground combat against the Imperial Army.

While experience afforded an important overall framework, Truman had demanded a projection into the future. This was neither easy nor customary. Casualty predictions are a treacherous business at best because critical elements—such as the intentions, strength, equipment, skill, expertise, and morale of the opponent—are unknown or imperfectly understood. Of these factors, relative numerical strength weighs heavily ("God," said Napoleon, "is on the side of the big battalions"). A point validated repeatedly over history and well understood by 1945 is that the greater the disparity in overall combat power between the attacker and the defender, the lower the casualties the attacker will incur. A rough rule of thumb is that to ensure success at a reasonable cost the attacker should outnumber the defender three to one. The Downfall plan projected that on X-Day on Kyushu, nine American divisions would face three Japanese.

Senior officers factored in concerns over casualties through broad, subjective judgments, however, not hypothetical balance sheets. If any reliable model for projecting casualties in the Pacific existed (and this is doubtful), the Joint Chiefs of Staff had not formally recognized it. Actual attempts to project figures for casualties normally occurred only after the operation was ordered and then became the provenance of those charged with providing medical care for wounded, disposition for the dead, and replacements to maintain unit strengths.

Besides the bewildering complexities and uncertainty of casualty estimates, lay parties must be wary of the nuances of the military lexicon. For Truman and the Joint Chiefs of Staff, "casualties" meant not only servicemen killed but also those wounded and those who become classed as "missing." The missing are those unaccounted for after battle, who either turn up later as prisoners of war or who are never accounted for and are ultimately presumed dead. The proportions of casualties among the killed, wounded, and missing vary radically among battles on land, those at sea, and those in the air. In World War II, the ratio of American battle casualties in ground combat was about four wounded or injured to one killed, with the missing accounting for only a few percentage points. In naval and aerial combat, however, the ratios tended to run closer to one wounded or injured to one killed. The number of missing was more substantial, but more of the missing ended up as presumed dead.

When Truman's orders for a review of invasion strategy arrived, the Joint Chiefs of Staff already had at hand at least two authoritative sources from which to begin estimating prospective invasion casualties. A series of papers prepared for and reviewed by the Joint Chiefs of Staff in the latter half of 1944 had mentioned casualties only in general terms. But the issue was too important to evade. Thus, the draft in this series dated April 25, 1945, and adopted by the Joint Chiefs of Staff as the basis for planning the invasion finally confronted the issue but still found it too contentious and speculative to resolve. This paper incorporated a table based on data compiled by the Surgeon General of the Army that compared casualty experience in seven Pacific amphibious campaigns (Guadalcanal, New Georgia, Leyte, Attu, the Marshalls, the Marianas, and Palau) with the casualty experience in protracted war in Europe, both in rates per thousands of men committed per day:*

	Pacific Amphibious Campaigns	European Protracted Campaigns
Killed in action	1.78	.36
Wounded in action	5.50	1.74
Missing in action	.17	.06
Total	7.45	2.16

The Joint Chiefs of Staff could have taken these ratios, plugged in a troop list and a projected duration for each campaign of the invasion, and secured a range of potential losses. The forces projected to be ashore on Kyushu for Olympic in MacArthur's order of May 28 totaled 766,700, but the most recently updated troop list stood at 681,000. Washington planners requested that MacArthur's headquarters generate a casualty estimate assuming a ninety-day campaign. Running the troop lists and a ninety-day campaign through an equation with the ratios in the April 25 paper produces the following:

Projected Casualties for Olympic for a Ninety-Day Campaign

	Pacific Experience		European Experience	
Troop list	766,700	681,000	766,700	681,000
Killed and missing	134,556	119,516	28,981	25,472
Total casualties	514,072	456,611	149,046	132,386

As for the overall prospects in an invasion of Japan, at 766,700 committed troops for Olympic and 1,026,000 committed troops for Coronet, both for ninety-day campaigns, projections would run as follows:

---

* There is no explanation as to why the topic of casualties was approached via these ratios rather than in the form of a specific number, or even the "Saipan ratio" of one U.S. serviceman killed to every seven Japanese killed or captured. One obvious factor was that no one had confidence in any single formula for projecting casualties and this method thus allowed for the wide variance of experience. Another consideration was that obtaining a number through application of these ratios required a specific scenario for the duration of the fighting and the number of U.S. servicemen ultimately committed against Japan. No one was prepared to hazard such projections because no one knew whether an organized capitulation of Japan could be secured.

Projected Casualties for Olympic and Coronet for a Ninety-Day Campaign

	Pacific Experience	*European Experience*
Troop list	1,792,700	1,792,700
Killed and missing	314,619	67,764
Total casualties	1,202,005	348,501

As awful as these numbers appear, they are not a comprehensive range. The troop list comprised only those men who would be physically on Kyushu; it did not include any of the other tens of thousands of men crewing naval vessels offshore or airmen not based on Kyushu. They, too, would sustain casualties, especially the naval personnel. A second projection for the invasion of Kyushu, however, also sat in files in Washington and could fill part of this gap. On May 13, Nimitz issued a draft edition of his Joint Staff Study for Olympic. This estimated casualties for only the first thirty days but contained the following table, breaking the losses down by service:

	Killed and Missing	*Returned to Duty Wounded*	*Evacuated Wounded*	*Total*
Navy	2,150	570	2,280	5,000
Marines	2,400	3,780	5,820	12,000
Army	6,400	10,080	15,520	32,000
Total	10,950	14,430	23,620	49,000

Nimitz's study was apparently the sole contemporary estimate of naval casualties for any part of Olympic. Planners could have attempted to factor in the projection from Nimitz—or better yet, they could have asked Nimitz to supply estimates for naval losses in the invasions of both Kyushu and Honshu. They did neither. Truman did not see any figures based on these authoritative documents, which were prepared before he told the Joint Chiefs of Staff that his approval of the invasion strategy was contingent upon casualty estimates.

Meanwhile, officers in MacArthur's command generated a projection of cumulative battle casualties among ground and perhaps some air units (but not naval units) as follows:

X-Day to X plus 15	9,727
X-Day to X plus 30	22,576
X-Day to X plus 60	55,906
X-Day to X plus 120	124,935

Although one authority reports that this estimate predated Truman's request for a casualty estimate, more likely it was the product of MacArthur's medical authorities in July 1945. In either event, this estimate allowed for only 22,576 casualties over the first thirty days, less than half the 49,000 figure advanced by Nimitz's staff for the same time frame. It is impossible to believe that an estimate from CINCPAC for the full campaign would have failed to significantly exceed this set of numbers from MacArthur's command, whatever its actual date.

To respond to the President's demand for specific information, Marshall requested that MacArthur submit an estimate for "battle casualties in OLYMPIC up to D+90" (that is, for a 90-day campaign). The expeditious response, passed as a reply from MacArthur and representing "estimated total battle casualties from which estimated return to duty numbers are deducted," indicated the following:

D-Day to D plus 30	50,800
D-Day plus 30 to D plus 60	27,150
D-Day plus 60 to D plus 90	27,100

The estimate also noted that another 4,200 nonbattle casualties (deaths, injuries, and disease) should be anticipated for each thirty-day period.

This second projection yielded a battle casualty total of 105,050, less than the other set of complete campaign figures by about 20,000. What is not clear is how the planners adjusted for the difference in the projected duration of the campaign. Did they expect fewer casualties because of a briefer campaign, or the same casualties compressed into a shorter period? The latter approach is suggested by the fact that projected losses over the first thirty days had more than doubled and the fine-print caveat that the new enumeration excluded the wounded who were returned to duty. The precise formula employed by MacArthur's staff to calculate this is unknown. What is known is that in the projection prepared by Nimitz's staff for just thirty days, the same category amounted to a hefty 29 percent of the 49,000 total. If the same percentage is applied to MacArthur's estimate, total casualties reach about 149,000.

MacArthur's amended set of numbers deeply disturbed Marshall. Only a few hours before the meeting with the president, the chief of staff urgently queried MacArthur whether the numbers were "based on plans for medical installations" (that is, intended to ensure that adequate provision had been made for the treatment and evacuation of casualties) or whether it represented "your best estimate of the casualties you anticipate from the operational viewpoint." He stressed that Truman was "very much concerned" about the casualties in Olympic. MacArthur instantly apprehended the subtext in the message from Marshall and promptly replied that the estimate "had not come to my prior attention" and represented no more than a "purely academic and routine" exercise for "planning alone." The figures had been extracted from experience at Normandy and Okinawa, which represented the highest casualty experience of the war for American forces. MacArthur disavowed that he expected such casualties.

Ultimately, the numbers set before Truman originated from neither MacArthur nor Nimitz but from staff officers in Washington. A draft paper prepared by the Joint Staff Planners on June 15 projected a combined total for both Olympic and Coronet of 193,500 casualties with 43,500 dead and missing. Twenty-four hours later, a revised version of this paper abruptly dropped any quantification whatsoever for a paragraph that began, "The cost in casualties of the main operations against Japan are not subject to accurate estimate." This edition stressed that "the scale of Japanese resistance in the past has not been predictable" and found it difficult to assess whether Kyushu would more closely resemble Okinawa or Leyte. But none of this work was placed before Truman either. Instead, the Operations Division of the Army rewrote the paragraph on casualties in the paper prepared by the Joint Staff Planners, and this carefully tailored variant—signed in its final form by Major General John Hull—armed General Marshall for the rendezvous with the president.

The June 18, 1945, White House Meeting

The one-hour meeting called by the President convened at 3:30 P.M. on June 18. Present were the Joint Chiefs of Staff, with the Secretaries of the Army and Navy, Assistant Secretary of War John J. McCloy, and Lieutenant General Ira C. Eaker, who was substituting for General Arnold. Truman called on Marshall first, and the Chief of Staff read a digest of the paper prepared by the Joint Staff Planners with the section by Hull on casualties. The paper outlined the forces to be employed and the strategic calculations that produced the strategy to end the war. Marshall strongly emphasized the need to launch the Kyushu assault on November 1 because weather conditions thereafter might delay the operation for six months. According to the paraphrase in the minutes of the meeting, Marshall stressed that Olympic was

> essential to a strategy of strangulation and appears to be the least costly worth-while operation following Okinawa. The basic point is that a lodge-

ment in Kyushu is essential both to tightening our strangle hold of blockade and bombardment of Japan, and to forcing capitulation by invasion of the Tokyo Plain.

If the Japanese were ever willing to capitulate short of complete military defeat in the field, stated Marshall, they would do it when faced by the completely hopeless prospect occasioned by (1) the destruction resulting from the air and sea blockade coupled with (2) a landing on Japan underscoring the firmness of American resolve and also perhaps coupled with (3) Soviet entry or threat of entry into the war. Having thus warned that an organized Japanese surrender might not be obtainable, he stated that American objectives should include Soviet involvement in "clean-up" operations in Manchuria and perhaps Korea, while the Chinese, assisted by United States airpower and supplies, cleared their own country.

Marshall read Hull's digest, which approached the critical subject of casualties obliquely, observing that "our casualty experience in the Pacific war is so diverse as to casualties that it is considered wrong to give any estimate in numbers." Having jettisoned the formulas featured in the April 25 planning paper by the Joint Staff Planners, the more recent calculations of the Joint Staff Planners, and the projections of the theater commanders, and noting that "General MacArthur has not yet accepted responsibility for going ashore where there would be disproportionate casualties," the digest illustrated this "diverse experience" in a table as follows:

Campaign	U.S. Casualties: Killed, Wounded, and Missing	Japanese Casualties: Killed and Prisoners	Ratio, U.S./Japan
Leyte	17,000	78,000	1:4.6
Luzon	31,000	156,000	1:5.0
Iwo Jima	20,000	25,000	1:1.25
Okinawa	39,000 (ground)	119,000	1:3
	7,000 (navy)	n/a	—
Normandy	42,000 (first thirty days)	—	—

Then Marshall pointed to the record of MacArthur's operations from March 1, 1944, to May 1, 1945, in which it was claimed that 13,742 U.S. servicemen were killed to 310,165 Japanese, or a ratio of 22.6 to 1.* Cit-

---

* The numbers supplied by the Army in this table are not accurate. For example, the postwar U.S. official histories gave Japanese total strength on Leyte at only 59,400 to 70,000, not all of whom became casualties, and U.S. Army battle casualties alone, without nonbattle losses, at 15,584. On Luzon, because the Japanese strategy was to tie down American forces for the longest possible time to delay attack on the Homeland, the Imperial Army evaded decisive engagements, and consequently the bulk of

ing the theory that Kyushu offered "maneuver room" for both land and sea forces, Marshall pointed out that casualties for the first thirty days would probably be on the model of Luzon, which represented the most favorable ratio.[†] Truman was told to expect 350,000 defenders on Kyushu. The minutes do not reflect that anyone worked this out in front of Truman, but this method would project between 70,000 and 280,000 American casualties on Kyushu if, as was normal in the Pacific, virtually the entire Japanese garrison had to be annihilated.

Unlike the paper prepared by the Joint Staff Planners, which estimated that naval casualties would approximate the rate at Okinawa (hardly a bright prospect, as the Okinawa campaign was the most costly of the war for Navy personnel with over 4,900 killed—40 percent of all American deaths at Okinawa), Marshall did not incorporate any figures for naval losses. It is a grim fact, he told Truman, that there is not an easy, bloodless way to victory in war and it is the thankless task of the leaders to maintain their firm outward front which holds the resolution of their subordinates. Marshall noted that the impact of Russian entry on the already hopeless Japanese might well be the decisive action levering them into capitulation at that time or shortly thereafter if the Americans landed in Japan. Finally, he ended by quoting MacArthur:

> I believe the operation presents less hazards of excessive loss than any other that has been suggested and that its decisive effect will eventually save lives

---

the Japanese garrison died of disease and starvation rather than in combat. U.S. losses were about 37,900. On Okinawa, the number given for Japanese casualties clearly exceeded postwar information on the garrison, which actually numbered no more than about 76,000 Japanese; the balance of the 100,000 or so defenders were impressed Okinawans. Given these discrepancies, the supposed 22.6 to 1 casualty ratio should be taken with a large grain of salt. Indeed, in the final revised version of this paper of July 11, 1945, while the 22.6 to 1 claim remained, it was acknowledged that the overall Japanese-U.S. casualty ratio achieved by MacArthur was no more than 5 to 1. See M. Hamlin Cannon, *Leyte: The Return to the Philippines* (Washington, D.C.: Government Printing Office, 1954), p. 368; Robert Ross Smith, *Triumph in the Philippines* (Washington, D.C.: Government Printing Office, 1963), Appendixes H and H-2; Thomas M. Huber, *Japan's Battle of Okinawa, April–June 1945,* Leavenworth Papers, no. 18 (Fort Leavenworth, Kans.: Combat Studies Institute, U.S. Army Command and General Staff College, 1990); and J.C.S. 1388/4, 11 July 1945, details of Campaign Against Japan, RG 218 (Geographic File 1942–45), 381 Japan (6-14-45), Box 118. There is no evidence that J.C.S. 1388/4 was shown to Truman.

[†] The claim of "maneuver room" simply does not withstand scrutiny. Luzon possesses a plain forty miles wide and 120 miles long, extending from Manila north to Lingayen Gulf with a hard-surfaced road suitable for mobile warfare. The mountainous target area in southern Kyushu (described further in Chapter 11), had only three narrow, soggy plains with no hard-surfaced roads. Louis Morton, *The Fall of the Philippines* (Washington, D.C.: Government Printing Office, 1953), pp. 6–7; CCS 417/11, 22 Jan 45, appendix A, Kyushu Terrain Estimate, pp. 18–19; 381 Pacific Ocean Operations 6-10-43, Sec. 11, RG 218, Box 686.

by eliminating wasteful operations of nondecisive character. I regard the operation as the most economical one in effort and lives that is possible. In this respect it must be remembered that the several preceding months will involve practically no losses in ground troops and that sooner or later a decisive ground attack must be made. The hazard and loss will be greatly lessened if an attack is launched from Siberia sufficiently ahead of our target date to commit the enemy to major combat. I most earnestly recommend no change in OLYMPIC. Additional subsidiary attacks will simply build up our final total casualties.

Admiral King then added his concurrence, highlighting the point that Kyushu also offered a key to success in siege operations. We should do Kyushu now, stated King, after which there would be time to judge the effect of possible operations by the Russians and the Chinese. Likewise, he added, preparations needed to commence for an invasion of Tokyo Plain. If preparations did not go forward, he emphasized to Truman as he had in April to his colleagues, they could not be arranged later; once started, however, they could always be stopped if desired. Marshall seconded the point that a decision on action subsequent to Kyushu could be made later. Truman asked if a later decision would not depend on Russian actions, and according to the minutes "it was agreed that this would have considerable influence."

Leahy then spoke at the President's bidding. He reminded everyone that the President had asked a specific question about the price in casualties of taking Kyushu. He expressed his view that, since he expected the fighting to be similar to that on Okinawa, where losses reached 35 percent of the committed forces, application of this percentage to the forces earmarked for Kyushu would provide a good estimate. King interrupted to reiterate Marshall's observation that unlike Okinawa, Kyushu offered maneuver room and thus was more akin to Luzon as a model. He opined that the cost of Olympic would fall somewhere between casualty experience on Luzon and Okinawa (that is, between 31,000 and about 41,000). Marshall then answered Leahy by giving the total assault troops as 766,700.

The issue of Japanese opposition on Kyushu provoked a comment by Truman later much cited but probably to the wrong effect. Marshall estimated Japanese opposition on Kyushu would be ultimately built up to eight divisions and 350,000 men. Although reinforcement beyond this number was possible, Marshall and King reassured Truman that destruction of Japanese communications probably would foreclose that threat. Leahy stressed that Kyushu was an island, and moreover one divided by a mountain range difficult for either side to cross. Leahy likened the operation to the "taking of another island from which to bring increased air power against Japan." The minutes record that Truman then commented that this "was practically creating another Okinawa closer to Japan, to which the Chiefs of Staff agreed." Truman's analogy to Okinawa thus seems to refer to its function for air-base sites rather than to its casualties.

General Eaker and Secretary of the Navy James Forrestal now spoke to support King's observation that Kyushu would be vital to the air and sea blockade of Japan. Secretary Stimson, after recording his agreement with the chiefs that "there was no other choice," ventured that there was "a large submerged class in Japan who do not favor the present war," whom he hoped to mobilize. Truman interjected that this possibility was being worked on all the time. This was a veiled reference to the President's meeting that very morning on a diplomatic strategy with Acting Secretary of State Joseph Grew. Truman then asked if the invasion of Japan by white men would not have the effect of more closely uniting the Japanese. Stimson thought there was every prospect of this, and added that this is why he still hoped for some fruitful accomplishment through other means. McCloy seconded this point.

Leahy pressed this opening. Unconditional surrender was unnecessary, he said, as Japan would pose no menace for the foreseeable future. Truman commented that he had "left this door open for Congress to take appropriate action," which is likely a garble in the minutes for his leaving the door open "before Congress," but he did not feel that he could take any action at this time to change public opinion on the matter.

The minutes then primly comment that "the President and the Chiefs of Staff then discussed certain other matters." McCloy later insisted that it was only as the meeting was breaking up that he lifted the shroud of silence on the atomic bomb. The minutes are far more likely to be correct than McCloy's memory and probably indicate that the bomb was discussed, although there is a weak possibility of some exchange on the use of poison gas, a matter Marshall had been pressing within the Joint Chiefs of Staff immediately before this meeting.

As the conference waned, the minutes show, Truman remarked that he had called it because "he had hoped there was a possibility of preventing an Okinawa from one end of Japan to the other. He was clear on the situation now and was quite sure" the Kyushu invasion should go forward and they could then decide "final action later." While the presentation had achieved its aim of reassuring Truman that the next step in the sequence of operations to end the war would likely not involve inordinate cost, Truman withheld sanction for any further operations. These comments are sometimes construed to show that Truman's decision to approve Olympic was based on the information he received on casualty projections. But the min-

utes show that Truman was shrewd enough to document in the record another ground for his decision. The President summarized that "the Joint
Chiefs of Staff, after weighing all the possibilities of the situation and considering all possible alternative plans were still of the unanimous opinion
that the Kyushu operation was the best solution under the circumstances."
The minutes reflect that the chiefs dutifully concurred with this.

On June 20, only two days after this meeting, Admiral King sent a memorandum to his peers on the Joint Chiefs of Staff on the briefing presented
to Truman. King protested that the information on casualties was "not satisfactory" and pointed out that Admiral Nimitz had estimated casualties at
49,000 over just the first thirty days. Moreover, admonished King, "it appears to me that the Chiefs of Staff will have to give an estimate of casualties expected in the operation." He believed a "fair estimate" of naval
casualties would be that they would continue "at approximately the same
rate" as at Okinawa. This memorandum should still any lingering argument that the estimates given Truman on June 18 were evenhanded or definitive.

Marshall replied to King's challenge on June 26. "In view of the fact
that casualties were discussed at the meeting on 18 June, it seems unnecessary and undesirable for the Joint Chiefs of Staff to make estimates,
which at best can be only speculative." Marshall did apparently allow that
King's point on Navy losses should be folded into a revised version of the
brief provided Truman, but there is no evidence that this revised version
was shown to Truman.

What did or did not happen at this fateful meeting forms a critical flash
point of debate. Charges came later that the numbers set out by the Joint
Chiefs of Staff for this meeting were the only contemporary official casualty estimates for an invasion of Japan, and that thus there was no authentic basis for the huge casualty estimates mentioned after the war by
Stimson and Truman as justification for the use of atomic bombs. Some go
so far as to maintain that the "real" estimate provided to Truman was Marshall's figure of 31,000 casualties—either omitting the qualification that
this was only for the first thirty days or arguing without warrant that thirty
days represented Marshall's expectation of the entire duration of the campaign.

None of this is correct. A plain reading of the minutes of this meeting
discloses that King was right: Truman *never* got an unambiguous or unanimous answer to his fundamental question about casualties, even for
Olympic. Marshall insisted at the outset that it was "wrong to give any estimate in numbers." At least four, and perhaps five, separate and markedly
varied means of projecting casualties passed before Truman. One method

centered on the set of casualty ratios based on actual campaign experience.

Leahy pushed the second method: a simple equation that ignored the number of defenders and anticipated that a fixed percent of the committed American troops would become casualties. Leahy believed that rate would parallel that on Okinawa: 35 percent. No one apparently made that calculation out loud, but it took no great mental mathematical effort to see that 35 percent of 766,700 works out to well over 200,000 casualties. A third documented method delivered only a partial figure: Marshall's opinion that the casualties of the first thirty days would equal the 31,000 of Luzon. King added a fourth: Casualties would fall somewhere between Luzon (31,000) and Okinawa (about 41,000).

The fifth casualty projection is not found in the minutes. According to Admiral Leahy's diary entry for this day, at some point Marshall estimated that the casualties would total 63,000 out of 190,000 "combatant troops." It is probable that these numbers emerged after Leahy mooted the 35 percent rate of loss and that Marshall sought to counter with this set of numbers (which equate to 33 percent of the "combatant troops"). The source for Marshall's 190,000 figure is puzzling. If by "combatant troops" Marshall meant a strict but conventional definition of "combat troops" as excluding all but those assigned to the infantry, field artillery, armor, and combat engineers, contemporary troop lists yield about 218,000. Broader definitions give larger numbers. Leahy's diary entry raises another question: Were there other numbers discussed but not noted in the official minutes? Finally, with regard to Truman's purported ease with the invasion plan, he only endorsed Olympic. An invasion of the Tokyo Plain was left for future decision, and the President was warned that an organized capitulation of Japan might not be obtainable.

More troubling than what happened during this meeting is what transpired before it took place. The documentary record shows that Truman was systematically denied information about the huge projections inherent in the April 25 paper of the Joint Staff Planners, which carried the imprimatur of the Joint Chiefs of Staff. The President was also shielded from the estimates prepared by the men charged with carrying out Olympic. As commander in chief, Truman represented the formal point where American military and political strategy fuse. His personal experience in World War I and in the army reserve gave him insight into military matters. But the men facing him that afternoon not only held formal title to mastery of military considerations but were the leadership team that had led the nation to triumph in the greatest war in its history. Thus, their views carried tremendous authority, and they represented themselves as unanimously behind the invasion plan. Finally, American strategists had long tied the maintenance of American political support for a fight to complete victory to casualties and time, but Truman had discounted the importance of time. Therefore, when he was never given a firm number and denied access to a number of sobering estimates, he was left without tangible facts in which to anchor a veto of Olympic.

The lead figure in this was Marshall. He actively sought to quash the 100,000-plus casualty estimates for Olympic from MacArthur's headquarters. Indeed, immediately after the meeting Marshall sent a message to MacArthur thanking him for the prompt response and advising him that his statement "had [a] determining influence in obtaining formal presidential approval for OLYMPIC." Reconciling Marshall's matchless overall record of probity with his conduct here is troubling, but only part of his thought process appears clear. First, Marshall held a conviction that only an invasion of Japan would secure a peace from which Japan would not emerge later as a threat, thus making worthwhile all the sacrifices already made. Second, European experience had erased in his mind any prospects of airpower securing peace, a point he made to Truman at this meeting.

Beyond these certainties, several strong inferences can be drawn about Marshall's reasoning. As of the date of the meeting, there was no objective basis upon which to believe that the ultimate Japanese deployment against Olympic would exceed the eight divisions and 350,000 men Marshall estimated for Truman. On the other hand, it was conceivable that if Kyushu was isolated and if the Japanese felt compelled to maintain two or three divisions in northern Kyushu due to its strategic importance, Olympic might well face substantially less. Further, Luzon had housed a Japanese garrison (287,000 men and seven divisions) that approximated the anticipated Japanese strength on Kyushu. This might explain its attraction as an analogy. Thus, it is very likely that Marshall refused to place high projections for Olympic losses before Truman because he did not believe casualties would reach such magnitudes. Even so, his tactics were questionable, and the failure even to mention naval casualties is not excusable.

But Marshall was not alone. Admiral King's role here in some respects is even more disturbing. No doubt King continued to believe, as he had told his fellow members of the Joint Chiefs of Staff in writing on April 30, that Japan's defeat would not require an invasion but that it remained prudent to maintain the option. King took care to point out to Truman that the invasion could always be canceled, but his desire to maintain the invasion option disarmed him from challenging the casualty estimates placed before the President. Moreover, it is reasonable to assume that King's views were known to his subordinates among the secretariat of the Joint Chiefs of Staff, and thus they too muted their disputes with their Army colleagues over the numbers. It was only after the meeting that King raised a formal protest to the numbers that had been waved before Truman, which occasioned Marshall's rejoinder that any estimates could be only "speculative."

King's failure to press the casualty issue more vigorously probably stemmed from the fact that he knew he held a trump card he could ultimately play against the invasion strategy. The minutes of the June 18 meeting reflect that Truman recorded for posterity that the Kyushu invasion strategy carried the unanimous support of the Joint Chiefs of Staff. The President was also told that the plan was backed by both Pacific theater commanders. This was certainly true of MacArthur, but King knew it was no longer true of Nimitz. Nimitz had concurred explicitly with Olympic in a message on April 28, but "after further experience in fighting against Japanese forces," he effectively withdrew his support. In a May 25 message to King, noting the slow progress of fighting on Okinawa against prepared defenses—notwithstanding overwhelming and unprecedentedly heavy air and sea support and artillery firepower—Nimitz stated that "it would be unrealistic to expect that such obvious objectives as southern Kyushu and the Tokyo Plain will not be as well defended as Okinawa." He emphasized the powerful and accelerating effect of the air and sea blockade and concluded:

> Unless speed is considered so important that we are willing to accept less than the best preparation and more than minimum casualties, I believe that the long range interests of the U.S. will be better served if we continue to isolate Japan & to destroy Jap forces & resources by naval and air attack.

This message had been sent "eyes only" to King, a category reserved for the most sensitive personal communications that would not be seen by anyone but King and Nimitz, save for a handful of discreet communications personnel or trusted staff officers. There does not appear to be any evidence that King shared it with any of his Navy subordinates or the other members of the Joint Chiefs of Staff, much less Truman. But King knew that he now possessed the power to halt the invasion by informing the President that he and Nimitz no longer supported it. If the Navy broke the consensus, American strategic planning would at a minimum be tossed into turmoil, and Truman would likely veto the invasion.

Looming over all of these factors that influenced Marshall and King was one other: the profound uncertainties of military operations in the distant future. Thus, while it is clear that Marshall and King molded the presentation to Truman in ways that raise troubling questions, they no doubt believed at the time that they were simply guiding decision making down a path of prudence—a path future developments could change. Starting about two weeks after the June 18 meeting, radio intelligence vindicated this caution by beginning to expose the startling fact that Japanese strength on Kyushu and before Tokyo was burgeoning at a furious pace, kicking over all the assumptions behind the earlier casualty estimates and posing a threat to the viability of the whole Downfall plan. Thus, though the casualty estimates at this meeting were inconclusive, they became obsolete. Truman's conference with the Joint Chiefs of Staff was by no means the last chapter in American strategic planning on how to end the war with Japan.

10

Pummeling and Strangling: Bombardment and Blockade, June to August

*"They . . . stuck in a knife into the living brains
to see what would happen"*

Bombardment

After the fighting on Okinawa ended on June 21, despite the fact that the invasion of Kyushu was still four months away, there was no respite in the Pacific war. Attacks by land- and sea-based aircraft fell with an accelerating fury upon the Homeland. Not only did Allied naval forces squeeze an ever tighter blockade around Japanese shores, they also punctuated their incursions with bombardments. No longer was the direct impact of the campaign of blockade and bombardment confined to big cities and selected coastal locations; now its effects spread across the whole of Japan.

With the June 15 attack on Osaka, Marianas-based B-29s completed the destruction or damaging of all the built-up areas on the initial list of thirty-three "Selected Urban Industrial Concentrations" issued by Washington. XXI Bomber Command planners anticipated that bad weather conditions from the middle of June would preclude precision bombing. Therefore, to maintain pressure on the Japanese war economy, they scheduled incendiary night attacks against urban industrial areas. The airmen hoped that "air power, as never before, [would] be given its chance to achieve a decisive effect on the enemy's ability to continue the war."

Using the 1940 census, staff officers created a list of the 180 largest Japanese cities by population. Of the first nine cities on the list, they crossed off seven as destroyed or substantially destroyed and two, Kyoto and Hiroshima, as "out of bounds by direction of high authority"—Kyoto for cultural reasons and Hiroshima (as of July 3) as a potential target for an atomic weapon. Of the remaining 171 cities, Niigata and Kokura shared Hiroshima's status, and seventeen were beyond range of aircraft based in the Marianas, pending development of Iwo Jima as a staging base. Limitations of the standard Superfortress AN/APQ-13 radar precluded attacks on fifteen other cities.

This left 137 cities, each of which was evaluated on the basis of three factors. Of greatest importance was the projected "congestion/inflammability" of each target. The success of the program hinged on the relative ease with which the cities could be torched and industries thus destroyed or damaged. Second came the incidence of war industries, both in or near the inflammable area. The incidence of transportation facilities ranked as a distant third criterion. Further blows at these facilities aimed to expand upon the devastating impact of the mining campaign and the prior disruption of transportation systems caused by incendiary attacks.

With these priorities established, detailed planning commenced. By mid-August, strikes ("burn jobs" in the common tongue of the XXI Bomber Command) were projected for each operational day on no fewer than sixteen urban industrial-area targets. Typical was the draft order for the Hachinohe urban area. Two groups of the 58th Wing—about eighty to one hundred aircraft—would dump 640 to 800 or more tons of high explosives and incendiaries on this modest city of 73,494. None of these city missions required more than three groups.

The program began with four typical targets on the night of June 17–18. The 314th Wing drew Kagoshima (population 190,259) in southern Kyushu, a major port and railway terminus. The city, one of the most easily identified and bombed radar targets in Japan, also housed lesser industries such as a silk mill and oil-storage facilities as well as four electric-power plants.

Bombardiers of the 58th Wing studied maps of the Omuta urban area, also on Kyushu. This target with 177,000 inhabitants claimed importance for its complicated chemical industries, coke manufacture, and allied products, such as synthetic oil, explosives, and fertilizer. It also ranked first as a port for shipping coal.

The Hamamatsu urban area on Honshu measured only 4.4 square miles but had a population of 165,000. A target of several earlier missions, it attracted continued attention as one of the six most important workshops for locomotive repair in Japan. It also produced aircraft propellers, ordnance, and machinery. Owing to uncertainties about bombing accuracy with radar at night against such a relatively small target, Hamamatsu drew a maximum effort by the veteran 73rd Wing.

The fourth small urban area struck that night was Yokkaichi, with only 102,000 souls. Described in briefings to 313th Wing crews as a "complemental town of Nagoya," its port was used by the whole region, and it had the largest oil refinery in Japan. Although the urban area covered seven square miles, the bulk of the population was squeezed within only 1.5 square miles. Antiaircraft defenses of all four of these targets were light—from thirty-two heavy guns in Kagoshima to zero in Yokkaichi—so bombing altitudes were set low, at seven to eight thousand feet.

A total of 477 strike aircraft took off for these four cities. Of these, 117 314th Wing aircraft dropped 809.6 tons of incendiaries on Kagoshima, 116 58th Wing aircraft struck Omuta with 769.2 tons, 130 73rd Wing aircraft released 911.7 tons on Hamamatsu, and 89 313th Wing aircraft hit Yokkaichi with 567.3 tons. Opposition to these raids was pathetic: Flak nicked only four Superfortresses. The eleven men from one 314th Wing B-29 were the only American casualties of the night.

The city of Omuta escaped lightly with the destruction of only 4.1 percent of its built-up area, but elsewhere bombs spread severe damage. At Kagoshima, flames burned out 44.1 percent of the urban area; at Hamamatsu 70 percent of the city was incinerated; and at Yokkaichi 60 percent of the city was destroyed. Postwar accounting compiled only total casualty lists for lesser Japanese cities throughout the war, thus precluding complete precision as to how many died in these raids. It is highly likely, however, that the great majority of the 6,509 wartime deaths in these cities (except Hamamatsu) occurred this night. During the rest of June, the XXI Bomber Command staged two series of night incendiary raids on the nights of June 19–20 and June 28–29. At a cost of only three aircraft, seven middling Japanese cities were burned, with probably 8,371 inhabitants killed.

Forecasts of reasonable weather prompted General LeMay to attempt a pair of daylight missions in the second half of June as counterpoint to the night attacks. On June 22, planners parceled out forces of between 21 and 186 aircraft for visual bombing attacks on six aircraft-industry targets on Honshu. The four wings put up an aggregate of 447 strike aircraft for these targets, but deteriorating weather between Iwo Jima and Japan canceled a fighter escort. The 73rd, 314th, and 58th Wings inflicted heavy damage on the Kure arsenal, the Mitsubishi aircraft plant at Tamashima, and the Kawanishi Aircraft Company plant at Himeji (which was virtually obliterated), while the 313th Wing targets at Akashi and Kagamigahara escaped with lesser damage. The price was five B-29s.

The prospect of more favorable weather on June 26 prompted a repetition of the tactics and techniques of the strikes on June 22. This time, four wings lofted 510 aircraft divided up into forces of between 32 and 120 planes. The weather, however, went sour, and the nine selected targets, mostly aircraft related, escaped with modest damage. Total losses for the mission came to six Superfortresses, including one "surveyed" due to flak damage after its landing at Iwo Jima, and one Mustang.

By the end of June, LeMay's command increased by a fifth wing, the 315th under Brigadier General Frank Armstrong. Its B-29s rolled off the assembly line without any defensive armament except tail guns, but each aircraft sported the AN/APQ-7 Eagle radar. If employed in a very long, straight bomb run of seventy miles or so, which was feasible only at night or in bad weather, this system permitted far more accurate blind bombing than could be achieved with the standard AN/APQ-13 set in other Super-fortresses.

LeMay assigned the 315th the mission of destroying the Japanese petroleum industry. The entire campaign was founded on an intelligence estimate that Japan could "struggle along" for another year on current stockpiles and production, but that a decrease in production could trigger a fuel crisis much sooner. Beginning with only thirty-five sorties on June 26, and ending with 132 on the night of August 14–15, the 315th destroyed six of its nine assigned targets in fifteen missions at a cost of only four aircraft. The skilled crews of this wing demonstrated remarkable ability and relative precision in destroying in darkness targets with known locations and clear radar signatures. But ultimately this was the least effective component of the strategic attack upon Japan because the loss of these processing facilities had almost no impact due to the overall lack of crude oil to refine.

During July, only the forecast for July 24 offered the chance to strike visually at seven targets in the Osaka-Nagoya region, but the actual weather grounded the Mustang escort. Of the 625 airborne bomb-carrying B-29s, 573 released 3,539.1 tons of bombs. The 58th Wing sustained the only loss but achieved excellent results, with poststrike photographs demonstrating damage to 77.5 percent of the roof area of a critical aircraft-propeller plant and 85 percent of the roof area of the Kawanishi aircraft plant, both in Osaka. The 73rd Wing ended up bombing a radar target, the city of Kuwana, where 416 residents died.

All the other strike operations in July were directed at Japanese cities at night. Over nine nights, Superfortresses rained incendiaries on thirty-five cities. The towns of Ichinomiya and Uwajima gained the dubious distinction of being raided twice because the first raids failed. Although the great majority of these cities contained targets that were clearly linked to Japan's war economy, the mission report was unable to identify such facilities in Choshi, which was hit by 705 tons of bombs and incendiaries on the night of July 19–20. A total of twelve Superfortresses were lost on these night attacks.

With a massive increase in the strength of Army Air Forces units in the Pacific in prospect, General Arnold issued orders for a major reorganization, effective July 16. Despite his stellar performance, LeMay was still only a two-star general, and a junior one at that. To command the United States Army Strategic Air Forces (USASTAF) in the Pacific, Arnold sent General Carl A. "Tooey" Spaatz, who had performed the same job in Europe. Under Spaatz, General Nathan Twining was given the Twentieth Air Force (as the XXI Bomber Command was redesignated); General James Doolittle brought over from Europe the reequipped Eighth Air Force, to be based in the Philippines and Okinawa. Sir Hugh Lloyd represented an anticipated British Lancaster bomber effort, also from Okinawa. LeMay continued to exercise effective operational control as Spaatz's chief of staff.

Shortly after Spaatz arrived, LeMay unveiled for the first time a potent psychological weapon: announcing targets in advance by leaflet drop. The purpose of the effort, noted one report, was "to present to the Japanese people an underlying reason for the acts of war that were being wrought against Japan . . . [and to move] some force in Japan . . . to take action to terminate the war." The principal source of the leaflets was the Psychological Warfare Branch of Nimitz's headquarters, which worked with the OWI in generating ideas for the leaflets. The actual drafting of the leaflets, however, was entrusted to a specially segregated group of intellectual and political Japanese prisoners of war who, "because of their very recent participation in the Japanese mentality, are best able to appeal to their compatriots." Generally, the dropping of leaflets became part of the duties of individual aircraft routinely dispatched each night on weather reconnaissance and solo strike missions all over Japan.

There was obvious unease among aircrews to this alerting of Japanese defenses, but it was attenuated by dispensing warnings to ten or a dozen cities and then bombing four. On the other hand, observed one American report, "naming one's targets or objective in the face of opposition was a grand gesture and displayed great strength and self-confidence." Further, "warning the cities and the residents of them to leave would give concrete support to the essential propaganda theme that America was not fighting the Japanese people." It was also anticipated that the warnings would reduce Japanese worker productivity. On the night of July 27–28, six aircraft scattered 660,000 leaflets on eleven Japanese cities. Through August 5, thirty-one cities were notified, and fourteen were subsequently bombed.

The series of attacks on August 1 posted a horrifying record. The 58th Wing reduced to ashes 80 percent of the city of Hachioji, a major rail terminus twenty-three miles west of Tokyo. Superfortresses of the 313th Wing burned out 65.5 percent of the rail center of Nagaoka (population 67,000). Sixty miles northeast of Tokyo, the 314th Wing destroyed 65 percent of Mito, another rail center. Toyama, the "third largest city on the west coast of Honshu," drew attention for its ball-bearing and machine-tool industries and the largest aluminum company in Japan. The attack by 182 Superfortresses of the 73rd Wing set an appalling mark for the entire strategic-bombing campaign. The 1,466 tons of bombs and incendiaries dropped in the raid destroyed an astounding 99.5 percent of the city. Of the 127,860 citizens of Toyama, 2,149 died, which is undoubtedly severe in absolute numbers but remarkably low for the near-total annihilation of an urban area. One 58th Wing crew of twelve went missing.

Of fifteen groups dispatched for another set of urban attacks on August 5, those of the 73rd and 314th Wings headed for Nishinomiya-Mikage, the three available groups of the 313th Wing set course for Saga on Kyushu, while those of the 58th Wing split their effort by sending two groups to Maebashi and two to Imabari on Shikoku. Japanese deaths in these cities totaled 1,964; in one crash landing and one ditching, only one American was injured this night.

The General Assault on Japanese Transportation

From feeble beginnings in 1942, U.S. efforts to cripple Japan by destruction of its transportation swelled at an ever increasing pace. In the climactic phase of this campaign from the later part of June to August 1945, American sea and air forces stripped away the last sanctuaries for Japanese shipping and commenced pummeling Japanese land transportation. At the beginning of July, all Japanese vessels capable of open-sea navigation were being withdrawn from the Yellow Sea and the East China Sea to the Sea of Japan. "This," observed an American appreciation, "is the most important change in the enemy's overall merchant shipping practices since the abandonment of Empire [to] Singapore convoying in March of this year." It meant that aluminous shale, which formerly was carried on bottoms across the Yellow Sea, would now have to go by railway to Korean ports, but it was "extremely doubtful" whether the rail system was up to this task. Without aluminous shale, essential for the manufacture of aluminum aircraft construction, the Japanese aviation industry would halt.

By husbanding their shipping within the Sea of Japan, the Japanese aimed to exploit the fact that from 1943 to the summer of 1945, minefields and other defenses at its narrow apertures to the Pacific had made it a lake secure from U.S. submarines. American electronics wizards, however, devised a special FM sonar that was thought to be accurate enough to permit a submerged submarine to navigate a minefield. Rear Admiral Charles Lockwood, commander of the Pacific Fleet submarines, sent a task unit of nine submarines fitted with the new device through the southern entrance at the Tsushima Straits between June 4 and 6. The *Tinosa*'s crew endured the excruciating torture of listening as the cable of a mine dragged along the hull from bow to stern; "How close the mine came to us, we'll never know," reported her skipper. These nine submarines swiftly slaughtered twenty-eight ships of 54,784 tons, including the submarine *I-122.* One boat, *Bonefish,* was caught in the shallow waters of Toyama Bay on June 18 and lost with all hands. On June 24, the remaining eight boats made a daring night exit at La Perouse Strait, where they remained on the surface because Ultra had forewarned of new Japanese subsurface mining efforts in the strait.

This sortie and another that followed it forced the Japanese to reroute ships, initiate convoying, and abandon the practice of anchoring outside ports. As an Ultra summary observed, the convoying of vessels in the Sea of Japan, besides decreasing the number of trips of individual ships,

> should greatly increase the strain on the west coast ports of Honshu. These ports, considered to be operating at peak capacity, will be faced with the problem of handling at irregular intervals groups of ships, instead of individual ships arriving on planned schedules.

In July, aircraft were also brought increasingly into play against Japanese transportation. Moreover, aviators broadened the attack to include for the first time vital inland rail communications on the continent and within Japan. Okinawa-based aircraft could range over the Tsushima and Shimonoseki Straits and assail shipping as far as Nagasaki and Sasebo. Aircraft from Iwo Jima could perform similar depredations in the Tokyo region, while the Third Fleet struck in raids with both aircraft and surface ships aimed at the shipping connections at the northern end of Honshu as well as at the communications with Hokkaido.

A Japanese message recovered in July acknowledged that shipping losses and damage in June amounted to nearly 600,000 tons, of which ninety ships of 290,000 tons were sunk or badly damaged and another twenty-three of 118,000 tons sustained "medium" damage. This message demonstrated that the mine campaign was even more successful than supposed. Further, as an American report astutely pointed out, the success of the mining program cannot be assessed alone on loss or damage to vessels. The reduction in efficiency of shipping caused by closed channels, the diversion to poorly serviced and ill-equipped harbors, are effects inherent in mining which do not equally apply to attacks by other agents.

At this rate, the report concluded, "shortly the enemy will find his merchant marine inadequate to carry the minimum of imports necessary for the prosecution of the war."

With the abandonment of the Yellow and East China Seas to oceangoing traffic, the Japanese became more dependent upon Korean ports, particularly Rashin and Seisen. The vulnerability of both the ports themselves and the rail lines leading to them forced a massive increase in antiaircraft and fighter defenses in these locales. The Japanese also directed the stockpiling of supplies, mostly foodstuffs and salt, in southern Korean ports by July 10, particularly Pusan.

As the Japanese feared, B-29s mined Pusan, Seisen, and Rashin for the first time on July 11 and 13. But American naval aircraft gave a foretaste of far worse things to come. Patrol planes of Fleet Air Wing One disrupted Korean rail lines and halted traffic for five days in early July. Continued attacks compelled considerable changes in plans for shipping raw materials from northern China and Manchuria to Korean ports. An extensive study of rail bridges highlighted the vital role of the bridge at Seisen. On July 31, six PB4Y Privateers destroyed one span of the bridge. As an American intelligence summary explained, this one stroke "effectively cut off Southern Korea, except for branch lines of comparatively small capacity." This episode served notice of how readily bulk-commodity shipment could be drastically reduced or halted on a limited rail net. This had dire implications for the Homeland itself.

The massive losses of Japanese shipping in the last five months of the war and the relative contributions of mines, submarines, and aircraft are documented in the following table (in number of ships/tonnage):

Month	Mines	Submarines	Land-based Aircraft	Carrier-based Aircraft	Miscellaneous Causes
April	17/33,500	19/68,164	11/19,743	35/92,173	4/3,386
May	65/163,683	16/31,194	35/68,467	55/107,020	2/7,359
June	59/122,546	46/91,339	11/23,806	64/123,384	7/8,239
July	65/154,681	14/29,497	18/30,634	80/155,221	1/1,892
August	16/37,129	5/15,433	15/18,511	33/62,840	1/2,230
Total	222/511,539	100/235,627	90/161,161	267/540,638	15/23,106

Halsey Hits Japan

Boiling out of Leyte on July 1 came the most potent element of the U.S. Pacific Fleet, designated Task Force 38, unchained from an Okinawa support role and bending knots northward to satisfy Admiral William Halsey's itch to smite the enemy in his Homeland. Halsey's armada comprised eight of the big *Essex*-class carriers and six of the low-slung *Independence*-class light carriers, altogether embarking almost one thousand planes. The task force operated in three groups, each squired by battleships, cruisers, and destroyers. The task force refueled near Iwo Jima and then dashed in to launch position off Tokyo on July 10. The Japanese resisted exclusively with antiaircraft fire. U.S. claims ran to one hundred Japanese aircraft, all on the ground.

The next set of strikes were strategic attacks over northern Honshu and Hokkaido on July 14 and 15. American intelligence well understood that coal powered most of Japan's industry; Honshu in particular imported five sixths of its coal needs. Analysis further indicated that a really "decisive reduction in the availability of coal" on Honshu would result only from immobilization of rail lines. The most vital inter-island rail and sea connection was the Honshu-Hokkaido rail ferries, which hauled 200,000 metric tons per year, 80 percent of them coal. Photographic coverage also exposed northern Honshu and Hokkaido ports "clogged with shipping diverted from the [mine] interdicted harbors to the south," with Hakodate alone overflowing with nearly 100,000 tons.

On July 14, Task Force 38 lashed these rich targets despite poor weather. One Japanese destroyer and two frigates succumbed, but more critically, Halsey's fliers sank a score of merchantmen. By the end of further strikes on the fifteenth, eight of the twelve large rail ferries rested on the bottom; damage rendered the other four unusable. With this stroke, the movement of coal extracted on Hokkaido to the industries on Honshu plummeted to 18 percent of its prior level. This blow by carrier planes ranks as the most devastating single strategic-bombing success of all the campaigns against Japan. On July 16, Task Force 37, the British Pacific Fleet, joined Task Force 38, adding three fleet carriers.

The Navy conducted a series of ship bombardments of shore targets during what proved to be the closing weeks of the war. On July 14, the battleships *South Dakota, Indiana,* and *Massachusetts* dumped 802 sixteen-inch shells on Kamaishi. The next day, 860 shells of similar caliber from the *Iowa, Missouri,* and *Wisconsin* rained on Muroran. On July 18, the *Iowa, Missouri,* and *Wisconsin,* plus the *North Carolina* and *Alabama,* loosed 1,207 sixteen-inch shells on Hitachi while the newly arrived British battleship *King George V* struck a nearby target. This same day, despite threatening weather, carrier planes raided Yokosuka, where the main target was the battleship *Nagato.* It survived in an unserviceable state to become a postwar target in the atomic-bomb test at Bikini.

Between July 24 and 28, Task Force 38 pummeled the surviving major units of the Imperial Navy in and around Kure. Halsey firmly directed Task Force 37 to attend to other targets, thus creating a distinct impression that the U.S. Navy regarded this operation as specific retaliation for Pearl Harbor. The directive from Admiral Nimitz, however, placed these attacks into the broader strategy. They were to eliminate the last major surface combatants of the Imperial Navy so that heavy units of the Allied fleets would not have to escort prospective convoys of Russia-bound supplies scheduled to be sent across the Northern Pacific upon Soviet entry into the war. On July 24, U.S. planes sank the battleship *Hyuga,* the heavy cruiser *Tone,* and the carrier *Amagi* while British aircraft discovered and severely damaged the escort carrier *Kaiyo.* On July 28, both task forces again lashed at Kure, this time sinking the battleships *Haruna* and *Ise,* the cruisers *Aoba* and *Oyodo,* and the escort destroyer *Nashi.* These operations produced one unintended consequence: With the Imperial Navy deprived of its last battleships and cruisers, Soviet naval forces also gained far more open range in the Sea of Japan.

During the night of July 29–30, the *South Dakota, Indiana,* and *Massachusetts* raked Hamamatsu with 810 rounds, and the task force returned on August 9 to Kamaishi for an encore with 850 sixteen-inch shells. According to at least one distinguished American scholar who participated in the occupation, foreign nationals reported that the Japanese finally realized the war was lost upon the visible appearance of Allied warships just off Japan's shores.

Replenishment at sea and a minuet with typhoons kept Halsey away from Japan from July 28 to August 9. Then he struck, this time at northern Honshu. For some time, Ultra had carefully pieced together a Japanese plan to send a raiding party of over three thousand Imperial Army and Navy troops on a one-way mission to the Marianas to wreak havoc on the Superfortress bases. Once about two hundred transport aircraft had assembled on northern Honshu bases and the operation appeared imminent, Nimitz ordered Halsey to attack. Two days of strikes completely broke up the planned grand suicide raid, dubbed Operation Damocles in American reports.

"It is my intent," Halsey reported on July 21, "to tighten blockade and keep pressure on the enemy by throwing light force sweeps against Empire coast and outlying islands at every opportunity. Objective denial of coastal sea lanes to enemy, destruction shipping and bombardment of shore targets." During the last month of the war, Task Force 38 regularly spun out detachments of cruisers and destroyers to conduct close nocturnal sweeps of inshore waters. While they did not achieve much destruction during this interval, they gave promise that American sea power would soon preclude nearly all shipping traffic along the Pacific coasts of the Home Islands.

Only Japanese undersea forces mounted any challenge to the bombardment and blockade during these waning days. The Imperial Navy had constructed several classes of very large submarines, each conceived originally to carry three special catapult-launched seaplane bombers that would attack and disable the Panama Canal. In June 1945, however, Imperial Headquarters directed the four boats of Submarine Flotilla One to abandon that mission and hurriedly mount Operation Arashi, a suicide-plane attack on American carriers at Ulithi. One boat, *I-13,* fell victim to an antisubmarine group directed to it by radio intelligence, which had exposed the whole mission. At the end of the war, the remaining three boats were still preparing for the attack.

Other Japanese submarines, fitted with *Kaiten* suicide torpedoes, also sortied, and two of these were successful. On July 24, the destroyer escort *Underhill,* shepherding a small convoy in the Philippine Sea, made a sound contact. In the ensuing skirmish, as the ship reported it was about to ram a midget submarine, *Underhill*'s forward half disappeared in a great flash, together with 112 men. Consorts removed 116 survivors from the remaining half before it was scuttled. Much worse was to come.

The destruction of the *Underhill* should have alerted all hands to the presence of Japanese submarines in the waters between the Marianas and the Philippines, but it did not. In the last thirty minutes of July 29, the heavy cruiser *Indianapolis,* having just deposited components of the atomic bombs at Tinian, cleaved through those waters and straight into the sights of Commander Mochitasura Hashimoto of the *I-58.* Hashimoto fired six torpedoes, at least two hit, and the *Indianapolis* went down within about fifteen minutes. Loss of electric power prevented transmission of a distress signal. It is believed that about eight hundred men got off the ship, only to endure terrible horrors of exposure and shark attack. Through a chain of errors, no one noticed that the *Indianapolis* failed to show up on time in Leyte Gulf. The fortuitous sighting of men in the water by a patrol plane on August 2 halted these travails, but there were only 316 survivors from the cruiser; 883 were lost.

Killing and Dying

It is easy to conclude from many depictions of the end of the Pacific war
that the tempo of killing and dying between the end of the Okinawa campaign on June 21 and the scheduled date of Olympic on November 1 was
set almost wholly by aerial bombardment, including the use of atomic
bombs. This is wrong. For two groups, one large and the other immense,
this period marked a continuation of a protracted immersion in mass death.
One of these groups was Allied prisoners of war; the other was a mass of
Asian peoples trapped by Japan's aggression.

Forrest Knox, an American soldier captured at Bataan and a survivor of
the death march, was typical. In the summer of 1945, he was at Toyama, in
desperate straits—"a human balloon full of fluid" due to beriberi. "If he
lay on one side," reported historian Gavan Daws, "his face would swell up,
and the guards would point at him and laugh and turn him over so they
could laugh at him swelling up on the other side." Knox was only one of
originally over 140,000 Caucasian prisoners of war, the overwhelming
majority of whom had been captured by Japan in the first six months of the
war. Nearly one third would die in captivity.

The record Japan created in her treatment of prisoners of war and civilian internees still appalls. Prisoners were starved and brutalized systematically. They were murdered by deadly purpose or on momentary whim.
They were beaten to death, beheaded, burned alive, buried alive, crucified,
marched to death, shot, stabbed, strangled, and simply abandoned to die.
Among U.S. Army personnel alone, the Japanese captured 24,992, of
whom 8,634 (35 percent) died in captivity. By contrast, only 833 of 93,653
Army personnel held by Germany died in captivity, a rate of 0.9 percent.
"To be a prisoner of the Japanese," explained Daws, the Dante of this hell,
"was like being caught in a twentieth century version of the Black Plague,
a Yellow Death."

Allied civilians interned by the Japanese numbered 130,895, and fared
somewhat better—only 14,650 died, or 11.2 percent. But a far worse fate
befell peoples of the regions overrun by Japan. From these populations
the Japanese ruthlessly extracted the *romusha:* slave laborers who were
impressed by the hundreds of thousands and died by the hundreds of
thousands. No one knows the totals for certain, but a fair approximation is
that 600,000 or so were dragooned as workers, of whom about 290,000
perished.

Romusha and POWs became ensnared together in the greatest death machine spawned by Japan's conquests, the Burma-Siam railroad. Of a POW
workforce that by Japanese count numbered 68,888, it is believed that

12,399 died. It was proportionately worse for the *romusha,* of whom perhaps 200,000 found themselves consigned to work there and about 70,000 died. Besides starvation rations, heat, brutality, and hideously exhausting labor, the railway workers became the victims of disease, particularly cholera. To deal with the masses of dead, cremations became a fixture of daily life for work parties. Bodies were laid across teak logs and then layered alternately with bamboo. Those dead of beriberi had to be speared first to drain so their fluid would not put out the fire. Then the pyres were ignited. Again, Daws: "When the bodies started to char, their arms and legs twitched, and they sat up as if they were alive. Smoke came out of their burned-out eyes, their mouths opened, and licks of flames came out; their lungs were full of steam, and noises came out."

When the tide of war turned, Japan began to move POWs from regions likely to be retaken by the Allies to Japan or the Asian continent. But when the Japanese shipped POWs, they did so in unmarked vessels without notice, so when Allied airmen and submariners destroyed Japanese shipping, they sank also thousands of POWs. By Japanese count, 10,800 POWs died out of 50,000 transported.

By 1945, the war had already turned up ample evidence that the Japanese would kill any prisoners if there was threat of liberation. In October 1942, a Japanese garrison in the Gilbert Islands had lopped off the heads of twenty-two prisoners after an Allied bombing raid. The same thing occurred at Ballale (ninety bayoneted) and Wake (ninety-six machine-gunned). At Palawan in the Philippines, a local commander feared an invasion. He had 150 American prisoners herded into air-raid shelters, poured gasoline over them, ignited it, and then machine-gunned those who tried to escape being burned to death.

Nearly to a man, Allied POWs believed the Japanese would kill them if the Homeland was invaded. Surviving written documentation to support this belief is limited but highly suggestive, as Daws records:

At Taihoku on Formosa, an entry in the Japanese headquarters journal recorded *extreme measures* to be taken against POWs in *urgent situations: Whether they are destroyed individually or in groups, or however it is done, with mass bombing, poisonous smoke, poisons, drowning, decapitation, or what, dispose of the prisoners as the situation dictates. In any case, it is the aim not to allow the escape of a single one, to annihilate them all, and not to leave any traces.*

A much smaller group of POWs were airmen. Of the eight captured fliers from Doolittle's raid in April 1942, three were executed. This set the tone for what followed, but the Japanese vented the greatest wrath on Super-fortress crews. Captured B-29 airmen were shot, bayoneted, decapitated, burned alive, or killed as boiling water was poured over them. Other air-crew members were beaten to death by civilians and shot with bows and arrows and then decapitated. The grisliest episode, however, came when

> The Western Japan military command gave some medical professors at Kyushu Imperial University eight B-29 crewmen. The professors cut them up alive, in a dirty room with a tin table where students dissected corpses. They drained blood and replaced it with sea water. They cut out lungs, livers, and stomachs. They stopped blood flow in an artery near the heart, to see how long death took. They dug holes in a skull and stuck in a knife into the living brains to see what would happen.

Vastly more numerous than the POWs and the *romusha* but kindred in suffering were the hundreds of millions of Asians trapped in the effects of Japan's aggression. While most Americans and Westerners in general carry at least some knowledge of Hitler's Holocaust—with its mechanical, bureaucratized extermination of six million (of a planned toll of eleven million) Jews—and perhaps an understanding that millions of other Europeans died of systemized neglect or slavery, few recall the costs of the Japanese march of conquest in the 1930s and 1940s. "Asia under the Japanese," charged Daws, "was a charnel house of atrocities."

Any accounting of the charnel house must begin with China—the original cause that drew America into war. No one can provide a certified figure for Chinese deaths in the war that engulfed that nation from July 1937 to August 1945 due to the tremendous difficulties created by the tumult of both the war with Japan, which generated huge numbers of refugees, and the subsequent Chinese civil war. Besides such fundamental problems as fixing original population totals in each province of China, there is also the issue of selecting a cutoff date for latent fatalities. The devastating effects of the Japanese blockade and its disruptions continued to produce what a United Nations report termed "an enormous number" of deaths in China by starvation into 1946, well after hostilities had officially ceased. Despite these problems, a believable range for Chinese losses appears to be ten to fifteen million dead, although recent research in Chinese archival holdings has yielded figures of eighteen million civilian and four million military fatalities.

China was not alone. According to one careful accounting by historian Robert Newman, deaths attributable to the Japanese empire from 1931 to 1945 reached the following staggering total:

China	10,000,000
Java (Dutch Indies)	3,000,000
Outer Islands (Dutch Indies)	1,000,000
Philippines	120,000
India	180,000
Bengal famine	1,500,000
Korea	70,000
Burma-Siam railroad	82,500
Indonesian, Europeans	30,000
Malaya	100,000
Vietnam	1,000,000
Australia	30,000
New Zealand	10,000
United States	100,000
Total	17,222,500

Controversy surrounds several of these numbers. There seems to be no reason to doubt that there was a vast sum of fatalities on Java, and on the Outer Islands, though whether it reached the millions is less certain. The incorporation of deaths in the Bengal famine is based on the fact that it could have been averted if the war had not barred shipment of the usual food relief from Burma. Even if these figures are discounted, however, it is entirely possible that they are more than offset by the ravages of the war in China, where significantly more than ten million probably perished.

Whatever the precise figures, they lead to another critical consideration. For China alone, depending upon what number one chooses for overall Chinese casualties, in each of the ninety-seven months between July 1937 and August 1945, somewhere between 100,000 and 200,000 persons perished, the vast majority of them noncombatants. For the other Asians alone, the average probably ranged in the tens of thousands per month, but the actual numbers were almost certainly greater in 1945, notably due to the mass death in a famine in Vietnam. Newman concluded that each month that the war continued in 1945 would have produced the deaths of "upwards of 250,000 people, mostly Asian but some Westerners." What is clear beyond dispute is that the minimum plausible range for deaths of Asian noncombatants each month in 1945 was over 100,000 and more probably reached or even exceeded 250,000. Any moral assessment of how the Pacific war did or could have ended must consider the fate of these Asian noncombatants and the POWs.

11

Ketsu Operation on Kyushu

"Diabolic"

Commands and Concepts

The American decision to target Kyushu for the initial invasion of the Japanese Homeland and the chosen code name for Kyushu both harbored remarkable symbolism. Historically, mountainous Kyushu, agriculturally poor, thrived from tribute paid by the king of the Ryukyus and from trade with the Ryukyus and China. Kyushu housed the Satsuma clan, with its capital at Kagoshima. Mountainous ramparts enforced independence—affirmed by the preservation of an archaic dialect—and bred warriors who were counted among the toughest in all of Japan. From the ranks of the Satsuma clan stepped key founders of both the Imperial Army and modern Japan. If the soul of the Japanese state rested in the cultural capital of Kyoto and the commercial heart pulsed in Tokyo—both on Honshu—the soul of the Imperial Army reposed in Kyushu. The American code name for Kyushu might have alluded to this: Diabolic. But *diabolic* also described the uncanny prescience with which Imperial Headquarters laid a deadly trap for the expected initial American invasion.

Kyushu wears a coarse fringe of smaller islands and peninsulas that soften its roughly quadrilateral outline. Nearly 200 miles separate its north and south coasts, while the span from east to west measures only 125 miles. According to the 1944 census, Kyushu held 10,041,290 people, most residing in the northern and northwestern industrial regions. Mountains dominate the eastern and central sections, but farmers tilled the patchy, level coastal plains and basins in the north, west, and south. Mountains partition southern Kyushu from northern and channel main communication arteries along the coasts.

According to an American terrain analysis, southern Kyushu "is a complex jumble of small lowlands and low but rugged uplands." It is marked by three long, narrow plains extending three to ten miles east to west and twenty to thirty miles north to south. These plains possess military significance as both real or potential airfield sites and as natural avenues of movement, though unfriendly to vehicles due to terracing and a paucity of roads. Two of these plains abut the southeastern coast of Kyushu, one north of Miyazaki and a second from the headland of Ariake Bay and past Miyakonojo. A third plain lies along the southwest coast near Kushikino. Long, narrow corridors, one to five miles wide, link these plains.

Kyushu loomed as the most likely major battleground for the Second General Army, which opened its headquarters on April 18 at Hiroshima on western Honshu. Field Marshal Shunroku Hata, sixty-six years old in 1945, commanded the Second General Army. Commissioned as an artillery officer in June 1901, Hata graduated with "top scholarly rank" from the war college nine years later and filled cosmopolitan billets in Europe, including at the peace conference after World War I. He served as the senior aide-de-camp to the Emperor in 1939, as army minister between 1939 and 1940, and was one of the final three candidates for premier when Koiso was tapped. Hata's background ensured that he would not miss the political ramifications implicit in his official military mission.

Immediately under the Second General Army were the Sixteenth Area Army, which defended Kyushu, and the Fifteenth Area Army, which guarded Shikoku and western Honshu. In its initial estimate of the situation, the staff of the Second General Army surmised that the United States would seek to end the war quickly after Okinawa by a direct thrust into the Homeland. The southern ranges of Kyushu around Miyazaki, Ariake Bay, and the Satsuma Peninsula formed the obvious targets for airfield sites and naval bases from which the Americans could mount an invasion of the Kanto (Tokyo) plain. The staff of the Second General Army conceded, however, that southern Shikoku also offered opportunities for an attacker, since it could provide good airfield sites around the Tosa plain—and as a bonus would be difficult for the Japanese to defend and reinforce.

Hata's staff found the timing of the American attack more difficult to predict. They calculated that it was highly probable at any time after June. While in July the Americans could mount a ten-division thrust, the size of the attacking force would increase by two to three divisions each month thereafter. Hata's planners considered the possibility of a simultaneous attack on northern and southern Kyushu, but they believed this would take more time to prepare and require the arduous seizure of several fortress areas along the Tsushima Straits approaches to northern Kyushu. The staff also glumly considered the possibility that an attack on Shikoku would be accompanied by a thrust along the Inland Sea around the Okayama area on Honshu, where they recognized "our preparations are almost nil." For purposes of operational guidance and planning, Hata's staff identified three periods of preparation time. The first extended to the end of July; the second was August and September; and the third was from October onward.

The gallant and protracted fight of the Thirty-second Army on Okinawa convinced the staff of the Second General Army that there would be a significant lull before an invasion of the Homeland. But while this hiatus conferred much-needed time for the Japanese to gird for battle, it also allowed the Americans to redeploy substantial forces from Europe to the Pacific. The Second General Army sought to grasp this opportunity to enhance preparations and enforce their concept of a decisive battle with the main emphasis on Kyushu and southern Shikoku and gradually to extend those preparations into the Inland and Japan Sea areas.

Meanwhile, Imperial Headquarters perceived that some field commands failed to grasp Tokyo's vision concerning the conduct of Ketsu-Go. On June 20, therefore, Tokyo issued in the name of the vice chief of staff of the Imperial Army a directive titled "A Matter Concerning the Thorough Understanding of the Concept of Decisive Engagement in the Homeland." This edict emphasized the total discarding of deep-inland defense tactics adopted for remote Pacific islands. The decisive engagement first required mass-suicide attacks by naval vessels and planes in order to destroy as much of the invasion convoys as possible. All ground forces must be concentrated in the coastal area to ensnare Allied forces in close, intermingled battles that would negate the enemy's firepower advantages. By daring and rapid action, the enemy must be destroyed between the time of the landing and when the bridgeheads were firmly established. These admonitions from Imperial Headquarters rippled deeply across the First General Army, compelling wholesale readjustment of defense positions. It had much less effect in the Second General Army, which was generally in compliance with the strategic concept from the outset.

On April 19, the Sixteenth Area Army issued its "Division Fighting Training Guidelines." These set the goal for completion of basic training of the static coastal-combat divisions in late May and the mobile decisive-battle divisions by the end of July. All soldiers were admonished to bear foremost in mind that the battlefield would be the sacred Imperial soil itself and that their goal was to see that all of the foreign invaders perished.

Between April and June, Field Marshal Hata and his staff repeatedly inspected their subordinate units. From late June into early July, Hata spent ten days on Kyushu. He found the tempo of work swift, but only 20 to 40 percent of the program of fortifications complete in Ariake Bay, and less elsewhere. He instructed the Sixteenth Area Army to regard the Miyazaki, Ariake Bay, and Satsuma Peninsula areas as one strategic theater; it was dangerous to concentrate just on Miyazaki.

In the words of Major General Joichiro Sanada, the deputy chief of staff of the Second General Army, Hata and his staff believed that the struggle for Kyushu would be "the last chance to change the war situation in our favor." They intended to reinforce Kyushu when the enemy landed with three to five divisions from the Fifteenth Area Army and the First General Army, but this was neither sufficient to deal with multiple landing sites nor certain, since these units would have to traverse long distances while under aerial and naval bombardment. Obviously, it would be far better to have crack counterattack units immediately on hand.

In May and again in June, the Second General Army beseeched Imperial Headquarters to release to Kyushu at least four divisions (two armored and two infantry) of the Thirty-sixth Army, the most powerful and efficient in the Homeland. This request confirms that Hata and his staff anticipated concurrent American amphibious assaults. Further, the expected severing of communication lines by American aircraft added urgency to the need for an early decision. Imperial Headquarters effectively rejected this plea with silence. Tokyo did shift additional airpower but resisted what might well have been an irreversible gamble by sending the heart and soul of effective Tokyo defenses to Kyushu, where they could be stranded by the destruction of communications.

The Sixteenth Area Army commander and staff on Kyushu generally agreed with the Second General Army that the Americans would most likely target Miyazaki, Ariake Bay, and the Satsuma Peninsula. Intense air and naval bombardment to isolate Kyushu from Honshu, to disconnect communications within Kyushu, and to obliterate coastal defenses would precede a landing. Japanese staff officers had extracted a number of lessons about American techniques from prior campaigns: Large forces would land simultaneously along broad fronts, proximate to ultimate objectives. The capture and use of airfields very early in the operations would be a high priority. The Americans would prefer areas where their superiority in heavy equipment could be brought into play. Relatively small emphasis would be placed upon surprise, and they would not avoid strong defenses if their other requirements were met.

Ariake Bay and Miyazaki matched these general criteria. Ariake offered four distinct advantages: excellent landing beaches, Kanoya and other airfields in proximity, a good anchorage and access to the better Kagoshima Bay, and easy access to the Miyakonojo plain. Ariake suffered from two distinct disadvantages: a somewhat constricted landing front that, moreover, could be reached only by running a gauntlet of close shoreline that framed the anchorage.

The Japanese initially evaluated the advantages and disadvantages of Miyazaki as nearly even. It afforded the twin cardinal advantages of wide beaches and airfield sites immediately inland, but it suffered from two major deficits: no protection from wind and wave, and terrain that limited access to the Miyakonojo plain and somewhat isolated the area.

Given these assessments and judgments as to the scale of American efforts, up to April 1945 the Japanese deemed Ariake Bay as the most threatened region and so deployed there the only field division on the island. From about the middle of April 1945, however, the broad Miyazaki beaches looked more likely to attract an American assault estimated at six to eight divisions. By July, judgments again shifted. It appeared that the onset of the typhoon season would dictate further delay in the date of the landings, but this in turn meant that the scale of the U.S. attack would burgeon to fifteen or sixteen divisions. The Sixteenth Area Army believed such a massive assault would strike several areas and include a landing along the Satsuma Peninsula in order to seize the protected anchorage of Kagoshima Bay. Thus, the Japanese became convinced that Ariake, Miyazaki, and the Satsuma Peninsula were all likely American targets.

On May 15, the Sixteenth Area Army issued its multipart operational plan, designed to cover seven scenarios all around the Kyushu coast. They emphasized construction of fortifications, starting at the coast and moving inland; training to secure "certain victory"; attention to transportation and communications matters; and close cooperation with the naval and air units. For construction of fortifications and transportation networks, the Army envisioned large-scale use of civilian labor.

The Army sternly advised the garrisons of isolated islands off Kyushu that, while they would enjoy whatever naval and air support might be available, they could entertain no hope for any ground reinforcements. Japanese commanders assumed as a matter of course that airborne assaults—modeled after those used by the Allies at Normandy—would accompany the beach landings and ordered thorough preparations for this

eventuality. While the Sixteenth Area Army staff contemplated the theoretical possibility of two enemy landings, they realistically believed that
available resources would enable them to confront only one landing; a second landing could be dealt with only by reinforcements from Honshu.

With the addition of units from the third-stage preparations, on June 28
the Sixteenth Area Army issued its last major directive on preparations
for the Ketsu operation, redistributing units and missions and clarifying
its plans for the mass counterattack. The Army's command and staff focused on how to deal with a simultaneous landing on multiple fronts and
how to move units to the battlefields under very intense enemy bombardment.

The nature of the topography and the poor mobility of counterattack
units due to their lack of vehicles required that command and coordination
of the counterattack be devolved from the Sixteenth Area Army to the
Fifty-seventh Army (a large corps by American standards) in southern
Kyushu and the Fifty-sixth Army in northern Kyushu. Perhaps the most
difficult challenge was determining where to mount the main Japanese
counterblow if more than one landing occurred. In the event of landings in
northern and southern Kyushu, counterattacking in the north would be
deemed most important, reflecting the superior political and strategic
value of that area. But by the time the Sixteenth Area Army formulated its
final rules for selecting the locale for the major counterattack, however,
southern Kyushu figured most prominently. The hierarchy was: wherever
the enemy main force landed; if the main-force landing could not be identified, then the first area the enemy landed; if the enemy landed simultaneously at Ariake, Miyazaki, and the Satsuma Peninsula, then Ariake. The
counterattack would be mounted within ten days of the landing. Forces
would march to the site of the decisive battle at night, in increments of fifteen to twenty kilometers.

The coastal units would fight to the death where they stood. They must
conduct "strenuous and daring" operations to contain and punish superior
enemy landing forces and airborne units for a protracted period. The one
counterattack regiment per division would strike at enemy units that broke
the crust of the defenses. The coastal divisions must intermingle the front
lines to create a chaotic situation that would nullify the enemy's vastly superior air, sea, and artillery firepower. Tanks would be employed only in
direct support of infantry in the counterattacks and as mobile artillery. Artillery would execute flanking fire on landing units and then engage in direct support of attacking Japanese infantry. Firing would be conducted at
short range, and massing would not be attempted. Particular emphasis was

placed on guarding Kagoshima Bay with coastal batteries. Careful preparations would be made for enemy airborne assaults in the Kanoya,
Miyazaki, and Miyakonojo areas.

The decisive battle divisions would be the "spear of the army" to
break through enemy lines. They must be prepared to move with alacrity
and discipline under enemy air superiority. They would lash their brav-
ery and fighting power together by using all their arms to pierce the outside shell of the enemy front, which they were warned would be swept
by intense American firepower. They must be prepared to face enemy armored vehicles and fierce artillery and air bombardment, including napalm.

The Sixteenth Area Army's June 28 order outlined a plan for a counteroffensive in each major area in southern Kyushu: Miyazaki, the I (A)
Operation; Ariake, the RO (B) Operation; and Satsuma Peninsula, the HA
(C) Operation. These three scenarios rested on an assumption that there
would be only one landing but two waves of counterattacks (the First
Echelon and the Second Echelon)—hence, the same units formed the
counterattack force for several scenarios. This table sketches those plans:

Sixteenth Area Army Counterattack Operations—June 28, 1945

		Coastal Divisions	Counter-attack Divisions	Brigades	Tank Brigades
Miyazaki,	First Echelon	3	4	—	3
I Operation	Second Echelon	—	2	—	—
Ariake,	First Echelon	2*	3	—	3
RO Operation	Second Echelon	—	2	—	—
Satsuma Peninsula,	First Echelon	3	5	1	3
HA Operation	Second Echelon	—	2	—	—

* Counts the heavily reinforced 86th Division as equivalent to two divisions.

Defending the Invasion Beaches

Imperial Headquarters packed Kyushu with defenders ultimately totaling
fourteen divisions and eleven brigades. These were far too many units for
the Sixteenth Area Army to control directly, so three intermediate headquarters were created. The Japanese styled these headquarters as armies,
but they were closer in size to American corps.

The vital strategic importance of the key industrial and population areas
in northeastern Kyushu, as well as the critical Shimonoseki-Moji Strait,
tied down a significant fraction of the Sixteenth Area Army's resources.

The March 31, 1945, order from Imperial Headquarters creating many new headquarters also assigned the Fifty-sixth Army to take charge of the defense of northern Kyushu. By August 1945, major elements of the Fifty-sixth Army comprised four divisions, one independent mixed brigade, and one tank brigade.* Upon an American landing in southern Kyushu, the Fifty-sixth Army expected to detach one division and the tank brigade to meet the invaders.

Also mobilized on March 31 was the Fifty-seventh Army under Lieutenant General Kanji Nishihara, charged with the defense of southern Kyushu. By August 1, army strength stood at the formidable total of 150,189 officers and men in five infantry divisions, two independent mixed brigades, the Fourth Antiaircraft Division, two tank brigades, and a host of other units.† One of these independent mixed brigades, the 109th, was heavily reinforced to a strength of 5,901 men and detailed to hold the substantial island of Tanegashima off Kyushu's south coast.

Like its superior headquarters, the Fifty-seventh Army focused originally on the Ariake Bay area, but as its chief of staff, Major General Yasumasa Yoshitake later recalled, by July they also believed that a simultaneous attack at Miyazaki, Ariake Bay, and Satsuma Peninsula was probable.

The 156th, 154th, and 212th Divisions were to defend the long expanse of beaches on the Miyazaki front. Lieutenant General Keishichiro Higuchi, the 156th Division commander, articulated a sophisticated and illustrative concept of operations. He enjoined his command about the weight of their responsibilities and the need for strict discipline, solidarity, and confidence in victory. Above all, he adjured, everything must be viewed as a battle against tanks. This represented the salient battle lesson passed on by several Japanese garrisons, most notably the Thirty-second Army on Okinawa, whose directive for defense summed up the Japanese view: "Fighting against the American land army is practically the same thing as fighting against . . . M4 [Sherman] tanks."

The Sherman by 1945 was underarmed and thinly armored by European standards, but in the Pacific it far outclassed its Japanese counterparts. The Japanese possessed many 37-mm antitank guns that were virtually useless against the Sherman, but they also fielded a very handy 47-mm gun that could readily perforate one. Unfortunately for the Japanese on Kyushu,

---

* Specifically, its main units were the 57th, 145th, 312th, and 351st Divisions, the 124th Independent Mixed Brigade (IMB), the 4th Tank Brigade, and the 46th Tank Regiment.

† The Fifty-seventh Army comprised the 25th, 86th, 154th, 156th, and 212th Divisions, the 98th and 109th IMBs, and the 5th and 6th Tank Brigades.

there were few antitank guns available, and only a fraction of them were 47 mm. More ominous still, the new American M26 tank was nearly impervious to even the 47-mm guns. The M26, however, possessed significantly less mobility than the Sherman—a serious detriment to its utility on Kyushu. Nevertheless, arrangements were in train in July to ship enough M26s to reequip two Sixth Army tank battalions in time for Olympic.

Though the Japanese lacked quantities of antitank artillery and effective handheld antitank weapons such as bazookas, they intended to compensate for these deficits with comprehensive suicide attacks. Japanese soldiers trained with hand-carried explosives: a hand-thrown mine, rigged on the hollow-charge principle and capable of penetrating two to three inches of steel; a "lunge" version of the same with a long handle that increased accuracy but guaranteed the death of the user; and improvised explosive charges weighing ten kilograms, carried by men who threw themselves at or under tanks. On Okinawa, these tactics had been devastating against Shermans. After two months of fighting, losses came to 221 tanks, which amounted to 57 percent of the strength of the four army battalions. The Japanese were quite correct to believe that if they could inflict unacceptable attrition on tank units, they could stymie the American assault.

The 156th Division, which by August 1 numbered 16,163 of its authorized 17,266 men, deployed its four regiments in the standard fashion: three along the coast and one in reserve. The tactical scheme used by this unit demonstrates how the Japanese intended to minimize the exposure of their units to a crushing prelanding bombardment. Along what the Japanese termed the "beachfront positions," each coastal regiment deployed only about one platoon (roughly forty men) in the dunes about one kilometer from the water's edge. Approximately one or two kilometers to the rear of the dunes was the "advanced frontal area" of checkerboard positions holding about three companies. The "main resistance" position was four or five kilometers from the water and contained the main forces of the coastal regiments. Behind the main-resistance positions were the artillery and the reserve positions. There would also be many fake positions to attract enemy fire amid the actual deployments. Moreover, the division constructed its beach positions at night to conceal them from American planes. By the time the war ended, the 156th had completed its basic position construction and had finished about two thirds of its storage facilities for its supplies.

To the left (north) of the 156th Division was the 154th, which was similarly organized but had a significant problem. The division commander, General Mori, still in the thrall of past battle lessons, thought in terms of a sustained defense from superior positions far back from the beaches. Consequently, he initially ordered deployments that violated the concept of defense near (but not on) the beach and that left uncovered not only airfield sites but also the left flank of the 156th Division. A visit by the chief of staff of the 156th Division to discuss this deficiency proved fruitless, and map exercises with the commanders of the Fifty-seventh Army provoked criticism but left Mori figuratively and literally unmoved. An inspection by Field Marshal Hata in June finally produced tangible results. The division was reassigned to Major General Asisaburo Futami and set about conforming to superior directives. By the end of the war, Futami's soldiers had completed all of the protected firing positions as well as shelters for about half the personnel, about 80 percent of the shelter for command and communication facilities, and about 50 percent of the ammunition storage.

Although the 212th Division was a "decisive battle" (that is, counterattack) division, owing to the extremely broad expanse of the beaches at Miyazaki, five of the division's nine infantry battalions sat along the coast to the left (north) of the 154th Division. While furious construction of defenses progressed in this area, the rest of the division reserve followed a rigorous training program stressing antitank defense and night attacks.

Two tank brigades were assigned to the Fifty-seventh Army. The 5th Tank Brigade, which by August 1 possessed 112 of its 118 authorized armored fighting vehicles, trained as vigorously as the extremely limited fuel situation permitted.* The brigade also lacked a full stock of ammunition, particularly critical armor-piercing rounds for the 47-mm guns. The 6th Tank Brigade fielded half the strength of the 5th, since its 37th Regiment had been detached to serve with the Fortieth Army.

In the Ariake Bay area, the 86th Division had been training and building fortifications since August 1944. In February 1945, the 98th IMB was mobilized for defense tasks on the Osumi Peninsula (the area west of Ariake Bay and just east of Kagoshima Bay) and assigned to the 86th Division. Then in May 1945, the 364th Infantry Regiment and the 765th, 766th, and 767th Independent Infantry Battalions were mobilized and also attached to the 86th Division. The addition of these units gave the combined division and brigade a strength of 28,796 men by August 1.

The division commander, Lieutenant General Wataro Yoshinaka, believed his nineteen battalions of infantry and eight of artillery could smash an initial enemy landing at the water's edge. Field Marshal Hata agreed.

---

* The brigade organizational tables called for fifty-six medium, twenty-six light, and thirty "gun" tanks, plus six self-propelled guns. On August 1, the brigade possessed all save six gun tanks. Although its original equipment was new, upgrading was in progress—by the war's end, the brigade boasted at least a partial issue of the Type 3, Chi Nu medium tanks with a long, 75-mm gun. This vehicle equaled the Sherman, but Japan produced only about sixty, while Sherman production ran to 49,234.

He extolled the Ariake Bay defenses as an example for the whole country. In one typical location, where a cliff overlooking the beach permitted actual water's-edge defense, a single battalion had excavated sixteen kilometers of tunnels with firing positions allowing direct fire by field guns, antitank guns, and heavy machine guns on the shore.

The 86th Division had achieved impressive progress in the construction of fortifications by the end of the war. By Japanese calculations, they were 80 to 90 percent completed around Ariake Bay and 30 to 50 percent complete around Kanoya. Considerable effort had also been expended on the road network to make it passable for counterattack units. But while the 98th IMB had made major strides in construction of fortifications, its situation with respect to supplies was the least satisfactory of major units in the Fifty-seventh Army, notably in ammunition.

The Fifty-seventh Army also had available two other units, the 25th Division and the First Advanced Tank Corps (really a light tank company). Solely assigned to the decisive counterblow against a landing, the well-trained 25th Division performed some fortification work in the Miyazaki area to create positions from which to launch its counterattack. Owing to the tremendous concern over the likelihood of an American airborne landing, the Fifty-seventh Army ordered the 86th, 154th, and 212th Divisions to prepare to meet this threat in their respective areas. The Army also detailed the twenty-seven light tanks of the First Advanced Tank Corps in the Miyakonojo plain for this duty and alerted the 37th Tank Regiment to be prepared for such tasks.

Fortieth Army Formation and Dispositions

The original defense scheme thus provided only two Army headquarters, one each for northern and southern Kyushu. By May 1945, however, the Army Division of Imperial General Headquarters concluded that the command arrangements for the decisive battle over the vast expanse of southern Kyushu needed adjustment. Initially, staff officers in Tokyo thought in terms of creating another geographical command to direct operations on the Satsuma Peninsula and the western half of southern Kyushu, as well as an army command that would control units of a mobile army to be deployed in the great counterattack. The mobile army would be immediately under the Sixteenth Area Army and not tied to any geographic responsibilities. The formation of the mobile-army headquarters proved abortive, but a new geographic army command was created for southern Kyushu.

Imperial General Headquarters extracted the existing Fortieth Army headquarters of Lieutenant General Mitsuo Nakazawa from Taiwan and redeployed it to Kyushu. The Fortieth Army assumed command of its new responsibilities along Fukiage Beach and Satsuma Peninsula on June 13.*

Coincident with the Fortieth Army's transfer, the Sixteenth Area Army focused increasingly on the degree to which the Kagoshima Bay area suited presumed American objectives. Accordingly, to shield Kagoshima Bay, the Fortieth Army's dispositions emphasized defense of the west and south coast of the Satsuma Peninsula, as well as the effective blockade of the mouth of the bay. The Sendai area and the inside of the bay were listed as second and third in priority, respectively.

On June 12, the Fortieth Army issued its operational plan. The 146th Division, with the 125th IMB attached, continued the mission to defend the south coast of the Satsuma Peninsula. For this purpose, the 146th Division was considerably reinforced. The 206th Division was also reinforced and covered the area from the Manose River, the western boundary of the 146th Division, to the boundary it initially shared with the 77th Division. This was essentially the Fukiage beachfront along the western side of the Satsuma Peninsula. Subsequently, the 303rd Division, reinforced with a field-gun battalion, assumed responsibility for the coastal frontage further north near Sendai, while the 77th Division reverted to a reserve role.

In the area of the 146th Division, all field fortifications in the close coastal zone were complete by early August 1945, as were about half of the planned tunnels. While the division itself possessed nearly a complete set of authorized equipment, the attached 125th IMB lacked about a third of its machine guns. The 303rd Division, formed during the third-stage mobilization with many older men, was placed under the Fortieth Army on June 19 and ordered to take over the beachfront area defended by the 77th Division by early August. It was severely deficient in equipment. The 77th, in contrast, had received all of its equipment, and its supply status was deemed satisfactory for its intended role to counterattack a landing along Fukiage Beach.

Although assigned to the general area of southern Kyushu in May, the 206th Division did not reach its final deployment area opposite Fukiage Beach until June and July. By the end of the war, about half of the division's fortification plan was complete, but the division also suffered severe equipment deficiencies.

By postwar American accounting, in August 1945 the Fortieth Army with attached units had on hand at least 84,622 of its authorized 96,363

---

* The major combat units assigned to the army were the 77th, 146th, 206th, and 303rd Divisions, the 125th IMB (formerly the Third Amphibious Brigade), and the 37th Tank Regiment.

personnel in combat units. It is manifest, however, from the serious equipment and supply shortfalls that this army enjoyed a significantly lower priority than the Fifty-sixth and Fifty-seventh Armies. This must be taken as a conscious reflection of how Japanese officers assessed the probability of an American landing in its operational area.

In addition to the three field armies, several other commands on Kyushu answered to the Sixteenth Area Army. The Kurume and Kumamoto Division Districts, originally administrative commands, assumed tactical control of three independent mixed brigades and the 216th Division.* Also under the Sixteenth Area Army were the 107th IMB in the Goto Islands and the Tsushima fortress. Of these various units, the 216th Division was earmarked for counterattack of any invasion, and the other units formed a reservoir of twenty-six additional infantry battalions (the equivalent of the number of riflemen in nearly three more infantry divisions).

Logistics

Overall, the Imperial Army faced severe logistical shortfalls for the Ketsu operation, notably in ammunition and weapon supplies. The Imperial Army enumerated ammunition stockpiles in a unit called a *Kaisenbun,* which can be translated as a "Division Battle." Derived from experiences in the Russo-Japanese War and since 1937 in the "China Incident," this measure nominally represented the amount of ammunition a typical division would consume in four months of fighting—assuming that there were only twenty days of active combat ("firing days") per month.[†] While this allotment proved quite adequate against modestly supplied Chinese or Russian units, recent experience had taught that double or treble this amount was required to match lavishly provisioned American forces. Moreover, if the fifty-five divisions and thirty-one independent mixed and tank brigades stationed on the Home Islands are counted as roughly the equivalent of sixty-five divisions (not to mention the levies of civilians requiring arms), there were only thirty *Kaisenbun* in all of Japan. Further, the Imperial Army employed a parallel set of tabular strength and equipment figures to calculate the amount of equipment required to fully outfit one division. There were only forty of these available.

---

* The Kurume Division District had the 118th IMB along the Bungo Strait in southeastern Kyushu and the 122nd IMB in the Nagasaki area. The Kumamoto Division District had the 126th IMB in the Amakusa Islands off southwestern Kyushu and the 216th Division. To deal with airborne attacks, the Kurume Division District also had several reserve infantry units.

[†] The components of a *Kaisenbun* are listed in Appendix A.

These acute shortages placed a premium on selecting priorities in distributing available equipment and ammunition. From the outset, Imperial Headquarters effectively staked its fortunes on Kyushu. Moreover, Imperial Headquarters prudently aimed to pack Kyushu with ample supplies and arms well before a landing, and discounted the prospect of substantial replenishment after an invasion. As a result of these priorities, the general equipment situation on Kyushu was adequate in terms of what had been authorized—and sumptuous compared with other regions save Tokyo.

By the end of the war, while some units, notably in the Fortieth Army, still experienced shortages, the large bulk of the forces on Kyushu were fully outfitted, and it is very likely that any shortages would have been made good before Olympic commenced. The most serious shortages were in transport. As of August 1, the Fifty-seventh Army had on hand only 943 of its 1,255 trucks and only 7,801 of its 25,673 horses. The Army also fielded only 114 of its 168 antitank guns, which illustrates both a shortage and the basically inadequate level of authorized vital weapons. In a postwar statement, the supply officer for the Sixteenth Area Army insisted that by the end of July Kyushu held twelve *Kaisenbun* of ammunition (for roughly the equivalent of seventeen divisions), 7,750 kiloliters of fuel (94 percent of goal), rations for 2.1 million soldiers for a month (164 percent of goal), but only 20 percent of the forage needed for horses. There remained shortages of certain types of artillery ammunition, signal equipment, vehicles, and special equipment.

With respect to ammunition, this supply officer's figures show that Kyushu held fully 40 percent of all the ammunition in the Home Islands. Inventory reports submitted early during the occupation provide alternative numbers and indicate that even if the Sixteenth Area Army did not control that much ammunition, it possessed about that portion of total firepower. While the Japanese faced distinct limitations in their capacity to conduct protracted battle even with their best-equipped units, their plan was to essentially decide the campaign within the first two to three weeks. Gauged by that purpose, equipment and ammunition levels on Kyushu appear sufficient. Indeed, the logistics situation was one of several compelling reasons for the Japanese to recklessly mount the quickest and most savage battle they could against Olympic.

12

Kamikazes, Civilians, and Assessments

"We were absolutely sure of victory"

Special Attack

The attack on Pearl Harbor was just over two hours old when a Japanese pilot deliberately crashed his damaged plane into an American ship—the first instance of what was to become an indelible feature of the Pacific war. Until late 1944, sporadic episodes occurred of what the Japanese called *kesshi,* or "dare-to-die decisions," in which Japanese aircraft were crashed intentionally into American planes or ships. But waning numbers and above all the precipitous decline of the combat effectiveness of Japanese airpower transformed the random and occasional into the systematic and regular beginning in October 1944.

The aircraft inventory in the tactical units of the Imperial Army and Navy swelled from about 2,600 when the war began to a peak of approximately 5,500 in January 1944; it remained around 4,100 by January 1, 1945. Behind these raw numbers stood another story. During 1942 and 1943, Allied forces, while securing only modest advances across the Pacific, embraced the Japanese in voracious aerial struggles in the South Pacific and on New Guinea. These high-attrition battles dramatically degraded the quality level of the fliers in Imperial Army and Navy combat units. Loss rates accelerated in 1944, with dire effects. While in December 1941 the average number of accumulated flight hours of frontline aviators totaled 500 in the Imperial Army and a formidable 700 in the Imperial Navy, by January 1, 1945, the corresponding numbers were 130 hours for the Army and 275 for the Navy. Thus, ostensible numerical increases in Japanese airpower did not offset enfeebled combat capability.

From 1943, some Japanese officers advocated organized suicide attacks to remedy this grim actuality, but others balked at such methods. In the spring of 1943, two officers completed design work on the *Kaiten* ("Heaven Shaker"), a piloted ("human") torpedo. Initially, senior officers flatly rejected it because it incorporated no provision for the pilot to escape, but such inhibitions soon crumbled. On May 27, 1944, an Imperial Army officer crashed his fighter into an American ship in what the Army deemed the first planned suicide attack of the war. Within a month, suicide tactics were sanctified at the highest level.

With Saipan about to fall, the Emperor summoned a conference on June 25, 1944. Ostensibly, this event produced just another pledge of improved cooperation between the Imperial Army and Navy. But after the Emperor withdrew, Fleet Admiral Prince Hiroyasu Fushimi, the former chief of the Naval General Staff, spoke:

> In present day wars, both friend and enemy use almost identical weapons and other essentials of war. In matters such as radar, our enemy is superior to us qualitatively and quantitatively. Results favorable to us cannot be expected unless improvements are effected in these matters. Both the Army and Navy must think up some special weapons [the usual Japanese euphemism for suicide weapons] and conduct the war with them. This is urgent.

To execute "body-hitting" or "sure-hit, sure-death" aerial suicide tactics, the Japanese developed a stubby, rocket-propelled aircraft, the nose of which was packed with explosives. It was to be launched from a mother plane near Allied vessels and guided to impact by a pilot. The Japanese dubbed this device *Oka,* or "Cherry Blossom"; the tart American targets baptized it the *baka* bomb—*baka* meaning stupid. The *Oka* was not ready in time to defend the Philippines in October 1944, and this, combined with a severe shortage of aircraft, forced the Japanese to improvise kamikazes.

Vice Admiral Takijiro Onishi, the newly appointed commander of the First Air Fleet, formed the first Imperial Navy kamikaze unit with twenty-four relatively well trained Zero fighter pilots drawn from the 201st Air Group. The initial organized attacks occurred on October 25 in the midst of the Battle of Leyte Gulf. Eighteen kamikazes took off; six returned, having failed to find a target—a common feature of such missions. The remaining twelve, each clutching a 250-kilogram bomb, managed to score damaging hits on the escort carriers *Santee* (sixteen killed) and *Kitkun Bay* (one killed) and sank the *St. Lô* (114 killed). Thus, in exchange for twelve planes, the Japanese sank one ship; more significant, the casualty ratio was 12 Japanese to 131 Americans, almost eleven to one.

Following this inaugural, the kamikaze effort flourished. During the remainder of the war, according to two sources, the following kamikaze sorties were flown:

Kamikaze Sorties

Month	Source 1	2	Month	Source 1	2
October 1944	55	50	April 1945	1,162	1,264
November 1944	143	160	May 1945	596	711
December 1944	232	202	June 1945	210	202
January 1945	230	133	July 1945	20	22
February 1945	196	40	August 1945	59	59
March 1945	37	263	*Total:*	2,940	3,106

Many kamikazes had more than one crew member. Thus, a total of 3,913 Japanese airmen died in the kamikaze effort, 2,525 from the Imperial Navy and 1,388 from the Imperial Army.

The kamikaze onslaught proved extremely costly to the United States Navy. Suicide attackers killed at least 763 Americans around Leyte from October to December 1944, and kamikazes added 470 American soldiers and sailors to their toll during the invasion of Mindoro in December. Then came January 6, 1945, later known as "One Helluva Day" at Lingayen Gulf, Luzon. With thirty-two aircraft manned by just thirty-four aviators, kamikazes killed 167 Allied personnel, including fourteen Australians, one American rear admiral, a *Time* magazine correspondent, and Winston Churchill's personal representative, Lieutenant General Herbert Lumsden. "Should suicide bombers attack [troop] transports," urgently signaled an admiral, "results might be disastrous." In total, up to the beginning of the Okinawa operation, kamikaze attacks killed at least 2,200 Americans.

Five months of bloody experience taught that the first and most effective line of defense against the kamikaze was an intercepting fighter. Within slightly more than a month from the first organized kamikaze attacks, the fast carriers markedly increased their complements of fighter planes, at the expense of attack planes. These reallocated resources permitted new tactics, collectively named "The Big Blue Blanket" (navy planes were painted in blue camouflage shades), which aimed to destroy kamikazes at their bases or to shoot them down before their dives.

For targeted ships, the kamikaze was deadly. Long war experience against conventional air attack had demonstrated two basic defense methods: radical maneuvering and massive gunfire. Once committed to a steep dive, a kamikaze was locked into a narrow path. A handy ship could theoretically maneuver out of that path, much as a dive-bombing attack could be evaded. But the skipper of the escort carrier *Ommaney Bay,* sunk by a kamikaze in the Philippines, spoke for those who sailed in unwieldy ships when he observed: "For a steeply diving suicide plane a ship is practically helpless." Further, as an official narrative of battle lessons from the Philippines noted, radical maneuvering offered much less chance of avoiding a plane attacking from a low level in a shallow dive or glide attack, the common situation when ships operated close to land—such as when supporting an amphibious operation.

"The delivery of a maximum volume of effective gunfire from all [anti-aircraft] batteries within range is the primary essential" to survival, counseled this same report. Radical maneuvering, however, was inimical to the delivery of the "maximum volume of effective gunfire." Abrupt maneuvers disrupted both radar and simpler gyroscopic gun sights, a special problem for machine gunners, for a kamikaze screaming down to impact typically traversed the effective range of automatic weapons within a mere twenty seconds.

Furthermore, experience showed that the 20-mm and 40-mm anti-aircraft guns that had been venomously effective against conventional bomb and torpedo attackers lacked the "stopping power" to handle a kamikaze. Only a shell from a standard five-inch gun guaranteed both the destruction and deflection of a kamikaze, but a Navy document pointed out that "at least four 5-inch guns were needed to provide enough [anti-aircraft] fire to give the ship a fair chance of defeating an incoming suicider." All the fleet carriers (except light carriers), battleships, cruisers, and destroyers scheduled for Olympic met this basic requirement and also enjoyed sophisticated, radar-fitted gun-director systems. Amphibious ships, such as the extremely vulnerable transports embarking 800 to 1,400 troops each, or lesser craft were well equipped if they boasted one five-inch gun with no sophisticated controls.

Isolation increased vulnerability, so ships drew together in tight antiaircraft formations to concentrate fire in mutual support. This effort, and the fact that kamikazes flew directly into their targets, produced a serious problem with "friendly fire" casualties as stray antiaircraft rounds inevitably struck nearby vessels. "A certain amount of wild firing and fire into other vessels," observed one report, "will have to be accepted in the defense tactics against suicide planes." With the advent of kamikazes, there was a marked increase in the number of documented deaths from "friendly" fire, totaling at least sixty-five killed and 368 wounded in 1945.

At Okinawa, the raw numbers of the kamikaze effort peaked, with 1,900 sorties, or nearly two thirds of the total for the war. They inflicted at least the following fatalities on American naval personnel:

March	192
April	1,430
May	1,499
June	199
July	69
Total	3,389

This made the casualty ratio 1.78 Americans for each Japanese kamikaze sortie. In addition to these losses, the British Pacific fleet sustained damage to the carriers *Indefatigable, Formidable* (two occasions), and *Victorious,* but their armored flight decks significantly protected them, so that their fatalities totaled only twenty-six.

It should not be overlooked that there were major losses from other causes at Okinawa. A conventional dive-bombing attack on March 19 during preliminary strikes on Kyushu inflicted monumental damage to the carrier *Franklin,* which sustained far more damage and casualties (798 killed in the ship's complement and air group) than any carrier that sank. Mines killed 172 bluejackets, shore batteries killed ninety-six, and suicide boats killed eight. All together, 4,907 United States Navy personnel died during the Okinawa campaign.

The actual number of Japanese aircraft available for operations at the end of the war remains in question. According to the postwar accounting by the United States Strategic Bombing Survey, Japanese airpower was as follows:

	Army	*Navy*	*Total*
Planes assigned to suicide units			
Combat types	900		900
Advanced trainers	1,750		1,750
Primary trainers		2,700	2,700
Total	2,650	2,700	5,350
Combat types assigned to units not yet designated for suicide missions	2,150	3,200	5,350
Grand Total	4,800	5,900	10,700

The Japanese were also said to have on hand another 7,200 aircraft in need of repair. While the Strategic Bombing Survey numbers appear sound, there is conflicting evidence for numbers both higher and lower. An officer at Imperial General Headquarters charged with planning aircraft availability calculated that in July the Imperial Army had 6,355 aircraft and that this total would grow to 7,346 by October. On the other hand, an Imperial Navy officer reported the Imperial Navy had 2,826 aircraft for conventional attack and 2,218 "trainers" (presumably suicide versions) for a total of 5,044, significantly below the Strategic Bombing Survey estimate.

The Strategic Bombing Survey also calculated that there were 18,600 pilots: 8,000 in the Imperial Army and the balance in the Imperial Navy. The Imperial Army ranks included 2,000 pilots with seventy hours of experience for flying kamikazes. Another 5,000 filled the tactical units, and 1,000 served in training units, many as instructors, an occupation that was about to end. The Imperial Navy fielded about 2,450 pilots capable of day and night missions, 1,750 rated capable of dawn and dusk missions, and 5,950 rated as less skilled. By the reckoning of the Imperial Navy, a pilot needed a mere thirty to fifty hours of flying time to pilot one of the kamikazes that had been converted from training aircraft.

Overall, the Strategic Bombing Survey found that Japan had on hand about one million barrels of aviation fuel at the end of the war. This represented a seven-month supply at the consumption rates of June and July 1945, and Japan still managed to produce about 25 percent of this low level of consumption. Fuel was not a limiting factor for the foreseeable future, as all of the planned 5,350 kamikaze sorties required only about 50,000 barrels of aviation gasoline.

In addition to aircraft, the Imperial Navy was busy manufacturing and deploying an array of nautical suicide vehicles. These included two types of midget submarines, which were not, strictly speaking, suicide vessels, but war experience demonstrated their survival rate would be minuscule. The original version, the sixty-ton *Koryu,* carried two torpedoes. Five hundred seventy of these were to be constructed by the end of September and 180 more per month thereafter, but bombing left only about 110 complete at the end of the war. The diminutive version was the *Kairyu,* of less than twenty tons, alternately armed with two torpedoes or six hundred kilograms of explosives packed into the bow for suicide ramming attacks. Production goals totaled about 760 by the end of September, but available *Kairyu* numbered only about 250 at the end of the war. About one thousand *Kaiten* were on hand at the end of the war. To offset their very limited range, two remaining cruisers, twenty-three destroyers, and many submarines (of forty-six available) were converted to carry them. Elsewhere, launching sites were prepared in caves along the coasts of Kyushu and Honshu. In addition to these, the Imperial Navy was busy recruiting men as suicide swimmers in the Water's Edge Surprise Attack Force. These individuals, garbed in diving suits, were to wait with explosive charges in the shallows off landing beaches to blow up themselves and landing craft.

Meanwhile, the Imperial Army contrived its own aquatic suicide squadrons. On May 23, the Army ordered mobilization of twenty Marine Advanced Units. Each of these comprised about one hundred *Shinyo* single-crewman suicide boats, each designed to carry two 120-kilogram depth charges. By the end of the war, the Imperial Army possessed about 6,200 *Shinyo*. On July 11, about eight hundred suicide boats were assigned to the Sixteenth Area Army. Experience in both Pacific and Atlantic theaters suggested these weapons would have limited success, but nonetheless they could be expected to kill some Americans, especially if one hit a packed transport.

Tactically, the Imperial Army envisioned dispatching waves of 300 to 400 planes about every hour, consistent with an objective of destroying troop transports before the landing. The Army desired that the Navy fly on an equal schedule. Under these projections, the Japanese would saturate the invasion fleet with as many kamikazes in three hours as they sent against Okinawa in three months. The Imperial Navy, however, expected to obtain better results by employing its planes at twilight periods.

Key staff officers gathered in early July at Sixth Air Army Headquarters at Fukuoka to delineate Japanese expectations about kamikazes. The conference limited its examination to resources available in July: 4,300 training planes converted for kamikaze attack and 700 conventional attack aircraft (no conventional fighter aircraft counted). The Imperial Navy projected that only 60 percent of the available aircraft would be operational for Ketsu-Go, and in the special-attack missions only one plane in six would achieve a hit. Thus of 4,000 kamikaze planes available in July, 2,400 would fly a mission and only 400 would score hits. (The Imperial Army maintained that one kamikaze in three would score a hit.) With regard to naval suicide craft, one of ten of each type would be destroyed at its base and the survivors of the original seven hundred *Shinyo* and twelve *Kairyu* would contribute a total of 67 more hits, making a grand total of 467 hits. These officers assumed that each hit would sink one vessel, for aggregate damage equal to the shipping of five divisions (at 120 ships per division). Thus, the Imperial Navy projected destruction of about one third of the invasion force. Since this exercise did not account for increases in strength in suicide units prior to October or the contributions of mines, submarines, destroyers, or shore batteries, the summary report projected that under favorable conditions up to 50 percent of the invasion force would be destroyed at sea. The assessment emphasized that it was "strategically important" to employ all fighting power against the first enemy landing forces. This obviously looked to the political impact of inflicting huge casualties in minimum time for maximum shock effect.

It must be noted that, since they planned to throw their entire air strength into the decisive battle on Kyushu, the Japanese recognized that "absolutely no display of air power could have been expected in Kanto [Tokyo] operations." Although they envisioned continued aircraft production between battles on Kyushu and Kanto, shortages of fuel, training deficiencies, and American countermeasures were expected to negate any effect from these aircraft.

Were Japanese expectations realistic? Looking over the entire kamikaze chronicles, the three critical factors in their success were pilot skill, topographic or hydrographic advantages (the degree to which terrain masked the approach of kamikazes), and efficiency of American defenses. Of these, pilot skill stood preeminent. Relatively skilled pilots in the Philippines attained a high ratio of hits to sorties, whereas the rudimentary capabilities of their peers at Okinawa dramatically lowered the success rate. For Ketsu-Go, the Japanese aimed to counter low overall quality with massive quantity.

Experience in the Philippines also illustrated the enormous advantages in stealth and surprise that suicide pilots could extract from favorable topographic or hydrographic factors. Okinawa, by contrast, demonstrated the deadly perils of long flights over water, through rings of radar-controlled defenses. Kyushu promised to reprise the Philippines with short flights and, more important, the chance for kamikazes to hug the landmass before banking out to sea. Moreover, the tactical environment at Kyushu might well cure one of the fundamental defects of the whole kamikaze effort: Few pilots crashed into transport-type vessels. Off Okinawa, only about twenty-three of nearly four hundred vessels struck by kamikazes were transport types. This was due partly to poor or nonexistent ship-recognition skills but more to the fact that other targets (such as carriers) initially had priority and that kamikazes had to pierce screening vessels to get to the transports. At Kyushu, if the invasion fleet lay in conventional disposition, the packed transports would be close to the coast, so that they would be immediately at hand as a kamikaze burst from land to sea, looking for a target. This factor portended a marked increase in the casualties caused by kamikazes.

There is no doubt that American defenses would have been much stronger against Ketsu-Go. Ultra identified most of the kamikaze bases, which thus could be subjected to heavy air attack. Experience at Okinawa, however, showed that neither tactical aircraft nor B-29s could wholly quell the kamikaze effort. The Japanese fully expected severe aerial pummeling of their bases and mounted what an American report labeled "extremely ingenious and painstaking" efforts at dispersal and concealment (as far as five miles from the air base) that very sharply reduced losses on the ground from June onward. One Japanese officer realistically estimated that no more than 20 percent of the kamikaze aircraft would be destroyed on the ground.

In light of Okinawa experience, the counter-air campaign to protect Olympic would likely have disrupted Japanese efforts at mass attacks but could not have destroyed more than 20 percent of all kamikazes on the ground. Much of the impressive bomb tonnage expended at kamikaze bases would have been wasted when weather compelled radar drops. Moreover, the trainer aircraft that constituted the bulk of the kamikazes did not require elaborate runway facilities. While they lacked the speed and carrying capacity of frontline aircraft, trainers actually presented a difficult target for fighters because they were smaller and more difficult to see. Finally, the wood construction and configuration of trainers made them far less vulnerable to the standard proximity-fuse antiaircraft shell.

American commanders fully appreciated how vulnerable the invasion fleet would be to kamikazes that used Kyushu to mask their approaches. Admiral Nimitz designed an elaborate radar air-warning net that included shore-based stations manned by Marines with equipment mounted in landing vehicles, destroyer and submarine radar-picket teams, and, to plug the deadly gap in coverage of land approaches, airborne radar pickets. This involved conversion of Navy B-17s (PB-1Ws, officially) with radar and facilities for fighter controllers—the ancestor of current AWACs aircraft. Four of these airborne pickets, each with its own fighter escort, would be continuously on station sixty to one hundred miles north of the landing beaches. In mid-July, when it appeared that the conversions could not be completed in time for Olympic, Nimitz proposed the emergency conversion of two squadrons of PB4Ys (Navy B-24s) for the job.

Postwar investigation disclosed one other important factor in the equation. While the Strategic Bombing Survey showed 5,350 planes earmarked for suicide attacks, the Imperial Army fully intended to commit *all* of its planes for kamikaze missions. This would bring total kamikaze sorties to as high as 7,500. The senior Imperial Navy officer in charge of opposing Olympic, Vice Admiral Matome Ugaki, did not reveal his intentions, but the fact that more Navy than Army aviators died as kamikazes, as well as the general unwillingness of the Navy to fall behind the Army in such competitions suggests an answer. A stronger clue comes from the fact that Ugaki's inability to comment arose because upon receiving orders to surrender (from the type of individuals he described as "selfish weaklings"), he flew a kamikaze mission—"to live" in his words "in the noble spirit of the special attack"—and disappeared at sea.

Though Japanese plans to dispatch kamikazes in massed waves appear to have been unrealistic, it is highly probable that for five days or more Olympic would have been subjected to a continuous torrent of determined suicide planes. The Strategic Bombing Survey noted that at Okinawa, about 18.6 percent of kamikazes hit or scored damaging near misses, but only 1.8 percent actually sank ships. At these rates, the 5,350 predesignated kamikaze aircraft for Ketsu-Go would have sunk approximately 95 ships and damaged about 995. These figures represented about one third of the invasion fleets. A more refined estimate of the effectiveness of kamikazes against Olympic is set forth in the table below, which incorporates a projection for total losses of American personnel afloat caused by Ketsu-Go. The effective sorties ratio (60 percent) represents the portion of total available aircraft that actually get off the ground. The ratio of American fatalities per effective sortie reflects Okinawa experience and would increase with better pilots and more hits on transports. "Other American fatalities" is based on the very conservative assumption that all other naval fatalities (from mines, submarines, shore batteries, conventional air attack, other suicide vehicles, Navy medical personnel serving in Marine units, and air-crew losses) would only equal American nonkamikaze losses at Okinawa.

**Estimated Effectiveness of Kamikazes
in Ketsu-Go and American Naval Personnel Losses**

Available Aircraft	Effective Sorties	At 1.78 American Fatalities per Sortie	Other American Fatalities	Total American Fatalities
5,350	3,210	5,714	1,514	7,228
7,500	4,500	8,010	1,514	9,524
10,700	6,420	11,428	1,514	12,942

This loss, the great bulk of it in the opening days of Olympic, would carry strong shock value, but the Japanese could reasonably expect it to be far overshadowed by events ashore.

Preparations for Internal Defense and Resistance

After their experience on Saipan, American planners incorporated the prospect of facing a "fanatically hostile population" into their situation estimates for an invasion of Japan. Two subsequent events fortified this expectation. The Philippines harbored about 38,280 Japanese civilians, including government officials, businessmen, farmers, and their families, as well as civilian employees of the Japanese armed forces. The United States Army official history on the campaign notes: "Except for the extremely aged and the very young, almost all of these Japanese civilians came to serve the armed forces in one way or another." Almost exactly two thirds of the 381,550 Japanese in the Philippines (not counting Leyte) died, but there is no explicit numbering of civilian losses. Then much worse came on Okinawa. As described earlier, at least 62,000 and perhaps as many as 100,000 to 150,000 civilians perished.

In March 1945, Imperial Headquarters moved to make this American nightmare a reality and to establish a seamless fusion of the military, the government, and the people. On March 24, Imperial Headquarters directed the formation the following month of Area Special Policing Units under the area commanders. These organizations would represent the practical mergers of the governmental and civilian spheres. Every village or town was to form its own units, which would be aggregated into formations of about three hundred. The only full-time members were the six members of the headquarters staff, with the remainder called up as needed. Ideally, each headquarters was to include one officer trained in guerrilla-warfare tactics, while another officer was to lead the local veterans' organizations. These formations were to provide a pool of auxiliary combat or combat-support units, as was soon illustrated by their direct attachment to operational units, usually in coastal areas. The members were scheduled for call-up in May, June, and July for three to four days each for rudimentary but morale-boosting instruction (bayonet, grenade, and antitank combat were mentioned specifically in training guidelines).

On March 27, Public Law Number 30 mobilized all citizens in the coastal areas to perform fortification, transportation, construction, or other efforts to assist the decisive-battle strategy. This followed upon the adoption by the cabinet on March 18 of the Decisive Battle Educational Measures Guidelines, which suspended all school classes, except grades one to six, from April 1, 1945, to March 31, 1946. All of these students and their teachers were to be mobilized for the production of food and military supplies, air-raid work, and other tasks to facilitate the decisive battle.

On March 23, the cabinet ordered the formation of the Patriotic Citizens Fighting Corps across the whole nation. This corps constituted a mechanism for inducting the whole body of citizens. The entire public, in effect, became subject to call-up under the Volunteer Enlistment Law, which applied to all men ages 15 to 60 and all women ages 17 to 40. They were organized into Volunteer Fighting Units and subject to military discipline and control through the local area commands. The scale of these organizations was formidable: A tabular representation of these units in Kumamoto prefecture on Kyushu, for example, gives a breakdown by subjurisdiction and then notes that the figures represented all the citizens in the age groups, a total of over one million persons.

What this sea of civilians lacked besides training were arms and even uniforms. A mobilized high-school girl, Yukiko Kasai, found herself issued an awl and told: "Even killing just one American soldier will do. You must prepare to use the awls for self-defense. You must aim at the enemy's abdomen." Many civilians found themselves drilling with sharpened staves or spears. Japan lacked the cloth to put those civilians into uniforms—one senior general spoke of his hope to provide them with patches on their civilian clothes. This lack of distinguishing identification would undoubtedly have made it impossible at normal combat range for a soldier or Marine to identify which civilians represented the Japanese armed forces and which did not, a sure prescription for vast numbers of deaths. At least one Fifth Air Force intelligence officer took the Japanese at their publicly broadcast word of total mobilization and declared in a July 21 report, "The entire population of Japan is a proper Military Target. . . . THERE ARE NO CIVILIANS IN JAPAN."

The prospect of turning the Homeland itself into a battleground provoked unease among even hardened professional Imperial Army officers. Most troubling was the issue of whether to evacuate the civilians from the battle area when the invasion came. The chief of staff of the Fifty-seventh Army believed initially that the correct course was to clear the battle area before the landings, which would preserve discipline, free up every inch of ground for military use, and concentrate the thoughts of the troops on military matters. He began to set the stage for this order by trying to enforce nonfraternization between soldiers and civilians.

But evacuation presented severe problems. First, because of ominous food shortages, Japan could not abandon even the smallest parcel of land. Then there was the problem of how and where to send the evacuated civilians without disrupting military operations. In May, General Inada of the Sixteenth Area Army planned to move civilians up into nearby mountains in each prefecture, but this scheme was abandoned in June after staff studies confirmed that lack of facilities, transportation, and provisions would founder the effort. The new plan directed civilians to remain where they were; if the battle began, they would be moved in accordance with the desires of each division. Moreover, the enrollment of all healthy men and women into Volunteer Fighting Units drastically reduced the number of people who would have to be redeployed.

In the Fortieth Army area, the operative directive declared: "The inhabitants will dedicate their lives along with the Army to the defense of the nation." Only those whose presence might present an obstruction were to be evacuated. Each local commander would employ his civilian unit so as to maximize his combat effectiveness.

The significance of these designs cannot be exaggerated. This mobilization was intended to create a huge pool of men and women to perform direct combat support and, ultimately, combat jobs. This would literally add tens of millions to the strength of the ground combat units, albeit of little formal combat power for lack of training and equipment. It would also guarantee huge civilian casualties and make the disturbing American nightmare of a "fanatically hostile population" into a reality. By mustering millions of erstwhile civilians into the area swept by bombs, artillery, and small-arms fire, Japan's military masters willfully consigned hundreds of thousands of their countrymen to death. Moreover, by deliberately eliminating any distinction between combatants and noncombatants, they would compel Americans to treat all Japanese as combatants or fail to do so at their peril. It was a recipe for extinction.

Ketsu–Go Versus Olympic

American officers subjected the massive amphibious assault on Kyushu that never occurred to several postwar assessments. The most comprehensive of these was a survey by the staff of the V Amphibious Corps. This study, while allowing that the struggle would have been "costly," overall deprecated Japanese prospects. The compilers of this report, however, acknowledged that they secured copies of very few enemy plans and orders; that demobilization had disorganized and dispersed Japanese units; and that they confronted many conflicts in the testimony of Japanese officers. This analysis likewise was skewed by the fact that the Japanese units facing the V Amphibious Corps—the Fortieth Army and particularly the 303rd Division—were the weakest Imperial Army detachments on Kyushu. Even with the far better perspective offered with more comprehensive Japanese material, the assessment that Ketsu-Go could not defeat Olympic still appears sound. But a brief examination of prospects for a landing on Kyushu is required here not only to provide context for what befell Olympic in the summer of 1945 but also to highlight the real significance of how Ketsu-Go figured in how the war ended.

Any evaluation of Ketsu-Go must commence with acknowledgment of several broad matters. First, the Japanese never formally elected to stake absolutely everything on any one permutation of Ketsu-Go. But in a series of decisions, Imperial Headquarters dispatched scarce equipment and supplies to Kyushu, albeit often in the hope that later production would make good the deficits elsewhere. By these actions, the Japanese made what historian John Ray Skates has aptly labeled a de facto choice, staking their fate on the battle on Kyushu. Therefore, the logic of Japanese strategy held that it made no sense whatsoever to hold in reserve any available air or ground forces capable of intervening on Kyushu.

Another preliminary factor concerns "Pastel," a sophisticated U.S. deception plan to support Olympic. At the strategic level, Pastel sought to mislead the Japanese into believing that the American targets were along the China coast—Shikoku or Hokkaido rather than Kyushu. But shrewd Japanese planning had already defeated Pastel's major aims. Imperial Headquarters anticipated that Kyushu would be the American objective. Moreover, the Japanese packed Kyushu with virtually everything they intended to use against Olympic and planned no reinforcement from the continent. Pastel's operational ruse to fake an airborne threat against Kyushu would have played to keen Japanese sensitivities and might have affected local Japanese arrangements to face an invasion, but to what extent we cannot say. Overall, it appears that Pastel would not have materially affected Olympic.

Some 900,000 Japanese servicemen awaited Olympic. How many would actually have confronted Olympic on the ground is not stated explicitly in Japanese material. Combat units certainly included the Fortieth Army (84,622 men), Fifty-seventh Army (150,198), plus the 57th (20,429) and 216th (21,736) Divisions and the 4th Tank Brigade (3,103), totaling a minimum of 280,088 trained fighting troops. Support and service troops, including aviation units, would have easily brought the total committed Japanese forces to 500,000 or more. American combat troops destined for Kyushu totaled about 380,000 out of a committed force list of about 680,000.

While chances of major reinforcement from Honshu to southern Kyushu appear slim, the Japanese, consistent with a now-or-never resolve, likely would have committed many if not all units in northern Kyushu against Olympic. The Japanese could also rely on the fact that at least four divisions (25th, 57th, 77th, and 86th) and two brigades (98th and 125th) in or committed to southern Kyushu were first-class. Finally, it is particularly important to contemplate the fact that the Japanese units on Kyushu still had at least seventy-six days to train, assimilate supplies and equipment, and, most of all, dig between the end of the war and November 1. The Japanese units that made Okinawa a byword for tenacious resistance were in their final positions only fifty to one hundred days before the landing. Thus, the Japanese would have strengthened their preparation, significantly beyond the state they were in when the war actually ended.

The ability of the Sixth Army to prevail over such heavy resistance would have hinged on the combination of tremendous firepower and the resolve of its riflemen. Vice Admiral Richmond K. Turner's amphibious forces incorporated thirteen old battleships, nine heavy and fifteen light cruisers, and thirty-eight destroyers dedicated to fire support. Another two fast battleships, one heavy and three light cruisers, and six destroyers from Task Force 58 would also have bombardment roles. In addition, 255 amphibious craft converted for fire support (LCS, LCI[G], LCI[M], LCI[R], LSM[R]) would drench the assault beaches with barrages of rockets and direct gunfire immediately ahead of the landing crafts bearing troops. The Japanese, however, generally located their main defenses well behind the area that the initial bombardment would have pulverized, with the exception of Ariake Bay. Once ashore, Sixth Army combat units would enjoy the support of twenty-seven artillery battalions (in addition to more than sixty attached to divisions and regimental teams) plus twelve tank and three tank-destroyer battalions.

The ground phase of Olympic would commence on X minus four with initial operations against the islands south and southeast of Kyushu. On Tanega Shima, a hornet's nest would have confronted the 158th Regimental Combat Team, its three infantry battalions facing six Japanese. The preliminaries presumably would have prompted the Sixteenth Area Army to move reserve units to the beaches. But Japanese staff officers correctly forecast the tremendous difficulties their reserve units faced in slogging long distances under severe aerial and naval bombardment. The more likely results would have been the piecemeal arrival of frayed units that would have been committed to plug gaps and replace the horrendous losses inflicted by the superior combat power American forces could bring into play. Ironically, while this problem alone may have negated any realistic prospect at military victory, it also may have aided the achievement of political goals since any attempt at a massed counterattack would likely have been shredded by American firepower at disproportionate cost to the Japanese. Thus, rather than vainly sacrificing reserves in futile counterattacks, the reserves would have sustained costly attrition, precisely as at Okinawa.

At the main landing areas, the V Amphibious Corps of 98,933 men would have achieved tactical surprise. The Japanese expected landings either on the southern end of the Satsuma Peninsula or along the Fukiage Beaches well south of the actual American target. Only the weak and poorly trained 303rd Division, which had a total strength of 11,634, would have faced the V Amphibious Corps. Once ashore, however, the Marines would have confronted the task of traversing daunting terrain to capture Sendai and Kagoshima. The corridors to each city limited military movement to the railroad and highway. The former was marked by deep cuts and tunnels. Japanese positions defended every turn. The continuous terracing of farmlands reinforced these obstacles with rises too steep for tracked vehicles and impossible for wheeled vehicles. The corridor to Kagoshima in particular narrowed in places to only one hundred yards, flanked by vertical cliffs up to three hundred feet high—a frontage suitable for less than one rifle company. Marine officers labeled this as "ideal terrain for a stubborn defense in depth."

The I Corps, assaulting Miyazaki with 93,266 men, would have outnumbered the 55,044 Japanese defenders, but the odds were far worse for the XI Corps at Ariake. Although the 112,648 attackers would have initially struck only the 28,160 men—albeit heavily reinforced and well trained—of the 86th Division, the Japanese had designated Ariake as the focus for their great counterattack. X-Day likely would have dawned with the Japanese 77th, 25th, 57th, and 216th Divisions, as well as the 4th, 5th, and 6th Tank Brigades—a combined strength of more than 86,000 men—marching for Ariake Bay. While it is probable that at least some of these units would have been diverted to confront the V Amphibious Corps—and perhaps the I Corps at Miyazaki—it appears nearly certain that Ariake Bay would have been the site of the severest and most costly battle on Kyushu.

The American IX Corps, numbering 79,155 soldiers, constituted the Sixth Army reserve. Its assigned mission was either to reinforce other elements of the Sixth Army or to execute a separate landing on the south coast of Kyushu from X plus three. The careful General Krueger probably would have employed the IX Corps in reinforcement, as he likewise would have committed the 11th Airborne Division (14,641 men) and most if not all of the 40th Infantry Division (21,897 men). If the IX Corps landed on southern Kyushu, it would have confronted heavy opposition from the 146th Division, the 125th IMB, and probably the 206th Division, totaling about 41,256 men.

What kind of casualties would such a titanic confrontation have produced? The short answer is that only reasonable estimates can be suggested. If the Japanese committed at least a half-million men in southern Kyushu and resolved to do or die there, it is hard to image that their fatalities would have been less than 200,000 to 250,000. The civilian population in the three prefectures over which fighting would have raged totaled 3,804,570 by the 1944 census. A mere 10 percent fatality rate among civilians would equate to another 380,000 deaths. Japanese military and civilian deaths on Kyushu thus would approximate 580,000 to 630,000 at the very low end.

Likewise, only a tentative projection of American losses in Olympic can be offered. While postwar information clarifies many calculable factors affecting casualties, there is at least one crucial intangible element to weigh: The partial demobilization had stripped a disproportionate share of the experienced combat leaders from American units and materially degraded their effectiveness. This undoubtedly would have produced significantly increased losses in subtle ways that cannot be measured. Assuming that casualties ashore merely equaled the lower ratio proposed by the Joint Chiefs of Staff planners in April 1945, and the campaign lasted no more than ninety days, casualties from the troop list of 681,000 would have reached 132,385, including 25,741 killed and missing. To these would be added naval casualties ranging from 7,228 to 12,942 killed and 16,809 to 30,098 wounded. This brings combined land and sea losses to the vicinity of 156,422 to 175,425, of whom between 32,969 and 38,683 would have been killed. These figures, of course, are projections, but they are based on assumptions that consistently bias the result to the low range. Moreover, this estimate excludes from consideration Army Air Forces losses or the large numbers of Allied prisoners of war and civilian internees who would have perished from abuse or starvation if the war had continued.

But a military yardstick is not the critical historical measurement of Ketsu-Go versus Olympic. The Japanese comprehended astutely that they need not repulse Olympic to attain their overarching political objective: to find the American threshold in casualties that would induce American policy makers to parley for terms to the taste of Japanese militarists. Moreover, they correctly perceived that this threshold comprised not just the raw number of losses in Olympic but also the implications those casualties carried. The Japanese did not have to reach the ultimate American threshold; they needed only to convince U.S. policy makers and the public that the bloodletting on Kyushu foretold an unbearable ultimate cost.

The American tolerance for casualties was never thus tested, so it cannot be certified, but there are several benchmarks from which it can be judged. First, with total battle deaths for the war at 292,751, each additional 29,275 dead increased the war's cost by 10 percent. Moreover, and perhaps more telling, the highest death total for any one month of the war—20,325 in March 1945—could have been exceeded easily in the first thirty days of Olympic. Because battle casualties fell in great disproportion on combat troops, battle casualties ashore of only 92,500—a number well within Japanese capabilities—would double the losses for the entire war among the assault divisions. This carried dire implications for combat effectiveness and morale. Any soldier or Marine infantryman slated for Olympic who believed the atomic bomb saved him from death or wounds had solid grounds for this belief. The other men earmarked for Olympic, whatever their job, would have become unwilling participants in a gigantic and deadly game of kamikaze roulette where random chance determined who lived and who died.

There is at least one contemporary suggestion that a key policy maker deemed the projected losses unacceptable: Marshall recoiled sharply at estimates from MacArthur's headquarters of casualties exceeding 100,000. Indeed, Marshall's message inviting MacArthur to disavow such projections explicitly cited President Truman's sensitivity to casualties, plainly a matter with heavy political freight. By these measures, if Ketsu-Go had produced casualties in the 140,000 to 160,000 range, that might well have been enough to secure Japanese political objectives.

Japanese field commanders had a sound grasp of Ketsu-Go's purely military prospects. After an inspection trip in June, Major General Joichiro Sanada remarked to Field Marshal Hata, the commander of the Second General Army:

> The morale of all front-line forces, from army and division commanders on down, is excellent. In view of their advantages of ample equipment, naval strategy and favorable terrain, I believe that the first wave of enemy troops could surely be pushed back into the sea. If the enemy attempts a second and a third landing, however, it is highly doubtful that he can be completely repulsed.

Hata replied: "You are probably correct. As long as we lack powerful general second and third line reserves, we cannot be certain of repulsing a second and third enemy landing."

The key opinions on Ketsu-Go, however, were those in Tokyo, where political implications were preeminent. A postwar statement by Major General Masakazu Amano, Chief of the Operations Section, Imperial General Headquarters, assessed the outlook for Ketsu-Go as follows:

We were absolutely sure of victory. It was the first and the only battle in which the main strength of the air, land and sea forces were to be joined. The geographical advantages of the homeland were to be utilized to the highest degree, the enemy was to be crushed, and we were confident that the battle would prove to be the turning point in political maneuvering.

Likewise, the chief of the intelligence section, Lieutenant General Seizo Arisue, explained to his American interrogators:

If we could defeat the enemy in Kyushu or inflict tremendous losses, forcing him to realize the strong fighting spirit of the Japanese Army and people, it would be possible, we hoped, to bring about the termination of hostilities on comparatively favorable terms.

The most critical attitude of all was that of Army Minister Anami, and the evidence on his views is overwhelming. According to his close subordinate Lieutenant General Masao Yoshizumi, Anami embraced the conviction that there were "considerable chances of victory in the decisive battle in the homeland." Indeed, Yoshizumi related that Army officers universally believed in Japan's victory in the "first decisive battle" (that is, against the first landing attempt). Anami's military secretary, Colonel Saburo Hayashi, flatly reported that the army minister "believed that the initial landing of the American invasion forces could be repulsed." Moreover, Anami thought that if Japan inflicted heavy damage in Ketsu-Go, it might be able to continue the fight, or at least come to a peace other than unconditional surrender. Even in the final *extremis,* he continued to believe that Japan should insist on something other than unconditional surrender or continue the war, reflecting his confidence in Ketsu-Go to the very end.

In the debates over the end of the Pacific conflict, Americans customarily relate the invasion of the Home Islands to the decision to use nuclear weapons to halt the war. This perspective, however, misses the role the invasion played in continuing the war. The leaders of the Imperial Army held the reasonable conviction that American morale could be broken in an invasion. Ending the war thus demanded that the Imperial Army's faith in Ketsu-Go must be shattered.

13

The Eclipse of Olympic

"Not the recipe for victory"

The Numbers

Foremost among the many elements contributing to Japanese confidence in Ketsu-Go was the conviction that they would surprise the American attackers with such massive forces that they would either defeat or severely bloody the invaders. What the Japanese did not anticipate, however, was that Ultra would unmask their carefully wrought plans. Newly declassified Ultra information now provides a radically different story of the dramatic challenge to the entire strategy of invasion during the last eight weeks of the war.

The ability of a defender to meet a seaborne assault has two components: what strength can immediately oppose the landing and what strength can ultimately be brought against any beachhead. On the first question, American intelligence had originally projected that only three of the six expected Japanese combat divisions on Kyushu would be available in the target area on X-Day. In May, MacArthur credited the Japanese with the capacity to meet the invasion ultimately with eight to ten divisions. On June 18, when briefing Truman, Chief of Staff Marshall stated that eight Japanese combat divisions could eventually be deployed at Kyushu, among an aggregate of 350,000 troops. Moreover, Marshall, backed by Admiral King, the commander in chief of the Navy, assured the President that American air and sea power would preclude further reinforcement. Truman was not briefed on Japanese air capabilities, but a May intelligence summary for MacArthur estimated that only 2,500 to 3,000 enemy aircraft would contest the invasion.

In one of its greatest but least known feats of the war, radio intelligence destroyed these assumptions. Intercepted messages detailed the general understanding of the Japanese strategy, unmasked the formidable Japanese buildup in the Homeland, particularly on Kyushu, as well as the amazing recovery of Japanese airpower, including vast numbers of kamikazes. These revelations thrust senior American military leaders into an agonizing and divisive debate that was on the verge of dramatically revising U.S. strategy as the war ended.

By the summer of 1945, Allied radio intelligence had reached peak efficiency. Each month, a million Imperial Army messages were intercepted and processed, as well as a lesser volume of Imperial Navy traffic. Important discoveries from this abundant harvest of military communications circulated daily among top War and State Department policy makers as the Magic Far East Summary side by side with the Magic Diplomatic Summary covering political developments.* At the same time, MacArthur's intelligence chief, Major General Charles A. Willoughby, published a daily summary, supplemented by twice-monthly reviews. In Pearl Harbor, Nimitz's superb intelligence staff likewise issued several sophisticated appreciations covering different facets of the intelligence picture. Willoughby's and Nimitz's publications did not circulate widely in Washington.

Three American and two British centers intercepted and exchanged the raw material for these major publications, and each center performed interpretation. Generally, these summaries reflect little if any dispute about Japanese naval strengths. MacArthur's intelligence chief and Washington, however, conducted low-grade bureaucratic skirmishes over the identification and location of Imperial Army units. In these conflicts, the Military Intelligence Service (MIS) of the War Department in Washington stood over Willoughby as the official arbiter of the Imperial Army ground order of battle (that is, the identification and location of formations); thus, its publication, the Far East Summary, represented the ultimate authority on this topic. Sharp divisions persisted among all three American centers over Japanese air strength. Despite the creation of a joint Army-Navy board in Washington devoted specifically to assessing Japanese aviation capability, no one source carried supreme authority on Japanese air strengths. Finally,

---

* Neither contemporary intelligence users nor historians have settled on strict definitions of Magic and Ultra. The convention followed here is that the term *Magic* is reserved for the deciphering of Japanese diplomatic messages, while the deciphering of Japanese military and naval communications is termed *Ultra*. By this classification system, the Magic Far East Summary would be styled *Ultra*. For sake of simplicity, it is referred to hereafter as the Far East Summary.

as the events over these two months illustrated, senior officers could choose to formulate opinions and plans that ignored the input of their intelligence staffs.

Radio intelligence very promptly laid out the basic Japanese organization for the defense of the Homeland and then unraveled the master strategic plan. By the end of April, MacArthur knew that the Japanese had created two army groups assigned to defend the Homeland. The First Army Group (First General Army), under Field Marshal Sugiyama in Tokyo, guarded northern Honshu and Tokyo. The Second Army Group (Second General Army), believed (correctly) to be under Field Marshal Hata in Hiroshima, supervised defense of central and western Honshu as well as Kyushu. Imperial Headquarters retained direct control of the Fifth Area Army, which defended Hokkaido and the Kuril Islands. Almost simultaneously with the discovery of the command arrangements came information of a definite plan for defense of the Homeland. "Perhaps significantly," noted Willoughby, "the plan [is] termed *Ketsu* (Decisive)."

During July and August, radio intelligence amassed a picture of the critical elements of the Ketsu operation. A message from the Imperial General Staff on July 6 revealed a major change in Japanese doctrine: "It is fundamentally contradictory for the Corps [armies] along the coast, whatever tactical difficulties may arise, to reckon on any continuation of this battle by retreat." Willoughby questioned initially whether this "no withdrawal" exhortation was simply a "pep talk," but he acknowledged that "if true," it "represents a complete reversal of present Jap[anese] defense doctrine." Willoughby accurately perceived this as the third change of Japanese defense policy. Having abandoned the initial tactic of water's-edge defense after experience with pulverizing Allied prelanding bombardments, the Imperial Army had adopted a doctrine of defense in depth in mid-1944. Now, however, it was reverting to a water's-edge defense. (Willoughby's surmise erred to the extent it pictured a defense scheme anchored directly on the beaches rather than some distance inland.)

Another July message from Imperial General Headquarters stressed that tanks were the "back bone" of Allied warfare and a "cardinal point" of Ketsu must be the destruction of armored vehicles, by suicide attack if necessary. On July 16, intelligence analysts noted the first messages referring to a numerical subdivision of the overall Ketsu operation (that is, Ketsu Number 5, Ketsu Number 6, etc.). Since these particular references emerged in the context of the movement of air units to Shikoku from Kyushu, they suggested the numerical subdivisions were linked to specific geographic regions. A message broken on August 7 finally confirmed the exact geographic distribution of Ketsus 1–7.

While an understanding of overall Japanese strategic plans and operational concepts was important, the most critical questions involved the actual numbers and capabilities of the Homeland's defenders. The multiplication of Japanese ground forces in the Homeland comprises two separate but related stories: One is of the aggregate growth of forces; the second is of their distribution. As of January 1, 1945, American order-of-battle specialists had identified eleven divisions in the Homeland. No one doubted that the Japanese would substantially expand this number during 1945. But predicting the extent of this expansion was complicated, since the Japanese created additional formations both by assembling entirely new units at depots (effectively large training centers, of which fourteen existed in the Homeland) and by upgrading existing units (typically by amalgamating one of the Imperial Army's numerous separate brigades with other units). During all of 1944, the MIS believed the Japanese had formed thirty new divisions, but of these only nine were created in the Homeland, all at depots.

Willoughby's early estimates illustrate the gross degree to which Army analysts underestimated the growth of Japanese forces in the Homeland, which in turn goes far toward explaining why the Army displayed such sanguine attitudes about the prospects for the invasion of Japan in general and the assault on Kyushu in particular up to July. In March, two months before the Joint Chiefs of Staff ordered the invasion, Willoughby assessed Japanese ground strength in the Homeland at 937,000 men, of which only 466,000 were combat troops organized in eleven combat (field) and fourteen depot (training) divisions. Willoughby, in a small but emblematic dispute with the MIS, had credited the Japanese with the creation of twenty-nine new divisions in 1944 (one less than the MIS had), and he projected a like increase in combat divisions in the Home Islands in 1945. Thus, by the fall, Japan would have as many as thirty-four combat and fourteen depot divisions.

As the weeks passed by, the ambitious Japanese mobilization plan spawned more and more units, which radio intelligence gradually detected. In the middle of July, Willoughby estimated Japanese troop strength in the Homeland had virtually doubled since January 1 to 1,865,000. By the end of July, the MIS had identified twenty-seven new divisions in the Homeland since the beginning of the year. With Ultra detecting startling numbers of additional Imperial Army units weekly, by mid-August the MIS estimated that the Japanese were capable of forming yet another fifteen to twenty-nine divisions before the end of the year. This assessment concluded that the Japanese would have between fifty-four and seventy divisions by January 1, 1946—a considerable increase over the forty-five to forty-eight Willoughby had predicted in March 1945.

More alarming than the aggregate increase of new Japanese units was their actual distribution. The key area was Kyushu, the target of Olympic, the only scheduled invasion that carried Truman's sanction. At the beginning of 1945, the island was defended by only one field division, the 86th. By the time the President met with the Joint Chiefs of Staff on June 18, the Japanese had begun to reinforce Kyushu. Analysts believed correctly that the Japanese were redeploying the seasoned 25th and 57th Divisions from Manchuria to Kyushu. Just three days before the meeting with Truman, a radio message linked the 77th Division with Kyushu. Moreover, associations disclosed the presence of the Fifty-seventh Army headquarters and one other unidentified army headquarters. Thus, when Truman reviewed the invasion plans, Kyushu was known to be garrisoned by four divisions and two army headquarters.

In July came the deluge. Traffic analysis fingered a new brigade on Kyushu in early July, then intelligence officers found a fifth division (the 206th). By July 9, estimates of total Japanese strength on Kyushu had already reached the 350,000 total Marshall had predicted would be the maximum the invasion would face. By mid-July, Willoughby noted that the traffic had identified major units only suspected previously, providing "a revealing picture of the enemy's feverish activity." Most identifications came in a swath from central Honshu to Kyushu, indicating the Japanese assessment of Allied intentions. While Willoughby stated that the "outstanding trend" in the entire Empire was the buildup on the Tokyo plain, he also pointed to a "tremendous influx and organization of mobile combat units" pouring into Kyushu, with positive identification of six divisions, as well as code names for at least two unidentified major units plus an artillery command.

During the second half of July, Willoughby identified three more divisions, two brigades, and two or three tank brigades on Kyushu, but the MIS surpassed him. By July 21, a map in the Far East Summary positioned eight Japanese field divisions on Kyushu, seven in the Olympic target area. Then, on July 25, the Far East Summary printed a table representing a tremendous revelation:

Division	Code name	Code number	Estimated location
*141?	GO TO	22,050	Tokyo Area
*142	KO SEN	22,200	Sendai?
143	GO KO	22,250	Nagoya

Division	Code name	Code number	Estimated location
*144	GO HAN	22,300	Osaka?
*145	GO SHU	22,350	N. Kyushu?
146	GO NAN	22,400	Kyushu
147	GO HOKU	22,450	Tokyo Plain
150	GO CHO	22,500	S. Korea
*151	GO O	22,550	Tokyo?
*152	GO SAWA	22,600	Tokyo Plain
*153	GO KYO	22,650	??
*154	GO RO	22,700	Miyazaki
155	GO DO	22,750	Shikoku
156	GO SEI	22,800	Miyazaki
*157	GO HIRO	22,850	N. Honshu?
160	GO SEN	22,900	S. Korea

In order to avoid disclosing the actual name of units in radio communications, the Imperial Army employed a dual system of code names and code numbers. Washington sleuths had discovered a pattern of fifteen code names all involving *GO,* meaning "to defend," and a second character that denominated a geographic area (for example, GO CHO meant "Defend Korea"). These fifteen code names (as well as KO SEN) lined up neatly in ranks with a series of code numbers, at intervals of fifty except 22,100 and 22,150. Once parts of this "definite pattern" were confirmed, it was relatively simple to fill in the blanks. The units marked * represented identifications of no fewer than nine new Japanese divisions, a huge and shocking increase. Willoughby initially sniffed that he was withholding his concurrence, but by the end of the month he too had picked up these additional units in his report. In a somewhat similar pattern, the MIS located the Fortieth Army headquarters on Kyushu on July 27, but Willoughby again dallied with his agreement until the end of the month. The discovery of an additional army-level headquarters in southern Kyushu, with only one remaining in northern Kyushu, signaled the demise of a key premise of American planning: that the Imperial Army would be constrained to balance its defenses at both ends of the island.

By August 2, the MIS reported three Japanese armies, eleven divisions, one brigade, and one regiment on Kyushu. Total estimated Japanese strength stood at 545,000, including 445,000 ground-combat troops. Further, one more division was reported moving to Kyushu, and there had been indications of two other divisions on the island. Just five days later, the MIS officially picked up two more divisions on Kyushu, making a total of thirteen, nine of which sat close to invasion beaches in southern Kyushu. In addition, the MIS located on Kyushu two depot divisions, three tank brigades, one IMB, one amphibious brigade, and one raiding (airborne) regiment. According to this tally, 560,000 men, including 460,000 ground-combat troops, stood vigil on Kyushu. The total Japanese order of battle on the Home Islands now counted forty-two divisions. By August 10, the Joint Intelligence Committee (JIC) of the Joint Chiefs of Staff estimated that by October 15, the Home Islands would house fifty-six field divisions (including three armored), fourteen depot divisions, and army troops with a combined strength of 2.6 million men. Of these, Kyushu would be packed with 600,000 men in thirteen field divisions. In the final revision of this estimate on August 20, the total on Kyushu reached 625,000 men and fourteen field divisions. (This total was exactly correct as to field divisions, but the actual number of Japanese servicemen on Kyushu was much greater: 900,000.) At least nine of these divisions were in southern Kyushu, triple the original estimate, and the aggregate total of defenders far exceeded the 350,000 figure Marshall provided to Truman on June 18.

Ultra yielded excellent quantitative information on the Japanese order of battle, but the qualitative picture remained obscure. The three major intelligence summaries for this period produced in Washington and the Pacific contain virtually no direct evidence about the equipment and training of individual units. The best contemporary record of the state of Allied understanding of the capabilities of the units mobilized to confront an invasion resides in the report of the special Pacific Order of Battle Conference, which convened in Washington in August. The collaborative reports generated by this assembly of intelligence officers from many commands credited the Imperial Army with 4.5 million men, out of a total Japanese ground force numbering 5.7 million. The Japanese were expected to form between forty-two and fifty-six new divisions, the equivalent of three to five armored divisions, and many smaller units in the Homeland during 1945. While manpower imposed no limit on this expansion, the report credited the Japanese with equipment sufficient to fully outfit only thirty divisions. Ammunition, particularly for larger caliber weapons, was deemed tight. In terms of combat efficiency, the report concluded that the eleven divisions in Japan on January 1, 1945, and the sixteen formed from depots in Japan in the 140 to 160 series should "all be considered first line, fully equipped and trained," but those in the 200 or 300 series were substandard.*

Although the Japanese were expected to have eight million males between the ages of fifteen and forty-five fit for some form of military ser-

---

* Based on postwar information, this assessment missed the higher quality of the 200 series divisions and overrated the 140 to 160 and 300 series divisions.

vice, they lacked anything like the equipment for mass militias. Intelligence analysts correctly deduced that the special guard (policing) units could tender "fairly effective fighting units." The independent companies of reservists and the Patriotic Citizens Fighting Corps could render service functions, but their "haphazard" training and arms endowed them with minimal combat effectiveness, "other than of a guerrilla or suicide nature in defense of their home districts." The report commented pointedly that "in view of their previous indoctrination in fanatical patriotism, the Japanese forces probably will have high morale," except for units of Koreans or Formosans. The massive force of reservists would make a major contribution to Japan's defenses by releasing the maximum number of trained soldiers to face the invaders.

Meanwhile, radio intelligence had demonstrated that whatever their shortcomings in combat effectiveness, the Japanese expressly intended to transfer the Patriotic Citizens Fighting Corps into combat as needed. Tokyo explicitly tied the formation and mobilization of such masses to demands of its diplomats and attachés to provide detailed information on the defense of Berlin, the death of the high command, and the formation of home guard units. This was yet another sobering indication of Japanese intentions to fight to the end.

Allied intelligence confirmed the obvious: Japan was weakest at sea. Having started the war as the third largest fleet in the world, the remnants of the Imperial Navy made a last desperate sortie in early April when the superbattleship *Yamato* and most of her crew perished in a suicide mission to defend Okinawa. Thereafter, the Imperial Navy did what any institution does in such circumstances: It reorganized. Admiral Soemu Toyoda became the supreme commander of the combined naval forces. In a commentary reprinted in the Far East Summary, senior American naval intelligence officers in Washington saw the elevation of Toyoda and his deputy, Admiral Jisaburo Ozawa, as freighted with political significance. This pair not only would lead a "toughened and more aggressive naval high command" but also would work well with more "extremist" Army officers (such as Hata and Sugiyama). This shift suggested more accord between the Army and Navy and "undoubtedly" strengthened the hand of those who wished to continue the war.

"On the eve of [Ketsu-Go]," Toyoda remarked in a July 29 general exhortation to his sailors, "my fondest hopes have been strengthened by the fact that we have been able to perfect our preparations and in the face of the enemy's determination to reduce this effective strength." All hands, he said, must contribute the utmost cooperation in this "finish fight," and when the enemy attacked, air, sea, and ground units must be concentrated

Plan for Operation Olympic
and Actual Japanese Dispositions as of August 1945

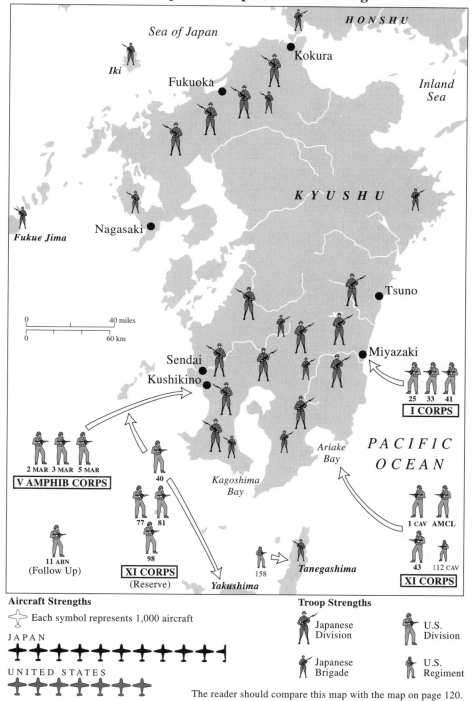

Aircraft Strengths

Each symbol represents 1,000 aircraft

JAPAN

UNITED STATES

Troop Strengths

Japanese Division

Japanese Brigade

U.S. Division

U.S. Regiment

The reader should compare this map with the map on page 120.

"on the threatened point and defeat and destroy the enemy force." While such messages indicated that Toyoda possessed firm resolve, they also confirmed the paucity of his material resources. When he took command in late April, the Imperial Navy's estimated operational resources included two battleships, two carriers (sans air groups), three cruisers, and thirty-four destroyers. By June, however, a message disclosed fuel oil allocations to units no larger than destroyers, thus implying the larger warships were nonoperational. After Halsey's strikes in July and August, CINCPAC projected the total operational units in home waters at one light carrier, twenty-nine destroyers, and forty-two submarines. Of these forces, the most significant was the Surface Forward Force of about sixteen destroyers, largely, if not all, fitted as *Kaiten* carriers.

A series of intercepts disclosed to American intelligence officers a fairly accurate portrait of the Imperial Navy's attempts to conjure up a host of diminutive suicide vehicles: midget submarines, *Kaiten,* and various suicide boats. One such message, for example, showed production of 388 torpedoes for midget submarines, of which 352 were earmarked for Kyushu. The sinking of the *Underhill* by a *Kaiten* prompted naval intelligence to warn that these weapons, believed to total 1,000, posed a "deadly threat to Allied surface craft." On the other hand, these devices possessed far less inherent capacity for dispersal than aircraft, and decoded messages gave fairly accurate locations for all their bases.

Messages also illustrated other ways in which the Imperial Navy was bracing to actively partake in the Ketsu operation. One series demonstrated the organization of surplus naval personnel into ground combat units. Another series disclosed Japanese plans to lay mines along the coast of Kyushu at Tachibana, Ariake, and Kagoshima bays, as well as off Miyazaki, thus demonstrating an acute assessment of probable American landing sites. Still another series disclosed requests for volunteers (68 officers and 570 men) of "high physical condition and outstanding morale." These were tied to the formation of the Water's Edge Surprise Attack Force. (See Chapter 12.)

Overall, the estimates composed in Washington and the two theater commands ran closely in accord as to Japanese forces ashore and afloat, but they diverged sharply on Japanese air capabilities. In his very first estimate in March 1945, Willoughby predicted that total Japanese airpower to oppose Downfall would number only 2,500 aircraft. The estimate appended to MacArthur's Downfall order on May 28 allowed for total Japanese aviation strength on X-Day of only 2,500 to 3,000 aircraft.

Radical but by no means equal alterations in all projections occurred between June and August. One reason for the universally acknowledged increase in Japanese aircraft strength was the effect of what one report called Japan's "extreme conservation" strategy, whereby aircraft were preserved simply by keeping them in widely dispersed and concealed hiding places on the ground, heavily protected by antiaircraft guns. One intercepted message, for example, contained orders from the 72nd Air Flotilla to subordinate units demanding that aircraft be dispersed "at least" three kilometers from airfields. A CINCPAC intelligence summary noted that photographs taken during July carrier strikes revealed planes concealed in villages, cemeteries, and wooded areas as far as five miles from airfields. A mid-July Imperial Army message touted the success of the dispersal and concealment program.

The more fundamental reason for the massive increase in Japanese aircraft strength, however, was a basic decision to use Japan's entire air force to oppose an initial invasion of the Homeland. American intelligence analysts gradually realized that the Japanese lacked plans for any operations beyond confronting an invasion, had abandoned training of new aircrew, and were pressing forward energetically to equip training planes for suicide attacks, organize them into units, and deploy them to prepared and concealed bases within range of expected invasion sites. This raised disturbing possibilities. An early estimate credited the Japanese air forces with 7,265 aircraft in a training role, and thus available for kamikaze missions, including 1,110 fairly modern and capable "combat type" planes used for advanced operational training.

Ultra identified three major Imperial Navy air commands involved in the kamikaze buildup. One order directed the 10th Air Flotilla, originally a training command, to build ten airfields in central Honshu, each fitted with fifty concealed dispersal sites. The 12th Air Flotilla, another former training unit with a strength in late June of 940 aircraft, was deployed to eighteen bases, nearly all on Kyushu. The 13th Air Flotilla, with a strength of 600 aircraft, occupied bases on Kyushu, Shikoku, and western Honshu.

By late July, Willoughby credited the Imperial Navy with 2,660 suicide training planes; he placed 775 of these on Kyushu and 70 percent between Tokyo and Kyushu. A message from the 13th Air Flotilla on July 31 asking for photographs of American troop transports for training suicide-attack aircrews resolved any lingering doubts about the prime targets of these aircraft. Other confirming messages contained references to the suitability of certain types of bombs for attacking troopships. Numerous messages identified and located at least two hundred previously unknown concealed air bases. As to tactics, messages disclosed that the Imperial Navy intended to make interception of its kamikazes as difficult as possible by using searchlight beams as beacons to guide suicide planes in night attacks. The Imperial Navy was not neglecting its hundreds of conventional aircraft, and messages documented intense training for conventional nighttime torpedo-plane attacks.

While messages linked the Sixth Air Army (headquartered at Fukuoka) with the Second General Army, and the First Air Army with the First General Army, initially Ultra offered little information on the numbers, organization, and intentions of Imperial Army aviation units. In early June, the use of the designator *TO* for suicide units was noted and matched to a January 1945 message indicating intentions to equip each TO unit with ten aircraft. As the weeks went by, Ultra yielded more and more information, such that by August 9, analysts credited the Imperial Army with about 205 TO units, eighty outfitted with operational types and the remaining 125 with trainers. It was also recognized then that the Imperial Army was preparing to manufacture aircraft in Manchuria, out of range of American bombers, and was withdrawing some tactical units to the continent for training and safety.

Messages also disclosed significant problems the Japanese faced with aviation units. The senior Imperial Navy commander acknowledged a drop in production due to bombing, as well as an "extremely constricted" aircraft-fuel situation. Summer messages disclosed special efforts to transport aviation-grade gasoline to Japan, cuts in fuel allocations, and preoccupation with fuel-conservation efforts, including use of alcohol fuel and a program to produce aviation-grade combustibles from pine-root oil. By late July, a CINCPAC summary observed that the Japanese aviation-fuel situation "showed no signs of becoming less acute." By August, allocations were down 31 percent from June figures. Traffic from more senior Japanese units disclosed that bomb damage to manufacturing plants had scotched plans to fit suicide planes with radios, while traffic from lower units carried complaints about engine malfunctions. Meanwhile, attacks on base facilities prompted the Japanese to temporarily abandon use of southern Kyushu airfields. Another message revealed that it took ten hours to extract concealed suicide trainers from their hiding places and launch them on Shikoku, which prompted CINCPAC analysts to comment that dispersal and concealment would make it more difficult for the Japanese to launch coordinated attacks.

There were also mixed indications of quantity and quality problems with aircrews. The Imperial Army ordered nine hundred flying personnel transferred from southern areas to the Homeland by August 31 for urgent use as replacement pilots. One Imperial Army suicide-unit commander complained that his pilots needed thirty hours of flight per month to stay proficient. A status report on three Imperial Navy fighter groups in the Homeland showed that only 32 percent of pilots qualified for daylight interception and that 51 percent of fighters were operational. There were slightly fewer qualified pilots than operational aircraft. During July, however, there was also an indication that aviation trainees were being reassigned to other duties, thereby suggesting that there was an excess of personnel to man available suicide trainers.

On the other hand, by late June, a CINCPAC intelligence summary, citing MIS figures, scoffed that a slackening bombing effort was permitting the Japanese to continue near-normal production levels, estimated to run at 1,490 combat aircraft per month, which promised an increase in Japanese air strength. While little evidence pointed to Japanese deployment of jet aircraft, Ultra betrayed the program to manufacture a modified version of the *baka* rocket bombs (the Model 43 Cherry Blossom) for use against the invasion fleet.

The mass conversion of training units and assets to the suicide role forced each intelligence producer to reexamine its estimate of Japanese air strength. An MIS estimate of Japanese air strength on May 10 provides a benchmark. As of that date, total Japanese air strength was thought to rest at 3,391, but of these only 1,247 constituted actual operational fighters and bombers. By June 14, however, the MIS acknowledged that the distinction between tactical and training units "has largely broken down," and adjustments began. Willoughby admitted that use of Imperial Navy training planes alone could add four thousand aircraft to combat rolls, though he deprecated their combat effectiveness and commented that numbers "have ceased to be the measure of the enemy's air capability." Washington finessed this quandary by incorporating only the tactical aircraft assigned to training units, not the elementary or advanced training planes, into estimates of Japanese air strength. This boosted the MIS total to 4,862. In late June, the new Joint Army-Navy Committee on the Japanese Air Forces still believed that losses exceeded production by about 250 aircraft per month, thus leading to the comforting projection that Japanese air strength would fall to around four thousand by October or November. Strict Japanese adherence to conservation policies, however, forced even these skeptics to admit that Japanese strength was actually rising in July; by August 9, their estimate stood at 5,911.

Meanwhile, other intelligence sources came into play. Aerial photographic coverage of all 243 known airfields in the Home Islands (excluding twenty-two minor ones) was completed at the end of the first week of July, thus providing the first visual count of aircraft. The fruits of this effort compared with Ultra as follows:

	Aircraft Photographed	Ultra Estimate		
		Total	*Combat*	*Training*
Tokyo	3,757	2,890	1,440	1,450
Nagoya-Osaka	2,446	2,090	890	1,200
Kure-Kyushu	1,807	1,885	1,005	880
Totals	8,010	6,865	3,335	3,530

By now, Willoughby recognized that his projections for Japanese air strength were low. While the staggered photography led to some duplication, overall Willoughby found these images confirmed the higher Ultra estimates, after deduction of transport and miscellaneous types. He allowed that the Japanese conservation policy would permit the numbers to increase still more over the next few months, despite a falling rate of production.

The intelligence analysts at CINCPAC differed markedly from the MIS and Willoughby over both the numerical strength and the threat posed by Japanese airpower. The comparison of the aerial photography with Ultra generated this commentary at CINCPAC:

It is interest[ing] to note that, of this figure [8,010], 40% were combat-types, and 45% were trainer-type aircraft which must be considered as available for combat use as suicide planes in the KETSU Operations. MIS, War Department, estimates Japanese production of trainer-type aircraft as at least 550 per month, and with the current plane hoarding policy, the number of Japanese trainer planes available for KETSU Operations can be expected to increase unless large numbers can be destroyed by air attacks on the fields where they are dispersed.

Beginning in a table published first on July 16, CINCPAC incorporated all trainers in its figures for Japanese air strength. With this action, CINCPAC refused to agree with the MIS and Willoughby that the threat of suicide training planes was negligible. Accordingly, the July 16 CINCPAC recapitulation figured total enemy air strength at 11,190, of which 8,750 were in the Japan-Korea region and thus available for Homeland defense. By the time the last table in this series was published on August 13, total Japanese air strength in CINCPAC's eyes stood at 11,930, of which 10,290 were available for Homeland defense. Of those available for the Ketsu operations, 4,880 were combat types and 5,410 were trainers.

Given this sharp split between the Army and the Navy, the opinion of a new entrant among the intelligence authorities, General Spaatz's United

States Army Strategic Air Forces headquarters, is significant. Spaatz's intelligence officer came down with CINCPAC, placing total Japanese aviation strength by August 10 at 10,210.

This controversy between the Army and Navy extended into the postwar debate over the prospects for Olympic. The Navy found persuasive evidence of the lethal capabilities of such aircraft in the sinking of the destroyer *Callaghan* with forty-seven of her crew on the night of July 28–29 off Okinawa. In this small skirmish, a handful of biplane twin-float Japanese seaplanes, similar or even inferior to the average training plane, overwhelmed the destroyer. The Navy ensured that this episode reverberated all the way to the President. The July 30 White House Map Room daily summary informed Truman that the "very maneuverable" and expertly piloted but "flimsy" Japanese planes of "wood and fabric with some plywood" construction sank the destroyer. Moreover, the detailed account of the incident underscored how the old-fashioned construction of such aircraft degraded the performance of key radars: Warning radar had picked up the aircraft belatedly, and gunfire proved ineffective because the supersecret VT-fused (for Variable Time, a code reference to the miniature radar-triggering device) projectiles were ineffective. This report parroted closely the analysis at CINCPAC, which noted the planes were "probably obsolete or trainer planes." If such aircraft could sink a well-armed, fast, and maneuverable warship, they clearly posed a severe danger to a lightly armed, slow, and unwieldy troop transport.

The Upheaval Begins

The intelligence revelations about Japanese preparations on Kyushu emerging in mid-July transmitted powerful shock waves both in the Pacific and in Washington. On July 29, Willoughby published "Amendment 1" to his April 25 "G-2 Estimate of the Enemy Situation with Respect to Kyushu." He noted first that the April estimate allowed for the Japanese capability to deploy six divisions on Kyushu, with the potential to deploy ten. "These [six] divisions have since made their appearance, as predicted," he observed, "and the end is not in sight." If not checked, this threatened "to grow to [the] point where we attack on a ratio of one (1) to one (1) which is not the recipe for victory." At Sixth Army Headquarters, Krueger's intelligence staff issued an estimate on August 1 that noted the Japanese had the equivalent of seven divisions in southern Kyushu as of July 21 and predicted that ten or eleven would await the landings. Krueger's intelligence chief shortly projected that Japanese strength on

X-Day would total 680,000, a number that almost matched the current troop list for Olympic and made Willoughby's one-to-one ratio appear all too real.

Ultra disclosures could serve only to reinforce Admiral Nimitz in the view he expressed as early as May 25: Olympic was unwise. On June 4, a weekly intelligence summary at CINCPAC noted the Japanese were "definitely anticipating [an American] invasion of Kyushu," with top priority being given to the southern part of the island. By June 18, the weekly summary noted the Japanese had drafted a priority list for defensive installations, with northern and southern Kyushu and the Tokyo plain in the top positions. The calendar barely showed July when a CINCPAC estimate declared flatly that Kyushu "has been receiving the enemy's most concentrated attention in troop reinforcement and build-up of defenses against invasion." Nimitz clearly implied that he remained very pessimistic about the prospects for an invasion of Kyushu in an August 3 message to King concerning the proposed transfer of one of his key subordinates, Rear Admiral Forrest Sherman. Nimitz insisted that Sherman must remain at CINCPAC Headquarters until the completion of planning for Olympic, but he could then be released because Olympic "might drag indefinitely."

Olympic also seemed in doubt to senior staff officers of the Joint Chiefs of Staff. "There is every indication that the Japanese have been giving the highest priority to the defense of Kyushu and particularly to southern Kyushu," noted the JIC in an early August report, "Defensive Preparations in Japan." On the Japanese priority list, southern Kyushu was followed by Shikoku, northern Kyushu, and the Kanto plain. Fully anticipating the destruction of their communication lines, the Japanese were toiling relentlessly to "concentrate the greatest part of the forces to be used for the defense of these vital areas in close proximity to the most threatened points of probable Allied assault." By the JIC recapitulation, from early 1945 Japanese ground strength on Kyushu had swelled from about 150,000 troops, 75 percent on the north end of the island, to about 545,000 men, 60 percent in the southern part of the island.

The JIC emphasized the massive buildup of Japanese air strength, particularly kamikazes. Fifty special bases for suicide planes had been identified on Kyushu, Shikoku, and Honshu, within range of Olympic. Deployment of conventional combat planes also showed tactical emphasis on Kyushu-Shikoku. The report noted the creation of an array of aquatic suicide vehicles and their deployment, as well as the laying of mines, pointing to high priority for Kyushu.

The report also highlighted a buildup on Shikoku from no active divisions at the start of the year to four active and one depot division, with support troops totaling about 150,000 men. The air deployment that covered Kyushu also substantially covered Shikoku. While the Japanese clearly appeared to believe that the initial assault would come in the south, they had not neglected the Kanto plain. There, strength had burgeoned from four active and three depot divisions (with other troops totaling 300,000 men) to a total of nine active divisions (one armored), three depot divisions, and other troops, for a total of 560,000. Aircraft and suicide-craft deployment, however, notably trailed that on Kyushu.

MacArthur's and Nimitz's intelligence staffs and the JIC all could only gather and analyze data; policy making rested elsewhere. But as senior American leaders including Marshall, King, MacArthur, and Nimitz turned to face the implications of the Ultra revelations about Kyushu, the whole context of events was in turmoil. As the intelligence picture for the invasion underwent upheaval, Magic also disclosed significant developments on the diplomatic front, Allied leaders issued the Potsdam Declaration to set forth the terms of unconditional surrender, atomic bombs were unleashed, and the Soviet Union intervened in the war. The ways in which this cataract of events severely buffeted leaders on both sides during the last two months of the war are inseparable from the debate over the fate and prospects of Olympic.

14

Unconditional Surrender
and Magic

"We are unable to consent to it under any circumstances whatever"

Unconditional Surrender

Just as Ultra betrayed the startling picture of burgeoning Japanese forces massed to defend Kyushu, the issue of "defining" or modifying the demand for unconditional surrender came to a head. Both Churchill at Yalta in February 1945 and the Joint Chiefs of Staff in April had urged that the Japanese be apprised of what it entailed. During the June 18 meeting with the Joint Chiefs of Staff to review plans to invade Japan, Secretary of War Henry L. Stimson and Assistant Secretary of War John J. McCloy raised the prospect of using means other than arms to secure Japan's capitulation, and the minutes note that Truman replied at one point that this was being worked on "all the time."

In fact, that very morning Truman had discussed with Acting Secretary of State Joseph C. Grew a diplomatic approach that Grew hoped might end the war. Grew's strategy involved fashioning a definition of *unconditional surrender* that incorporated a guarantee to the Japanese of preservation of the Imperial system and the current incumbent. In his estimation, this would deal a trump card to peace advocates within Japan who might then terminate the war before an invasion. Grew's aspirations extended well beyond an immediate end to the war, and others shared his hopes. How policy makers viewed changing or standing pat on "unconditional surrender" depended heavily on how they saw the ramifications.

By the summer of 1945, the policy of unconditional surrender, enunciated at Casablanca in 1943, reiterated often thereafter, and enforced upon

Germany represented not only the official war aim but also the goal to which the American populace subscribed overwhelmingly. In a June 1, 1945, poll, Americans favored prosecuting the war into the Homeland with its attendant costs over yielding to a compromise peace by a margin of nearly nine to one. Moreover, a May poll had disclosed that a very large majority of Americans held the Emperor personally responsible for the war. When asked to pass on his fate, 33 percent favored execution, 17 percent trial, 11 percent imprisonment, and 9 percent exile. Only 4 percent viewed him as a figurehead, and an almost imperceptible 3 percent viewed him as a potential asset in managing Japan after the war. No wonder, then, that Truman emphasized in his memoirs that in his address to Congress only four days after becoming president, "when I reaffirmed the policy of unconditional surrender, the chamber rose to its feet."

Joseph Grew was a career diplomat and the government's preeminent Japan specialist. He believed he possessed special insight from his "intimate experience with Japanese thinking and psychology." That insight bred the conviction that Japanese surrender was "highly unlikely" without a provision for retaining "the present dynasty." Grew further foresaw the postwar Soviet-American rivalry as leading to a new conflict. ("A future war with Soviet Russia is as certain as anything in the world can be certain," he remarked once.) He believed that Japan might be an important asset for America in such a confrontation.

The role of the Emperor was central in this scenario. If the Emperor's authority could facilitate terminating the war before Soviet entry, an important advantage could be seized. Further, if America could exercise its occupation via Japanese authorities acting under the aegis of the Emperor, both the need for massive American forces or the potential complications and frustrations of a shared occupation with other Allies could be avoided. Grew's vision thus encompassed the possibility of halting the war without an invasion.

Grew was not alone among high officials in perceiving virtue in the retention of the Emperor or the Imperial system. The retentionists essentially believed that all significant Japanese decision makers must clearly see their nation's utter defeat and that "moderates" within this group were struggling to end the war. But, since all Japanese revered the Emperor's unique cultural and religious status, in the words of historian Robert J. Maddox, "the unconditional surrender formula undermined the peace advocates [in Japan] because it guaranteed neither Hirohito's personal inviolability nor continuation of the imperial system," the minimal conditions the "peace" advocates could accept.

The retentionists argued that such guarantees could secure the United

States more than just a peace agreement with Tokyo. The authority of the Emperor might be the only force capable of ensuring the surrender of Japan's far-flung legions—no small matter since this involved over two million armed Japanese scattered across a vast expanse of the globe. The Emperor could also serve to stabilize a demoralized postwar Japan and legitimize Japanese officials acting at the behest of occupation authorities. Retentionists tended to minimize the possibility of a revanchist Japan striking again in the near future on the grounds that the severity of the defeat would discredit the militarist forces who had led her astray. They also posited that any attempt to depose the incumbent Emperor, much less to jettison the whole Imperial system, would embitter the Japanese, make the occupation far more difficult to enforce, and quite possibly plant the seeds for future conflict.

The opposite camp, the abolitionists, regarded Grew's arguments as a siren song guaranteed to lure America to folly. Fundamentally, abolitionists viewed Japanese militarism and the warrior system as rooted in the Imperial system; the two could not be sundered. A failure to extirpate the Imperial system would assure an eventual regrowth of a political culture bent on conquest. Of so-called Japanese moderates, one typical abolitionist text observed that they "do not materially differ in their national ambitions, their idea of Japanese destiny, and their ruthlessness from the so-called militarists." Assistant Secretaries of State Dean Acheson and Archibald MacLeish and former Secretary of State Cordell Hull were among those most closely identified with this view.

Given the aura surrounding the Roosevelt legacy of unconditional surrender, it would have taken a powerful argument, backed by firm evidence—not speculation—about Japanese internal political dynamics, and supported by a strong majority of senior advisers to sway Truman. None of these prerequisites transpired. Instead, events cast the cleavages within the administration in deep relief. In late May, Grew pressed for modification of the unconditional-surrender formula and received some encouragement in a meeting with Truman on May 28 when the President, reported Grew, "said that he was interested in what I said because his own thoughts had been following the same line." Truman, however, ordered Grew to discuss the proposal with the service secretaries and chiefs of staff.

Grew wasted no time and scheduled the meeting for the very next day. There, Stimson, Marshall, and James Forrestal expressed agreement with the concept in principle but challenged the timing. Ostensibly, they articulated concern that Japanese militarists would seize upon an initiative in the midst of the bloody Okinawa campaign as proof of crumbling American resolve. In his diary, Stimson noted that "the real feature that would govern the situation" was the atomic bomb, a supreme secret that could not be mentioned to all of those present. Moreover, Elmer Davis, head of the Office of War Information, objected passionately that Grew's proposal would be interpreted domestically as opening the door to a negotiated settlement. It is noteworthy that the most outspoken opposition emanated from Davis, Acheson, and MacLeish, all of whom held portfolios responsible for monitoring public and congressional attitudes.

Grew reported his failure to secure agreement to his proposal to Truman on May 30. That same day, Truman learned that another important constituency remained fervently committed to unconditional surrender. The closer the defeat of Germany approached, the more diplomatic rather than military issues came to the center of Soviet-American relations. As the Red Army overran central Europe, it unpacked from its baggage client governments. Quite apart from any matter of principle enunciated in the Atlantic Charter about granting peoples the right to freely choose their governments, the President also faced the important domestic consideration that many of these peoples had vocal kin within the American electorate. Foremost among them were the Poles.

The details of the Polish dispute are beyond the scope of this work, but the conflict already bubbled near or at a boil when President Roosevelt died. While Stimson and Marshall counseled caution, not least because of the perceived need for Soviet intervention against Japan, the crudity of Soviet actions to impose control animated advisers who persuaded Truman to take a strong stand. But after confrontation failed, Truman shifted to a more conciliatory approach. He dispatched Harry Hopkins to Moscow to defuse the crisis and to set up the summit conference with Stalin and Churchill that ultimately occurred in July at Potsdam. Hopkins, a symbol of Soviet-American cooperation, also probed for the Soviet dictator's position on entering the Pacific war. On May 29 and 30, Hopkins relayed Stalin's contemporaneous pledge to have Soviet forces ready in Manchuria by August 8. The American envoy also forwarded Stalin's report of Japanese peace feelers and conveyed the Soviet dictator's strong commitment to unconditional surrender. But Hopkins's cables also divulged Stalin's expectation that "Russia will share in the actual occupation of Japan."

Facing this alarming specter, Grew renewed his effort to have the United States issue a statement upon the conclusion of the Okinawa campaign modifying unconditional surrender. Grew presented a draft to Truman on the morning of June 18. Truman again appeared receptive to such a statement, but he indicated that it should appear as part of the fruit of the upcoming Potsdam conference.

Another cabinet officer advocating a modified unconditional surrender was Secretary of War Stimson. Unlike Grew, Stimson mixed conciliatory inducement with the unmistakable outlines of an ultimatum, timed to be early enough to forestall invasion but contemporaneous with punishing conventional and perhaps atomic bombing. Stimson prepared the ground by discussing a draft version with his colleagues, but he detoured around a formal approval process, probably for fear that opponents would leak to the public word that the administration was contemplating any softening of unconditional surrender. Stimson submitted a memorandum, "Proposed Program for Japan," to Truman on July 2. After forecasting that a fight to the end with Japan would be even bitterer than the endgame in Germany, Stimson characterized his plan as "an alternative to such forceful occupation of Japan which will secure us the equivalent of an unconditional surrender of her armed forces." He proposed an ultimatum to "warn of what is to come and [to provide a] definite opportunity to capitulate." Stimson also advised that a warning of Soviet intervention, if used, must come before the "Russian attack if actual" had "progressed too far." He alluded to mentioning the atomic bomb—once it was proven.

The Secretary of War drew liberally from Grew's array of inducements and included an explicit promise that the Japanese would be permitted to retain the throne. He stressed his confidence in Japan's reconstruction "as a responsible member of the family of nations" and pointedly observed, "her liberal leaders (although now submerged by the terrorists)" had "yielded only at the point of the pistol and, so far as I am aware, their liberal attitude has not been personally subverted in the way which was so general in Germany." But Stimson's draft had an exceedingly stern tone, warning of utter devastation and announcing: "Following are our terms. We shall not deviate from them. They may be accepted or not. There are no alternatives."

Stimson's draft soldiered on among the working papers for the American delegation headed for Potsdam. This delegation, which conspicuously lacked specialists on Japan, included Stimson and the new Secretary of State, James F. Byrnes, a man who retained political ambitions and who was keenly attuned to public opinion. With his State Department advisers sharply split on the issue of tampering with unconditional surrender, Byrnes sought counsel from Cordell Hull. By telephone, the former Secretary of State said he found that Stimson's draft sounded "too much like appeasement." In a following memorandum, he warned that prospects for acceptance by Japan were uncertain and that its failure would heartily encourage militarists at the cost of "terrible political repercussions" at home.

At Potsdam, this issue emerged first in the strategy sessions of the Combined Chiefs of Staff. The American and British chiefs formally reported to Truman and Prime Minister Churchill that the defeat of the Japanese armed forces in the Homeland "will establish the optimum prospect of capitulation by Japanese forces outside the main Japanese islands," but they could not guarantee that this would necessarily "obviate the necessity of defeating Japanese forces elsewhere." Thus, the specter of the fearsome task of the piecemeal annihilation of Japanese forces scattered all across Asia and the Pacific remained alive. Moreover, an intelligence estimate propounded the view to the Combined Chiefs that

> for a surrender to be acceptable to the Japanese Army it would be necessary for the military leaders to believe that it would not entail discrediting the warrior tradition and that it would permit the ultimate resurgence of a military in Japan.

Ending the war with Japan in this posture was unacceptable to any Allied policy maker. Sir Alan Brooke, speaking for the British chiefs, questioned whether "there might be some advantage in trying to explain [unconditional surrender] to the Japanese in a manner which would ensure that the war was not unduly prolonged in outlying areas." The explanation, Brooke ventured, might include preservation of the throne. Admiral William Leahy interjected that this was a political question and that it would be helpful if Churchill raised this with Truman.

The meeting the next day of the Joint Chiefs of Staff alone, without their British counterparts, again addressed the issue of securing the compliance of outlying Japanese garrisons with a surrender. Marshall stated:

> From a purely military point of view the attitude of the Joint Chiefs of Staff should be that nothing should be done prior to the termination of hostilities that would indicate the removal of the Emperor of Japan, since his continuation in office might influence the cessation of hostilities in areas outside Japan proper.

The minutes of this session show that the Joint Chiefs of Staff recognized a fine distinction between this position and recommending that the United States promise to retain the throne and its incumbent. The former involved military considerations and thus was a legitimate subject for their counsel to the President; the latter they viewed as a political matter beyond their competence. Leahy reported that consideration was being given on "a political level" to removal of the explicit promise in the draft ultimatum that the Japanese people could retain the throne. The "political level" was, of course, the President and Secretary of State Byrnes.

The upshot of this meeting was a memorandum to the President recommending changes in the proposed declaration. The memorandum argued that the language in the Stimson draft that allowed for the establishment of "a constitutional monarchy under the present dynasty" housed dangerous ambiguity. It was susceptible to a reading either that the United Nations was preparing to "depose or execute the present Emperor and install some other member of the Imperial family" or that it was "a commitment to continue the institution of the Emperor and Emperor worship." In place of these phrases, the Joint Chiefs of Staff proposed language conforming to the Atlantic Charter: "Subject to suitable guarantees against further acts of aggression, the Japanese people will be free to choose their own form of government." Stimson uneasily added his concurrence to this change and similar verbiage became part of the Potsdam Declaration issued on July 26.*

While formal deliberation of the modification of unconditional surrender culminated in the Potsdam Declaration, in a separate effort Captain Ellis M. Zacharias maneuvered a plan through the Navy Department and then secured White House approval for "a strategic plan to effect the occupation of Japan" without invasion. Zacharias believed that schisms between the Imperial Army and Navy had spawned a peace faction in the Japanese government centered on disgruntled naval leaders who could induce surrender before an invasion. To activate this faction, Zacharias, a fluent Japanese linguist, intended to beam personal broadcasts as an official spokesman for the United States government directly at this group. He further aimed to energize them by defining unconditional surrender as nothing more than the "complete cession of hostilities and yielding of arms" and "emphasize with authority what we will not do."

Once he got his commission in hand, however, Zacharias slipped the leash of official policy. In a radio broadcast to Japan on July 7, he blandished his rogue interpretation of American policy that unconditional surrender represented only "a technical term which refers to the form in which hostilities are terminated," while "the exact conditions of peace are something to be settled in the future." He coupled this with the observation that the Atlantic Charter guaranteed peoples the right to choose their own form of government. In an anonymous but much noted letter to *The Wash-*

---

* One of the fundamental tenets held by critics of Truman is that he succumbed to the blandishments of Byrnes and removed the original language from Stimson's draft against the virtually unanimous advice of his senior advisers. This memorandum from the Joint Chiefs, long of record but customarily ignored by critics, illustrates the weakness of this charge.

ington Post on July 17, Zacharias beckoned the Japanese government to simply ask through diplomatic channels "whether or not unconditional surrender goes beyond the conditions" already set forth by the President. He specifically noted that this included the status of the Emperor. Clearly, the explicit or implicit promises in these broadcasts undercut American policy.

Magic

Much is known and much more has been made of the internal American debate over the unconditional-surrender policy and the Zacharias broadcasts. But this focus misses the central reality that the ultimate decision as to when and how the war would end rested with Japan's leaders. Understanding this central reality of the end of the Pacific war requires an examination of the Magic intercepts and the evidence from Japan.

Prior to mid-July, Magic had exposed the want of authority of any Japanese peace entrepreneur overseas and the lack of any diplomatic initiative by the Japanese government. The one exception was a series of talks between former Premier Hirota and Soviet Ambassador Malik in Tokyo that aimed at opening negotiations with the Soviets. In Foreign Minister Togo's reports to Ambassador Sato in Moscow, it was clear that these approaches elicited no Soviet interest, even in Hirota's scarcely veiled offer of an alliance.

On June 30, Togo wired Sato a proposal to present to Soviet Foreign Minister Molotov that essentially aimed to establish "firm and lasting relations of friendship . . . [so that] they shall both cooperate in the maintenance of peace in East Asia." As bargaining chips, Togo laid on the table the neutralization of Manchuria, renunciation of fishery rights (provided the Soviets supplied Japan with oil), and an open-ended invitation for discussion of "any matter which the Russians would like to bring up." Togo admonished Sato to learn and report the Soviet reaction "with all possible speed, if possible by the beginning of July." Sato saw no prospect for success of the initiative and said so, but Togo's peremptory orders compelled him to meet with Molotov on July 11. As Sato predicted, the Soviet foreign minister swirled to the tunes of diplomatic evasion.

With this initiative at a stalemate, on July 11 Togo radically upped the stakes in a radio cable to Sato. This message and all those that follow were intercepted and deciphered within hours by Allied code breakers. Intelligence officers then quoted these exchanges in detail in the Magic Diplomatic Summary. This system was so efficient that American policy makers sometimes actually perused the dispatches before they had reached their intended Japanese recipients. The quoted excerpts hereafter are exactly as they appeared in the Magic Diplomatic Summary and thus are precisely as they appeared before key American policy makers. Togo notified Sato that:

> We are now secretly giving consideration to termination of the war because of the pressing situation which confronts Japan both at home and abroad. Therefore, when you have your interview with Molotov . . . you should not confine yourself to the objective of a rapprochement between Russia and Japan but should also sound him out on the extent to which it is possible to make use of Russia in ending the war. . . .
>
> While we naturally hope[d] to obtain a treaty through negotiations between Hirota and Malik, those talks are also intended to find out the extent to which it is possible to make use of Russia in ending the war.
>
> We should like to know the views of the Russian government on this subject with all haste. . . .
>
> While there is no question of your skill, please be careful in your conference to avoid giving the impression that our plan is [to] make use of the Russians in ending the war.

Later that same day, Togo sent another dispatch:

> Despite the last statement in my previous message, it would appear suitable to make clear to the Russians our general attitude with regard to termination of the war. Therefore, please tell them that:
>
> "We consider the maintenance of peace in East Asia to be one aspect of the maintenance of world peace. Accordingly, Japan—as a proposal for ending the war and because of her concern for the establishment and maintenance of lasting peace—has absolutely no ideas of annexing or holding the territories occupied as a result of the war."

Before July 12 passed, Togo was on the air again with a "Very Urgent" cable:

> I have not yet received a wire about your interview with Molotov. Accordingly, though it may smack a little of attacking without sufficient reconnaissance, we think it would be appropriate to go a step further on this occasion and, before the opening of the Three Power [i.e., Potsdam] Conference, inform the Russians of the Imperial will concerning the ending of the war. We should, therefore, like you to present this matter to Molotov in the following terms:
>
> His Majesty the Emperor, mindful of the fact that the present war daily brings greater evil and sacrifice upon the peoples of all the belligerent powers, desires from his heart that it may be quickly terminated. But so long as

England and the United States insist upon unconditional surrender the Japanese Empire has no alternative but to fight on with all its strength for the honor and existence of the Motherland. His Majesty is deeply reluctant to have any further blood lost among the people on both sides, and it is his desire, for the welfare of humanity, to restore peace with all possible speed. . . .

It is the Emperor's private intention to send Prince Konoe to Moscow as a Special Envoy with a letter from him containing the statements given above. Please inform Molotov of this and get the Russians' consent to having the party enter the country. . . .

Although it will be impossible to have this delegation get there before the big men in Moscow leave for the Three Power Conference, we must arrange for a meeting immediately after their return. Accordingly, I should like to have the trip made by plane, if possible.

The significance of this message and a handful of others between mid-July and early August forms a crucial part of the postwar debate on whether Japan's surrender could have been obtained without use of atomic weapons. Besides the plain text of the decrypted messages, American policy makers also relied on interpretation by the very experienced Magic analysts. An American naval-intelligence commentary of limited distribution on these cables observed:

Although the above traffic does not reveal definitely whether or not the Japanese Chiefs of Staff participated with the Foreign Office in "secretly giving consideration to termination of the war," the fact that the move is stated to be an expression of "the Emperor's will," would appear to be of deep significance.

This qualified and tentative interpretation stood in contrast to the views generated by the MIS. On July 12, Brigadier General John Weckerling, Deputy Assistant Chief of Staff, G-2, forwarded a message to General Thomas Handy, Deputy Chief of Staff, who was in charge in Washington while General Marshall was at Potsdam. Weckerling characterized Togo's messages as containing "the long awaited Japanese peace offer." He noted the three components of the Japanese plan were (1) a proffer of "attractive terms of peace, including withdrawal of Japanese troops from all occupied territory, to appeal to U.S. and British War weariness"; (2) prevention of occupation of Japan; and (3) "propitiation of Russia by offering renunciation of Japanese rights under [the] Portsmouth Treaty" and territories, such as the Kurils and Karafuto, as well as concessions in Manchuria.*

---

* The Portsmouth Treaty ended the Russo-Japanese War of 1904–1905.

The next day, Weckerling submitted to Handy a memorandum on the Japanese peace offer and requested that it be forwarded to Marshall. It merits quoting in full:

> Weckerling believes there are a number of interesting deductions suggested by Message 893 [Togo's "Very Urgent" cable]:
>
> (1) That the Emperor has personally intervened and brought his will to bear in favor of peace in spite of military opposition;
> (2) That conservative groups close to the Throne, including some high ranking Army and Navy men, have triumphed over militaristic elements who favor prolonged desperate resistance;
> (3) That the Japanese government clique is making a well coordinated, united effort to stave off defeat believing
>   (a) that Russian intervention can be bought by the proper price, and (b) that an attractive Japanese peace offer will appeal to war weariness in the United States.
>
> Of these (1) is remote, (2) a possibility, and (3) quite probably the motivating force behind the Japanese moves. Mr. Grew agrees with these conclusions.*

A notation on the memorandum indicates it was transmitted to Marshall.

The Weckerling-Grew analysis is crucial evidence in the great debate over American policy in the summer of 1945. Critics have selectively chosen raw text of Japanese diplomatic messages for evidence that Japan was near to surrender. But when the full series of messages are put into context, and contemporary interpretations—both American and Japanese—are considered, a very different picture emerges. Obviously, the Weckerling-Grew analysis discounted the Emperor's initiative as a ploy to play on "war weariness in the United States" and "stave off defeat," not as a seri-

---

* There is clear evidence that Grew's reported concurrence is consistent with his thinking at this time. On July 7, Secretary of the Navy Forrestal noted in his diary that Admiral Nimitz requested authorization for release of an article prepared by an American journalist, in which three Japanese newspaper publishers on Okinawa predicted that Japan would surrender provided she was reassured that only token occupation forces would be deployed in the Homeland. Forrestal referred the question to Grew, who responded:

> that it was precisely the kind of overture which he had predicted would come from Japan at some time prior to the actual assault on the homelands. He said he thought it would be most dangerous to have it published at this juncture because it was propaganda to weaken our determination to carry out the complete defeat of Japan. He said that this effect could only be prejudicial to the all out prosecution of the war by Americans and he therefore was strongly opposed to its appearance in print.

See James V. Forrestal, *The Forrestal Diaries,* ed. Walter Millis (New York: Viking Press, 1951), July 7, 1945.

ous effort to end the war on terms acceptable to the United States. This judgment by the sophisticated analysts who had been studying Magic for years and Grew, the most experienced Japanese expert in the government, carried great weight.

But it was not solely American analysts who challenged the bona fides and efficacy of the Emperor's reported intervention to send a special envoy to the Soviet Union. Only after his conference with Molotov did Ambassador Sato finally receive Togo's "Very Urgent" wires of July 11 and 12. Sato responded with a scathing lecture:

> How much of an effect do you expect our statements regarding the nonannexation and non-possession of territories which we have already lost or are about to lose will have on the Soviet authorities?
>
> As you are well aware, the Soviet authorities are extremely realistic and it is extremely difficult to persuade them with abstract arguments. We certainly will not convince them with pretty little phrases devoid of all connection with reality. . . .
>
> If the Japanese Empire is really faced with the necessity of terminating the war, we must first of all make up our own minds to terminate the war. Unless we make up our own minds, there is absolutely no point in sounding out the views of the Soviet Government.

Sato urged the government "to make the great decision" to end the war but advised that Japan could expect only "virtually [the] equivalent to unconditional surrender." He concluded: "I send this telegram in the belief that [it] is my first responsibility to prevent the harboring of illusions which are at variance with reality. I beg your indulgence."

Sato dutifully attempted yet once more to secure approval for the Konoe mission, but the Soviets once again proved evasive. Sato's report of this Soviet rebuff concluded with the comments that while he "kne[lt] in veneration before the exalted solicitude of His Majesty for the restoration of peace," he admonished that if Konoe came armed with nothing beyond the framework of the Hirota-Malik exchanges,

> we shall uselessly disappoint the expectations of the authorities of this country. More than that, we shall generate feelings of dissatisfaction at our Government's lack of good faith and thus bring evil even upon the Imperial Household. I feel very serious anxiety on this point.
>
> It is my firm conviction that, once we have resolved to send a special and important Envoy on a long trip, he can have no function except to propose an armistice and peace.

Sato warned that if the Soviets inquired about the precise commission of the envoy, he must be able to promise them something significant.

Magic showed that on July 15, Sato informed Tokyo that

> it appears that Stalin and Molotov left Moscow for Berlin in the evening of the 14th. Therefore, so far as I can surmise, despite the fact that they probably had at least a half a day remaining before their departure, they avoided making any reply other than the tentative statement that they were delaying their answer.

Sato again expressed his view that Japan "in the long run . . . has indeed no choice but to accept unconditional surrender or terms closely equivalent thereto." He then added:

> I would like to point out, however, that even on the basis of your various messages I have obtained no clear idea of the recent situation. *Nor am I clear about the views of the Government and the Military with regard to the termination of the war.* Moreover, I have been of the opinion that, if it were finally decided to bring the war to an end, it would be necessary to obtain a new formal resolution which would be sufficient to overrule the decision reached at the conference held in the Imperial Presence on 8 June. [emphasis added]

Sato's message pierced to the heart of matters: Was Togo acting with authorization of the government and the military or on some lesser warrant? That the Japanese ambassador on the spot, having heaped ridicule on the original proposed negotiating stance and the very notion that the Soviets would bestir themselves on Japan's behalf, now challenged the bona fides of Togo's instructions speaks volumes about how much significance American readers of these exchanges could reasonably attach to the initiative.

Togo sent a fateful response to Sato on July 17:

> We have been fully aware from the outset that it would be difficult under existing circumstances either to strengthen the ties of friendship between Japan and Russia or in making effective use of Russia in ending the war. The present situation, however, is such that we have no recourse but to make efforts along those lines and we cannot be satisfied merely with keeping Russia from entering the war against Japan. We have therefore decided to recognize the Russians' wishes on a broad scale in order to obtain their favor. Negotiations for that purpose are necessary—[word uncertain, possibly "prerequisite"] for soliciting Russia's good offices in concluding the war and also in improving the basis for negotiations with England and America.

Although the directing powers, and the government as well, are convinced that our war strength still can deliver considerable blows to the enemy, we are unable to feel absolutely secure peace of mind in the face of an enemy who will attack repeatedly. If today, when we are still maintaining our strength, the Anglo-Americans were to have regard for Japan's honor and existence, they could save humanity by bringing the war to an end. If, however, they insist unrelentingly upon unconditional surrender, the Japanese are unanimous in their resolve to wage a thorough-going war.

The Emperor himself has deigned to express his determination and we have therefore made this request of the Russians. *Please bear particularly in mind, however, that we are not seeking the Russians' mediation for anything like an unconditional surrender* [emphasis added].

This message evaded a direct answer to Sato's fundamental question. Togo did not allege broad support from the Imperial Army and Navy for peace, because no such commitment existed. Only the uniformed members of the Big Six had sanctioned efforts to open negotiations, and they had not disclosed their action to more than a tiny handful of their subordinates.

Togo had hinted that beyond approaching the Soviets, "the directing powers, and the government" remained divided as to terms for peace. This was in fact the case. In a postwar statement, the foreign minister admitted that the Big Six never agreed on terms, and one of General Umezu's key subordinates quoted Umezu to the same effect. Indeed, a July 14 meeting witnessed a very heated confrontation. Army Minister Anami again insisted that any terms must be formulated on the basis that Japan was not defeated. Navy Minister Yonai intervened to curtail the confrontation before a breakdown occurred within the Big Six. Premier Suzuki and Admiral Toyoda later confessed that there never was agreement on the concessions to be made to the Soviets to secure mediation, much less on the terms Japan would propose as the basis of mediation with the Allies. Above all, Togo's message underscored that nothing approaching unconditional surrender was acceptable even within the limited circle that was contemplating peace negotiations.

Furthermore, two key sources, one available only after the Emperor's death in 1989 and a second that came to light shortly after the war, disclose the Emperor's real intentions with this initiative. The Emperor's narrative in *Showa Tenno Dokuhakuroku* related that by July 7 he had become distressed that the government had achieved no progress at all with the Soviets since his meeting with the Big Six on June 22. He was anxious to commence mediation before the Potsdam Conference and to improve Japanese-Soviet relations. Most telling of all, however, is what he did not claim: Nowhere did he suggest that his proposal to dispatch an envoy was for the purpose of securing an immediate peace, although making such an assertion would have been enormously to his interest in war-crime trials or for purposes of posterity.

That *Showa Tenno Dokuhakuroku* correctly reflected the Emperor's limited horizons in July 1945 is confirmed by Koichi Kido's contemporary diary. Immediately after Prince Konoe met with the Emperor on July 12, he told Kido that the Emperor had asked his opinion on terminating the war. Konoe had replied that while the Army insisted that the war could be continued and that their reasoning might not be "wholly groundless" if their calculations were correct, the Navy discounted the validity of Army figures. Konoe spoke of declining public morale, early signs of resentment toward the Emperor, and the people's last hope for deliverance "in some way or other" by the Emperor. Accordingly, he told the Emperor that it was "imperative to terminate the war as early as possible." "Thereupon," reported Konoe, "His Majesty remarked that He has the intention eventually to send me to the Soviet Union as a special envoy, and asked me to be prepared for it."

The Emperor then provided Kido with a report of the interview as follows:

> After outlining my intentions, I asked Konoe his opinion related to the outlook for the war. He replied that it was imperative to bring the war to an end at this juncture. When I told him that I might ask him to go to [the] Soviet Union on a mission, he accepted the proposal, claiming that he would give his utmost, at the risk of his life, were it the imperial command.

While these entries show Konoe believed the war must be swiftly "terminated," they do not document that the Emperor saw things the same way. The distinction is critical. When the Emperor ordered the Big Six to begin negotiations on June 22, and later when he actually ordered a halt to the war on August 10 and 14, Kido's diary faithfully recorded those facts. By contrast, Kido's immediate account of the Konoe interview conspicuously contains no evidence the Emperor issued such decisive orders. Moreover, it is exceedingly hard to credit that the Emperor could have delivered momentous instructions sealing the fate of Japan in this session that lasted just fifteen minutes. Viewed in light of *Showa Tenno Dokuhakuroku* and Kido's diary, Weckerling and Grew's belief that messages showing the Emperor's personal interest in sending a special envoy most likely signaled just a ploy was too harsh, but they were correct to question whether Japan had resolved to end the war on terms acceptable to the Allies.

On July 19, Sato again disparaged Tokyo's diplomatic acumen. He reported a blunt Soviet challenge to the purpose of the Konoe mission and added that "it is . . . hard to deny that the Japanese authorities are out of touch with the atmosphere prevailing here." Togo responded two days later:

> Special Envoy Konoe's mission will be in obedience to the Imperial Will. He will request assistance in bringing about an end to the war through the good offices of the Soviet Government. In this regard he will set forth positive intentions, and he will also negotiate details concerning the establishment of a cooperative relationship between Japan and Russia which will form the basis of Imperial diplomacy both during and after the war.
>
> Please make the above representations to the Russians and work to obtain their concurrence in sending of the special Envoy. Please understand especially my next wire.

That wire was transmitted the same day. To understand its profound importance, we must backtrack slightly. After perusing Togo's message of July 17 affirming that Japan could not accept "anything like" unconditional surrender, Sato responded immediately. The Magic Diplomatic Summary described Sato's July 18 message as "obscurely worded" in parts, but reported its key contents as follows:

> a. It goes without saying that in my earlier message calling for unconditional surrender or closely equivalent terms, I made an exception of the question of preserving our national structure [i.e., the Imperial system]. Although I have no fear that you misunderstood what I said in the last part of my 8 June message, I am wiring this for your information.
>
> b. In connection with the question of preserving our national structure . . . we must create a strong impression [with the Soviets] that our proposals represent the positive demands of Japan's 70 million people [i.e., presumably their maximum concessions].
>
> c. Except for the matter of maintenance of our national structure, I think that we must absolutely not propose any conditions. The situation has already reached the point where we have no alternative but unconditional surrender or its equivalent.

Togo's July 21 response noted that he had been informed of Sato's message, which the editors of the Magic Diplomatic Summary reminded policy makers showed that Sato "advocated unconditional surrender provided the Imperial House was preserved." To this proposal, the Foreign Minister declared:

With regard to unconditional surrender we are unable to consent to it under any circumstances whatever. Even if the war drags on and it becomes clear that it will take much more than bloodshed, the whole country as one man will pit itself against the enemy in accordance with the Imperial Will so long as the enemy demands unconditional surrender. It is in order to avoid such a state of affairs that we are seeking a peace, which is not so-called unconditional surrender, through the good offices of Russia. . . .

Therefore, it is not only impossible for us to request the Russians to lend their good offices in obtaining a peace without conditions, but it would also be both disadvantageous and impossible, from the standpoint of foreign and domestic considerations, to make an immediate declaration of specific terms.

Togo ended this cable by acknowledging that he had also read a long message from Sato on July 20 that had contained an extended and impassioned plea for surrender on Allied terms save for preservation of Japan's "national structure," but he was transmitting the cabinet's decision and Sato must proceed accordingly.

By any reasonable standard, these exchanges between Sato and Togo from July 17 to 21 are authoritative, contemporaneous, and decisive evidence concerning the argument that an offer to retain the Emperor would have secured Japan's surrender without resort to atomic bombings or perhaps even Soviet intervention. In his message of July 18, Sato placed exactly this set of terms on the table as the best Japan could expect. Togo's response was not even that the government would give such an offer serious consideration. Rather, Togo in unambiguous language and in the name of the cabinet absolutely rejected such terms: "We are unable to consent to it under any circumstances whatever." Further, not only was the substance of this exchange clear on the actual Japanese diplomatic stance and thus the proximity of Japan to peace on terms acceptable to the United States, this vital information was equally clear to American readers by the text of these messages and the commentary in the Magic Diplomatic Summary.

Sato secured an interview with Soviet Vice Commissar Alexander Lozovsky on July 25, but lacking the "concrete plans" he needed, he found himself resorting to "fancy phrases" to cloak Konoe's mission yet obtain permission for it to proceed. He weathered a difficult interrogation by Lozovsky, managed to highlight Konoe's direct commission from the Emperor, and implied that Konoe would bear the sort of "concrete plans" the Soviets were so anxious to scrutinize. Lozovsky promised a rapid response from his government. Togo commended the minister for his "tenacity in the face of the ups and downs of this matter."

Even before Togo received Sato's report on this interview, he sent new instructions. The Potsdam Conference had recessed for the British elec-

tions, which were to replace Churchill with Clement Attlee. Togo anticipated that during this recess Molotov would return to Moscow. Therefore,
Togo wanted Sato to secure an interview with the Soviet Foreign Minister
in which Sato should emphasize that the Japanese sought to "permit Stalin
to acquire the reputation of an advocate of world peace, and, further, that
we are prepared to meet fully the Russian demands in the Far East." The
Japanese foreign minister then addressed the recent broadcasts by Captain
Zacharias. In Togo's words, Zacharias had set out Japan's options as either
submission to "a dictated peace after being destroyed" or unconditional
surrender, with "the attendant benefits stipulated by the Atlantic Charter."
Togo added:

> The fact that the Americans alluded to the Atlantic Charter is particularly
> worthy of attention at this time. It is impossible for us to accept uncondi-
> tional surrender, no matter in what guise, but it is our idea to inform them by
> some appropriate means that there is no objection to the restoration of peace
> on the basis of the Atlantic Charter.
>
> In all likelihood the difficult point is the attitude of the enemy in insisting
> on the form of an unconditional surrender. If America and England stick to
> this, the whole thing will break down over this one point. On the other hand,
> although the governments of Russia, England and America may be cool
> toward our proposal of a Special Envoy on the ground that it may be a peace
> stratagem on our part, this—as I have stated repeatedly—is not merely a
> "peace feeler."

Togo's ruminations about the Zacharias broadcasts have been seized
upon by postwar critics who insist that they demonstrate that more might
have been attempted via diplomacy to secure the surrender of Japan. These
critics read every Japanese comment that unconditional surrender was unacceptable as though it meant that unconditional surrender with the proviso that the Imperial institution would be retained was acceptable. But
Togo had expressly rejected such an offer. Critics have also asserted that
the Zacharias broadcasts "confused" the Japanese about the real American
stance. The official history prepared by Japan's Self Defense Agency,
however, states flatly that while the Zacharias broadcasts attracted attention within the cloisters of the Foreign Ministry, which had no legal and
little persuasive power to secure peace, they had no impact at all on the Imperial Army, the dominant political force in Japan. Nor is there evidence
that any other key policy maker was attracted by Zacharias's efforts. Thus,
Zacharias did not "confuse" anyone whose opinion counted.

Meanwhile, in Washington on July 27, naval intelligence circulated an
assessment of the Japanese political situation that wove together the Ultra

and Magic evidence. War Department analysts decided to reprint this as-tute assessment in detail in the Magic Diplomatic Summary, thus assuring that it could be seen by all top policy makers:

> An analysis of Japan's situation, as revealed through Ultra sources, suggests her unwillingness to surrender stems primarily from the failure of her other-wise capable and all-powerful Army leaders to perceive that the defenses they are so assiduously fashioning actually are utterly inadequate. There is nothing in the Japanese mind to prevent capitulation per se, as demonstrated by the advocacy of virtual unconditional surrender by an increasing number of highly placed Japanese abroad.* However, until the Japanese leaders re-alize that an invasion can not be repelled, there is little likelihood that they will accept any peace terms satisfactory to the Allies.

This same day, Sato advised Tokyo that it was "most difficult" to predict the Russian response to the Konoe mission, but it was "not at all unlikely that the Soviet government will refuse to consider it" and that such refusal "will place us in a most embarrassing position and may even involve the Imperial House itself."

The Potsdam Declaration; Time Runs Out

The United States, Great Britain, and China, but not the Soviet Union (which was still officially neutral in the Pacific war), publicly released the Potsdam Declaration on July 26, 1945, to give Japan "an opportunity to end this war." After warning of the inevitable "utter devastation of the Jap-anese homeland," the declaration called upon Japan to choose between "annihilation" or "the path of reason" and sternly announced: "The fol-lowing are our terms. We will not deviate from them. There are no alterna-tives. We shall brook no delay."

The essential terms then itemized included: elimination "for all time the authority and influence of those who have deceived and misled the people of Japan into embarking on world conquest"; occupation of "points" in Japan until the new order is established and "convincing proof" is pro-vided that war-making power has been destroyed; limitation of Japan's sovereignty to basically the Home Islands; and complete disarmament of Japanese military forces, after which the soldiers and sailors may "return to their homes with the opportunity to lead peaceful and productive lives."

---

* This is a reference to the many messages from Japanese diplomats and some military and naval at-tachés in Europe who had attempted without official sanction to become peace entrepreneurs. Note, however, the analysis does not cite any messages originating from Japan.

Additionally, while the Allies did not intend that the Japanese "be enslaved as a race or destroyed as a nation . . . stern justice shall be meted out to war criminals."

If Japan acceded, the Allies guaranteed the establishment of freedom of speech, religion, and thought, "as well as respect for the fundamental human rights." Japan would retain her industries, pay just reparations in kind, be granted access to raw materials, and gain eventual access to world trade relations. Finally, the Allies promised that "the occupying forces of the Allies shall be withdrawn from Japan as soon as these objectives have been accomplished and there has been established in accordance with the freely expressed will of the Japanese people a peacefully inclined and responsible government."

The term *unconditional surrender* appeared in the Potsdam Declaration just once, in the last paragraph, where the Allies "call upon the government of Japan to proclaim now the unconditional surrender of all Japanese armed forces." Given the affirmations that neither the Japanese race nor Japan would perish, the promises that ordinary soldiers and sailors could return home, the pledge that commerce and industry would be restored, and that the Japanese people would obtain basic rights long denied them, the Potsdam Declaration had indeed proffered to Japan terms "much more lenient than those imposed on Germany," as the appalled Australian external-affairs minister, Herbert Evatt, declared.

In Japan, Foreign Minister Togo attempted to take the lead in formulating a response. He cautioned the Supreme Council for the Direction of the War on the morning of July 27 that "it would [be] extremely impolitic for Japan to reject the Potsdam Declaration." Over some opposition, he secured agreement, both from the Big Six and then at a cabinet meeting that afternoon, not to dismiss publicly the declaration and to pursue "clarification" through the Soviets—or so he thought.

The facts of what happened next are not disputed; the causes and consequences are. The cabinet decision not to reject but to use the Potsdam Declaration to Japan's advantage led to another dilemma. There could be no reasonable expectation that the Allies would not alert the Japanese public of the declaration by radio or leaflet. Thus, some acknowledgment of the declaration was a necessity, but any acknowledgment in turn mandated a choice, as Robert Butow elegantly described it, between "unsatisfactory alternatives and dangerous ones." An emphatic rejection might scuttle negotiations with the Allies, but anything less might incite diehards to scuttle the government. An awkward compromise provided for release to newspapers of an expurgated version of the declaration, coupled with a ban on editorial commentary.

The next morning, however, the Japanese media trumpeted the rejection of the Potsdam Declaration by Japan's rulers. For example, the newspaper *Asahi Shimbun,* under the headline LAUGHABLE MATTER, sneered that the proclamation was, according to the government, "a thing of no great moment." It was only in the afternoon of July 28, after this disastrous public spurning of the Potsdam Declaration, that the Chiefs of Staff of the Army and Navy, as well as the Army Minister, pressed Prime Minister Suzuki to pronounce a yet more definitive rejection. Suzuki meet with the press at 4:00 P.M., and in response to a planted question he replied: "The government does not regard [the Potsdam Declaration] as a thing of any value; the government will just ignore [*mokusatsu*] it. We will press forward resolutely to carry the war to a successful conclusion." Literally, *mokusatsu* meant "kill with silence," but idiomatically it housed an array of meanings: "take no notice of it," "treat with silent contempt," or "ignore." These connotations prompted the foreign press to report that the Japanese had rejected the declaration, as *The New York Times* commented, with contempt. Secretary of War Stimson later wrote that once the Japanese rejected the proclamation as "unworthy of public notice," the United States was bound to demonstrate what the threat of "prompt and utter destruction" meant.

Despite later efforts by Togo and others to pin the blame on the militarists for this folly, the indisputable fact is that the rejection of the Potsdam Declaration blared out from the front pages of Japanese morning papers on July 28, before any military spokesmen even mentioned it. Moreover, there is no record of an effort by the Japanese government to overtly or covertly transmit to the Allies any hint that *mokusatsu* did not precisely reflect its attitude.

Many Japanese viewed *mokusatsu* as a colossal error by their government that triggered the atomic bombs and Soviet entry into the war. Initial postwar assessments generally ascribed it to inadvertence or misjudgment. But, in fact, *mokusatsu* accurately mirrored the underlying outlook of key Japanese leaders. Contemporaneous evidence indicates that perhaps the root of the fallacious calculations within the Big Six was a gross misjudgment of the element of time. Rear Admiral Takagi, Yonai's secretary, asked the navy minister why the prime minister had been allowed to blurt out something so absurd as *mokusatsu.* "If one is first to issue a statement," replied the "moderate" Yonai, "he is always at a disadvantage. Churchill has fallen. America is beginning to be isolated. The government therefore will ignore it. There is no need to rush." In a similar vein, Togo defended his preference for an indirect and time-consuming approach through the Soviets to seek clarification of the Potsdam Declaration, on the basis that "we wanted to wait and see how things would develop, at least until we received a reply from the Russians."

Most telling of all, however, are Prime Minister Suzuki's own words. On July 30, he learned at a meeting with the Cabinet Advisory Council that the nation's leading businessmen had urged that Japan accept the Potsdam terms. To this news, Suzuki retorted to Kainan Shimomura, the director of the Cabinet Information Bureau, that

> for the enemy to say something like that means circumstances have arisen that force them also to end the war. That is why they are talking about unconditional surrender. Precisely at a time like this, if we hold firm, they will yield before we do. Just because they have broadcast their Declaration, it is not necessary to stop fighting. You advisers may ask me to reconsider, but I don't think there is any need to stop [the war].

And what of the Emperor? He acknowledged in *Showa Tenno Dokuhakuroku* that he had embraced fully the "decisive battle doctrine" until June, before he advocated a démarche through the Soviets to mediate an end to the war. He discoursed in *Showa Tenno Dokuhakuroku* on many failures of his advisers during the war but conspicuously omitted the *mokusatsu* response from his list of deficiencies. On the other hand, straddling this period are two events that disclose his priorities. On July 25, he instructed Kido that the three sacred regalia must be safeguarded to protect the Imperial house and *kokutai*. These comprised a mirror, a curved jewel, and a sword passed down solemnly by his ancestors for thousands of years, which stood as core symbols of the legitimacy of the Imperial line. On July 31, the Emperor again emphasized to Kido the need to make the regalia absolutely secure. The contrast between his concern with the sacred regalia and his silence then and subsequently about *mokusatsu* indicates he gave primacy to the Imperial institution, not to statesmanship vital to the fate of millions of his subjects.

On July 29, Sato, that sturdy and wise voice of reason, had forwarded to Tokyo his assessment of the Potsdam Declaration. The ambassador reiterated that if Japan surrendered unconditionally, it would reap the benefits of the Atlantic Charter, terms never offered to Germany. Meanwhile, Togo had perused the Potsdam Declaration and presumably concluded that the silence of the Soviet Union represented its concurrence. Further, he had confessed to Sato on July 28 that he could not be certain whether the Soviets had communicated his proposals to the Western Allies or what future actions the Soviets might take. Togo advised Sato that the official position of the Japanese government was that it would give careful study to the Potsdam Declaration. Togo, however, secured no authority to communicate this stance to the Allies, and thus it remained the mere proposal of the Foreign Ministry.

Sato again wired blunt counsel to Togo on July 30. He believed the Soviets must have passed on the proposals of July 11–12 concerning the special envoy to the United States and the British and that the joint declaration represented the Allied response. Sato further reasoned:

> The important point in connection with the Joint Declaration is that America and England have demanded Japan's immediate unconditional surrender and have stated clearly that they have no intention of softening the terms set forth in the Proclamation. If it is to be understood that Stalin was completely unable to influence the intentions of America and England on this point, the fact is that he will be unable to accept our proposal to send a Special Envoy. . . . There is no alternative but immediate unconditional surrender if we are to prevent [Russia's] participation in the war. . . .
>
> Your way of looking at things and the actual condition in the Eastern Area [meaning the Soviet Union] may be seen as being completely contradictory.

Sato attempted once more to present to the Soviets a brief issued by Togo on July 30, but yet again they evaded a response. In a "Very Urgent" cable on August 2, Togo continued to impress upon Sato the importance of his mission:

> I have been fully apprised of Your Excellency's views by your successive wires, and I am well able to understand them as the opinions of the Ambassador on the spot. However, it should not be difficult for you to realize that although with the urgency of the war situation our time to proceed with arrangements of ending the war before the enemy lands on the Japanese mainland is limited, on the other hand it is difficult to decide on concrete peace conditions here at home all at once. At present, in accordance with the Imperial Will, there is unanimous determination to ask the good offices of the Russians in ending the war, to make concrete terms a matter between Japan and Russia, and to send Prince Konoe, who has the deep trust of the Emperor, to carry on discussions with the Russians. . . . It has been decided at any rate to send a special envoy in accordance with the views of the highest leaders of [this] Government, and along with this [decision] we are exerting ourselves to collect the views of all quarters on the matter of concrete terms. (Under the circumstances, there is a disposition to make the Potsdam Three Power Declaration the basis of our study concerning terms.)
>
> Accordingly, the most urgent task which now confronts us is to persuade the Soviet Government to accept the mission of our Special Envoy. His

OKINAWA: PREVIEW OF THE BATTLE IN THE HOMELAND

American soldiers close in on a fortified cave, the distinctive feature of Japanese defenses on Okinawa that was being replicated manyfold on Kyushu.

The Japanese recognized that the chief threat to the cave was the tank, and they countered effectively with mines, antitank guns, and suicidal individual sorties. More than half the American tanks landed on Okinawa were destroyed.

Perhaps the most ominous feature of Okinawa was the integra-
tion of the civilian population
into the defense; this led to the
deaths of, at minimum, 62,000
noncombatants.

More than 12,000 U.S. servicemen died seizing the island or on ships subjected to withering kamikaze
attacks. Combined battle and nonbattle casualties totaled about 72,000—a number almost equaling
that of the 76,000 trained Japanese defenders—an extremely ominous indicator as the invasion of the
Homeland was prepared.

BLOCKADE: THE CRESCENDO OF THE CAMPAIGN AGAINST JAPANESE SHIPPING

The destruction, by carrier planes from Admiral William F. Halsey's fleet, of the train ferries connecting Hokkaido and Honshu was the single most devastating blow to the Japanese economy during the war.

In a series of July attacks, Halsey's fliers also sought out and destroyed the remaining major Japanese warships—ironically, eliminating one of the last deterrents to a Soviet landing in the Homeland.

Radio intelligence unmasked a Japanese plan to fly thousands of suicide commandos to attack the B-29 bases in the Mariana Islands; U.S. Navy planes aborted this scheme with an attack on the Japanese transport aircraft.

BOMBARDMENT: THE FIRE BY NIGHT AND DAY

Because of the technical immaturity of the B-29s, adverse weather, and adherence to high-altitude attacks, Brigadier General Haywood S. Hansell, the initial commander of the Twenty-first Bomber Command, failed to produce quick results.

General Henry Arnold (left), the commander of the Army Air Forces, counted on the B-29s to make the final case for an independent air force. He replaced Hansell with Major General Curtis LeMay (right) in January 1945.

The justification for the incendiary attacks was the Japanese system of using workers' homes around each industrial complex as a feeder system, complete with machine tools, for supplying parts and components.

After two months of further failure, LeMay switched to massive incendiary attacks on Japanese cities. The first of these, against Tokyo on the night of March 9–10, 1945, killed upwards of 90,000 and left scenes of utter devastation.

B-29s release incendiaries over Yokohama on May 29, 1945.

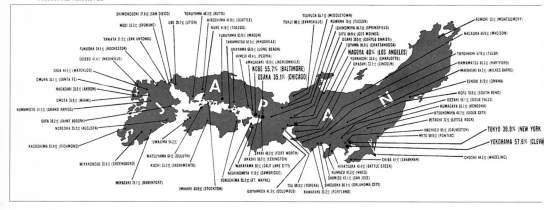

This map from a 1945 report by General Arnold shows the cities of Japan struck by B-29 incendiary or atomic attacks. The extent of the destruction of each city is given, and each is paired with a U.S. city of comparable size.

Only the end of the war forestalled a shift of the strategic bombing campaign to an attack on the Japanese rail system that would have caused a catastrophic rupture of Japan's means of distributing food.

THE IMPERIAL ARMY PREPARES OPERATION KETSU-GO

The Japanese deduced that the obvious American target within the Homeland was southern Kyushu, because it was within range of large numbers of Okinawa-based fighters. Moreover, examination of a topographic map of Kyushu readily identified the probable landing areas (see arrows).

KAMIKAZES: MORE THAN 5,000 SUICIDE PLANES AWAIT THE INVASION

Vice Admiral Takijiro Onishi, the "father" of the kamikaze effort. "If we are prepared to sacrifice twenty million Japanese lives in a special attack [kamikaze] effort," said Onishi, "victory will be ours!"

More than 2,900 Japanese aircraft, bearing 3,913 crew members, were lost in kamikaze attacks.

A kamikaze a split second before crashing the carrier *Essex* (CV-9) on November 25, 1944.

The impact a second later, as seen from the carrier *Ticonderoga* (CV-14).

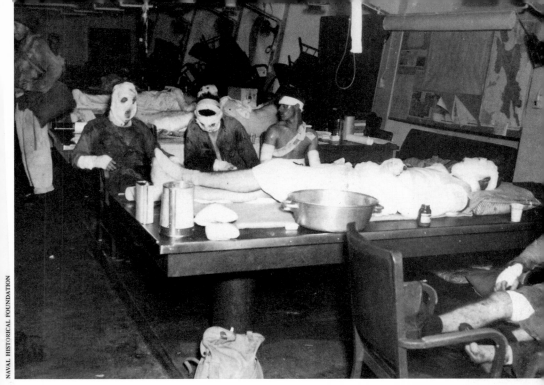

The Japanese planned to pummel the packed troop transports of the Homeland invasion fleet with more than 5,000 kamikazes so as to produce massive numbers of dead as well as hideous burn casualties, like these crewmen of the escort carrier *Suwanee*.

THE CIVILIANS

For Ketsu-Go, Japanese leaders aimed to repeat the sacrifice of civilians as at Saipan (here depicted by a Japanese artist) on a gigantic scale, with participation of the whole adult population of Japan in the defense of the Homeland.

U.S. ARMY LEADERS

General George C. Marshall, Chief of Staff, was convinced that only an invasion would secure a victory assuring enduring peace.

General Douglas MacArthur commanded all U.S. Army forces (except the strategic air force) slated for the invasion of Japan. He dismissed radio intelligence evidence that Japanese forces defending Kyushu were far larger than American plans projected.

General Walter Krueger commanded the Sixth Army, slated to attack Kyushu in Operation Olympic. By August 1, 1945, his intelligence officer was projecting that Japanese strength by X-Day on Kyushu would total 680,000—equal to the strength of Krueger's forces.

U.S. NAVY LEADERS

Fleet Admiral Ernest King, the Commander in Chief and Chief of Naval Operations. He was poised to play his secret trump card against any invasion strategy just as the war ended.

Fleet Admiral Chester W. Nimitz, Commander in Chief of the Pacific Ocean Areas and MacArthur's naval counterpart—a brilliant leader in war and a magnanimous victor.

THE PRESIDENT

President Harry S. Truman meets former President Herbert Hoover on May 28, 1945. Hoover's memoranda probably sparked Truman to examine the invasion strategy in June.

CODE BREAKING: THE CRITICAL ELEMENT

Among the leaders who controlled Japan's fate, Foreign Minister Shigenori Togo was the most zealous advocate of quickly ending the war.

Ambassador Sato—himself a former foreign minister—delivered scathing assessments of Japan's attempts to enlist the Soviet Union as a mediator to end the war.

The cover page of the Magic Diplomatic Summary for July 22, 1945, which contained Togo's rejection of Sato's advice that the best terms Japan could hope to secure were unconditional surrender modified only to the extent of retention of the Imperial Institution.

Total pages—29
(incl. TABS A and B)

ULTRA
TOP SECRET

Copy No. **MI-3**

No. 1214 — 22 July 1945

By Auth.   A. C. of S., G-2
Date   22 July 1945
Initials   C. W. C.

WAR DEPARTMENT
Office of A. C. of S., G-2

"MAGIC"—DIPLOMATIC SUMMARY

NOTE: No one, without express permission from the proper authorities, may disseminate the information reported in this Summary or communicate it to any other person.

Those authorized to disseminate such information must employ only the most secure means, must take every precaution to avoid compromising the source, and must limit dissemination to the minimum number of secure and responsible persons who need the information in order to discharge their duties.

No action is to be taken on information herein reported, regardless of temporary advantage, if such action might have the effect of revealing the existence of the source to the enemy.

The enemy knows that we attempt to exploit these sources. He does not know, and must not be permitted to learn, either the degree of our success or the particular sources with which we have been successful.

<u>MILITARY</u>

    1. <u>Tokyo again says no unconditional sur-</u>   (197837
<u>render; Sato pleads for peace</u>: On 19 July Ambassador   197845
                                              WLMR)
Sato forwarded to Tokyo a letter from Vice Commissar
Lozovsky which stated that since "the mission of Prince
Konoye, the Special Envoy, is in no way made clear" the
Russian Government could not give a "definite reply" to
the Japanese proposal (DS 20 Jul 45).

TOP SECRET
ULTRA

THE ATOMIC BOMBS

"Little Boy" struck Hiroshima on August 6, 1945.

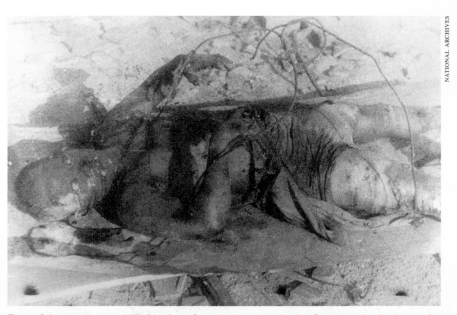

Tens of thousands were killed by heat from the bomb or by the firestorm that broke out in the devastated city.

Many survivors suffered permanent thermal burns.

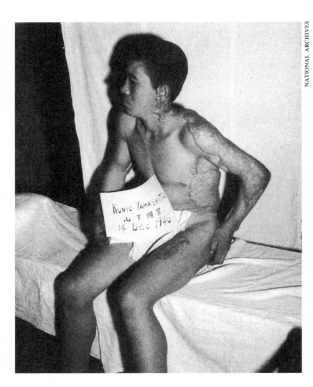

"Fat Man" struck Nagasaki on August 9, 1945. The twin nuclear blows demolished the Ketsu-Go strategy.

THE BIG SIX AND MARQUIS KOICHI KIDO

The fate of Japan rested in the hands of only eight men. Six of them comprised the Supreme Council for the Direction of the War; the other two were Lord Keeper of the Privy Seal Marquis Koichi Kido and the Emperor.

Prime Minister
Baron Kantaro Suzuki

NATIONAL ARCHIVES

Chief of the Naval General Staff
Admiral Soemu Toyoda

NAVAL HISTORICAL FOUNDATION

Foreign Minister
Shigenori Togo

NATIONAL ARCHIVES

Lord Keeper of the Privy
Seal Marquis Koichi Kido

NATIONAL ARCHIVES

Chief of the Army General
Staff General Yoshijiro
Umezu

NATIONAL ARCHIVES

Army Minister
General Korechika Anami

NATIONAL ARCHIVES

Navy Minister
Admiral Mitsumasa Yonai

NATIONAL ARCHIVES

THE EMPEROR

Japan approached the abyss of war against the United States in 1939 as Emperor Hirohito strode the decks of the battleship *Nagato*. Six years later, his intervention to halt the war caught Japan on the edge of a precipice of catastrophe.

Majesty, the Emperor, is most profoundly concerned about the matter and has been following developments with the keenest interest. The Premier and the leaders of the Army are now concentrating all their attention on this one point. . . . Whatever happens, if we should let one day slip by, it might have [results?] lasting for thousands of years.

The commentary on this message in the Magic Diplomatic Summary observed pointedly that it "contain[ed] the first statement to appear in the traffic that the Japanese Army is interested in the effort to end the war with Soviet assistance." Given the governing American perception that the militarists exercised ultimate control of Imperial Japan, the fact that no message prior to August 2 presented any concrete evidence of a desire by Japan's military masters for a démarche through the Soviets plainly undermined the weight attributable to Togo's diplomatic overtures. But now, even with this revelation, Togo again admitted that Japan's ruling elite still could not agree on "concrete" terms.

Sato replied to Togo's cable the following day with an "Extremely Urgent" response affirming that he would strive to secure an interview with Molotov immediately upon the commissar's return to Moscow, but again he predicted that the Soviets would demand "a concrete plan" prior to receiving the special envoy. Sato feared that even if the Soviets accepted the envoy, the absence of meaningful terms would frustrate the mission. He feared as well the prospect of invasion, followed after "innumerable sacrifices" by the Japanese people by surrender, which would focus the "ill will of the people . . . upon the Government and the Military, extending its evil influence even to the Imperial House."

Sato urged that his cable be presented to both the Supreme Council for the Direction of the War and the Emperor, and he followed up the next day with a forthright dispatch arguing that since the Potsdam Declaration "already provides the basis for ending the Greater East Asian War," even if Soviet good offices were obtained the terms would be the same. The earliest possible surrender would produce additional amelioration, but he warned:

Even though there may be some amelioration, it is already clear, even without looking at the example of Germany, what the peace terms will be and we must resign ourselves beforehand to [giving up?] a considerable number of [so-called] war criminals. However, the state is now [on the verge of] ruin, and it is entirely inevitable that these war criminals [must] make the necessary sacrifice to save their country as truly patriotic warriors.

In Washington, naval intelligence officers prepared a review for the chief of naval operations of the Japanese-Soviet diplomatic developments through August 6. "Although not yet agreed on the method" (except that there was "unanimous determination to ask the good offices of the Russians"), there was a disposition to make the Potsdam Declaration the basis of study—"possibly in the hope (or determination) of finding in its terms a sufficiently effective emollient for the tortured pride which still rebels at the words 'unconditional surrender.' " Notwithstanding Sato's warnings that the Soviets would not alter the terms of the Potsdam Declaration, the summary characterized Togo as still blindly bent on "fly[ing] into the arms of Russia," despite "the possibility that Russia might not be there to catch him. What course will be taken in [this] event, probably no one in Japan yet knows." If, however, conditions had reached such a state that Sato's warning of a threat to the Imperial House was real, then "it may be assumed that a definite move of some kind will not be long delayed."

Those who argue that American policy makers recognized that Japan was near surrender when they chose to unleash atomic weapons rest the core of their case on selected excerpts of these diplomatic exchanges from July 11 to August 3. The first important defect with this critique is that it simply ignores the fact that there were two streams of decrypted Japanese messages. Military Ultra showed without exception Japan's armed forces girding for Armageddon. If, as American leaders correctly believed in 1945, the Imperial Army held the dominant position in Japan, then the Ultra reports carried an unmistakable political import. Indeed, naval intelligence expressly identified the fundamental obstacle to peace as the Imperial Army's belief that it could achieve success against an invasion, and this assessment was reiterated in the Magic Diplomatic Summary of July 27 for Army and State Department readers.

More fundamentally, the full series of Magic Diplomatic Summaries demonstrates just how illusory is the image that Japan was near to capitulation before atomic weapons were employed. As the Magic interpreters underscored, not a single diplomatic message originating from Japanese authorities in Tokyo indicated any disposition for peace prior to mid-July. Even after the Emperor intervened to propose a special envoy to the Soviet Union, Magic revealed that neither he nor the government had agreed on the terms they would accept, much less terms that were acceptable to the Allies. Since the Emperor and the government of Japan remained at sea on these fundamental questions, the dismissal of these desultory efforts was amply merited.

The most often repeated condemnation of American diplomacy in the summer of 1945 is that policy makers understood that a promise to retain the Imperial institution was essential to end the war, and that had the United States communicated such a promise, the Suzuki cabinet would likely have promptly surrendered. The answer to this assertion is enshrined in black and white in the July 22 edition of the Magic Diplomatic Summary. There, American policy makers could read for themselves that Ambassador Sato had advised Foreign Minister Togo that the best terms Japan could hope to secure were unconditional surrender, modified only to the extent that the Imperial institution could be retained. Presented by his own ambassador with this offer, Togo expressly rejected it. Given this, there is no rational prospect that such an offer would have won support from any of the other five members of the Supreme Council for the Direction of the War.

A further crucial point about the Magic evidence is what it actually reveals about Togo's authority. In 1945, Americans of all ranks remembered very well the image of Japanese diplomats in ostensible parleys for peace in Washington at the moment bombs rained on Pearl Harbor. Thus, Americans were not disposed to accept the words of Japanese diplomats as definitive proof of their nation's intentions. And Ambassador Sato validated this skepticism. The Magic Diplomatic Summary establishes that both Ambassador Sato in Moscow and American analysts asked for whom Togo spoke. With his customary bluntness, Sato on July 15 had demanded to know whether diplomatic efforts to end the war carried any legal sanction in the face of the decision in the Imperial presence on June 8 to battle to the end. In his waffling response of July 17, Togo made no claim of support from the Imperial Army and Navy, nor did he report any legal warrant behind the move. Without such sanction, could Togo's cables be deemed evidence that the Japanese government had embarked on a serious effort to end the war?

Beyond this, over and over Sato came back to the theme that Japan must present "concrete terms." Togo could not provide them. Over and over again, Togo conceded that no agreement on terms to secure Soviet mediation had been reached, much less terms to end the war. Even in the August 2 message where Sato reported that the "leaders of the [Imperial] Army" were devoting rapt attention to opening a negotiating channel with the Soviets, the foreign minister again confessed the lack of agreement on peace terms—and the use of the plural *terms* is telling. Finally, we now have available the Emperor's own account of this period. Nowhere in *Showa Tenno Dokuhakuroku* does the Emperor even claim that he intended for Konoe to immediately terminate the war or that terms for an end to the war had been formulated. Nor did the Emperor criticize the *mokusatsu* response to the Potsdam Declaration. In the face of this evidence, it is fantasy, not history, to believe that the end of the war was at hand before the use of the atomic bomb.

15

Magic and Diplomacy
with the Soviets

"A most important session"

The information disgorged by Ultra unmasking the huge Japanese buildup in the Homeland began to swell after July 9, while the first intercepts of major diplomatic messages commenced several days later. By those dates, and for the next month, President Truman and many of his principal subordinates were at, or in transit to or from, the Potsdam Conference. This fact, plus the extraordinary security veiling the decoded enemy communications, raises an important question about what policy makers, particularly Truman, learned from radio intelligence. This question, in turn, is linked to the evolution of relations with the Soviet Union.

As commander in chief of the armed forces, President Roosevelt had established the White House Map Room as his military command post. There, a small staff organized and condensed for his review the stream of incoming messages describing the daily activities of American forces (that is, reports describing bombing missions and aircraft dispatched, tons of bombs dropped and aircraft losses, damage and sinking of ships, and actions over the past day by divisions and higher commands). These reports often contained casualty totals. The White House Map Room was also the destination of couriers who delivered Ultra and Magic material from the radio-intelligence centers in Washington. This arrangement continued under Truman.

The daily operational summaries, which Truman definitely received during his trip, reveal no reference to the Homeland buildup. Remarkably, the mobile version of the Map Room traveling with Truman to Potsdam was not outfitted with an Ultra or Magic radio link. A July 13 message from the White House Map Room urgently queried the detachment with Truman whether they had received "MR-Out-105" (that is, Map Room Out[-going Message No.] 105). The text of message 105 is not contained in the message files, but from context it obviously concerned Foreign Minister Togo's wires to Ambassador Sato in Moscow of July 11 and 12, disclosing the Emperor's attempt to open a negotiation channel with the Soviet Union. The following day, the detachment with Truman reported that "105 is one of the messages that we get by locked pouch and cannot be transmitted here." Couriers consumed three days transporting these pouches from Washington to Potsdam.

By July 17, a new delivery system was in place. General Marshall and Admiral King had Ultra radio communications links in place. One or both of them provided radio intelligence material to Colonel Frank McCarthy, who held a number of formal titles but effectively was General Marshall's personal aide. McCarthy gave the information to Admiral Leahy, Truman's chief of staff. These arrangements were deemed "satisfactory." Admiral Leahy played the crucial role of a filter, choosing what Truman did or did not see. To date, however, no documentary evidence has emerged of what Ultra or Magic material McCarthy passed on to Leahy or what he in turn provided to Truman. Therefore, barring discovery of new information, we cannot know with assurance how much Truman saw of the Ultra revelations about Kyushu or the Magic reports of Japanese diplomatic exchanges.

The puzzle involves not only what Truman actually saw but also what conclusions he extracted from whatever he did learn. This historical dilemma is not unique to the end of the Pacific war. The extraordinarily stringent security guarding Ultra and Magic required, for example, that all but the record copy of the Magic summaries be destroyed after being read by the recipient. None of the top wartime leaders—Churchill, Roosevelt, Truman, or their most senior military subordinates—are known to have maintained a written record of the impact of radio intelligence on their decision making, and none of them referred to Ultra in their memoirs or postwar writings. Only a handful of clipped references to radio intelligence from this period by policy makers are known to exist. But, as a recent Air Force history observed, "as these MAGIC reports were going directly to major decision makers, one must assume a degree of influence."

What the available evidence establishes is that radio intelligence was forwarded swiftly to Truman. There is contemporary evidence (discussed below) that Truman was aware of diplomatic messages from Magic. But

there is also decades-old evidence suggesting either that Truman did not
see the full stream of Ultra and Magic messages or more probably that his
memory of what he saw faded with the passage of time. Here, it must be
borne in mind that the Magic Diplomatic Summary between April 12 and
August 15, 1945, alone totaled 2,068 pages. Truman saw this material
once and could retain no written records to confirm or refresh his memory.
When the editors of the *Foreign Relations of the United States* series met
with Truman in 1956 to ask him about his recollection of certain intercepted messages, Truman responded that he was familiar with the content
of these particular messages. Truman's phrasing might reflect that the contents had been relayed to him, rather than that he personally had read the
actual messages. But his cautious words more likely stemmed from his
difficulty long after the event to recall his immediate reaction or conclusions. Moreover, the editors had just the texts of the Japanese messages,
not the Magic Diplomatic Summary with its commentary.

After Truman died in 1972, some private papers emerged that included
what now is referred to as his Potsdam diary. These handwritten notes reflect ten entries between July 7 and August 5. These and his private letters
provide glimpses of Truman's immediate reaction to a series of important
revelations, notably about the atomic bomb and apparent Japanese diplomatic intercepts. Truman reached Potsdam on the evening of July 15, but
he did not meet Stalin and Churchill until two days later. At that encounter,
Stalin declared that the Soviets would enter the Far East war on August 15.
To this news, an exuberant Truman scribbled "Fini Japs when that comes
about" in his diary, adding "I can deal with Stalin. He is honest—but smart
as hell."

The following day, Truman lunched with Churchill and recorded in his
diary:

> Discussed Manhattan [the atomic bomb project] (it is a success). Decided to
> tell Stalin about it. Stalin had told [Churchill] of telegram from Jap Emperor
> asking for peace. Stalin read his answer to me. It was satisfactory. Believe Japs
> will fold up before Russia comes in. I am sure they will when Manhattan ap-
> pears over their homeland. I shall inform Stalin about it at an opportune time.

This entry illustrates the difficult interpretive problems rampant in evalu-
ating this diary. For example, Truman attributes his reference to "telegram
from Jap Emperor asking for peace" to information provided by Stalin, not
to Magic. Moreover, the Emperor had only proposed to send a special
envoy; he had not actually asked for peace, although that was a fair infer-

ence of his probable ultimate goal. Further, the Japanese had yet to specify any peace terms. Truman's belief that the "Japs will fold up before Russia comes in" could imply he had seen Magic material, which was feasible by this date. But Truman's account also conveys an optimism about the significance of the Emperor's intervention well beyond what was warranted in light of the Weckerling-Grew assessment of July 13 that this was simply a ploy. Bearing in mind that no specialists on Japan, or apparently on the interpretation of Magic, accompanied Truman to Potsdam, and that he might not have read personally the Magic Diplomatic Summary, Truman's diary entries probably represent no more than his initial reaction to incomplete intelligence information.

On July 18, Truman wrote his wife: "I'll say that we'll end the war a year sooner now, and think of the kids who won't be killed!" This letter is a simultaneous rejoinder to two postwar arguments. First, it reflects that, up to that point in time, Truman thought in terms of the Pacific war continuing into mid-1946. This rebuts the subsequent assertion that Truman believed the Pacific war was nearly over before he journeyed to Potsdam and thus steered his decisions about the atomic bomb by how it related to diplomacy with the Soviets, not ending the war with Japan. It also counters the allegation that, after the White House meeting on June 18, Truman harbored no fear that an invasion of Japan would involve heavy loss. Indeed, this same day, Churchill cabled home of how earnestly Truman spoke "of the terrible responsibilities that rested upon him in regard to unlimited effusion of American blood."

The only diary entry between July 18 and July 25 contains nothing indicative of Ultra or Magic. But on July 25, Truman wrote: "At 10:15 I had Gen. Marshall come in and discuss with me the tactical and political situation. He is a level headed man—so is [British Admiral Lord Louis] Mountbatten." This entry almost certainly refers to a critical meeting, but both Truman's terse description and the available collateral information is maddeningly ambiguous as to precisely what transpired. Secretary of War Stimson's diary shows that over the prior two days Truman had solicited Marshall's views on the continued necessity for Soviet intervention in the Pacific war, but only through Stimson. The diary entry indicates Truman summoned Marshall, which suggests the President was anxious for information and advice. The presence of Mountbatten, the commander in chief of the Southeast Asia Command, signals that the meeting addressed Pacific matters, at least in part. Truman's use of the phrase *tactical and political situation* strongly implies that Marshall addressed the tactical prospects for Olympic. (American troops were nowhere engaged in any significant active combat on this date and, from the American perspective, the military aspects of Soviet intervention were "strategic," not "tactical.") It would be incredible if any review of the outlook for Olympic by July 25 neglected the Ultra revelations about the Japanese buildup on Kyushu.

By contrast, the reference to the "political" situation raises multiple possibilities. It could imply discussion of either the political ramifications and necessity for Soviet intervention or the significance of the Magic diplomatic intercepts. It might indicate that Marshall informed Truman about the Weckerling-Grew interpretation of the Emperor's intervention. It is, of course, entirely possible that discussion covered both topics.

Mountbatten's personal diary reveals that he had been briefed on what he described as "the greatest secret of the war" the evening before by Marshall and General Arnold, under conditions of extreme secrecy. After being told that the atomic bomb was so powerful that it would likely kill all human beings within a radius of a mile or two, Mountbatten recorded that he said, "This will surely mean the end of the war within the next few days, or anyway within the next few weeks." Marshall and Arnold essentially agreed with him but hedged that "they couldn't possibly visualize the war going on beyond the end of 1945 in any case."

Mountbatten's two-paragraph account of his extended meeting with Truman is totally devoted to the atomic bomb. He pointed out to Truman that neither he nor MacArthur had been informed of this development, which would profoundly affect their plans. The President, in Mountbatten's words,

> agreed that this should be given consideration, but his view of course was that the war should not continue for one unnecessary day . . . he felt the sooner the war could be brought to an end, both from the point of view of human life and economy, the better. . . .

Mountbatten's diary entry contains no reference to Soviet relations as a consideration in the decision to use the bomb.

Two other factors in the background to this meeting may be significant. As of this date, the Ultra and Magic information came to Truman through Leahy, who received it from Colonel McCarthy, Marshall's aide. Thus, it appears Marshall had to know what Leahy had available to pass to Truman, but Marshall had had an unsettling experience with Leahy's discharge of identical responsibilities with President Roosevelt. On February 12, 1944, Marshall had discovered that the Ultra material being forwarded to the White House was not being seen directly by Roosevelt. Instead, one officer initially screened all the material and then forwarded "a very few portions" to the attention of Admiral Leahy, who, in turn, "very seldom" shared anything with the President. Marshall reorganized the system to make sure a daily distribution of "Black Book" pamphlets went directly to very senior officials, including the President, and briefed Roosevelt on the new arrangement. Now, at Potsdam, Marshall's concern may have been aroused by the similarly jury-rigged system. Thus, Marshall might have deemed it essential that he assure that Truman was aware of the latest Ultra and Magic disclosures. Then, too, Marshall might also have felt personal responsibility because Ultra was demolishing the assumptions upon which he had based his low casualty estimates for Truman in June.

There is also a memorandum dated July 25 from Marshall to the President addressing the problems following a "Japanese capitulation in the near future," an event Marshall characterized as not expected "in the next few weeks." This memorandum indicates that the initial occupation of Japan would have to be executed by U.S. forces. Russian divisions would be available, but the United States would have to assist in their supply and transport "if it is decided to use them anywhere except on the mainland." Marshall also advised that it appeared "desirable that the Chinese participate in the occupation of Japan." Whether this memorandum was delivered or discussed at this meeting is unknown.

All of the above discussion is based on evidence reasonably contemporaneous with this meeting and thus of inherent credibility. In 1952, however, Truman asserted that he met with Marshall during the Potsdam Conference and that Marshall told him that an invasion of Japan could cost a minimum of a quarter-million American casualties. Truman's remote recollection does not carry the same weight as documentation proximate to the event. Moreover, records from the Potsdam Conference appear to demonstrate that this exchange could not have occurred, as Truman recalled, in a large meeting with many other senior U.S. officials present. But if Truman's basic memory that he met with Marshall on Olympic at Potsdam is correct—and it quite probably is—it relates to the meeting of July 25. And if Olympic was discussed on that date, it is hard to believe that Marshall would not have mentioned the Ultra disclosures.

Truman's diary entry for July 25 further notes the intention to use the "most terrible bomb in the history of the world" but to first issue a warning. Truman wrote:

Even if the Japs are savages, ruthless, merciless and fanatic, we as the leader of the world for the common welfare can not drop this terrible bomb on the old capital or the new. . . . The target will be a purely military one and we will issue a warning statement asking the Japs to surrender and save lives. I'm sure they will not do that, but we will have given them the chance.

In view of the more optimistic July 17 entry, the July 25 comments can be read as evidence of deflated expectations about a Japanese surrender. Whether this is related directly to this briefing by Marshall or other information cannot be resolved by the current evidence. One thing is clear about this session on the morning of July 25: Truman himself deemed it "a most important session."*

Truman was back at sea, en route home when Admiral Leahy received the following message on August 3:

> The distribution of MAGIC material concerning matter contained in MR-OUT-317, and others on same subject, has been strictly limited. General Marshall has asked that all messages on this subject be marked for your eyes only and that further distribution be only such as you deem absolutely necessary.

This message very likely indicates that Togo's cable of August 2 (which contained the disclosure that the Imperial Army was interested in the Soviet negotiation channel) had reached Leahy. Notes prepared by Walter Brown, an aide to Byrnes, contain the following for this date: "President, Leahy, [Byrnes] [agreed] Japs looking for peace. (Leahy had another report from Pacific) President afraid they will sue for peace through Russia instead of some country like Sweden." This notation is significant because it provides contemporary confirmation that Leahy definitely had been sharing radio intelligence information with Truman. At the same time, while it was obvious that Japan was "looking for peace" by August 3, no American knew Japan's ideas save that Suzuki had rejected, apparently with ridicule, the Potsdam Declaration. That Truman hoped Japan would choose a non-Soviet channel is understandable since, like the Japanese, Truman could see that such a role would permit the Soviets to extract a middleman's price for services, and experience with Soviet occupation in Europe scarcely recommended its repetition in Japan.

Several other key policy makers have left some evidence on Ultra and Magic information and how they interpreted it. On July 16, Secretary of War Stimson noted in his diary that he received "a very important paper"

---

* When Truman's Potsdam diary and letters to his wife first appeared, some soon argued that they "proved" Truman knew the use of atomic weapons was unnecessary since he realized that Soviet intervention alone would end the war and that atomic bombs were not the only alternative to the invasion, but that the bombs would end the war before Soviet entry. Thus, the diary and the letters have been taken as key evidence establishing that the bombs were dropped primarily with anti-Soviet motives. Truman's diary entries are simply too abbreviated and elliptical to support firm conclusions. His comment that he believed the Japanese might surrender before Soviet entry is ambiguous because it is not clear when he thought the first atomic bomb would be employed and how many he believed would be necessary to secure Japan's surrender. (Truman had yet to learn of the successful test of the atomic bomb.) Truman's remarks on July 25 indicating he knew the Japanese would not accept the Potsdam

on "Japanese maneuverings for peace." Heretofore, it may have seemed obvious that Stimson's entry referred to Magic intercepts. Now, however, it appears most likely that he was alluding to the Weckerling-Grew assessment, which had been transmitted to Marshall, who presumably shared it with Stimson. On July 18, Stimson spoke to Allen Dulles of the OSS about "something which recently came to him with regard to Japan," which presumptively must have been about Dulles's encounters with Japanese peace entrepreneurs in Europe.

What impact the intercepts, the Weckerling-Grew assessment, or the Dulles conversation had on Stimson is not articulated. On the one hand, he declined to reverse his earlier veto of a proposal to add Kyoto to the target list for an atomic bomb, commenting that he saw "no new factors for reversing myself but on the contrary the new factors seem to confirm it." He also continued to press to have the Potsdam Declaration include a guarantee of the Imperial system. On the other hand, his diary entries recounting his many conversations with other senior American and British officials, including Truman, neither state nor imply that he believed a Japanese surrender was imminent or that he attached special significance to diplomatic intercepts. Further, his diary entries in August show he foresaw an armistice and then negotiations prior to a Japanese surrender and that Byrnes and Truman anticipated a guarantee about the Imperial institution at that juncture.

On August 7, in a memorandum to Secretary of State Byrnes, Joseph Grew reported:

> We have good reason to believe that important elements in Japan, including some of their elder statesmen as well as high officers in the Army and Navy, are trying to bring about an acceptance of the terms proposed in the Potsdam Proclamation. We know, for instance, from secret but unimpeachable information that Sato, the Japanese Ambassador to Moscow, formerly Minister of Foreign Affairs, has been earnestly recommending this course and we believe it possible although by no means certain that this movement may gain headway to a point where the advocates of peace will be able to overcome the opposition of the military extremists *and their present control of the Emperor* [emphasis added].

Declaration have been represented as evidence that he realized the lack of guarantee of the Imperial institution would trigger certain rejection, but it is far more likely that they reflect new radio intelligence information Truman had received, either from Marshall or through Leahy, indicating that the Japanese were nowhere as near to surrendering as he had believed on July 17. See Robert L. Messer, "New Evidence on Truman's Decision," in *Hiroshima's Shadow,* ed. Kai Bird and Lawrence Lifschultz (Stony Creek, Conn.: Pamphleteer's Press, 1998), pp. 90–98; Gar Alperovitz, *The Decision to Use the Atomic Bomb* (New York: Alfred A. Knopf, 1995), pp. 302, 546–47, 631, 663.

This passage appears in new light with the benefit of knowledge that Grew had concurred with Weckerling on July 13 that the messages about the Emperor's intervention represented merely a diplomatic ploy. Clearly, Grew's comments to Byrnes demonstrate that he did not regard the Emperor as an independent force but as one still controlled by the "military extremists." Moreover, Grew's cautious language betrayed his very tentative stance on how near Japan was to peace on terms acceptable to the Allies.*

Another important official maintaining a diary was Secretary of the Navy James Forrestal, who remained in Washington when Truman went to Potsdam. On July 13, Forrestal recorded, obviously after reading the Magic revelations about the Emperor's proposal for a special envoy to the Soviet Union, that "the first real evidence of a Japanese desire to get out of the war came today." Forrestal noted, however, that Sato's response to Togo blasted the proposals as "quite unrealistic." Forrestal used the heading "Japanese Peace Feeler" in six more entries through July 30 where he emphasized Sato's condemnation of the rampant fallacy in Japan's diplomacy. On July 24, Forrestal underscored Sato's advice that Japan must "accept . . . any terms, including unconditional surrender, on the basis that this was the only way of preserving the entity of the emperor and the State itself." Forrestal then recorded the response to Sato:

> The Cabinet in council had weighed all the considerations which he had raised and that their final judgment and decision was that the war must be fought with all the vigor and bitterness of which the nation was capable so long as the only alternative was the unconditional surrender.

Forrestal then embarked on a trip to Europe, where he arrived on July 28, after the Potsdam Declaration was issued. He met with Truman on July 28 and 30. Although he wrote down in detail the subjects of their conversation on the twenty-eighth, there is no indication he advised the President or anyone else that he believed Japan susceptible to surrender by diplomacy alone, or even that Japan was on the cusp of surrender.

---

* Both Grew and Stimson advised Truman that a guarantee of the Imperial institution would prove essential to obtaining Japan's surrender. After the war, Grew highlighted his efforts in his memoirs and may have persuaded Stimson to suggest in his own memoirs that such a guarantee might have obtained a surrender without the use of atomic weapons. Grew, *Turbulent Era, II,* pp. 1421–73; Stimson and Bundy, *On Active Service in War and Peace,* p. 629. These memoirs form the foundation for an argument alleging that use of atomic bombs actually *delayed* the surrender because the U.S. government chose to wait to use them rather than issue such a guarantee, coupled perhaps with other modifications of unconditional surrender, at some point between around June and August 1945. Sherwin, *A World Destroyed,* pp. 236–37; Sherwin, "Hiroshima and Modern Memory," *The Nation* (October 10, 1981); 329, 349–53.

Running in parallel with the issue of Ultra and Magic disclosures and their impact on the strategy to end the war is the question of Soviet intervention against Japan. By the time of the Potsdam Conference, Soviet intervention was linked to use of the atomic bombs and the unconditional-surrender policy. Postwar debates have focused intensely on the nature of those links. Originally, American strategists viewed Soviet intervention as vital in order to tie down Japan's Kwantung Army and prevent the transfer of its manpower to the Homeland. Even before the successful test of the atomic bomb, however, the threat posed by the Kwantung Army to American strategy had dissipated due to the precipitous decline in the quality of its formations and the severance of Japanese communications with the mainland.

Truman directed Stimson to secure Marshall's views on the military necessity of Soviet intervention on July 23. The next day, Marshall responded that the massing of Soviet forces along the Manchurian border had pinned down the Kwantung Army, but that

> even if we went ahead in the war without the Russians, and compelled the Japanese to surrender to our terms, that would not prevent the Russians from marching into Manchuria . . . thus permitting them to get virtually what they wanted in the surrender terms.

Stimson acknowledged that Marshall's response was not explicit, but interpreted it as indicating that "with our new weapon we would not need the assistance of the Russians to conquer Japan." He conveyed this to Truman.

Stimson devoted much of his energies to the issues raised by the atomic bomb. He initially saw the secret of the bomb as a bargaining counter to trade for liberalization of the Soviet regime, which he saw as vital for long-term peace. In June, Truman indicated he shared this thought that the secret of the bomb could be traded for a quid pro quo, and news of the suc-

---

Accepting this argument requires the supposition that the Japanese government or the Emperor would have terminated the war upon such an initiative. There is no contemporary Japanese evidence to support this belief, but there is clear Magic evidence to the contrary. Moreover, an examination of Grew's actual prognostications in the summer of 1945 reveals a very different story from his postwar assertion. On July 7, he predicted that the United States must anticipate a Japanese diplomatic offensive to stave off defeat, and six days later he joined Weckerling in interpreting the Emperor's intervention as most likely representing just such a ploy. Even as late as the above memorandum on August 7, Grew was still far from firm about the proximity of a Japanese surrender and he was flatly wrong on the position of the Emperor. Grew's memoirs also demonstrate that he was beguiled by his Japanese postwar contacts into the erroneous belief that "surrender minded elements" in Tokyo would have seized a guarantee to end the war and that Prime Minister Suzuki was "surrender minded even before May, 1945."

cess of the atomic-bomb test buttressed the President. At the Potsdam Conference, however, direct observation of the Soviet system sobered Stimson on this idea.

The interplay between the handling of unconditional surrender, the Potsdam Declaration, the bomb, and the Soviet-American relationship creates a complex picture. Stalin expressly reaffirmed his support for unconditional surrender to Truman not only through Hopkins in May but also face-to-face at Potsdam on July 18. Stalin presumably sought to neuter Japan and prevent it from restraining Soviet postwar ambitions in the Far East and to foreclose the chance that Japan might capitulate before the Soviets obtained the spoils promised at Yalta. Jettisoning unconditional surrender thus would not be viewed benignly by the Soviets. Indeed, on this last point the Forrestal diary provides telling evidence. In discussing the proposed Potsdam Declaration, Grew commented on July 6 that

> he was afraid it would be ditched on the way over by people who accompany the President—[Charles] Bohlen, among others—who reflect the view that we can not afford to hold out any clarification of terms to Japan which could be construed as a desire to get the Japanese war over with before Russia has an opportunity to enter.

Stimson's diary illustrates the American perception at Potsdam that various Soviet demands revealed unrestrained ambitions. Though Truman told Stimson he saw much of this as bluff, James Byrnes played a more important role than Stimson in formulating foreign policy. We have less direct contemporary evidence on Byrnes's thinking, but Forrestal recorded in his diary on July 28 that "Byrnes said he was most anxious to get the Japanese affair over with before the Russians got in, with the particular reference to Dairen and Port Arthur. Once in there, he felt it would not be easy to get them out."

No doubt some American policy makers, especially Byrnes, hoped that the atomic bomb would prove a useful diplomatic tool. But even before the Ultra revelations about the Japanese buildup on Kyushu became known, the solid consensus of the historians has been that the diplomatic fruits of the atomic bombs were at best a bonus or reinforcing reason, not the underlying one, for their employment.

Finally, recognition that the bomb had important political implications in the relations of the United States and the Soviet Union did not suddenly come upon Stimson, Byrnes, and Truman in 1945. President Roosevelt perceived this from the start when he set the United States on a course to an atomic bomb. Further, in a December 31, 1944, meeting, Stimson had advised Roosevelt that the Soviets had spies working to unravel the secrets of the atomic-bomb project. Stimson wrongly thought the spies had not secured any "real knowledge," and he counseled both against taking the Soviets officially into confidence and to look forward to securing a quid pro quo for the secrets of atomic weapons. Roosevelt continued to withhold the secret from the Soviets, and Stimson recorded no objection from the president to linking the bomb and political concessions.

16

Hiroshima

"Horrible catastrophes"

The Manhattan Project and "Targets"

Profoundly alarmed by progress toward an atomic bomb in Nazi Germany, émigré and American scientists had convinced President Franklin Roosevelt of the urgent need to beat Hitler to possession of such a weapon. Roosevelt sanctioned the enterprise, later christened the Manhattan Project, in 1941. There is no evidence that Roosevelt ever questioned the legitimacy of such weapons, but there is evidence he saw their colossal political implications and decided to deny Stalin knowledge of the project because, as historian Barton Bernstein observed, "the bomb might well give the United States future leverage against the Soviets."

By virtually every measure, the atomic-bomb program was mammoth. The price—over two billion dollars—was camouflaged among other appropriations and hidden, as were nearly all other aspects of the program, from the legislative branch and all but a select circle within the executive branch. Major General Leslie Groves steered the program around an archipelago of secret research and production sites, most notably in Tennessee, Washington State, and New Mexico. To direct the research of a galaxy of enormously gifted scientific talent, he recruited Dr. J. Robert Oppenheimer. Groves mordantly observed that while Oppenheimer lacked the Nobel Prize credential of many of his subordinates, he was "a real genius."

The terrifying fear of atomic weapons in Hitler's arsenal propelled the frantic Allied effort well into 1944, but the Germans stumbled at the outset by, among other things, grossly overestimating the amount of uranium required to sustain a chain reaction. Therefore, they deduced that producing a bomb demanded greater quantities of fissionable material than they could manufacture. Moreover, this perceived difficulty pointed inescapably to the corollary that even if a bomb program succeeded, the resulting weapons would be few in number, limited in power, or both.

In Japan, both the Imperial Army and the Imperial Navy had supported programs of research on atomic weapons, and in early 1943 a study by the Army Aeronautic Technology Research Institute had declared that an atomic bomb was feasible. Prime Minister Tojo, believing Japan's fortunes could be decided by the atomic bomb, took personal interest and ordered that Nishina Laboratories be granted unlimited budgets and resources for this effort.

The laboratories were run by Dr. Yoshio Nishina, a world-class physicist, but the Imperial Army–sponsored project sauntered rather than marched under his direction. The first and fundamental problem the Japanese confronted was securing an adequate supply of uranium ore. They contracted for shipment by submarine of two tons of ore from a Czechoslovakian mine, but none of this reached Japan.

The Japanese programs achieved relatively little through late 1944, and in the spring of 1945, B-29 raids effectively halted them. The April 13 Tokyo incendiary raid consumed the main research facility, and another raid eliminated a centrifuging separator.

Prior to actual testing and employment of atomic bombs, projections of their destructive capabilities varied markedly. An August 1944 report predicted that uranium bombs would equal about 20,000 tons of TNT, while plutonium bombs would equal at least 5,000 tons of TNT. By December 1944, however, the power of a uranium bomb was estimated as that of 10,000 tons of TNT. Projections for a plutonium bomb ranked its destructiveness as equal to five hundred tons of TNT; later estimates ranged up to 2,500 tons. To comprehend the thinking in 1945, it is essential to bear in mind that a single B-29 could deliver eight to ten tons of bombs, and thus a typical individual raid of five hundred Superfortresses unleashed four to five thousand tons of explosives. Accordingly, a single atomic explosion represented no order-of-magnitude increase in destructiveness over a conventional air raid.

The availability of the bombs was also uncertain. An August 1944 memorandum prognosticated that the first plutonium bomb would be available March 31, 1945, or possibly one month earlier. It would be July before a single uranium bomb would be ready. By December 1944, eroding expectations left scientists predicting that the first uranium bomb would be available about August 1, 1945, and a second by the year's end. Groves reported that "our previous hopes that [a plutonium] type of bomb might be developed in the late spring have now been dissipated by scientific difficulties." It was July before the first plutonium bomb was available, and thereafter "about 17" were expected to be produced by the end of the year.

Once the realistic prospect of these weapons dawned, attention shifted to target selection, a matter heretofore delegated to theater commands. Marshall decided that security requirements and unique technical considerations mandated guidance by the Manhattan Project leaders, which suited Groves's predilections. A target committee comprising both Groves's officers and scientists met in April and May. Two factors channeled their deliberations: There would be few bombs and thus few targets deemed worthy of such weapons. Given these constraints, as Groves later related:

> I had set out as the governing factor that the targets chosen should be places the bombing of which would most adversely affect the will of the Japanese people to continue the war. Beyond that, they should be military in nature, consisting of either important headquarters or troop concentrations, or centers of production of military equipment or supplies. To enable us to assess accurately the effects of the bomb, the targets should not have been previously damaged in air raids. It was also desirable that the first target be of such size that the damage would be confined within it, so that we could definitely determine the power of the bomb.

This ordering of priorities fit the strategy of shock favored by Secretary of War Stimson, General Marshall, and other project leaders. The first meeting of the target committee agreed that each bomb must be dropped under visual conditions, not by radar, to assure that the effect of each bomb would not be squandered by aiming error, despite the prospect of extremely few clear days during Japan's notoriously poor summer weather. (The violation of this guideline on the second atomic mission led to wholly unexpected consequences.) Given the direction of aerial bombardment in Europe and against Japan, the committee left no recorded qualms about describing the preferred target as one of the "large urban areas of not less than three miles in diameter existing in the larger populated areas."

At the next gathering of the target committee in May, Oppenheimer took charge of the meeting by plunking down an eleven-item agenda. Most of these dealt with technical issues. Oppenheimer impressed the assembly that the fissionable material in the bomb contained a billion deadly radiation doses and that "will, of course, have an effect on exposed personnel in the target area." Would this kill many or few "exposed personnel"; would the radioactivity linger and in what amount; or would the potential lethal doses of radiation be moot because victims would die first of heat or blast? Oppenheimer did not say, and the skimpy record does not show that anyone pressed the point.

The meeting pursued Oppenheimer's themes of "psychological factors in target selection" and "use against military objectives." These tied initially to the expected power of the bombs, which remained uncertain. By this time, estimates projected that the uranium bomb, code-named "Little Boy," might be equivalent to 5,000 to 15,000 tons; the plutonium bomb, "Fat Man," was "anybody's guess: 700, 2,000, 5,000 tons," as one writer noted. It was agreed that confining use to a purely military objective would diminish the full impact of the weapon and that "it should be located in a much larger area subject to blast damage." The minutes further show that the desired "psychological objectives" not only concerned Japan but also were hoped to be "sufficiently spectacular for the importance of the weapon to be internationally recognized when publicity on it is released."

From a number of candidates, the target committee distilled a list of four: the cites of Kyoto, Hiroshima, and Yokohama, and the Kokura arsenal. Niigata was left as an alternative. Kyoto's place at the head of the list stemmed from its large size (over one million population) and the fact that it had been thus far untouched due to its recognized cultural importance. The committee noted that "from the psychological point of view there is the advantage that Kyoto is an intellectual center for Japan and [thus] the people are more apt to appreciate the significance of such a weapon." During discussions, Tokyo and even the Emperor's palace itself fell under scrutiny. The city was ruled out on the basis that it was already "practically rubble." As to targeting the palace (a euphemism presumably for killing the Emperor), it was "agreed that we should not recommend it but that any action for this bombing should come from authorities on military policy." At a third meeting on May 28, the committee members refined their recommendations to three targets, in order: Kyoto, Hiroshima, and Niigata. They confirmed the city centers as the aiming point, not a specific industrial area, because the bomb might "miss" the intended point of impact by up to a fifth of a mile and they wanted no waste of power.

Still another committee became involved in targeting. Secret development of the bomb under sole aegis of the executive branch during wartime could be justified, but many issues on atomic energy in peacetime had emerged that demanded immediate attention. To lay the groundwork on these postwar issues, Secretary of War Stimson created the Interim Committee. He astutely chose this title to avoid the implication that the executive branch intended to deny the legislative branch the right to exercise its oversight functions on atomic policy once the wartime emergency had passed. The Interim Committee comprised Stimson, his assistant George Harrison, Vannevar Bush (the czar of the wartime science effort), Harvard President James Conant, physicist and M.I.T. president Karl T. Compton, Assistant Secretary of State William L. Clayton, and Under Secretary of the Navy Ralph A. Bard. Joining the committee as Truman's personal representative was Secretary of State Designate James F. Byrnes. Stimson also appointed an advisory scientific panel composed of Oppenheimer, Enrico Fermi, Ernest Lawrence, and Arthur H. Compton.

Apparently ignorant of the full costs of the Hamburg, Dresden, or Tokyo fire raids, Arthur Compton wrote that since the bomb "introduces the question of mass slaughter, really for the first time in history" and carried with it "the question of possible radioactive poison over the area bombed," it was perhaps inevitable that this committee would examine methods of use. George Marshall had been meditating on this and told Stimson on May 29 that he believed the bomb should be used first on a military target, not civilians, and then on a large war plant only after civilians were warned to leave.

The Interim Committee's formal mandate did not include explicit review of the decision to use the bomb. By now the presumption that the bomb would be used as soon as available (a point explicitly memorialized by Oppenheimer in the minutes) possessed a tremendous momentum of its own. But this was probably the last moment where policy makers could have opted for alternatives with reasonable prospect of success, and indeed such alternatives were reviewed. The bomb, said Stimson in his opening remarks on May 31, represented a "new relationship of man to the universe. This discovery might be compared to the discoveries of the Copernican theory and the laws of gravity, but far more important than these in its effects on the lives of men."

When the committee began to examine the effects of the bomb on the Japanese, someone questioned whether the impact of the bomb really would be distinguishable from "any current air corps strike of current dimensions." Oppenheimer responded that there would be signal differences: "The visual effect of an atomic bombing would be tremendous. It would be accompanied by a brilliant luminescence which would rise to a height of 10,000 to 20,000 feet." The bomb's power would range between the equivalent of two thousand and twenty thousand tons of TNT; its radiation "would be dangerous to life for a radius of at least two-thirds of a mile." He ventured that the bomb would kill twenty thousand Japanese.

The minutes conclude:

After much discussion concerning the various types of targets and effects to be produced, the Secretary expressed the conclusion, on which there was general agreement, that we could not give the Japanese any warning, that we could not concentrate on a civilian area, but that we should seek to make a profound psychological impression on as many Japanese as possible. At the suggestion of Dr. Conant the Secretary agreed that the most desirable target would be a vital plant employing a large number of workers and closely surrounded by workers' houses.

Byrnes passed this recommendation to Truman on June 1. The President concurred that "the only reasonable conclusion was to use the bomb."

In this chronology, two important matters must be noted. First, as the distinguished scholar of these events, Barton Bernstein, so lucidly demonstrated, from the outset a presumption that the bomb would be used when ready was embedded in the shared understanding of Roosevelt and those directing the Manhattan Project. This presumption represented a key bequest in Roosevelt's potent legacy to Truman. Thus, any notion that these policy makers agonized over the question of use or that Truman made a personal and lonely decision to use the bomb misconstrues the decision process. Later, Groves stated that Truman's "decision was one of noninterference—basically, a decision not to upset the existing plans." But Truman's noninterference transpired in the context of a policy that arrived before him carrying the unanimous sanction of his principal advisers on the issue, all of whom save Byrnes had similarly served Roosevelt. None of these advisers had been moved to reexamine the issue of use, and thus there was no catalyst for Truman to do so.*

A second point concerns the deliberate decision to target large numbers of noncombatants. The men who unanimously concurred with the description of the target experienced no sensation that their choice vaulted over a great divide. This moment culminated a long policy-making process that had begun with stubby bombs wiggling down from the Kaiser's zeppelins and bombers in World War I, then incubated as a theory between the wars, first tried by Axis nations in Asia and Europe, and then brought to a crescendo by Britain and the United States in Europe and finally against Japan. But its implications were understood and acknowledged in the uneasy cosmetic formulation dutifully recorded for posterity. The target de-

* It is probably significant that Truman ordered no formal gathering with his advisers to review use of the atomic bomb, while he did insist on such a meeting to examine the invasion strategy. He ordered that meeting, however, only after receiving the critical Hoover memorandum. Of course, it does not follow from this that Truman would have delved into the plans to use the bomb even if a scientist, who would not have held standing with Truman comparable to that of Hoover, had raised the question.

scription squared with the evolution of American bombing doctrine that persisted in demanding that the intended aiming point must be a legitimate military objective ("a vital plant"). But while Stimson observed that "we could not concentrate on a civilian area," these men admitted their deliberate design that the atomic bomb should do more than lay waste to a war production facility. As Barton Bernstein observed, these men "all knew that families—women, children, and even in the daytime, during the bombing attack, some workers—dwelled in 'workers' houses.' "

It is more the express acknowledgment that the atomic bombing would produce huge civilian casualties than the actual effect that sets this formulation apart from what had gone before. Those with access to Magic and Ultra knew from intercepted messages that the March fire raid on Tokyo reportedly had killed up to 100,000 Japanese. Stimson, for one, was troubled by the incendiary campaign against Japanese cities, and sharply if very belatedly questioned Arnold about it in early June. He was assured that the Army Air Forces were attempting as much precision as possible but that the Japanese system of dispersal explained and justified the burning out of huge neighborhoods.

Truman recorded in his diary on July 25 that the target would be a "purely military one," but this might have reflected either Truman's lack of understanding of the power of the bombs or his reluctance to admit the consequences of what he had failed to halt. Despite describing it as "this terrible bomb," Truman, like Roosevelt and probably all advisers save the scientists, did not truly grasp the real horror of these weapons. On the other hand, Bush and Conant, the two senior scientists, actually believed that unless the huge and hideous effects of the weapons were graphically demonstrated on cities, people and leaders would not accede to the surrender of national sovereignty necessary to enforce an international control system for nuclear weapons.

Sometime during the May 31 conference, the question of a demonstration of the bomb on an unpopulated area was explored, perhaps informally. The concept was rejected for several reasons: There was still no guarantee the weapon would work, and a failure would have a diametrically opposite effect from that sought; the Japanese might intercept the bomber; Japanese militarists might refuse to be impressed; or the Japanese might move Allied prisoners of war into the designated target zone. But the issue of noncombat use did not end there and merged with another matter: postwar nuclear dangers.

Niels Bohr, the great Danish physicist, met rude rebuff when he attempted to persuade Churchill to notify Stalin of the atomic-bomb project. Bohr then won an interview with Roosevelt in August 1944. Roosevelt seemed to indicate, as he had three times earlier with Supreme Court Justice Felix Frankfurter, that he placed international control above military use. But not only did the President fail to move to implement such concepts, he in fact ordered action to the contrary. He signed an agreement with Churchill the following month expressly rejecting the proposal that "the world should be informed regarding [the atomic-bomb project], with a view to an international agreement regarding its control and use."

Another scientist with a postwar vision was Leo Szilard, who possessed not one but many conceptions that veered radically, from the conviction that the bomb must be used in combat to shock the public into sacrifices (a view similar to that of Bush and Conant), to preemptive war to secure uranium deposits, to approaching the Soviets after the bombs had been used on Japan, to a plea that the United States must eschew even a test and keep the secret until it had an "overwhelming and unapproachable" advantage from which to dictate a well-conceived blueprint for peace.

Szilard also believed scientists, notably himself, must be accorded a role in cabinet-level policy making. He first arranged to see Roosevelt (with the proposal in hand to consult the Soviets *after* using the bombs), but the President's death canceled the appointment. He next tried to meet with Truman, but found himself redirected to James F. Byrnes. Szilard did not know that Truman intended to make Byrnes his Secretary of State but surmised that Byrnes would have some major role in atomic policy. What exactly happened at the meeting is not clear, beyond the fact that each party emerged with a low opinion of the other. Byrnes probably alluded to the political implications of the bomb in dealing with the Soviets and displayed profound ignorance of many nuclear energy matters. When Szilard spoke emphatically of both keeping research going and retaining complete secrecy, Byrnes attempted to administer a dose of reality by pointing out that Congress was unlikely to appropriate vast sums of money without being advised of the expenditure's purpose. Byrnes recalled the unfavorable impression created by his visitor's "general demeanor" and alluded to Szilard's condescending tone and insistence on participating in policy making. Nothing beneficial came of this exchange.

Another font of ideas about policy on atomic weapons was the Chicago Metallurgical Laboratory, where a group, including Szilard, prepared what later became known as the Franck Report, after its leader, James Franck. The report favored eventual international control ("based on mutual trust and willingness on all sides to give up a certain part of their sovereign rights") of atomic energy as the only safe solution. The authors raised the specter that use of an atomic bomb against Japan, without warning, would both arouse great international animosity against the United States and greatly complicate the establishment of international controls. Demonstrate the bomb on an uninhabited area before an international audience, they recommended; thereafter, use it against Japan under United Nations sanction. Franck and his colleagues slipped in a curious non sequitur at one point as they dismissed the weapon as too puny to shock the Japanese to surrender but then argued that it would impress the despotic Soviet government into granting free access to roving foreign inspectors.

The Franck Report prompted George Harrison, acting on behalf of Stimson, to request the scientific panel advising the Interim Committee to look again at the demonstration idea, apparently only in the limited context of securing an early Japanese surrender. The panel reported:

> The opinions of our scientific colleagues on the initial use of these weapons are not unanimous . . . We can propose no technical demonstration likely to bring an end to the war; we see no acceptable alternative to direct military use.

The members of the panel further noted pointedly that "as scientific men" they had "no claim to special competence" in solving military, social, or political problems created by atomic power. On June 21, based on this report, the Interim Committee confirmed that there was no alternative to military use of the weapon.* At the same time, the Interim Committee, reversing its position from May, recommended that the Soviets be advised of the bomb before its use, "if suitable opportunity arose."

Under Secretary of the Navy Ralph Bard, shortly before his scheduled departure from the government on July 1, likewise expressed reservations in a memorandum on using the weapon without warning. Bard did not, as sometimes reported, have an interview with Truman on June 27 in which the President allegedly said that "the question was whether we wanted to save many American lives and Japanese lives or whether we wanted to . . . win the war by killing our young men." Bard, a committed believer that blockade and bombardment would end the war, maintained later that he counseled Truman not to invade and "kill a million people." Like many other postwar recollections, Bard's statements should be taken with considerable reservation.

To resolve lingering doubts about the workability of the plutonium-implosion concept, a test had been scheduled, code-named Trinity. At 5:30

---

* Szilard continued to agitate and got sixty-eight signatures on a petition calling for no use until Japan was advised in detail of surrender terms and had refused. This petition never got beyond Stimson, and in view of the Ultra disclosures of the Japanese buildup against Olympic, later theories that the petition could in any way have altered events are far-fetched, to say the least.

A.M. July 16, a statically rigged implosion device detonated in the desolate Jornada del Muerto valley northwest of Alamogordo, New Mexico. Brigadier General Thomas F. Farrell, Grove's deputy, reported:

> The whole country was lighted by a searing light with the intensity many times that of the midday sun. It was golden, purple, violet, gray and blue. It lighted every peak, crevasse and ridge of the nearby mountain range with a clarity and beauty . . . the great poets dream about but describe most poorly and inadequately. Thirty seconds after, the explosion came first, the air blast . . . followed almost immediately by the strong, sustained, awesome roar which warned of doomsday and made us feel that we puny things were blasphemous to dare tamper with the forces heretofore reserved to The Almighty.

Following terse, cryptic reports of the success of the test, a detailed report from Groves reached Truman at Potsdam on July 21. Groves euphorically reported that the power of the bomb was "conservative[ly]" calculated as between fifteen and twenty thousand tons of TNT. It was heard at a distance of one hundred miles and seen up to 180 miles away. Groves advised Truman that "here and there" the radioactivity on the ground was fairly high, but in no place would it have required evacuation of the population. The report incorporated a narrative by Farrell describing graphic examples of the power of the bomb and the pervasive reactions of those who had worked on it. He included this comment: "As to the present war, there was a feeling that no matter what else might happen, we now had the means to insure its speedy conclusion and save thousands of American lives." The die was cast.

The mission of actually dropping atomic bombs fell to the 509th Composite Group. It was commanded by a young but extraordinarily capable Army Air Forces officer, Colonel Paul W. Tibbets, Jr., a B-29 test pilot with extensive combat experience in Europe. Tibbets, who was originally told to prepare two bomb groups to drop bombs in Europe or against Japan, ultimately organized only the hybrid 509th Group—a single squadron of specially modified B-29s to actually carry and deliver the bombs, supported by service and supply elements to make the group independent of normal channels. In July 1945, the group deployed to Tinian.

The 509th mounted twelve practice missions to simulate as near as possible the special techniques required for their role. Each B-29 released a single large demolition bomb, dubbed "pumpkins," on a run into the wind over selected targets from altitudes of at least thirty thousand feet. The pilot then executed a dramatic turn of at least 150 degrees away from the drop point, thus adding the thrust of a tail wind to the power of the engines to place as much distance as possible between the aircraft and the explosion. Scientists calculated that even at a distance of ten miles from the blast, a B-29 would be subjected to a sudden two G acceleration. The B-29 was designed to handle a four G acceleration.

General Spaatz demanded a written directive to drop the atomic bombs. President Truman approved a draft plan July 24, and the orders to Spaatz were issued the following day, in the name of Secretary of War Stimson and Chief of Staff Marshall. These stipulated use of "the first special bomb" when weather permitted visual release after August 3. Targets were listed in the sequence Hiroshima, Kokura, Niigata, and Nagasaki. Spaatz was further told that "additional bombs will be delivered on the above targets as soon as made ready." Obviously, a sustained effort was anticipated.

The 509th Group report identified the lack of prior damaging attacks as the principal factor in the selection of the target cities. The conspicuous absence of Kyoto from the list was the result of direct intervention by Secretary of War Stimson, who deleted the city over vigorous and protracted efforts by Groves. Stimson had traveled to Japan and appreciated the cultural significance and splendor of the old capital and insisted that its artifacts, if not its one million inhabitants, be spared. Even so, the 509th continued to launch practice missions to the vicinity of Kyoto, which occasioned some erroneous postwar suggestions that it had remained a target. The city substituted for Kyoto was Nagasaki, despite pointed messages from both Spaatz and Nimitz to their superiors in Washington reminding them of the presence there of Allied prisoner-of-war camps.

Mission number thirteen of the 509th Group designated the Hiroshima "urban industrial area" as the primary target. The Kokura arsenal and city ranked second, followed by the Nagasaki urban area. The mission report described Hiroshima correctly as the largest city in the Japanese Homeland (except Kyoto) that had remained undamaged by the B-29 incendiary strikes. With a 1940 population of 344,000, Hiroshima fairly earned its description as an "army city." It featured the headquarters of the Fifth Division and was a primary port of embarkation, as the mission report declared:

> The entire northeast and eastern sides of the city are military zones. Prominent in the north central part of the city are the Army Division headquarters marked by the Hiroshima Castle, numerous barracks, administrative building and ordnance storage houses. In addition, there are the following military targets: Army Reception Center, large Military Airport, Army Ordnance Depot, Army Clothing Depot, Army Food Depot, large port and dock area, several

shipyards and ship building companies, the Japan Steel Company, railroad marshalling yards and numerous aircraft component parts factories. . . .

The size of the city was another important factor in the selection. According to preliminary data, it was believed that the radius of damage that would be inflicted by the atomic bomb was 7,500 feet. By placing the aiming point in the center of the city, the circle of prospective damage covered almost the entire area of Hiroshima with the exception of the dock area in the south.

Not identified in the mission report but known to American intelligence was that the city housed the headquarters of Field Marshal Hata's Second General Army. Counting Hata's headquarters, about 43,000 soldiers crowded into Hiroshima amid perhaps as many as 280,000 to 290,000 civilians. This almost certainly gave Hiroshima the highest density of servicemen to civilians among Japan's large urban areas. But even if Hiroshima played a very prominent role in Japan's war-making potential, it could not be classified as wholly a military installation.*

Weather dashed hopes to use the first atomic bomb on August 3; only on August 5 did meteorologists offer prospects of the requisite clear visibility the next morning. With Tibbets at the controls, *Enola Gay,* the B-29 named for his mother and carrying "Little Boy," the uranium bomb, commenced

---

* Why had Hiroshima, the seventh largest city by population in Japan, and Nagasaki (the twelfth largest) not been bombed earlier? The directives that Hansell and then LeMay operated under to June 15 specified as targets only thirty-three "Selected Urban Industrial Concentrations," exclusive of both these cities, and important aircraft-manufacturing concerns, which both cities lacked. The Joint Chiefs of Staff issued a formal order on July 3 precluding any form of attack on Kyoto, Hiroshima, Kokura, and Niigata. Thus, for Hiroshima the only window in which an attack could have occurred prior to the atomic bombing was between June 15 and July 3. During that interval, the XXI Bomber Command operated on only six days. Two of these, June 22 and 26, provided opportunities for daylight visual bombing, and thus were used to attack aircraft-manufacturing targets. Night urban-area attacks were mounted on the other four days against fourteen cities. These cities ranged widely over the spectrum of the largest sixty cities in Japan, but generally they were satellites of the Tokyo and Nagoya industrial regions or independent ports and industrial regions. It is likely Hiroshima was not targeted because, while it was a huge training, storage, and transportation center for the Imperial Army, it lacked significance in manufacturing of war material, particularly aircraft production. Nagasaki, on the other hand, was mainly a major shipbuilding center and thus redundant in view of the mine-laying campaign. More important, it was found to be one of fifteen cities that could not be readily attacked at night or under inclement conditions by aircraft fitted with the standard APQ-13 radar. Joint Chiefs of Staff to Commander in Chief, Army Forces Pacific, Command . . . WARX 26350, 3 July 1945 (message placing Kyoto, Hiroshima, Kokura, and Niigata off-limits to attack without authorization of the JCS), RG 218, Geographic File, 1942–1945, 373.11 Japan (8-20-43), Pt. 13, Box 117; USAF HC File 760.01, 1 Jul–2 Sep 1945, v.14, Headquarters Twentieth Air Force, Office of the A-3, Subject: Attacks on Small Urban Industrial Areas, 21 July 1945, AFHC; USAF HC File 760.01, Narrative History, Headquarters Twentieth Air Force, 1 Jul–2 Sep 45, v.1; XXI BC MR, Nos. 206–9, 210–12, 215–20, 223–31, 234–37, 240–43.

its takeoff roll at 2:45 A.M., August 6. Two more planes bearing scientific instruments and observers followed, while ahead three weather planes scouted the targets. Navy Captain William S. Parsons, the bomb commander, armed Little Boy during the uneventful flight to Japan.

Hiroshima

"Shimmering leaves, reflecting sunlight from a cloudless sky, made a pleasant contrast with shadows in my garden as I gazed absently through wide-flung doors opening to the south," wrote Dr. Michihiko Hachiya in Hiroshima. Recently, he had confided his pessimism about the course of the war to a young cousin, an army doctor. The cousin retorted that "the chief of staff has said that no matter how much the nation criticizes the army, the army will reply with victory!" An approaching weather plane crossed Hachiya's cloudless sky and tripped the air-raid alert at 7:09. The plane passed, and the all clear sounded. People emerged from shelters to go to work; brigades of mobilized schoolchildren resumed the task of tearing down swaths of buildings to make firebreaks. "You could say that it was the sound of this siren that killed the great majority of citizens of Hiroshima," accurately observed Susumu Kimura, a schoolgirl. Even minimal sheltering would have saved innumerable lives.

Upon hearing the changed pitch of the engines as the *Enola Gay* banked violently into its evasive turn, many looked up to see the "dazzling gleam from its mighty flank, and . . . a fleecy white cloud trail across the blue sky." Little Boy detonated at 8:16, after a forty-three-second fall to an altitude of 1,900 feet over the courtyard of the Shima Hospital, 550 feet southeast of the Aioi bridge aiming point. The power of the bomb later was calculated as equivalent to 12,500 tons of TNT. It created a blinding pulse of light for perhaps only a tenth of a second, but the center of that pulse reached 5,400 degrees Fahrenheit.

On a hillside two kilometers northwest of the city, P. Siomes, a German Jesuit missionary, was gazing out the window toward Hiroshima when "a garish light which resemble[d] the magnesium light used in photography" filled the whole vista. Behind it surged an intense heat wave. He jumped to the window but saw only "brilliant yellow light" and heard only a "moderately large explosion." An Imperial Army medical-investigation team reported that the flash appeared yellow to those nearby and blue to those farther away. Distant witnesses described it as a red radiant sunset. Two words became fixed to the event: *pika* and *don*—*pika* meaning a glitter, sparkle, or bright flash of light; *don* meaning a boom or loud sound. Many who had been close in later recalled hearing no sound of an explosion and spoke only of the *pika;* those like Father Siomes who saw the flash and heard a rumble called it the *pika-don,* flash-boom.

Close in, the *pika* signified more than brightness. At a stone bridge about four hundred yards from ground zero, an American officer later found the etched shadow of a man with one foot in the air pulling a laden two-wheeled cart. The man's shadow had shielded the blacktop from the heat, but elsewhere the surface melted to tar and absorbed dust. The only vestige of another man idling at a bank building was his shadow on the granite. Both had been vaporized at or near the speed of light, passing from being to nothingness faster than any human physiology can register. Among those who died from the bomb, they were the lucky ones and presumably knew nothing.

The light waves traveled in straight lines so that persons farther away showed patterns of burns perfectly reflecting their exposed surfaces. For a radius of two miles, the flash inflicted "primary burns," noted a detailed study, "[which] are injuries of a special nature and not ordinarily experienced in everyday life." Among those not vaporized, the skin characteristically took on a dark brown or black hue, and most victims died in agony within a few minutes or hours. Nearly all objects, not only flesh, took on this tone, so that Hiroshima's ruins appeared "brown, the color of unfired pottery."

The *pika-don* caught Michiko Yamaoka, a fifteen-year-old mobilized high-school student, ambling toward her job as a telephone operator, about eight hundred meters from what became the hypocenter, the theoretical point directly below where the bomb burst. She understood that "Japan was winning, so we still believed. We only had to endure." In the bright sunlight, she put her hand above her eyes to glance up to the faint sound of an aircraft, then Little Boy exploded. "There was no sound. I felt something strong. It was terribly intense. I felt colors. It wasn't heat. You can't call it yellow, and it wasn't blue." She sensed the heat wave envelop her as the blast lifted her up and tossed her aside. She lay under rocks, unable to see but able to hear "moans of agony and despair." Then she heard, "Fire! Run away! Help! Hurry up!" The heat wave had ignited a firestorm that overran the injured and the trapped, hugely increasing the death toll. Yamaoka's mother found her, and soldiers dug her out as crackling flames encroached near, charring her skin and clothes and leaving her hair "like a lion's mane." Nearby were people trying to push intestines back into their bodies; headless bodies; legless bodies; seared, swollen faces. She encountered a friend and called out. The friend at first did not respond, then she exclaimed: "Miss Yamaoka, you look like a monster." Only then did she know how badly she had been burned.

Shin Bok Su was a Korean and a Hiroshima resident since 1937. Her family had emerged from its shelter with the all clear, then "'PIKA!' a brilliant light and then 'DON!' a gigantic noise," then blackness. She heard her mother-in-law call out and found her lying protectively across a thirteen-month-old son but trapped by fallen debris. She finally freed them, but the terrified older woman bolted away. Her husband appeared, and they began frantically digging to find their other two children as the fires marched toward their house; finally, soldiers tugged them away. They spent the night on city sports fields with people dying all around them. The next day, they returned to the site of their once large house, where fires still burned, as did "the corpses of my children. When I approached, I saw a line of buttons from my son's white shirt. Akiko, my girl, was curled up next to Takeo. Flames were still licking up from them."

For Dr. Hachiya, in an instant a vision of shimmering leaves vanished; the garden shadows disappeared; a stone lantern brilliantly ignited; a blast removed his clothes and inflicted multiple wounds. With his injured wife, he fled into the street, tripping over the head of a dead officer crushed beneath a massive gate. "Excuse me, excuse me, please!" he cried hysterically to the dead man. Motionless in the street, their stunned gazes beheld their neighbors' house sway and then crash with a rending sound into the street, followed shortly by a swirl of dust as their own house collapsed. Hachiya staggered to his workplace, the Ministry of Communications Hospital, a modern building. He passed others—all completely silent—walking with arms held out, forearms dangling. A young girl who also witnessed this behavior described more graphically how she saw

> three high school girls who looked as though they were from our school; their faces and everything were completely burned and they held their arms out in front of their chest like kangaroos with only their hands pointed downward; from their whole bodies something like thin paper is dangling—it is their peeled off skin which hangs there, and trailing behind them the unburned remnants of their puttees, they stagger exactly like sleep walkers.

Hachiya and his wife found the streets deserted except for the dead. Some looked as if they had been frozen by death while in the full action of flight, others lay sprawled as though some giant had flung them to their death from a great height.

The hospital quickly became packed with the dying and injured. They came seeking "so much as a glimpse of a white robed doctor or nurse," wrote Hachiya. Broken bodies literally filled every space; the floors and grounds soon became coated with feces, urine, and vomitus. A coworker, Dr. Hanaoka, arrived to report that he saw reservoirs filled to the brim with people who looked as though they had been boiled alive. Another colleague, Mr. Katsutani, bore more eyewitness descriptions of horrors, the worst of which were the injuries to soldiers he passed, their skin burned from the hips up, "their flesh wet and mushy" where the skin peeled, "and they had no faces! Their eyes, noses and mouths had been burned away, and it looked like their ears had melted off." Little Boy caught thousands of soldiers doing morning calisthenics. It totally flattened the headquarters of the Second General Army at Hiroshima Castle, and an intercepted message later disclosed that the entire army staff, from Field Marshal Hata on down, had been injured. The bomb killed the commander of the Fifty-ninth Army, Lieutenant General Yoji Fujii, whose "burnt sword was found alongside his charred remains."

In the following days, months, and years, the catastrophe was dissected by Japanese and Allied studies. On August 13, the Imperial Army Medical Committee ascribed the mass death at Hiroshima to two causes: the majority by the collapse of buildings due to blast and resultant fires, and a minority to burns due to heat radiation from the bomb. No fewer than 95 percent of a group of patients examined had burns, and about two thirds of them were burned on the face, forearms, and hands. This same report found that the bomb destroyed all Japanese-style dwellings within a radius of two kilometers, and all stone buildings within five hundred meters, though reinforced concrete buildings still stood. A postwar British mission report agreed and noted that a material number of those killed sustained, in theory, multiple lethal injuries.

But heat and blast did not account for all the fatalities. Starting on August 7, Dr. Hachiya watched as patients began to vomit and have diarrhea; they had no appetite. The symptoms resembled bacillary dysentery, and at first Hachiya suspected the bomb had thrown off a deadly gas or perhaps a germ. More mystifying still were those who appeared over the next several days with no apparent injury but complaining of weakness and nausea. By the ninth, patients began to display small subcutaneous hemorrhages and commenced coughing, vomiting, or defecating blood. The husband of Shin Bok Su initially appeared to have suffered only a scratch, but by August 25 his hair began falling out. By the time he died, "his body had turned black. Blood seeped from his skin. He smelt awful." "People were dying so fast," confessed Hachiya, "that I had begun to accept death as a matter of course and ceased to respect its awfulness."

What Hachiya and his colleagues grappled with was radiation sickness caused by the gamma rays unleashed by the bomb that perforated the skin without leaving visible traces. The British mission report dryly explained these horrors:

> The gamma rays do not attack the cells in the bloodstream, but the primitive cells in the bone marrow, from which most of the different types of cells in the blood are formed. Therefore serious effects begin to appear only as the fully-formed cells already in the blood die off gradually and are not replaced as they would be normally by new cells formed in the bone marrow. In severe cases, it was apparent that the gamma rays had virtually killed the entire bone marrow. In such cases, all three types of cells formed in the marrow became deficient: red cells, platelets, and white cells. As red cell formation ceased, the patient began to suffer from progressive anaemia. As platelet formation ceased, the thin blood seeped in small and large haemorrhages into the skin and the retina of the eye, and sometimes into the intestine and the kidneys. The fall in the number of white cells, which was useful in diagnosing mild cases because it could be detected by taking blood counts, in severe cases lowered resistance, so that the patient inevitably fell prey to some infection, usually spreading from the mouth and accompanied by gangrene of the lips, the tongue, and sometimes the throat. . . . Deaths probably began in about a week after the explosion, reached a peak in about three weeks, and had for the most part ceased after six to eight weeks.*

Tokyo

American radio operators listened carefully to fourteen Imperial Army radio circuits with a terminal at Hiroshima on the morning of August 6. Except for one message, no traffic originated from Hiroshima between 7:38 and noon. By midnight, eight circuits were back in operation. At 9:55, a message was intercepted from the 12th Air Division (headquartered eighty

---

* Hiroshima was one of the few major metropolises in Japan not known to have a prisoner-of-war camp. According to Japanese military commanders in October 1945, a total of twenty American prisoners of war, all recently captured aircrew, were killed by the first atomic bomb. Headquarters Sixth Army, October 9, 1945, Subject: Deceased Allied Prisoners of War, to Commanding General, X Corps; Headquarters Sixth Army, October 9, 1945, Subject: Missing Air Crew, to Commanding General Japanese Second General Army; same parties, October 9, 1945, Subject: Casualties Among American Prisoners of War; Chief of the General Staff, Second Demobilization Headquarters, October 16, 1945, to Chief of General Staff, U.S. Sixth Army, all in RG 407 Entry 427, World War II Operations Reports, Sixth Army 106-1.3, Box 2410, NARA. There is other evidence, however, that at least one and possibly two or three of these men were killed by the Japanese after the bombing. Daws, *Prisoners of the Japanese,* pp. 333–34. These deaths form a tiny fraction of the ten thousand or so American prisoners of war who perished in Japanese captivity, nor were they the only ones caused by "friendly fire." The average number of Allied prisoners of war or civilian internees who died each day of the effects of captivity at the hands of the Japanese easily doubled this toll.

miles southwest of the city) reporting that "a violent, large, special-type bomb, giving the appearance of magnesium," exploded above the center of the city with a "blinding flash and violent blast," leveling everything within a two-mile radius, with one third of the residents "seriously or slightly injured." An amplifying message estimated casualties as 70 to 80 percent of the population and added:

> As a result of the horrible catastrophes brought about by the recent air raid, there appears to be a gradual increase in the circulation of wild and fantastic rumors. Moreover, there have been an increasing number of cases in which the fighting spirit of victims or eyewitnesses has been broken.

Civil authorities were busily countering this, pointing out that "those who took refuge immediately in the safe underground shelters escaped injury completely."

In Tokyo, the most senior Japanese leaders groped to comprehend what had happened. Japanese radio-intelligence operators had sorted out from American traffic indications of the presence of the 509th Composite Group and its unusual operations. At 8:30, fifteen minutes after the bomb detonated, the Kure Navy Depot flashed a message to Tokyo that an enormously destructive bomb had struck Hiroshima. Shortly after 10:00, a message from Hiroshima to the Army Ministry referred to information that the United States had been working on a new type of bomb and stated "this must be it." Nearly four hours passed before a Domei News Agency telegram clicked out in Tokyo to report an attack on Hiroshima, but it also failed to impress the magnitude of the event. Near dusk, a senior civil-government administrator arrived to report vast destruction in an attack by "a small number of enemy planes." Only on the morning of August 7 did the bolt strike in a single message to the Vice Chief of the Imperial Army General Staff: "The whole city of Hiroshima was destroyed instantly by a single bomb."

But government radio monitors had by then picked up the broadcast of President Truman's statement of August 6, announcing the use of an atomic bomb on Hiroshima, that warned:

> We are now prepared to obliterate rapidly and completely every productive enterprise the Japanese have above ground in any city. We shall destroy their docks, their factories and their communications. Let there be no mistake; we shall completely destroy Japan's power to make war.
>
> It was to spare the Japanese from utter destruction that the ultimatum of July 26 was issued at Potsdam. Their leaders promptly rejected that ultimatum. If they do not now accept our terms they may expect a rain of ruin from the air, the like of which has never been seen on earth.

While senior Japanese officers did not dispute the theoretical possibility of such weapons, they refused to concede that the Americans had vaulted over tremendous practical problems to create an atomic bomb.

Delayed by aircraft problems, the seven-man Imperial Army investigation team dispatched from Tokyo, headed by Lieutenant General Seizo Arisue and including Dr. Nishina, reached Hiroshima only on August 8. As their plane circled the city, the vista of destruction told Nishina "at a glance that nothing but an atomic bomb could have inflicted such damages," while Arisue allowed that the Americans must have employed "an unconventional type of bomb." An officer charged up to their plane with a harlequin face—half burned, half not—to exclaim: "Everything which is exposed gets burned, but anything which is covered even only slightly can escape burns. Therefore it cannot be said that there are no countermeasures."

Arisue's team knew of Truman's announcement that the weapon was an atomic bomb but examined several competing theories. One was that the Americans had worked secretly from the night of the fifth to the morning of the sixth to scatter in the sky above Hiroshima an explosive material, such as magnesium. Then, they used some method to ignite that substance and cause a huge explosion (or explosions—certain witnesses reported two or three of them). Other competing theories were that this was some new, powerful incendiary bomb, or perhaps a liquid oxygen bomb, with strong incendiary material. But after two days of study, the panel reported back to Tokyo that it was "no exaggeration to say that the whole city of Hiroshima" had been destroyed by an atomic bomb.

Back in Tokyo, the Empress Dowager insisted that a far stronger shelter should be excavated at her palace. The Imperial Army explained that a sturdy shelter already existed at the nearby Imperial Palace. Nonetheless, her request signaled that the bomb had shaken the Imperial family.

Initial news of the atomic bomb failed to cow most leaders of the Japanese armed forces. Some simply denied the existence of an atomic weapon. But the Chief of the Naval General Staff, Admiral Toyoda, was already formulating a second line of defense. He argued that the United States could not possess more than a limited amount of radioactive material, which could produce only a few bombs. Further, he believed that world opinion would intervene to bar the United States from perpetrating another such "inhuman atrocity." Toyoda's stance illustrated the irony that while Japan's own atomic program did not yield a bomb, it did breed knowledge wielded to minimize the significance of the American weapons. Toyoda's assessment is also critical evidence of how easily Japanese military leaders could have inoculated themselves against being swayed by a mere demonstration of a single atomic device.

Moreover, news of Hiroshima competed at the Army Division of Imperial Headquarters with intense focus on plans to withdraw forces into a redoubt comprised of Japan, southern Manchuria, and Korea. The Vice Chief of the General Staff, Torashiro Kawabe, acknowledged in his diary on August 7 that he was "shocked tremendously" by the reports from Hiroshima. He noted wistfully that this reflected Japan's scientific weakness but insisted defiantly that the Imperial Army must remain tenacious even in the face of this new setback.

Foreign Minister Togo tried simultaneously to unearth the facts and to exploit the stunning news of Hiroshima in an emergency cabinet meeting. Togo extracted from the American statements about the "new and revolutionary increase in destruct[ive]" power of the atomic bomb a reason to accept the Potsdam Declaration. But the Army countered forcefully, minimizing the effects and insisting that no conclusions could be drawn before completion of an investigation.

With concern already gnawing about eroding civilian resolve, the issue of a public statement about the bombing split the government and the military. This very day, August 7, new reports reached Tokyo about nose-diving morale and even panic not only over the actual series of incendiary attacks against medium and smaller cities but also because the Americans now announced their targets in advance, thus piteously exposing the impotence of Japan's defenses. The sole conventional attack on August 7 sent 131 Superfortresses to the massive Toyokawa naval-ammunition plants. The raid illustrated that even strikes at indisputably military objectives could generate heavy loss, for the attack inflicted 2,699 casualties, of which 1,408 were fatalities, many of them girl workers. At 3:30 Imperial Headquarters released a terse announcement conceding that an attack by a small number of B-29s with a "bomb of a new type" had inflicted considerable damage on Hiroshima; an investigation was in progress.

Meanwhile, Marquis Kido received the report that "the United States used an atomic bomb against Hiroshima, causing extremely serious damage and 130,000 casualties." In an audience with the Emperor at 1:30 P.M. on August 7, Kido observed the worried countenance of his sovereign, who had learned about Hiroshima from court circles on the sixth. Kido's diary documents that the Emperor displayed concern, and he posed many questions. What the diary does not record, however, is what four years later Kido reported the Emperor stated: "Now that things have come to this impasse, there is no other way. I don't care what happens to me personally, but we should lose no time in ending the war so as not to have another tragedy like this." This is the first of a series of incidents over the next tumultuous days where postwar evidence offered by Kido and others that places the Emperor in a favorable light lacks contemporary confirmation in circumstances where it might be expected to exist. Thus, it is not clear that the Emperor spoke in such dramatic and decisive terms at this juncture. But there is no doubt that the bomb unsettled Hirohito: His aide-de-camp's diary documents almost hourly questions about Hiroshima after Kido departed.

On the morning of August 8, the Emperor received a detailed report on Hiroshima from the foreign minister. Togo called for immediate termination of the war on the basis of the Potsdam Declaration. According to Togo, the Emperor then stated that the "new weapon" made it "less and less possible to continue the war" and that Japan must "make such arrangements as will end the war as soon as possible." Hirohito bade Togo to "do his best to bring about an early termination of the war" and to inform Prime Minister Suzuki that this was his desire. Whether the Emperor expressed his desires with such clarity, however, remains debatable. Once again, Kido's detailed diary fails to reflect such decisiveness, and the erratic course recorded by Kido over the next forty-eight hours suggests that, even if the Emperor accepted the need for a speedy termination of the war, he either still balked personally at simple acceptance of the Potsdam Declaration or perhaps he doubted whether the Imperial Army would comply with his command to end the war.

As night came to Tokyo on August 8, the government of Japan had still not met formally to reassess the situation with the advent of the atomic bomb. On Tinian, Americans labored frantically to prepare a second atomic bomb, while in Manchuria massive Soviet forces coiled to strike.

17

Manchuria and Nagasaki

"I would appreciate your personal estimate"

Olympic Under Assault

As Japan grappled with Hiroshima and the advent of atomic weapons, American military leaders simultaneously struggled with the ultimate implications of the Ultra evidence for the massive Japanese buildup to confront Olympic. On the day the first atomic bomb was dropped, the Joint War Plans Committee of the Joint Chiefs of Staff forwarded a report, "Alternatives to 'OLYMPIC,' " to the Joint Staff Planners, a body just below the Joint Chiefs themselves. Noting the alarming fresh intelligence estimates of Japanese preparations on Kyushu, the committee observed that

> the possible effect upon OLYMPIC operations of this build-up and concentration is such that it is considered commanders in the field should review their estimates of the situation, reexamine objectives in Japan as possible alternates to OLYMPIC, and prepare plans for operations against such alternate objectives.

An attached draft message to MacArthur and Nimitz observed that while the dramatic increase in Japanese strength did not yet require a change of the directive, it did compel focus on the prospects for Olympic and mandate that commanders formulate "alternate plans and submit timely recommendations." It advised that "operations against extreme northern Honshu, against the Sendai area, and directly against the Kanto Plain are now under intensive study [in Washington]."

The Joint Staff Planners formally reviewed these reports on August 8. During late July and early August, this body had been assessing a wide spectrum of future developments. These ranged from the darkly pessimistic, including the distinctly unappetizing prospect of operations after an invasion of the Kanto plain (Coronet), assuming the Japanese did not surrender, to the very sanguine, including preparations for a possible sudden Japanese collapse and surrender. The majority of the papers they reviewed contemplated the continuation of the war into 1946, including the possibility of an attack on northwest Kyushu in the event that Coronet was "found to be not feasible."

The committee's reports reached the Joint Staff Planners two days after Hiroshima and one day before Nagasaki. Probably because of this timing, the minutes of their meeting show that the planners temporized. They "took note of . . . the fact that the Joint War Plans Committee is preparing studies on alternate objectives with a view to presentation to the Joint Chiefs of Staff."

But General Marshall had already acted. On August 7, Washington time, he sent the following dispatch to MacArthur:

> Intelligence reports on Jap dispositions which have been presented to me and which I understand have been sent to your Staff are that the Japanese have undertaken a large buildup both of divisions and of air forces in Kyushu and Southern Honshu. The air buildup is reported as including a large component of suicide planes which the intelligence estimate here considers are readily available for employment only in the vicinity of their present bases. Concurrently with the reported reinforcement of Kyushu, the Japanese are reported to have reduced forces north of the Tokyo plain to a point where the defensive capabilities in Northern Honshu and Hokkaido appear to be extraordinarily weak viewed from the standpoint of the Japanese General Staff. The question has arisen in my mind as to whether the Japanese may not be including some deception in the sources from which our intelligence is being drawn.
>
> In order to assist in discussions likely to arise here on the meaning of reported dispositions in Japan proper and possible alternate objectives to OLYMPIC, such as Tokyo, Sendai [northern Honshu], Ominato [extreme northern Honshu], I would appreciate your personal estimate of the Japanese intentions and capabilities as related to your current directive and available resources.

Marshall provided a copy of this message to Admiral Leahy, Truman's chief of staff.

"I am certain," intoned MacArthur in his expeditious "personal estimate" of August 9, "that the Japanese air potential reported to you as accumulating to counter our OLYMPIC operation is greatly exaggerated." He pointed out the feeble Japanese reaction to Third Fleet strikes, including coastal bombardments and daily air operations. He insisted that he had been through this situation before in the Philippines, where prior to the Luzon landing there were reports of massing Japanese air strength that proved false. "As to the movement of ground forces," he concluded,

> the Japanese are reported as trying to concentrate in the few areas in which landings can be effected from Tokyo southward, and it is possible that some strength may have been drawn from the areas of northern Honshu. I do not credit, however, the heavy strengths reported to you in southern Kyushu. The limited capacity of railroads and the shipping losses discourage belief that large forces can be concentrated or supported effectively in southern Kyushu.

MacArthur insisted that Allied tactical airpower, in addition to the B-29 force, would "quickly seek out and destroy" Japanese air potential and "practically immobilize" and "greatly weaken" Japanese ground forces in southern Kyushu.

"In my opinion," declared MacArthur, "there should not be the slightest thought of changing the OLYMPIC operation." The purpose of Olympic, he pointed out, was to obtain air bases to cover a strike into "the industrial heart of Japan." Olympic was "sound and will be successful." To leap immediately to Tokyo, he warned, would mean abandoning the benefits of land-based air cover, other than the B-29s, "and for that reason alone would be fraught with the greatest danger." As to the other alternatives, only limited study had so far been conducted, but the prospective weather alone, for both landing and subsequent use as air-base sites, appeared to rule out Ominato. While Sendai offered "somewhat greater potentialities," its proximity to Tokyo offered a chance of "heavy infiltration of ground troops" from the capital. MacArthur ended with a peroration that selectively recalled history and played up to Marshall's own admitted doubts that perhaps the Japanese had cleverly managed to hoodwink Ultra:

> Throughout the Southwest Pacific Area campaigns, as we have neared an operation intelligence has invariably pointed to greatly increased enemy forces. Without exception, this buildup has been found to be erroneous. In this particular case, the destruction that is going on in Japan would seem to indicate that it is very probable that the enemy is resorting to deception.

MacArthur's conclusion contained an extraordinarily brazen lie. "MacArthur consistently dismissed ULTRA evidence that failed to accord with his preconceived strategic vision," concluded historian Edward Drea in the best study of the general's use of Ultra. MacArthur's dismissal of such evidence was facilitated by his intelligence chief, Charles Willoughby, who consistently underestimated Japanese strength. The classic example of this, and the most devastating demonstration of the mendacity of MacArthur's assertion, is Luzon. Willoughby's final prelanding estimate of Japanese strength was 195,000 (up from an original projection of 137,400), whereas actual Japanese strength was 287,000.

But behind this lie was something else. Marshall had observed to Secretary of War Stimson in December 1944 that MacArthur was "so prone to exaggerate and so influenced by his own desires that it is difficult to trust his judgment." It is almost impossible not to believe that MacArthur's resort to falsehood was motivated in large measure by his personal interest in commanding the greatest amphibious assault in history.

After receipt of MacArthur's self-serving estimate late on August 9 (Washington time), Admiral King moved to intervene decisively in the controversy over Olympic. He gathered both Marshall's original query and MacArthur's reply into a package, and sent both "Eyes Only" to Nimitz, asking for his comments. While King required that Nimitz send a copy of his comments to MacArthur, he did not set a deadline.

King clearly aimed to bring on an explosive interservice confrontation over Olympic and probably the whole invasion strategy. On April 30, he had informed his colleagues on the Joint Chiefs of Staff that he only agreed to permit orders to be issued for an invasion so that the necessary preparations could be put in train to maintain that option. But he also had warned that the Joint Chiefs would be revisiting this issue in August or September. Now, precisely as he had predicted, this had come to pass.

Nimitz had advised King "Eyes Only" on May 25 that he no longer supported an invasion of Japan, and thus no Army officer was aware of this fact. King now forced Nimitz either to avow support of Olympic (an action that can be safely ruled out, given the intelligence developments since May 25) or to break the apparent interservice consensus. It was obvious that if Nimitz withdrew his endorsement of Olympic, he would create a major confrontation with the Army institutionally, as well as personally with MacArthur. By the time Nimitz received King's order, however, a second atomic bomb had been dropped and the Soviet Union had entered the war. Moreover, very shortly thereafter, evidence appeared for the first time that Japan might be seriously contemplating peace. Indeed, the next major message from King to Nimitz, only some thirteen hours later, began, "This is a peace warning." Nimitz understandably hesitated to see if events would deliver him from the onerous duty of igniting what was certain to be a firestorm over American strategy to end the war.

In an interesting coincidence, August 9 should have marked the end of the use of Olympic as a code name for the invasion of Kyushu. The Joint Chiefs of Staff notified MacArthur, Nimitz, and Spaatz that administrative errors had permitted the Olympic code name to be published in a memorandum classified only as restricted. Accordingly, the Joint Chiefs ordered that henceforth *Majestic* should be substituted for *Olympic*.

Meanwhile, with no response from Japan after the bombing of Hiroshima, the conventional air campaign continued. Yawata, a highly industrialized major city of 261,300 with the largest steelworks in the Japanese Empire, had been a priority B-29 target since June 1944, but its poor radar characteristics had shielded it from a fire raid. With a forecast of clear weather for August 8, the Twentieth Air Force sent three wings to bomb Yawata while the 314th Wing dispatched its Superfortresses to attack aircraft plants in Tokyo. The 245 B-29s targeting Yawata burned out 22 percent of the city. The Yawata mission cost four B-29s and one escorting P-47. Three B-29s from the 314th Wing were downed on the Tokyo mission.

On the Eve

As evening descended on August 8, complacent Japanese soldiers in eastern Manchuria huddled against the patter of rain as their commanders gathered for a tabletop maneuver exercise at Fifth Army Headquarters, miles from the border. At 1:00 A.M., August 9, the Soviet onslaught began. Rain masked not only the sound of advanced infantry units infiltrating through gaps, but also the roars, clanks, and metallic squeals of tanks and heavy self-propelled guns. The attackers either overran Japanese defenders before they could properly man their positions or obliterated them by massed close-range tank and self-propelled gun fire.

What happened in eastern Manchuria represented in microcosm August Storm, the Soviet code name for the massive assault on Japanese forces on the continent: the deft exploitation of terrain by massive and heavily armored forces and paralyzing surprise. As early as March 1945, Soviet staff officers had commenced drafting plans for the Manchurian offensive. In April, the Soviets began a flow of 136,000 railcars to move 403,355 men and 2,119 tanks and self-propelled guns over the fragile 10,000-kilometer rail link connecting Europe to Manchuria. This great influx doubled Soviet forces in the Far East from forty to more than eighty divisions. For the first time in the war, the Soviets created a full-fledged separate theater of operations. It was placed under fifty-year-old Marshal Aleksandr Mikhailovich Vasilevsky, who commanded more than 1.5 million men assigned as follows:

1. The Trans-Baikal Front of Marshal Rodion Y. Malinovsky, with 654,040 men organized into one tank army (Sixth Guards), four combined-arms armies (each of about 80,000 to 100,000 men), a Soviet-Mongolian Cavalry-Mechanized Group, the Twelfth Air Army, and a small reserve.
2. The First Far Eastern Front of Marshal Kirill A. Meretskov. This front fielded 586,589 men formed into four combined-arms armies, one mechanized corps (about 16,000 men), an "operational group," the Ninth Air Army, and a reserve.
3. The Second Far Eastern Front under General Maksim A. Purkayev, who directed 337,096 men formed into eleven rifle divisions, four rifle brigades, and eight tank brigades.

The Red Army of 1945 was much bloodied but vastly wiser after four years of titanic struggle in Europe. Battle-tested Soviet commanders, trained in a cauldron that killed over ten million members of the Soviet armed forces, now instinctively relied upon maneuver, firepower, and machines, not on simple numbers. But of all the elements of the Soviet combat power arrayed against the Japanese, the most vital was the quantity and quality of its armored vehicles, totaling 3,704 tanks and 1,852 self-propelled guns, welded to the Soviet determination to use them to the utmost.

Marshal Vasilevsky's Far East headquarters defined its goal as the seizure of Manchuria and the destruction of a major portion of the Japanese Kwantung Army. This would be achieved in a strategic double envelopment along three separate axes. The Trans-Baikal Front marching from the west and the First Far Eastern Front thrusting from the east would converge in the Mukden, Changchun, Harbin, and Kirin areas of south-central Manchuria. In northeastern Manchuria, the Second Far Eastern Front would mount a supporting attack, pushing southward to Harbin and Tsitsihar. In addition to these three onslaughts on the continent, the Soviets also planned a fourth thrust with a potentially yet more ambitious aim: seizures of southern Sakhalin Island and the Kuril Islands as prerequisites to a landing on Hokkaido, the northernmost of the Home Islands.

From its formation in 1919, the Kwantung Army, once the "most prestigious and powerful unit of the Japanese Army," represented the burnished shield of Japan's conquests in Manchuria and the potential sword for further expansion. During the 1930s, it not only functioned as a state within the state but usurped the mantle of the state itself in initiating war, first in Manchuria and then in China. In August 1945, sixty-four-year-old General Otozo Yamada commanded the Army, numbering 713,000 soldiers in Manchuria, organized into twenty-four infantry divisions, nine infantry

August Storm:
Soviet Offensive in Manchuria, August 1945

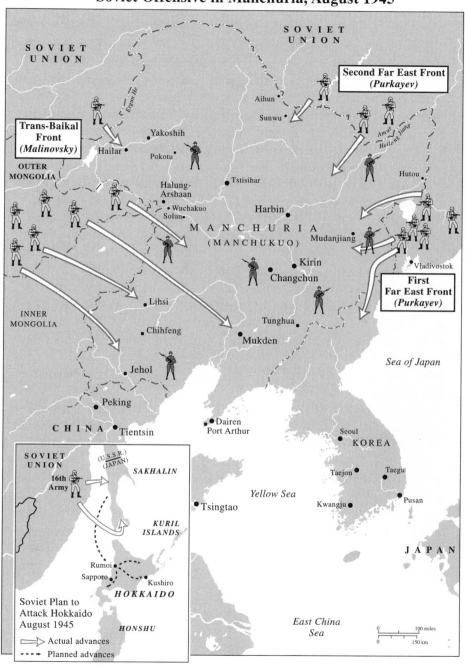

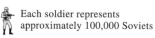
Each soldier represents approximately 100,000 Soviets

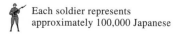
Each soldier represents approximately 100,000 Japanese

brigades, and two tank brigades. Japanese soldiers deployed elsewhere in the theater (Southern Korea, Sakhalin, and the Kurils) numbered 280,000 organized into ten infantry divisions and three infantry brigades. Supplementing these forces were local auxiliary forces with a roster of 170,000 in the Manchukuoan Army of eight infantry and seven cavalry divisions and double that number of infantry and cavalry brigades. Another 44,000 auxiliaries formed five or six cavalry divisions and brigades in Inner Mongolia.

In the summer of 1945, there was little glint left in the swords of the Kwantung Army. On paper, the Kwantung's numerical strength stood at a peak, but this was belied by the fact that its combat effectiveness languished at a nadir. Between January 1942 and August 1945, no fewer than nineteen infantry and two armored divisions, as well as a long roll call of lesser combat and support units, had been stripped from the Army and redeployed to Pacific fronts. Their replacements lacked so much equipment, experience, and training that the Army was now a mere shell of its former self. Not only were Japanese tanks hopelessly outnumbered (1,155 versus 5,556 Soviet armored fighting vehicles), they were also woefully outclassed. Moreover, Japanese soldiers lacked any weapons that were effectual against most Soviet armor. The grandiloquent title of Air Army was a fraud; it fielded only fifty first-line aircraft. Japanese staff officers calculated that compared with the standard of 1937, the twenty-four divisions and nine brigades deployed in 1945 equaled the combat effectiveness of only six and two-thirds divisions.

To accommodate this steep decline in combat effectiveness, new plans modestly called for delay at the borders by a fraction of the Army while the main forces gathered to hold a mere quarter of southeastern Manchuria in the Tunghua area. The Japanese counted upon the raw terrain, vast distances, impoverished communications, and determined resistance to exhaust the Soviets before they reached the Tunghua redoubt. This final plan was issued only in June, too late to complete all of the required redeployments and fortifications. Worse yet, the Kwantung Army's lower-echelon commanders remained ignorant of the new plan, nor were the millions of Japanese civilians in Manchuria warned that they largely would be abandoned.

Exacerbating the vulnerability of the Kwantung Army was faulty intelligence. Ostensibly, Imperial Army intelligence officers wrestled simply with the question of when, not if, the Soviets would strike in Manchuria. They mistakenly believed that the bloody losses in the war with Germany would prompt the Soviets to minimize their casualties by withholding an attack until Japan was weakest—that is, after an American invasion. Japanese officers also considered climate (which ruled out a winter offensive), and some apparently even believed the Soviets would honor the neutrality pact, which technically did not expire until April 1946. The most decisive misconception, however, stemmed from the thesis that the Soviets would attack only when they had at least fifty-five rifle divisions available in the Far East. Japanese couriers, passing under diplomatic immunity along the Trans-Siberian Railroad between Moscow and Vladivostok in May and June, reported massive movements of troops and armaments eastward toward Japanese-occupied Manchuria. One courier alone between May 12 and 18 counted 195 military trains, which he estimated were laden with 64,000 troops, 120 tanks, about 2,800 trucks, 500 fighter aircraft, and over 1,000 guns of various calibers. Nonetheless, Japanese intelligence refused to believe that the Soviets had amassed the necessary rifle divisions by August 1945. Consequently, Kwantung Army leaders slumbered under the delusion that the Soviets would not attack until September or October 1945 or even the spring of 1946. They were not alone. When the Soviets ominously recalled embassy personnel on July 24, Tokyo alerted the Kwantung Army of only a slight possibility of attack.

The Soviet Assault

The scale of the Soviet attack on Manchuria was vast but concentrated in three main regions, each corresponding to a Soviet front. By far the bulk of the most ferocious fighting occurred in eastern Manchuria. There, Marshal Meretskov designated the vital communications center of Mutanchiang as the objective of his First Far Eastern Front. He planned to seize it with a converging attack from east to west by his Fifth and First Red Banner Armies. The northern flank of this thrust would be protected by the Thirty-fifth Army, the southern flank by the Twenty-fifth Army. The Fifth Army under Lieutenant General Noritsume Shimizu faced the main Soviet attack. Shimizu's three divisions were spread thinly across huge sectors.

The onslaught of the First Far Eastern Front relied more upon surprise and maneuver than on numerical preponderance to crush the Japanese defenders. The Soviet Fifth Army, for example, with twelve divisions and 692 armored vehicles, shattered the Japanese 124th Division by rapidly penetrating the border along avenues the Japanese had deemed impassable, rather than butting against defended localities. Only on the southern flank of the First Far Eastern Front attack did the Japanese enjoy something like nominal parity in numbers (though not quality), but here, too, the Soviets eschewed head-on assaults for flank movements that propelled spearheads far to the west, deep behind Japanese lines by sundown of August 9.

In western Manchuria, geography conferred a tremendous advantage upon the Japanese defenders. The broad Grand Khingan mountain range forms a traditional rampart to rebuff an invader from the west. The value of the Grand Khingans is multiplied in modern times by the fact that an invader must first move forces and then supplies across a wide sweep of desert and steppe to the west of the mountains. This geography and recent history led the Imperial Army strategists to two fatal miscalculations. First, they concluded that the Grand Khingan range, though only of moderate height and ruggedness, constituted a formidable barrier that would funnel an attacker into two approaches, both in northwestern Manchuria: one parallel to the rail lines from Halung and Arshaan to Solun, the other parallel to the rail line from Hailar and Yakoshih to Pokotu. The Japanese deployed their forces to block these avenues and heavily fortified key areas. Second, the trauma of the August 1939 large-scale border battle at what the Soviets victors called Khalkhin-Gol and the Japanese losers named Nomonhan inculcated a belief among the Japanese that the upper limit of manpower the Soviets could sustain in this area was 200,000 men. The actual figure proved to be more than three times this number.

Marshal Malinovsky's Trans-Baikal Front struck on the western sectors of the Manchurian border. The Thirty-sixth Army—seven rifle divisions under Lieutenant General Alexsandr A. Luchinsky—attacked from the north-northwest toward Hailar. Lieutenant General Uemura Mikio's Fourth Separate Army defended Hailar and its approaches with the well-equipped 119th Infantry Division and the 80th IMB. But Luchinsky's blow in dense fog and darkness was so swift that a Soviet armored brigade had motored into the outskirts of Hailar before the day was out.

From northwest of the Manchurian border, Soviet General I. I. Lyudnikov's Thirty-ninth Army struck southeast along the Handagai-Wuchakou-Solun axis with nine rifle divisions, a tank division, and two tank brigades. The Japanese manned their heavy fortifications along this obvious route of advance with the weakly equipped 107th Division. Behind the 107th Division waited the other two divisions of the Forty-fourth Army. The quick-stepping Soviets flowed easily around the Japanese defenders and soon cut off the 107th Division.

This assault constituted only part of Malinovsky's main blow. Farther along his center and right, to the west of the Manchurian border, Malinovsky arranged the Sixth Guards Tank Army and the Seventeenth Army along a line from northeast to southwest, and placed the Fifty-third Army in reserve. The Seventeenth Army and a Soviet-Mongolian Cavalry-Mechanized Group were to deliver a supporting attack southeasterly toward Linhsi and Chihfeng, while the Sixth Guards Tank Army delivered the principal blow at the deep objectives of Changchun and Mukden. On

August 9, on Malinovsky's right and center, massive forces of men, horses, and armored vehicles surged unopposed, save for some small-scale cavalry clashes, for as many as ninety miles from their starting points. The Sixth Guards Tank Army reached the foothills of the Grand Khingan range and without pausing commenced to negotiate the steep passes.

While the main Soviet attacks in Manchuria emanated from the east, west, and northwest, the Soviet Second Far Eastern Front of General Maksim A. Purkayev mounted a secondary attack from the northeast to preclude Japanese forces from intervening against the main attacks. Purkayev's mission compelled him to overcome an extremely formidable lacework of rivers that divides the Soviet Maritime Territories from Manchuria and then a wall of mountains barring passage into central Manchuria.

Purkayev mounted his main effort with Lieutenant General Stepan K. Mamonov's Fifteenth Army of three rifle divisions down the Sungari River, which constituted the obvious avenue of movement across the vast marshy tracks along the borders, and into central Manchuria via a gap in the mountains to Harbin. The Imperial Army defenders—the First Area Army and Manchurian auxiliaries—easily recognized the significance of the Sungari and dotted its banks with prepared defenses. But Mamonov's forces encountered no initial resistance as the Japanese defenders withdrew. Meanwhile, Purkayev's Sixteenth Army waited on northern Sakhalin Island to attack Japanese forces holding the southern half of the island. By sundown of August 9, the Soviet assault was at full tilt in every sector.

Nagasaki

A second atomic bomb was available: Fat Man, the plutonium-implosion weapon of the type tested at Trinity.* The original schedule devised on Tinian slated Fat Man for use over Japan on August 11, but a forecast of deteriorating weather starting on the tenth and extending for five days ignited a rush to execute the mission on August 9. "Everyone felt," recalled Ensign Bernard J. O'Keefe, a member of the bomb-assembly team, "that the sooner we could get off another mission, the more likely it was that the

---

* The untested Little Boy had been used first on Hiroshima for reasons both theoretical and practical. Scientists and engineers had great confidence that the triggering arrangements for the uranium bomb would function properly, but they believed a test was essential to verify the reliability of the much more adventurous implosion trigger for the plutonium bombs. A successful test of a plutonium weapon would also validate expectations about the power of a uranium bomb. Moreover, there was a very small supply of fissionable U-235 uranium compared with the much more plentiful quantities of plutonium. See Vincent C. Jones, *Manhattan: The Army and the Atomic Bomb* (Washington, D.C.: Center of Military History, 1985), pp. 488–91, 504–14.

Japanese would feel that we had large quantities of the devices and would surrender sooner. . . . We knew the importance of one day; the *Indianapolis* sinking also had a strong effect on us."

But the route to Nagasaki remained a complex one. Fat Man was secured into the bomb bay of a B-29 named *Bock's Car*, to be flown by Major Charles W. Sweeney. His primary target was Kokura, a city that had 168,000 inhabitants in 1940. Situated in northern Kyushu, near Yawata, the city held a huge arsenal. This made Kokura the closest approximation of the type of military target Marshall had recommended in May.

Sweeney's secondary target was Nagasaki on western Kyushu. Roughly five miles square, with a population in 1940 of 253,000, Nagasaki was the third largest city on Kyushu. It contained the Mitsubishi shipyard, the biggest and most productive in Japan, which in November 1944 had employed 36,391 workers. The city sprawled across reclaimed land from the waterfront to the lower slopes of the surrounding hills. Small strips of built-up areas nestled in the valleys to the east and abutted the banks of the Urakami River to the north. Four rivers and canals and a few wide streets constituted natural firebreaks.

Before takeoff, Sweeney's crew discovered that the fuel pump for the reserve gasoline tanks did not work, a serious fault that would have aborted a normal mission. They were ordered to proceed by Brigadier General Farrell, but the effort continued to labor under a tenacious jinx. Storms buffeted the flight all the way to Japan. After a delay awaiting an escort plane that ultimately missed the rendezvous, Sweeney steered *Bock's Car* for Kokura because of reports of good weather there and bad weather over Nagasaki. Three attempted bomb runs over Kokura failed because heavy ground haze and smoke obscured visual sighting. This left *Bock's Car* with only enough fuel for one pass over Nagasaki, but there weather also precluded visual bombing. Nonetheless, Frederick Ashworth, the bomb commander, and Sweeney elected to execute the run in contravention of the stringent rule against radar bombing. They did not want either to attempt to land on Okinawa with the bomb on board or to jettison it.

Because of the inaccuracies of the radar-directed bomb run, Fat Man widely missed the aiming point over the metropolitan center. Instead, it detonated about a mile distant, over the Urakami district, a place that symbolized two facets of the city's history. Near to hand was the Mitsubishi torpedo factory, which manufactured weapons wielded so effectively at Pearl Harbor. But also in proximity was the Urakami Catholic Cathedral, the largest of its kind in eastern Asia and a symbol of Nagasaki's role as Japan's tightly controlled portal to European contact. Fat

Man wiped out the cathedral and probably more than half of the fourteen thousand Catholics in Nagasaki.

Fate dealt the population of Nagasaki at least a small measure of fortune. Fat Man landed where ridges and valleys shielded a wide swath of the city from heat, blast, and radiation, and there was no firestorm. Thus, by most accounts the number of dead was half that at Hiroshima, despite Fat Man's much greater power. (Later assessments credited Fat Man as equivalent of 22,000 tons of TNT and Hiroshima's Little Boy to only 12,500 tons.)

Two sets of problems confront any effort to quantify the deaths due to the atomic bombs. The first stems from the general deterioration of Japanese civil administration in 1945, the second from the stupendous power of the weapons. The Japanese proved unable to produce a certifiable count of the numbers of persons present in the two cities on the days of the atomic bombings. Thus, there was no base from which other calculation might be derived.* According to Japanese sources, for example, the number of individuals registered to receive a rice ration in Hiroshima as of June 30, 1945, was 245,423. The same report, however, notes that workers pouring in from the surrounding area significantly raised the daylight population of Hiroshima above this figure. In addition, there were more than 40,000 soldiers present, many newly drafted whose families had journeyed to Hiroshima to see them off. Making these allowances, one Japanese estimate placed 370,000 persons in Hiroshima on August 6, 1945, though this number is very probably high.

Perhaps the best contemporaneous report is that from the police department of the Hiroshima prefecture, which calculated that by the end of November 1945 Little Boy had inflicted the following casualties:

Deaths	78,150	60.3 percent
Seriously injured	9,428	7.3 percent
Slightly injured	27,997	21.6 percent
Missing	13,983	10.8 percent
Total	129,558	100.0 percent

The official Japanese history of Imperial General Headquarters, from which this narrative draws heavily, states the number of deaths is "difficult

---

* Unlike Hiroshima, Nagasaki was known to house Allied prisoners of war, but so did any alternative target. After the war, it became known that about sixty to eighty POWs were killed, while another four died in a camp five miles from the hypocenter on the islet of Koyagi. Gavan Daws, *Prisoners of the Japanese* (New York: William Morrow and Co., 1994), p. 334.

to ascertain," and gives a range for Hiroshima between 70,000 and 120,000.* The following table provides some indication of the ranges of the more noteworthy estimates made over the years:

				Dead	
	Population 1945	*MED, June 1946*	*USSBS, March 1947*	*Japan Economic Stabilization Board, April 1949*	*OSW (Japan) and USNR, April 1966*
Hiroshima	255,000	66,000	80,000	78,150	70,000
Nagasaki	195,000	39,000	45,000	23,753	36,000
				Injured	
	Population 1945	*MED, June 1946*	*USSBS, March 1947*	*Japan Economic Stabilization Board, April 1949*	*OSW (Japan) and USNR, April 1966*
Hiroshima	255,000	69,000	80–100,000	151,000	70,000
Nagasaki	195,000	25,000	50–60,000	55,000	40,000

MED: Manhattan Engineering District, "The Atomic Bombings of Hiroshima and Nagasaki."

USSBS: Strategic Bombing Survey, *The Effects of Atomic Bombs on Health and Medical Services in Hiroshima and Nagasaki* .

Japan Economic Stabilization Board, April 1949.

OSW (Japan) and USNR: *Analysis of Japanese Nuclear Casualty Data.*

Decades afterward, revised estimates were put forward of much higher numbers for total deaths attributed to the bombs. These estimates worked backward from two dubious premises. First, they assumed the accuracy of a count of atomic-bomb survivors in 1950 numbering 158,597 for Hiroshima and 124,901 for Nagasaki (plus ten individuals present for both bombs). These numbers were then subtracted from a conjectured population of each city on the dates of the bombings. This process yielded a count of deaths by 1950 that totaled 200,000 for Hiroshima and over 140,000 for Nagasaki. While the very earliest low numbers of casualties should be approached with skepticism, these extremely high revised figures are at least equally subject to challenge.[†]

---

* In the face of this mass death, material destruction seems irrelevant, but an August 1946 report from Hiroshima city officials indicated that the bomb destroyed 70,147 of 76,327 homes in the metropolis, or 92 percent. See *Daihon'ei Rikugun-Bu (10)*, p. 418.

† For example, the 1950 total of identified survivors was 283,498, at a time when they often were shunned. Subsequently, the complex and highly politicized definition of a *hibakushka* (atomic-bomb victim) became anyone who was within two kilometers of the epicenter of the bombs at the time or

The postwar revisions do suggest plausible higher numbers for one category of individuals. The USSBS counted Hiroshima casualties among Second General Army personnel up to December 10, 1945, at only 6,087 dead, 687 missing, and 3,353 injured. The Second General Army, however, did not have command responsibility for even half the servicemen in the city. Revised figures, based on Mid-Japan Veterans Association lists, pushed total estimated military fatalities to possibly as high as 20,000. Military fatalities at Nagasaki were vastly fewer and ran perhaps as low as 150. The actual total of deaths due to the atomic bombs will never be known. The best approximation is that the number is huge and falls between 100,000 and 200,000.

---

within a few days thereafter. In March 1995, no fewer than 328,629 living Japanese qualified by this definition. Furthermore, whenever such an individual dies, from any cause whatsoever, they become officially classified as a deceased *hibakushka.* As of August 1994, the deceased *hibakushka* for Hiroshima numbered 186,940 and for Nagasaki 102,275. John Dower, "Three Narratives of Our Humanity," in Edward T. Linenthal and Tom Engelhardt, eds., *History Wars: The Enola Gay and Other Battles for the American Past* (New York: Metropolitan Books/Henry Holt and Company, 1996), p. 79 and especially Note 28.

18

The Decisive Day

*"I have given serious thought
to the situation prevailing at home and abroad"*

Chain Reaction

August 9 became the "day that [Japan's] future course was charted," observed Foreign Minister Togo. *Charted* is the correct term, for it remained uncertain for days whether Japan could hold that course. The Soviets formally delivered a declaration of war to Japanese Ambassador Sato in Moscow at 11:00 P.M. (Tokyo time), August 8; first word of hostilities reached Tokyo via a Soviet radio broadcast about 4:00 A.M., August 9. Both Foreign Minister Togo and Chief Cabinet Secretary Sakomizu greeted the news with utter incredulity.

Prime Minister Suzuki is said to have accosted Sumihisa Ikeda, an officer just transferred from Manchuria, and asked him: "Is the Kwantung Army capable of repulsing the Soviet Army?"

Ikeda responded, "The Kwantung Army is hopeless."

"Is the Kwantung Army that weak?" sighed Suzuki. "Then the game is up." This exchange, often cited to establish the decisive importance of Soviet intervention, is based on Ikeda's recollection several years after the event. It conflicts with evidence from August 1945 demonstrating that Suzuki, far from resigning himself to a swift capitulation, vacillated sharply over the next critical days on the terms and timing of the war's end.

The Soviet entry did not panic the Army's leaders. Army Minister Anami commented calmly to an aide, "The inevitable has come." As recently as the June Imperial conference, Vice Chief of the General Staff Kawabe had declared Soviet neutrality was one of the "fundamental conditions" for prosecuting the war, but now he vowed to carry on. He soon learned that the Vice Minister of the Army shared this view. Kawabe briskly drafted a plan of action to pursue the war with the United States. The first step was the declaration of martial law throughout Japan. "If necessary," he added, "we will change the government and the Army and Navy will take charge." As one Army Ministry officer observed, martial law was aimed explicitly at quelling any initiative by those disposed to peace.

Kawabe urged his views on Chief of Staff Umezu, but Umezu kept his own counsel. Undaunted, Kawabe turned to the Army Minister. After listening to Kawabe's recitation, Anami snapped, "Good. I'll take your opinion as representative of the entire Army General Staff." Anami set War Ministry officers to work implementing martial law.

A key factor influencing events this day and for some time thereafter was Tokyo's ignorance of the dimensions and progress of the Soviet onslaught. This sprang directly from the Kwantung Army's drastically erroneous initial estimate of Soviet forces in eastern Manchuria:

	Estimate	*Actual*
Infantry divisions	3	15
Tank brigades	2–3	8

Moreover, during August 9, the Kwantung Army and Tokyo had *no* inkling of the huge Soviet mechanized thrust into western Manchuria. No wonder that on that afternoon Imperial General Headquarters stated that the "scale of these attacks is not large."

While the Imperial Army stood unified and belligerent, Japanese civilian leaders were divided and hesitated. Foreign Ministry officials gathered at Togo's residence and concurred that the war must be terminated immediately, with the sole condition of preserving the national polity. Togo then sped to Prime Minister Suzuki's residence. There, the Foreign Minister insisted that "because the Soviets have now joined the war, I think it is necessary for us to decide to terminate the war quickly." Togo conveyed the same opinion to Navy Minister Yonai and Prince Takamatsu, the Emperor's younger brother. Although Togo gained the impression that Suzuki agreed with his analysis, the official Japanese military history characterizes Suzuki's reaction as "vague," and Cabinet Secretary Sakomizu insisted later that Suzuki only resolved to abide by the decision of the Emperor.

Suzuki soon learned the Emperor's wishes. Kido's diary discloses that, in a brief audience at 10:00, the Emperor demanded Suzuki's assessment of the situation and a response from the government. Only ten minutes later, Suzuki arrived, as though on cue. Kido told the prime minister that the war should be terminated quickly "by immediately taking advantage of the Potsdam Declaration." He added that the Emperor wished to obtain the views of the senior statesmen.

Grand Chamberlain Hisanori Fujita recalled a mood of "impatience, frenzy and bewilderment" when the Supreme Council for the Direction of the War assembled at 10:30. The fevered atmosphere was intensified by the rumor that Tokyo would be the next target for the atomic bomb. The source for this story was Lieutenant Marcus McDilda, a captured P-51 pilot. After a day of repeated beatings and torture, a Japanese officer threatened McDilda with death if he failed to divulge details about the atomic bomb. McDilda, who knew nothing, fabricated a description of an atomic weapon in his heavy southern drawl. When his interrogators demanded to know the next target for an atomic bomb, McDilda reflected a moment and named Kyoto and Tokyo. The capital, he said, would be bombed "in the next few days."

Prime Minister Suzuki opened the meeting by announcing that the great shock of the Hiroshima bomb and now the Soviet intervention made it impossible to continue the war. Therefore, they must accept the Potsdam Declaration. Togo declared that the sole exception to the Potsdam terms would be a "guarantee of the Emperor's position." There was no response to this for a long time. Finally, the famously reticent Yonai said simply, "We can't get anywhere by keeping silent forever." The navy minister then deftly delineated the boundaries of the debates that followed. Japan must either accept the Potsdam terms, with the exception of preservation of the Imperial system, or it must attempt substantive negotiations over additional terms.

In his memoirs, Admiral Toyoda reported that "a rather bullish atmosphere" dominated as the meeting began. "To be sure," he stated, "the damage of the atomic bomb was extremely heavy, but it is questionable whether the United States will be able to use more bombs in rapid succession." Then the news arrived of the atomic-bomb blast over Nagasaki. The governor of Nagasaki prefecture swiftly informed Tokyo that Nagasaki had been attacked with a bomb like that used on Hiroshima, but the weapon seemed much less potent and damaging. The number of dead was "small," he reported, and he observed pointedly that it included none of the senior officials in the prefecture. Thus, misinformation from the Nagasaki governor dissipated the shock effect of the second atomic bomb. Still, however, the three-day interval between the bombings seemed to foretell that the Americans were locked into a relentless rhythm of atomic strikes, and it clearly undermined Toyoda's argument that the American supply of nuclear weapons must be sparse.

After two hours of intense debate, the Big Six remained split. Togo, Yonai, and Suzuki favored the single Imperial condition, while Anami, Umezu, and Toyoda insisted on adding three more conditions first identified by Yonai: self-disarmament, Japanese control of any war-crimes trials, and, above all, no Allied occupation of Japan. These terms would permit, at some later and better moment, Japan's warriors to inculcate a myth that they were never really defeated and only of their own volition laid down arms to spare the world more ravages of war. In shorthand, these positions can be labeled the "one-condition offer" and the "four-conditions offer."*

Japanese officials took great pains to distort the postwar version of the next key episode of this day because it was too revealing about the true attitudes of all the critical Japanese decision makers in 1945, not least the Emperor. At 1:00, Prince Konoe reached the Imperial Palace and huddled with Kido. According to Kido's diary, after the Big Six meeting broke up, at about 1:30, Suzuki came to announce that the Big Six had agreed to accept the Potsdam Declaration, but with four conditions. Precisely what Suzuki meant is susceptible to different interpretations. The least likely explanation is that he honestly believed the Big Six had reached unanimous agreement during the morning. The much more probable explanation is that he simply promoted the lowest common denominator of agreement within the Big Six. Kido acquiesced to this pronouncement as the decision of the government. ("It can't be helped," he remarked.) Moreover, this scheme fairly matched the terms set out in Kido's June 8 "Draft Plan."

Konoe, however, correctly perceived this as an incipient disaster. He advised Prince Takamatsu that the Allies would regard such a response as tantamount to a refusal to surrender. Kido's diary shows Takamatsu telephoned him at 2:45, and then Kido met with the Emperor at 3:10. Konoe also secured intervention by former Foreign Minister Mamoru Shigemitsu, who was on extremely close terms with Kido. Kido recorded Shigemitsu's warning by telephone at 4:00 as "strongly [urging] that a proper measure be adopted to meet the situation, asserting that a rupture would be inevitable if we should lay down the four conditions." Kido then saw the Emperor again between 4:35 and 5:10. This may have been the critical moment not only of this day but of the whole process, for thereafter Kido supported Togo's one-condition offer.

During the Tokyo war-crimes trials after the war, Kido (with Togo's support) insisted lamely that he "found out recently" that his diary entry wrongly depicted Suzuki as reporting that the Big Six had endorsed the

---

* Later recollections by Toyoda and Togo depicted Yonai as siding with the foreign minister and Suzuki, but a contemporaneous report by Anami indicated that the navy minister initially stood aligned with the other military chiefs.

four-conditions offer. Kido's contemporary diary entry carries far more credibility than the postwar attempt to explain it away. But Kido's postwar version aimed to do more than protect the Big Six. If Kido's diary entry was correct, it provided hard evidence that the Big Six still believed they commanded the discretion to deviate markedly from unconditional surrender. Beyond that, if Kido's ready acquiescence to this was also fact, then he obviously either perceived Japan's options in the same light or believed that the armed forces would not comply with more stringent conditions. And if Kido was the trusted alter ego of his Sovereign, then his diary entry also gives a powerful inference of the Emperor's stance as late as three days after Hiroshima.

While the drama of the phone calls to Kido and his meetings with the Emperor unfolded, the full cabinet met at 2:30. This proved a reprise of the morning arguments, with Togo and Anami assuming the opposing leadership roles. Anami conceded that Japan could not prevail based on simple numerical ratios of strength and acknowledged that the attitude was spreading among the population that there was no hope to win the war. Nonetheless, he adamantly maintained that the country would fight when the decisive battle came. According to the minutes of the session reprinted by the Foreign Ministry, the Army Minister then blurted out to the cabinet:

> One atomic bomb could destroy 6 square miles, which was equivalent to 2000 B-29s each with 300 conventional bombs of 500 pounds each. . . . the Americans appeared to have one hundred atomic bombs . . . while they could drop three per day. The next target might well be Tokyo.

It is astounding that Anami chose to relate this horrifying (and grossly exaggerated) scenario to civilian ministers in the midst of a debate on the rationality of continuing the war.

At 8:00 P.M., Suzuki finally summoned the cabinet to a vote. Togo had gained a few adherents, but so had Anami. A substantial fraction remained undecided. Since the unwritten but ironclad rule was unanimity, not a simple plurality, the deadlocked ministers recessed. Togo and Suzuki headed to the Imperial Palace, where the Emperor received them immediately. Togo recounted the events of the day in detail, organizing his talk around the clear point that no unanimous decision to terminate the war was forthcoming from either the Supreme Council or the cabinet. According to the rigorous protocol of Imperial Japan, this impasse left no role for the Throne and required that the cabinet resign. Suzuki then proposed convening an Imperial conference that night. With a grave nod, the Emperor gave his sanction, which all present recognized as extraordinary, since it created an opportunity for direct intervention by the Throne.

In the last minutes of August 9, the key decision makers in Japan assembled in the underground air-raid shelter adjoining the Imperial library, which had become the Emperor's home. Present were the Big Six, Baron Hiranuma (the president of the Privy Council), and five aides. Each man found on his desk a draft copy of Togo's proposed one-condition offer.

At ten minutes to midnight, August 9, the Emperor quietly entered the room. The Premier took the floor and proceeded to recount the day's events as though the Emperor knew nothing of them. Both of the officers recording the contents of this session show Suzuki presenting the four-conditions offer as the "general agreement" of the Supreme Council for the Direction of the War, thus confirming Kido's contemporary diary entry with all of its implications. Suzuki reiterated the major points and recapitulated the vote in the cabinet. With the deadlock thus described, Suzuki gave the floor to Togo who insisted that any attempt to broach additional terms would preclude peace. Yonai succinctly supported Togo's position.

Generals Anami and Umezu mounted the counterattack. Anami "absolutely opposed" the foreign minister's views and returned to the potent themes the military had long mastered: It was only necessary for the Japanese people to resolutely persevere in a battle in the Homeland itself to achieve the additional terms. Umezu marshaled the specifics: The military confidently anticipated dealing an invasion force a smashing blow; while Soviet entry was unfavorable, it did not affect the plan to fight in the Homeland; and it would be unthinkable to now accept unconditional surrender after so many had given their lives for His Majesty. Umezu announced that he personally would accept the Potsdam Declaration, but only with the four additional terms.

Inadvertently skipping Admiral Toyoda, who was next in precedent, Suzuki turned to Baron Hiranuma. Hiranuma applied his incisive mind and legalistic style in a Socratic seminar on Japan's predicament, ranging first over diplomacy and then onto Japan's military situation. He paraded the blatant manifestations of Japan's impotence and vulnerabilities: relentless bombing from the air; brazen bombardment by warships of the Homeland's coasts; the want of means of retaliation, much less defense; the destruction of transportation facilities; the oppressive doubts eroding the fighting spirit of the people; the entry of the Soviets into the war; and, "above all," the unleashing of the atomic bomb.

Hiranuma then spoke of the general deterioration of the domestic situation, particularly the shortage of food. He predicted that the "continuation of the war will create greater domestic disturbances than would termination of the war." Suzuki interrupted to support this thought and added that the people "cannot withstand the air-raids any longer."* Perhaps by design, this interjection prompted Hiranuma to move to the climax of his argument. While he basically agreed with the foreign minister, he seemed to suggest that there should be further probing of the Allies on the four conditions. Anami found Hiranuma's ultimate opinion so convoluted that he was not certain where Hiranuma actually stood. The Emperor, however, counted Hiranuma in Togo's camp.

There is no dispute about the clarity of one of Hiranuma's criticisms. Togo's draft, he insisted, fundamentally erred by stating that Japan should accept the Potsdam Declaration on the understanding that it did not include any demand for a change in the status of the Emperor under the national laws. Hiranuma maintained that since the nation and the sovereignty of the Throne were created at the same moment, the legitimacy of the Throne existed independently and was not contingent upon formal recognition under the national laws. Accordingly, the reservation should encompass the understanding that the Allied proclamation would not comprise any demand that would prejudice the prerogatives of His Majesty as a Sovereign Ruler.

Lurking beneath what might appear to be an abstruse obsession with theoretical precision was something far more ominous. This was not simply an effort to secure an Allied pledge to preserve the Imperial institution with a "symbol" emperor, as Grew and Stimson perceived it. Rather, as American scholar Herbert Bix observed,

> The Japanese Government . . . was asking the Allies to guarantee the emperor's political power to rule the state on the theocratic premises of state Shinto. It was not constitutional monarchy that the Suzuki cabinet was seeking to have the Allies assure, but monarchy based on the principle of oracular sovereignty. In the final analysis, the *kokutai* meant to them, in their extreme moment of crisis, the . . . retention of real, substantive political power in the hands of the emperor, so that he and the "moderates" might go on using it to control the people.

After observing that on this very grave matter it was appropriate to seek the opinion of the Throne, Hiranuma wheeled to face the Emperor and

---

* It is astonishing to note that these comments by Suzuki and one other isolated reference in May are the only documented references by a member of the Big Six to the strategic air campaign, despite the fact that B-29s burned down half of Tokyo and killed about 100,000 citizens.

said, "In accordance with the legacy of Your Imperial Forefathers, Your Imperial Majesty is also responsible for preventing unrest in the nation. I should like to ask Your Majesty to make Your decision with this point in mind."

When Hiranuma finally sat down, Suzuki at last turned to Admiral Toyoda. The Chief of the Naval General Staff remained in ranks with Anami and Umezu. If Japan could not disarm her own troops, Toyoda pointed out, he could not be sure orders would be obeyed. Some present took this as a threat. "We cannot say that final victory is certain," intoned the Admiral, "but at the same time we do not believe that we will be positively defeated."

Suzuki announced that the hours of discussion had provoked no consensus, and therefore he had no recourse but to submit the issue to His Majesty for a "decision." Facing the Emperor, Suzuki said, "Your Imperial Majesty's decision is requested as to which proposal should be adapted—the one stated by the Foreign Minister or the one containing the four conditions."

"Without the slightest hesitation," reported Suzuki, the Emperor rose from his seat at the head of the table. The councillors leaped as one up to attention and bowed in his direction, as the Emperor, emotion visible on his face, spoke. No verbatim transcript exists of the Emperor's words, but the following is part of the meticulous re-creation by Robert Butow, modified by the items in brackets from the official Japanese military history series:

I have given serious thought to the situation prevailing at home and abroad and have concluded that continuing the war can only mean destruction for the nation and prolongation of bloodshed and cruelty in the world. I cannot bear to see my innocent people suffer any longer. Ending the war is the only way to restore world peace and to relieve the nation from the terrible distress with which it is burdened.

I was told by those advocating a continuation of hostilities that by June new divisions would be placed in fortified positions at Kujukuri-hama [the beaches east of Tokyo] so that they would be ready for the invader when he sought to land. It is now August and the fortifications still have not been completed. Even the equipment for the divisions which are to fight there is insufficient, and reportedly will not be adequate until after the middle of September. Furthermore, the promised increase in the production of aircraft has not progressed in accordance with expectations.

There are those who say that the key to national survival lies in a decisive battle in the homeland. The experiences of the past, however, show that there has always been a discrepancy between plans and performance. I do not believe that the discrepancy in the case of Kujukuri can be rectified. Since this is the shape of things, how can we repel the invaders? [At about this point, he also made specific reference to the greatly increased destructiveness of the atomic bomb.]

It goes without saying that it is unbearable for me to see the brave and loyal fighting men of Japan disarmed. It is equally unbearable that others who have rendered me devoted service should now be punished as instigators of the war. Nevertheless, the time has come when we must bear the unbearable. . . .

I swallow my own tears and give my sanction to the proposal to accept the Allied proclamation on the basis outlined by the Foreign Minister.

As the Emperor then slowly exited the conference room, Suzuki alone spoke: "His Majesty's decision *should* be made the decision of this conference as well." The Prime Minister's comment betrayed the extralegal standing of what was at that moment no more than an expression of the Emperor's personal opinion before an assembly without constitutional authority and thus also lacking legal writ to effect such a policy, even had the councillors concurred. Only the cabinet held the legal power to enforce the Imperial will, and now word passed that there would be a cabinet meeting at the premier's official residence. Sometime between 3:00 and 4:00 A.M., the ministers officially adopted the "Imperial decision," therefore swaddling the Emperor's words spoken only an hour before in legal force.

But Anami had not yet wholly yielded. He specifically demanded to know if the Prime Minister was braced to continue the war if the Allies rejected the one condition. In a low voice, Suzuki answered that he was. Yonai then asked Anami if he, too, stood ready to fight on in that event, and the Army Minister replied in the affirmative.

Foreign Ministry officials labored furiously before dawn to dispatch cables (the first at 6:45 A.M.) through Sweden and Switzerland to the Allies announcing that Japan would accede to the Potsdam Declaration "with the understanding that the said declaration does not comprise any demand which prejudices the prerogatives of His Majesty as a Sovereign Ruler."

Japan's government had reached a momentous decision, yet two complementary threats remained very much alive. The first was the distinct possibility that the military would not obey the decision to surrender. Despite inculcating the concept of Imperial infallibility and sanctity since the Meiji Restoration, the Imperial Army had ignored and sometimes brazenly contravened governmental decisions on occasions far less threatening to warrior-class sensibilities than this one. The second threat bore a label lifted from many chapters of recent history: "government by assassination." Since under the theoretical edifice erected by the militarists and ultranationalists, the Emperor personally could do no wrong, any error of policy must be the product of evil, crooked, and traitorous advisers. These individuals deserved a traitor's fate, which fanatical assassins provided without tarrying for judicial process. Suzuki still carried a bullet within his body from a 1936 episode of such tactics.

The story of events in Tokyo during the remainder of August 10 revolves primarily around the delicate task of communicating the Emperor's decision to the armed forces, senior officials, and the nation. Anami reached the Army Ministry about 3:00 A.M. and briefed Vice Chief of Staff Kawabe, who confided to his diary that the principal reason for the Emperor's decision was his loss of confidence in the armed forces in general and the Army in particular. The Emperor's decision, recorded Kawabe with "acute pain," sprang from his conviction that there was no prospect for success in the Ketsu operation and his belief that continuing the war would enfold the Japanese people in disaster.

At Anami's summons, senior staff officers at the Army Ministry gathered for a briefing at 9:30 A.M. The Army Minister transmitted the events of the past day. With his audience in consternation, Anami tried to explain:

> I do not know what excuse I can offer but since it is the decision of His Majesty that we accept the Potsdam Proclamation there is nothing that can be done. The really important consideration is that the army act in an organized manner. Your individual feelings and those of the men under you must be disregarded.
>
> Since the imperial decision is predicated upon the assumption that the Allies will guarantee the preservation of our national polity, it is too soon to say that the war has already ended. The army must therefore be prepared either for war or for peace.
>
> If there is anyone here who is dissatisfied and who wishes to act contrary to His Majesty's decision, he will have to do so over my dead body.

The Japanese history of Imperial Headquarters observes that officers were "greatly shocked," particularly because the Emperor's statements disclosed his loss of faith in the Army. But if the Emperor's pronouncement thunderstruck the general staff, the Army Minister himself was reeling from the Prime Minister's role in it. Anami confided to his secretary, Colonel Hayashi, that he had never suspected that Suzuki entertained any disposition for peace.

American commanders, completely ignorant of the Japanese peace proposal, launched air attacks in the morning hours of August 10. From shortly after dawn, carrier planes swarmed over the Tokyo region, and at 10:20 A.M. seventy B-29s struck the Tokyo arsenal. The raid killed 232 people. Meanwhile, from Okinawa the Far Eastern Air Forces launched nearly five hundred fighter and bomber sorties at Kumamoto and at shipping targets.

In Manchuria, Japanese reconnaissance planes belatedly detected the massive onslaught by the Trans-Baikal Front as the Sixth Guards Tank Army reached the highest point in the Grand Khingans. The Japanese ability to counter this thrust, however, was further compromised when General Ushiroku of the Third Area Army directed all his units that had not been cut off to withdraw. Ushiroku intended to concentrate his men north and south of Mukden for the purpose of protecting his soldiers' families. But his decision contravened the plans of General Yamada to construct a defense further to the rear, thus exacerbating the confusion in Japanese ranks.

In mid-afternoon, the Emperor met with the seven former prime ministers. Most agreed that the Potsdam Declaration would be acceptable, if the Emperor's position remained assured. Only Generals Koiso and Tojo demurred. Tojo spoke in allegory that the national polity was like a conch; if it lost the protective shell of its armed forces, it must die.

There remained the task of notifying the Japanese people. Here, too, a fissure appeared in the cabinet. The demands of those who advocated an immediate announcement were countered by the reservations of those who believed it premature to say anything before the Allied response was in hand. The compromise statement published in the newspapers on August 11 delivered yet another sermon on the fighting spirit and effectiveness of the armed forces and denounced the indiscriminate slaughter of the innocent young, old, and female by a "new-type bomb" in the hands of the "diabolical enemies" of the Empire. But the statement concluded in phrases intended to prepare the population to "bear the unbearable":

> In truth, we cannot but recognize that we are now beset with the worst possible situation. Just as the government is exerting its utmost efforts to defend the homeland, safeguard the polity, and preserve the honor of the nation so too must the people rise to the occasion and overcome all manner of difficulties in order to protect the polity of their Empire.

The vast majority of the population assumed, however, that this announcement meant accepting the duty to fight to the last man across every meter of the Homeland. This impression was strengthened by the fact that the communiqué appeared in conjunction with a statement quoting Army Minister Anami: "Even though we may have to eat grass, swallow dirt, and lie in the fields, we shall fight on to the bitter end, ever firm in our faith that we shall find life in death." Anami ended with the words, "Follow the illustrious examples of Masashige Kusunoki [a symbol of eternal loyalty to the dynasty] and Tokimasa Hojo [the shogun who defeated the Mongol invasion of 1281] and surge forward to destroy the arrogant enemy!"

To those in inner circles of power, the Army Minister's statement could be read only as a declaration that the military would not accept the Emperor's decision. The peace faction fell into disarray: Some advocated having the foreign minister or other high authority command that the presses be stopped, while others merely wanted to seek "clarification" from Anami. Only after the event did the full story of Anami's statement emerge—a tangled tale wherein his principal speechwriter, Lieutenant Colonel Inaba, interpreted the Army minister's remarks as indicating that units in Manchuria must continue to struggle and that others maintain their determination to fight until the surrender was a fact. Through a complex chain of events, Inaba's combative text was published without Anami's personal sanction.

There was, however, something of a tit for tat to the Anami proclamation. Concerned that a third atomic bomb might be dropped while the official announcement of Japan's conditional acceptance of the Potsdam ultimatum passed along diplomatic channels—and with the more hopeful thought that public release of the announcement might trigger such an outpouring of public rejoicing in Allied countries that the governments would have no choice but to acquiesce in Japan's reservation—Foreign Ministry officials managed to leak such a statement past the censors via the Morse code broadcasts of the Domei News Agency. It was also published side by side, in obvious contradiction, to the Army Minister's statement to illustrate to the public, said one editor later, "that the General trend in the government was towards the termination of war . . . while on the other hand, the insistence of the militarists to continue the war was very strong."

Tremendous tension gripped the Imperial Household on August 10 and 11 as the Emperor and his advisers awaited the Allied response. Relays of high-level officials and senior statesmen trooped through to see Marquis Kido. Kido and Imperial Household Minister Ishiwata conceived a unique (and perhaps desperate) solution to the perplexing problem of how to minimize both the peril and the confusion that a sudden announcement of defeat could generate. They boldly proposed to break precedent by having the Emperor personally broadcast the stunning news by radio throughout the nation.

The American Response

The international date line and the intervening time zones belied the measured pace of diplomatic exchanges to create the illusion of blinding speed: Japan's official, conditioned acceptance of the Potsdam Declaration reached Washington on the same day and at almost the precise hour of its dispatch. Later assumptions that officials in Washington anticipated a prompt Japanese surrender after the initial use of atomic weapons are disproved by the contemporary evidence. For example, President Truman had known by at least mid-July that the smooth transition from a wartime to a peacetime economy without depression, massive unemployment, or inflation was crucial to his domestic political fortunes. Yet he never dispatched any orders to energize action along these lines, a step he surely would have taken if he believed for more than a few minutes that the end of the war was imminent.

On August 2, Under Secretary of War Robert Patterson had queried George Harrison as to whether the War Department should begin cutting back on war contracts. Not only was Harrison against such action then, he still maintained on August 9 that events must advance further before Patterson should embark on a "resurvey" of procurement programs. On August 8, Secretary of the Navy Forrestal wrote to Truman requesting that Admiral Nimitz, General Eisenhower, or General Marshall replace MacArthur as the commander for the final operations against Japan in order to assure "common direction and command." It is impossible to believe that Forrestal would have taken this audacious action, certain to provoke uproar between the services and perhaps ignite a political storm, if he seriously thought the end of the war was near.

The arrival of the Japanese response on August 10 clearly surprised Stimson. He had been about to depart on a vacation when the message arrived, an eloquent indicator of how far official Washington believed Japan remained from surrender even after two atomic bombs. General Marshall provided another striking reaction, and one linked to a vital underlying issue: the treatment of captive American and Allied servicemen. Marshall drafted a response demanding that "precedent to a discussion of the proposal of the Japanese government" all Allied prisoners of war must be transported "immediately forthwith and without delay" to designated points for release to Allied representatives. The estimated number of Allied prisoners of war in Japanese hands totaled 168,500 in mid-June, including 15,000 Americans. Meeting Marshall's precondition would consume many days, again illustrating how a major American policy maker anticipated a delayed surrender at best.

Truman, too, shared a "deep concern" for prisoners of war. Before the day was out, Marshall's proposal metamorphosed into a "solemn warning" to be jointly issued by Allied governments placing Japan and its people "individually and collectively" on notice not to harm prisoners of war. The cover memorandum to Truman on this noted, "This matter is presented at this time with the thought that if the Japanese Government continues to wage war it may engage in acts of violence against Allied prisoners-of-war."

Stimson hurried to an impromptu White House meeting with Truman, Byrnes, Leahy, and Forrestal to discuss the Japanese response. There, Stimson reiterated his consistent position that the Emperor should be retained so that his unrivaled symbolic authority could be deployed to serve American interests. The Secretary of War, a man careful with his words, warned that this was vital "in order to save us from a score of bloody Iwo Jimas and Okinawas all over China and the New Netherlands [Indonesia]." Stimson's comments again raised the ultimate nightmare scenario where no organized Japanese surrender could be obtained, leaving the Allies with the task of defeating Japanese legions piecemeal all over Asia and the Pacific. A score of Iwo Jimas translated to 634,160 casualties, including 171,720 killed or missing, while twenty Okinawas equals 982,660 casualties, including 250,400 killed or missing. And Stimson's comment did not address losses in the Home Islands. Forrestal supported Stimson. Leahy likewise advocated immediate acceptance of the Japanese proposal. But Secretary of State Byrnes checked the building momentum by insisting that the demand for unconditional surrender had been issued even before the use of the atomic bomb or Soviet entry into the war. Therefore, the United States should accept nothing less. If, indeed, other terms were to be offered, the United States, not Japan, should do the proposing. Forrestal suggested that they draft an acceptance in which they defined the terms in a manner effectively equivalent to the Potsdam Declaration. Forrestal's stratagem won Truman's approval, and Byrnes departed to draft the necessary message.

Despite his adamant position, Secretary Byrnes displayed considerable sensitivity to both potentially volatile American public opinion and equally delicate Allied sensibilities. Simple acquiescence to the Japanese terms would trigger outrage and might create a precedent that would hobble the authority of an occupying force. Flat rejection of the opportunity for peace might also ignite public outcry. He also had to ensure that his message did not appear as a unilateral American effort to redefine or rewrite the terms agreed upon at Potsdam with the Allies.

Given these challenges, the draft was completed with remarkable speed by Byrnes, aided by an assistant, Truman, Leahy, and Stimson. Regarding the Japanese reservation, they noted:

> From the moment of surrender the authority of the Emperor and the Japanese Government to rule the state shall be subject to the Supreme Commander of the Allied powers who will take such steps as he deems proper to effectuate the surrender terms. . . .
>
> The ultimate form of government of Japan shall, in accordance with the Potsdam Declaration, be established by the freely expressed will of the Japanese people.
>
> The armed forces of the Allied powers will remain in Japan until the purposes set forth in the Potsdam Declaration are achieved.

As intended, the message implied much but firmly promised nothing. The careful phrases allowed for the continuance of the Imperial institution, if the Japanese people so chose. The Emperor, not necessarily the incumbent, would reign, however, while the Supreme Allied Commander, cast in a role not unlike a shogun, would rule during an occupation of indefinite duration. By no means was this an explicit guarantee that the Imperial institution would continue, much less that Hirohito would remain on the throne.

Although British and Chinese concurrence followed without significant conflict, the Soviet response proved Byrnes's concern about Allied sensibilities to be well-founded. Foreign Minister Molotov initially balked, maintaining that leaving the Japanese the possibility of retaining the Emperor did not comport with unconditional surrender. Ultimately, however, the Soviet government formally concurred. With this news, Byrnes quickly transmitted the response to Japan.

Conjoined to this complex issue was the equally vexing question of what military operations, if any, should Truman authorize while the diplomatic exchanges unfolded. Stimson and Forrestal urged suspension of all air attacks, conventional and atomic. Certainly another atomic bomb, they argued, might embitter the Japanese enough to drive them into Soviet arms. Truman halted further use of atomic weapons, except on his express order. According to the diary of Henry Wallace, Secretary of Commerce, the President said that "the thought of wiping out another 100,000 people was too horrible. He didn't like the idea of killing 'all those kids.' " Truman did not extract that figure from thin air—it was precisely the number of casualties in Hiroshima reported in an Imperial Navy message that had appeared in an Ultra summary the day before.

Truman knew that another bomb was not ready anyway. Marshall and Groves had delayed transport of critical bomb components from the

United States to Tinian, making it impossible to ready a third bomb until about August 21. Groves and Marshall took this action because they believed two bombs would move the Japanese to capitulation, concurring with Stimson's policy that the bombs should be used only to end the war. Pacific commanders nevertheless transmitted recommendations on targets for the third weapon. General Farrell and Captain Parsons had met with General Twining, Admiral Nimitz, and General Spaatz, and by the afternoon of August 9 they urged Washington to review target lists since the "effects at Trinity and Hiroshima . . . [had] far exceeded optimistic expectations." They "expressly recommended" that the next bomb be dropped in the "region of Tokyo" to achieve maximum psychological effect. On August 14, Twining submitted a new list of six targets in order of priority: Sapporo, Hakodate, Oyabu, Yokosuka, Osaka, and Nagoya.

As for conventional weapons, Truman ordered that military operations continue at "present intensity," because of their "different nature and purpose." This suggests that the president was mindful of the Ultra evidence of the Japanese buildup on Kyushu. Such actions also did duty as a reminder of American resolve intended to discourage Japanese diehards (assuming they were susceptible to rational persuasion) and to energize advocates of peace.

Strategic bombing by B-29s continued only briefly. During the night of August 9–10, the 315th Wing had struck at one of its oil targets. The 314th Wing attacked the Tokyo arsenal on August 10, though deteriorating weather compelled Spaatz to cancel attacks on the eleventh. Unfortunately, news correspondents publicly translated his remark, "The Superforts are not flying today," as evidence of a cease-fire order. This aroused Truman's concern that if Spaatz launched a further attack, it would be interpreted as a signal that peace negotiations had broken down. Accordingly, the President halted all bombing by B-29s.

The New Air–Target Directive

No American leader could rest assured that the sudden appearance of a serious and authoritative Japanese peace proposal would secure a Japanese surrender. Nor was it certain that a surrender would be obeyed by the Imperial Army and Navy. Hence, plans for both an invasion and the campaign of blockade and bombardment evolved hand in hand with diplomatic developments.

On August 11, coincident with Truman's suspension of B-29 attacks, Spaatz ordered a momentous reorientation of the entire strategic air war against Japan, away from massive urban incendiary bombing. The decision stemmed from the findings of the United States Strategic Bombing Survey (USSBS) concerning the effects of bombing on Germany. Between June 11 and 15, a USSBS team presented its informal findings to the Joint Target Group, a special planning organization under General Arnold that directed and evaluated strategic air attacks on Japan.

The USSBS report concluded that air bombardment had pitched German war production downward from mid-July 1944, "in an almost unbroken decline until the end of the war," and that this "contributed in decisive measure to the early and complete victory which followed." This result was achieved by concentrating on two target systems: oil and transportation. The assault on transportation, primarily the railway system, resulted in the "total disintegration of the economy, largely through paralysis of coal movements," because "without coal almost all other types of basic production became impossible." The report further observed that "the Germans were even concerned as to their ability to move sufficient food to avoid widespread starvation in their predominantly industrial communities." The USSBS account deprecated the effectiveness of raids aimed at classic precision targets such as factories for airframes, ball bearings, and motor transport, and it labeled purely urban attacks as "relatively indecisive" in their effect on war production. The central lesson of bombing in Europe, concluded the report, was the selection of a few decisive target systems and their full and sustained destruction.

The Joint Target Group generally concurred with the recommendations of the USSBS team on the priority for transportation targets, radar, and aircraft plants but rejected USSBS recommendations for emphasis on nitrogen plants (for explosives), synthetic-oil plants, and refineries. USSBS representatives had pressed particularly for attacks on the Japanese rice crop using a chemical (TN8), though admittedly this could not take place prior to 1946. The Joint Target Group rejected this because "rice production is not considered a profitable target in view of the currently accepted strategy" and added pointedly, "indigenous food supplies may be very important to the commander charged with occupation." General Spaatz, who was then en route to assume his duties in the Pacific, was in turn impressed by a briefing from the USSBS party. Spaatz received a directive that reordered bombing priority to targets other than Japanese cities. On August 11, LeMay, acting now as the chief of staff of the USASTAF, Pacific, issued parallel sets of operational directives to the Eighth and the Twentieth Air Forces reflecting the priorities set by the new target directive. LeMay defined the overall mission as "the progressive destruction and dislocation of Japan's military, industrial and economic systems." The operational directive then went over the list of objectives, in order of priority:

USASTAF Operational Directive
11 August 1945

	Number of Individual Targets	
	Eighth Air Force	Twentieth Air Force
Primary Objectives		
1. Transportation system		
Railroad yards and facilities	8	46
Bridges	9	4
2. Aircraft industry	2	15
3. Munition storage	11	30
4. Urban industrial areas	2	33
Secondary Objectives		
1. Arsenals	1	6
2. Aircraft industry	2	17
3. Oil storage	3	14
4. Chemical plants (nitrogen)	3	13
Total	41	178

The assignment of more than four times as many targets to the Twentieth Air Force reflected the relative strengths of the commands. As of August 1, the Twentieth Air Force in the Marianas numbered 76,539 personnel, 1,002 Superfortresses, and 1,228 crews. The Eighth Air Force was then in the process of a planned redeployment to Okinawa, in increments between August and early 1946. It was to ultimately comprise a total of five full B-29 wings and two fighter groups with very long range fighters (P-47Ns) and bring the personnel strength of the USASTAF to 182,237. Planners anticipated the following strength in aircraft:

Aircraft	Sept. 45	Oct. 45	Nov. 45	Dec. 45	Jan. 46	Feb. 46
B-29	992	1,217	1,355	1,534	1,546	1,648
P-47N	444	444	444	666	666	666
P-51	333	333	333	333	333	333

Figures represent unit establishment and reserve. The September 1945 figure had already been exceeded by August 1.

Numbers alone do not convey the full measure of the actual destructive power of the USASTAF. Strike photographs showed that the percent of bombs in daylight precision raids that fell within one thousand feet of the target soared from 12 to 40 percent between January and June. This meant that thirty aircraft could accomplish a task previously requiring 250. During July and August, deployment of sophisticated new electronic bombing aids foretold enhanced accuracy and destructive power. David T. Griggs, a scientific consultant to the Office of the Secretary of War, wrote on July 13 that "since the majority of the bombs dropped on Japan by B-29s in the next few months will be dropped by radar, no stone may be left unturned to insure that our radar bombing is as effective as we know how to make it."

Except for the 315th Wing, the standard B-29 in the Twentieth Air Force was fitted with the AN/APQ-13 radar. In July 1945, scientists rated radar bombing with it as capable of inflicting about 20 percent of the damage of the average visual bombing technique. With several technical enhancements, the scientists believed the APQ-13 might be capable of 40 to 45 percent efficiency, but it would never be capable of true precision attack on a target as small as an individual factory. By contrast, the APQ-7 radar fitted to 315th Wing aircraft scored 50 to 60 percent accuracy. Individual aircraft attacks by well-trained and -briefed crews, exploiting reconnaissance data, permitted still greater efficiency.

The most important of the prospective enhancements was Shoran, officially designated AN/APN-3. Basically, a Shoran permitted very precise blind bombing by use of radio signals transmitted from ground stations to an aircraft. Scientific advisers believed this instrument alone would increase the effectiveness of the B-29 force "by a factor of three" and would "permit the execution of missions against precision targets almost independent of weather, and night missions would be just as accurate as day missions."

Shoran was further expected to achieve great things with a group of B-29s soon to be specially fitted to carry huge Tall Boy and Grand Slam bombs. This group would attack targets such as the Shimonoseki Tunnel and "other targets requiring high penetration and highly concentrated destructive capacity."

Between November 1944 and August 1945, aircraft based in the Marianas unleashed 157,000 tons of bombs on Japan. By mid-August, it was clear that the growing strength of B-29s would enable the USASTAF to unleash an equal amount of tonnage within the next eleven weeks. Staff officers made the following projections:

Month	Sorties	Ratio IC: HE	Bomb-load/aircraft capacity (tons)		Estimated total expenditures (tons)
July	6,350	80 20	7.25	7.25	46,038
August	7,100	80 20	7.5	7.75	53,605
September	7,430	70 30	7.75	8.25	58,697
October	8,060	50 50	8.0	8.75	66,495
November	8,860	30 70	8.0	9.0	77,256
December	9,370	30 70	8.0	9.0	81,519

IC: incendiary
HE: high explosive

Despite these projections, Deputy Chief of Staff for Operations Colonel J. B. Montgomery believed crew fatigue and lack of replacements would have leveled off the ability of the Twentieth Air Force to deliver bombs at a rate of about 50,000 tons per month.

Spaatz had more on his mind on August 11 than the new target directive and the burgeoning power of his command. This same day he wrote in his diary that he intended to "write [Assistant Secretary of War Robert] Lovett repeating my views towards [canceling the] invasion":

> When the atomic bomb was first discussed with me . . . it was pointed out to me however that the use of the atomic bomb would certainly mean that an invasion would be unnecessary and that thousands of American lives would be saved. The invasion is still planned in spite of this—and only the surrendering of the Japanese after attacks on their homeland by Air only will cancel the invasion.

Thus, as August 11 closed, not only was the strategic air campaign poised to move in a radically new direction but the senior army aviator in the Pacific was about to counsel Washington against an invasion.

19

Surrender

"The war situation has developed not necessarily to Japan's advantage"

Waiting

Senior Imperial Army field commanders learned of the Emperor's decision on August 11. Meanwhile, in an atmosphere explosive with potential for a coup d'état, Army Vice Chief of Staff Kawabe met repeatedly with high-ranking officers who either frankly doubted that senior field commanders would comply with the surrender or demanded that Japan insist upon more favorable terms. Kawabe confessed in his diary that he shared these same thoughts. The fact that soldiers like the Vice Chief of Staff questioned whether the Imperial Army would obey the Emperor's command illustrates how uncertain remained the path to peace.

Early on August 12, as diplomats transmitted the official copy of the Byrnes note to Tokyo, the Japanese monitored a public-radio broadcast of the text at 12:45 A.M. Vice Minister of Foreign Affairs Sunichi Matsumoto, Chief Cabinet Secretary Sakomizu, and other officials were disappointed and dismayed over the absence of an express guarantee of the status of the Emperor. Nonetheless, Matsumoto and Sakomizu set out to persuade Foreign Minister Togo and Prime Minister Suzuki that Japan must immediately and unequivocally accept the terms.

At the Army Ministry, Byrnes's note engendered rage in junior officers. Chief of Staff Umezu and Army Minister Anami resolved that the cabinet should reject it but pursue further negotiations. Meanwhile, they deluded themselves that Japan could prosecute the war against the United States, Britain, and China while eschewing a formal declaration of war with the

Soviet Union during efforts to "improve the situation" by wedging the Soviets away from their allies. They provided no reasons as to why the Soviets, now having officially entered the war on the side of the Allies, would be susceptible to any blandishments from Japan. Imperial Headquarters reassured field commanders of the Army's persistence.

Anami left a fairly clear record—at least on the surface—of what impelled him. As he had admitted to the cabinet on August 9, the simple calculation of odds showed Japan must yield or perish. But again and again, he returned to an adage that represented the source of his tenacious refusal to capitulate in any guise: "A road to success will somehow be revealed to us if we carry on with strong determination." As historian Edward Drea observed:

> Warfare, Anami insisted, came down to a clash of wills, and the human spirit
> or esprit in combat, or *seishin,* outweighed any material factors and could
> turn the tide of battle. According to Anami, the decisive battle would pre-
> serve *kokutai.* The Army, he was convinced, could fight such a battle, but it
> required firm leadership to keep morale from plummeting.

The royal family, including the Emperor's brothers Takamatsu and Mikasa, met at 3:00 P.M. The Emperor, underscoring his loss of faith in the military, obtained pledges of support for his decision. This transformed the princes of the blood from potential rallying symbols for fanatics to valuable assets in ending the war. To officers within the Army Ministry and General Staff, this meeting underscored the Emperor's determination to end the war and was proof, one noted bitterly, that "in any age the upper classes were always the first to crumble."

At another extraordinary cabinet meeting, Suzuki dismissed Sakomizu's advice that they must proceed with caution. Japan, he said, must reject Byrnes's note, and the war must continue if the Allies declined to back down. Emboldened by Suzuki's pronouncement, Anami exhorted his colleagues that Japan must not only insist on a guarantee of the Imperial system but also demand self-disarmament and no occupation of the Homeland. With sentiment flowing Anami's way, Togo managed to secure a postponement pending receipt of the official copy of the note.

Following this meeting, Togo castigated Suzuki for his defection. The Prime Minister was then intercepted by Matsumoto, who handed him a sobering dispatch from Japan's embassy in Sweden: The Allies would stiffen, not soften, their terms if Japan spurned the note. Suzuki was then confronted by Kido. Not only would "millions of innocents" die of bombing and starvation if the war continued, counseled the Lord Keeper of the

Privy Seal, it was "His Majesty's wish that we advance on the basis of the views held by the Foreign Minister." These intercessions drove Suzuki back into the ranks of those seeking to end the war.

Suzuki feared that defeat might eliminate the Throne, but on this same date Navy Minister Yonai confessed his deep foreboding over another peril to the Emperor:

> I think the term is inappropriate, but the atomic bombs and the Soviet entry into the war are, in a sense, gifts from the gods [*tenyu,* also "heaven-sent blessings"]. This way we don't have to say that we have quit the war because of domestic circumstances. Why I have long been advocating control of the crisis of the country is neither from fear of an enemy attack nor because of the atomic bombs and the Soviet entry into the war. The main reason is my anxiety over the domestic situation. So, it is rather fortunate that now we can control matters without revealing the domestic situation.

Yonai was referring to the danger that Japan's home front might actually revolt and topple the Throne. Even suggesting the possibility that the Japanese people would destroy the Imperial institution was too painful for Yonai to put into direct words, but alarm at this prospect steeled the resolution of not only the Navy Minister but also Kido and the Emperor.

In Tokyo, the end of August 12 was punctuated by a somber situation report from the Kwantung Army. It described limited Soviet penetrations in the north but severe fighting in eastern Manchuria, with the situation ominously obscure. To the west, Soviet mechanized units were depicted as advancing slowly (actually, most had halted due to lack of fuel), but, noted the Emperor's military aide-de-camp, they threatened to sever the key rail line between Dairen and Changchun within a week. On Sakhalin, Japanese defenders were holding their own.

After radicals placed public posters in Tokyo exhorting "Kill Lord Keeper of the Privy Seal Kido," the Lord Keeper prudently moved his residence to his suite of rooms at the Imperial Household Ministry, inside the palace grounds. There, at 7:10 A.M. on August 13, he received General Anami. The Army Minister warned yet again that agreement to the Potsdam Declaration would doom the Throne, and that a battle in the Homeland might still secure better terms. Kido responded that the Emperor had sanctioned the diplomatic decision to end the war; to alter Japan's stance now would make the Emperor appear a fool or madman, which was intolerable. Kido was firm: "We must abide by the wishes of His Majesty, we must accept the Allied reply in its present form."

Anami left unconvinced and proceeded to yet another meeting of the

Big Six. Here, joined by Umezu and Toyoda, he still blocked the government from acceptance of Byrnes's note. Suzuki transferred the venue to a full cabinet session. When a new vote was taken, twelve ministers sided with Togo for immediate acceptance, three stood opposed, and one remained undecided. Suzuki announced that he would report the cabinet deadlock to the Throne and seek a decision from the Emperor.

As these meetings transpired, reports from the Kwantung Army acknowledged that Soviet forces in eastern Manchuria had closed in on Mutanchiang in heavy fighting. On Sakhalin, too, bitter combat continued, and in western Manchuria, Soviet mobile forces had resumed their relentless advances.

Anami and Umezu possessed the legal as well as the practical power to continue the war. By simply resigning his post, Anami could collapse the cabinet, forestalling any action. Either officer might also orchestrate a coup d'état, perhaps with an overture of assassinations. But the velocity of events wore on both men. Moreover, since August 9 the frequency and length of the meetings demanding concentration and perseverance had precluded the sort of careful collaboration and preparations between Anami and his staff that might have bolstered Anami's advocacy. At the same time, his restraint from resignation may well have stemmed from his conviction, shared by even the virulent diehards who were prepared to see Japan perish before surrender, that the cycle of changing governments must cease because it degraded Japan's position internally and presented a spectacle of vulnerability to her enemies.

Just how easily Anami and Umezu could have harnessed forces to continue the war is illuminated in another incident on this evening of August 13. Umezu and Toyoda met at 9:00 P.M. with Togo in yet another fruitless effort to find common ground. As this conference drew to a close, Admiral Takijiro Onishi, now Vice Chief of Naval General Staff, burst in. From the mouth of the "father" of the kamikazes came this chilling sentiment, rampant among Navy and Army officers:

> Let us formulate a plan for certain victory, obtain the Emperor's sanction, and throw ourselves into bringing the plan to realization. If we are prepared to sacrifice 20,000,000 Japanese lives in a special attack [kamikaze] effort, victory will be ours!

At roughly the same time, in Washington U.S. Army leaders were experiencing growing doubts that Japan was actually near surrender. Magic had revealed that on August 11 Foreign Minister Togo advised his representatives to Japan's client governments in Asia that he had not yet "received the agreement of the Army and Navy on [the surrender offer]." Apparent confirmation of Togo's caution came from an intercepted message from Imperial General Headquarters on the same day. This general dispatch instructed all commands to prosecute the war "to preserve the Fatherland as well as complete annihilation of the fanatic enemy and not to be affected by the numerous reports on the progress of the war."

These intercepts are undoubtedly responsible for the remarkably wary estimate provided to General Marshall on August 12 by Major General Clayton Bissell, his chief intelligence officer. Bissell pointed out that although Japan was impotent at sea and in the air,

> large, well disciplined, well armed, undefeated Japanese ground forces have a capacity to offer stubborn fanatic resistance to Allied ground operations in the homeland and may inflict heavy Allied casualties. . . . Japanese stockpiling has established food and munitions in all areas of expected invasion in sufficient quantities to support operations for from about four to six months despite expected serious disruption of Japanese rail, road and water transportation systems. Adverse weather and heavy cloud cover during the next month may reduce the effectiveness of Allied air power in disrupting the Japanese rail and road system. . . . Atomic bombs will not have a decisive effect in the next 30 days.

Bissell predicted that a surrender emanating from Tokyo would likely be obeyed in Manchuria and southern regions, but he doubted the Japanese would surrender to any Koreans and would not venture a guess as to what would happen in "chaotic" China. He foresaw "probable" continued armed resistance by "some irreconcilable military forces" in the Homeland.

On August 13, Major General John E. Hull, the Assistant Chief of Staff for Operations at the War Department, telephoned Colonel L. E. Seeman of the Manhattan Project at the express direction of General Marshall. Hull explained that the Chief of Staff believed the two atomic bombs "have had a tremendous effect on the Japanese as far as capitulation is concerned," but Marshall doubted that further atomic bombing would influence any Japanese decision to end the war. Therefore, Marshall commissioned Hull to examine an alternative strategy to reserve all additional atomic-weapon production and then deploy them in direct support (that is, "tactical" support) of the invasion "rather than [on] industry, morale, psychology, etc."

Seeman, affirming that he had studied possible tactical use "a good deal," reported that at least seven bombs probably would be ready for use by October 31. The great hazard, he stressed to Hull, was that of a bomb that failed to explode. He advised a "safety factor" of "48 hours" before soldiers advanced into areas hit by atomic weapons, but at no point did See-man warn of any explicit radiation risks to American servicemen. This was congruent with his conclusion in his report to Groves of August 4 address-ing such tactical use. Seeman had warned emphatically of lethal radiolog-ical effects from an atomic explosion out to 3,500 feet at detonation, but predicted the ground would be safe within one hour, although he proposed to form special "monitoring teams" to scan ahead of advancing troops. Seeman's report dovetailed with Groves's submission to Marshall on July 30 in which Groves advised that gamma rays from the bomb would be fatal to unshielded humans at 3,500 feet but would have no damaging ef-fects on the ground. This evidence, of course, illustrates all too sadly how little was understood about radiation hazards in 1945, even among those who had considered the danger.

Truman, like Marshall, had profound doubts about the proximity of a Japanese surrender. Although the Japanese had been informed that an un-qualified acceptance could be transmitted in plain, uncoded text, Secretary of the Navy Forrestal noted in his diary on August 13 that they apparently were replying in code. This appeared to be evidence of a qualified re-sponse.* In addition, radio intercepts showed increased traffic between Japanese command units, which was interpreted as a probable indicator of an "all-out banzai attack." Consequently, army air commanders in the Pa-cific received a message that "the President directs that we go ahead with everything we've got," and parallel orders reached Admiral Halsey.

The next day, August 14, for the first time since August 10, B-29s took to the air on missions against three precision targets and two cities. The 58th Wing struck the Hikari Naval Arsenal at Tokoyama; the 73rd Wing hit the Osaka Army Arsenal; three groups of the 313th Wing bombed the Marifu railway yards in Iwakuni; and the 314th Wing divided its attention between Kumagaya, population 49,000, and Isesaki, with only 40,000 residents. Altogether the Twentieth Air Force lofted 779 air-craft, of which 709 bombed the primary targets with 4,463 tons of explo-sives. There were no B-29 losses, but four of 186 escort and strike fighters failed to return. The city of Kumagaya lost 334; only twenty-one died in Isesaki.

For Koichi Kido, August 14 commenced with perils literally raining from the sky. It was the assessment of Allied psychological-warfare ex-perts that it would be advantageous to inform the Japanese public directly of the dramatic diplomatic developments. During the previous day, B-29s

* With what appears in retrospect to be incredibly poor judgment, the Japanese Foreign Ministry se-lected this tense moment to send two coded messages on extraneous matters to Bern (SRH-090, pp. 11–12; SRH-092, pp. 30–31).

had released leaflets in Japanese with the full text of the government's conditional-surrender offer of August 10, along with Byrnes's response. After Kido's chamberlains shoved one of the leaflets into his hands, his face was "stricken with consternation," and for good reason. Kido feared that the leaflets would rip off the veil of relative secrecy over events of the last few critical days and spark a convulsion in the public and in the military rank and file that would destroy the government.

Kido recognized that swift action was mandatory. Within minutes, he met with the Emperor; subsequently, Suzuki joined them. The Emperor agreed to order an Imperial conference at which he would "command" the cabinet to accept Byrnes's note without alteration and to draft an Imperial rescript codifying that decision. Moreover, according to *Showa Tenno Dokuhakuroku,* the Emperor rejected Suzuki's original proposal to wait until 1:00 P.M. because it granted too much time for military officers to assemble a coup d'état; the Emperor personally set the meeting for 11:00 A.M.

At Anami's urging, the Emperor received the most senior military and naval officers at 10:20 A.M. The key figure in this assembly was Field Marshal Hata, who had just arrived from Hiroshima that morning. Anami expected Hata to minimize the impact of the atomic bomb; younger officers counted upon the respected and forceful Hata to persuade the Emperor to fight on. After Admiral of the Fleet Nagano and Field Marshal Sugiyama pleaded that Japan still possessed the material and spiritual resources to carry on the struggle, Hata spoke. He carried the unmatched credentials of command of what was expected to be the decisive battlefront on Kyushu and direct experience with the atomic bomb. With his eyes full of tears, Hata spoke forthrightly: He had no confidence in repulsing the enemy landing, he said, and he did not dispute the Emperor's decision to accept the Potsdam Declaration. The Emperor replied that the Soviet intervention and the enemy's "scientific power" could not be checked even with "special attack" forces, and he requested that his field marshals and fleet admirals cooperate with him to end the war. It was tantamount to an order.

Then, shortly before 11:00 A.M., the Emperor, flanked by an aide-de-camp, entered the same air-raid shelter where the first Imperial conference of August 9 had transpired to face the assembled cabinet, the supreme councillors, and other senior officials. Suzuki announced the purpose of the meeting, then wheeled to face Anami, Toyoda, and Umezu. He bid them to rise and unfold their case to His Majesty. Little of what these officers said was recorded, but their manner was; powerful emotions buffeted the self-control of all three. Neither general spoke at length, but the admiral managed to recite his arguments once again. When they finished, the Emperor pronounced his verdict:

I have listened carefully to each of the arguments presented in opposition to the view that Japan should accept the Allied reply as it stands and without further clarification or modification, but my own thoughts have not undergone any change. I have surveyed the conditions prevailing in Japan and in the world at large, and it is my belief that a continuation of the war promises nothing but additional destruction. I have studied the terms of the Allied reply and have concluded that they constitute a virtually complete acknowledgment of the position we maintained in the note dispatched several days ago. In short, I consider the reply to be acceptable.

He lamented "how difficult it will be for the officers and men of the army and navy to surrender their arms to the enemy and to see their homeland occupied," as it was onerous for him to issue such an order and to face the prospect that his loyal servants would be tried as war criminals. But these considerations were outweighed by the devastation the Japanese people would face if the war continued. Then he concluded:

In order that the people may know of my decision, I request you to prepare at once an imperial rescript so that I may broadcast to the nation. Finally, I call upon each and every one of you to exert himself to the utmost so that we may meet the trying days which lie ahead.

These words left both the Emperor and his audience in tears, which "flowed unceasingly," recalled Minister of State Shimomura.

The cabinet convened immediately after the conference and unanimously ratified and thus made legal the Emperor's wishes. The Foreign Ministry began transmitting official word to the Allies through Sweden and Switzerland. The first semiofficial confirmation to reach Washington arrived at 2:49 A.M., August 14, in a Domei shortwave news report.

Seizing War from the Jaws of Peace

History will never know with certainty whether or when Imperial Japan might have accepted Allied terms of surrender without the Emperor's intervention. But even the Emperor's command was not sufficient to guarantee peace. The war would end only if Japanese uniformed leaders complied with the Imperial decision. Moreover, due to the corrosive precedents set during the past two decades, the Emperor's decision also required the armed forces to maintain discipline sufficient to quash any effort to halt the march to peace.

The uncertain prospects for compliance, even at the highest levels of the Imperial Army, were illustrated swiftly and dramatically. Immediately following the Imperial conference, Anami, the most powerful figure in Japan besides the Emperor himself, had three remarkable conversations. He called on Umezu with a question: "Do you believe that the war should be continued even at the risk of launching a coup d'état?" Umezu's answer was unequivocal:

> No, it is impossible, because the decision of His Majesty the Emperor has already been given. Launching a coup d'état in complete defiance of the Emperor's decision will, first of all, invite a split within military circles. Moreover, the nation will not follow us. There is nothing we can do now but to comply with the Emperor's decision.

At about the same time, Anami ducked into a washroom and asked Colonel Hayashi about the possibility of attacking a large American convoy rumored to be outside of Tokyo. Hayashi pronounced, "Your idea is absolutely mistaken," and pointed out that not only had the Imperial decision already been made, but that the convoy's presence was merely a rumor.

The Army Minister then encountered Lieutenant Colonel Masahiko Takeshita, his brother-in-law. Takeshita urged Anami to resign, an act that normally would have halted any official government decision. Anami replied that it was too late, the Imperial edict would be issued regardless. Takeshita continued to press for a coup d'état and suggested—probably without basis—that Umezu was receptive to such a plan. Anami replied that he wished to go to the Army Ministry first.

Anami returned to the Army Ministry, his face pale but composed. When he spoke to the staff at about 3:00 P.M., "all were dumbfounded and their bodies seemed to stiffen," recorded a witness. When one officer demanded to know why he was prepared to comply with the Emperor's request, Anami replied,

> I could not refute the Emperor's own belief any longer. Especially when he asked me in tears to forebear the pain, however trying it might be I could not but forget everything and accept it. Moreover, His Majesty was confident that the maintenance of the national polity would be guaranteed.

At the suggestion of Major General Suichi Miyazaki, Kawabe linked up with Vice Minister of the Army Lieutenant General Tadaichi Wakamatsu and went to the room where the most senior officers of the Army had gathered. There were Field Marshals Sugiyama and Hata and two of the three members of the Army's "Big Three": Umezu and Inspector General of

Training Doihara. (The other member of the Big Three was Anami.) Kawabe spoke earnestly of the need for the five top-ranking officers to reach accord, and Hata immediately concurred that "this is of the utmost importance."

For several interminable seconds there was silence as those present weighed the fatefulness of their decisions. Then Kawabe spoke: "Under the present circumstances, I do not think that the situation calls for any discussion or consideration. I think the only thing for the entire army to do is to loyally obey the Imperial Decision." The personality of each officer was mirrored by his response. The ever sphinxlike Umezu merely nodded, Doihara murmured, "That's right," but Hata looked straight at Kawabe and clearly pronounced, "I agree with you." Sugiyama presented a silent, impassive countenance, but Kawabe detected within it no disagreement.

Seizing the initiative further, Kawabe proposed they all sign an agreement, and Wakamatsu left to secure writing implements. When Wakamatsu fumbled at the phrasing, Kawabe dictated, "The Army will act in accordance with the Imperial Decision to the last." The name of each officer was written and the date; each signed and placed his seal. Anami entered at just this moment, and he, too, affixed his seal without objection. Umezu then voiced concern that air units were likely to cause trouble, and Wakamatsu took the document next door to the headquarters of the Air General Army, where he secured the seal of its commander, Masakazu Kawabe (the brother of the vice chief of staff).

This written accord by the most senior officers in the Army, in addition to Anami's announcement, created an apparently formidable firebreak against any attempt to ignite a coup d'état in Tokyo. Anami is often credited as the linchpin in the process, but the record shows that Umezu, Kawabe, and Wakamatsu also played critical roles. Just how wavering Anami's real attitude may have been was soon demonstrated.

The concord of the most senior officers of the Army failed to foreclose others from embarking on revolt and testing whether discipline in Tokyo would hold. As early as August 11, a group of field-grade officers had huddled in an air-raid shelter in the bowels of the Army Ministry to plot a coup d'état. Their goal was to part the Emperor from his peace-seeking advisers and install a new government, the objective of which would be literally victory or extinction. A conviction gripped the plotters that the Japanese people could not and must not outlive the destruction of the national polity. They embraced a vision of an entire people etching a sublime place in history with the fire of their heroic, loyal, and total self-immolation.

Non-Japanese—as well as many Japanese—observers must immediately ask: If the Emperor's expressed will was to terminate the war, what

conceivable justification existed for such actions? For the plotters, ultimate loyalty rested not in the current incumbent but to the Imperial institution. Thus, "acting in compliance with the wishes of the imperial
ancestors constitutes a wider and truer loyalty to the Throne."

The plotters meant to replace the current structure of government with
one where every circuit of power and decision was connected to the office
of the Army Minister. To achieve their goal, they knew they must first win
over an ascending series of incumbent senior officers: Lieutenant General
Takeshi Mori of the Imperial Guards Division; General Shizuichi Tanaka,
the commander of the Eastern District Army; and ultimately Umezu and
Anami.

Anami's role in these events seems to have been central but remains unclear. In a hurried interview on the afternoon of August 12 with some officers, Anami lent what seemed a passive ear to a veiled reference to a coup
and sanctioned a proposal to have the Eastern District Army prepare for
disturbances, preparations that might equally well serve to execute a coup.
The next day, at 8:00 P.M., Anami again met with the conspirators. After
sitting impassively through a presentation, Anami pronounced their plans
and their grasp of the situation incomplete, but he did not specifically reject their ideas, and, indeed, he left the tantalizing suggestion behind his
careful words that he might join them.

This encounter thoroughly alarmed Colonel Hayashi, who pointed out
that word of acceptance of the Potsdam Declaration was already leaking
out; this would complete the collapse of public morale. Therefore, it was
useless for the army to propose to fight on "because the people will not follow." According to Hayashi, Anami returned to the Army Ministry and
confronted a key conspirator, Colonel Okikatsu Arao, with this argument.
Precisely what transpired at this rendezvous is unknown, but within a few
hours its significance appeared grave.

On August 14, the plotters panicked, and they struck during that night.
When General Mori parried their request to join a revolt, he was murdered
by Major Kenji Hatanaka, a key leader of the revolt. Hatanaka and his
comrades drafted an order to the Imperial Guards Division and "authenti-
cated" it with Mori's seal—or so the tale was long told. The Emperor's account in *Showa Tenno Dokuhakuroku,* however, contained a bombshell.
The Emperor insisted that the order was also signed by Colonel Arao. Arao
was not just a clever staff colonel at the center of all policies and military
plans, he was a man trusted above all others by Army Minister Anami. His
participation implied strongly that the scheme to seize the Imperial Palace
was "not the fleeting dream of a few young officers but a plan in which

some central figures in the Army were participants," observed Kazutoshi Hando, a Japanese historian who provided commentary on *Showa Tenno Dokuhakuroku*. Who else was involved and to what degree? The record is now and may forever remain incomplete.

Nevertheless, the fact is that a small group of Imperial Army officers assembled a coup d'état within a mere seventy-two hours, with or without the complicity of higher officers. With the forged order, the plotters dispatched the soldiers of the Imperial Guards Division, who proceeded to occupy the Imperial Palace. It is sobering to reflect on what the results might have been had the plotters enjoyed more time to subvert loyalties or assassinate more recalcitrant officers like Mori.

Incredibly, the Emperor's chamberlains reported later that the Emperor slept through all of this, but according to *Showa Tenno Dokuhakuroku* he was very much awake and observed the seizure of the palace through the armored shutters on his quarters. The immediate objective of the coup plotters was to seize a phonograph record of the Emperor announcing the end of the war, set for an unprecedented national radio broadcast that day. But the soldiers failed to pry it from its hiding place. Then the high tide of the hasty revolt ebbed as swiftly as it rose. General Tanaka dashed to the Imperial Palace, determined to quash the revolt or die trying. His courageous and pugnacious actions restored control of the Imperial Guards. With their plot thwarted, Hatanaka and his fellow main conspirator committed suicide in front of the Imperial Palace. By 8:00 A.M., August 15, Tanaka could deliver an assurance to the Emperor that there was no further cause for concern. After one final inspection to satisfy himself that order was present and danger was past, Tanaka departed the palace. On August 24, stricken by what he regarded as his own heavy responsibility for enforcing surrender, General Tanaka also committed suicide.

As Tanaka exited the palace, yet another scene in this drama played out. At the urging of Hatanaka, Masahiko Takeshita went to Anami's residence to ask him one last time to join the revolt. There, he found Anami writing what appeared to be a will, obviously intent on suicide. They talked, and after considerable consumption of sake the Army Minister slashed open both his belly and his throat and toppled forward, toward the Imperial Palace. He left two scrolls. One contained the words, "Believing firmly that our sacred land shall never perish, I—with my death—humbly apologize to the Emperor for the great crime." The other held a thirty-one-syllable poem of cryptic content: "Having received great favors from His Majesty, the Emperor, I have nothing to say to posterity in the hour of my death."

Anami both atoned for his acts and left a riddle: What was the great crime? Did it involve the role of the Imperial Army in plunging Japan into war or only Anami's personal role? If Colonel Arao's endorsement on the order to seize the Imperial Palace is legitimate, there is the distinct possibility that the great crime involved Anami's flirtation with defiance of the Emperor's command.

All over Japan, soldiers and civilians alike gathered to listen to the Emperor's words at noon, August 15. In his Hiroshima hospital, Dr. Hachiya awaited the broadcast, convinced in his heart that it would disclose the enemy invasion and orders to fight to the "bitter end." In a voice never heard before by his subjects and employing an archaic Japanese of official court circles, barely comprehensible to ordinary citizens, the Emperor announced that Japan would accept the Potsdam Declaration. Japan had taken up the sword only to "ensure Japan's self preservation and the stabilization of East Asia, it being far from Our thought either to infringe upon the sovereignty of other nations or to embark upon territorial aggrandizement." In the key passage, the Emperor explained that:

> Despite the best that has been done by everyone—the gallant fighting of military and naval forces, the diligence and assiduity of Our Servants of the State and the devoted service of Our one hundred million people, the war situation has developed not necessarily to Japan's advantage,* while the general trends of the world have all turned against her interest. Moreover, the enemy has begun to employ a new and most cruel bomb, the power of which to do damage is indeed incalculable, taking the toll of many innocent lives.

Japan would now capitulate, continued the Emperor, not only to prevent the "ultimate collapse and obliteration of the Japanese nation" but also "the total extinction of human civilization." Mournfully, he sought to solace those who had fought Japan's battles and borne the cruel weight of the war in death, wounds, and bereavement, but he explained that "We have resolved to pave the way for a grand peace for all the generations to come by enduring the unendurable and suffering what is insufferable." He cautioned all to turn away from any act that could lead to "needless complications, or any fraternal contention and strife" and instead to bend to "work with resolution so as ye may enhance the innate glory of the Imperial State and keep pace with the progress of the world."

---

* The original draft had acknowledged Japan's loss of the war with the phrase "the war situation has deteriorated day by day," but Anami had objected that this was too strong and obstinately insisted on the circumlocution of "the war situation has developed not necessarily to Japan's advantage."

The Emperor's broadcast was followed by an announcement advising the Japanese people that the atomic bomb was the greatest reason for the surrender. In the Hiroshima hospital, now overflowing with hideously afflicted victims of that bomb, Dr. Hachiya stood stunned.

> Like others in the room, I had come to attention at the mention of the Emperor's voice, and for a while we all remained silent and at attention. Darkness clouded my eyes, my teeth chattered, and I felt cold sweat running down my back. . . . By degrees people began to whisper and then to talk in low voices until, out of the blue sky, someone shouted: "How can we lose the war!"
> Following this outburst, expressions of anger were unleashed.
> "Only a coward would back out now!"
> "There is a limit to deceiving us!"
> "I would rather die than be defeated!"
> "What have we been suffering for?"
> "Those who died can't go to heaven in peace now!"
> The hospital suddenly turned into an uproar, and there was nothing one could do. Many who had been strong advocates of peace and others who had lost their taste for war following the *pika* were now shouting for the war to continue. . . .
> The one word—surrender—had produced a greater shock than the bombing of our city.

Continuing War

Even after the Emperor's broadcast, spasms of insubordination and incipient insurrection still flared within the Homeland. Both Army and Navy airmen actively contemplated launching suicide attacks on the Allied fleet as it moved to accept the surrender in Tokyo Bay. General Masao Yoshizumi, chief of the Military Affairs Bureau, ordered the disarming and defueling of Army aircraft to bar fanatics from seizing them. This seems to have foreclosed action by Imperial Army units, but it took extraordinary actions, including intervention by the Imperial family, to foil another potentially disastrous plot.

At Atsugi airfield southwest of Tokyo, where MacArthur was slated to land in his new capacity of supreme Allied commander for the occupation, Navy Captain Ammyo Kosono orchestrated an insurrection for several days. He defied all authority, including Prince Takamatsu, while his airmen showered leaflets on Tokyo calling for true patriots to revolt. Ultimately, however, Kosono literally lost his senses and was carted away in a straitjacket. Soldiers arrived and, after a fight with pistols, furniture, and fists, they removed the propellers from all aircraft. Little wonder that Admiral Yonai later recounted that the most anxious days of his stint as Navy Minister passed between August 14 and 23.

Outside the Homeland itself, Japanese forces were actively engaged in war in Manchuria and China; elsewhere, they garrisoned Imperial conquests. Whether these units would obey the Emperor's command was as much in doubt in Tokyo as it was in Allied capitals. On August 15, two Soviet armies brought the intense battle around Mutanchiang in eastern Manchuria to a climax. Even at the end, there was an episode epitomizing the pervasive ferocity of Japanese resistance. Soviet tanks had penetrated all the way to the headquarters of the Japanese 126th Division. There, recorded David Glantz, "a squad of firemen from the transport unit, each armed with a 15 kilogram explosive, attacked the leading five tanks in a suicide charge, one tank per man, and successfully demolished all five tanks." The awed Soviets called such suicide attackers *smertniks.*

The battle before and around Mutanchiang was the most ferocious but not the only pitched battle of the campaign. The Soviet Second Far Eastern Front drove down the Sungari River from the northeast, toward the center of the country, encountering stiff resistance from well-alerted Japanese defenders at two border towns. The Soviet Trans-Baikal Front advancing from the west faced stout defenders around Hailar and Arshaan, but its huge mechanized units essentially conducted a massive motor march against very slight resistance into the heart of Manchuria. It was August 18 before the Kwantung Army ordered its subordinate units to cease fire, but this by no means stilled all combat. It was August 22 before the Hutou Fortified Region along the eastern Manchurian border finally fell.

Korea, Sakhalin, the Kurils, Hokkaido, and Points South

One of many important revelations to emerge after the collapse of the Soviet Union was that Stalin's ambitions in the Far East in 1945 extended from the outset not only to Manchuria and Korea but also to Japan proper. In the Manchurian-Korean border region, I. M. Chistyakov's Twenty-fifth Army faced Japanese units under the First Area Army and the Third Army. Chistyakov launched part of his forces westward to sever any link between Japanese forces in Korea and Manchuria. He also dispatched rifle units with naval support to stake out Soviet claims along the northeastern face of the Korean peninsula through a series of overland marches and amphibious landings. By the end of August, Red Army units had reached the

Thirty-eighth Parallel, the previously agreed demarcation line of the shared Soviet-American occupation of Korea.

The Soviet strategy for the campaign also featured a two-pronged thrust to Hokkaido. On August 11, the Red Army had launched an attack from due north of Hokkaido via the huge Sakhalin Island. This endeavor made very slow progress against fanatical Japanese resistance. On August 18, the Soviets added an advance toward Hokkaido from the northeast, starting with an amphibious assault on Shimushu, the northernmost of the Kuril Islands, which formed a natural set of stepping-stones. Here, too, Japanese defenders put up determined resistance. Some Imperial Army units began to comply with the capitulation order on August 19 and 20; others fought until August 29. Soviet occupation of the southern Kuril Islands was completed by September 3. It was only on this very late date that the last Japanese units on Sakhalin ceased their resistance.

For the invasion of Hokkaido, the Soviet First Far Eastern Front intended to assault from Sakhalin. The lead division would seize a beachhead initially with only one rifle regiment. The rest of that division would follow, and then two more divisions would land. With these forces, the Soviets aimed both to seize all of Hokkaido and to attack the Kurils from the south. They believed only three Japanese infantry divisions and a brigade—about fifty thousand men under arms—plus the Fifth Area Army Headquarters, defended the entire island. Given the vast size of Hokkaido and its mountainous terrain, the Soviets expected that the Japanese could oppose their landing with only one division. The seizure of Hokkaido would confer important military and political rewards: a springboard for attacks on Honshu and a right to participate in the occupation of Japan.*

A combination of stiff Japanese resistance and diplomatic action by President Truman saved Hokkaido from otherwise certain Soviet invasion. The Potsdam agreement included a demarcation line that placed Hokkaido within the American sphere, but it permitted contingency planning for military operations across the line. On August 15, Truman provided Stalin with a copy of MacArthur's General Order Number One, setting out procedures for the occupation of Japan. The next day, Stalin proposed that So-

---

* The Soviets overestimated Japanese strength, as the Fifth Area Army defenses on Hokkaido comprised only two divisions and one brigade. They were oriented toward the American threat from the east, not the Soviet plan to land on western Hokkaido. Japanese airpower in this region was very weak, as was the Imperial Navy's capability. The Soviet Navy's amphibious shipping resources were limited but sufficient to transport the three assault divisions in several echelons. The Red Army intended to seize the northern half of Hokkaido. If resistance proved strong, reinforcements would be deployed to aid the capture of the rest of Hokkaido. Given the size of Hokkaido, the Japanese would have been hard-pressed to move units for a concerted confrontation of the Soviet invasion. The chances of Soviet success appeared to be very good.

viet forces accept the Japanese surrender on northern Hokkaido, on the grounds that Japanese occupation of Soviet territory in 1919–1921 justified it and Soviet public opinion demanded it. Truman shot back a terse message on August 18, rejecting the proposal as a change in the Potsdam agreement. This same day, Soviet theater commander Marshal Vasilevsky formally sought authorization from Moscow for the seizure of Hokkaido. (The continued resistance of Japanese units provided a rationale for further Soviet operations.) When no immediate reply was forthcoming, Vasilevsky sent a second message on August 20, stating that he planned to land on Hokkaido on August 22. Stalin finally replied but only to sanction preparations. Vasilevsky directed his subordinates to be ready in all respects to attack on his personal order no later than the end of August 23. At midday on August 22, Stalin abruptly ordered the operation suspended indefinitely. In retrospect, it appears that Japanese resistance on Sakhalin would have precluded readiness before August 24 or 25 in any event, but Truman's firm reply on August 18 was crucial. Moreover, events soon showed that Truman's refusal to permit Soviet advances to Hokkaido saved hundreds of thousands of Japanese from death.

The Reckoning

When the Soviet columns neared Harbin in central Manchuria, they brought to a close one of the more egregiously inhumane operations of the twentieth century. The main source of this horror was a Japanese military physician, Shiro Ishii, who thought doctors could provide Japan with devastating and unmatched new biological weaponry. His cheeky persistence created a network of research and development stations in China, Manchuria, Burma, Thailand, and Singapore, the largest of which, the Ishii Unit near Harbin, became internationally infamous under its alternate designation, Unit 731.

Ishii knew that Japan was not alone in research on biological weapons, but he believed it could seize one absolutely critical advantage over potential adversaries. Instead of basing plans solely on theoretical work supported by animal studies, Ishii tested his developments secretly in a program of human experimentation. At Ping Fan, south of Harbin, Ishii erected a huge, seventy-six-building flagship installation. Sheldon H. Harris, the foremost authority on this subject, reports that the Japanese explained this massive facility to local inhabitants as a lumber mill, "and with the exquisite sarcastic 'humor' for which Ishii and his colleagues were famous, they referred among themselves to their human subjects as *murata,* or logs."

The human fodder for these experiments came as early as 1932 from Harbin. Japanese security forces provided Ishii with a minimum of three thousand condemned prisoners, and likely many more. Groups of *muratas* were studied in "controlled" experiments with cholera, tuberculosis, typhoid, botulism, gas gangrene, glanders, influenza, meningococcus, plague, smallpox, tetanus, tularemia, anthrax, syphilis, gangrene, frostbite, pressure chambers, and bullets. Every *murata* was "sacrificed." Most underwent exquisitely detailed autopsies, though some experiments called for vivisection—dissection of live human bodies—to trace the path of infections. Like his German counterparts, Ishii used crematoriums to dispose of the mass of remains created by his industrial-scale death machine.

No one knows the exact toll of Japanese biological-warfare experimentation. Besides the deaths of many thousands in the various experimental stations, of which Ping Fan was only the largest and most elaborate, the Japanese tested various methods of biological warfare on the Chinese population. Diseases unleashed by the Japanese continued to recur after the war. The release of plague-infected mice when Ping Fan was destroyed by Ishii as Soviet columns closed in was probably linked to a deadly outbreak around Harbin in 1947 that alone killed thirty thousand. Harris therefore believes the total number of deaths ran well into the tens of thousands.

While the Soviets did not capture all of Ishii's records, they did seize most of the records of the Kwantung Army, which since have remained inaccessible. The lack of these records effectively precludes precise calculations of Imperial Army losses against the Soviets. After the war, the Japanese claimed only 21,000 dead in the Kwantung Army. This is grossly too low and obviously omits many thousands of Japanese casualties, besides ignoring losses among the Manchurian and Mongolian auxiliaries recruited to Japan's cause, plus an indeterminate number of Japanese reservists and civilians. On the other hand, the Soviets claimed to have killed 84,000 and captured 594,000 Japanese soldiers during the campaign. These numbers apparently include both Manchurian and Mongolian auxiliaries and Japanese reservists and civilians. There is a significant and unexplained difference between the Soviet sum of 678,000 and the Japanese figure for their forces in the theater (not including auxiliaries), 713,000. Initially, the Soviets admitted the loss of 8,000 killed and 24,000 wounded in the campaign, but with release of archival material after 1989, the actual totals proved to be 12,103 killed and 24,550 wounded.

Whatever the number of Japanese dead during the campaign, this figure is immensely overshadowed by the toll from Soviet captivity. According to the best American study of the subject, the Soviets captured 2,726,000 Japanese nationals in northern Asia and Manchuria, about one-third military and two-thirds civilian. Ultimately, the Soviets repatriated 2,379,000; of the balance, 254,000 were confirmed as dead, and 93,000 were presumed dead. By a Japanese estimate, in Manchuria alone during the first winter of captivity, 179,000 civilians and 66,000 military personnel perished. Other sources give the total of dead and missing as high as 376,000.

David Glantz, the leading American student of the Manchurian campaign, has observed: "At every level in every sector, Soviet commanders in Manchuria took great risks, planned bold operations, and executed their plans with abandon." While ample credit is due to Soviet commanders, Glantz added:

> A certain casualness, if not haughtiness, prevailed in the Japanese camp, reflecting to a degree Japanese faith in their predictions and their capabilities to resist such an attack. Mixed with this casualness was perhaps a tendency to denigrate Soviet capabilities. As for the argument that the Japanese lethargy reflected a low quality of their troops and poor esprit de corps, the combat record of units in the ensuing campaign dismisses that charge.

Furthermore, there is a long list of now forgotten places—Hailar, Halung, Arshaan, Aihun, Sunwu, Pokotu, and Sakhalin—where Japanese soldiers fought and died with the same devotion they had shown on countless battlefields between 1937 and 1945.

Ultra and Surrender

As Tokyo gradually gained assurances that the armed forces in the Homeland and Manchuria would comply with the surrender, the dispositions of the Imperial legions across the Pacific and in other regions of Asia still remained at issue. Washington shared this concern. For American officials from Truman on down, Japan's surrender divided into two questions: Would the central government formally capitulate; and if so, would the armed forces obey such an order? For answers Washington and the theater commanders looked to Ultra and Magic, not diplomatic notes.

The information conveyed by code breaking was at first mixed. As noted earlier, on August 10, the Japanese foreign minister admitted that the Imperial Army and Navy had not formally concurred with the Emperor's decision. An August 11 intercepted message from Field Marshal Terauchi, the commander of the Southern Army (which directed units in Burma, present-day Indonesia, the Philippines, and the South Pacific), underscored the uncertainty over obedience to a general surrender. Terauchi declared: "The plans of the Southern Army have changed in no way whatever. Each Army . . . will go ahead to strengthen its war preparations more and more."

That very day, the Chief of the Imperial Army General Staff commanded that: "The Imperial Army and Navy shall by no means return the sword to the scabbard."

The Far East Summary quoted U.S. Navy analysts who cautioned that, while these sorts of messages suggested the possibility of a treacherous attack following the surrender announcement, it was more likely that the operations ordered were for the "purpose of maintaining discipline and morale through the crisis of Japan's surrender."

Support for that interpretation could be read between the lines of an August 14 joint message from the Vice Minister of the Navy and the Vice Chief, Naval General Staff, announcing that the Imperial Navy retained "firm determination to prosecute our holy war to the last man . . . although it is expected that the enemy's war of stratagems will create many complications, we will not be taken in by them and wish everyone to carry out his duties to the very end in a thorough manner."

The tide of belligerent traffic from the Japanese armed forces along with diplomatic silence sent Truman's oscillating hopes for a speedy surrender downward again. On August 10, Truman had expressed confidence to his advisers that the "negotiations" could be wrapped up in three days. But days of silence passed, and on August 13 and again on the fourteenth news of the delivery of two Japanese messages to Bern inflated his hopes, only to have them burst by word that neither was the Japanese response he expected. At noon August 14, Truman met with the Duke of Windsor, who was en route back to the United Kingdom, and British Ambassador John Balfour. According to Balfour, Truman, after confessing glumly that the latest Japanese telegram "did not contain the message awaited by the whole world . . . remarked sadly that he now had no alternative but to order an atomic bomb dropped on Tokyo." It was only at 4:05 P.M. that Truman learned officially of Japan's decision to surrender.

Ultra did not confirm cease-fire orders from the Imperial Army and Imperial Navy to subordinate commands until the early hours of August 16. In accordance with requests from senior military leaders, the Foreign Ministry dispatched a message on August 15 through the Swiss government that was "a statement of our wishes, and they are not presented as conditions of acceptance of the [Potsdam Declaration], but they are vitally important in order to make smooth the coming delicate and difficult task of carrying into effect the actual terms of the Joint Declaration. (Our requests are particularly necessary in terms of our internal political situation.)" These requests were primarily for advance notification of Allied entry into Japan "so that arrangements can be made for their reception."

This message implied that obedience to the surrender order might be in doubt even within the Homeland. This might explain a message to the entire Imperial Navy on August 15 that tried to establish the bona fides of the capitulation and simultaneously provided incontrovertible proof of the role of the Emperor in the surrender. The Navy Minister "respectfully submit[ted] a report on the events which led to the Empire's acceptance of the Potsdam Declaration." He revealed what had transpired after the deadlocks at the Supreme Council for the Direction of the War and in the cabinet proved unbreakable.

The Navy Ministry found it necessary to send out another message on August 16 insisting on obedience to the Emperor's wishes and coupled this with a disturbing addendum:

> Since the outbreak of the conflict, all hands have bent every effort toward attaining the goal of the holy war. In spite of this, however, the fortunes of war were not with us. . . . Words cannot express our humiliation and it can only be borne when we are convinced of its temporary nature.

This same day, the Navy Ministry ordered that the intentional destruction of weapons, supplies, and material must be halted because of its ramifications for future payment of indemnities, but it also provided a "specially ordered" exemption:

> All papers relating to prisoners and interrogation (particularly those such as the ones published in December 1944 which refer to interrogation of American pilot prisoners), and confiscated————, together with this despatch are to be immediately and positively disposed of in a manner that will offer the enemy no pretext.*

Outside Japan, Ultra disclosed disturbing initial responses to the surrender. On August 15, a message to the Chief of the General Staff from the Japanese ambassador in Nanking relayed the incredulous objections of China Expeditionary Army Commander General Okamura:

> Such a disgrace as the surrender of several million troops without fighting is not paralleled in the world's military history, and it is absolutely impossible

---

* This dispatch suggests strongly that orders to annihilate POWs were issued but destroyed before they fell into Allied hands.

to submit to unconditional surrender of a million picked troops, in perfectly healthy shape, to the Chunking forces of defeated China.

While General Okamura did issue an order for "cease fire" at 5:00 A.M., August 17, he was by no means alone in initially protesting any surrender.

During these days of uncertainty, indirect evidence of the surrender taking hold came in a series of messages describing units burning documents and codes. Orders from the Army Ministry indicated that "unit commanders will burn them i.e., Emperor portraits, rescripts, regimental colors and writings in the Emperor's hand on the spot and in the same reverence as if they were returning them." Some air units continued reconnaissance, but by August 18, traffic showed that all units accepted surrender, with "a few minor exceptions."

Intercepts did provide "numerous" pieces of evidence that "certain of Japan's leaders fail to grasp the full significance of their surrender or to comprehend the fact that Japan has become already a conquered nation," as one American summary noted. Among the messages intercepted were invitations to various officials of client governments to take refuge in Japan, as if they would be beyond the reach of Allied authorities or their own peoples. On August 14, the Greater East Asia Ministry exhorted its representatives to "guide" Japanese citizens to prepare them "to face all hardships and witness the renewal of fighting spirit over the long period of the future."

On August 15, a message revealed a cabinet decision for "the direction of all public opinion." The basic theme was "to support the unification of the whole people and to prepare for the difficulties we will face in maintaining our national structure." The directive emphasized that all people shared responsibility for the "disaster" and that "arguments assigning responsibility for the war to the Government, the Army, or other quarters, will be treated suitably." Minister Kase warned from Bern on August 17 that broadcasts declaring that the conclusion of peace "was due to a shortage of material and failure in the war of science, but [that] this was only a temporary condition" had aroused "considerable attention" in Allied radio and newspaper reports.

There now would be an end, mostly, to the fighting, but not to the dying. More than three hundred thousand Japanese were to perish in Soviet captivity, and thousands more from the lingering effects of the blockade and the atomic bombs. Hundreds of thousands of Chinese and other Asians were to continue to expire from disease and starvation produced by Japan's aggression. But hundreds of millions, including several million

Allied servicemen, believed they had been delivered from suffering and death.

The formalities of the surrender transpired on September 2 on the decks of the battleship *Missouri* in Tokyo Bay. There, in a brisk but subdued ceremony, a delegation of Japanese signed the instrument of surrender in front of MacArthur. Admiral Nimitz swiftly set the tone for the peace to follow. In a message to his vast fleets immediately upon the end of the war, Nimitz displayed his magnanimous character:

> It is incumbent on all officers to conduct themselves with dignity and decorum in their treatment of the Japanese and their public utterances in connection with the Japanese. The Japanese are still the same nation which initiated the war by a treacherous attack on the Pacific Fleet and which has subjected our brothers in arms who became prisoners to torture, starvation and murder. However, the use of insulting epithets in connection with the Japanese as a race or as individuals does not now become the officers of the United States Navy. Officers in the Pacific Fleet will take steps to require of all personnel under their command a high standard of conduct in this matter. Neither familiarity nor abuse and vituperation should be permitted.

This message also proved to reflect on the character of President Truman. Of the dozens of messages and hundreds of operational reports he received from theater commanders, he took particular care to see that this message was culled out and preserved separately in his papers.

20

Assessing Realities

*"A score of bloody Iwo Jimas and Okinawas all across China
and the New Netherlands"*

The Pacific war ended in September 1945. Amid shattered cities, the Japanese people faced lean years beyond their imagining. Occupation authorities under MacArthur treated Japan's surrender as indeed unconditional and moved briskly to extinguish Imperial Japan. They recognized no guarantee to preserve the Imperial institution, much less the incumbent, beyond the promise in the Potsdam Declaration that the Japanese people would be free to choose their form of government. For American leaders, the abrupt halt of the war delivered them from a double quandary. On the political level, they had been wrestling the contradictions of the public's insistence on complete victory with its fading stamina. Meanwhile, on the military level, the Japanese capitulation snuffed out an incipient confrontation over strategy ignited by Ultra revelations.

The seemingly self-evident proposition that swiftly gained ascendancy in the United States was that the atomic bombs not only caused the Japanese surrender but also obviated the horrifying costs of an invasion. Opinion polls showed overwhelming support (about 85 percent) for use of the bombs. The minuscule number of Americans who thought the bombs should not have been employed were outnumbered six to one in an October 1945 poll in which 23 percent of the respondents would have favored dropping *more* than two bombs. Millions of American servicemen believed that they personally had their lives spared by the bombs. This attitude, later labeled the "patriotic orthodoxy" by one of its critics, secured an invulnerable hold on the generation that fought the war.

Dissenting voices at first were few and faint, but over several decades a body of scholarship grew to assail this orthodoxy. The varied arguments of these critics had distilled into recurrent themes: Japan was thoroughly defeated by August 1945 and her rulers understood this; Japanese leaders were actively moving toward surrender; American policy makers knew that a guarantee of the Imperial system was essential in obtaining Japan's capitulation and that such a pledge would have ended the war without an invasion or atomic bombs.

Other critics have complemented or supplanted these dominant themes with assertions that conventional blockade or bombardment alone would have ultimately induced Japan's surrender as well. Still others have argued that at least a demonstration of atomic weapons should have been attempted before they were used on cities. The most provocative charge has been of some ulterior purpose in the use of atomic weapons: intimidating the Soviets, justifying the enormous expenditure of funds, satisfying (perverse) intellectual curiosity, or perpetuating the Manhattan Project as a bureaucratic empire.

This barrage of challenges seeped into the public discourse, aided by growing public cynicism since the 1960s. By November 1994, one poll disclosed that the majority of Americans favoring the use of the atomic bomb had slipped to 55 percent, while those opposed swelled from 4 percent to 39 percent. Within these broad numbers, there were sharp divisions, with 72 percent of men in favor and 53 percent of women against. There was another schism by age groups with the 18–44-year-olds split almost evenly (48 percent "pro" and 46 percent "anti"), while those 45 and above remained strongly supportive (64 percent "pro" and 31 percent "anti").

These debates over the end of the war in the Pacific intermingle arguments about the course of actual events with suppositions. This chapter begins to address these issues by disentangling the essential factual realities from the speculative alternatives.*

---

* The standard postwar canon condemning the use of atomic bombs now asserts routinely that General Dwight D. Eisenhower told Secretary of War Stimson at a July 1945 meeting that the use of an atomic bomb ("that awful thing") was not necessary and that Japan ("already defeated") would surrender. There is only one source for this episode, Eisenhower's own postwar recollections—the first in 1948 and a second variant in 1963 that somehow gained much additional detail (for example, Stimson is described as "furious"). The strongest refutation of this recollection is Stimson's own contemporaneous account. Stimson maintained a detailed diary that is an unfailing record of all his discussions on the atomic bomb, yet both entries reflecting meetings with Eisenhower in July 1945 contain no hint of such an exchange, nor do the official or semiofficial records of the period or the diaries of Leahy, Arnold, or any other relevant party.

Beyond Eisenhower's flawed memory, there is the fundamental question of his knowledge of military and political developments in the Pacific. In a letter of July 12, 1945, to an old friend, Eisenhower confessed he had not the "slightest idea of what is going to happen in the Pacific." Eisenhower does

The Military Components:
Blockade and Bombardment

Perhaps the most basic misconception of the military realities in 1945 is that American policy makers viewed their choice as a stark one between the use of atomic bombs or an invasion. The Joint Chiefs of Staff set the official twofold American strategy in May 1945. First, the ongoing campaign of blockade and bombardment would continue at an accelerating tempo through October. Second, there would be a two-phase invasion of Japan, commencing in Kyushu in November 1945 followed by a "knockout blow" at the Kanto plain in March 1946. Once her cities were ravaged and her capital was captured, Japan would then capitulate and foreclose the necessity of further campaigns to defeat the several million Japanese soldiers and sailors spread across much of Asia and the Pacific.

Only the blockade/bombardment strategy carried the unanimous endorsement of senior American officers, and only this part of the overall U.S. strategy reached partial completion. Between blockade and bombardment, the former was the more potent force. Japan's war economy collapsed for lack of vital raw materials, especially oil. The end of the war found the Japanese system of maritime transport at or near extinction.

After the war, critics focused intense moral scrutiny on aerial attacks, including atomic bombs. They frequently cited a postwar declaration by Admiral Leahy:

> The use of this barbarous weapon at Hiroshima and Nagasaki was of no material assistance in our war against Japan. . . . In being the first to use it, we had adopted an ethical standard common to the barbarians of the Dark Ages. I was not taught to make war in that fashion, and wars cannot be won by destroying women and children.*

Leahy asserted—as did many critics—that nuclear weapons were both immoral and unneeded because the blockade could have secured Japan's ca-

---

not seem to have received Pacific-theater Ultra or Magic during this period. It thus requires a remarkable amount of credulity to believe that Eisenhower would exhibit such a cavalier attitude.

This matter is, however, highly instructive on the issue of historical methodology. Eisenhower's recollection is offered by critics as proof of an authoritative contemporary American appreciation of the military and political situation in the Pacific. Eisenhower, however, effectively spent the entire war in the European theater, including the summer of 1945. Why then should he be deemed to possess any expertise on the state of the war in the Pacific? Moreover, how can critics accept Eisenhower's unsupported account while simultaneously insisting that postwar statements from Truman or Stimson must be discounted for lack of contemporary documentation?

* This statement is often quoted in a context that asserts or implies that Leahy made such views known during the war, but there is no record he did so. There is a theoretical point that the Japanese govern-

pitulation. But if one accepts his moral criteria, how can the firebombing and atomic bombs be condemned yet the blockade pass muster? The type of total blockade imposed upon Japan had, until as recently as World War One, itself been deemed a "barbarous" form of warfare because its effects did not discriminate between combatants and noncombatants. Beyond logical rigor, there is also a utilitarian consideration that undermines this moral argument. Aerial bombardment inflicted civilian deaths in Japan measured in hundreds of thousands, but the direct and indirect effects of the blockade in China killed noncombatants by the millions, and the blockade against Japan aimed for the same ghastly results.

The bombardment program included attacks by Navy and Army Air Forces tactical aircraft, as well as naval shelling of coastal sites, but the centerpiece was the strategic air campaign. (The important operational statistics of that campaign are contained in Appendix B.)

The strategic air campaign inflicted enormous damage upon Japan, but the precise measure of death remains elusive. Air attacks destroyed about 20 percent of Japan's housing in five months and rendered 15 million homeless. The most widely cited figures from the United States Strategic Bombing Survey are 333,000 dead and 472,000 wounded, including 120,000 from the atomic bombs. According to computations in 1949 for the Japanese government, the total number of deaths on the "home front," the vast majority from air attacks, was 323,495. This included 92,133 who perished at Hiroshima and 25,677 at Nagasaki, constituting 36 percent of the total dead.

By one Japanese count, there were at least 126,762 deaths in the six largest cities hit by incendiary raids from March to mid-June 1945. The series of fire raids on smaller "urban areas" between June 17 and August 14 inflicted 47,408 fatalities. Both the American and the Japanese figures for casualties from air attack may be somewhat low due to the confusion stemming from administrative disruptions in Japan in 1945 and as a result of latent atomic-bomb fatalities. An adjustment upward to a total of about 410,000 deaths from all air raids would probably account for both these

---

ment could have chosen between permitting either its soldiers or its civilians to starve to death in a blockade, whereas the atomic bomb left no autonomy to the Japanese. From the viewpoint of the Japanese population as a whole, however, this distinction is meaningless. There is no prospect that the Imperial Japanese government would have favored noncombatants in a blockade. Indeed, Ketsu-Go implicitly anticipated the sacrifice of huge numbers of Japanese civilians. Furthermore, this argument neglects the fact that Japan's choice to continue the war in the face of blockade also condemned to death masses of noncombatants in other Asian countries, as well as Allied prisoners of war and civilian internees. Thus, championing the blockade is to perversely grant higher sanctity to the lives of noncombatants in the aggressor nation than to those in victim nations.

considerations. Whatever the total, all but about 100,000 died in only three raids: the fire raid on Tokyo of March 9–10 and the two atomic attacks.

The efficacy of the systematic bombing campaign by B-29s deservedly remains a matter of controversy. The explicit wartime justification for it was the peculiar nature of the Japanese industrial economy, in that the typical plant was surrounded by buildings that served not only as residences but also as a network of individual workbenches, complete in some cases with machine tools. The existence of this system was a fact. Dr. Karl T. Compton sent these observations about Tokyo to President Truman in October 1945:

> Standing in the ashes of a substantial portion of the burned homes are various types of machine tools like lathes, drill presses, etc. Here family groups were manufacturing repetitive parts like nuts, bolts, or coils which were delivered to the manufacturing centers for use in the assembly of military weapons. In the area we examined, approximately one fifth of the homes showed evidence of such activities.

It was asserted after the war that the Japanese had displaced the home-feeder system, thus vastly undermining the utility of fire bombing for idling war industries. No specific contemporary intelligence confirming this development supports this claim, and it is unlikely that it could have been detected by photographic or radio intelligence. Indeed, a major factor affecting the air campaign was the dismal lack of specific knowledge concerning the industrial fabric of Japan.

Critics have also argued that most of the bombing campaign was redundant, since the blockade alone would have eventually halted Japanese production. As historian Michael S. Sherry aptly phrased it: "Much of LeMay's bombing simply made the rubble of Japan's war economy bounce." This is certainly true in a cumulative sense. It is also fair to conclude that evidence of this was available in 1945. But the B-29 bombing campaign was executed as part of a larger American strategy that built toward an invasion. Viewed in this context, the question was not whether bombing would be ultimately redundant but whether in the short run it would decrease the number of weapons and supplies available to kill invading Americans.

Much has been written about LeMay's switch from precision to incendiary area attacks, particularly on the question of the degree to which it was his decision. The first obvious point is that if LeMay, the preeminent operational technician of his era, could not orchestrate precision bombing of the Japanese aviation industry, no one else could. Precision bombing of a target as small as an individual factory simply exceeded the capabilities of the B-29 force in the first half of 1945. Only very large, but relatively distinct targets such as ports or railroad marshaling yards otherwise remained feasible. While such attacks might have reduced the number of Japanese urban areas targeted, they would not have shielded civilians wholly. As in Europe, weather and the limited discrimination of available radar equipment would have resulted in substantial civilian casualties.

LeMay's actions comported with expectations in Washington. Targeting directives up to March 1945 and the development of the M-69 firebomb both pointed unmistakably toward urban attacks. The fact that bomb dumps in the Marianas already housed huge inventories of incendiaries also betrays the anticipated course of the campaign. But probably the single most important factor influencing LeMay was his knowledge that General Arnold wanted tangible and quick results from the XXI Bomber Command. LeMay was undoubtedly correct in thinking that if he had not switched to urban-area fire attacks when he did, he would have been replaced by someone who would. Thus, no one in Washington had to issue a direct order to LeMay; he needed only to conclude that precision bombing was unworkable and that another strategy was urgently required. The responsibility that can be credited or charged to LeMay is not that he switched to area incendiary bombing but that he made the fire raids far more destructive.

Moral challenges to the bombing of Japan arise from the undeniable fact that incendiary bombing inflicted horrific losses on civilians and their property. That the Army Air Forces did not employ incendiary bombing widely in Europe has prompted the charge that race figured in the use of such tactics against Japan. Race might have eased the switch in tactics, but it did not cause it. Strategic bombing in the Pacific, including the atomic bombs, marked the culmination of strategic thinking, not an abrupt departure. Once it became acceptable to bomb a wide expanse of land surrounding a target in Europe, it was no great leap to inflict vast destruction on many square miles of urban area in Japan containing a latticework of factories and supporting cottage industries. Moreover, if German cities had possessed such marked vulnerability to fire, or if the intelligence on the German industrial system had been as abysmal as was the knowledge of Japan's war-production facilities, it is extremely doubtful that the Army Air Forces would have eschewed use of incendiaries in Europe.

Final responsibility for conduct of the armed forces, including bombing policy, rests with civilian authority in America. Postwar scholarship so far has unearthed no indication that President Roosevelt intervened at any point to halt the gradual casting off of inhibitions on bombing in Europe.

Of the civilian leaders, only Stimson challenged the incendiary campaign, and he accepted Arnold's explanations that the Japanese industrial organization justified the tactic.

It would be wrong to view Roosevelt and other civilians as simply neglectful. Roosevelt had maintained initially that the German and Japanese peoples were not inherently evil, but he privately believed that the German people had been "Prussianized." After Yalta, he told the Germans that they must "realize that only with complete surrender can they begin to reestablish themselves as people whom the world might accept as decent neighbors." In addressing occupation policy, he affirmed that

> it is of the utmost importance that every person in Germany should realize that this time Germany is a defeated nation. . . . The fact that they are a defeated nation, collectively and individually, must be so impressed upon them that they will hesitate to start any new war.

Viewed in this light, massive urban bombing complemented the aim of unconditional surrender. It was not just a handful of men in rogue governments who flaunted vile ideologies; whole populations imbibed these beliefs and acted as willing acolytes. Unconditional surrender and vast physical destruction would sear the price of aggression into the minds of the German and Japanese peoples. No soil would be left from which myths might sprout later that Germany and Japan had not really been defeated. These policies would assure there would be no third world war with Germany, nor would Japan get a second opportunity.

The Military Components: Invasion Strategy

The intense postwar American debate about how the war ended has distorted the role of the prospective invasion by viewing it in parochial terms. Under the dual track adopted by U.S. decision makers, invasion formed only half the American strategy to end the war. But either defeating or inflicting severe casualties on the enemy during the invasion of the Homeland not only provided the core rationale of the military strategy embraced by Japan's rulers but also was the foundation of their political strategy toward a negotiated peace. So long as the leaders of the Imperial Army, including Army Minister Anami, remained convinced that Ketsu-Go offered the prospect of success, they had no incentive to acquiesce in any serious diplomatic efforts to end the war sooner. From their perspective, any Allied attempt to offer terms before Ketsu-Go had extracted its blood price would betray cracking American resolve. Moreover, while some critics have argued that the Japanese leaders viewed the Potsdam Declaration as fatally deficient because of its failure to explicitly guarantee the Imperial institution, evidence from Japan reveals that even "moderates" such as Prime Minister Suzuki and Navy Minister Yonai instead saw the declaration as a harbinger of weakening Allied morale.

No discussion of invasion strategy can evade the ongoing obsessive and misplaced American controversy over casualty projections. Both Secretary of War Stimson and President Truman wrote after the war that the use of atomic bombs saved huge numbers of American lives by obviating the need for an invasion. In 1947, Stimson stated that he "was informed that such operations might be expected to cost over a million casualties, to American forces alone." In 1953, Truman reported to Air Force historians that at Potsdam General Marshall gave him an estimate of 250,000 to 1,000,000 American invasion casualties. In his memoirs in 1955 and again to a biographer in 1959, Truman maintained that the decision to use the bomb saved "a half million" American "boys." These statements provided a utilitarian justification for the bombs.

When archival evidence became available decades later, critics attacked these numbers on the basis that they lacked authoritative contemporary support. Specific questions also arose about how Truman's statement to Air Force historians in 1953 evolved.*

The utilitarian moral calculus regarding atomic weapons involves far more than just the issue of invasion casualty estimates because the relevant human costs are not confined to American military personnel. But even this narrow issue is far more complex than either critics or defenders of Stimson and Truman have allowed because of the inherent uncertainty of any projection and because the estimates passed through at least three distinct phases: the period prior to June 14, 1945, when Truman ordered a meeting on the invasion strategy; the subsequent June 18 meeting; and the radically changed situation disclosed by Ultra after June 18.

The Joint Chiefs of Staff never agreed on what level of American effort would be required to secure unconditional surrender or its equivalent. Nei-

---

* In his original handwritten draft, Truman recalled a meeting at Potsdam with many advisers at which Marshall mentioned a "minimum" quarter-million casualty figure. Circumstantial evidence appears to rule out any such large gathering; in fact, several individuals mentioned by Truman could not have been present. Moreover, an aide pointed out that while a quarter-million casualties "sound[ed] more reasonable" to him, he reminded Truman that Stimson had publicly used the million figure. The version dispatched to the historians attributed the higher range to Marshall. This interplay could show that Truman had changed his recollection to fit Stimson's statement and thus avoided raising questions about the rationale Stimson provided for the decision to use the atomic bombs. But it could also simply show that Truman's memory was fuzzy for specifics though correct for the larger proposition.

ther they, nor any other American, knew if a Japanese government would surrender, or if the Japanese armed forces would comply with a capitulation order. Indeed, the Joint Chiefs justified combining an invasion strategy to the campaign of blockade and bombardment on the basis that invasion not only was most likely to secure a capitulation, but also because it would position the United States to enforce the ultimate defeat of Japan if there was no organized surrender of Japan's armed forces. Experience on Saipan and Okinawa added the dreadful specter that the Japanese civilian population would be no less staunch in defending the Homeland. Given the record Japan had created, every American could foresee an unimaginably bloody finish fight requiring not only an invasion, but a further interminable struggle against Japanese armed forces elsewhere in Asia and the Pacific and unbending warriors across the Homeland amid a fanatically hostile civilian population.

Not only did the Joint Chiefs of Staff lack a consensus about how the war would end; they also lacked a reliable method of predicting casualties. The closest they came to an enumeration of prospective American casualties was with the adoption of the April 25, 1945, paper of the Joint Staff Planners. That paper featured formulas for projecting casualty ranges based on analogies to broad Pacific and European experience. Admiral King immediately perceived that those ratios could not support an invasion strategy; and even applied just to the two-phase invasion strategy, the ratios yielded immense casualty figures. That these numbers were taken seriously is confirmed by the fact that the Selective Service and the War Department were implementing induction call-ups for the Army and replacement training programs that could handle huge numbers of casualties, and the War Department was developing radical new replacement policies for infantry units. These actions support one central conclusion: The Army was making comprehensive preparations to confront both the severe practical and morale problems of dealing with potentially immense losses. It was against this backdrop that the assumption the atomic bomb

---

What sounded "reasonable" to an aide who knew nothing of the Ultra evidence Truman could not cite and what Truman concluded on reflection could be very different. Critics further pointed out that before 1953 Truman made a series of varying estimates. What critics do not dwell upon, however, is that if the number wounded had exceeded the number dead by the usual factor of four, a quarter-million lives saved—as Truman mentioned at the Gridiron Dinner in December 1945—translates into a million casualties averted. In sum, critics have implied or charged that the large numbers cited by Stimson and Truman were fabricated after the event. While this alone raised questions about the rationale for the use of the atomic bombs, some insist that since Truman could not have feared huge casualties in an invasion, there must have been some ulterior reason to use the atomic bomb, such as intimidating the Soviets with "atomic diplomacy."

would be used passed through the Interim Committee and gained President Truman's sanction.

When Truman ordered a meeting to review the invasion strategy, he explicitly identified casualties as the decisive criterion. The handful of methods of casualty projection placed before Truman that day were designed to convince him to approve Olympic. It is arguable that the low-end number endorsed by Marshall for ground casualties (31,000 during the first 30 days) was a reasonable projection, but not the only reasonable projection, given the current intelligence assumptions. But the silence on air and naval casualties—not challenged by King—as well as the systematic suppression of estimates from the theater commanders, cannot be justified. Marshall warned Truman that it might not be possible to obtain a formal capitulation of Japan, that an invasion aimed at Tokyo might be necessary, and that he looked to Allied nations to assist in the defeat of Japanese forces outside the Homeland even following a surrender. No casualty estimates for alternatives beyond Olympic were set forth at the meeting, and only projections for Coronet were prepared before the meeting.

For many critics of the figures offered by Stimson and Truman, the story of prospective invasion casualties ends there. The reality was different. Only two days later, Admiral King expressed his unease to General Marshall that Truman had not been informed of Nimitz's projection of 49,000 casualties in the first thirty days alone. This same day, the results appeared of a study Stimson had authorized that confirmed the wisdom of maintaining induction and replacement-training capacity at levels adequate to deal with massive casualties.

Meanwhile, one of Stimson's aides, Edward L. Bowles, commissioned a scientist, W. B. Shockley, to estimate the blood price of conquering Japan. Shockley reported that defeating Japan would cost the Japanese five to ten million deaths and the United States between 1.7 and 4 million casualties, including 400,000 to 800,000 fatalities. Shockley's report appeared in July, just as Ultra began destroying the assumptions underlying all the prior projections. Ultra demonstrated that the Japanese defenses of Kyushu exceeded the original estimates by more than three times in combat divisions and two to four times in aircraft. As MacArthur's intelligence officer Charles Willoughby phrased it, these numbers showed that the Americans would be going in at odds of one to one, which assured very high casualties. Faced with these revelations, however, senior officers did not request new casualty projections. Instead, the end of the war found the top American military leaders grappling with the questions of whether Olympic was still feasible at an acceptable cost. It was against this backdrop that the actual orders to use atomic weapons were issued.

In the immediate postwar period, two significant efforts were made to address what the costs of invading Japan would have been. In mid-September 1945, General Arnold, disturbed by what he deemed Japanese propaganda about the atomic bomb and its alternatives, requested an official statement on potential invasion losses. This prompted correspondence between Lieutenant General John E. Hull (who signed the brief read by Marshall at the June 18 meeting) and Lieutenant General Ira Eaker, deputy commander of the Army Air Forces. Hull pointed out that MacArthur's staff had estimated losses for the first month at 55,000 and MacArthur himself had said that this was too high. Hull cautioned that a claim that the atomic bombs had saved 200,000 lives was "open to argument." Therefore, Hull proposed a very elastic estimate of "tens of thousands of American lives, possibly 200,000 lives" saved. Hull implied that he favored smaller numbers, but these words leave room for casualty numbers of up to "possibly" one million. Given Hull's role in preparing the low estimates placed before Truman on June 18, it is not surprising that he continued to resist admitting that the Army's invasion strategy could carry a very high price in blood. What is not understandable, however, is why Hull failed to acknowledge the implications of the Ultra evidence about Japanese strength on Kyushu and continued to use the projections prepared in June 1945 by MacArthur's staff as his basis.*

Yet another postwar opinion on likely casualties in an invasion of Japan came from Willoughby. In an article in a military publication in June 1946, he wrote that "two to two and a half Japanese divisions [could] extract . . . approximately 40,000 American casualties on land." Using this yardstick, Willoughby calculated that taking Kyushu would have cost 200,000 American casualties, while the price of clearing the Kanto plain would have reached 400,000. This opinion never secured the endorsement of a senior policy maker.†

---

* In April 1946, another Army Operations Division study was completed by Colonel R. F. Ennis, based on the premise that the United States either possessed no atomic bombs or chose not to use them. Half of the six-page memorandum concentrated on the effects of a huge typhoon in October 1945. The other half was a hasty, error-filled discussion of Japanese preparations and plans and a badly mangled description of Japanese internal politics. Ennis projected that Kyushu could have been occupied in two months at a cost of 75,000 to 100,000 U.S. casualties. This report, which apparently never circulated beyond the Operations Division, cannot be deemed a serious effort to project casualties.

† Medical authorities under MacArthur, projecting from Luzon figures, calculated Olympic casualties at 394,859 over 120 days, of which 125,935 would be battle casualties. This estimate is sometimes wrongly cited as though all were battle casualties. These numbers do not reflect any adjustment for Ultra revelations, and there is no evidence that either Truman or Stimson was aware of them. Thus, they are of limited value in the casualty controversy. See Mary Ellen Condon-Rall and Albert E. Cowdrey, *Medical Services in the War Against Japan* (Washington, D.C.: Government Printing Office, 1998), pp. 414–17.

Where does this complex tangle lead? The postwar debate approaches the casualty issue as a matter of certainty: Either there was or there was not a firm contemporary estimate to support the later assertions of the President and the Secretary of War. The reality was that no one knew how much fighting still remained to obtain the defeat of Japan and military leaders disavowed their ability to project losses accurately. Marshall flatly termed the exercise "speculative." But though contemporary studies stress that casualty projections must be regarded as equivocal, they acknowledge potential ranges that reach the large numbers cited by Truman and Stimson. The April 1945 planning paper approved by the Joint Chiefs of Staff was indisputably authoritative, and its range of projections would have yielded the one million figure that has assumed talismanic significance. It is also likely that at Potsdam on July 25 General Marshall did give Truman a figure or a basis to believe that casualties would substantially exceed earlier projections. We simply have no information on what intelligence Truman was shown at Potsdam and what conclusions he might have derived at that time. It is hard to believe, however, that Truman was not advised of the Japanese buildup, which carried obvious implications. But there is no current evidence that Truman or Stimson saw Shockley's paper, and there is no other known basis for Truman's figure of a half-million deaths.

We do have firm evidence that the specter of huge casualties was a real concern before the war ended. On the morning of August 10, Stimson stressed to Truman that the Emperor would prove indispensable in securing the compliance of Japan's armed forces. Absent the Emperor's assistance, America would face "a score of bloody Iwo Jimas and Okinawas all across China and the New Netherlands [Indonesia]." This comment is significant on three counts. First, it was couched in terms of the costs of defeating soldiers and sailors who would not comply with a surrender order from Tokyo. Thus, Stimson again raised the worst fears of American strategists by implying not simply the high price of an invasion but the huge cost of defeating in detail all of Japan's men under arms. Second, it shows that the Secretary of War, a man not given to hyperbole or exaggeration in debate, was even at this point thinking in terms of immense American casualty totals. And Stimson's projection (twenty Okinawas is a number just under one million) did not include casualties incurred within the Home Islands. Third, it shows that such prospects were mentioned in Truman's presence in the summer of 1945 by an official in his government. While Stimson made the comment after the atomic bombs were used, his orders for review of the Army's plans for replacements demonstrates his concern about vast casualties had existed before Hiroshima.

Moreover, his remarks occurred in private, long before the great casualty controversy commenced, and cannot be challenged as after-the-fact justification.

All the emphasis on precise casualty figures, however, obscures the decisive question: What casualties did American policy makers believe the American public would abide in order to achieve an enduring peace? The shrewder critics of Truman and Stimson have pointed out that overall American losses for the war were about one million (including 290,907 battle deaths). It is extremely difficult to believe that Truman and his advisers, already concerned about public morale, would have embarked on any strategy likely to double that number. But what they perceived the upper limit of public tolerance to be must remain in the realm of conjecture. It is perhaps significant that General Marshall, who was keenly attuned to public morale, balked at pressing numbers over 100,000 for Olympic alone to Truman. In any event, the Japanese buildup on Kyushu was sufficient to threaten to make the cost of invasion unacceptable. Thus, the Japanese were correct to believe that—in a nonnuclear arena—they could secure bargaining leverage to force a negotiated peace. But once American leaders learned of the odds facing Olympic, there is no prospect that any other consideration could have stayed the use of atomic weapons.

The Political Components

The fundamental political reality is that it was Japanese, not American, leaders who controlled when and how the Pacific war would end. Those insisting that Japan's surrender could have been procured without recourse to atomic bombs cannot point to any credible supporting evidence from the eight men who effectively controlled Japan's destiny: the six members of the Supreme Council for the Direction of the War, Lord Keeper of the Privy Seal Kido, and the Emperor. Not only has no relevant document been recovered from the wartime period, but none of them, even as they faced potential death sentences in war-crimes trials, testified that Japan would have surrendered earlier upon an offer of modified terms, coupled to Soviet intervention or some other combination of events, excluding the use of atomic bombs. Nor does *Showa Tenno Dokuhakuroku* contain any indication that a different Allied policy might have brought about an earlier surrender.

Certainly, Japan's leaders recognized that the war ultimately must end, but as Edward Drea has pointed out, "When Hirohito and the peace faction or any other Japanese who mattered talked about ending the war, they meant by negotiated settlement, not a capitulation and certainly not an unconditional surrender." There is abundant documentation to support this assessment. The formal policy of the Suzuki government adopted in June 1945 was the Ketsu-Go fight to the finish, which contained no explicit role for negotiations. The sole diplomatic initiative carrying any legitimacy was the démarche to the Soviet Union, which, Foreign Minister Togo conceded, unmistakably signaled an intent to mediate an end to the war. This maneuver, however, demanded services of the Soviets as mediators and a negotiated termination with the Allies. Both steps required concessions. The Supreme Council for the Direction of the War never reached consensus on the incentives to dangle before the Soviets; before Hiroshima, they never even engaged in substantive discussion of what conditions they would accept.

Only on August 9, after withstanding months of blockade and bombardment, obvious preparations for invasion, two atomic bombs, and Soviet intervention, did the Big Six formulate terms for ending the war. Even then, Army Minister Anami and Chiefs of Staff Umezu and Toyoda insisted on maintaining the old order—a position completely unacceptable to the Allies.

Nor does the record leave any doubt, reasonable or otherwise, that an American offer to retain the Imperial institution would have obtained an earlier Japanese surrender. In the Magic Far East Diplomatic Summary for July 22, Togo expressly rejected the advice of Ambassador Sato to accept such an offer. If Togo, the most vigorous advocate within the inner eight of ending the war promptly, dismissed such a proposal, there is no rational prospect that it would have won support from any of the other members of the Supreme Council.

Although there was no realistic chance that diplomacy could have halted the war prior to the use of atomic weapons, there still remain several contentious issues concerning exactly why Japan surrendered. The end of hostilities required both a decision by a legitimate authority that Japan must yield to Allied terms and compliance by Japanese armed forces with that decision. The Suzuki cabinet, the legal government of Japan, never agreed on its own to surrender on terms acceptable to the Allies. We cannot know whether this cabinet ever would have reached consensus on such terms. More fundamentally, we cannot know whether the Suzuki government would have even survived had Imperial Headquarters executed its plan to declare martial law.

The legitimate authority that determined Japan must capitulate was the

Emperor. The contemporary evidence and the Emperor's own voice in *Showa Tenno Dokuhakuroku* demolish the postwar myth that the Emperor was eager for surrender throughout 1945 and thus could have been mobilized to end the war by American diplomacy. The Emperor was in fact a vigorous advocate of Ketsu-Go until the final defeat loomed on Okinawa. His instinctive choice even then of an alternate strategy was to launch a new offensive in China. Only after this proposal was rejected by the Imperial Army did he look to diplomacy as a way to extricate Japan from its predicament. And still his aim was Soviet mediation to avoid anything like unconditional surrender. There is no evidence he ever contemplated terms less favorable for Japan than the ones Kido drafted in early June, which resembled the Treaty of Versailles. Neither Kido's contemporary diary nor the Emperor's own recollections support the belief that the Emperor instructed Prince Konoe to stop the war immediately upon any terms. Tellingly, Suzuki's disastrous *mokusatsu* rejection of the Potsdam Declaration passed without criticism from the Emperor. Nor did his alter ego Kido object initially to the proposal of the Suzuki cabinet on August 9 to submit an offer of surrender congenial to Army Minister Anami and the other military leaders that would have been wholly unacceptable to the Allies. Since Kido was the man most intimately aware of the Emperor's mind-set, this episode is further compelling evidence of the Emperor's actual thinking.

Why did the Emperor finally intervene? He consistently gave three reasons. When he first announced his decision in the early morning hours of August 10, he said that he had "given serious thought to the situation prevailing at home and abroad." The allusion to Japan's internal situation is significant. There is a great deal of direct and indirect evidence demonstrating that fear (perhaps exaggerated) of a domestic upheaval provided Konoe, Yonai, and ultimately Kido and the Emperor with a powerful impetus to end the war. This collapse of domestic morale arose from the general trajectory of the war but became much more marked in the summer of 1945 due to blockade and the bombing. The Emperor also explicitly cited two military considerations: inadequate preparation to resist the invasion and the vast destructiveness of the atomic bomb and the air attacks. He did not refer to Soviet intervention.

The Emperor did cite both Soviet intervention and the enemy's "scientific power" when he met early on August 14 with Japan's most senior military officers and reaffirmed his determination to end the war. This appears to be the only contemporary instance where the Emperor saw Soviet intervention as significant, and even then he coupled it with the atomic bomb.

In the Imperial Rescript ending the war, the Emperor spoke explicitly on one point: the enemy's employment of a "new and most cruel bomb, the power of which to do damage is indeed incalculable, taking the toll of many innocent lives."

Just a week after the surrender ceremony the Emperor wrote to his eldest son, the crown prince, his reflections on the causes of Japan's defeat. In what historian John Dower calls "this most private of communications, at this extraordinary moment," Hirohito explained that Japan had lost because "our people" regarded the British and Americans too lightly and exalted fighting spirit while ignoring science. Had the war continued, he would not have been able to safeguard the "three holy regalia," and most of his subjects would have perished. He conspicuously made no mention of Soviet intervention.

Six months later, when he prepared *Showa Tenno Dokuhakuroku,* he repeated the same explanation. After describing how graphic reports of the unpreparedness of the armed forces to repel invasion had convinced him that continuing the war was impossible, he cited the two explicit reasons that prompted him to end the war: He feared the Japanese race would perish if the war continued; and he believed that the national polity was threatened, that if the Americans landed at Ise Bay, the three sacred treasures of the Imperial line would be lost. According to the national myth, these regalia dated back to, and thus symbolized, the divine origins of the Imperial line from the sun goddess Amaterasu. As Dower points out, the regalia thus not only served as "symbols of legitimacy and majesty," but also were integral to the Emperor's sense of being the "inheritor of a sacred kingship."

Thus, the contemporaneous evidence clearly places concern for public order, fear of the results of bombardment, and the loss of confidence in the ability of Japan's armed forces to resist an invasion.

But the Emperor's decision alone did not end the war. Halting hostilities required disciplined compliance by the armed forces. The entries in the diary of Vice Chief of the Imperial Army General Staff Kawabe, which confirm open discussion at Imperial Headquarters that Japan's overseas legions would not obey the surrender order, the attempted coup d'état, and Ultra messages demonstrate that neither Tokyo nor Washington could lightly assume such compliance.

We know much less about why almost all Japanese officers ultimately obeyed the surrender order. Some key leaders emphasized the effect of Soviet intervention. In 1948, Kawabe told American interrogators that "it was with a nervous heart filled with fear that [senior Army officers] expected Russia to enter the war." Reports reaching Tokyo described Russian forces as "invading in swarms," said Kawabe, and officers imagined gigantic Soviet forces from Europe deployed against them.*

In another much-cited postwar statement addressing Soviet intervention, Admiral Toyoda told American interviewers in 1949 that "the atom bombing was a cause for the surrender but it was not the only cause." He recalled that "the Russian participation in the war against Japan rather than the atom bombs did more to hasten the surrender."

Like much other evidence that should be approached with circumspection, the recollections of Kawabe and Toyoda were only set down years after the events. Far more credible is the extended and compelling explanation provided by Premier Suzuki in December 1945:

> The Supreme War Council, up to the time [that] the atomic bomb was dropped, did not believe that Japan could be beaten by air attack alone. They also believed that the United States would land and not attempt to bomb Japan out of the war. On the other hand there were many prominent people who did believe that the United States could win the war by just bombing alone. However the Supreme War Council, not believing that, had proceeded with the one plan of fighting a decisive battle at the landing point and was making every possible preparation to meet such a landing. They proceed[ed] with that plan until the Atomic Bomb was dropped, after which they believed the United States . . . need not land when it had such a weapon; so at that point they decided that it would be best to sue for peace.

Suzuki's assessment goes to the heart of the matter: Soviet intervention did not invalidate the Ketsu-Go military and political strategy; the Imperial Army had already written off Manchuria.

In a postwar commentary, Kido reinforced Suzuki's analysis with the insight that the atomic bombs served not only as an important cause but as an indispensable excuse for the surrender: "If military leaders could convince themselves that they were defeated by the power of science but not by lack of spiritual power or strategic errors, they could save face to some extent."

---

* Kawabe's statement became evidence for the thesis that Soviet forces were the central reason for the surrender. But the Emperor made the decision to surrender only about twenty-five hours after the Soviet attacks commenced. At that moment, the Kwantung Army had yet to even detect the "swarms" of Soviet soldiers on the march from the west. Tokyo, of course, knew no more. Thus, the Emperor's decision could not have been based on the spectacle of "swarms" of attackers or a rout of the Kwantung Army. Moreover, at the very meeting where the Emperor first announced his determination to surrender, no less an authority than General Umezu affirmed that Soviet intervention did not invalidate Ketsu-Go.

Likewise, Cabinet Secretary Sakomizu noted, "In ending the war, the idea was to put the responsibility for defeat on the atomic bomb alone, and not on the military. This was a clever pretext."

In summary, the Soviet intervention was a significant but not decisive reason for Japan's surrender. It was, at best, a reinforcing but not fundamental reason for the intervention by the Emperor. It shared with the atomic bombs a role in securing the compliance of the Imperial Army and Navy, but the atomic bomb played the more critical role because it undermined the fundamental premise that the United States would have to invade Japan to secure a decision.*

---

* It is often argued in the United States—and it is an article of faith among the Japanese—that the atomic bombing of Nagasaki was gratuitous because it made no contribution to ending the war. The premise of this argument is that once Japan learned the United States had a usable atomic weapon, surrender was inevitable. Yet key Japanese decision makers offered no such assertion. The second and more fundamental defect of this belief lies in the reality that Japan's militarists had a second line of argument: Even if the Americans had a bomb, they would either have few of them or they would be deterred by moral outrage from using additional ones. Thus, waiting for Japanese leaders in Tokyo to confirm that Hiroshima had been destroyed by an atomic bomb could not have guaranteed capitulation with compliance because this fact alone could not have convinced the militarists. It took Nagasaki to demolish this second line of argument. In this regard, Toyoda's postwar account that on the morning of August 9 the Big Six had a "bullish" attitude toward continuing the war—until word of Nagasaki arrived—is significant evidence.

21

Alternatives and Conclusions

"Immediately after the defeat, some estimated that 10 million people were likely to starve to death"

Disputes concerning the military and political realities of the summer of 1945 are only part of the great historical controversy over the conclusion of the Pacific war. The horrors of Hiroshima and Nagasaki center the debate as much upon what might have happened as upon what did. The understandable desire to explore alternatives all too often merges with a presumption that any termination of the conflict that avoided the use of nuclear weapons would have been preferable. But an exploration of paths history did not take casts sobering illumination over both this presumption and the actual outcome.*

The prospects of halting the Pacific war without use of atomic weapons demand at the very least consideration and evaluation of the major events in progress on August 15, 1945:

1. The strategic air attack on Japan's railroad system as the crescendo of the overall blockade-and-bombardment strategy;
2. The Soviet intervention;
3. The ongoing review of the American invasion strategy; and
4. The impact of the continuing war on Chinese and other Asian peoples.

---

* The effects of these events on the development of the cold war is beyond the scope of this work. See instead David Holloway, *Stalin and the Bomb* (New Haven: Yale University Press, 1994), which profits from access to important new Soviet material. Holloway is skeptical "that changes in American policy would have elicited significant shifts in Soviet policy" (p. 370).

Of this quartet, without the atomic bombs, the new strategic-bombing directive of August 11 would have had the most significant effect. At first glance, the new directive, which substituted selective attacks on transportation targets for the area-incendiary campaign appears far more humane. Civilian casualties would diminish markedly both because only thirty-five cities were among the 221 total targets and because the recent policy of dropping leaflet warnings prior to attacks prompted many civilians to decamp immediately for the countryside.

In the long term, however, the new directive would have caused far more loss of life by starvation than the atomic bombs exacted. Simply stated, Japan in 1945 was facing mass famine brought on by the destruction of her transportation system. While three out of four Japanese resided on Honshu—and half of them in the southwestern part of the island—Japan harvested the great bulk of its food on Hokkaido, parts of Kyushu, and in northern Honshu. Tokyo, to take the most extreme case, required delivery of 97 percent of its rice supply.

During the course of the war, Japan's rice production fell from 10,027,474 metric tons in 1942 to 8,783,827 tons in 1944. This decline became a disaster in 1945 as wet and cold weather during the growing season coupled with typhoons and floods in September and October depressed the rice crop by 20 percent and caused serious losses of other crops as well. In November 1945, the government estimated that there would be only 6,355,000 metric tons of rice available for the coming year. Compounding the hardships brought by plummeting rice production was a steep decline in the seafood catch, which normally supplied about 10 percent of human caloric intake as well as the bulk of animal food.

Imports of food had long filled the gap between Japan's needs and domestic production; they now became still more critical. Starting in April 1945, importation of nonfood items from the continent virtually ceased. In Korea, Japanese colonial authorities confiscated one million tons of rice, 20 to 25 percent of indigenous production, thereby placing the Korean populace in grave danger. By August, the amount of food reaching Japan reached "insignificant levels," noted one American scholar.

The Japanese government coped with the supply shortage through conservation and rationing. During 1945, however, the whole ration-distribution system plunged into a precipitous spiral as shortages created a thriving black market that increased scarcity by siphoning resources from official channels. By August 1945, the distribution system had completely broken down.

Individual Japanese watched their food rations dwindle to alarming levels. In 1941, the average citizen consumed about 2,000 calories daily, just

6.4 percent above subsistence levels. (Americans in 1941 each had a diet of about 3,400 calories.) By 1944, the Japanese daily average fell to 1,900 calories; by 1945 it sank to only 1,680. The incidences of tuberculosis, beriberi, and digestive, skin, and vitamin-related diseases soared. By the end of the war, about 20 to 25 percent of the urban population suffered from serious nutritional deficiencies. Even in Kyoto, which was not targeted by LeMay's bombers, weight loss per capita was ten pounds.

The disasters affecting the 1945 rice crop compelled government officials to progressively revise downward the per-capita food ration. By November 9, 1945, the government reported that, under ideal conditions, food supplies would suffice for an average daily diet of only 1,325 calories. This proved optimistic. By February 1946, normally the end of the food collection cycle from the fall harvest, government requisitions stood at only 60 percent of quotas. To overcome this desperate situation, the government started a deficit-transfer program to better distribute the available supplies of food. Aided by an appeal from the Emperor, this program managed to postpone the food-supply crisis until May and June of 1946. The government also augmented the 1946 food supply with 150,000 metric tons of "food substitutes": stems and leaves of sweet potatoes, mulberry leaves, acorns, residue of starch manufacture, seaweeds, leaves of garden radishes, mugworts, residue from apple and grape presses, pumpkin seeds, water oats, arrowroot, silkworms, and locusts were dried, ground, and mixed with wheat flour. Even though some of these things were known to be indigestible, the mixture was used as "stomach filler" for "the underprivileged urban population." Conceived as a stopgap for 1945, this program became a fixture during the first years of occupation.

In the spring of 1946, these measures, too, faltered, pushing the occupation to a crisis. Daily shipments to Tokyo fell to one third of need. Rather than reduce the official ration, on May 14 the Japanese government simply stopped delivering the daily allotment. The official daily ration now stood at only 1,042 calories per person in Tokyo, but the amount actually issued averaged approximately 800 calories. On May 19, a crowd of 150,000 demonstrated at the Imperial Palace for emergency rations.

"Immediately after the defeat, some estimated that 10 million people were likely to starve to death," noted Daikichi Irokawa, a Japanese historian. He believed that "if the people who died of sickness and general physical deterioration are classified among those who died of starvation, the [actual] death toll comes to several hundred thousand."

MacArthur (now effective ruler of Japan) released 8,705 tons of imported cereals in the Tokyo-Yokohama area and 7,768 tons on Hokkaido. He had warned of desperate peril since January, had 80,000 tons of food shipped in from Pacific stockpiles, and built a reserve of 100,000 tons of foodstuffs and 5,000 tons of salt. In Washington, skeptics questioned the seriousness of the situation and dispatched an investigative commission headed by Herbert Hoover. The former president validated the crisis and recommended shipment of 600,000 tons more. But even in the face of Hoover's report, other voices asked why the United States should help its recent hated enemy. MacArthur, in one of his finest hours, silenced them by observing that the Allies had just tried and executed Imperial Army commanders for their responsibilities in "ill treatment, including starvation" of American prisoners of war; with the situation reversed, America had to do better. During the next year, the United States shipped about 800,000 tons of food to Japan.

An economist wrote of the postwar years, "It is quite clear . . . that Japan's food situation was saved from chaos only by . . . imports of American grains." A contemporary American report was more blunt: "It was evident from the onset of the occupation that imports of foodstuffs were needed not only to stave off disease and unrest but also to prevent actual starvation."

The redistribution of the fall 1945 harvest staved off the food-supply crisis to mid-1946. If bombing had disrupted this process, mass starvation would have been unleashed far earlier. As the new air-targeting directive promised to shatter Japan's rail system—the only means of gathering and distributing the harvest—this outcome appears likely.

When Japan entered the war, she was singular among industrialized nations in that the great bulk of her internal transportation customarily moved over wave rather than along rail. But the war crippled Japan's merchant marine and with it established internal transportation patterns. By mid-August 1945, American aircraft, submarines, and ships were destroying merchant vessels at a rate that theoretically would have annihilated Japan's merchant marine within weeks, but in fact any semblance of a systematic water-transportation system was near an end.

Once deprived of shipping, Japan could turn only to the railways for bulk commodity movement. The nationalized rail network comprised 12,000 miles of line and 5,800 miles of sidings and yard track in 1945. Except within the four major industrial concentrations—Tokyo, Nagoya, Osaka-Kobe-Kyoto, and Moji-Shimonoseki—the lines were all short-haul routes appended to coastal shipping facilities. Trains had normally brought agricultural products harvested in the interior to the nearest seaports for domestic shipping to redistribute them to population centers.

The United States Strategic Bombing Survey described the Japanese railway system as "one of the most vulnerable of any size to be found anywhere." On account of a backbone of mountains stretching longitudinally across the Home Islands, the main rail lines stuck to the coasts. The lines that crossed the mountainous backbone of Honshu were few and limited in capacity. Only the section from Tokyo southwest through the Inland Sea ports to Shimonoseki was developed for heavy traffic. Once the railways were cut, there would be no adequate substitute for the bulk movement of commodities. The primitive Japanese highway system—97 percent unpaved—could not sustain serious movement of goods. Thus, the importance of the rail system to Japan in 1945 was fundamental, as acknowledged in a postwar American report: "In view of the disrupted condition of coast-wise shipping and the shortage of trucks, the railways are the backbone of the entire transportation system."

The August 11 targeting directive listing fifty-four railroad yards and facilities and thirteen bridges probably represented what a later era called overkill. The Strategic Bombing Survey estimated that blocking the links from Honshu to Kyushu at the Kanmon tunnel and from Honshu to Hokkaido at the rail ferries, coupled with a mere half-dozen well-selected line cuts would have "disposed effectively of the Japanese rail system as an economic asset." The Japanese had made virtually no provision for recuperation of the rail system; neither plans nor materials—even elementary items such as bridge timbers—were ready to deal with any major gap.

Buried in one segment of the multipart United States Strategic Bombing Survey is the conclusion that had the strategic air forces aimed their efforts at forcing the Japanese to surrender, rather than facilitating invasion, "there is very good reason to believe that an effective railroad attack might have brought about a very rapid capitulation." The question naturally arises of why an attack on Japan's rail system was not mounted earlier. The answer appears to be that the Strategic Bombing Survey investigators enjoyed a far clearer picture of Japan's food situation and her dependence on her rail system than American planners obtained during the war. A series of messages in the Magic Diplomatic Summaries from March to June contained many nuggets indicating a food-supply shortage and concerted efforts to increase imports from Asia. But, as the Magic Far East Summary of June 18 acknowledged, the available evidence was susceptible to two different interpretations. While messages suggested an overall shortage of food, they could also have indicated merely a "maldistribution rather than a general lack of food or . . . that the Japanese are holding stocks against future eventualities" (that is, an invasion).

Without critical hard data from Ultra and Magic on Japan's food production and reserves, wartime analysis was far off the mark. A master assessment of Japan's situation by the Military Intelligence Service on June

30 concluded that Japan would not experience any "serious overall food shortage" in 1945. This was because the War Department figured that Japan would harvest nine million tons of rice and winter grain to add to a rice reserve of two million tons. Both these estimates are now known to have grossly exceeded reality.

American intelligence did, however, possess a much sharper understanding of the role of Japan's railroads. A special report in the Far East Summary of August 8 noted that "Japan's war economy now depends heavily on large rail movement of bulk commodities to and within Honshu." All of the food shipped to southwestern Honshu moved by one of ten rail lines, and these shipments provided half the total supply in that key area. The report further noted the great vulnerability of the Japanese rail system to air attack and even ship bombardment.

The timing of the assault on Japan's railways came at precisely the moment when it could do by far the most damage. Postwar information has made it clear that Japan reached November 1, 1945, with only enough rice in government hands for four days of consumption (133,000 tons). Japan depended on the distribution of the fall crop to food-deficient areas to see her on to 1946 without a disaster. Had the war continued for even only a few more weeks, the destruction of Japan's rail network would have quickly caused a food-supply crisis in late 1945. And once this catastrophe began, it would have required massive repair and replacement of rail infrastructure to remedy, far beyond the capacity of Japan's resources, even after hostilities ceased.

Such a catastrophe would likely have ruptured the key fault line between Japan's military and civilian decision makers. Imperial Army and Navy leaders as a group perceived foreign occupation as the sole lethal threat to the Imperial institution. What set the civilians, including Kido and the Emperor, apart from all but a few of the uniformed decision makers was the conviction that the Imperial institution could also perish by internal upheaval. This fear was a major factor in the Emperor's decision to end the war after Hiroshima, Soviet intervention, and Nagasaki, but before destruction of the rail-transportation system. It is reasonable to assume that even without atomic bombs, the destruction of the rail-transportation system, coupled to the cumulative effects of the blockade-and-bombardment strategy, would have posed a severe threat to internal order and subsequently thus impelled the Emperor to seek to end the war.

When precisely this would have occurred and whether it would have led to an organized capitulation are the next key questions; both are difficult to answer. Timing presumably would have revolved around what reserves, if any, Japan's urban population could draw on once the rail system collapsed. Surely by the beginning of November 1945 the actual crisis would have commenced. The anticipation of the crisis, however, might have unsettled the civilian population some weeks sooner. Whether the Emperor would have acted to forestall the crisis or moved only after it began is conjectural. Equally speculative is whether his efforts would have weathered opposition and whether military discipline would have held in check potential rebellions against the surrender order. But if the timing and circumstances of a Japanese surrender as a result of rail bombing remains unclear, it is certain that vastly more noncombatants would have perished.

A central premise of the critical literature on the end of the Pacific war has been that the Emperor's intervention under different circumstances would have led inevitably to the type of swift and organized surrender that followed the use of the atomic bombs. This assumption emerged as early as the summary report of the United States Strategic Bombing Survey, which pronounced emphatically:

> Based on a detailed investigation of all the facts and supported by the testimony of the surviving Japanese leaders involved, it is the Survey's opinion that certainly prior to 31 December 1945, and in all probability prior to 1 November 1945, Japan would have surrendered even if the atomic bombs had not been dropped, even if Russia had not entered the war, and even if no invasion had been planned or contemplated.

In addition, a number of air and naval leaders in the United States, joined by General MacArthur, also offered testimonials after the war that conventional attacks could have ended the war without atomic bombs.

The date set down so authoritatively by the Strategic Bombing Survey has not fared well under scrutiny. The actual evidence provided by surviving Japanese political leaders did not support such a date, nor did the survey examine "all the facts." Although survey investigators were in an excellent position to pursue the significance of the new bombing directive of August 11, they did not do so. Furthermore, the contemporary record is conspicuously lacking in such confident predictions to Truman.*

Moreover, these affirmations of the effectiveness of sea- and airpower appeared in the midst of conflicts over service roles and budgets, particularly those connected to the creation of a single Department of Defense with a separate Air Force. While naval leaders such as Leahy may have ex-

---

* On the other hand, we do know that Truman was told the opposite. The minutes of the June 18, 1945, White House meeting reflect that Marshall informed him that bombing could not end the war. None of the other military or civilian officials dissented. "Minutes of Meeting Held at White House on Monday, 18 June 1945 at 1530," Xerox 1567, George C. Marshall Library.

perienced moral revulsion over atomic weapons, their arguments arose while counteracting the thrust for ascendancy of air leaders. The airmen, not surprisingly, wished to burnish the image of the decisive nature of air warfare and thus had an institutional interest in proclaiming the effectiveness of conventional, as well as atomic, attack. Accordingly, these statements packed a lot of baggage behind their superficial representations of sound military judgment. Furthermore, neither the Strategic Bombing Survey nor these military leaders addressed the contingency of the Japanese political situation and, more significant, neither compared the human costs of these alternatives with the toll exacted by atomic weapons.

Soviet intervention would very likely have shaped the prospects for success of any intervention by the Emperor to end the war, but in which direction is not certain. Without the impetus provided by atomic weapons, the Soviet attack might have come one or two weeks later in August, but delay would have eased, not diminished, the Soviet triumph on the continent. Under an optimistic scenario, a later Soviet attack grants more time for the Japanese to assess the implications of the rail bombings, thus increasing the impact of the Soviet intervention and enhancing the chances of surrender. Further, the spectacle of Soviet troops landing on Hokkaido, with the possibility that they could reach Honshu, would significantly increase the incentive for capitulation.

But Soviet intervention might also have triggered a reaction from the Imperial Army that could have foreclosed peace. The bolt from Manchuria galvanized Japan's soldiers to commence plans to declare martial law, terminate civilian government, and rule from Imperial Headquarters. Had the Imperial Army seized a position of such absolute ascendancy, it is by no means obvious that the war would have terminated in an organized Japanese surrender.

Any examination of Soviet intervention must also come to grips with its horrific cost in deaths of noncombatants. The Soviets captured about 2.7 million Japanese nationals. The dead and permanently missing among this group, only one third of whom were members of the armed forces, numbered at least 347,000, and perhaps as many as 376,000. This exceeds all but the most exaggerated tolls attributed to the atomic bombs. Moreover, Soviet seizure of Hokkaido would have jeopardized another three million Japanese noncombatants. If Japanese civilians on Hokkaido perished at the same rate as their compatriots in Manchuria, then nearly another 400,000 would have died. Further, Soviet advances into northern Honshu were conceivable, adding still more potential victims.

Soviet intervention might well have transformed the convulsive debate in American councils on the invasion strategy. The war ended with Admiral Nimitz poised to announce to Army and civilian officials that he no longer supported an invasion of Japan. Such a message from Nimitz would have sundered the strategic consensus between the Army and Navy, which civilians, including Truman, were hard pressed to challenge.

At this juncture, the key interaction would likely have been between Marshall and Truman. There is strong evidence that Marshall remained committed to an invasion as late as August 15. In his August 7 message to MacArthur, Marshall suggested the substitution of other locations for Kyushu, not cancellation. On August 13, General Hull, on Marshall's behalf, explored the use of atomic weapons to support a landing. But tempering Marshall's personal commitment to invasion would have been his comprehension that civilian sanction in general, and Truman's in particular, was unlikely for a costly invasion that no longer enjoyed consensus support from the armed services.

Two forces presumably would have tugged at the American debate. Once the rail system collapsed, it would have been impossible for the Japanese to conceal the consequences. The halt of military production, the urgent need to distribute and ration food, and the multitude of problems generated by masses of refugees would have emerged in Magic and Ultra. All of this would bolster arguments by the Navy that there was no need for invasion.

On the other hand, a Soviet landing on Hokkaido might have revived interest by uniformed and civilian American policy makers in a U.S. invasion of extreme northern Honshu or southern Hokkaido. On August 9, the Joint War Plans Committee of the Joint Chiefs of Staff sketched just such a landing on northern Honshu as an alternative to Olympic, albeit not in reaction to Soviet intervention since Soviet designs on Hokkaido were unknown. The advantages of this plan were that Japanese defenders were far less numerous (two field divisions and other forces numbering only one hundred thousand men) than those braced on Kyushu, and the location was only 350 miles from Tokyo, versus the 600 miles separating southern Kyushu and the Japanese capital. The disadvantages were that the location was beyond the range of any land-based aircraft except the B-29s, and that the plan offered no chance to destroy major Japanese forces.

The projected date of this attack also fell within the typhoon season. Both Japanese and American planners viewed a typhoon as a deadly threat to an invasion fleet, and avoiding such danger clearly influenced the original target date for Olympic. These fears were realized in Typhoon Louise, which struck Okinawa on October 9 in full fury. Beneath a black sky, winds gusted to 120 knots and pounding waves thirty-five feet high slammed ship and shore. Twelve vessels sank, and 222 grounded, of which only about eighty returned to duty. Virtually all the tents on Okinawa were shredded, but miraculously only eighty-three men were lost and about one hundred were seriously injured. By a postwar estimate, this event alone would have set back Olympic by thirty to forty-five days. Had an invasion of northern Honshu been on order for October 15, Louise would have intersected the course of the invasion convoys at sea. Would they have escaped? What damage would have been sustained? No one can say.

American planners also considered at least two other invasion targets. Shikoku possessed useful airfield sites and lacked the strong defenses Ultra had betrayed on Kyushu. But while Shikoku lay within range of land-based air cover from Okinawa, it lacked the political value of northern Honshu. The obvious alternative was Operation Coronet, a strike directly at Tokyo. MacArthur's assent to this plan might have been obtained if the alternative was no invasion at all.

On August 15, MacArthur's headquarters issued a staff study on Coronet that mapped out dual thrusts: one from western Tokyo Bay by the Eighth Army, with nine infantry and two armored divisions; and a second by the First Army from the east across Kujikuri Beach, with nine infantry (including three Marine) divisions. Five divisions would form an immediate reserve, while three others in the Philippines would constitute a strategic reserve. Total troop commitment reached 1,171,646 men.

Even this revised Coronet was plagued by two profound problems: It was beyond reach of land-based air support, save the B-29s and P-51s from Iwo Jima, and it faced Japanese defenses of intimidating density. If potential casualties precluded Kyushu, then there was nothing to recommend Coronet, save for the prospect of a less severe kamikaze onslaught (most kamikazes were positioned to defend Kyushu and lacked fuel to redeploy to the Tokyo region and then conduct an attack). MacArthur's study allowed for initial Japanese defenses of six infantry and one and one-third armored divisions, plus support forces, including 160,000 naval-base troops and large numbers of civilian volunteer units. This estimate was already grossly outstripped by the contemporary Joint Intelligence Committee estimate that identified Japanese forces as eight infantry, one armored, and three depot divisions, as well as other forces, aggregating 560,000 men. Another disquieting issue was troop morale and readiness due to the severe problems generated by partial demobilization and redeployment. This alone, quite apart from casualty projections, might well have ruled out Coronet. In the midst of this debate, there might have been yet another sobering reminder of the steep cost of amphibious assaults. The British had slated an attack on the approaches to Singapore, Operation Zipper, for September 9. This likely would have encountered ferocious

Japanese opposition and thus struck a strong cautionary chord against attacks into formidable defenses. If any invasion at all remained in prospect, the northern Honshu venture, with political considerations dominant, stands as the most probable. It is also conceivable that this change in military strategy could have been accompanied by diplomatic efforts to soften the terms offered by the Potsdam Declaration in order to induce a Japanese surrender and avoid a joint occupation of Honshu with the Soviets.

Looming over all the debate of these military and political considerations is the reality of what Japan's war of aggression was doing to the Chinese and other Asian peoples. There is no way to assess with assurance the monthly price exacted from them in death and suffering. It might have exceeded one hundred thousand per month in China alone. Arguments that alternative means could have ended the war without atomic weapons in "only" three months need to be held against this reality.

The explicit or implicit premise underlying much of the great controversy over the end of the Pacific war is that the actual termination was the worst possible outcome and that some other course could have brought peace earlier, or at least without the use of atomic weapons. But the real question about this historical moment is why the Japanese government surrendered as early as it did and why Japan's armed forces capitulated in an organized fashion at all. In the summer of 1945, the dominant Japanese military leaders held the conviction that Ketsu-Go promised to salvage at least the survival of the old order. They thus had no incentive to accept a mere dilution of unconditional surrender. American leaders started the summer unsure whether even an invasion of the Home Islands could induce an organized surrender. They then discovered to their horror that Japan had raised new armies and prepared six to ten thousand aircraft for a final Armageddon exactly where American soldiers and Marines were slated to land. Skilled intelligence analysts, seconded by the recognized authority in the American government on Japan, Joseph Grew, pronounced the new Japanese diplomatic initiative with the Soviets, backed by the Emperor, as simply a ploy to play upon American war weariness. Moreover, they could point to explicit language from Japan's foreign minister rejecting out of hand the concept that the Empire would surrender unconditionally save for the retention of the Imperial system.

Given the abrupt change in the military calculus and the sterile prospects for diplomacy, the chance that atomic weapons would not have been employed is nil. Without atomic weapons, the Emperor's intervention would have been delayed. His action was essential to obtain an organized surrender, and it caught Japan on the edge of the precipice of a series of events that would have plunged its people into catastrophe. The decisions made by Truman and his subordinates to add nuclear weapons to the campaign of blockade and bombardment cost the lives of between 100,000 and 200,000 Japanese at Hiroshima and Nagasaki, on top of the many tens of thousands of others who died in the incendiary raids or due to the ultimate effects of the blockade. Those Japanese noncombatants, however, held no stronger right not to be slaughtered than did the vast numbers of Chinese and other Asian noncombatants, the Japanese noncombatants in Soviet captivity in Asia, or the Japanese noncombatants (not to mention Allied prisoners of war and civilian internees) who would have perished of starvation and disease in the final agony of the blockade. Thus, alternatives to the atomic bombs carried no guarantee that they would end the war or reduce the amount of human death and suffering.

Finally, the deaths actually incurred in ending the war were not gratuitous. American goals were not simply victory but peace. Had American leaders in 1945 been assured that Japan and the United States would pass two generations in tranquillity and still look forward with no prospect of future conflict, they would have believed their hard choices had been vindicated—and so should we.

Appendix A

Standard *Kaisenbun* Allowances

Weapons	Rounds per Weapon	Notional Divisional Strength	Total per Kaisenbun	Rounds per Day
Rifles	300	9,000	2,700,000	3.75
LMG	8,000	350	2,800,000	100
AT Gun	1,200	14	16,800	15
Bn Gun	1,500	18	27,000	18.75
Reg Gun	1,300	12	15,600	16.25
Artillery	2,000	24	48,000	25

Abbreviations

LMG: light machine gun
AT Gun: antitank gun
Bn Gun: battalion gun (70 mm)
Reg Gun: regimental gun (75 mm)
Artillery: field and mountain guns (75 mm)
Rounds per day is based on eighty "firing days."

Source: USSBS no. 64, pp. 65, 89 (Exhibit T), 91 (Exhibit V), 97. The totals for the *Kaisenbun* in USSBS are from a translation of a Japanese staff-officer logistics manual, dated October 10, 1943, captured on Saipan. A *Kaisenbun* weighed 2,500 to 3,000 metric tons.

Appendix B
Strategic Air Bombardment
of Japan

	XX Bomber Command (from China)	XXI Bomber Command (from the Marianas)
Total Sorties	4,669	28,258
Bomb Tonnage		
Total	11,244	156,501
Incediaries	3,296	103,068
High Explosives	8,395	54,917
Mines	528	9,751

Source: USAF HC File 760.308-1.

The material price to the United States in the strategic bombing of Japan was remarkably modest. Superfortress losses for all operations totaled 414. USAF HC File 760-308-1, pp. 13–15. Air crew casualties numbered 2,897, of which 2,148 were deaths. Another 334 aviators were listed as captured or interned, of whom 262 survived. USAF HC File 760-308-1, pp. 12–13; *Army Battle Casualties and Nonbattle Deaths in World War II, Final Report, 7 December 1941–31 December 1946,* pp. 90–91, 93. (The later source also had a category designated the "Air Offensive against Japan," presumably including tactical missions flown against Japan, which resulted in 4,578 casualties, including 3,602 deaths. A total of 437 airmen were known to have been captured or interned, of whom 99 died.) Behind the gross numbers, statisticians calculated that a total of 2,048 crews joined XX and XXI Bomber Commands. Of these 317, or 15 percent, became casualties. The early crews, however, faced a rate of loss of 34 percent, but by the end of the war the rate had dropped to a quarter of that figure.

To place these losses in perspective, Britain's Bomber Command lost 8,953 aircraft with 55,500 aircrew killed between 1939 and 1945. Crew losses in the two American strategic air forces in Europe, the Eighth and the Fifteenth, were never computed officially but must easily have exceeded 25,000 killed. American heavy bomber losses from all causes in Europe numbered 10,152. Middlebrook and Everitt, *The Bomber Command War Diaries,* pp. 707–708; Davis, *Carl A. Spaatz,* Appendix 11 (for heavy bomber losses). Total Army Air Forces fatalities in the European theater have never been explicitly totaled by the Air Force, and were approximately 36,320. *Army Battle Casualties and Nonbattle Deaths in World War II, Final Report, 7 December 1941–31 December 1946,* pp. 92–95.

Notes

Abbreviations for Record Sources

CMH   Center for Military History, Washington, D.C.
HSTL   Harry S. Truman Library, Independence, Missouri
MCHC   United States Marine Corps Historical Center, Washington, D.C.
NARA   National Archives and Records Administration, Washington, D.C.
NHC   Naval Historical Center, Washington, D.C.
USAF HC   United States Air Force Historical Research Agency, Maxwell, Alabama
USSBS   United States Strategic Bombing Survey

1. Tokyo Burns: Raid of March 9–10

P. 3   Weather on the night of March 9–10, 1945: Boeicho Boei Kenshujo Senshi Shitsu (War History Office, Defense Agency) *Senshi Shosho* (War History Series) No. 82, *Daihon'ei Rikugun-Bu (10)* (Army Division, the Imperial General Headquarters, vol. 10) (Tokyo, 1975), pp. 40–42 [hereafter *Daihon'ei Rikugun-Bu (10)*]; Thomas R. Havens, *Valley of Darkness: The Japanese People in World War Two* (Lanham, Md.: University Press of America, 1986), p. 178 (Havens erroneously says it was Armed Forces Day); Masuo Kato, *The Lost War: A Japanese Reporter's Inside Story* (New York: Alfred A. Knopf, 1946), pp. 200, 208–9; Robert Guillain, *I Saw Tokyo Burning: An Eyewitness Narrative from Pearl Harbor to Hiroshima* (Garden City, N.Y.: Doubleday, 1981), p. 178.

P. 3   Reports on approach of B-29s: Hoito Edoin, *The Night Tokyo Burned* (New York: St.

Martin's Press, 1987), pp. 58–59, 96; Gordon Daniels, "The Great Tokyo Air Raid, 9–10 March 1945," in W. G. Beasley, ed., *Modern Japan: Aspects of History, Literature and Society* (London, 1975), pp. 121, 124; Guillain, *I Saw Tokyo Burning,* p. 181; Kato, *The Lost War,* p. 200.

P. 4   Reaction of civilians and appearance of B-29s: Haruko Taya Cook and Theodore Cook, *Japan at War: An Oral History* (New York: New Press, 1992) p. 344; Lars Tillitse, "When Bombs Rained on Us in Tokyo," *Saturday Evening Post,* January 12, 1946, p. 82; Guillain, *I Saw Tokyo Burning,* p. 176.

P. 4   Tillitse's observations: Tillitse, "When Bombs Rained on Us in Tokyo," p. 82.

P. 4   Air-raid protection facilities: Daniels, "Great Tokyo Air Raid," p. 123; Harold N. Martin, "Black Snow and Leaping Tigers," *Harper's,* February 1946, p. 152; Havens, *Valley of Dark-*

ness, p. 157; Tillitse, "When Bombs Rained on Us in Tokyo," p. 34.

P. 5   Air-raid preparations: Michael S. Sherry, *The Rise of American Air Power: The Creation of Armageddon* (New Haven: Yale University Press, 1987), chap. 1; Daniels, "Great Tokyo Air Raid," pp. 120–22; United States Strategic Bombing Survey [USSBS], no. 4, Civil Defense Division *Field Report Covering Air Raid Protection and Allied Subjects Tokyo,* pp. 5–6.

P. 5   "Furs and jewels" and reaction to Doolittle raid: Tillitse, "When Bombs Rained on Us in Tokyo," p. 34; Daniels, "Great Tokyo Air Raid," pp. 120–21.

P. 5   Decisions on air-raid precautions: Tillitse, "When Bombs Rained on Us in Tokyo," p. 34; Edoin, *The Night Tokyo Burned,* p. 118.

P. 6   Decisions on partial evacuation: Havens, *Valley of Darkness,* pp. 162–63.

P. 6   Evacuation and firebreaks: Edoin, *The Night Tokyo Burned,* p. 25; Daniels, "Great Tokyo Air Raid," p. 123; Havens, *Valley of Darkness,* pp. 162–63, 165; USSBS, *Air Raid Protection and Allied Subjects Tokyo,* p. 155; Target Information Sheet, Tokyo Urban Industrial Area, Obj. Area 90-17, Target Section, A-2, Twenty-first Bomber Command, 9 March 1945, United States Air Force History Center [USAF HC], reel A7805, pp. 406–10 [hereafter Target Information Sheet, Tokyo].

P. 7   Bitter's observation and geography of Tokyo: Martin, "Black Snow and Leaping Tigers," p. 152; Tillitse, "When Bombs Rained on Us in Tokyo," p. 82; USSBS, *Air Raid Protection and Allied Subjects Tokyo,* p. 3; Kato, *The Lost War,* p. 210; Guillain, *I Saw Tokyo Burning,* pp. 176, 183.

P. 7   "Inflammability was probably the chief qualification" and features of building construction: Daniels, "Great Tokyo Air Raid," p. 117; USSBS, *Field Report Covering Air Raid Protection and Allied Subjects Tokyo,* pp. 3, 72; Edoin, *The Night Tokyo Burned,* p. 96.

P. 7   Incendiary munitions and their appearance: Martin, "Black Snow and Leaping Tigers," p. 155; Guillain, *I Saw Tokyo Burning,* p. 184; Twenty-first Bomber Command Mission Report, no. 40, Consolidated Statistical Summary, "Disposition of Bombs" [hereafter XXI BC MR, no. 40]; E. Bartlett Kerr, *Flames over Tokyo: The U.S. Army Air Forces' Incendiary Campaign Against Japan, 1944–1945* (New York: Donald I. Fine, 1991), p. 340.

P. 8   Firefighting organization and capabilities: USSBS, *Air Raid Protection and Allied Subjects*

Tokyo, p. 2; Havens, *Valley of Darkness,* pp. 157–58; Daniels, "Great Tokyo Air Raid," pp. 123, 125; Guillain, *I Saw Tokyo Burning,* p. 184.

P. 9   Official description of raid, density of targeted area, and incendiary totals: Edoin, *The Night Tokyo Burned,* p. 59; Target Information Sheet, Tokyo, USAF HC, reel A7805, pp. 406–10; XXI BC MR, no. 40; Daniels, "Great Tokyo Air Raid," p. 124. The total bomb tonnage represents the figure the Twenty-first Bomber Command calculated as actually dropped in the target area.

P. 9   Firestorm begins and its appearance: Edoin, *The Night Tokyo Burned,* p. 77; Martin, "Black Snow and Leaping Tigers," p. 152; Guillain, *I Saw Tokyo Burning,* p. 183; Tillitse, "When Bombs Rained on Us in Tokyo," p. 82.

P. 9   "Their long glinting wings, sharp as blades": Guillain, *I Saw Tokyo Burning,* p. 182; Martin, "Black Snow and Leaping Tigers," p. 152.

P. 9   Reaction time and abandonment of homes: Martin Caidin, *A Torch to the Enemy* (New York: Bantam Books, 1960), p. 153; Martin, "Black Snow and Leaping Tigers," p. 152; Guillain, *I Saw Tokyo Burning,* p. 185; Edoin, *The Night Tokyo Burned,* pp. 74–75.

P. 10   Escape paths: Edoin, *The Night Tokyo Burned,* pp. 73–74; USSBS, *Air Raid Protection and Allied Subjects Tokyo,* p. 71.

P. 10   "People panicked": Cook and Cook, *Japan at War,* pp. 345–46.

P. 10   "People's clothes were on fire": Edoin, *The Night Tokyo Burned,* pp. 67–68.

P. 11   Account of Kimie Ono: Ibid., p. 64.

P. 11   Neighborhood cohesion: Kato, *The Lost War,* p. 211.

P. 11   Fleeing citizens trapped, "the spirit of *shikada ga nai*": Kato, *The Lost War,* p. 212; Martin, "Black Snow and Leaping Tigers," p. 152.

P. 12   Account of Masatake Obata: Edoin, *The Night Tokyo Burned,* pp. 69–72.

P. 12   Buddhist temple in Asakusa: Guillain, *I Saw Tokyo Burning,* p. 186.

P. 12   Account of Hidezo Tsuchikura: Caidin, *A Torch to the Enemy,* pp. 170–74.

P. 13   Account of Kinosuke Wakabayashi: Edoin, *The Night Tokyo Burned,* pp. 73–74; Kato, *The Lost War,* p. 211; Daniels, "Great Tokyo Air Raid," p. 125; USSBS, *Air Raid Protection and Allied Subjects Tokyo,* p. 63.

P. 13   Account of Miwa Koshiba: Edoin, *The Night Tokyo Burned,* pp. 61–62.

P. 13   All-clear signal and vista: USSBS, *Air-Raid Protection and Allied Subjects Tokyo,* Exhibit D; Edoin, *The Night Tokyo Burned,* p. 87; Guillain, *I Saw Tokyo Burning,* p. 176; Kato, *The Lost War,* p. 215.

P. 14   "The people who came back were like ghosts": Cook and Cook, *Japan at War,* p. 348.

P. 14   Account of Masuko Harino: Edoin, *The Night Tokyo Burned,* pp. 77–78, 84–86.

P. 14   Account of Masatake Obata: Ibid., pp. 86, 91.

P. 14   Account of Captain Shigenori Kubota: Ibid., pp. 95–99; USSBS, *Air Raid Protection and Allied Subjects Tokyo,* Exhibit D.

P. 15   "The entire river surface": Edoin, *The Night Tokyo Burned,* p. 100.

P. 15   "Stacked in neat precision": Ibid., pp. 100–101.

P. 16   Medical condition of survivors: Havens, *Valley of Darkness,* p. 180; Edoin, *The Night Tokyo Burned,* pp. 103–5; Daniels, "Great Tokyo Air Raid," p. 126.

P. 16   "On some broad streets": Kato, *The Lost War,* p. 215; USSBS Morale Division, *The Effects of Strategic Bombing on Japanese Morale,* Jun 47, pp. 36–37 (statement by unidentified official of the Police Bureau, Ministry of Home Affairs).

P. 16   Calculations of material destruction: Edoin, *The Night Tokyo Burned,* pp. 101–2, 106; USSBS, *Air Raid Protection and Allied Subjects Tokyo,* p. 1, Exhibit D, report of Archives Section of Ministry of Home Affairs; XXI BC MR, no. 40, pp. 33–38; Daniels, "Great Tokyo Air Raid," pp. 126–27.

P. 17   Appearance and handling of survivors: Guillain, *I Saw Tokyo Burning,* p. 177; USSBS, *Air Raid Protection and Allied Subjects Tokyo,* p. 156; Daniels, "Great Tokyo Air Raid," pp. 127–29; Tillitse, "When Bombs Rained on Us in Tokyo," p. 85.

P. 17   Impact on civil authorities: Daniels, "Great Tokyo Air Raid," p. 128.

P. 17   Calculations of deaths: USSBS, *Air Raid Protection and Allied Subjects Tokyo,* p. 83; Magic Diplomatic Summary, no. 1110, 9 Apr 45, SRS-1632, RG 457, NARA. The same figure is also in the Magic Far East Summary, SRS-383, 7 Apr 45, RG 457, NARA.

P. 18   Later estimations of deaths: Daniels, "Great Tokyo Air Raid," pp. 127–28, the best sin-

gle study, uses a figure of over 90,000. Edoin, *The Night Tokyo Burned,* p. 106, uses 100,000, as do Kato, *The Lost War,* pp. 215–16, and Tillitse, "When Bombs Rained on Us in Tokyo," p. 85. Daniels (p. 129) points out these totals presumably exceed the toll from the 1923 earthquake of 73,000 in Tokyo and represent (by his numbers) half of those killed at Hiroshima and equal the deaths at Nagasaki. The death tolls in Hiroshima and Nagasaki remain controversial and are discussed in Chapter 17. See also USSBS, *Tokyo Field Report,* p. 3, which gives a figure for March 9–10 of 83,793.

P. 18   Disruption of Tokyo and spread of news of raid: Edoin, *The Night Tokyo Burned,* pp. 106–7.

P. 18   "The victims, who had been digging through the rubble": Herbert Bix, "Japan's Delayed Surrender: A Reinterpretation," *Diplomatic History,* 19. 2 (spring 1995): 211.

P. 18   Emperor's tour of the devastated areas: Alvin Coox, *Japan: The Final Agony,* Ballantine's Illustrated History of World War II, Campaign Book no. 9 (New York: Ballantine Books, 1970), p. 28; Edoin, *The Night Tokyo Burned,* p. 107.

P. 19   "Thinking of the people dying endlessly in the air raids": Daikichi Irokawa, *The Age of Hirohito: In Search of Modern Japan* (New York: Free Press, 1995), p. 97.

P. 19   Effect of raid on the Emperor: Evidence that this did not change the Emperor's view that Japan must fight on to one last decisive battle until at least May will be developed in Chapter 6. For a contrary view representative of the early postwar history of these events, which held that this event influenced the Emperor's decision for peace later in the year, see Edoin, *The Night Tokyo Burned,* p. 108.

2. Strategies Old, Strategies New

P. 20   Origins of War Plan Orange: Edward S. Miller, *War Plan Orange* (Annapolis: Naval Institute Press, 1991), p. 4.

P. 20   Superior American air and sea forces: Ibid.

P. 21   Phase 3 of War Plan Orange: Ibid., p. 150; Martin Gilbert, *The First World War: A Complete History* (New York: Henry Holt, 1994), pp. 46–47, 84–85, 102–3, 391–92, 395, 511; Michael Walzer, *Just and Unjust Wars: A Moral Argument with Historical Illustrations,* 2d ed. (New York: Basic Books, 1977), pp. 172–75.

P. 21   "It was an article of faith": Miller, *War Plan Orange,* p. 165. Interestingly, however, when pressed to identify invasion sites, Army G-2 put forward the Kagoshima Bay area on Kyushu and the Tokyo Bay area on Honshu, which were close to the sites projected for invasion in 1945.

P. 22 Concern about American public morale and patience: Ibid., p. 29.

P. 22 Airpower in Phase 3: Ibid., p. 164.

P. 22 The approach to war and the German threat in prewar planning: Stetson Conn, Rose C. Engelman, and Byron Fairchild, *Guarding the United States and Its Outposts* (Washington, D.C.: Center of Military History, 1989), chap. 1; Mark S. Watson, *Chief of Staff: Prewar Plans and Preparations* (Washington, D.C.: Government Printing Office, 1950); Louis Morton, *Strategy and Command: The First Two Years* (Washington, D.C.: Government Printing Office, 1962), chap. 3; Robert Dallek, *Franklin Roosevelt and American Foreign Policy, 1932–1945* (Oxford: Oxford University Press, 1979), pp. 373–76.

P. 23 Institutional viewpoints of U.S. Army and U.S. Navy: The propositions stated are implicit in the myriad plans and decisions of the two services. The distinguished historian is Russell Weigley, describing the experiences of Major General Charles H. Corlett, who was sent by General Marshall to England to share his practical experience gained in Pacific amphibious operations and found his advice ignored. *Eisenhower's Lieutenants* (Bloomington: Indiana University Press, 1981), pp. 46–47. For Stimson's admission, see the Diary of Henry S. Stimson, February 27, 1945, Yale University Library [hereafter Stimson Diary]. The value judgments about combat with the Japanese held within the Army is particularly exemplified in postwar promotions, where officers with European service dominated the office of chief of staff. Just the opposite was true in the Navy in selections of chiefs of naval operations. It is important to note, however, that the frequent arguments of naval leaders about resource allocations to the Pacific did not represent a fundamental dispute about the overall priority of Europe. Indeed, it was Admiral Harold Stark, then chief of naval operations, who articulated the "Europe First" strategic emphasis as early as November 12, 1940. As one volume of the official U.S. Army history series acknowledged, "Admiral Stark's study constitutes perhaps the most important single document in the development of World War II strategy." Morton, *Strategy and Command,* p. 81.

P. 23 American and British skepticism about the Soviet Union: Bradley F. Smith, *Sharing Se-*

crets with Stalin (Lawrence: University of Kansas Press, 1996), chap. 2.

P. 23 "To welcome Russia as an associate": Dallek, *Franklin Roosevelt,* p. 298.

P. 23 "The Nazi regime is indistinguishable": Winston S. Churchill, *The Second World War,* vol. 3, *The Grand Alliance* (London: Houghton Mifflin, 1950), p. 331.

P. 23 "A stark contrast between freedom and totalitarianism": Dallek, *Franklin Roosevelt,* p. 298. The extent to which the British Ministry of Information was prepared to go to present a positive image of the Soviets is noted in Richard Overy, *Why the Allies Won* (New York: W. W. Norton, 1995), pp. 296–97. Overy devotes an entire chapter to the moral dimension of the war.

P. 24 Mass deaths in the Soviet empire: That millions died during the Soviet reign is, with rare exceptions, no longer seriously disputed. Russians now commonly refer to "the twenty million." Robert Conquest, "The Evil This Time," *New York Review of Books,* September 23, 1993, pp. 24, 27. There is also a growing body of evidence that a substantial fraction of the huge number of deaths that occurred in the Soviet empire during World War II were due to Stalin, not Hitler. Norman Davies believes this number totals six million. "The Misunderstood Victory in Europe," *New York Review of Books,* May 25, 1995, pp. 7, 8.

P. 24 Guadalcanal: Richard B. Frank, *Guadalcanal: The Definitive Account of the Landmark Battle* (New York: Random House, 1990), chap. 1.

P. 26 Battle of Manila: Robert Ross Smith, *Triumph in the Philippines* (Washington, D.C.: Government Printing Office, 1963) pp. 211–307; Richard Connaughton, John Pimlott, and Duncan Anderson, *The Battle for Manila* (Novato, Calif.: Presidio Press, 1995), pp. 123, 174–75, chap. 7. With the exception of Warsaw, Manila was the most devastated Allied capital of the war in terms of physical destruction and casualties. American losses were 1,010, Japanese 16,665 (counted dead), while 100,000 of Manila's inhabitants perished. Connaughton, Pimlott, and Anderson place responsibility on the Japanese commander for making Manila a battleground and for provoking the rampant rape and murder by the men under his command, but they find American use of firepower very excessive. They posit that "tentative estimates suggest" that for every six Filipinos murdered by the Japanese, four died in the attempt to liberate the city (p. 123). Most Filipinos believed, however, that absent the American effort, the Japanese would have wiped out still more civilians.

P. 26 King outlines Pacific grand strategy: Grace Pearson Hayes, *The History of the Joint Chiefs of Staff in World War II: The War Against Japan* (Annapolis: Naval Institute Press, 1982), pp. 280, 293–94, 367–68.

P. 26 Unconditional surrender: Bix, "Japan's Delayed Surrender," p. 204; see also Michael D. Pearlman, *Unconditional Surrender, Demobilization, and the Atomic Bomb* (Fort Leavenworth, Kans.: Combat Studies Institute, U.S. Army Command and General Staff College, 1996), pp. 1–8.

P. 27 Background of unconditional-surrender policy: Dallek, *Franklin Roosevelt,* pp. 373–76; Martin Gilbert, *Winston S. Churchill,* vol. 7, *Road to Victory, 1941–1945* (Boston: Houghton Mifflin, 1986), pp. 300–301, 309–10.

P. 27 The goal of defeating Japan within one year of Germany: Edward S. Miller, "Savvy Planning," *Military History Quarterly* 7.3 (spring 1995): 52–53; Hayes, *History of the Joint Chiefs of Staff,* pp. 431–32, 466–67.

P. 28 American battle casualties to mid-1944: *Army Battle Casualties and Nonbattle Deaths in World War II, Final Report, 7 December 1941–31 December 1946,* Statistical and Accounting Branch, Office of the Adjutant General, p. 10; *The History of the Medical Department of the United States Navy in World War II, The Statistics of Diseases and Injuries,* The Division of Medical Statistics, Bureau of Medicine and Surgery, Navy Department, Navmed P-1318, vol. 3 (Washington, D.C.: Government Printing Office, 1950), pp. 178–79. These figures include the Army (inclusive of the Army Air Forces), Navy, Marine Corps, and Coast Guard. They do not include merchant marine losses.

P. 28 "Attempting to describe the other side of the moon": Meirion Harries and Susie Harries, *Soldiers of the Sun: The Rise and Fall of the Imperial Japanese Army* (New York: Random House, 1991), p. 4.

P. 28 "The bravest people I have ever met": John Masters, *The Road Past Mandalay* (New York: Harper and Brothers, 1961), p. 155.

P. 28 Fighting at Guadalcanal: Frank, *Guadalcanal,* pp. 78–79, 149–56. During the initial landings, 347 of the 350 Japanese stationed on Tulagi perished, as did 516 of 536 defenders of Gavutu-Tanambogo. The Ichiki Detachment annihilated at the Tenaru originally numbered 917 men. Of these, an unidentified number remained at the landing site, 33 were killed in a patrol action, and

777 died along the Tenaru, with an undisclosed number escaping to rejoin the rear party.

P. 28 "I have never heard or read of this kind of fighting": Ibid., p. 157.

P. 28 Japanese casualties at Attu: Conn, Engelman, and Fairchild, *Guarding the United States,* p. 295. At Attu, the American invasion force numbered about 15,000, of whom 459 were killed and 1,148 wounded. Attu was second only to Iwo Jima with respect to the proportions of Americans killed and wounded to Japanese killed.

P. 29 Casualties on Tarawa: Joseph H. Alexander, *Utmost Savagery* (Annapolis: Naval Institute Press, 1995), pp. 71, 125.

P. 29 Japanese casualties at Makin: Philip A. Crowl and Edmund G. Love, *Seizure of the Gilberts and Marshalls* (Washington, D.C.: Office of the Chief of Military History, 1955), p. 125. Besides the three hundred combat troops, Makin held about eight hundred laborers. Of the latter, 104 were captured.

P. 29 Japanese casualties in the Marshalls: Ibid., pp. 301, 331. On Roi-Namur forty and at Kwajalein 127 additional prisoners were taken, but these were impressed Korean laborers.

P. 29 Marianas operations: Philip A. Crowl, *The Campaign in the Marianas* (Washington, D.C.: Office of the Chief of Military History, 1960), pp. 265–66; Samuel Eliot Morison, *History of United States Naval Operations in World War II,* vol. 8, *New Guinea and the Marianas, March 1944 to August 1944* (Boston: Little, Brown, 1964), pp. 338–39; Robert Sherrod, *On to Westward* (New York: Duell, Sloan, and Pearce, 1945), pp. 145–49; Carl W. Huffman, *Saipan* (Washington, D.C.: Historical Division, Headquarters, U.S. Marine Corps, 1950), p. 245; John W. Dower, *War Without Mercy* (New York: Pantheon, 1986), pp. 45, 298. The overall totals are from Crowl, the details of American deaths and Japanese prisoners and civilian internees from Morison. Sherrod provides the eyewitness accounts of the civilian deaths.

P. 30 Saipan suicides and Marshall's remarks: For the real story of the Saipan suicides, see Haruko Taya Cook, "The Myth of the Saipan Suicides," *Military History Quarterly* 7.3 (spring 1995): 12–19. Marshall's comments are in CCS, 167th Mtg., 7-14-44, CCS 381 Pacific Ocean Area (6-10-43), Sec. 6, RG 218, NARA.

P. 30 New Pacific strategic policy: CCS 417/3, 7-11-44 (adopted as CCS 417/9 and approved by Roosevelt and Churchill in CCS 680/2), ibid.

P. 30   Joint Strategic Survey Committee paper: JCS 924/2, 30 Aug 44, CCS 381 Pacific Ocean Area (6-10-43), Sec. 7, RG 218, NARA.

P. 31   Allied participation in final assault on Japan: Hayes, *History of the Joint Chiefs of Staff,* pp. 654–55, 633; CCS 900/3, Combined Chiefs of Staff Report to the President and Prime Minister, 24 July 1945, Naval Aide Files, Box 4, Folder: Berlin Conference, vol. II, Joint Chiefs HSTL.

P. 31   Collapse of confidence in China: Hayes, *History of the Joint Chiefs of Staff,* pp. 643–50; Barbara W. Tuchman, *Stilwell and the American Experience in China, 1911–45* (New York: Macmillan, 1970), pp. 501–3; Memo, Sub: Future Operations, 5 Feb 45, Strategic Plans Division, Box 166, Operations Southern Kyushu Olympic, NHC. For a lucid explanation of this important Japanese offensive, see H. P. Willmott, *June 1944* (Poole, Dorset: Blandford Press, 1984), pp. 165–73.

P. 31   American visions of Soviet role: Hayes, *History of the Joint Chiefs of Staff,* pp. 668–69.

P. 31   Meeting at Tehran: CCS 417, CCS 381 Pacific Ocean Areas (6-10-43), Sec. 10, RG 218, NARA; Hayes, *History of the Joint Chiefs of Staff,* pp. 521–33.

P. 31   Stalin's intentions: Hayes, *History of the Joint Chiefs of Staff,* pp. 668, 670–71. Stalin's supply demands amounted to 860,420 tons of dry cargo and 206,000 tons of liquid cargo to be delivered by June 30, 1945.

P. 32   Soviets renege on air-base plans: Ibid., pp. 672–733.

P. 32   JCS favoring Soviet entry: Ibid. A corollary American commitment under this plan was the opening of direct air and sea communications to the Soviet Maritime Territories promptly upon Soviet entry. This was deemed vital since the Trans-Siberian railroad would be fully occupied moving Soviet forces. Admiral Nimitz designed a two-step operation, code-named Operation Keelblocks, to occupy Kamchatka and then to seize southern Paramushiru. Planners for the Joint Chiefs of Staff picked at this plan, but it remained on the table.

P. 32   Yalta agreements: Ibid., pp. 682–84; Dallek, *Franklin Roosevelt,* pp. 516–18.

P. 33   "Intermediate" and "contributory" operations: "Operations for the Defeat of Japan," JCS 924/5, 27 October 1944, pp. 125–47; CCS 381 Pacific Ocean Area (6-10-43), Secs. 9–10, RG 218; JCS 924/7, 6 Nov 44, JPS, 176th Mtg., 10-25-44; Operations for the Defeat of Japan, JPS

404/15; for Hokkaido and Kyushu comparisons see "Operations for the Defeat of Japan," JCS 924/5, 27 October 1944, pp. 154–55; CCS 381 Pacific Ocean Area (6-10-43) Sec. 9, RG 218, NARA.

P. 33   Contributory operations considered: "Operations for the Defeat of Japan," JCS 924/5, 27 October 1944, pp. 154–55; CCS 381 Pacific Ocean Area (6-10-43), Sec. 9, RG 218, NARA; Hayes, *History of the Joint Chiefs of Staff,* pp. 161–65. There was one other factor at play against King's preference for an enclave in China: Stimson's absolute opposition to any scheme that had American troops fighting on the continent of Asia. Stimson Diary, February 27 and April 5, 1945. It appears, however, that staff studies killed the China scheme for the reasons cited in the text before Stimson had to confront the strategy at the political level with Truman.

P. 33   European developments: JPS 605, "Alternatives to the Campaign for Defeat of Japan," 21 January 1945; CCS 381 Pacific Ocean Operations (6-10-43), Sec. 11, RG 218, NARA. Stimson compared the shock of the Ardennes offensive to that administered to American policy makers by the start of the war. Stimson Diary, March 3, 1945, "Notes After Conference with the President March 3, 1945." This led to a long struggle between Stimson and Marshall over whether they had underestimated the size of the army required to finish the war. Marshall insisted it was large enough and that in any event it would take a year to raise new divisions. Stimson argued the contrary and appeared to secure Roosevelt's approval for an increase on January 11, 1945, but, as was often the case, this was not borne out by events. Stimson Diary, particularly entries of December 27, 1944, and January 4 and 11, 1945. Stimson's diary contains a great many entries relating to this topic into April 1945, see notably January 11 and 18, February 15, 17, and 21, March 27, and April 4.

P. 33   Pacific command compromise: CM-OUT-63196, Marshall to MacArthur, 4 April 1945, Marshall Papers, Box 75, Folder 2, George C. Marshall Library; Hayes, *History of the Joint Chiefs of Staff,* pp. 687–95. Marshall characterized the setup as "a major retreat by the Navy from their original stand." Hayes notes that these command arrangements were not finally formalized until July 2. Also of note is the fact that Hayes observes that the record on precisely how thinking developed and decisions were made by the Joint Chiefs of Staff during late 1944 and 1945 presents a problem. There were progressively fewer meetings of the Joint Chiefs, and "the system of keeping and publishing minutes was almost entirely abandoned" (p. 653). As part of this command agreement, the Twentieth Air Force, the B-29 effort, continued to operate as a separate command directly answering to General H. H. Arnold, the commander of the Army Air Forces. The airmen converted the former Twentieth Air Force headquarters into the United States Army Strategic Air Forces and began arrangements to send General Carl Spaatz to the Pacific to reprise the role he exercised in Europe.

P. 34 Views of Nimitz: COMINCH to CINCPAC 112045 April 45, CINCPAC Command Summary; CINCPAC ADV to COMINCH 28 0235 April, CINCPAC Command Summary, p. 3,216, NHC. For Nimitz's views in January 1945, see Memo, Sub: Future Operations, 5 Feb 45, Strategic Plans Division, Box 166, Operations Southern Kyushu Olympic, NHC. About this same time, Admiral Halsey sent his assessment of the strategic options, and he reported he was studying an attack on Kyushu and Tangeshima as the "best answer to the overall strategic problem." COM3rdFLT to CINCPAC ADV 090314 Apr 45, CINCPAC Command Summary, p. 3,208.

P. 34 Marshall-MacArthur exchange: COMINCH 211920 Apr 1945, CINCPAC Command Summary, pp. 3,211–12 (this retransmitted Marshall to MacArthur War 67098, 12 Apr, and MacArthur to Marshall, 014442 of 20 Apr).

P. 34 Joint Staff Planners April paper: JCS 924/15, 25 April 1945; CCS 381 Pacific Ocean Operations (6-10-43), Sec. 11, RG 218, NARA.

P. 34 JCS adopt April paper: On May 2, 1945, in a paper labeled JCS 924/16, Admiral King, subject to criticism of "quoted figures on casualties," formally concurred with the strategy recommendation in JCS 924/15. On May 10, 1945, the JCS by "informal action" approved the recommendation in JCS 915/16 (a memorandum from Admiral King) that the JCS "note" JCS 924/15. The staff records indicate that the "decision on JCS 924/15 circulated." On May 25, the JCS by "informal action" approved the draft directive for the invasion, which was issued in Joint Chiefs of Staff to MacArthur, Nimitz, and Arnold, WX 87938 25th (May) (Signal Corps Message form for MacArthur is dated 26 May 1945), RG 4, Box 17, Folder 4, MacArthur Archive.

P. 36 Final JCS posture as victory for the Army: For an excellent review of the development of American strategy and the role of George Lincoln, see Charles F. Brower IV, "Sophisticated Strategist: General George A. Lincoln and the Defeat of Japan, 1944–45," *Diplomatic History* 15 (summer 1991): 317–37, esp. p. 327.

P. 37 Final JCS posture as only a revokable compromise: Memorandum for the Joint Chiefs of Staff, Subject: Campaign Against Japan, 30 April 1945, 381 Pacific Ocean Operations (6-10-43), Sec. 12, RG 218, Box 169, NARA. While Brower, "Sophisticated Strategist," presents JCS 924/15 as fundamentally a vindication of Army views and particularly those of Lincoln, he acknowledges that "King's tame acceptance of the [JCS] paper . . . was deceptive. In fact he was merely changing tactics and postponing any resolution of the debate. . . . Because King thought that Japan would fall before an invasion was necessary, he was prepared to allow the JCS to issue an operational directive to begin preparations for the invasion."

3. From Zeppelins to B–29s

P. 38 "The day may not be far off": Haywood S. Hansell, Jr., *Strategic Air War Against Japan* (Washington, D.C.: Government Printing Office, 1980), p. 1.

P. 38 Aviation visionaries: Ibid., pp. 1–2.

P. 39 Aviators' arguments and second Mitchell quote: Ronald Schaffer, *Wings of Judgment: American Bombing in World War II* (New York: Oxford University Press, 1985), p. 20; Stephan L. McFarland, *America's Pursuit of Precision Bombing, 1910–1945* (Washington, D.C.: Smithsonian Institution Press, 1995), p. 76.

P. 39 "Targets" and civilian views: Hansell, *Strategic Air War Against Japan,* pp. 4–12; Schaffer, *Wings of Judgment,* pp. 32–33.

P. 39 Air warfare in the 1930s: Sherry, *Rise of American Air Power,* pp. 69–71, is good for contemporary interpretations and the basic facts. Williamson Murray, *Luftwaffe* (Baltimore: Nautical and Aviation Publishing Company of America, 1985), chap. 1, esp. pp. 16–18, explores the actual course of development of German air doctrine and shows that early on the Luftwaffe was just as interested in strategic attack as the Royal Air Force and the Army Air Forces, but Germany's strategic placement in Europe, resource availability, and practical experience in Spain, as well as leadership changes, affected the ultimate path pursued. This strikes a major blow at Sherry's theory that "only England and America seriously developed the concept and instruments of strategic air war" (p. 72). Carrying Murray's thesis further and in more depth is James S. Corum, *The Luftwaffe: Creating the Operational Air War, 1918–1940* (Lawrence: University of Kansas Press, 1997), esp. pp. 199–200, which undermines the Guernica myth. Corum explains in detail why the Luftwaffe at the outbreak of World War II was the most sophisticated air force in the world in both tactical- and strategic-bombing doctrine and equipment. For a graphic example of the visual imagery from air raids in China, see Philip B. Kunhardt, Jr., ed., *Life: World War II* (Boston: Little, Brown, 1990), p. 137.

P. 40 German strikes at "morale" targets: Murray, *Luftwaffe,* pp. 21, 40; Steven Zaloga and Victor Madej, *The Polish Campaign 1939* (New York: Hippocrene Books, 1985), p. 141.

P. 40 United States Army Air Corps Tactical School doctrine: Hansell, *Strategic Air War Against Japan,* pp. 4–12; Schaffer, *Wings of Judgment,* pp. 32–33. For a thorough discussion of how much operational experience showed the fallacy of prewar expectations for the "precision" in "precision bombing" see McFarland, *America's Pursuit of Precision Bombing,* esp. chap. 10.

P. 40 Early efforts of the Eighth Air Force: Roger A. Freeman, *Mighty Eighth War Diary* (London: Jane's, 1981), pp. 10–64.

P. 41 RAF bomber doctrine: Martin Gilbert, *Winston S. Churchill,* vol. 6, *Finest Hour, 1939–1941* (Boston: Houghton Mifflin, 1983), pp. 655–56.

P. 41 RAF night area bombing: Max Hastings, *Bomber Command* (New York: Dial Press/James Wade, 1979), pp. 117–18; Martin Middlebrook, *The Battle of Hamburg: Allied Forces Against a German City* (New York: Charles Scribner's Sons, 1980), pp. 278, 281; John Terraine, *A Time for Courage* (New York: Macmillan, 1985), p. 677. Terraine, it should be noted, was by no means unsympathetic to the Royal Air Force.

P. 42 Eighth Air Force setbacks and use of radar: Middlebrook, *Battle of Hamburg,* pp. 145–97, 281; Freeman, *Mighty Eighth War Diary,* pp. 89–90, 126 (for mission figures for October 1943 and March and May 1944, see pp. 126, 195, 248); Richard G. Davis, *Carl A. Spaatz and the Air War in Europe* (Washington, D.C.: Center for Air Force History, 1993), p. 298; Ken Rust, *Eighth Air Force Story* (Temple City, Calif.: Historical Aviation Album, 1978), p. 47. An example of how dependent the Army Air Forces became on radar aids appears in a March 13, 1945, letter from Lieutenant General Carl Spaatz, commander of the United States Strategic Air Forces in Europe to General Marshall. Spaatz noted that only about five days per month permitted visual bombing, whereas the "all-weather program" (i.e., radar aids) permitted five times that tempo. Marshall Papers, Box 85, Folder 24, Marshall Library.

P. 42 Pantelleria, Rome, and Balkan bombing: Schaffer, *Wings of Judgment,* pp. 44–52, 54–59; Davis, *Carl A. Spaatz,* p. 261. Calculating the exact tonnage dropped on urban targets in the Balkans is impossible from the sources I examined. According to detailed tables provided by Richard Davis, the sum of all bombs dropped on Bulgaria was 2,600 tons and Romania was 26,415 tons. These totals represented about 3 percent of a grand total of 1,096,794 tons dropped by American bombers. Even 3 percent grossly exaggerates this figure because in Romania the overwhelming portion of the tonnage reflected the persistent campaign against Ploeşti oil complex (Appendix 18).

P. 43 Pre-Normandy bombing campaign: *After the Battle,* no. 42 (1983): 42; *Wings of Judgment,* pp. 38–43; Gilbert, *Road to Victory,* pp. 727–28; Davis, *Carl A. Spaatz,* p. 403, provides the "approximately 4,750" number, based on information from a French underground organization. Martin Middlebrook and Chris Everitt, *The Bomber Command War Diaries* (New York: Penguin Books, 1990), pp. 489–524, provides a very partial accounting of deaths in occupied countries caused by Bomber Command attacks that totals 1,763 between April 1 and June 6–7, 1944. The single worst episode was on the night of April 18–19, when 464 died at Noisy-le-Sec. Since Bomber Command was only one of the four major Allied air components in this campaign, the 12,000 figure seems within reach. I could not locate any comprehensive report on the actual number of deaths, and it is likely that no one ever attempted an accurate tabulation.

P. 43 Oil and transportation attacks in 1944: Davis, *Carl A. Spaatz,* pp. 346–47, 398; Alfred C. Mierzejewski, *The Collapse of the German War Economy, 1944–45: Allied Air Power and the German National Railway* (Chapel Hill: University of North Carolina Press, 1988), esp. pp. 99–100 and chaps. 4 and 9. This is a critical work on the European air war.

P. 44 Technical limitations: Davis, *Carl A. Spaatz,* pp. 346–47, 386–87, and chaps. 14 and 15.

P. 44 The "V" weapons attacks, Thunderclap, and the Quesada Plan: Gilbert, *Road to Victory,* pp. 839–43; Schaffer, *Wings of Judgment,* pp. 80–84, 89–91; Davis, *Carl A. Spaatz,* pp. 342–49, 548–49. Schaffer gives the numbers under the Quesada Plan as 1,500, but the text follows the figures in Davis.

P. 45 Arnold and Clarion: Schaffer, *Wings of Judgment,* pp. 86–87.

P. 45 Establishment of USSBS: Ibid., pp. 87–89.

P. 46 Bombing policy, the Battle of the Bulge, and Dresden: Freeman, *Mighty Eighth War Diary,* pp. 432, 439–40; Middlebrook and Everitt, *Bomber Command War Diaries,* pp. 663–64; Schaffer, *Wings of Judgment,* pp. 95–97, 101; Terraine, *Time for Courage,* p. 678; Davis, *Carl A. Spaatz,* pp. 543–49, 556–59. Terraine notes that David Irving, in *The Destruction of Dresden,* originally argued that the death toll in the city was in the region of 135,000 but subsequently admitted this was in error and that the most authoritative evidence supported the conclusion that the figure more likely was 25,000 dead and 35,000 missing.

P. 46 Clarion and Pforzheim: Freeman, *Mighty Eighth War Diary,* pp. 447–48; Middlebrook and Everitt, *Bomber Command War Diaries,* p. 669. The raid on Toyama is described in chap. 10.

P. 46 German civilian casualties: The 300,000 figure is from Sherry, *Rise of American Air Power,* p. 260. The 593,000 figure is provided by Max Hastings, citing work by the West German Federal Statistical Office. See Hastings, *Bomber Command,* p. 410.

P. 46 "The most striking moral paradox": Overy, *Why the Allies Won,* p. 296.

P. 46 Shock of the Battle of the Bulge: Stimson diary, March 3, 1945, "Notes After Conference with the President, March 3, 1945."

P. 47 "At no time after the fall of France": Hastings, *Bomber Command,* p. 200.

P. 47 Support of the switch to more indiscriminate bombing: Ronald Schaffer states that "the most important factor moving the AAF toward Douhetian war [i.e., unrestricted bombing of civilians] was the attitude of the country's top civilian and military leaders." He then describes the support and the rationale for such bombing policies by Arnold, Marshall, Eisenhower, Stimson, Robert A. Lovett (the Assistant Secretary of War in charge of air matters), and Roosevelt. Schaffer, *Wings of Judgment,* p. 106.

P. 47 "The triumphs of technological fanaticism": Sherry, *Rise of American Air Power,* chap. 9; Davis, *Carl A. Spaatz,* p. 529.

P. 48 Mitchell and Marshall quotes: Sherry, *Rise of American Air Power,* pp. 31, 58, 109.

P. 48 Committee of Operations Analysts: Hansell, *Strategic Air War Against Japan,* p. 21; Kerr, *Flames over Tokyo,* pp. 22–23.

P. 49 Lack of accurate intelligence on Japan: John F. Kreis, *Piercing the Fog* (Washington, D.C.: Government Printing Office, 1996), pp.

51–52, 364–71. This account describes how for decades before the war Japanese secrecy restricted the ability of attachés to collect data and constrained commercial contact, severely limiting the information available to American officials charged with planning an air assault on Japan. To a large extent, the planning of the air campaign against Japan was guided by European experience.

P. 49 Roosevelt backs air campaign from China: Hayes, *History of the Joint Chiefs of Staff,* pp. 343–44, 383–85.

P. 49 Matterhorn concept: Hansell, *Strategic Air War Against Japan,* pp. 21–23.

P. 50 Twentieth Air Force created: Ibid., pp. 26–27, 30.

P. 50 Early operations of the Twentieth Bomber Command: Ibid., pp. 26–27; Thomas M. Coffey, *Iron Eagle* (New York: Crown Publishers, 1986), p. 113.

P. 50 LeMay replaces Wolfe: Coffey, *Iron Eagle,* p. 134.

P. 50 LeMay's background: Ibid., pp. 185–86, 330–31.

P. 50 LeMay's early military career: Ibid., pp. 185, 200–213, 215, 244.

P. 50 LeMay's performance in Europe: Ibid., pp. 49–50.

P. 51 Statistical tallies: Ken Rust, *Twentieth Air Force Story* (Temple, Calif.: Historical Aviation Album, 1979), pp. 17, 41.

P. 51 LeMay's experience in China: Coffey, *Iron Eagle,* pp. 114–15, 121–23, 127–28.

P. 51 End of B-29 operations from China: Ibid., pp. 113, 128.

P. 52 Japanese industrial concentration: USSBS, no. 55, Urban Areas Division, *The Effects of Air Attack on Japanese Urban Economy,* p. 1.

P. 52 "Extreme pressure to perform." Hansell, *Strategic Air War Against Japan,* p. 31.

P. 53 Hansell's arrival: Ibid., pp. 31, 141.

P. 53 Target priorities: Ibid., p. 50.

P. 53 "Of particular interest to me": Ibid., pp. 50–51.

P. 53 November 24 mission to Tokyo: XXI BC MR, no. 7; William Green and Gordon Swanborough, *Japanese Army Fighters,* Part 2, *World War II Aircraft Fact Files* (New York: Arco Publishing, 1978), p. 47; Boeicho Boei Kenshujo Senshi

Shitsu (War History Office, Defense Agency) *Senshi Shosho* (War History Series), No. 19, *Hondo Boku Sakusen* (Home Air Defense Operations) (Tokyo), table 41 [hereafter *Hondo Boku Sakusen*].

P. 54 Late November and December missions: XXI BC MR, nos. 8–10, 12–14, 16; Hansell, *Strategic Air War Against Japan,* pp. 40–44, 48–49.

P. 54 Arnold's criticism: Hansell, *Strategic Air War Against Japan,* p. 136.

P. 54 New target directive and Hansell quote: Ibid., p. 51.

P. 55 Hansell's protests: XXI BC MR, no. 14; Hansell, *Strategic Air War Against Japan,* p. 51.

P. 55 Origins of new target directive: Schaffer, *Wings of Judgment,* pp. 110–19.

P. 55 Incendiary tests: Kerr, *Flames over Tokyo,* pp. 29–30.

P. 55 Results of incendiary tests: Ibid., pp. 14–15, 31–32.

P. 55 The M-69 incendiary: Ibid., pp. 13–14.

4. LeMay Takes Command

P. 57 "General Arnold": St. Clair McKelway, "A Reporter with the B-29s," *The New Yorker,* June 16, 1945, p. 32.

P. 57 McNamara's report: USAF HC File 760.308-4, Memorandum 4 Feb 45, Lt. Col. Robert S. McNamara.

P. 58 Change of command: Curtis E. LeMay with MacKinlay Kantor, *Mission with LeMay* (Garden City, N.Y.: Doubleday, 1965), p. 338; XXI BC MR, no. 18.

P. 58 Nagoya attack: XXI BC MR, no. 19; Rust, *Twentieth Air Force Story,* p. 25.

P. 58 Akashi raid: XXI BC MR, no. 20. According to the USSBS, in point of fact 94 percent of the factory's machine tools and other machinery were still serviceable after the raid. As a result of foresight in converting what had been component plants at Futami and Takatsuki to final assembly works, much of the Akashi machinery was moved to them. The Futami plant was able to turn out 1,300 engines between January and August 1945, but Takatsuki only thirteen. USSBS, *Effects of Air Attack on Japanese Urban Economy,* p. 37.

P. 58 Nagoya raid: XXI BC MR, no. 22.

P. 58 Tokyo raid: XXI BC MR, no. 24 (including the Consolidated Statistical Summary); Rust, *Twentieth Air Force Story,* p. 26; *Hondo Boku Sakusen,* table 41.

P. 59 Kobe raid: XXI BC MR, no. 26, pp. 1–2, 4–7. One of the losses was a 73rd Wing plane that developed an engine fire after landing and was surveyed.

P. 59 Ota raid: XXI BC MR, no. 29; USAF HC 313th Wing, reel CO141, p. 577, Memorandum, Subject: XXI Bomber Command Critique of Mission 29, 12 Feb 45.

P. 60 Attacks on Nagoya, February 15–17: XXI BC MR, no. 34; *Hondo Boku Sakusen,* table 41; Samuel Eliot Morison, *History of U.S. Naval Operations in World War II: Victory in the Pacific 1945* (Boston: Little, Brown, 1960), pp. 20–25.

P. 60 "One thousand other reasons": Coffey, *Iron Eagle,* pp. 137, 144–45.

P. 60 Tokyo attack: XXI BC MR, no. 37, pp. 1, 3, 5–7, Consolidated Statistical Summary. Losses included a damaged 500th Bomb Group aircraft that crashed and collided with a parked plane of the 497th Bomb Group, destroying them both.

P. 60 Iwo Jima: General background from Morison, *Victory in the Pacific,* pp. 3–7, 9–19, 67–75; and George C. Dyer, *The Amphibians Came to Conquer* (Washington, D.C.: Government Printing Office, 1969), p. 997.

P. 61 American casualties on Iwo Jima: As is common for tabulations of American casualties in Pacific operations, different accountings have produced different numbers. The number used in the text is a composite. For Marine Corps losses, the source is the official Marine Corps history, which only includes losses explicitly attributed to Iwo Jima. This source also provides totals of personnel lost on aviation duty (227 killed and 303 wounded) and sea duty (137 killed and 150 wounded) for several operations, but does not segregate out those casualties sustained during the seizure of Iwo Jima. George W. Garand and Truman R. Strowbridge, *Western Pacific Operations, History of U.S. Marine Corps Operations in World War II,* vol. 4 (Washington, D.C.: History Division, Headquarters, U.S. Marine Corps, 1971), Appendix H. To the total of Marine casualties reported in the official Marine Corps history, I have added the Navy casualties reported in *History of the Medical Department of the United States Navy,* vol. 3, p. 173. This source also gives numbers for Marine casualties significantly lower than the official Marine history totals: 19,043 casualties including 5,521 dead.

P. 61   Japanese captured on Iwo Jima: Garand and Strowbridge, *Western Pacific Operations,* pp. 711–12.

P. 61   Iwo Jima as haven: The statistics are from USAF HC File 760.078-1, "20th Air Force Combat Staging Center (Provisional)." Of the 3,092 landings, 2,331 involved aircraft on bombing missions and 125 were on mining missions. How many crewmen Iwo Jima saved cannot be calculated with precision. Although some sources treat all such landings as saving the aircrew, and thus project up to 20,000-plus lives saved, there is no doubt that some aircraft made precautionary landings, though they might have struggled on to the Marianas, and that many who would have been forced to ditch might have been saved by the air-sea rescue program, whose efficiency much improved from about the date of the capture of Iwo Jima. There is no doubt, however, that the numbers of lives saved would have run into the thousands, and no airman who used Iwo Jima could know for sure whether he would or would not have survived a flight onward to the Marianas with perhaps a sojourn at sea, particularly as the weather deteriorated during the summer.

P. 61   Tokyo raid: XXI BC MR, no. 38, pp. 1–2, 4–7, Annex A, pp. 2, 4, Consolidated Statistical Summary; Coffey, *Iron Eagle,* p. 277.

P. 61   Day of Black Snow: Martin, "Black Snow and Leaping Tigers," pp. 151–52.

P. 61   Tokyo raid: XXI BC MR, no. 39, pp. 1, 5–6, Consolidated Statistical Summary.

P. 62   LeMay quotes: Sherry, *Rise of American Air Power,* p. 279; LeMay and Kantor, *Mission with LeMay,* pp. 343, 345.

P. 62   Decision to shift targeting: Sherry, *Rise of American Air Power,* pp. 31, 58; Coffey, *Iron Eagle,* p. 149.

P. 62   LeMay analysis and radar: LeMay and Kantor, *Mission with LeMay,* pp. 344–46.

P. 63   "His decision to avoid introducing these methods piecemeal": Sherry, *Rise of American Air Power,* p. 272; Kenneth P. Werrell documents that, after the fact, several others claimed to have recommended to LeMay that he lower bombing altitudes. These included Colonel John Montgomery (a staff officer), Colonel Paul Tibbets (who commanded the atomic-bomb unit), General Thomas Power (commander of the 314th Wing), and General Emmett O'Donnell (commander of the 73rd Wing). In addition, Werrell notes that a secondary source gave credit to advisers from Boeing for the idea, and General Barney Giles, Arnold's deputy, maintained that he approved the idea. LeMay, however, later stated that while ideas for other components of the plan came from others, "the low altitude part . . . was my own thinking." *Blankets of Fire* (Washington, D.C.: Smithsonian Institution Press, 1996), pp. 152–54. I believe that to the extent others spoke of lower altitudes, it is not clear they specified the radically lower altitudes LeMay ordered. Moreover, as Werrell notes, the heavy responsibility for this potentially disastrous decision rested wholly on LeMay.

P. 63   Dangers of light flak: LeMay and Kantor, *Mission with LeMay,* pp. 345, 347; McKelway, "A Reporter with the B-29s," *The New Yorker,* June 23, 1945, p. 32.

P. 64   Decision to remove defensive armament: LeMay and Kantor, *Mission with LeMay,* p. 349.

P. 64   "You know General Arnold": Ibid., pp. 345–48.

P. 64   "[Arnold's] on the hook": Ibid., p. 348; W. F. Craven and J. L. Cate, eds., *The Army Air Forces in World War II,* vol. 5, *The Pacific: Matterhorn to Nagasaki* (Washington, D.C.: Office of Air Force History, 1953), p. 614 n. 25.

P. 64   LeMay's knowledge of atomic bomb: LeMay and Kantor, *Mission with LeMay,* pp. 228–42, 348, 379.

P. 64   Aircraft strengths and target planning: 73d Wing Mission Report, No. 29, pp. 1–2, USAF HC, reel B0034; XXI BC MR, no. 40, pp. 1–2, "Aircraft Participating Chart," XXI BC Field Order 43.

P. 65   Bomb tonnage: XXI BC MR, no. 40, pp. 3–4; Roger A. Freeman, *The Mighty Eighth War Manual* (London: Jane's, 1984), pp. 153, 159.

P. 65   Altitude bands: XXI BC MR, no. 40, XXI BC Field Order 43.

P. 65   "The primary difficulties encountered": XXI BC MR, no. 40, pp. 5–7, 14; 313th Wing, MR, p. 2, USAF HC, reel C0141, p. 1575.

P. 65   "I walked the floor": Coffey, *Iron Eagle,* p. 162.

P. 65   McKelway and LeMay await the reports: McKelway, "A Reporter with the B-29s," June 23, p. 35.

P. 66   Returning aircraft: XXI BC MR, no. 40, pp. 6–7.

P. 66 B-29 losses: Ibid., pp. 8, 32–33, 35, "Aircraft Lost and Damaged Chart."

P. 67 "It was a hell of a good mission": Coffey, *Iron Eagle,* pp. 164–65.

P. 67 "As one of my first acts": LeMay and Kantor, *Mission with LeMay,* p. 353; Coffey, *Iron Eagle,* p. 166.

P. 67 "We were going after military targets": LeMay and Kantor, *Mission with LeMay,* p. 384.

P. 67 "If I had done a better job": Ibid., pp. 383, 390.

5. Fire and Mud

P. 68 Damage to Tokyo on March 9–10: XXI BC MR, no. 40, pp. 8, 36–37.

P. 68 Much-increased striking power: Ibid., p. 7; LeMay and Kantor, *Mission with LeMay,* p. 353.

P. 68 Erroneous crew reports: USAF HC File 760.551, 1944–45, pp. 15–16; 73d Wing MR, no. 29, p. 32; LeMay and Kantor, *Mission with LeMay,* p. 354.

P. 68 Attack on Nagoya of March 11: XXI BC MR, no. 41, pp. 1–8.

P. 68 Attack on Osaka of March 13–14: XXI BC MR, no. 42, pp. 1–9.

P. 69 Attack on Kobe of March 16–17: XXI BC MR, no. 43, pp. 1–3, 7–8, 18, 32–36, Consolidated Statistical Summaries. In addition to the attractions listed in the text for the target planners, there was the further fact that the city drew its meager water supply from only three reservoirs.

P. 69 Attack on Nagoya of March 18–19: USAF HC File 760.551, 1944–45, p. 15; XXI BC MR, no. 44.

P. 69 Attack on Nagoya of March 23–24: XXI BC MR, no. 45, esp. p. 8.

P. 69 Statistical summary: USAF HC File 760.309-3, Bombing Activities, 20th Air Force, p. 7.

P. 69 LeMay runs out of incendiaries: USAF HC File 762.13, HQ XXI Bomber Command Diary, entries for 12, 19, and 30 March, 16 April, and 20 and 29 May. On March 12, the Twenty-first Bomber Command issued an emergency order for 21,000 tons of incendiaries to arrive within 30 to 45 days, with another 14,000 tons to follow within another 30 days. By March 19, the Twenty-first Bomber Command advised its logistical supporters that it needed 15,000 tons per month per wing, or 75,000 tons per month by June. But in a conference with Navy officers on May 20, airmen learned that the prior orders had not been forwarded because the responsible navy officer suspended processing the requisitions based on his assessment that the Marianas lacked sufficient storage facilities for that amount of bombs.

P. 70 "The situation was bad enough": E. B. Sledge, *With the Old Breed at Peleliu and Okinawa* (Novato, Calif.: Presidio Press, 1981), pp. 259–60. Little heralded upon initial publication, Sledge's work has grown in reputation over the years until it is now recognized as one of the finest, if not the finest, of all the memoirs of an American participant in World War II.

P. 71 Okinawa: There are many excellent accounts of the fighting on Okinawa, starting with the official historians of the Army and the Marine Corps, but the factual details in this text are extracted from Thomas M. Huber, *Japan's Battle of Okinawa, April–June 1945,* Leavenworth Papers, no. 18 (Fort Leavenworth, Kans.: Combat Studies Institute, U.S. Army Command and General Staff College, 1990). Naval and ground artillery expenditures are from Roy E. Appleman, James M. Burns, Russell A. Gugeler, and John Stevens, *Okinawa: The Last Battle* (Washington, D.C.: Government Printing Office, 1948), Tables 8 and 9. The *Time* magazine quote is noted in George Feifer, *Tennozan: The Battle of Okinawa and the Atomic Bomb* (New York: Ticknor and Fields, 1992), p. 251.

P. 71 Casualties on Okinawa: Huber, *Japan's Battle of Okinawa,* pp. 118–20; Appleman, Burns, Gugeler, and Stevens, *Okinawa,* p. 473. Marine and Navy losses for Iwo Jima and Okinawa are from *History of the Medical Department of the United States Navy,* vol. 3, pp. 84, 173. It is difficult to find a final count of prisoners that clearly breaks out Okinawans from the other prisoners. The CINCPAC Command Summary for June 15 shows that as of 2400, 14 June, prisoners numbered only 953 military and 604 laborers. CINCPAC Command Summary, p. 2,698. A report for Admiral King for the week of June 24–30 notes that as of midnight, June 28, the Tenth Army counted 10,578 prisoners of war, of which "labor troops" numbered 3,300. "Labor troops" were probably overwhelmingly Okinawans, but there also should have been Okinawans among the other 7,000-plus prisoners. "Pacific Theater 24–30 June 1945," RG 38, Box 123, Folder: Week Review, NARA.

P. 72 Civilian casualties on Okinawa: Huber, *Japan's Battle of Okinawa,* p. 13; Feifer, *Tennozan,* pp. 532–33; Morison, *Victory in the Pa-*

cific, p. 82, no. 5. The text follows Morison for the Okinawa population per the 1940 census of 463,000, rather than Huber's number of 435,000. The report to Truman is in the Map Room file daily-situation report for August 2. Naval Aide Files, Map Room, Box 6, Berlin Conference, Communications from Map Room, 26 July to 2 August 1945, Folder 1, HSTL.

P. 72   Twenty-first Bomber Command support of Okinawa: XXI BC MR, nos. 46, 50, 60–61, 70–75, 76–81, 82–90, 91–95, 97–125, 127–38, 140–45, 147–49. Admiral Nimitz's headquarters believed that the B-29 attacks, as well as strikes by the carriers on Kyushu, did help. A report for Nimitz made this point in noting that the longest gap between massed suicide attacks was between May 4 and May 25. Joint Intelligence Center, Pacific Ocean Area, Analysis of Enemy Shipping, Mining and Mine Countermeasures, Report "F," 4 April 1945, p. 48, RG 457, NARA [hereafter SRMD-008], p. 233 (May 28, p. 1).

P. 72   Attacks, March 30–April 3: XXI BC MR, nos. 48, 50, 55–57; USAF HC File 703.651-1, Ltr 27 Nov 45, LTG Barney M. Giles to Gen. H. H. Arnold.

P. 73   Attacks of April 7: XXI BC MR, nos. 58–59, pp. 1, 5–7, 29–31, Consolidated Statistical Summaries; USSBS, no. 15, Aircraft Division, *The Japanese Aircraft Industry,* p. 126; XXI BC MR, nos. 58–59 (esp. pp. 6–7, 29–31), Consolidated Statistical Summaries.

P. 73   Attacks on aircraft industry: April 12 attacks: XXI BC MR, nos. 63–65, pp. 1–2, 10–12, 47, Consolidated Statistical Summaries; April 24 attack: XXI BC MR, no. 96, pp. 1, 4–7, 35–37, Consolidated Statistical Summary; April 30 attack: XXI BC MR, no. 126, pp. 1–2, 7, 9; May 5 attack: XXI BC MR, no. 146, pp. 1–6, 9–10, 26–27; May 11 attack: XXI BC MR, no. 167–71, pp. 3–6; no. 172, pp. 1–2, 5–7; USAF HC File 760.01, 1 Jul–2 Sep 45, v. 14.

P. 73   April 13–14 attack: XXI BC MR, no. 67, pp. 1–2, 4–6, 8, 31–34, Consolidated Statistical Summary; USAF HC File 760.551, 1944–45, p. 10. Fires presumably ignited by the raid destroyed the main Imperial Army research facility, extinguishing Japan's major atomic-bomb project. John W. Dower, *Japan in War and Peace: Selected Essays* (New York: New Press, 1993), pp. 78–79.

P. 73   April 15 attack: XXI BC MR, nos. 68–69, pp. 6–9, 33, Consolidated Statistical Summaries.

P. 73   May 14 attack: XXI BC MR, no. 174, pp. 5–8; USAF HC File 760.551, 1944–45, p. 16.

P. 74   May 17 attack on Nagoya: XXI BC MR, no. 176, pp. 1–3, 5–7, 35–37, Consolidated Statistical Summary; USAF HC File 760.551, 1944–45, p. 16.

P. 74   Damage to Nagoya: XXI BC MR, no. 176, pp. 9, 38; USAF HC File 760.551, 1944–45, pp. 16–17.

P. 74   "One of the most difficult cities": USAF HC File 760.511, 1944–45, p. 17.

P. 74   Attack on Tokyo, May 23–24: XXI BC MR, no. 181, pp. 1–6, 28, Consolidated Statistical Summary.

P. 74   POWs in Tokyo: Kerr, *Flames over Tokyo,* pp. 250–51; XXI BC MR, no. 181, p. 41.

P. 74   Attack on Tokyo, May 25–26: XXI BC MR, no. 183, pp. 1–2, 6, 8, 32, 37–39.

P. 74   Losses and damage, May 25–26: XXI BC MR, no. 183, pp. 8–9, 41, Consolidated Statistical Summary. The recapitulation in this mission report shows the total destruction was distributed as follows:

Missions	Date	Square Miles Destroyed
37, 38, 40	February 19 and 25 and March 9	15.1
67	April 13	10.3
69	April 15	5.4
181, 183	May 24 and 26	20.0

By the arbitrary boundaries set by American analysts, Tokyo had 110.8 square miles of built-up area and 7 square miles of parks.

P. 75   "A fine night with a strong southerly wind": Coox, *Japan, The Final Agony,* p. 30.

P. 75   "Something like a religious faith": Ibid., p. 33.

P. 75   Attack on Yokohama of May 29: XXI BC MR, no. 186, pp. 1–7, 9, 17–19, Consolidated Statistical Summary. The number of attacking B-29s counts only those loaded with bombs.

P. 76   Attack on Osaka of June 1: XXI BC MR, no. 187; VII FC Consolidated Mission Report, 1 June Osaka. Of the three pilots recovered, two survived a midair collision, and a third was found by a submarine on June 6. Weather caused at least one other major loss during the Pacific war. On April 16, 1944, the Fifth Air Force launched a large strike in marginal weather to support the landings at Hollandia. Because of a heavy weather front on return, a total of thirty-one aircraft bearing thirty-two crewmen failed to return.

Steve Birdsall, *Flying Buccaneers* (Garden City, N.Y.: Doubleday, 1977), pp. 164–67.

P. 76   Attack on Kobe of June 5: XXI BC MR, no. 188, pp. 1–3, 5, 8, 27, Consolidated Statistical Summary.

P. 76   June 7 attack on Osaka: XXI BC MR, no. 189.

P. 76   Attacks of June 10: XXI BC MR, nos. 195–200, pp. 1–3, 9–12, Consolidated Statistical Summary; USAF HC File 760.1621, 22 Nov–11 June 45, Cdr 20th AF to Cdr XXI BC, USAF HC; VII FC MR, attached to XXI BC MR, nos. 195–200, pp. 23–26.

P. 76   Attacks on June 15: XXI BC MR, no. 203.

P. 76   Losses in major Japanese cities: USAF HC File 762.398-3, "Statistical Data on Incendiary Missions, June–August 1945"; *Hondo Boku Sakusen*, table 63.

P. 77   Background on the minelaying campaign: The two principal sources are Craven and Cate, *The Pacific,* pp. 662–66, and Ellis A. Johnson and David A. Katcher, *Mines Against Japan* (Washington, D.C.: Government Printing Office, 1973), chap. 4.

P. 77   Operation Starvation: Johnson and Katcher, *Mines Against Japan,* pp. 40–42, 110.

P. 77   Japan's shipping vulnerability: H. P. Willmott, *Empires in Balance: Japanese and Allied Pacific Strategies to April 1942* (Annapolis: Naval Institute Press, 1982), pp. 88–89; Mark P. Parillo, *The Japanese Merchant Marine in World War II* (Annapolis: Naval Institute Press, 1993), pp. 242–43. Willmott makes the fundamental point about Japan's shipping needs, but the text reflects basically Parillo's numbers for captured shipping, with some rounding.

P. 78   Japanese shipping, 1941–1944: Parillo, *Japanese Merchant Marine,* pp. 242–43. There are small discrepancies between the sources used for these tables, but this data is the best available.

P. 78   Severing of Japanese shipping: SRMD-008, p. 48; Parillo, *Japanese Merchant Marine,* p. 143, tables A.4 and A.5, pp. 238, 239.

P. 78   Japanese shipping situation: Johnson and Katcher, *Mines Against Japan,* p. 110; Gregory K. Hartmann, *Weapons That Wait: Mine Warfare in the U.S. Navy* (Annapolis: Naval Institute Press, 1979), pp. 73, 78.

P. 78   Japanese maritime communications: Johnson and Katcher, *Mines Against Japan,* pp. 110–12, 116.

P. 79   Aerial mines: Ibid., pp. 114–15.

P. 79   Statistics of mine campaign: Ibid., pp. 129–30, tables 7-1, 7-2.

P. 80   Code breaking and the mine campaign: SRMD-008, various dates (see, for instance, pp. 166–67, 178). For more specific instances but no narrative, see SRH-105, Japanese Swept Channels and Sunken Vessels as Indicated in Ultra (Maps), 18 August 1945, RG 457, NARA. Code breaking was not the sole source of information that facilitated the campaign. Minefield charts purloined from sunken vessels, notably the heavy cruiser *Nachi* resting on the bottom of Manila Bay, disclosed many secrets of channels and shipping routes. SRMD-008, pp. 76, 83, 27 April p. 4, 4 May p. 2.

P. 80   "Neither extensive, efficient, nor adequate": USSBS, no. 78, Naval Analysis Division, *The Offensive Mine Laying Campaign Against Japan,* pp. 27, 37, 39, 46; Parillo, *Japanese Merchant Marine,* pp. 198–201. Captain Kyuzo Tamura, one of the key Japanese officers in the countermine effort, recalled that it took one month to develop a counter for the needle-type magnetic mine, two months for the ship-propeller acoustic mine, and three months to complete research on the hull-vibration acoustic mine and the pressure mine, but no counter was found to these last two.

P. 80   Countermeasures: Parillo, *Japanese Merchant Marine,* p. 201; USSBS, *Offensive Mine Laying Campaign,* pp. 28, 40–41, 45, 47; Johnson and Katcher, *Mines Against Japan,* p. 131; SRH-203, 26/27 Jun, No. 74; SRMD-008, p. 214, 3 Aug p. 6.

P. 81   "The Americans overrated Japan's economic potential": Havens, *Valley of Darkness,* p. 91; USSBS, *Effects of Air Attack on Japanese Urban Economy,* pp. 3, 14.

P. 81   Decline of imports: Parillo, *Japanese Merchant Marine,* table A.10, pp. 244–47.

P. 81   Japan's oil needs: USSBS, *Effects of Strategic Bombing on Japan's War Economy,* pp. 46–47; Parillo, *Japanese Merchant Marine,* pp. 42–45. As an example of the demands of a synthetic-oil program, estimated steel requirements alone numbered 2.5 million tons, or 44 percent of the entire annual output for 1941.

P. 81   Oil transportation demands: Parillo, *Japanese Merchant Marine,* pp. 45–46. As Munitions Minister Teijiro Toyoda commented later, "The shipping shortage and the scarcity of oil were the two main factors that assumed the utmost importance in Japan's war effort."

P. 81   Cutoff of oil imports: Ibid., pp. 143, 213, 205, 237, 247, tables A.1, A.4, A.11.

P. 82 Raw material shortages: USSBS, *Effects of Air Attack on Japanese Urban Economy,* pp. v, 2.

P. 82 Factors affecting war production: USSBS, no. 42, Manpower, Food, and Civilian Supplies Division, *The Japanese Wartime Standard of Living and Utilization of Manpower,* pp. 72–73; Havens, *Valley of Darkness,* pp. 91–96; USSBS, *Effects of Air Attack on Japanese Urban Economy,* p. 24; USSBS, no. 53, Overall Economic Effects Division, *The Effects of Strategic Bombing on Japan's War Economy,* pp. 3, 49–50, 126.

P. 82 Collapse of war production: Jerome B. Cohen, *Japan's Economy in War and Reconstruction* (Minneapolis: University of Minnesota Press, 1949), pp. 108–9; USSBS, *Effects of Strategic Bombing on Japan's War Economy,* p. 51.

P. 82 Aircraft manufacturing: USSBS, *Effects of Strategic Bombing on Japan's War Economy,* pp. 2, 5, 126.

P. 82 Effects of blockade on aircraft industry: Ibid., p. 5.

P. 82 Collapsing aircraft production: Ibid., pp. 3, 126.

6. The "Fundamental Policy"

P. 83 Assessment at Imperial General Headquarters: See generally Boeicho Boei Kenshujo Senshi Shitsu (War History Office, Defense Agency) *Senshi Shosho* (War History Series) No. 57, *Hondo Kessen Junbi (2) Kyushu No Boei* (Preparations for the Decisive Battle on the Homeland [2] Defense of the Kyushu Area) (Tokyo), pp. 159–61 [hereafter *Hondo Kessen Junbi*]; *Reports of General MacArthur, Japanese Operations in the Southwest Pacific Area,* vol. 2, pt. 2 (Washington, D.C.: Government Printing Office, 1966), p. 577; and Statement of Baron Suzuki, 26 Dec 45, Interrogation No. 531, p. 308, CMH.

P. 84 January 20 strategic directive: *Hondo Kessen Junbi,* pp. 161–64; Drea, *MacArthur's Ultra,* p. 202.

P. 84 Reorganization of Japanese air units: *Hondo Kessen Junbi,* pp. 167–70; Office of the Chief of Military History, Department of the Army, *Japanese Monograph no. 25, Air Defense of the Homeland,* pp. 11–15, 19–20, 25; Leon V. Sigal, *Fighting to a Finish* (Ithaca: Cornell University Press, 1988), pp. 35, 38–39; *Reports of General MacArthur,* 2:2:588–89.

P. 85 Mobilization plan and organizational structure: *Hondo Kessen Junbi,* pp. 177–82, 211–16, 278–92; *Japanese Monograph no. 17, Homeland Operations Record,* appendix 7; *Reports of General MacArthur,* 2:2:591–92, 605–7.

P. 85 April 8 directive: *Hondo Kessen Junbi,* pp. 164–66, 264; *Reports of General MacArthur,* 2:2:601. A complete translated copy of this order is found in *War in Asia and the Pacific,* vol. 12, *Defense of the Homeland and End of the War* (New York: Garland Publishing, 1980) pp. 201–31.

P. 85 Operational policy and reinforcement plans: *Reports of General MacArthur,* 2:2:604–5, 607.

P. 85 Distinctive features of Ketsu-Go: Ibid., p. 612.

P. 86 First and second phases of mobilization: *Hondo Kessen Junbi,* pp. 211–25; *Reports of General MacArthur,* 2:2:608–11, 619–21, 623 n. 48.

P. 86 Emergency measures: *Hondo Kessen Junbi,* pp. 278–83; *Reports of General MacArthur,* 2:2:622. Among these steps, the 3rd Amphibious Brigade was shipped from the Kuril Islands to southern Kyushu, the 77th Division withdrew from Hokkaido and headed for Kyushu, and two rather than one of the infantry divisions in transit from Manchuria ended up in Kyushu. Also, a lone infantry regiment garrisoning the isolated island of Tanega Shima just south of Kyushu was upgraded to the status of the 109th IMB.

P. 86 Third-stage mobilization: Statement of Major Yasuji Komuratani, Doc. No. 61337, CMH; *Hondo Kessen Junbi,* pp. 242–46. Of the nineteen divisions and fifteen IMBs, one division and one IMB were mobilized in Korea; all the other units of this size were assigned to the Homeland.

P. 86 Legal authority of Imperial Army and Navy: Harries and Harries, *Soldiers of the Sun,* p. 65.

P. 87 Terror tactics: Irokawa, *Age of Hirohito,* pp. 83–84; Edward J. Drea, *In Service of the Emperor: Essays on the Imperial Japanese Army* (Lincoln: University of Nebraska Press, 1998), p. 186.

P. 87 Control of information: Robert J. C. Butow, *Japan's Decision to Surrender* (Stanford: Stanford University Press, 1954), pp. 78–80; Irokawa, *Age of Hirohito,* p. 24; Statement of Kiichiro Hiranuma, Former President of the Privy Council 1945, 16 Dec 49, Doc. No. 55127, p. 7, CMH.

P. 87 Constriction of real power: Butow, *Japan's Decision to Surrender,* p. vi; Irokawa, *Age of Hirohito,* pp. 9–10.

P. 88 Destruction of documents: Asada, "The Shock of the Atomic Bomb and Japan's Decision to Surrender: A Reconsideration," *Pacific Historical Review* 64.4 (November 1998), p. 484. Herbert P. Bix, "The Showa Emperor's 'Monologue' and the Problem of War Responsibility," *Journal of Japanese Studies,* 18:2 (1992); 295.

P. 88 Emperor's role in ending the war: There is a good description of the body of this evidence in Asada, "Shock of the Atomic Bomb." Asada urges particular caution with respect to the postwar "Interrogations" and "Statements" of Japanese military and civilian officials assembled by historians working for the G-2 sections of MacArthur's General Headquarters. He states that these documents demonstrate that the Japanese officials often contradicted themselves and "were obviously anxious to please their American questioners. They were also eager to defend the emperor and protect the imperial institution."

P. 88 Japanese officials protect the Emperor: This is acknowledged by Asada and well supported by the evidence. In particular, I would cite the discrepancy between Kido's contemporary diary and his postwar representations of events in the afternoon of August 9 when Kido received from Suzuki a report of the terms upon which the Big Six were prepared to terminate the war. This is discussed in detail in Chapter 18.

P. 88 The Emperor's statement: Hidenari Terasaki and Mariko Terasaki Miller, eds., *Showa Tenno Dokuhakuroku—Terasaki Hidenari Goyogakari Nikki* (The Showa Emperor's Monologue and the Diary of Hidenari Terasaki); *Bungei Shunjusha,* December 1990. The references in this text are to the version published originally in the journal that included besides the "soliloquy," or "monologue," commentary by the editors and by the Japanese historian Kazutoshi Hando. This was subsequently published as a book by *Bungei Shunjusha* in 1991 in a version with a different pagination; Irokawa, *Age of Hirohito,* p. 30.

P. 88 Motivations for *Showa Tenno Dokuhakuroku:* Drea, *In Service of the Emperor,* p. 171.

P. 88 Emperor's knowledge of military situation: Ibid., pp. 173–74, 187. The Emperor received 145 briefings on the military situation between September 1941 and December 1944 and more than one hundred presentations by the Imperial Navy between just October and December 1944.

P. 88 Imperial Headquarters overrules the Emperor: Ibid., pp. 200, 207. Drea cites as but one example the issue of the Okinawa garrison. Originally, three divisions defended the island, but one was transferred out in December 1944. The Emperor urged that this division be replaced, and a division was selected. The general in charge of the First (operations) Bureau of the Army General Staff, however, canceled the deployment. As Drea notes: "In other words, a bureau chief had overruled the emperor." Further examples are provided by the refusal of Chief of Staff Umezu to order the commander in the Philippines, General Yamashita, to comply with the Emperor's strategic concepts and the Emperor's proposal for a new attack in China around May 1945.

P. 89 Exaggeration of battle achievements: Ibid., pp. 187, 191, 192.

P. 89 Pursuit of the "decisive battle": Ibid., pp. 171–72, 190.

P. 89 Imperial Navy strategic thought: See generally the masterful work by David C. Evans and Mark R. Peattie, *Kaigun: Strategy, Tactics, and Technology in the Imperial Japanese Navy, 1887–1941* (Annapolis: Naval Institute Press, 1997), esp. chaps. 13 and 14.

P. 89 Imperial Army strategic concepts: Akira Iriye, *Power and Culture: The Japanese American War, 1941–1945* (Cambridge, Mass.: Harvard University Press, 1981), p. 41; Sigal, *Fighting to a Finish,* p. 29.

P. 89 Imperial Army attitude toward Americans: Drea, *In Service of the Emperor,* p. 32.

P. 89 "We can no longer direct the war": Irokawa, *Age of Hirohito,* p. 92.

P. 90 Selection of Koiso; Butow, *Japan's Decision to Surrender,* pp. 16, 30–31; Statement of Kiichiro Hiranuma, 16 Dec 49, Doc. No. 55127, pp. 1–5, CMH. The three generals recommended were Marshal Terauchi, General Koiso, and General Hata. By Hiranuma's account, Terauchi and Hata were ruled out due to their appointments at front commands, Terauchi with the Southern Army and Hata with the China Expeditionary Army. (Koiso, by contrast, was then Governor General of Korea.) Hiranuma insisted that Yonai's appointment signified a desire by all the *jushin* to rapidly restore peace. On the other hand, Lord Keeper of the Privy Seal Kido related that the *jushin* recommended Terauchi, but Tojo was "absolutely against" his selection, so Koiso, the second choice, got the nod. Statement of Koichi Kido, 17 May 49, Doc. No. 61476, p. 4, CMH.

P. 90 Creation of Supreme Council: Butow, *Japan's Decision to Surrender,* pp. 36–38.

P. 90 Koiso's military strategy and blunder in public statement: Ibid., pp. 42–43.

P. 90 Emperor meets with senior statesmen: Ibid., p. 44; Bix, "Japan's Delayed Surrender," p. 203. While Bix has much important factual material, I do not subscribe to his central theme as to the Emperor's dominant responsibility for a "delayed surrender." Kido, after the war, tried to depict this episode as evidence that the Emperor had become strongly desirous of terminating the war. Statement of Koichi Kido, 17 May 49, Doc. No. 61476, pp. 10–11, CMH.

P. 90 Konoe memorial, Emperor's response, and warning of Soviet intervention: Irokawa, *Age of Hirohito,* pp. 91–92, quoting directly and extensively from *Showa Tenno Dokuhakuroku;* Bix, "Japan's Delayed Surrender," pp. 201–2.

P. 91 Kido and Matsudaira support "decisive victory": Drea, *In Service of the Emperor,* p. 199.

P. 91 Koiso resigns: Statement of Koichi Kido, 17 May 49, Doc. No. 61476, p. 3, CMH; Statement of Kiichiro Hiranuma, 16 Dec 49, Doc. No. 55127, p. 5, CMH; Statement of Lt. Gen. Masao Yoshizumi, 22 Dec 49, Doc. No. 54484, p. 1, CMH; Statement of Mamoru Shigemitsu, 13 Jan 50, CMH; Iriye, *Power and Culture,* pp. 238–39; Bix, "Japan's Delayed Surrender," pp. 210–12; Butow, *Japan's Decision to Surrender,* pp. 59–61; Sigal, *Fighting to a Finish,* pp. 41–44. Shigemitsu's statement is of particular interest since it stresses that a key factor in Koiso's fall was that he lost the Emperor's confidence.

P. 91 Suzuki's character: Statements of Lt. Gen. Masao Yoshizumi, Doc. No. 54485, p. 1, and 22 Dec 49, Doc. No. 54484, p. 3, CMH; and Statement of Hisatsune Sakomizu, 20 May 49, Doc. No. 61339, p. 1, CMH.

P. 91 Haragei: Butow, *Japan's Decision to Surrender,* pp. 70–72; John Toland, *The Rising Sun: The Decline and Fall of the Japanese Empire, 1936–1945* (New York: Random House, 1970), p. 864; Statement of Hisatsune Sakomizu, 17 Aug 49, Doc. No. 62004, p. 3, CMH; Statement of Seizo Sakonji, 20 May 49, Doc. No. 61339, pp. 1–4, CMH. The subject of Suzuki's mind-set upon his appointment is both important and controversial. According to his private secretary, Sakomizu, who argued vigorously for the *haragei* interpretation, a major part of Suzuki's conduct early on can be attributed to the fact that, as he admitted to Sakomizu, even as a senior former naval officer, he had not been fully informed

of Japan's situation. But Sakonji reported that Suzuki was thinking in terms of peace after one more "splendid" military success. Sakonji also tellingly reveals that when he and two other state ministers sought to bring Navy Minister Yonai, who was known for his views that Japan must seek peace, together with Anami and Suzuki in late May, Yonai resisted because he believed neither Anami nor Suzuki were "ready to listen to the proposal to terminate the war" (Doc. No. 61339, p. 2). Further, as will be noted in Chapter 19, up to the very end, Anami never suspected Suzuki would ever come out in favor of surrender on anything approximating the terms Japan ultimately accepted.

P. 92 Significance of Suzuki's appointment: Butow, *Japan's Decision to Surrender,* pp. 65n., 68–69; Statements of Hisatsune Sakomizu, 20 May 49, Doc. No. 61339, pp. 1–3, and 17 Aug 49, Doc. No. 62004, p. 1, CMH; Statement of Seizo Sakonji, 20 May 49, Doc. No. 61339, pp. 1–4, CMH; Statement of Lt. Gen. Masao Yoshizumi, 22 Dec 49, Doc. No. 54484, pp. 1–2, CMH. Yoshizumi reported that Suzuki had affirmed for Army Minister Sugiyama his complete agreement with a three-point army plan, the first of which was "prosecution of the war to the bitter end." Sugiyama related this to Yoshizumi. Hiranuma insisted later based on "supposition" that Suzuki understood Japan's situation and would move to terminate the war immediately. Statement of Kiichiro Hiranuma, 16 Dec 49, Doc. No. 55127, p. 7, CMH, Statement of Seizo Sakonji, 20 May 49, Doc. No. 61339, pp. 1–3, CMH. Sigal, *Fighting to a Finish,* p. 47, notes correctly that Suzuki "was no dove."

P. 92 Anami's role: Drea, *In Service of the Emperor,* p. 203.

P. 92 Anami and Umezu; Anami's character and background: For a sketch of his general career, *Daihon'ei Rikugun-Bu (10),* pp. 146–47, and Fuller, *Shokan,* pp. 82–83; for views of his subordinates, see Statement of Lt. Col. Inaba, Doc. No. 57592, p. 3, CMH (describing Anami as a "simple and honest man who did not use tricks"); Statement of Maj. Gen. Yatsuji Nagi, 27 Dec 49, Doc. No. 54228, p. 1, CMH; Statement of Lt. Gen. Kawabe, 21 Nov 49, Doc. No. 52608, CMH; Statement of Lt. Col. Takeshita, 11 Jun 49, Doc. No. 50025-A, CMH; "the Ivory Mask" nickname: Drea, *In Service of the Emperor,* p. 195. Kawabe completely rejects the notion that Anami favored peace but only advocated continuation of the war to appease the strong demands of Imperial Army circles. A notable example of Umezu's behavior was that when he returned from his inspection trip to China with his pes-

simistic report to the Emperor, he did not share it
with his staff. On Umezu and Anami, see also
Colonel Takashi Nakayama, "Strategic Concept
at the End of the War and Defense of the Home
Islands," U.S.-Japan History Exchange Conference, October 25, 1987, pp. 34–37, CMH.

On Umezu's career, see Fuller, *Shokan,* pp.
225–26; on general character, see Kawabe
(Anami's "pure and transparent character" con-
trasts with that of Umezu, who "was very politically minded and a complex character"). See also
Statement of Ikeda, 16 Jun 50, Doc. No. 54479,
CMH, who described Umezu as "not a man of
firm conviction." It is notable that Ikeda had
served closely with Umezu for a very protracted
period.

P. 93   Suzuki's selection of cabinet: International Military Tribunal for the Far East, Library
of Congress (Law Library microfilm edition)
[hereafter IMTFE] Suzuki 35,590–92 (impressions of and recruitment of Togo); IMTFE Togo
35,778–80; IMTFE Matsudaira 35,595–97;
IMTFE Sakomizu 35,603–5; Statement by
Shigenori Togo, 17 May 49, p. 8, CMH; Statement of Hisatsune Sakomizu, 17 Aug 49, Doc.
No. 62004, CMH. See also Butow, *Japan's Decision to Surrender,* pp. 65–67; Sigal, *Fighting to a
Finish,* p. 48.

In one of a great many efforts to present the
Emperor as explicitly committed to seeking a
prompt peace from an early date, Marquis Kido
beguiled postwar interrogators with the tale that
he expressly told Suzuki of the Emperor's desire
for peace at the earliest moment. Statement of
Koichi Kido, 17 May 49, Doc. No. 61541, p. 2,
CMH. This is not in accord with Kido's other
statement this day, which describes the same
conversation but omits mention of instructions
from the Emperor (Statement of Koichi Kido, 17
May 49, Doc. No. 61476, p. 4, CMH). By contrast, to postwar American interrogators Suzuki
stated that he

> did not receive any direct order from the
> Emperor [to seek peace], but I understood
> clearly from what the Emperor said to me
> at that time that the Emperor was very
> much concerned over the situation that
> Japan faced in the war. . . . Therefore I
> was given to understand that it was the
> Emperor's desire for me to make every ef-
> fort to bring the war to a conclusion as
> quickly as possible.

The reader will note the indirection with
which Suzuki approaches these very vital issues:
the very ambiguous nature of how he understood
his supposed charter from the Emperor when
nothing was communicated directly and the very

vague and indefinite terms of bringing the "war
to a conclusion" and "as quickly as possible."
Statement of Baron Suzuki, 26 Dec 45, Interrogation No. 531, p. 306, CMH.

P. 93   Soviets revoke neutrality pact: Butow,
Japan's Decision to Surrender, pp. 58–59.

P. 93   Talks about approaching Soviets: Statement by Shigenori Togo, 17 May 49, pp. 7–8,
CMH; IMTFE Togo 35,782; Butow, *Japan's Decision to Surrender,* pp. 81–82.

P. 93   Discussions within Big Six: Butow,
Japan's Decision to Surrender, pp. 77–78; Statement by Shigenori Togo, 17 May 49, p. 7, CMH;
IMTFE Togo 35,782–83; Sigal, *Fighting to a
Finish,* pp. 49–51. Sigal's analysis is particularly
acute on the competing interests of the parties.
After the war, Togo was scathing about the conceptions of his colleagues and called the Imperial
Navy concept of alliance with the Soviets "even
more fantastic" than the Imperial Army's goal of
keeping the Soviets out of the war.

P. 94   Final agreement on the approach to the
Soviets: Butow, *Japan's Decision to Surrender,*
pp. 84–85; Iriye, *Power and Culture,* p. 248;
Statement by Shigenori Togo, 17 May 49, p. 11,
CMH. There is a conflict between Butow and
Iriye as to whether the Big Six expressly autho-
rized Togo to seek Soviet mediation to end the
war. Iriye appears to imply that they did, but
Butow firmly says they did not. I follow Butow.

P. 94   Negative reasons for picking Soviets:
Butow, *Japan's Decision to Surrender,* pp.
87–89. Statements of Koichi Kido, 17 May 49,
Doc. No. 61541, p. 3, and 11 Aug 50, Doc. No.
61476, pp. 9–10, CMH.

P. 94   Positive reasons for picking Soviets:
Statement of Koichi Kido, 11 Aug 50, Doc. No.
61476, pp. 9–10, CMH; Sigal, *Fighting to a Finish,* pp. 57–58.

P. 95   Flawed understanding of Soviet perspective: Butow, *Japan's Decision to Surrender,* pp.
88–90.

P. 95   Hirota-Malik talks: IMTFE Togo
35,783; Butow, *Japan's Decision to Surrender,*
pp. 90–92.

P. 95   Origins and purpose of "Fundamental
Policy": Statement of Col. Sako Tanemura, 21
Aug 50, Doc. No. 61977, CMH; Statement of
Hisatsune Sakomizu, 22 May 49, Doc. No.
62003, p. 3, CMH. *Hondo Kessen Junbi,* pp.
24–26, shows that the genesis of this draft dated
back to at least February, and its adoption was
postponed in anticipation of the formation of a

new cabinet. The assessment of the world situation prepared in the early draft anticipated that the Soviets would enter the war when they saw it to their advantage to earn a voice in the settlement in the Far East.

P. 95 "Present State of National Power": *Hondo Kessen Junbi*, pp. 582–83; Sigal, *Fighting to a Finish*, pp. 64–68; Butow, *Japan's Decision to Surrender*, pp. 93–96. Sigal points out that "The Present State of National Power" was not, as Butow reports, generated by the Army but was the product of the Togo-Suzuki agreement. In a secret session of the Special Committee of the Emergency Diet in June 1945, Vice Army Minister Shibayama revealed that the possible duration of time Japan could continue the war in terms of the food situation was one year. Statement of Col. Sako Tanemura, 21 Aug 50, Doc. No. 61977, p. 8, CMH.

P. 96 June 6 meeting and Suzuki's role: Butow, *Japan's Decision to Surrender*, pp. 96–99.

P. 96 June 8 meeting: Ibid., pp. 99–102; Statement of Soemu Toyoda, 10 Mar 50, Doc. No. 57669, p. 3, CMH.

P. 96 Kido's postwar version: Statements of Koichi Kido, 17 May 49, Doc. No. 61541, pp. 3–4, and Doc. No. 61476, pp. 5–6, CMH. See also Butow, *Japan's Decision to Surrender*, p. 113.

P. 96 Alternative version of Kido's thinking: *Showa Tenno Dokuhakuroku*, pp. 134–36, and Bix, "Japan's Delayed Surrender." Bix states that Kido's "plan" marked the end of his "long honeymoon relationship with the military hardliners" (p. 212). The Emperor's account rambles and contains some internal contradictions. At one point he says that he believed Okinawa would be the "the last decisive battle" and that failure there meant unconditional surrender at the end of the road. Then he says after Okinawa he believed that only an attack in Yunnan in China offered an alternative, but when the Army turned it down, he decided the only way out was to decide for peace.

P. 97 Seven professors from Tokyo University: *Showa Tenno Dokuhakuroku*, p. 139. As the commentary in the journal notes, it was a revelation to learn that the Emperor knew of this. Owing to their pledges of secrecy, however, the details of the professors' effort remain unknown.

P. 97 Kido's "Draft Plan": *The Diary of Marquis Kido, 1931–45: Selected Translations into English* (Frederick, Md.: University Publications of America, 1984), pp. 435–36. The same text in a somewhat different rendition appears in IMTFE Kido 31,146–51, and was further modified by the translation version of Kido's proposal in Bix, "Japan's Delayed Surrender," p. 212. See also Butow, *Japan's Decision to Surrender*, pp. 112–15.

P. 97 Kido's desire to approach the United States: *The Diary of Marquis Kido*, p. 436; Statements of Koichi Kido, 17 May 49, Doc. No. 61541, pp. 3–4, and Doc. No. 61476, pp. 5–6, CMH. See also Butow, *Japan's Decision to Surrender*, p. 113.

P. 98 Kido briefs the Emperor: IMTFE Kido 31,151–55, amended by translations by Butow, *Japan's Decision to Surrender*, p. 114. IMTFE shows Kido assigning part of the Emperor's willingness to agree to concern over distressing incendiary attacks on medium and small cities. As of this date (June 9), however, such attacks had not begun. On the Emperor's Imperial Rescript of June 9, see Bix, "Japan's Delayed Surrender," p. 213.

P. 98 Kido's meeting with Suzuki: Statements of Koichi Kido, 17 May 49, Doc. No. 61541, pp. 3–4, and Doc. No. 61476, pp. 6–7, CMH; IMTFE Kido 31,151–55; Butow, *Japan's Decision to Surrender*, p. 114.

P. 98 Kido talks with Togo and Anami: Statements of Koichi Kido, 17 May 49, Doc. No. 61541, pp. 3–4, and Doc. No. 61476, pp. 7–8, CMH; IMTFE Kido 31,155–58. See also Butow, *Japan's Decision to Surrender*, p. 114.

P. 99 Emperor expresses hope in Okinawa victory: Drea, *In Service of the Emperor*, pp. 199, 205.

P. 99 Emperor urges attack in Yunnan: *Showa Tenno Dokuhakuroku*, p. 134; Drea, *In Service of the Emperor*, p. 201. I follow Drea's rendering of the Emperor's statement.

P. 100 Emperor receives Umezu's report: *Showa Tenno Dokuhakuroku*, pp. 135–36; also cited in Butow, *Japan's Decision to Surrender*, p. 116, fn 13. In a statement after the war, the Emperor's aide-de-camp, Hasunuma, insisted that Umezu's report had little impact, which might explain why Butow placed it in a footnote. *Showa Tenno Dokuhakuroku* clearly attaches to it more significance. Statement by Shigeru Hasunuma, 31 Mar 50, Doc. No. 58225, pp. 4, 6, CMH. It is on p. 6 of Hasunuma's statement that the Emperor expresses doubts about the ability of the population to hold out under air attack. Confirmation of the significance of Umezu's report is also provided by Statement of Yasumasa Matsudaira, 15 Aug 49, Doc. No. 60745, p. 4, CMH.

P. 100 Report of Admiral Hasegawa: *Showa Tenno Dokuhakuroku*, p. 136; Statement Concerning Inspection Report [...] of Admiral Kiyoshi Hasegawa, 24 Mar 50, Doc. No. 57667, CMH.

P. 100   Report of Prince Higashikuni: *Showa Tenno Dokuhakuroku,* pp. 136–37; also cited in Irokawa, *Age of Hirohito,* p. 44. A specific date for this report is not given, but *Showa Tenno Dokuhakuroku* places it as "about that time" of the report of Admiral Hasegawa.

P. 100   Emperor decides on negotiated peace: *Showa Tenno Dokuhakuroku,* pp. 137–38; cited also in Irokawa, *Age of Hirohito,* p. 31.

P. 101   Plans to move the palace to Matsushiro: Drea, *In Service of the Emperor,* pp. 206–9.

P. 101   June 18 meeting of "Big Six": IMTFE Kido 31,155, 31,159–60, Togo 35,783–4.

P. 101   Togo meets with Hirota and Emperor: Statement of Togo, Doc. No. 50304, pp. 20–23, CMH. Here, Togo has the Emperor indicating that based on the reports of General Umezu and Admiral Hasegawa, the war must be ended "without delay." I believe this is an example of postwar statements attributing far stronger fervor to the Emperor's exhortations for swiftly moving to peace than *Showa Tenno Dokuhakuroku* indicates. Butow, *Japan's Decision to Surrender,* pp. 117–18.

P. 102   June 22 meeting: Asada, "The Shock of the Atomic Bomb and Japan's Decision to Surrender: A Reconsideration," p. 500; Statement of Togo, 17 May 49, Doc. No. 50304, p. 21, CMH; Statement of Toyoda, 29 Aug 49, Doc. No. 61340, pp. 4–5, CMH; IMTFE Suzuki 35,593, Kido 31,160–63, Togo 35,783–85, Sakomizu 35,607; Butow, *Japan's Decision to Surrender,* pp. 119–20. Butow's account included examination of the Kido "Nikki" (diary) and documents from the Japanese Foreign Ministry.

7. Magic Insights

P. 103   American success in decryption: David Kahn, *The Code Breakers* (New York: Macmillian, 1967), pp. 355–69. Yardley's book *The American Black Chamber* was published in 1931. See also Henry L. Stimson and McGeorge Bundy, *On Active Service in Peace and War* (New York: Harper and Brothers, 1947), p. 188.

P. 103   Magic in the Pearl Harbor investigations: Almost every work on the subject covers this. Good examples are Roberta Wohlstetter, *Pearl Harbor, Warning and Decision* (Stanford: Stanford University Press, 1962), and Gordon Prange, *At Dawn We Slept* (New York: McGraw-Hill, 1981).

P. 103   Intelligence from Oshima: Examples of the extremely valuable intelligence gleaned from Oshima leading up to the Normandy landings can be found in F. H. Hinsley, E. E. Thomas, C. A. G. Simkins, and C. F. G. Ransom, *British Intelligence in the Second World War,* vol. 3, pt. 2 (New York: Cambridge University Press, 1988), pp. 32–33, 45, 47, 51–52, 57, 61, 63, 215–16. See also Carl Boyd, *Hitler's Japanese Confidant: General Oshima Hiroshi and MAGIC Intelligence, 1941–45* (Lawrence: University Press of Kansas, 1993).

P. 104   Magic and Japanese intentions: A recent restatement of the thesis that Imperial Japan was actively seeking peace on terms acceptable to the Allies and that American policy makers, including President Truman, knew this is contained in Gar Alperovitz, *The Decision to Use the Atomic Bomb and the Architecture of an American Myth* (New York: Alfred A. Knopf, 1995), pp. 23–28, 292–93, 295–97. After listing a series of Magic messages, initiatives by Japanese diplomats, and OSS reports, Alperovitz comments:

> None of these approaches, of course, carried formal, official authorization, and, accordingly, they were treated with considerable caution: There was obviously an enormous difference between a general mid-level (or even high-level) probe and a true Japanese initiative. Moreover, experts in Washington differed as to the appropriate weight to attach to various moves at various points in time as the summer [of 1945] progressed.
>
> Nevertheless, the increasing pace of contacts involving important Japanese representatives was an obvious indication of Japan's deteriorating internal situation—and, too, of the clear trajectory of change.

The first paragraph characterizes the situation quite accurately as to the lack of any official sanction behind these contacts. I cannot concur that a whole series of meaningless episodes demonstrated a "clear trajectory of change."

P. 104   Postwar references to Magic: The first reference was apparently James V. Forrestal, *The Forrestal Diaries,* ed. Walter Millis (New York: Viking Press, 1951), and this was followed by Butow, *Japan's Decision to Surrender,* p. 130, and the discussion ranging to p. 141.

P. 105   Translations of Japanese messages: *Foreign Relations of the United States, Diplomatic Papers: The Conference of Berlin 1945, Volumes 1 and 2* (Washington, D.C.: Government Printing Office, 1960), passim [hereafter *FRUS, Berlin 1945*].

P. 105   References establishing the thirty governments or equivalents whose signals were being intercepted and read follow:

Government	"Magic" Diplomatic Summary Number	Date	SRS Number
Argentina	1026	15 Jan 45	1548
Belgium	1177	15 Jun 45	1699
Bolivia	1045	3 Feb 45	1567
Bulgaria	1141	10 May 45	1663
Chile	1045	3 Feb 45	1567
China (Chiang Kai-shek)	1172	10 Jun 45	1694
China (Japanese client)	1032	21 Jan 45	1554
Colombia	1140	9 May 45	1662
Cuba	1152	21 May 45	1674
France (de Gaulle)	1049	7 Feb 45	1571
France (Indochina)	1050	8 Feb 45	1572
Greece	1026	15 Jan 45	1548
Iran	1189	27 Jun 45	1711
Italy	1147	16 May 45	1669
Lebanon	1147	16 May 45	1669
Liberia	1146	15 May 45	1668
Luxembourg	1150	19 May 45	1672
Mexico	1023	12 Jan 45	1545
Mongolia (Japanese client state)	1181	19 Jun 45	1703
Netherlands	1097	27 Mar 45	1619
Nicaragua	1152	21 May 45	1674
Peru	1140	9 May 45	1662
Portugal	1029	18 Jan 45	1551
Saudi Arabia	1157	26 May 45	1679
Spain	1130	29 Apr 45	1652
Switzerland	1045	3 Feb 45	1567
Syria	1163	1 Jun 45	1685
Turkey	1030	19 Jan 45	1552
Uruguay	1152	21 May 45	1674
Venezuela	1076	6 Mar 45	1598

A comment is due here on methodology. Originally, my review was of the SRS series of Magic Diplomatic Summaries released in 1978. Subsequently, I reviewed the 1995 set. Since the SRS series was commonly used as a reference prior to 1995, I have retained citations to the SRS numbers. Researchers should also beware that photocopies of the 1995 set may appear to contain blanked-out sections. Examination of the originals, however, shows clearly that these areas are the product of formatting conventions, not censorship.

P. 106   OSS not privy to Magic: John F. Kreis, *Piercing the Fog* (Washington, D.C.: Government Printing Office, 1996), 3–4. There were limited exceptions to this general policy.

P. 106   "An influential member": Dip. No. 1142, 11 May 45, SRS-1664. The word replaced with Imperial Navy in the text was *Admiralty.* Alperovitz, *Decision to Use the Atomic Bomb,* pp. 29–30, notes that the commentary accompanying the text of the German attaché's message had been blocked out in text released prior to 1995. After acknowledging that the position of Imperial Army leaders was "absolutely critical, both at the time and in subsequent interpretations," he notes:

> Quite apart from the significance of this rather minor report on the attitude of army leaders in May, a decision to isolate a carefully defined passage of this kind points beyond general classification procedures to specific choices by specific officials as to what the public could and could not be permitted to know about the events of 1945.

This is a marvelous attempt to make lemonade out of lemons. The problem of implying some sinister intent to deceive the public in this incident is that the previously censored interpretive text severely undercut the significance of the diplomatic message suggesting a possibility of peace.

P. 106   Messages indicating impediment of unconditional surrender or general question of terms of surrender: Portuguese Minister Fernandes, Dip. No. 1110, 9 Apr 45, SRS-1632; Spanish Military Attaché, Dip. No. 1150, 19 May 45, SRS-1672; Swedish Minister Bagge via French Ambassador Catroux, Dip. No. 1150, 19 May 45, SRS-1672.

Besides the May 5 message and the trio on surrender terms, there were seven messages containing indications that civilian morale had declined. This number, however, represented five from one source, Swiss Minister Gorge. At least four dispatches affirmed the soundness of popular morale, and although three of them originated from Japanese officials, one came from Swedish Minister Bagge.

Messages indicating decline of popular morale (7): Swiss Minister Gorge, Dip. No. 1045, 3 Feb 45, SRS-1567; Messages of French Ambassador Cosme and Portuguese Minister Fernandes, Dip. No. 1081, 11 Mar 45, SRS-

1603; Swiss Minister Gorge, Dip. No. 1083, 13 Mar 45, SRS-1605; Swiss Minister Gorge, Dip. No. 1111, 10 Apr 45, SRS-1633; Swiss Minister Gorge, Dip. No. 1118, 17 Apr 45, SRS-1640; Swiss Minister Gorge, Dip. No. 1188, 26 Jun 45, SRS-1710.

Messages affirming the soundness of popular morale (4): "Weekly Intelligence" circular, Vice Chief Imperial Army General Staff, March 11, Dip. No. 1082, 12 Mar 45, SRS-1604; Foreign Minister Shigemitsu, March 13, Dip. No. 1084, 14 Mar 45, SRS-1606; French Ambassador Catroux, relating conversation with Swedish Minister Bagge returned from Tokyo, Dip. No. 1150, 19 May 45, SRS-1672; Vice Minister of Foreign Affairs Matsumoto, Dip. No. 1170, 8 Jun 45, SRS-1692.

P. 107   "Thinking people at the Court": Dip. No. 1041, 30 Jan 45, SRS-1563.

P. 107   "Are they sincere or are they intoxicated?": Dip. No. 1045, 3 Feb 45, SRS-1567.

P. 107   "Unrelieved pessimism on all aspects": Dip. No. 1040, 29 Jan 45, SRS-1562.

P. 107   "New Cabinet would probably be formed": Dip. No. 1043, 1 Feb 45, SRS-1565.

P. 107   "Is being criticized more and more": Dip. No. 1083, 13 Mar 45, SRS-1605; Dip. No. 1084, 14 Mar 45, SRS-1606; "Japanese Army and the circles it influences": Dip. No. 1101, 31 Mar 45, SRS-1623. (Interestingly, the German military attaché did not say the "Japanese Army and Navy.")

P. 108   "The fortification of coasts and mountains": Dip. No. 1143, 12 May 45; SRS-1665.

P. 108   "Japan does not expect to win": Dip. No. 1188, 26 Jun 45, SRS-1710.

P. 108   Other messages affirming Japan would fight on: Portuguese Minister Fernandes, Dip. No. 1049, 7 Feb 45, SRS-1571; Ambassador Cosme (no Japanese surrender foreseeable before defeat of Germany), Dip. No. 1066, 24 Feb 45, SRS-1588; Portuguese Minister, Dip. No. 1118, 17 Apr 45, SRS-1640; Spanish Minister (noting that Prince Konoe, a known pacifist, refused to join the government), Dip. No. 1130, 29 Apr 45, SRS-1652; Portuguese Minister, Dip. No. 1168, 6 Jun 45, SRS-1680; Portuguese Minister, Dip. No. 1151, 19 Jun 45, SRS-1703.

P. 108   Messages indirectly indicating plans for unremitting resistance: February 8 message (indicating a plan for synthetic aircraft-fuel production requiring two years to bear fruit), Dip. No. 1050, 8 Feb 45, SRS-1572; "Weekly Intelligence" Circular, Vice Chief of Imperial Army

General Staff (noting organization of regional government permitting continued resistance in a fragmented Japan), Dip. No. 1153, 22 May 45, SRS-1675; Message of Greater East Asia Ministry (noting plans to induct Japanese boys ages 14 and over in China), Dip. No. 1168, 6 Jun 45, SRS-1680.

P. 108   Damage in Tokyo fire raid: Dip. No. 1082, 12 Mar 45, SRS-1604; Dip. No. 1084, 14 Mar 45, SRS-1606; Dip. No. 1089, 19 Mar 45, SRS-1611; Dip. No. 1094, 24 Mar 45, SRS-1616; Dip. No. 1095, 25 Mar 45, SRS-1617.

P. 109   Damage in fire blitz: Dip. No. 1110, 9 Apr 45, SRS-1632; Dip. No. 1084, 14 Mar 45, SRS-1606; Dip. No. 1086, 16 Mar 45, SRS-1608; Dip. No. 1087, 17 Mar 45, SRS-1609. Specifically, the March 16–17 Kobe raid reportedly destroyed about 68,000 buildings and killed about 1,000 persons; the raid on Nagoya two nights later reportedly destroyed about 37,400 dwellings and killed 1,600 (Dip. No. 1096, 26 Mar 45, SRS-1618). The last raid of the series on Nagoya on March 24 reportedly destroyed 6,600 houses and left 2,200 persons killed or wounded . (Dip. No. 1104, 3 Apr 45, SRS-1626).

P. 109   "The new Cabinet is devoting itself": Dip. No. 1114, 13 Apr 45, SRS-1636; Dip. No. 1115, 14 Apr 45, SRS-1637.

P. 109   Gorge's initial optimism and "No perceptible difference": Dip. No. 1117, 16 Apr 45, SRS-1639 and Dip. No. 1141, 10 May 45, SRS-1663.

P. 109   "The military and the nation in general are not yet prepared": Dip. No. 1130, 29 Apr 45, SRS-1652. The characterization of Konoe as a "pacifist" (and his reputation as a "liberal") aroused the ire of the Magic editors, who retorted that Konoe had advocated laws giving the government control of capital and labor; had been premier when Japan attacked China and when it signed the Tripartite Pact with Germany and Italy; and had helped establish the rabid Imperial Rule Assistance Association.

P. 109   Deaths of Chinese laborers: Dip. No. 1102, 1 Apr 45, SRS-1624.

P. 110   Messages from Manchurian official: Dip. No. 1086, 16 Mar 45, SRS-1608; Dip. No. 1121, 20 Apr 45, SRS-1643; Dip. No. 1191, 29 Jun 45, SRS-1713.

P. 110   Message from Korean official: Dip. No. 1182, 20 Jun 45, SRS-1704.

P. 110   Hitler or Nazis to fly to Japan: Dip. No. 1128, 27 Apr 45, SRS-1650; SRH-075, pp. 10–11. The aircraft involved was a JU-290 with a

5,600-mile range, scheduled to take a polar route from Bardufoss in northern Norway to Paramushiro, a distance of 4,785 miles.

P. 110 April 28 query in Lisbon: Dip. No. 1131, 30 Apr 45, SRS-1653; SRH-075, p. 4.

P. 111 Sato and Shigemitsu on Soviet treaty: Dip. No. 1055, 13 Feb 45, SRS-1577; Dip. No. 1057, 15 Feb 45, SRS-1579; Dip. No. 1061, 19 Feb 45, SRS-1583; Dip. No. 1087, 17 Mar 45, SRS-1609.

P. 111 Sato gauges Soviet intentions: Dip. No. 1066, 24 Feb 45, SRS-1588; Dip. No. 1069, 27 Feb 45, SRS-1591 (quote on Molotov's "warmth"); Dip. No. 1070, 28 Feb 45, SRS-1592.

P. 111 Sato describes interview with Molotov: Dip. No. 1107, 6 Apr 45, SRS-1629.

P. 111 "Russia will carefully gauge the decline in Japan's military strength": Dip. No. 1116, 15 Apr 45, SRS-1638; Dip. No. 1141, 10 May 45, SRS-1663; Dip. No. 1156, 25 May 45, SRS-1678.

P. 112 Sato's strategic survey: Dip. No. 1143, 12 May 45, SRS-1665.

P. 112 "A spaniel in the presence of a mastiff": SRH-078, p. 10.

P. 112 "We are facing future trouble with Russia": Dip. No. 1164, 2 Jun 45, SRS-1686; SRH-078, p. 11.

P. 113 "In view of our situation": Dip. No. 1166, 4 Jun 45, SRS-1688; SRH-078, p. 12. Hirota's tenure as Premier extended from March 1936 to February 1937, and he had also served as Ambassador to the Soviet Union (1930–1932) and Foreign Minister (1933–1936, 1937–1938). American intelligence analysts noted that during the summer of 1944, Hirota had been the designated "Special Envoy" that Foreign Minister Shigemitsu had proposed to send to Moscow, ostensibly for the purpose of "improving relations," but there had been "various indications that something more was actually involved."

P. 113 "Absolute completeness of unconditional surrender": Dip. No. 1176, 14 Jun 45, SRS-1698.

P. 113 Japanese embassy in Stockholm: Dip. No. 1183, 21 Jun 45, SRS-1705; Dip. No. 1184, 22 Jun 45, SRS-1706; see also Dip. No. 1187, 25 Jun 45, SRS-1709. Butow, *Japan's Decision to Surrender,* p. 56, identifies the military attaché as Major General Makoto Ono. The Ultra sources use Onodera. In a postwar interview, Okamoto explained that on May 10, Wider Bagge, a

Swedish diplomat who had just returned from Tokyo, where Okamoto had known him, paid a call on Okamoto to discuss opening a channel for conducting negotiations with the United States and Britain, in accordance with conversations between Bagge and Foreign Minister Shigemitsu. To Okamoto's keen disappointment, his report of this contact brought a temporizing reply from Tokyo that he must await further instructions. Then Okamoto learned of Onodura's approach to Prince Karl, to open negotiations through a German national of dubious background and with the understanding that a fixed condition for peace would be retention of the Imperial Army. Since Okamoto was convinced that the Allies would never agree to retention of the Imperial Army and Navy, at the behest of Swedish Foreign Minister Gunther, Okamoto reported Onodura's freelance diplomacy to Tokyo. Statement of Suemasa Okamoto, 29 Jul 50, Doc. No. 61477, CMH. On the other hand, Foreign Minister Togo stated at the war-crimes trials that he learned of the Shigemitsu-Bagge arrangement for the first time from the Japanese minister to Finland, Tadashi Sakaya. Togo asserted that he gave his approval to the plan to have the Swedish government approach the Western Allies, but "nothing came of this scheme." IMTFE Togo 35,780.

P. 113 "Japan is firmly determined": Dip. No. 1189, 27 Jun 45, SRS-1711.

P. 114 Messages disclosing the probes at the Vatican and message from the former Japanese ambassador to France: Dip. No. 1143, 12 May 45, SRS-1665; SRH-075, pp. 14–15; Dip. No. 1167, 5 Jun 45, SRS-1689; Dip. No. 1177, 15 Jun 45, SRS-169; Dip. No. 1186, 24 Jun 45, SRS-1708; SRH-088, pp. 11–12.

P. 114 Fujimura's efforts at diplomacy: Dip. No. 1170, 8 Jun 45, SRS-1692; Dip. No. 1176, 14 Jun 45, SRS-1698; Dip. No. 1175, 13 June 45, SRS-1697; Butow, *Japan's Decision to Surrender,* pp. 103–9. Butow provides a fuller account than can be accessed through Ultra material. Fujimura misrepresented to Japan that Allen Dulles's OSS approached him first rather than vice versa, and he lied to the OSS representatives when he told them his government had not responded; in fact, he had been told to exercise extreme caution. Fujimura's German intermediary, Dr. Friederich Hack, was a bizarre German national who for twenty years had aided the Imperial Navy. See also a message from Minister Kase in Dip. No. 1136, 5 May 45, SRS-1658. Kase forwarded the wisdom ascribed to three Swiss banking officials that since "Japan is not an object of world-wide detestation like Nazi Germany," Japan should make a peace offer. Kase had previously nudged things along by warning Tokyo not to accept fleeing Nazi officials.

P. 114 Okamoto's efforts at diplomacy: Butow, *Japan's Decision to Surrender,* pp. 109–11. Reports of contacts by Fujimura and his intermediary, Per Jacobsson, were forwarded to Truman by the OSS. Whether Truman made anything of them, however, is another matter. See the series of OSS Memorandum for the President, 12 May, 4 and 22 June, 13, 16, and 18 July, and 2 and 9 August 1945, Papers of Harry S. Truman, Rose Conway File, HSTL. These contain commentary reflecting the OSS assessment of the authenticity of Fujimura's claims of high contacts and doubts about the Jacobsson conduit.

P. 114 Formosan exchange: Dip. No. 1192, 30 Jun 45, SRS-1714; SRMD-007, 7 July; SRMD-007, 7 July (Navy analysis).

P. 115 "We have received no peace offer": Quoted in Butow, *Japan's Decision to Surrender,* p. 111.

8. Downfall and Olympic Plans

P. 117 Downfall plan: DOWNFALL, Strategic Plans for Operations in the Japanese Archipelago, author's copy. A copy of the DOWNFALL plan may be found in OPD 350.05, Sec. 1, RG 165, NARA.

P. 118 Revised troop list: General Headquarters, SWPAC, Operational Instruction No. 1, 20 June 1945, Annex No. 2, Tentative Troop List; Steven J. Chamberlain Papers, Box 4, United States Army Military History Institute [hereafter USAMHI].

P. 119 Krueger's background: Interviews James F. Collins, sec. 2, p. 40; Clyde Eddleman, sec. 4, pp. 9–10, 11–13; George Decker, p. 20, USAMHI; William M. Leary, ed., *We Shall Return: MacArthur's Commanders and the Defeat of Japan* (Lexington: University of Kentucky Press, 1988), pp. 61–62.

P. 119 Sixth Army Field Order No. 74, 28 July 1945, provides the organization and missions for all of the subordinate units. Strengths are taken from Annex 3, Troop List.

P. 122 Battle casualties for units in Olympic: *Army Battle Casualties and Nonbattle Deaths,* pp. 80–81, 90–91; Personnel Strength Statistics, Personnel Accounting Office, U.S. Marine Corps, 3 April 1950, U.S. Marine Corps Historical Center. Figures for Army losses are adjusted to subtract from the wounded category those who died of wounds received. "Other" provides an accounting category recognized by the Army but without a Marine analogue.

P. 122 Redeployment plans: Robert W. Coakley and Richard M. Leighton, *Global Logistics and Strategy, 1943–1945* (Washington, D.C.: Center of Military History, 1986), pp. 585–86, Appendixes D-3, D-4, pp. 836–37; John D. Miller, *The United States Army in World War II: Organization and Role of the Army Service Forces* (Washington, D.C.: Center of Military History, United States Army, 1954), p. 89. Of the fifteen divisions scheduled for transfer to the Pacific, nine divisions formed the follow-up for Coronet and six were held in a garrison/reserve capacity.

The numbers of servicemen and their proposed routing involved in this mass redeployment were as follows:

Direct from Europe to the Pacific:	395,000
From Europe through the United States:	408,200
Originating in the United States to the Pacific (of which 102,500 were for the B-29 program):	138,500
Return from Europe to remain in the United States:	2,255,000

P. 124 Point system: Coakley and Leighton, *Global Logistics and Strategy,* pp. 594–95; John Ray Skates, *The Invasion of Japan: Alternative to the Bomb* (Columbia: University of South Carolina Press, 1994), pp. 63–65, citing "War Department Demobilization Plan after the Defeat of Germany," in John C. Sparrow, "History of Personnel Demobilization in the United States Army," DA Pamphlet 20-210 (Department of the Army, July 1952), pp. 302–5, 308, 312–13.

P. 124 Demobilization issues: Michael D. Pearlman, *Unconditional Surrender, Demobilization, and the Atomic Bomb* (Fort Leavenworth, Kans.: Combat Studies Institute, U.S. Army Command and General Staff College, 1996), pp. 3, 18–19.

P. 124 ASR scores and new rosters: Skates, *Invasion of Japan,* pp. 65–66. Skates provides by far the best treatment of this critical but neglected issue about the end of the war in the Pacific.

Not surprisingly or unreasonably, MacArthur objected to even partial demobilization of his combat units slated for Olympic, pointing out that "high point men" included a disproportionate share of battle-experienced noncommissioned officers and key specialists. This included an estimated 23,000 enlisted men from the Sixth Army. There was also an overall shortage of officers, which totaled 4,500 just for Olympic units. Marshall overruled MacArthur, and the chief of staff further asked that men with adjusted service ratings above 74 be placed on nonhazardous duty as soon as operations and replacements permitted. *Studies in the History of General Douglas MacArthur's Command in the Pacific,* Part 4, *Final Phase: Plans and Operations to 15 August 1945,* pp. 111–14, RG 4, Box 24, Folder 5, MacArthur Archive.

P. 125 Effects of readjustment: Robert R. Palmer, Bell I. Wiley, and William R. Keast, *The Procurement and Training of Ground Combat Troops* (Washington, D.C.: Office of the Chief of Military History, Department of the Army, 1948), pp. 638–39; Memo A.C. of S., G-1, 5 Jun 45, Enclosure: "Tentative Redeployment Schedule," Marshall Papers, Box 82, Folder 30, Marshall Library; Skates, *Invasion of Japan,* p. 67. The corps headquarters scheduled for redeployment to the Pacific in October 1945 were: the III, V, VII, XIII, and XVIII.

P. 125 Devastating effects of demobilization: Pearlman, *Unconditional Surrender,* pp. 18–19.

P. 125 "Professional heavy weight prize-fighter": Headquarters European Theater of Operations, United States Army, "Battle Experience Against the Japanese," 1 May 1945, p. 2, author's collection.

P. 126 Training program: Palmer, Wiley, and Keast, *Procurement and Training of Ground Combat Troops,* pp. 623–37.

P. 126 Army Air Forces and redeployment: Skates, *Invasion of Japan,* pp. 69–70.

P. 126 Navy and readjustment: Ibid., pp. 70–71; CINCPAC ADV to COMINCH 200729 Jul 45, RG 38, Box 141, Folder Pre-OLYMPIC Dispatches, NARA; *All Hands,* September, October, and November 1945.

P. 126 "The capitulation of Hirohito": Palmer, Wiley, and Keast, *Procurement and Training of Ground Combat Troops,* pp. 646–47.

P. 126 Concern for morale of public and Army: Brower, "Sophisticated Strategist," pp. 326–27; Stimson Diary, esp. January 11 and 18, 1945.

P. 127 "These men were weary": Stimson and Bundy, *On Active Service in Peace and War,* p. 632.

P. 127 50 percent survival rate: Palmer, Wiley, and Keast, *Procurement and Training of Ground Combat Troops,* pp. 232–37; "History of Mobilization," 7 June 45, pp. 29–31; Marshall Papers, Box 77, Folder 1, Marshall Library.

P. 128 The draft through 1944: *Selective Service and Victory: The Fourth Report of the Director of Selective Service* (Washington, D.C.:

Government Printing Office, 1948), pp. 156, 159, 590, 593, 596, tables 136, 138, 140. The total number of inductees in the continental United States from October 1940 to December 1945 was 9,838,691, of whom 8,108,531 went to the Army, 1,526,250 to the Navy, 188,709 to the Marine Corps, and 15,201 to the Coast Guard. The territories of Alaska, Hawaii, Puerto Rico, and the Virgin Islands contributed another 81,711 inductees, but it is not clear to which armed services they were assigned (tables 136 and 138, pp. 590, 593). All inductees prior to January 1943 were furnished to the Army.

P. 128 The draft in 1945: Ibid., pp. 160, 595, table 140.

P. 128 Learned-Smith Report: Palmer, Wiley, and Keast, *Procurement and Training of Ground Combat Troops,* pp. 234–37.

P. 128 Replacement training program in 1945: Ibid., Table No. 1, p. 224.

P. 128 Infantry crisis: *Army Battle Casualties and Nonbattle Deaths,* p. 5. Of 182,701 deaths among battle casualties in all branches save the air corps, the infantry sustained 142,962. On the replacement crisis, see Palmer, Wiley, and Keast, *Procurement and Training of Ground Combat Troops,* "The Provision of Enlisted Replacements."

P. 129 Projections of draft and replacement training: *Selective Service and Victory,* table 140, p. 595. The Navy calls ran at 15,000 to 33,000 and the Marine Corps at only 2,200 to 7,000 between January and July 1945. The percent of the call filled by the Navy was similar to the Army totals, but the Marine Corps met only 34.1 to 53.3 percent of the call. The Marines, however, continued to secure a substantial number of enlistees, particularly those age seventeen who were not yet subject to induction. Voluntary enlistments of men ages eighteen to thirty-seven had ceased on December 4, 1942. From January 1943, men were inducted into all branches of service. Ibid., pp. 160, 593 and table 138. As to what proportion of the inductees were expected to replace actual battle casualties, in a March 1945 study of redeployment the Army Service Forces projected battle casualties as approximately 40,000 per month for the anticipated eighteen months of redeployment. Army Service Forces, Office of Commanding General, 14 March 1945, Memorandum for Member of Ad Hoc Committee on Study of West Coast Problems, Tab "B," Summary of Redeployment Forecast, Atlantic and Pacific Sections, para. 27. Copy provided by Barton Bernstein.

P. 129 Material production plans: War Production Board, "Program for a One-Front War," *War*

Progress, no. 250 (June 30, 1945): 1–8; Confidential File, War Production Board, State Department, Box 36, Folder: War Production Board, 3 of 4 War Progress, April 14–July 14, 1945, HSTL.

P. 129   Logistical plans: Coakley and Leighton, *Global Logistics and Strategy,* pp. 595–97.

P. 130   Papers of Lt. Gen. Arthur Trudeau, USAMHI, Interview pp. 91, 134, 140. For Manila see also Col. N. B. Sauve, USAR Papers, USAMHI "A Personal Account of G-2, USAFIA 1942, USASOS 1942–45, AFWESPAC 1945," and Col. A. E. Schanze, Assistant Chief of Staff, G-1, Eighth Army, Memoir "This Was the Army," A. E. Schanze Papers, both USAMHI.

P. 130   Logistical arrangements: Coakley and Leighton, *Global Logistics and Strategy,* pp. 616–18.

9. The Invasion and the President

P. 131   "I feel like I have been struck": Alonzo L. Hamby, *Man of the People* (New York: Oxford University Press, 1995), p. 293.

P. 131   Truman as a public speaker: Robert J. Donovan, *Conflict and Crisis* (New York: W. W. Norton, 1977), p. 4.

P. 131   "The greatest of men had fallen": David McCullough, *Truman* (New York: Simon and Schuster, 1992), p. 349.

P. 131   Varied opinions on Truman: Donovan, *Conflict and Crisis,* pp. 13–14.

P. 132   "We shall not know what he is really like": Stimson Diary, April 13, 1945.

P. 132   Carrying on the Roosevelt legacy: McCullough, *Truman,* pp. 348, 359–60.

P. 132   Stimson's initial impression of Truman: Although Stimson noted with concern some vacillation and lack of force on seeing Truman on April 12 (Stimson Diary, April 12, 1945), his diary soon shows his satisfaction with the Truman style of governmental decision making, as reflected by Stimson's last comment on the Roosevelt style of cabinet meetings (Diary, April 6–11) referring to "this disorderly administration" versus April 18, 1945, which praises Truman's methodical and decisive approach.

P. 132   "Laboring with the terrific handicap": Ibid., April 13, 1945.

P. 132   Truman briefed on Ultra and atomic bomb: Christopher Andrew, *For the President's Eyes Only* (New York: HarperCollins, 1995), pp. 150–51; Stimson Diary, April 25, 1945. During

his work on what was called the Truman Committee, investigating war contracts, Truman had come across part of the Manhattan Project but had ceased probing as to its purpose at Stimson's request.

P. 132   "I have to decide Japanese strategy": Truman Diary, June 17, 1945, in Robert H. Ferrell, ed., *Off the Record: The Private Papers of Harry S. Truman* (New York: Penguin, 1980), p. 47.

P. 132   "An estimate of the time required": George C. Marshall Papers, Xerox 1567, Marshall Library. A copy is also contained in U.S. Department of Defense, *The Entry of the Soviet Union into the War Against Japan* (Washington, D.C.: Government Printing Office, 1955), p. 76.

P. 132   Public concern over casualties: John D. Chappell, *Before the Bomb: How America Approached the End of the Pacific War* (Lexington: University Press of Kentucky, 1996), chap. 3, pp. 80–82, 84, 104; Robert P. Newman, *Truman and the Hiroshima Cult* (East Lansing: Michigan State University Press, 1995), p. 8.

Besides the 500,000 to one million figure given by Kyle Palmer of the *Los Angles Times* in mid-May, Chappell cites articles warning of casualties of one million or more in such publications as *Newsweek, The New Republic,* and *Life.*

P. 133   Hoover memorandums: At least two memorandums from President Hoover reached the War Department. One, untitled, is attached to a cover memorandum dated June 1, 1945, from General Thomas T. Handy to General Hull, reflecting that Stimson requested the staff's reaction. A response to this dated June 4, 1945, was prepared by the Strategy and Policy Group, Operations Division. Hoover submitted a second and better-known memorandum, "Memorandum on Ending the Japanese War." A cover note dated June 7, 1945, from Fred M. Vinson recommended that President Truman submit it for comment to the State and War Departments and former Secretary of State Cordell Hull, which Truman did on June 9. At the War Department, General Marshall sent a response, "Memorandum of Comments on 'Ending the Japanese War,' " to Stimson on June 15, 1945, who forwarded his comments to the President on June 16. Both Acting Secretary of State Grew and former Secretary of State Hull replied on June 12 and Grew again the day after. Stimson, Hull, and Grew commented primarily on Hoover's proposal to soften terms of surrender and his belief that setting up a postsurrender military government in Japan would be nearly impossible. Copies of these exchanges are found in parts in White House Central Files, Confidential, HSTL, and George C. Marshall Papers, Box 84, Folder 29, and Microfilm Item 3073, Marshall Library. Stimson forwarded Marshall's June 15, 1945, memorandum to Truman on June 16. A copy of this exchange is also found in Memorandum for the Secretary of War from HST with enclosed "Memorandum on Ending the Japanese War," June 9, 1945, from Hoover; JAPAN (after December 7, 1941), Stimson Safe File, RG 107, NARA; Memorandum of Comments, "Ending the Japanese War," 14 June 45, ABC 387 Japan (15 Feb 45), Entry 421, RG 165, NARA. The "very much perturbed" quote is found in Memorandum for General Lincoln, June 16, 1945, from J. E. Hull, Microfilm Item 3073, George C. Marshall Papers, Marshall Library.

P. 133   Harris's comments: Richard G. Davis, *Carl A. Spaatz and the Air War in Europe* (Washington, D.C.: Center for Air Force History, 1993), p. 581.

P. 134   Table of battle deaths: *Army Battle Casualties and Nonbattle Deaths,* p. 10; *History of the Medical Department of the United States Navy,* pp. 3:178–79.

P. 134   Projection of casualties: Giangreco, "Casualty Projections for the U.S. Invasions of Japan, 1945–46: Planning and Policy Implications," *Journal of Military History* 61 (July 1997): 528–31.

P. 135   Ratio of killed to wounded and injured: *Army Battle Casualties and Nonbattle Deaths,* p. 5. The ratio of total battle casualties in wounded and injured in ground branches of the Army (820,877) to battle deaths (182,701) is actually about 4.5 to 1. Of these, the total captured, interned, and missing is 102,160 (12 percent), but this number is skewed by the large numbers of men captured or missing in the Ardennes campaign (26,612). Ibid., p. 92.

P. 135   Ratio of losses in naval and air combat: *History of the Medical Department of the United States Navy,* p. 3:170. Of 69,242 Navy casualties, those killed in action, died of wounds, or died in captivity totaled 36,488 (53 percent). Among naval aviation personnel (including the Marine Corps), deaths number 4,514 of 7,081 total casualties. Ibid., p. 175. The Army Air Forces sustained 115,382 battles casualties, of which 52,173 (45 percent) were deaths. *Army Battle Casualties and Nonbattle Deaths,* p. 5.

P. 135   Projection of casualties by JCS: JCS 924/15, 25 April 1945; CCS 381 Pacific Ocean Operations (6-10-43), Sec. 12, RG 218, Box 686, NARA. According to some contemporary documents, during the first fifteen days troop strength on Kyushu was 427,400 of 766,700 or 340,500 of 681,000. In that circumstance, projections would have worked out to 476,156 and 138,052 total casualties based respectively on Pacific and European experience. Admiral King had expressly objected to these projections with the words "it would be a particular mistake to support the invasion strategy with the quoted figures on casualties. Because of the many differences in the character of combat and enemies in the two theaters, such a comparison of casualties proves nothing." King's comment presumably was aimed mainly at the implication that Pacific operations were markedly more costly, which reflected adversely on the Navy. There was good reason for King to object to the methodology used to compile these numbers, but that would require an extended essay beyond the scope of this work. None of the other members of the JCS registered such disapproval of "the quoted figures on casualties," and when King's memorandum was reviewed by the JCS, the records pointedly indicate that his colleagues adopted the paragraph containing a recommendation to adopt the strategy recommendation in JCS 924/15, but they were silent on the paragraph containing his protest. JCS 925/16, 2 May 45, and the noted action by the JCS on 10 May 45, CCS 381 Pacific Ocean Operations (6-10-43), Sec. 12, RG 218, Box 686, NARA.

P. 137   Nimitz's estimate: Commander in Chief Pacific and Pacific Ocean Area, Joint Staff Study OLYMPIC Naval and Amphibious Operation, Preliminary Draft, 13 May 45, RG 165, Box 1842, NARA. This copy is in the files of the Army Operations Division. The final version of this staff study was issued on June 18. There is no message from King in RG 38 or in the CINCPAC Command Summary paralleling that of Marshall discussed below requesting casualty projections from the theater commander for the June 18 meeting. The presence of this draft might explain why King made no such special request to Nimitz on the casualty question. On the other hand, King might have deemed it the Army's business to explain the casualty projections for an invasion he did not really believe would ever take place.

P. 137   Projection of casualties: "From Olympic to Blacklist," (ms., U.S. Army Center of Military History, n.d.), p. 18, cited in Skates, *Invasion of Japan,* p. 79.

P. 138   Formal request from MacArthur: Marshall to MacArthur, 16 June 45, and MacArthur to Marshall, 17 June 45, RG 4, USAFPAC Correspondence WD, Folder 4, MacArthur Archive.

P. 138   Returned to duty numbers: Postwar medical statisticians calculated that overall, 73.2

percent of all wounded returned to duty in the Southwest Pacific Theater and 73.7 percent of all wounded returned to duty in the Pacific Theater in World War II. Perhaps surprisingly, these numbers are slightly higher than the 72.4 percent figure for all theaters. The average number of days lost to battle injury and wound admission in the Southwest Pacific Theater was 113; for Pacific Ocean areas it was 115. These figures exclude all wounded who were treated and immediately returned to duty. Clearly, that number would have been substantial, and the omission of this category materially depressed the total estimate. Office of the Surgeon General, Department of the Army, *Medical Statistics in World War II* (Washington, D.C.: Government Printing Office, 1975), pp. 56, 110–11, 120–22.

P. 138   Exchange of Marshall and MacArthur: Marshall to MacArthur, 19 Jun 45, and MacArthur to Marshall, 19 Jun 45, RG 4, USAF-PAC Correspondence WD, Folder 4, MacArthur Archive.

P. 139   Casualty estimates by JCS staff and Hull: JWPC 369/1, "Details of the Campaign Against Japan," June 15, 1945, ABC 385, RG 319; JCS 1388, 16 June 1945, "Details of the Campaign Against Japan," Report by the Joint Staff Planners, Geographic File 1942–45, 381 Japan (6-14-45), RG 218, Box 118, NARA. Hull's memorandum to General Eaker and Handy used by Marshall is dated June 17, 1945, and is noted to be a corrected copy of the memorandum prepared by General Lincoln (Marshall Library).

P. 139   Meeting of June 18: "Minutes of Meeting Held at White House on Monday, 18 June 1945 at 1530," Xerox 1567, Marshall Library. All subsequent notations of the exchanges in this conference are from this source.

P. 143   Use of gas warfare: For the background on Marshall's persistent efforts to have the JCS and president consider the use of gas against dug-in Japanese defenders, see OPD 385 TS 1945, Sec. 1, Cases 5–14, copies in George C. Marshall Papers, microfilm reel 119, item 2932, Marshall Library (see also Box 73, Folder 35); Leahy's memo of June 20, 1945, is also in Entry 419, RG 165, Box 166, NARA. Marshall actively pressed for use of poison gas against Japanese troops isolated in caves or bunkers. He had mentioned approaching the President "informally" on this matter within a few days of this meeting, but a memorandum from Leahy on June 20 seems to carry the clear implication that the matter had not been raised with the President by that date, which would rule out discussion on June 18. Leahy's memorandum also indicates that Truman had

stated he would not change American policy of use only in retaliation. Attention continued to be given to stockpiling gas munitions in the Pacific theater preparatory to carrying out the national policy of "immediate and overwhelming" retaliation, which, of course, also would have created a potential option to initiate gas warfare. There was a serious problem in procuring gas munitions, as the diversion of bomb cases to incendiary use absorbed much potential capacity.

P. 144   King's memorandum of June 20: JCS 1388/1, 20 June 1945, "Proposed Changes to Details of the Campaign Against Japan"; Marshall's response: JCS 1338/2, 26 June 1945, "Proposed Changes to Details of the Campaign Against Japan"; the "final" version of "Details of the Campaign Against Japan" was JCS 1388/4, 11 July 1945, which did include the comment on p. 34 that "naval casualties will probably be at about the same rate as for Okinawa." I located no evidence that this was shown to Truman (who as of that date was at sea en route to Potsdam). All of these items are in Geographic File 1942–45, 381 Japan (6-14-45), RG 218, Box 118, NARA.

P. 144   June 18 figures: Rufus Miles, "Hiroshima: The Strange Myth of Half a Million Lives Saved," *International Security* 10 (fall 1985): 121–40, and Barton Bernstein, "A Postwar Myth: 500,000 Lives Saved," *Bulletin of Atomic Scientists* 42 (June–July 1986): 38–40.

P. 144   The misuses of the 31,000 estimate: Recent examples include Adam Goodheart, "The Invasion That Never Was," in Kai Bird and Lawrence Lifschultz, eds., *Hiroshima's Shadow* (Stony Creek, Conn.: The Pamphleteer's Press, 1998), p. 138, and Alperovitz, *Decision to Use the Atomic Bomb*, pp. 518–19. Goodheart states that "Marshall's staff estimated that the invasion of Kyushu would result in about 31,000 casualties." He then adds that there was no formal estimate for Honshu but "that campaign was generally expected to be far less costly in American lives." This is grossly in error. Alperovitz argues that only the 31,000 figure was "actually presented personally and directly to the president." He then acknowledges that the figure was only for the first thirty days but argues that neither Marshall nor Truman expected the war to go beyond thirty days after a landing.

P. 145   Leahy's diary entry: Leahy Diary, June 18, 1945, Library of Congress. The "combat troop" calculations are drawn from: (1) Tentative Troop List "OLYMPIC," USAFPAC Staff Study Ops "OLYMPIC," 28 May 1945, RG 4, Box 40, Folder 2, MacArthur Memorial Archives; (2) General Headquarters, United States Army Forces Pacific, Operations Instructions No. 1, 20

June 1945, Annex No. 2, Tentative Troop List, RG 4, Box 41, Folder 1A, MacArthur Memorial Archives. The two troop lists, one prepared before and one after June 18, 1945, are almost identical as to the combat units and generally give unit strengths for shipping purposes very close to the Table of Organization Strengths in the sources cited below. The major exception is the 11th Airborne Division, which is given as 12,997 in the first troop list but as 8,858 in the second. Source (1) in the recapitulation lists Sixth Army (including V Amphibious Corps) combat total as 382,937. Source (2) lists the Sixth Army combat total as 250,245 (including headquarters, antiaircraft, military police, and signal units) and V Amphibious Corps total as 86,558, or 336,803 combined total.

Shelby Stanton, *Order of Battle U.S. Army World War II* (Novato, Calif.: Presidio Press, 1984), gives June 1945 Table of Organization Strengths for U.S. Army units; Benis M. Frank and Henry I. Shaw, *Victory and Occupation, History of U.S. Marine Corps Operations in World War II*, vol. 5, Historical Branch, G-3 Division, Headquarters, U.S. Marine Corps, 1968, Appendix H (4 September 1945 G-100 Series Tables). There are some very minor discrepancies between figures in troop lists and these strengths, but they are too small to make a material difference.

P. 146   Marshall to MacArthur, 19 June 1945, RG 4, USAFPAC Correspondence WD, Folder 4, MacArthur Archive.

P. 146   Marshall's conviction on need for invasion: Marshall made this explicit point in a film directed by Frank Capra, *On to Tokyo,* shown to millions of soldiers in the summer of 1945 to explain redeployment and strategy to end the war. The creation of this film is instructive. Marshall, ever aware of the importance of explaining to American soldiers the reasoning behind actions from grand strategy to petty details, ordered creation of this film so he could, in effect, speak personally to the millions of men under his command. He stressed that Japan's strategy was based on exhausting American will so that Japan could rise again to strike. He spoke of how American strategy looked to use overwhelming amounts of material rather than blood to defeat Japan.

P. 146   Japanese strength on Luzon: Drea, *MacArthur's Ultra,* p. 184. Smith, *Triumph in the Philippines,* appendixes C-2, H-2, puts Japanese strength at about 275,000, but I follow Drea's number of 287,000, as it is based on an authoritative Japanese source.

P. 147   "Unless speed is considered so important": CINCPAC to COMINCH, 28 Apr 45 and

CINCPAC to COMINCH, 051725 May 45, Command Summary, Book 6, January 1945 to July 1945, p. 3232, NHC. According to a postwar interview with Vice Admiral Bernhard H. Bieri, King's Chart Room operation, into which messages from Nimitz flowed, had extremely restricted access, as did the White House Map Room. This sheds light on how King could keep the May 25 message from Nimitz secret. Interview, VADM Bernhard H. Bieri, pp. 230–31, NHC.

10. Pummeling and Strangling: Bombardment and Blockade, June to August

P. 149   Strategic planning for incendiary raids: USAF HC File 760.01, 1 Jul–2 Sep 1945, vol. 14, Headquarters Twentieth Air Force, Office of the A-3, Subject: Attacks on Small Urban Industrial Areas, 21 July 1945. Although the date of this report is the later part of July, the analysis distilled in this document represents thinking evident from mid-June in individual mission reports.

P. 150   Detailed plans for incendiary attacks: USAF HC Files 760.309-3, Bombing Activities 20th Air Force, p. 12; File 760.302-1 10 Jul–24 Aug, 20th AF Weekly Activities Report, 25 Jul, for 15–22 July; File 760.322 Apr–Aug 1945, 21st Bomber Command Plans Book; Foreign Affairs Association of Japan (Tokyo), *The Japan Year Book 1943–44,* republished by the Interdepartmental Committee for the Acquisition of Foreign Publications (n.d.), p. 35, MCHC; USAF HC Files 7603.322, 760.302-1 10 Jul–24 Aug 20th AF Weekly Activities Report, week of 6–13 August, AFHC. "Burn jobs" is from p. 8 of a copy of an untitled draft article by Charles Murphy of *Time* magazine in Spaatz Papers, Library of Congress, Box 2, Folder: August (1945).

P. 150   Raids, night of June 17–18: XXI BC MR, nos. 206–9, pp. 1–3, 6–8.

P. 151   Results of raids: Ibid., pp. 9–11, Consolidated Statistical Summary; *Hondo Boku Sakusen,* Table 63. Figures from table 63 were based on the Comprehensive Report on the Damages in the Pacific War (published on April 7, 1947) by the Economic Stabilization Board. Hamamatsu had been used as a target of opportunity often in the past and was attacked again after June 17, as well as subjected to naval bombardment. Likewise, Yokkaichi was subject to several attacks during the war, but neither was subjected to concentrated area attacks as on this night.

P. 151   Raids of June 1945: XXI BC MR, nos. 210–12, pp. 1–3, 6–8; nos. 234–37, pp. 1–2, 4, 7–10, 14, 37, 39, Consolidated Statistical Summaries; *Hondo Boku Sakusen,* Table 63.

P. 151   Raid of June 22: XXI BC MR, nos. 215–20, pp. 1–3, 8, 10–11, 36–38, Consolidated Statistical Summaries.

P. 151   Raid of June 26: XXI BC MR, nos. 223–31, pp. 1–4, 16–21, 24–25, 27–28, 35–38, 52–53, 57–58, Consolidated Statistical Summaries.

P. 152   315th Wing campaign: 20th AF MR, nos. 232, 238, 245, 255, 261, 267, 270, 281, 283, 291, 303, 310, 315, 322, 328. For the intelligence estimate, see SRMD-008, p. 241, 11 June p. 1.

P. 152   Raid of July 24: 20th AF MR, nos. 284–90, Consolidated Statistical Summaries; *Hondo Boku Sakusen,* Table 63.

P. 152   Incendiary attacks on Japanese cities in July: July 1–2: XXI BC MR, nos. 240–43, pp. 1–4, 9–11, 14–15, Consolidated Statistical Summaries; July 3–4: XXI BC MR, nos. 247–50, Consolidated Statistical Summaries, *Hondo Boku Sakusen,* Table 63; July 6–7: XXI BC MR, nos. 251–54, pp. 1–10, 45–55, Consolidated Statistical Summaries, *Hondo Boku Sakusen,* Table 63; July 9–10: XXI BC MR, nos. 257–60, pp. 1–13, 36, 42–43, Consolidated Statistical Summaries, *Hondo Boku Sakusen,* Table 63; July 12–13: XXI BC MR, nos. 263–66, pp. 1–13, 29–31, Consolidated Statistical Summaries, *Hondo Boku Sakusen,* Table 63 (death tolls are from Tsuruga and Uwajima only); July 16–17: XXI BC MR, nos. 271–74, Consolidated Statistical Summaries, *Hondo Boku Sakusen,* Table 63; July 19–20: 20th AF MR, nos. 277–81, *Hondo Boku Sakusen,* table 63; July 25–26: 20th AF MR, nos. 293–95, Consolidated Statistical Summaries, *Hondo Boku Sakusen,* Table 63; July 28–29: 20th AF MR, nos. 297–302, pp. 13–14, USAF HC File 760.308-1, pp. 7, 31, USAF HC.

P. 153   Command changes: Washington (JCS) to MacArthur and Nimitz, WX-10463, 2 June 1945; Washington (JCS), WX-30438, 11 July 1945, RG 4, Box 17, Folder 4, MacArthur Archive; LeMay and Kantor, *Mission with LeMay,* pp. 386–87; Coffey, *Iron Eagle,* p. 178.

P. 153   Preattack warnings: 20th AF MR, nos. 297–302, pp. 13–14; USAF HC File 760.308-1, pp. 7, 31, USAF HC.

P. 154   Attacks of August 1: 20th AF MR, nos. 306–9, pp. 1–13, Consolidated Statistical Summaries; *Hondo Boku Sakusen,* Table 63. There are no death totals for Hachioji, but for the three other towns, including Toyama, the toll was 3,534.

P. 154   Raids of August 5: 20th AF MR, nos. 312–16, pp. 1–12, Consolidated Statistical Summaries; *Hondo Boku Sakusen,* Table 63; damage

to Saga and Maebashi from Craven and Cate, *The Pacific,* p. 675.

P. 154   "This is the most important change": SRMD-008, p. 156, 6 July p. 1.

P. 155   Submarine attacks in Sea of Japan: Clay Blair, *Silent Victory: The U.S. Submarine War Against Japan* (Philadelphia: J. B. Lippincott, 1975), pp. 832–40; *Warship XI* (Annapolis: Naval Institute Press, n.d.), p. 59; Johnson and Katcher, *Mines Against Japan,* p. 125; SRMD-008, p. 130, 15 June p. 1; 12 Jun 45, SRS-449.

P. 155   Aircraft attacks on shipping lanes: USSBS, *Offensive Mine Laying Campaign Against Japan,* pp. 3–4.

P. 156   "The success of the mining program cannot be assessed": SRMD-008, p. 191, 27 July p. 1.

P. 156   Korean ports and air attacks on railroads: SRMD-008, p. 160, 13 July p. 1; p. 162, 13 July p. 3; pp. 176–77, 20 July pp. 1–2; p. 198, 27 July p. 6, shows orders to remove twenty twin 25-mm machine-gun mounts from destroyers to defend vital Korean ports; SRMD-008, p. 209, 3 Aug p. 1; SRMD-008, 6 Aug p. 6; XXI BC MR, nos. 262, 268; Johnson and Katcher, *Mines Against Japan,* pp. 130, 190, 197–98.

P. 156   Losses of Japanese shipping: Joint Army Navy Assessment Committee (JANAC), *Japanese Naval and Merchant Shipping Losses During World War II by All Causes,* February 1947, NHC. JANAC was organized to make sure the apportionment of credit for sinking Japanese vessels was divided fairly between the services. The JANAC review did not extend to vessels below five hundred tons.

P. 157   July 10 fast carrier attack: ComSecond-Car Task Force, Pac, Serial 00242, 31 August 45, Subject: Action Report 2 July to 15 August [this was the report of Admiral McCain, Commander Task Force 38 and hereafter is cited as COMCTF 38 Serial 00242]; Naval Aviation Combat Statistics World War II, Air Branch, Office of Naval Intelligence, Office of the Chief of Naval Operations, 17 June 1946, p. 38. Copy in author's possession.

P. 157   Significance of rail ferries: COMCTF 38 Serial 00242; SRMD-008, pp. 160, 176, 200–202; 13 July p. 1; 20 July p. 1; 27 July pp. 10–12. According to American figures, of the total Japanese production of 40 million tons of coal, Kyushu supplied 26 million and Hokkaido 10 million, of which Honshu received 18.4 million tons—9 million tons by rail from Kyushu via Kammon, 4 million tons by water and 2 million tons by rail ferry from Hokkaido, and 2 million tons by sea. Karafuto supplied another 1.4 million tons. After the Third Fleet strike, rail-ferry movement from Hokkaido was suspended.

P. 157   Attacks on rail ferries: COMCTF 38 Serial 00242; USSBS, no. 54, Transportation Division, *The War Against Japanese Transportation, 1941–1945,* p. 95; David Brown, *Warship Losses of World War Two* (London: Arms and Armor Press, 1990), p. 154; Barrett Tillman, *Hellcat: The F6F in World War II* (Annapolis: Naval Institute Press, 1979), p. 222; Map Room Files 17 July 1945, Naval Aide Files, HSTL; Morison, *Victory in the Pacific,* pp. 311–12.

P. 157   Attacks of July 14–18: *Operational Experience of Fast Battleships: World War II, Korea, Vietnam* (Washington, D.C.: Naval Historical Center, 1989); COMCTF 38 Serial 00242.

P. 158   Attacks, July 24–30: CINCPAC ADV TO COM3rdFLT 11 2335 July 45, CINCPAC Command Summary, p. 3,488; *Operational Experience of Fast Battleships;* Brown, *Warship Losses of World War Two,* pp. 155–56. LeMay challenged the utility of striking Hamamatsu, a city southeast of Nagoya along the coast, which was for month after month "Hometown for the B-29's." If for any reason the primary target could not be hit, Hamamatsu was. LeMay says he did not give mission credit for this. LeMay and Kantor, *Mission with LeMay,* pp. 376–78. The Strategic Bombing Survey afforded a different view of these bombardments. While conceding that they had little economic effect before the end of the war, "there is considerable evidence . . . that the attack, in combination with other pressures, . . . had considerable influence in lowering the will to continue the war of the local populations which were subjected to gunfire from heavy ships." The American scholar is Gerhard L. Weinberg, author of *A World at Arms: A Global History of World War II* (Cambridge: Cambridge University Press, 1994), p. 499n.

P. 158   Operation Damocles: COMCTF 38 Serial 00242. The fascinating intelligence story is laid out in SRMD-008, pp. 271, 279, 288; 23 Jul p. 1; 30 Jul p. 1; 6 Aug p. 1. See also 14 Jul 45, SRS-481; 26 Jul 45, SRS-493; 4 Aug 45, SRS-502. See also *Air Defense of the Homeland,* Japanese Monograph No. 25, pp. 68, 73. The Japanese code name was "Katana," "Ken-Go," or "Operation Sword." Originally, intelligence analysts figured Iwo Jima or Okinawa as the targets, but the fitting of auxiliary fuel tanks to transport aircraft and the erection of a B-29 mock-up in the training area disclosed the Marianas objective. Weinberg, *World at Arms,* p. 876, reports this operation originally was conceived as an attack by submarine on the American West Coast to destroy aircraft factories.

P. 158   "It is my intent": Naval Aide Files, Map Room, Box 6, Berlin Conference, Communications from Map Room, 26 July to 2 August 1945, Folder 1, HSTL.

P. 159   Japanese submarine aircraft plan: Robert C. Mikesh, *Aichi M6A1 Seiran: Japan's Submarine Launched Panama Canal Bomber,* Monogram Close Up No. 13 (Boylston, Ala.: Monogram Aviation Publications, 1975); examples of the close watch on this operation by radio intelligence are found in SRMD-007, 5, 6, 24 July, 17 Aug; SRH-203, 8/9 Jul, no. 86; and SRMD-008, p. 256, 2 Jul. p. 1.

P. 159   Loss of *Underhill* and *Indianapolis:* Morison, *Victory in the Pacific,* pp. 315–30.

P. 160   "If he lay on one side": Gavan Daws, *Prisoners of the Japanese* (New York: William Morrow, 1994), p. 343. This work is a masterpiece of research and writing.

P. 160   Forrest Knox: Ibid., pp. 18, 30, 96, 343. Daws points out that the exact figures for Allied prisoners of war are hard to ascertain. He sets figures at about a total of 320,000 captured by Japan, of whom about 180,000 were other Asians: Filipinos serving with Americans, Indians and Chinese serving with British, and Indonesians serving with the Dutch. The Japanese released a great majority of the Asians serving with the Allies. Another study by Van Waterford, *Prisoners of the Japanese in World War II* (Jefferson, N.C.: McFarland and Co., 1994), p. 146, gives numbers for POW captives at plus or minus 193,000 and deaths at 60,600.

P. 160   U.S. Army POWs: Bernard M. Cohen and Maurice Z. Cooper, *A Follow-Up Study of World War II Prisoners of War* (Washington, D.C.: Department of Medicine and Surgery, Veterans Administration, 1954), Table 2, p. 4. A total of 1,416 naval personnel (Navy and Marine Corps) died in Japanese captivity (versus three held by Germany). I could not, however, locate a figure for the total number of U.S. naval personnel taken prisoner by the Japanese. *History of the Medical Department of the United States Navy,* vol. 3, pp. 170–71. E. Bartlett Kerr, *Surrender and Survival* (New York: William Morrow, 1985), pp. 339–40, gives total U.S. POWs (Army and Navy) at 25,600, of whom 10,650 were listed as killed or died, a ratio of 42 percent. These figures probably understate the number of naval personnel taken prisoner, thus somewhat increasing the percentage of deaths.

P. 160   "To be a prisoner of the Japanese": Daws, *Prisoners of the Japanese,* p. 361.

P. 160   *Romusha:* Ibid., p. 208; Waterford, *Prisoners of the Japanese in World War II*, p. 146.

P. 160   Burma-Siam railroad: The figures for fatalities among Allied POWs are from Daws, *Prisoners of the Japanese*, pp. 222–23. "The Death Railway" *After the Battle* 26 (1979): 1, gives the Japanese totals for "workers" cited in the text. As to deaths among *romusha*, "The Death Railway" puts the figures as between 80,000 and 100,000. The text figure is derived by subtracting the number of Allied POW dead from the total dead given in Newman, *Truman and the Hiroshima Cult.*

P. 161   "When the bodies started to char": Daws, *Prisoners of the Japanese*, p. 212.

P. 161   Deaths among POWs shipped by Japan: Ibid., p. 297.

P. 161   Killing of prisoners upon threat of liberation: Ibid., pp. 278–79, 324.

P. 161   "An entry in the Japanese headquarters journal": Ibid., p. 325.

P. 161   Killing of airmen: Ibid., pp. 277, 321–22.

P. 162   "A charnel house of atrocities:" Ibid., p. 363.

P. 162   Estimates of Chinese losses: The ten million figure is from Dower, *War Without Mercy,* pp. 295–96, while the fifteen million figure (a "reasonable approximation") is from Weinberg, *World at Arms,* p. 894. Dower subsequently set the death toll at "perhaps 15 million" in *Embracing Defeat: Japan in the Wake of World War II* (New York: W. W. Norton/New Press, 1999). The highest figures are from James C. Hsiung and Steven I. Levine, eds., *China's Bitter Victory* (New York: M. E. Sharpe, 1992), p. 295 and note. Hsiung reports he verified the eighteen million civilian and four million military figure in person at the "Nanking Second Archival Center, whose holdings of archival materials on the War of Resistance are considered unsurpassed in China today." The lowest figure mentioned by Dower and Newman is two million, the highest thirty million. The low-range figure appears to be based on statements about Chinese military losses alone.

P. 163   Deaths due to Japanese empire, 1931–1945: Newman, *Truman and the Hiroshima Cult,* pp. 134–39.

11. Ketsu Operation on Kyushu

P. 164   Symbolism of Kyushu: Harries and Harries, *Soldiers of the Sun,* p. 6.

P. 164   Kyushu terrain: CCS 417/11, 22 Jan 45, Appendix A, Kyushu Terrain Estimate, p. 18; 381 POA (6-10-43), Sec. 11, RG 218, Box 686; JWPC 363/1 27 Jun, Encl. B, p. 21; 381 POA (6-10-43), RG 218, Box 6; *Hondo Boku Sakusen,* Table 62, shows a combined population in 1944 for the seven prefectures on Kyushu of 10,041,290 (Fukuoka, 3,066,472; Oita, 973,707; Saga, 705,651; Kumamoto, 1,371,005; Nagasaki, 1,490,890; Miyazaki, 839,556; and Kagoshima, 1,594,009). Of six major cities, only one—Kagoshima with 190,257 inhabitants—was perched in the southern part of the island.

P. 165   Kyushu terrain features: CCS 417/11, 22 Jan 45, Appendix A, Kyushu Terrain Estimate, pp. 18–19; 381 POA (6-10-43), Sec. 11, RG 218, Box 686.

P. 165   Hata background: Richard Fuller, *Shokan: Hirohito's Samurai* (London: Arms and Armor Press, 1992), pp. 96–97; Butow, *Japan's Decision to Surrender,* pp. 32–33; Donald M. Goldstein, Katherine V. Dillon, and J. Michael Wenger, *Rain of Ruin: A Photographic History of Hiroshima and Nagasaki* (Washington, D.C.: Brassy's, 1995), p. 41. The headquarters of the Second General Army was the same building used by the Emperor Meiji as a command post during the Sino-Japanese war in the late nineteenth century.

P. 165   Organization and assessments of Second General Army: *Hondo Kessen Junbi,* pp. 273–76.

P. 166   Opportunity created by Okinawa: Ibid., p. 444. Contemporaneous plans at IGHQ reflected four reinforcing divisions.

P. 166   "A Matter Concerning the Thorough Understanding . . .": Imperial Headquarters directive of June 20, Ibid., pp. 445–46. According to Colonel Ichiji Sugita, the misconception as to the nature of the decisive battle in the Homeland arose because of the failure of Imperial Headquarters to initially clarify its concept, and because the field commanders, from battle lessons on Saipan and Leyte, "feared the enemy's bombardment, bombing and attacks by flame-throwing tanks. Thus, they slighted the coast and its important flat lands and constructed cave positions in the rear areas with altitude advantage, and went so far as to resort to passive defensive measures which lacked the greatest prerequisite for the decisive battle in Japan proper and the spirit to fight it out." Statement of Col. Ichiji Sugita, Doc. No. 58553, Statements of Japanese Officials on World War II, General Headquarters, Far East Command, Military Intelligence Section, Historical Division, CMH. The Sixteenth

Area Army discerned that topography precluded any further effort to advance positions toward the water's edge but did correct the dispositions of the Fifty-fifth Army on Shikoku.

P. 166 Division Fighting Training Guidelines: *Hondo Kessen Junbi,* pp. 302–3.

P. 167 Hata inspection: Ibid., pp. 447–49. Hata decided as a result of his inspection that the original goal of completing general preparations by the end of June was unobtainable, and he therefore moved the deadline back to the end of July.

P. 167 Reinforcement of Kyushu: The Second General Army's original reinforcement plan of three to five divisions is in ibid., p. 444. Contemporaneous plans at IGHQ reflected four reinforcing divisions. The story of the effort to secure a portion of the Thirty-sixth Army is covered in Maj. Gen. Joichiro Sanada, "Statement on the Operational Preparations for the Defense of Kyushu," Doc. No. 58513, CMH; Col. Ichiji Sugita, Statement Concerning Homeland Defense in 1945, Doc. No. 53241, CMH. The chief of the Imperial Army's intelligence section, Lieutenant General Arisue, commented after the war that the reason why Imperial Headquarters deferred a decision to dispatch "the decisive battle forces in the Kanto Area to the Kyushu Area" was lack of sound intelligence. Statement of Lt. Gen. Arisue, Doc. No. 61660, CMH.

There is also evidence that, had the war gone on, orders might have been issued to send part of the Thirty-sixth Army south. According to Colonel Hiromu Hosoda of the operations staff of Army Section, IGHQ, Chief of Staff Umezu favored redeployment of the Thirty-sixth Army over opposition from the operations staff. Movement of the Thirty-sixth Army was recognized as having "an extremely important effect" on the Homeland operation, and avoidance of interruption of the logistical buildup on Kyushu by diverting transportation facilities to move all or part of the army, as well as disruption of training of the army's units, also favored deferring the decision. Hosoda believed that a decision to transfer the Thirty-sixth Army would have been made at the end of August. Statement of Col. Hiromu Hosoda, Doc. No. 54477, CMH. Major General Amano stated that the transfer plan had been adopted but "was awaiting the proper time for the transfer." Statement of Maj. Gen. Masakasu Amano, Doc. No. 59617, pp. 1–2, CMH. It is extremely likely, however, that within a few days or weeks of when the war actually ended, the destruction of Japan's railways would have halted any effort to move units to Kyushu.

P. 167 Estimate of Sixteenth Area Army staff: *Hondo Kessen Junbi,* p. 294.

P. 167 Japanese appreciation of American landing tactics: Ibid., pp. 294–95; and Maj. Gen. Yasumasa Yoshitake, "Statement Concerning the Estimate of U.S. Army Plan of Invasion-Against Southern Kyushu During the Period from April 1945 to August 1945 and Changes in the Operational Plans and Preparations of the 57 Army," p. 5, CMH.

P. 168 Early assessment of American landing sites: *Hondo Kessen Junbi,* pp. 294–96, 458–59.

P. 168 May 15 Sixteenth Area Army plan: Ibid., pp. 298–300. Operation Number One had three subdivisions: I ("A"), the Miyazaki Area; Ro ("B"), the Ariake Area; Ha ("C"), the Satsuma Peninsula. Operation Number Two covered two areas in northern Kyushu: Ni ("D"), the Shimonoseki-Moji area, and Ho ("E"), the Nagasaki-Sasebo area. Operation Number Three looked to central Kyushu: He ("F"), the Amakusa area, and To ("G"), the Bungo Strait area.

P. 168 Sixteenth Area Army anticipates airborne assaults: Ibid., pp. 300–302.

P. 169 Sixteenth Area Army final directives: Ibid., pp. 460–65.

P. 169 Planning the major counterattack: Ibid., pp. 301, 465. Interestingly, an American assessment prepared in July 1944 likewise recognized the superior political and strategic value of northern Kyushu but ruled out an attack there due to the "grave disadvantages" of difficult and strongly defended sea approaches, lack of suitable beaches for landing and buildup, and the daunting prospect of substantial urban fighting amid a much larger hostile population. JWPC 235/1n 14 Jul 44, Plan for Operations Against Kyushu, Encl. B, p. 14, RG 218, Box 660.

P. 169 Coastal defense plans: *Hondo Kessen Junbi,* pp. 467, 470–71.

P. 170 Decisive battle-division plans: Ibid., pp. 305–6. These instructions for the counterattack divisions were actually issued on April 19 but are placed here for clarity and to avoid repetition.

P. 170 Sixteenth Area Army Counterattack Operations Plans: Ibid., pp. 467–69. On June 10, 1945, with the destruction of the Thirty-second Army on Okinawa, the 64th IMB located on the Amami Oshima islands (north of Okinawa) was assigned to the operational control of the Sixteenth Area Army.

P. 171 Fifty-sixth Army arrangements: Ibid., pp. 338–42, 350, 460, 552–56. The Fifty-sixth Army actually commenced to exercise command on April 26.

P. 171 Fifty-seventh Army organization and strength: Ibid., pp. 308–9, 353; Fifty-seventh Army Table of Strength and Equipment, August 1, 1945. The Army's artillery units included one heavy and two field-gun battalions, and three heavy or field heavy artillery regiments.

P. 171 Defenses of Tanega Shima: Japanese Plans for the Defense of Kyushu, pp. 2–3; John J. Tolson Papers, USAMHI; *Hondo Kessen Junbi,* pp. 313–15; and Maj. Gen. Yasumasa Yoshitake, "Statement Concerning the Estimate of U.S. Army Plan of Invasion," p. 4, CMH. The 109th IMB comprised six battalions of infantry mustering 4,590 men, supported by twelve field guns, a dozen 25-mm antiaircraft machine guns, and headquarters, engineer, communication, and medical units.

P. 171 Initial focus of the Fifty-seventh Army: *Hondo Kessen Junbi,* pp. 311–13.

P. 171 Final assessment of the Fifty-seventh Army: Ibid., pp. 458–60; Maj. Gen. Yasumasa Yoshitake, "Statement Concerning the Estimate of U.S. Army Plan of Invasion," pp. 6–7, CMH.

P. 171 Miyazaki front: *Hondo Kessen Junbi,* pp. 594–95.

P. 171 American tanks and Japanese antitank measures: Appleman, Burns, Gugeler, and Stevens, *Okinawa,* pp. 255–56, 386–87; 412; Huber, *Japan's Battle of Okinawa,* pp. 68–71; Charles M. Baily, *Faint Praise: American Tanks and Tank Destroyers During World War II* (Hamden, Conn.: Archon Books, 1983), pp. 1, 118; and Lt. Col. Yoshitaka Yoshinaga, "Statement Concerning Anti-tank Arms of the Japanese Army Forces in Preparation for the 1945 Homeland Operations," CMH. One source gives the penetration capabilities at 30 degrees obliquity of the Japanese Type 94 37-mm gun as 24 mm (about one inch) at 400 yards and of the Type 1 47-mm as 50 mm (about two inches) at 500 yards. Peter Chamberlain and Terry Gander, *World War 2 Fact Files: Anti-Tank Weapons* (New York: Arco Publishing, 1974), pp. 30–31. The armor of the M4 and the M26 was as follows:

	Hull front	Hull sides	Turret front	Turret sides
M4	2.5 inches	1.5 inches	3.0 inches	2.0 inches
M26	4.0 inches	3.0 inches	4.0 inches	3.0 inches

R. P. Hunnicutt, *Pershing: A History of the Medium Tank T20 Series* (Berkeley: Feist Publications, 1971), p. 217; R. P. Hunnicutt, *Sherman: A History of the American Medium Tank* (Belmont, Calif.: Taurus Enterprises, 1978), p. 545. Lieutenant Colonel Yoshinaga also mentions that

hollow-charge shells were being developed for many artillery weapons (such as the Type 92 70-mm infantry gun and the Type 41 mountain howitzer) as well as a 40-mm rifle grenade, and that superior high-velocity guns of 75 mm or greater bore were under development but not fielded. Mobility is strongly influenced by ground pressure. Ground pressure of the M26, at 12.5 pounds per square inch, was superior to early model Shermans (14.5 pounds per square inch) but inferior to late model Shermans (10.8 pounds per square inch). This mobility issue was to arise again in Korea, where the Sherman proved superior.

Orders were issued in July to ship 125 M26 tanks to reequip the 767th Tank Battalion at Hawaii with fifty-four (seventeen tanks in each of three companies) and the 706th Tank Battalion on Luzon with seventy-one (seventeen tanks in each of four companies). In lieu of the six 105-mm howitzer tanks on the M26 chassis (T26E2), each battalion would receive six M4A3 tanks with 105-mm howitzers. The 767th would receive seventeen M24 light tanks, but the 706th would not have a light tank company. George C. Marshall Papers, OPD 400 TS (30 Jun 45), Memo For Record, 2 July 45, Subject: Requirements for M 26 Heavy Tanks, reel 119, item 2945, Marshall Library. On the 767th Tank Battalion, see also CG U.S. Army Forces, Middle Pacific to War Department, No. RJ 67423, 4 Aug 45, RG 165, Box 39, Folder Top Secret Incoming Msgs OPD Jul 28–Aug 17, 1945, NARA.

P. 172 156th Division strength and defense scheme: Japanese Plans for the Defense of Kyushu, p. 19; John J. Tolson Papers, USAMHI; *Hondo Kessen Junbi,* pp. 316, 318–22, 519 (see particularly fig. 22, p. 318) and attachment, "Organization of Units of the Second General Army," which provides details of table of organization strength and equipment. The three large coastal "containment" regiments were authorized 3,850 men each, in three 889-man battalions plus an additional 537-man counterattack battalion. The fourth ("counterattack") infantry regiment fielded 3,207 men. There are some discrepancies between the deployments described in the document in the Tolson papers and *Hondo Kessen Junbi,* but they presumably arise from the fact that *Hondo Kessen Junbi* describes the deployments of the 156th in detail, whereas the other source is describing more general deployments. I believe that there is an implication in *Hondo Kessen Junbi* that the deployments of the 156th Division were particularly skilled.

P. 172 154th Division arrangements: *Hondo Kessen Junbi,* pp. 322–23, 519–20, Attached Table One, Units of the Second General Army.

P. 173 212th Division arrangements: Ibid., pp. 323–26. Specifically, the 212th was deployed with the entire 518th Infantry Regiment in the sector immediately adjacent to the 154th Division and the 516th Infantry Regiment (less one battalion) to the north of the 518th Regiment. The remaining forces of the division thus comprised only the 517th Infantry Regiment and one battalion of the 516th.

P. 173 Fifty-seventh Army tank brigades: Ibid., pp. 520–21; attachments "General Description of the Strength of the 57th Army, as investigated on August 1, 1945" and "Organization of the Units of the Second General Army"; Hunnicutt, *Sherman*, p. 513; Raymond Surlemont, *Japanese Armor* (Milwaukee: Z and M Enterprises, 1976), pp. 34–40. The "gun tank" was apparently the Type 2, Ho-I, fitted with a short-barrel 75-mm gun. The self-propelled guns presumably were among the small number of 150-mm guns mounted on a Type 97 tank chassis. Although the Japanese history series is not explicit on the numbers of Type 3 Chi-Nu tanks issued, Surlemont includes (p. 20) a photograph of a group of them on Kyushu, "outside Hakata," thus presumably the 4th Tank Brigade or en route to the 5th or 6th Tank Brigade in the southern part of the island. The presentation in "Organization of the Units of the Second General Army" expressly states that the brigades were receiving an upgrade of equipment.

P. 173 Status and preparations of the 86th Division and attached units: *Hondo Kessen Junbi,* pp. 327–38; ms., LTC Keisuke Matsumoto, Japanese Self Defense Forces Staff College, October 1987, "Preparations for Decisive Battle in Southern Kyushu in Great East Asia War," pp. 55–58, presented at the U.S.-Japan Military History Exchange Conference, CMH; Statement of Maj. Katsunori Kai, 15 Sep 49, Doc. No. 50732, CMH. The 98th IMB was technically less two of its four infantry battalions but had the 364th Infantry Regiment attached.

P. 174 Progress of 86th Division preparations: *Hondo Kessen Junbi,* 522–24.

P. 174 25th Division and I Advanced Tank Corps: Ibid., pp. 524–25. Surprisingly, *Hondo Kessen Junbi* is obscure about the I Advanced Tank Corps, but V Amphibious Corps, Operations Report, Occupation of Japan, Annex Charlie, Appendix 4, Detailed Order of Battle VAC Area, lists 1st "Special" Tank Unit of 350 men, which appears to be this unit, and the April 1946 report of the British Combined Observers states that it had twenty-seven light tanks. Report by British Combined Observers (Pacific), "Report of Operation OLYMPIC and Japanese Counter-measures," April 4, 1946, CAB 106, no. 97, Public Record Office Kew.

P. 174 Transfer of Fortieth Army and order of battle: *Hondo Kessen Junbi,* pp. 358–61, 460. The Fortieth Army had been activated in January 1945 under the then standard organization table of thirty-eight officers, ninety-nine enlisted men, and thirty-two horses. The decision to remove the army's headquarters from Taiwan likely also reflected the judgment that it was now very unlikely that the Americans would attempt to seize Taiwan and that the forces there could not play an active role in the war. On May 1, the 3rd Amphibious Brigade was ordered to the Sixteenth Area Army. It was redesignated on May 23 as the 125th IMB and subsequently subordinated to the 146th Division before both units were transferred to the Fortieth Army (ibid., pp. 350–51). The other significant units assigned to the Fortieth Army included one independent field-gun regiment, one regiment and one battalion of heavy artillery, one regiment and one battalion of field heavy artillery, one self-propelled gun battalion, three trench mortar battalions, and one independent light tank company.

P. 175 Emphasis on Kagoshima Bay: Ibid., pp. 362–63; Statement of Major Kinjiro Tokaji (Operations Officer, 40th Army), CMH.

P. 175 Fortieth Army operational plan: *Hondo Kessen Junbi,* pp. 362–65. Reinforcements of the 146th Division included the 435th Independent Infantry Battalion, two trench mortar battalions, an independent tank company, a field-gun regiment and several other field heavy and heavy artillery battalions. Reinforcements of the 206th Division included a field heavy artillery battalion and one company of a field-gun regiment.

P. 175 Status of 146th Division and 125th Brigade: Ibid., pp. 537–43.

P. 175 Status of 303rd and 77th Divisions: Ibid., pp. 544–45; Statement of Major Kinjiro Tokaji, pp. 3–4, CMH.

P. 175 Status of 206th Division: *Hondo Kessen Junbi,* pp. 545–46.

P. 175 Overall status of the Fortieth Army: Figures are from Appendix 4, Annex Charlie, Operations Report, Occupation of Japan, V Amphibious Corps, MCHC. The itemized list of units shows a few for which neither authorized nor on-hand strength was available, thus the figures for both were presumably somewhat, but not markedly, higher.

P. 176 Other units on Kyushu: *Hondo Kessen Junbi,* pp. 565–75.

P. 176 *Kaisenbun:* USSBS, no. 64, pp. 65, 89 (Exhibit T), 91 (Exhibit V), 97. The totals are from a translation of a Japanese staff officer logistics manual dated October 10, 1943, that was captured on Saipan. A *Kaisenbun* weighed 2,500 to 3,000 metric tons. In calculating division equivalents, three independent mixed or tank brigades are counted as one division.

P. 177 Supply priority to Kyushu units: Statement of Lt. Col. Kyoshi Ohta, pp. 1–2, CMH. By way of comparison, a staff officer at Imperial Headquarters reported that the First General Army possessed somewhat less than 50 percent of the calculated requirements for provisions, and this total was far better than the levels of accumulated arms, ammunition, and fuel. Statement of Lt. Col. Shinroku Iwakoshi, Doc. No. 62800, CMH. With respect to movement of supplies to Kyushu, the ambitious original scheme called for shipment of all supplies within one week of May 27, from main depots direct to the vicinity of frontline divisions. Eighty percent of this goal was completed, but deficiencies and erratic transportation continued to demand shipments through July.

P. 177 Supply status of Sixteenth Area Army: Statement of Lt. Col. Kyoshi Ohta, pp. 2–3, CMH. This statement also indicates that by the end of July the supply stockpiles were distributed equally between caves and schools or dwellings.

P. 177 Postwar inventories: G-2 Daily Intelligence Summaries, October 1945, RG 4, Box 28, Folder 3, MacArthur Archive. See particularly summaries 32-1280, 34-1282, 35-1283, 36-12844. The percentages in the text are based upon computations derived by dividing holdings of the Sixteenth Area Army into the total for the Imperial Army. Exact percentages are:

Rifles and light machine guns	24.6
Pistols and submachine guns	18.8
Heavy grenade dischargers ("knee mortars")	89.9
Mines	61.6
Battalion and antitank guns	48.8
Field and mountain guns	28.0
Mortars	66.0

Not all of these stocks were at the immediate disposition of field units. The Fifty-seventh Army had 3.5 *Kaisenbun* of ammunition for a strength that roughly equaled about seven divisions. The situation of the Fortieth Army was worse. The plan was for the Army to have 1.5 *Kaisenbun* for its nearly five division equivalents, but at the end of the war only 40 percent of this amount was on hand. *Hondo Kessen Junbi,* Attached Table. The

Japanese history series provides the following specific comments on immediately available supplies for units on Kyushu: The 156th Division had 0.5 *Kaisenbun* and two months of food (pp. 316, 318–22, 519); the 154th Division had 1.0 *Kaisenbun* and thirty days' provisions (pp. 322–23, 519–20); the 86th Division had 0.7 *Kaisenbun* and three months' supplies (pp. 522–24); the 98th IMB is described as the least satisfactorily supplied of the major units in the Fifty-seventh Army, notably with respect to ammunition (pp. 522–24); the 25th Division had one *Kaisenbun* "and supplies" (pp. 524–25); the 146th Division had about 0.7 *Kaisenbun* and fuel for one month (pp. 537–48); and the 206th Division had about three fifths the "desired amount"—about one month's provisions (pp. 545–46).

12. Kamikazes, Civilians, and Assessments

P. 178 First suicide crash and Japanese air strengths: Samuel Eliot Morison, *History of United States Naval Operations in World War II:* vol. 3, *The Rising Sun in the Pacific 1931 to April 1942* (Boston: Atlantic/Little, Brown, 1948), p. 115; USSBS, No. 62, Military Analysis Division, *Japanese Air Power,* pp. 28–29, 33, 35, 40. As the narrative of the USSBS notes, Japanese record-keeping methods precluded exact counts of available aircraft. The figures for strengths in tactical units are believed to be accurate to within 5 percent.

P. 179 "In present day wars, both friend and enemy": Denis Warner, Peggy Warner, and Sadao Seno, *The Sacred Warriors* (New York: Avon Books, 1982), pp. 52–53, 49, 56–57, 63–64, 69. The Japanese flier was Major Katsushige Takata, commander of the Fifth Air Regiment. He apparently aimed at the destroyer *Sampson* but hit the lowly *SC 699,* which was alongside.

P. 179 The *Oka:* Hatsuho Naito, *Thunder Gods: The Kamikaze Pilots Tell Their Story* (Tokyo: Kodansha International, 1989), pp. 23, 33–36, 44–47.

P. 179 Initial organized kamikaze attack: Rikihei Inoguchi and Tadashi Nakajima with Roger Pineau, *The Divine Wind: Japan's Kamikaze Force in World War II* (Annapolis: Naval Institute Press, 1958), pp. 3–13, 57–59, Appendix A; William T. Y'Blood, *The Little Giants: U.S. Escort Carriers Against Japan* (Annapolis: Naval Institute Press, 1987), pp. 206–15. October 25 marked the first major organized kamikaze mission, but these were not the first kamikaze attacks at Leyte. A freelance kamikaze crashed the Australian heavy cruiser *Australia* on October 21, killing thirty men; other isolated attacks sank the ocean tug *Sonoma* and *LCI 1065* on October 24. Warner, Warner, and Seno, *Sacred Warriors,* pp. 91–94.

P. 180   Sources for kamikaze statistics: R. J. Overy, *The Air War, 1939–45* (New York: Stein and Day, 1980), p. 99; *Special History of One Hundred Million Japanese During Showa Period,* History of Japanese Warfare, no. 4, *Special Attack Forces,* Tokyo *Daily News,* Sept. 1, 1979.

P. 180   Airmen lost in kamikaze attacks: Warner, Warner, and Seno, *Sacred Warriors,* Appendix 3.

P. 180   Early kamikaze attacks: Samuel Eliot Morison, *History of United States Naval Operations in World War II:* vol. 12, *Leyte, June 1944–January 1945* (Boston: Atlantic/Little, Brown, 1958), Chapters 13, 15, 16; Samuel Eliot Morison, *History of United States Naval Operations in World War II:* vol. 13, *The Liberation of the Philippines, Luzon, Mindanao, the Visayas, 1944–45* (Boston: Atlantic/Little, Brown, 1959), pp. 22–50, 104–11, Appendix 4; Warner, Warner, and Seno, *Sacred Warriors,* pp. 154–58, Appendix 1; *Special History of One Hundred Million Japanese;* CTG 77.2 to COM7THFLT 06 1210 Jan 45, CINCPAC Command Summary, pp. 3,195–96.

P. 180   American losses in early attacks: Y'Blood, *Little Giants,* pp. 332–38. The total number of fatalities represents a rough calculation from figures in Morison cited in the preceding note.

P. 180   New U.S. countertactics: Tillman, *Hellcat,* pp. 153–55, 158. In a typical *Essex*-class carrier, the number of embarked fighters soared from thirty-six to seventy-three starting in December 1944. Plans were afoot to convert the light carriers to all-fighter complements. The increase in fighter planes meant that the dive-bombing (SB2C) and torpedo-bombing (TBM) squadrons were reduced to fifteen planes each. Tillman points out that even the larger squadrons were not enough to satisfy Admiral John S. McCain, who wanted still more fighters and was prepared to eliminate all dive-bombers. In December 1944, *Essex* embarked an air group of fifty-four Hellcats and thirty-six Corsairs, leaving only fifteen TBM attack planes. Half the fighters doubled as dive-bombers.

P. 181   Battle lessons in the Philippines: COM-INCH P-008 Amphibious Operations: Invasion of the Philippines October 1944 to January 1945, pp. 3-7 to 3-11, NHC [hereafter COMINCH P-008].

P. 181   Gunfire effectiveness and vulnerability of transports: John C. Reilly, Jr., *United States Navy Destroyers of World War II* (Poole, Dorset: Blandford Press, 1983), p. 79; Y'Blood, *Little Giants,* pp. 318–19. Troop capacity for transports is from Memo for F-1, Subject: Troop Lift for OLYMPIC, 5 Jun 45, Box 166, Folder: Operations-S. Kyushu, OLYMPIC, Strategic Plans Division, NHC. As Y'Blood notes, one report, comprehensively comparing the defensive characteristics of a fleet carrier with an escort carrier, found the former was ten times as well protected as the latter.

Notwithstanding the known shortcomings of 20-mm and 40-mm guns against the kamikaze, in 1945 naval yards feverishly mounted massive additional quantities of these weapons as a counter to the kamikaze menace, particularly on destroyers. Weight considerations principally dictated why ships took on more of these automatic weapons rather than additional five-inch guns, despite a theoretical calculation that a five-inch gun was over eight times as lethal as even a 40-mm gun. Norman Friedman, *U.S. Naval Weapons* (Annapolis: Naval Institute Press, 1985), pp. 87–88. Friedman notes the lethal area from the burst of a five-inch shell was about fifty times as great as that from a 40-mm round, but the latter fired at about six times the rate of the former.

P. 181   "Friendly fire" casualties: Eleanor D. Gauker and Christopher G. Blood, "Friendly Fire Incidents During World War II Naval Operations," *Naval War College Review* 48.1 (winter 1995): 115–22. This source gives a combined total of "friendly fire" deaths for the war of 186 with 438 wounded. These totals include eighty-three dead on the submarine *Seawolf* in 1944. This overall subject remains a controversial topic. For example, the loss of the submarine *Dorado* in October 1943 under unknown circumstances while on passage from New London to the Panama Canal has led to many speculations about friendly fire. However, there is an equal possibility that she was a victim of a German mine. Vernon J. Miller, "An Analysis of U.S. Submarine Losses During World War II," in *Warship XI,* pp. 120–21. On the other hand, there is no doubt that there were significant losses, including Admiral Norman Scott, on the light cruiser *Atlanta* on November 13, 1942, from friendly fire from the *San Francisco.* It is impossible from source material to calculate how many of the 170 dead on the *Atlanta* were due to the nineteen-inch shells from the *San Francisco* that riddled her superstructure concurrent with many hits from Japanese guns. Frank, *Guadalcanal,* pp. 443–44, 459. Gauker and Blood do not record any losses on the *Atlanta* as due to "friendly fire."

P. 182   Naval losses at Okinawa: Morison, *Victory in the Pacific,* p. 212, Appendix 2; Appleman, Burns, Gugeler, and Stevens, *Okinawa,* p. 473. There remains some difficulty in calculating Navy casualties at Okinawa. The Bureau of Medicine and Surgery's official calculation shows a total of only 4,022 killed or died of wounds for what is described as "Bombing and landing on Okinawa." It also lists, however, a total of 1,031 killed, died of wounds, or died as prisoner of war for a category called "Bombardment of Kyushu Island and Japan." It appears clear that the latter category includes losses on the *Franklin,* which was hit while performing preliminary strikes for the Okinawa landings. Morison includes these losses for Okinawa, which seems more appropriate. Compare *History of the Medical Department of the United States Navy* 3:173, with Morison, *Victory in the Pacific,* Appendix 2. The losses on the *Franklin* are from Roy W. Bruce, "Done Blowed the Ship to Hell," *Naval History* 9.2 (March–April 1995).

P. 182   Overall Japanese air strength: USSBS, *Japanese Air Power,* pp. 24–25, 70. For Imperial Army alternative numbers, see Lt. Mikizo Takemura, Lt. Col. Kazumi Fujii, "Statement of Changes in Number of Army Aircraft Available in the Homeland After 31 March 1945," Doc. No. 57225, Statements of Japanese Officials on World War II, General Headquarters, Far East Command, Military Intelligence Section, Historical Division, CMH. A completely authoritative statement about the actual number of Japanese aircraft that would have been available to oppose Olympic is probably not to be had, primarily due to problems with Japanese record keeping and the end of the war. The number in the text from USSBS is neither the highest nor the lowest and represents my best judgment. It appears that the lower figures arise because some of the commonly noted figures actually represented strength as of about July 1 rather than August 15. For example, the low number quoted for Imperial Navy aircraft is provided by Toshiyuki Yokoi, "Kamikazes in the Okinawa Campaign," in David C. Evans, ed., *The Japanese Navy in World War II,* 2d ed. (Annapolis: Naval Institute Press, 1986), pp. 470–72. But according to a statement from Rear Admiral Katsuhei Nakamura of the Naval Aeronautical Department, the figure for July 1 was a total of 5,045 aircraft, of which 3,566 were available. This number is only one different from that in *The Japanese Navy in World War II.* See Statement of Admiral Nakamura, 20 Aug 49, Doc. No. 50565, CMH, which clearly appears to be based on documents in his possession. The highest number for availability I located was 12,725, in V Amphibious Corps, Op-

erations Report, Occupation of Japan, Annex Charlie, *The Japanese Plan for the Defense of Kyushu,* p. 10, MCHC (hereafter V Amphib, *Japanese Plan for the Defense of Kyushu*).

P. 183   Pilot availability: USSBS, *Japanese Air Power,* pp. 24–25, 42.

P. 183   Fuel availability: Ibid. Some of the Imperial Army officers interrogated after the war expressed conflicting views. Two officers who saw the Strategic Bombing Survey figures produced other numbers showing that the Imperial Army, at least, was in far more strained conditions. Lt. Col. Jiro Tsukushki and Lt. Col. Mikize Takemura, Report on the Survey of Army Aviation Fuel Situation in the Mainland Area During and After January 1945, Doc. No. 56826, Statements of Japanese Officials, CMH. Their numbers indicated that the Imperial Army had on hand 59,000 kiloliters (15,586,620 gallons) of fuel at the end of July and needed 40,000 (10,567,200 gallons) for the Ketsu operation. They anticipated absolutely no imports. Fuel production, of which only 20 percent was gasoline and the rest alcohol and wood turpentine, languished at only 7,000 to 10,000 kiloliters per month, while monthly projected consumption ran at 12,000 to 14,000 kiloliters. By the end of December, there would be only 43,000 kiloliters on hand.

Somewhat different numbers were provided by Lt. Col. Katsuo Kato, who stated that by July 1945 the Imperial Army stocks totaled about 70,000 kiloliters, of which 40,000 were reserved for the decisive battle. Consumption ran about 10,000 per month, but with use of substitute fuels, this reduced to 6,000. Lt. Col. Katsuo Sato, Statement on Ketsu Go Air Operations, Doc. No. 59402, Statements of Japanese Officials on World War II, General Headquarters, Far East Command, Military Intelligence Section, Historical Division, CMH.

Another knowledgeable Imperial Army officer, Lt. Col. Koji Tanaka, provided data that essentially supported the USSBS, but he admitted that "the fuel situation was our greatest worry in the Ketsu Operation."

P. 183   Nonaerial suicide weapons: "Water's Edge Surprise Attack Force," 17 Jul, SRS-484; SRMD-008, p. 275, 23 Jul p. 5.

P. 183   Japanese suicide craft: Shizuo Fukui, *Japanese Naval Vessels at the End of World War II* (Annapolis: Naval Institute Press, 1991), pp. 99–102; *Hondo Kessen Junbi,* pp. 474–75; *Japanese Suicide Craft,* S-02, U.S. Naval Technical Mission to Japan, January 1946, NHC; SRS-484 17 July 45, Far East Summary, pp. 2–3. Each Shinyo "Marine Advanced Unit" was supported by a "Marine Advance Unit Maintenance Unit," of about four hundred men under a captain or lieutenant.

Disposition of the suicide-boat detachments was as follows:

	Marine Advanced units	Maintenance Units
56th Army	33d, 34th, 38th (about 300 boats)	3d, 4th, 8th
57th Army	31st, 32d (about 200 boats)	1st, 2d
40th Army	35th, 36th (about 200 boats)	5th, 6th
Kumamoto Division District	37th (about 100 boats)	7th

P. 184 Suicide attack tactics: USSBS, *Japanese Air Power,* p. 71.

P. 184 Japanese expectations of suicide attack success: Statement of Table Maneuver of Air Operation Ketsu at Fukuoka, early July 1945, Document No. 56044, Statements of Japanese Officials, CMH. Major General Kazuo Tanikawa noted that the official Imperial Navy estimate was one out of six. While the Imperial Army version was more optimistic, Tanikawa thought the Navy "was about right." Maj. Gen. Kazuo Tanikawa, "Statement Concerning Preparations for Okinawa and Homeland Air Operations," Staff Officer Imperial General Headquarters Army Department and Combined Fleet Staff Officer, Statements of Japanese Officials on World War II, General Headquarters, Far East Command, Military Intelligence Section, Historical Division, CMH. According to one key staff officer, the Imperial Army estimated the success rate of special attack thus: of a six-plane unit, one destroyed before airborne, two destroyed en route, and 1 to 1.5 hit the target—thus a rate of ¼ to ⅙. Data Concerning the Ketsu Operation, Lt. Col. Koji Tanaka, Staff Officer, Imperial General Headquarters, p. 3. The hypothesis for this exercise was an attack on Kyushu in October that would unfold in three phases: (1) a preliminary landing by one regiment on the Koshiki Islands; (2) an attack, with six divisions landing on the western coast of Satsuma Peninsula; and (3) the main effort by ten divisions at Miyazaki. This hypothesis again illustrates that by July the Japanese anticipated at least two major landing sites. A senior Imperial Army aviator, Lieutenant General Sugawara, told American interrogators after the war: "I feel that if preparations had gone according to our plans, it would have been possible for us to defeat the Allied attempt to land on our shores." USSBS, *Japanese Air Power,* p. 71.

P. 185 Lack of suicide forces to defend Honshu: Lt. Col. Katsuo Kato, Statement on Ketsu-Go Air Operations, Statements of Japanese Officials on World War II, General Headquarters, Far East Command, Military Intelligence Section, Historical Division, CMH.

P. 185 Assessment of suicide threat: Maj. Gen. Kazuo Tanikawa, "Statement Concerning Preparations for Okinawa and Homeland Air Operations," Doc. No. 50570, Statements of Japanese Officials on World War II, General Headquarters, Far East Command, Military Intelligence Section, Historical Division, CMH; Commander TG 38.4, Serial 0779, Sept. 7, 1945, NHC. Lieutenant Colonel Koji Tanaka agreed that assembling massive waves of attackers appeared to be beyond realistic Japanese capabilities, while Major General Tanikawa wholly discounted the ability of Japanese fighters to establish even transient air superiority. Lt. Col. Koji Tanaka, Data Concerning Ketsu Operations, 5 May 49 Statements of Japanese Officials on World War II, General Headquarters, Far East Command, Military Intelligence Section, Historical Division, CMH.

P. 185 American preparations to meet kamikaze threat: For the series of messages on radar pickets, including airborne variants, see: CINCPAC to CNO 02 0816 Jun, reel TS-24, NHC (also found in RG 38, Box 141, Folder "Pre-Olympic messages," NARA); CINCPAC to CNO Jun 45, CINCPAC Command Summary, p. 3,171; CINCPAC 14 0332 Jul, reel TS-24, NHC; COMPHIBSPAC to CINCPAC 271435 Jun 45 (dated 1 July on Dispatch heading); CINCPAC to COMINCH 012212 Jul 45; COMPHIBSPAC to CINCPAC 170915 Jul 45; CINCPAC to COMINCH 132057 Aug 45, last five messages are all in RG 38, Box 141, Folder "Pre-Olympic messages," NARA. Other messages show that the War Department was enlisted to impress upon MacArthur the extreme importance the Navy attached to air warning. WARCOS to CINCAFPAC 02 1745 Aug 45; CINCAFPAC to WARCOS 04 0109 Aug 45, CINCPAC Command Summary, p. 3,427.

P. 186 Intentions of Japanese commanders: USSBS, *Japanese Air Power,* p. 69; Donald M. Goldstein and Katherine V. Dillon, eds., *Fading Victory: The Diary of Admiral Matome Ugaki, 1941–1945,* trans. Masataka Chihaya (Pittsburgh: University of Pittsburgh Press, 1991), pp. 659, 663–66. USSBS, *Japanese Air Power,* pp. 71–72, quotes Captain Inoguchi (IJN) as reporting that while he expected one per nine or ten kamikazes to score a hit, others thought in terms of one in six.

P. 187   Potential threat of kamikazes against Olympic: USSBS, *Japanese Air Power,* p. 25.

P. 188   Japanese civilians in the Philippines: Smith, *Triumph in the Philippines,* p. 694, Appendix H-2.

P. 188   Civilian losses at Okinawa: Huber, *Japan's Battle of Okinawa,* p. 13; Feifer, *Tennozan,* pp. 532–33; see also Chapter 5, p. 70.

P. 188   Imperial Headquarters moves to mobilize civilians: *Hondo Kessen Junbi,* pp. 406–9, 414–15. Some idea of the scale of this preparation can be gleaned from the organization within the jurisdiction of the Sixteenth Area Army:

Area (Prefecture)	
Kurume Division District	
Shikoku	30 Special Policing Units
Saga	11 Special Policing Units
Nagasaki	13 Special Policing Units
Kumamoto Division District	
Kumamoto	17 Special Policing Units
Oita	18 Special Policing Units
Miyazaki	15 Special Policing Units
Kagoshima	16 Special Policing Units

P. 188   Effects of civilian mobilizations: *Hondo Kessen Junbi,* pp. 410–13.

P. 188   Civilian training, American perception: Havens, *Valley of Darkness,* pp. 188–90; Statement of Lt. Gen. Masao Yoshizumi, 22 Dec 49, Doc. No. 61388, p. 3, CMH; Craven and Cate, *The Pacific,* p. 696.

P. 190   Fighting among civilian population: *Hondo Kessen Junbi,* pp. 420–23.

P. 190   American postwar critiques: V Amphib, *Japanese Plan for the Defense of Kyushu,* pp. 1, 39. Other important assessments include: (1) Report by British Combined Observers (Pacific), "Report of Operation OLYMPIC and Japanese Countermeasures," April 4, 1946, CAB 106, no. 97, Public Record Office Kew; (2) Report of Reconnaissance Southern Kyushu, IX Corps Zone of Operation, 3–5 Dec 45, RG 407, Entry 427, WWII Operations Reports, IX Corps 209-2.0; and (3) File: Intelligence Specialist School and Information, Edmund J. Winslett Papers, US-AMHI. Like the V Amphibious Corps officers, the British observers extracted a good deal of their detailed information from officers of the Fortieth Army. This was by far the weaker of the two armies in southern Kyushu. A detailed comparison of the data in *Hondo Kessen Junbi* and these reports shows the Japanese position overall was much stronger by virtue of the higher state of training and equipment of the Fifty-seventh

Army, a fact that does not come through in the V Amphibious Corps report or that of the British observers. Winslett actually walked the ground and conducted a detailed physical examination of the landing areas. The IX Corps reconnaissance was conducted within a three-day window, extracted information from a very limited number of Japanese officers at area army and army level, and borrowed from the V Amphibious Corps research.

P. 191   De facto choice: Skates, *Invasion of Japan,* p. 118. General Amano at Imperial Headquarters acknowledged an intention to commit the "maximum available strength of ground forces [and] needless to say the entire combat strength of the air and sea special attack units" on Kyushu. Statement of Maj. Gen. Masakasu Amano, Doc. No. 59617, p. 2, CMH. Lieutenant General Kawabe, Vice Chief of the General Staff, acknowledged after the war that there was no real hope that Japan could carry out either a simultaneous defense of the Kanto plain with Kyushu or defend Kanto after the Kyushu operation. Statement of Lt. Gen. Torashiro Kawabe, Doc. No. 54476, p. 1, CMH.

P. 191   "Pastel" deception plan: The best source is Dr. Thomas M. Huber, *Pastel: Deception in the Invasion of Japan* (Fort Leavenworth, Kans.: Combat Studies Institute, U.S. Army Command and General Staff College, 1988). See also General Headquarters, United States Army Forces Pacific, Operations Instructions No. 3, 5 Aug 45, RG 4, Box 41, Folder 3. The assessment that Pastel would not have had any material effect is shared by Skates, *Invasion of Japan,* p. 164.

There was one proposal pending at the end of the war that potentially could have had an impact. In a July 25 memorandum, C. D. Glover of Admiral Nimitz's staff noted that the diversionary threat to Shikoku timed for X minus 15 to X minus 2 "may draw out the kamikazi [*sic*] boys in force," and he deemed it highly advisable that the transports detailed for this feint not carry any troops and be accorded the maximum protection by carrier aircraft. Whether this would have worked is very uncertain, for the Japanese believed that an assault on Shikoku would not have constituted the sole or major operation. Strategic Plans Division, Memorandum 25 July 45, Subject: Tactical Cover and Deception Plan for OLYMPIC, Strategic Plans Division Box 160, File D-2, NHC.

P. 192   Naval firepower supporting Olympic: Amphibious Forces Pacific, A11-45, Serial 000344 10 Aug 45, particularly Annexes A, G.

P. 193   V Amphibious Corps faces 303rd Division: V Amphib, *Japanese Plan for the Defense*

of *Kyushu*, pp. 35–38; *Hondo Kessen Junbi*, Attached Table III, Organization of the Major Units of the 2d General Army.

P. 193 Terrain challenges to V Amphibious Corps: File: Intelligence Specialist School and Information, Speech 9 Mar 1948, pp. 8–9, 13; Edmund J. Winslett Papers, USAMHI; V Amphib, *Japanese Plan for the Defense of Kyushu*, pp. 22–25. Winslett commanded the Sixth Army's photographic unit, which supplied about 95 percent of all tactical intelligence, that is, the meticulous itemizing of where the Japanese had installed individual units and fortifications, which was below the Ultra horizon. General Krueger sent Winslett to survey the invasion beach areas and compare the preinvasion intelligence with an on-site survey.

P. 193 I and XI Corps assault: *Hondo Kessen Junbi*, Attached Table III, Organization of the Major Units of the 2d General Army; V Amphib, *Japanese Plan for the Defense of Kyushu*, pp. 20–21; Lecture notes, "Intelligence Information, Invasion of Japan, 3 June 1946," p. 6; Edmund J. Winslett Papers, USAMHI.

P. 193 IX Corps role: Sixth Army Field Order No. 74, 28 July 1945 and Annex 3, Troop List.

P. 195 Doubling of losses in assault divisions: American battle casualties were not spread evenly across all branches but were concentrated overwhelmingly in the infantry. For the war as a whole in the U.S. Army, the infantry accounted for 80 percent of fatalities in ground units. *Army Battle Casualties and Nonbattle Deaths*, p. 5, gives totals from which the percentage of infantry casualties is extracted. The same data show artillery sustained 5.2 percent and engineers 4.2 percent of all battle deaths for the war among ground branches. The assumption that 92,500 overall casualties results in a doubling of losses in the assault divisions is derived by multiplying this number by 80 percent to approximate the 74,239 casualties Olympic divisions had already sustained.

P. 195 "The morale of all front-line forces" and Hata reply: Maj. Gen. Joichiro Sanada, "Statement on the Crucial Battle of the Homeland," Doc. No. 52336, Statements of Japanese Officials on World War II, General Headquarters, Far East Command, Military Intelligence Section, Historical Division, CMH.

P. 196 "We were absolutely sure of victory": Statement of Maj. Gen. Masakasu Amano, 10 Jun 1950, Doc. No. 59617, CMH. See also statement 29 Dec 1949, Doc. No. 54480, CMH.

P. 196 "If we could defeat the enemy in Kyushu": Statement of Lt. Gen. Seizo Arisue,

Doc. No. 52506, CMH. In the same vein, Lieutenant General Kawabe spoke of how he did not expect Ketsu-Go to result in victory, but after his personal inspection of Kyushu in late June, he was confident of inflicting "staggering losses" on the attackers. Statement of Lt. Gen. Kawabe, 18 Jun 49, Doc. No. 50569, p. 3, CMH.

P. 196 Attitudes among the Big Six: Statement of Former Admiral Soemu Toyoda, 29 Aug 49, Doc. No. 61340, p. 3; Interrogation of Premier Baron Suzuki, 26 Dec 45, Interrogation No. 531, p. 308, CMH; Statements of Lt. Gen. Masao Yoshizumi, 22 Dec 49, Doc. No. 54484, p. 4, Doc. No. 54485, pp. 2, 3, and Doc. No. 61338, p. 3, CMH; Statement of Col. Saburo Hayashi, 23 Dec 49, Doc. No. 54482, p. 3, CMH.

There are a mass of statements attesting to Anami's confidence in the prospects for Ketsu-Go. In addition to the statements from General Yoshizumi and Colonel Hayashi, Hayashi related in another interview: "I think [Army] Minister Anami's ideas of continuing the war was that he wanted to make peace after dealing a heavy blow to the enemy" (23 Dec 49, Doc. 61436, p. 5, CMH). Colonel Sei Matsutani reported: "It seems to me that General Anami had hopes of concluding peace in early August on fairly advantageous terms after at least inflicting a blow in Japan proper upon the enemy" (Statement, 13 Jan 50, Doc. No. 54227, p. 2, CMH). Major General Yatsuji Nagai, Chief of the Military Affairs Section, Army Ministry, commented that Anami believed strongly in the idea that the tide of war could be turned by a decisive battle in the Homeland. Apparently, he thought that by taking advantage of this opportunity, an "honorable peace could be concluded" (Statement of 27 Dec 49, Doc. No. 54228, p. 2, CMH). In the mildest of these, Colonel Okikatsu Arao, also an important staff officer at the Army Ministry, stated that "[Army] Minister Anami was confident of victory to some extent (at least lessen the conditions in the Potsdam Proclamation)" (Statement of 27 Dec 49, Doc. No. 54226, p. 2, CMH).

13. The Eclipse of Olympic

P. 198 Estimates of Japanese ground and air forces: The initial capability of six divisions total with only three in southern Kyushu is mentioned repeatedly in planning documents from at least mid-1944 and reiterated in Downfall, Strategic Plans for Operations in the Japanese Archipelago, author's copy. (A copy of the Downfall plan may be found in OPD 350.05, Sec. 1, RG 165, NARA.) MacArthur's projection of ultimate Japanese capabilities is from the same Downfall plan. Marshall's estimate before Truman is found in "Minutes of Meeting Held at White House on Monday, 18 June 1945 at 1530," Xerox 1567, Marshall Library. These minutes make no mention of Japanese air capabilities. Locating an exact contemporary estimate of Japanese forces on Kyushu as of June 18 proved difficult. A figure of 298,000 appears in a CINCPAC estimate in SRMD-008, p. 242, Jun 11 p. 2, RG 457, NARA. This is considered authoritative, as CINCPAC followed MIS figures. Report of Pacific Order of Battle Conference (Ground forces), 15–18 August 1945, SRH-098, pp. 13–14, RG 457, NARA [hereafter Report of Pacific Conference, 15–18 August 1945]. On June 16, MIS issued an estimate placing 300,000 Japanese military personnel on Kyushu. "War Department (MID) Military Intelligence Service, Japanese Ground Order of Battle Bulletin, 16 June 1945," SRH-195, Part II, Entry 9002, Box 77, RG 457, NARA.

P. 198 Key intelligence summaries: GHQ, SWPA, Special Intelligence Precis, SRH-362, p. 8. These three major publications appear in the SRS series, SRH-203 and among the CINCPAC reports particularly SRMD-008, RG 457, NARA.

P. 199 Japanese strategic organization and plan identified: GHQ, SWPA, Military Intelligence Section, G-2 ULTRA Intelligence Summaries, Semi-Monthly Review No. 1, SRH-203, Part 6, p. 1,878.

P. 199 Ketsu-Go plan details: SRH-203, 14/15 Jul, No. 92, 15/16 Jul, No. 93, and 29/30 Jul, No. 107; SRMD-007, 16 July and 7 August; SRS-493, 26 Jul. Insight into Japanese expectations emerged from a message deciphered in early August betraying a communications exercise based on a hypothetical American invasion of southern Kyushu, with ten divisions landing from the sea and two airborne divisions dropping inland. SRH-203, 3/4 Aug, No. 112.

P. 199 Japanese methods of creating units: Report of Pacific Conference, 15–18 August 1945, pp. 33–34.

P. 200 Early projections of aggregate Japanese strength: G-2 Estimate of Enemy Situation with Respect to an Operation Against Kyushu-Honshu, 24 March 45, RG 4, Box 22, Folder 7, MacArthur Archive; G-2 Estimate of the Enemy Situation with Respect to an Operation Against Southern Kyushu, 25 April 45, RG 4, Box 22, Folder 8, MacArthur Archive. Willoughby believed the Japanese forces in southern Kyushu would be deployed so that they could bring 27,000 to 31,000 men in one division and one regiment initially against a landing at Ariake Bay, and within three to five days, another 20,000 to

23,000 men and one division. There would be the equivalent of a reinforced regiment at Makurazaki and at Miyazaki, not over one division.

P. 200 Ultra detects mobilization: Report of Pacific Conference, 15–18 August 1945, p. 36.

P. 200 Ultra projects mobilization: Ibid., pp. 34–40.

P. 201 Strength identified on Kyushu by June 18: SRS-431, 25 May; SRS-438, 1 June; SRS-452, 15 June; GHQ, SWPA, Military Intelligence Section, G-2 ULTRA Intelligence Summaries, Semi-Monthly Review No. 3, SRH-203, Part 6, p. 1991.

P. 201 Early July identifications: SRH-203, 2/3 Jul, No. 80; SRS-476, 9 July.

P. 201 Mid-July identifications: GHQ, SWPA, Military Intelligence Section, G-2 ULTRA Intelligence Summaries, Semi-Monthly Review No. 6, SRH-203, Part 6, p. 2197; SRH-203, 13/14 Jul, No. 91.

P. 201 Late July identifications: SRH-203, 15/16 Jul, No. 93 (154th Division), 23/24 Jul, No. 101 (156th Division and 122d IMB), 22/23 Jul, RG 100 (126th IMB), 21/22 Jul, No. 99 (37th and 40th Tank Regiments), 25/26 Jul, No. 103 (146th Division), and 27/28 July, No. 105 (unidentified tank brigade); SRS-488, 21 July 45.

P. 201 July 25 revelation: SRS-492, 25 July 45; SRH-203 28/29 Jul, No. 106.

P. 202 Fortieth Army identified: SRS-494, 27 July 45; SRH-203, 28/29 Jul, No. 106, and 29/30 Jul, No. 107.

P. 202 Military presence in northern and southern Kyushu: Drea, *In Service of the Emperor*, p. 160.

P. 202 Estimate by August 7: SRS-500, 2 Aug 45; SRS-505, 7 Aug 45.

P. 203 Updated intelligence as of August 10, 1945: Joint Intelligence Committee, "Japanese Reaction to an Assault on the Sendai Plain," JIC 218/10, 10 August 1945 (final revision August 20, 1945). The total for Kyushu includes the Tsushima Fortress, which was under the Fifty-sixth Army. Geographic File 1942-45, CCS 381 Honshu (7-19-44) Sec. 4, RG 218, Box 90, NARA.

P. 203 Lack of hard data on quality of Japanese units: There is, of course, no solitary or group citation that can be rendered for the absence of information in SRH-203, the SRS series, or SRMD-008 for the June to August time frame. Indirect evidence to support this proposition can be gleaned from the fact that intelligence officers referred to deductions based on general understandings of Japan's situation with respect to munitions in order to assess combat capability and readiness. For example, a master assessment of Japan's strategic situation by MIS on June 30 emphasized that Japan lacked heavy artillery but not light weapons or ammunition. The MIS estimated that Japan held 104 "division months" of ammunition and produced 24 "division months" per year. She could be expected to expend 100 "division months" against an invasion of Honshu or Kyushu. War Department, General Staff, Military Intelligence Service, G-2, Estimate of Enemy Situation 30 June 1945, COMINCH Strategic Plans Division, Box 176, NHC.

P. 203 Qualitative estimates: Report of Pacific Conference, 15–18 August 1945, pp. 4, 7, 15, 22–29, SRH-098.

P. 203 Home Defense forces: Ibid., pp. 45–53.

P. 204 Mobilization of civilians; requests for information from diplomats and attachés: SRH-203 27/28 Jun, No. 75; GHQ, SWPA, Military Intelligence Section, G-2 ULTRA Intelligence Summaries, Semi-Monthly Review No. 2, SRH-203, Part 6, p. 1932.

P. 204 Imperial Navy reorganization: SRMD-008, p. 215; April 30, p. 2; SRS-438, 1 Jun 45.

P. 206 Navy resources: SRH-203, 9/10 Aug, No. 118; SRMD-007, 4 August; SRMD-008, p. 215, April 30 p. 2; p. 243, Jun 11 p. 3; p. 291, 6 Aug p. 4; SRS-499, 1 Aug; SRS-501, 3 Aug. SRMD-008, p. 291, also listed one large, two light, and one auxiliary carrier as possibly operational, as well as one light cruiser.

P. 206 References to the Imperial Navy's suicide-weapon arsenal: Examples are SRS-440, 3 Jun; SRS-494, 27 Jul; SRMD-008, p. 243, 11 Jun p. 3; p. 253, 25 Jun p. 3; p. 282, 30 Jul p. 4; and SRS-501, 3 Aug. The "deadly threat" of Kaitens is from SRS-506, 8 Aug. References to suicide-weapon bases include SRS-483, 16 Jul; SRS-503, 5 Aug; and SRMD-008, p. 253, 25 Jun p. 3.

P. 206 Surplus personnel for land units: SRMD-008, p. 275, 25 Jun p. 2; minelaying messages include SRS-441, 4 Jun; for references to the "Water's Edge Surprise Attack Force," see SRS-484, 17 Jul; SRMD-008, p. 275, 23 Jul p. 5.

P. 206 Early estimates of Japanese airpower: G-2 Estimate of Enemy Situation with Respect to an Operation Against Kyushu-Honshu, 24 March 45, RG 4, Box 22, Folder 7, MacArthur Archive; GHQ, SWPA, Military Intelligence Section, G-2 ULTRA Intelligence Summaries, Semi-Monthly Review No. 2, SRH-203, Part 6, p. 1933.

P. 207 Conservation strategy: SRS-472 5 July 45, SRS-458, 21 Jun 45; SRS-444, 29 Jun 45 (use of antiaircraft guns); SRS-505 7 Aug 5 ("three kilometer order") see also SRS-476, 9 July 45; SRMD-008, p. 265, 16 Jul p. 1 (photographic evidence); SRH-203, 27/28 Jul, No. 105 (noting success of dispersal and concealment program but also noting increase in personnel casualties).

P. 207 Japanese decision to expend their air forces: The following are representative citations of a wealth of data: SRS-487, 20 Jul 45 (no plans for future operations, Imperial Navy has abandoned air training); SRS-430, 24 May (both Imperial Army and Imperial Navy converting training units to suicide role); SRS-444, 7 Jun 45, SRS-452, 15 Jun 45, and SRS-456, 20 Jun (conversion of Imperial Navy trainers for suicide role); SRS-481, 14 Jul 45 (similar conversion of Imperial Army trainers); SRMD-007, 5 Jul (conversion of navy trainers); SRMN-016, 17 July, p. 173 (navy abandons training); SRH-203, 28/29 Jun, No. 76 (Japan prepared to sacrifice whole air force); GHQ, SWPA, Military Intelligence Section, G-2 ULTRA Intelligence Summaries, Semi-Monthly Review No. 3, SRH-203, Part 6, p. 1992 (army abandons air training); SRMD-008, p. 229, 21 May p. 1 (trainers and training units converted to suicide role).

P. 207 Imperial Navy air commands: SRS-444, 7 Jun 45. For Tenth Air Flotilla see SRS-441, 4 Jun, and GHQ, SWPA, Military Intelligence Section, G-2 ULTRA Intelligence Summaries, Semi-Monthly Review No. 2, SRH-203, Part 6, p. 1991; for Twelfth and Thirteenth Air Flotillas, see SRS-478, 11 Jul, and SRH-203, 21/22 Jul, No. 99; for Willoughby's later July totals see SRH-203, 17/18 Jul, No. 95; for messages indicating targeting of troop transports, see SRS-502, 4 Aug 45, and SRMD-007, 26 Jul; reports identifying concealed suicide-plane bases include SRS-438, 1 Jun 45; SRS-497, 30 Jul 45; SRS-502, 4 Aug 45; SRH-203, 3/4 Jul 45, No. 81, and 9/10 Jul 45, No. 87 (minimum of two hundred air bases identified). For conventional training in night torpedo attacks, see SRS-483, 16 Jul 45; SRMD-007, 7 July and 15 Jul 45.

P. 208 Information on Imperial Army air units: SRS-444, 7 Jun 45; SRS-469, 2 Jul 45; SRS-499, 1 Aug; SRS-476, 9 Jul. For the gradual buildup of a picture of Imperial Army air units, see SRS-441, 4 Jun 45; SRS-472, 5 Jul 45; SRS-507, 9 Aug 45; SRH-203, 28/29 Jun 45, No. 76. For manufacture of aircraft and training and safety of units in the Manchurian sanctuary, see SRS-499, 9 Aug 45.

P. 208 Production drop: SRS-419, 13 May; for fuel constriction, see SRS-445, 8 Jun 45, and SRS-466, 29 Jun; for efforts concerning fuel, see

SRS-445, 8 Jun 45, and SRMD-008, p. 251, Jun 25, p. 1, and also SRH-203, 29/30 Jun, No. 77; SRMD-007, 7, 17, 24, 28 July; SRMD-008, 3 Aug, pp. 12–13; SRMD-008, pp. 220–21; for CINCPAC analysis, see SRMD-008, p. 281, 30 Jul, p. 3; on loss of radio equipment, see SRH-203, 27/28 Jun, No. 75; on problems with engines, see SRS-507, 9 Aug 45; on abandoning southern Kyushu airfields, see SRS-487, 20 Jul, and SRH-203, 8/9 Jul, No. 86; and on delays in launching suicide planes on Shikoku, see SRH-203, 25/26 Jul, No. 103, and analysis in SRMD-008, p. 261, 9 Jul p. 1.

P. 208 Replacement pilots and training time: SRS-493, 3 Aug; for status report on Imperial Navy fighter units, see SRMD-008, p. 271, 23 Jul p. 1; and on excess of trainees, see SRH-203, 5/6 Jul, No. 83.

P. 208 CINCPAC on bombing and Japanese aircraft production: SRMD-008, p. 251, Jun 25 p. 1; for the use of "Baka" bombs against invasion fleet see, e.g., SRH-203, 6/7 Aug, No. 115.

P. 209 May 10 figure: SRS-416, 10 May 45; for June 14 see SRS-451, 14 Jun (see also SRH-053); for Willoughby's calculation, see GHQ, SWPA, Military Intelligence Section, G-2 ULTRA Intelligence Summaries, Semi-Monthly Review No. 2, SRH-203, Part 6, pp. 1933–34; for Willoughby on numbers no longer measure of enemy air strength, see SRH-203, Semi-Monthly Review No. 7, 31 Jul/1 Aug; estimates of waste and falling air strength, see SRS-463, 26 Jun 45; on recognition of strict conservation policy and 9 August estimate, see SRS-486, 19 Jul 45, and SRS-507, 9 Aug 45.

P. 210 Willoughby revises estimate: SRH-203, 7/8 Jul, No. 85.

P. 210 CINCPAC commentary: SRMD-008, p. 256, 2 Jul p. 1.

P. 210 CINCPAC estimates: SRMD-008, p. 266, 16 Jul p. 2, and p. 297, 13 Aug p. 2. USASTAF estimates: USAF HC File 760.6315 7 Jun–10 Aug 45, AFHC. The quoted figures are from Enemy Air Order of Battle Report No. 14, 10 August 1945. USASTAF broke Japanese aviation strength into an interceptor force with gross total of 1,610 fighters, of which 805 were effective and 510 available for interception. The estimate also credited the Japanese with 1,100 bombers and 5,900 suicide planes available in Japan.

There is also a mysterious tally prepared at Admiral King's headquarters found in SRMN-045, pp. 259–67, RG 457, NARA. The copy of this document consists of a number of consecutively numbered pages without commentary on its sources or distribution. It appears obvious that the series runs in a chronological sequence, with the ups and downs roughly parallel to those of other headquarters, except for the fact that the totals remain notably low. This credited the Japanese with 4,600 to 4,800 aircraft on March 31 as the Okinawa operation commenced and contained early projections that the Japanese would have only 600 aircraft in Japan to oppose Olympic and but 350 to oppose Coronet. Even these low numbers were revised downward to 325 and 250 respectively. Subsequent revisions, however, boosted the estimate for Japanese air strength back up to 4,150 as of September 30, of which 2,030 would be fighters, 1,320 bombers, plus 800 "others." There is no cross-reference to this report in other intelligence documents or communications files, and it cannot be linked to any other documents or plans. It remains thus impossible to judge what influence, if any, these reports possessed.

P. 211 Loss of *Callaghan:* Map Room Summary 30 July, Naval Aide Files, Map Room Files, Box 6, Berlin Conference—Communications from Map Room, July 26 to Aug. 2, 1945, Folder 1, HSTL; CINCPAC Command Summary, daily summary 29 July, p. 3281. Ultra showed there were only eight aircraft in this attack group, and a detailed account appeared in the Far East Summary of 3 August, SRS-501.

P. 212 Revisions of estimates: General Headquarters, United States Army Forces Pacific, Military Intelligence Section, General Staff, "Amendment No. 1 to G-2 Estimate of the Enemy Situation with Respect to Kyushu," 29 July 1945, p. 1, Gen. John J. Tolson Papers, USAMHI (a copy is also in RG 4, Box 22, MacArthur Archive); Headquarters, Sixth Army, G-2 Estimate of the Enemy Situation OPERATION OLYMPIC 1 August 1945, RG 165, Box 1843, NARA; Walter Krueger, *From Down Under to Nippon: The Story of Sixth Army in World War II* (Washington, D.C.: Combat Forces Press, 1953), p. 333. It was probably no random happenstance that Willoughby's Daily Intelligence Summary for August 2–3 contained a detailed terrain analysis of the Sendai plain on northern Honshu, one of the rival landing sites to Kyushu. G-2 Daily Intelligence Summary, 2/3 Aug, Summary 1216, RG 4, Box 28, Folder 1, MacArthur Archive.

P. 212 CINCPAC revised views: SRMD-008, p. 238, June 4 p. 2; p. 247, Jun 18 p. 2; pp. 257–58, 2 Jul pp. 2–3.

P. 212 Nimitz on Olympic: CINCPAC ADVAN to COMINCH 030209 Aug 45, CINCPAC Command Summary, p. 3503.

P. 213 Joint Intelligence Committee: Joint War Plans Committee, JWPC 397 4 August 1945 (with attached copy of "Defensive Preparations in Japan"), JIC, RG 218, NARA.

14. Unconditional Surrender and Magic

P. 214 Diplomacy debate: Minutes of the Meeting Held at the White House on Monday, 18 June 1945 at 1530, pp. 5–6, HSTL; Joseph C. Grew, *Turbulent Era: A Diplomatic Record of Forty Years,* vol. 2 (Boston: Houghton Mifflin, 1952), pp. 1421–22.

P. 215 Poll data: Hadley Cantril, ed., *Public Opinion 1935–1946* (Princeton: Princeton University Press, 1951), p. 392; Sigal, *Fighting to a Finish,* pp. 89–95. Although the Gallup Poll on what to do about a peace offer was reported as June 29, 1945, Sigal cites another source for the actual date of polling as May 1945.

P. 215 "The chamber rose to its feet": Harry S. Truman, *Memoirs,* vol. 1, *Year of Decisions* (Garden City, N.Y.: Doubleday, 1955), p. 42. Truman's precise use of the term *unconditional surrender* between May and July has generated its own minicontroversy. At the time of Germany's surrender, Truman issued a statement that spoke of the "unconditional surrender of [Japan's] *armed forces,*" which also noted that "unconditional surrender does not mean the extermination or enslavement of the Japanese people." Papers of Harry S. Truman, White House Central Files, Confidential, HSTL. Then, in a statement for Congress on June 1, 1945, Truman noted "these are our plans for bringing about the unconditional surrender of *Japan.*" Papers of Harry S. Truman, Press Releases, HSTL. Alperovitz makes a good deal out of the alternating use of *armed forces* and *Japan* as the surface reflections of important subterranean policy shifts. Alperovitz, *Decision to Use the Atomic Bomb,* esp. pp. 39–41, 52–58, 304–17. I do not find such significance in the language used in these statements. Much more important, I found no evidence that these shifts in terminology had any measurable impact on the handful of Japanese in a position to decide Japan's fate.

P. 215 "Intimate experience," "highly unlikely," "present dynasty": Grew, *Turbulent Era* 2:1421; on considerations influencing Grew, see Sigal, *Fighting to a Finish,* pp. 96–98.

P. 215 Grew's analysis: Sigal, *Fighting to a Finish,* pp. 96–102.

P. 216 Views of the "retentionists": Robert James Maddox, *Weapons for Victory: The Hi-*roshima Decision Fifty Years Later* (Columbia: University of Missouri Press, 1995), pp. 14–15.

P. 216 Views of the "abolitionists": Ibid., p. 15.

P. 216 Grew approaches Truman: Grew, Memorandum of Conversation, May 28, 1945, *Foreign Relations of the United States, Diplomatic Papers 1945,* volume 6, *The British Commonwealth: The Far East* (Washington, D.C.: Government Printing Office, 1969), pp. 545–46 [hereafter *FRUS, 1945*]; Grew, *Turbulent Era* 2:1434.

P. 217 Grew's failure and Stalin's announcements: Messages from Hopkins and "Russia will share in the actual occupation of Japan," Hopkins to President, Nos. 4541, 291150 May 45, and 5364, 300930 May 45, Incoming messages, Box 1, Folder Incoming messages, exact translation (1945 April to May), File of Map Room, Papers of HST, HSTL; the synopsis of the Soviet-American dispute over Poland is drawn from Martin J. Sherwin, *A World Destroyed: Hiroshima and the Origins of the Arms Race* (New York: Vintage, 1987), pp. 139–40, 151–75, 180–85, supplemented by Maddox, *Weapons for Victory,* pp. 21–24, 26–28, 36–42. Sherwin's work is rich in explaining the complex and varied attitudes of Truman's advisers as to how to deal with the Soviets and Truman's oscillating policy.

P. 217 June 18 meeting of Grew and Truman: Grew, Memorandum of Conversation, June 18, 1945, *FRUS, 1945,* 1:177; Sigal, *Fighting to a Finish,* pp. 116–17.

P. 218 Stimson's July 2 memo to Truman: Memorandum for the President, July 2, 1945, and attached "Proposed Program for Japan," Harry S. Truman Papers, Naval Aide Files, Box 4, Folder: Berlin Conference, Vol. 11, Japan, HSTL. Also found in *FRUS, 1945,* 1:890–94. See also Sigal, *Fighting to a Finish,* p. 125. Stimson's position by the May–June period represented an evolution of his thinking. Earlier in January, Stimson had noted in his diary that John McCloy had showed him a paper from Admiral King proposing a modification of the unconditional-surrender formula, which McCloy endorsed. Stimson, however, believed at that time that it would weaken the American position and wished to talk it over with Marshall (Stimson Diary, January 22, 1945). By certainly the day after the White House meeting that sanctioned Olympic, Stimson was noting in his diary that while he and Forrestal agreed with the proposed military program, they believed it "would be deplorable if we have to go through with the military program with all its stubborn fighting to a finish" and that some way should be found to induce Japan to surrender. Stimson Diary, June 19, 1945; see also June 26–30, 1945.

P. 218 Hull's exchanges with Byrnes: *FRUS, 1945,* 2:1267–68; Sherwin, *A World Destroyed,* p. 225.

P. 219 Combined Chiefs report to Truman and Churchill: CCS 900/3, 24 July 1945, Combined Chiefs of Staff Report to the President and Prime Minister, Naval Aide Files, Box 4, Folder: Berlin Conference, Vol. 11, Joint Chiefs, HSTL.

P. 219 Combined Chiefs intelligence: "Estimate of the Enemy Situation," July 8, 1945, CCS 643/2, in U.S. Department of Defense, *Entry of the Soviet Union,* p. 88; *FRUS, 1945,* 2:36n.

P. 219 Brooke's recommendation: Minutes of the 193rd meeting, Combined Chiefs of Staff, July 16, 1945, *FRUS, 1945,* 2:36–37.

P. 219 "From a purely military point of view": Minutes of the 196th meeting, Joint Chiefs of Staff, July 17, 1945, in ibid., p. 2:40.

P. 219 Leahy's "political level" remarks: Ibid. Secretary of War Stimson's diary confirms that Truman and Byrnes explained the omission of a guarantee of the Imperial institution from the final version of the ultimatum as purely tactical: They assumed the war would end in negotiations and that at that juncture they would proffer an assurance as to the Imperial institution. Stimson Diary, July 23–25 and August 9–10, 1945.

P. 220 JCS recommendation to Truman: JCS, Memorandum to the President, July 18, 1945, *FRUS, 1945,* 2:1269; Memorandum for the President from the Secretary of War, July 20, 1945, Harry S. Truman Papers, Naval Aide Files, Box 4, Folder: Berlin Conference, Vol. 11, Japan, HSTL. The source of the concerns on the language in the Stimson draft appears to have emerged in JCS 1275/5 from the Joint Strategic Survey Committee. This is also noted in Memorandum for General Hull from H. A. Craig, Major General, Acting Assistant Chief of Staff, Subject: JSSC [Joint Strategic Survey Committee] on Proclamation Regarding Unconditional Surrender of Japan, 14 July 1945, OPD 387.4 TS, microfilm, Marshall Library.

P. 220 The Zacharias broadcasts: Sigal, *Fighting to a Finish,* pp. 132–34; Alperovitz, *Decision to Use the Atomic Bomb,* pp. 394–404, 440. As Alperovitz points out, it is unclear whether Zacharias's broadcast about the Atlantic Charter had sanction of the OWI or the Navy Department. He finds indirect evidence of support from Forrestal, which might well be the case.

P. 221 Togo's reports to Sato: Togo's message of 25 June, Magic Diplomatic Summary, No. 1188, 26 Jun 45, SRH-079, p. 9; Togo's June 28 message, ibid., No. 1195, 3 July 45.

P. 221 Togo's June 30 message to Sato: Ibid., No. 1201, 9 July 45, and No. 1202, 10 July 45; SRH-084, pp. 2–3.

P. 221 Sato disparages initiative; Togo's order: 5 July message from the Foreign Ministry: Ibid., No. 1199, 7 July 45; Sato's July 5 message: Ibid., No. 1201, 9 July 45; Sato's July 6 message, Foreign Minister's July 9 message: Ibid., No. 1202, 10 July 45; SRH-084, pp. 6–7.

P. 221 Sato's report of meeting with Molotov: Magic Diplomatic Summary, No. 1205, 13 July 45; SRH-084, pp. 2–4. Sato had a preliminary meeting on July 10 with another Soviet Foreign Ministry official, Lozovsky: Magic Diplomatic Summary, No. 1204, 12 July 45.

P. 221 Togo's messages of July 11: Magic Diplomatic Summary, No. 1204, 12 July 45.

P. 222 Togo's message of July 12: Ibid., No. 1205, 13 July 45.

P. 223 American naval-intelligence commentary: SRH-084, pp. 9–10; Magic Diplomatic Summary, No. 1219, 27 July 45.

P. 223 Weckerling and Grew memos: Memorandums for the Deputy Chief of Staff, from Deputy Assistant Chief of Staff, G-2, 12 Jul 45 and 13 Jul 45, reel 109, item 2581, Marshall Library. Grew does not mention his participation in this assessment in his memoirs. It is therefore difficult to discern whether the omission can be attributed to the high security classification of such material or because it does not track well with his main argument that, with clarification of the status of the Emperor, Japan's surrender might have been readily procured. Grew, *Turbulent Era* 2:1421–41.

P. 225 Sato's responses to Togo's messages: Magic Diplomatic Summaries, No. 1206, 14 July 45, and No. 1207, 15 July 45; SRH-085, pp. 5–6.

P. 225 Reports: Ibid.

P. 225 Sato's "veneration" message: Ibid., No. 1206, 14 July 45, and No. 1207, 15 July 45; SRH-085, pp. 7–9.

P. 226 Sato's July 15 message: Ibid. No. 1208, 16 July 45; SRH-085, pp. 10–12.

P. 226 Togo's message of July 17: Magic Diplomatic Summary, No. 1209, 17 July 45; SRH-085, pp. 12–13.

P. 227 Big Six never agree to terms: Statement by Foreign Minister Shigenori Togo, 17 May 1949, pp. 24–27, CMH. Umezu's comments: Statement of Lt. General Masao Yoshizumi, 6 Jun 49, Doc. No. 61338, pp. 2–3, CMH. Admiral Toyoda said the Big Six "never discussed" actual terms to induce the Soviets to arrange a negotiated surrender. Statement of Admiral Soemu Toyoda, 29 Aug 49, Doc. No. 61340, p. 5, CMH. Premier Suzuki commented first that the government was split between those who "wanted to end the war by a *negotiated peace* and those who wanted to fight it out to the last, and no matter how many arguments and meetings we had, we could never get complete agreement anywhere in the government" (emphasis added). Statement of Baron Suzuki, 26 Dec 45, Interrogation No. 531, pp. 311–12, CMH. Suzuki's definition of the range of options under consideration is instructive. He then went on to indicate that the "only way was to negotiate with a neutral country such as Russia to bring the war to a close, with understanding that Japan would have to accept certain terms to effect that negotiation." When asked what specific concessions Japan was prepared to accept as a basis for negotiations through the Soviets, Suzuki said "Japan had not actually been able to make a decision regarding what terms it would accept." Thus, he was conceding there was not even agreement on what concessions had to be made to secure Soviet mediation, much less the terms Japan would present as the basis for mediation with the Allies. Ibid., p. 307.

P. 227 Emperor's stance on a special envoy: *Showa Tenno Dokuhakuroku,* pp. 136–38.

P. 228 Meeting of July 12 of Konoe and the Emperor: IMTFE Kido 31,164–71. The IMTFE version is used here in preference to the rendition in *Diary of Marquis Kido,* p. 440, because of some telling additional details in the former.

P. 228 The Emperor's account: *Diary of Marquis Kido,* p. 440, is used here in preference to the variant in IMTFE Kido 31,164–71, on the basis of the richness of the translation.

P. 228 Significance of the Emperor's meeting with Konoe: From this episode both Suzuki and Konoe (or more properly those invoking his name) spun deceptive tales designed to prove or suggest that the Emperor was far closer to accepting peace than the credible contemporary evidence shows. Premier Suzuki told American interrogators that there was no agreement as to what terms Japan would accept:

> Principally because it didn't know what demands would be made. There was no way of knowing what the United Nations

wanted since no declaration had been made and Japan itself naturally under the circumstances was prepared to accept almost any terms in order to achieve peace. Prince Konoye was on the point of going to Moscow *with Japan's decision regarding what terms it would accept* when the Potsdam conference began, and since the negotiation was still at a point where it wasn't even clear whether Russia would act as intermediary or not, we were in a quandary as to what the general situation was and what demands we would have to meet. Just at that time the Potsdam Declaration came and that was the end of attempted negotiation [emphasis added].

Statement of Suzuki, 26 Dec 45, Interrogation No. 531, p. 307, CMH. Clearly, the contemporary evidence from Kido's diary shows this statement grossly misrepresents the facts, since no agreement was ever achieved on terms for opening Soviet negotiation, much less peace, a fact Suzuki himself had conceded in the same statement as noted above.

Konoe allegedly told USSBS authorities that "he received direct and secret instructions from the Emperor to secure peace at any price, notwithstanding its severity." USSBS, no. 2, Office of the Chairman, *Japan's Struggle to End the War,* p. 44. The first problem with this assertion is that, as Robert Newman pointed out, a review of the material from which this report was derived discloses no such statement from Konoe. Newman, *Truman and the Hiroshima Cult,* p. 55. The second major problem is that neither Kido's contemporary diary nor the Emperor's own postwar statement provides any sustenance to such a proposition. The third problem is that it is directly challenged by Togo's 1949 interview. Statement of Shigenori Togo, 17 May 49, CMH.

On the topic of the Konoe mission, Herbert Bix describes a letter drafted at the Foreign Ministry for Konoe aimed at securing a Soviet guarantee for preservation of the throne and its incumbent. Bix also notes a document Konoe and his advisers drafted titled "Essentials of Peace Negotiations." This set the preservation of the emperor system as the rock-bottom condition for peace but allowed for the possibility of conceding all overseas possessions and disarmament, though only for a fixed period of time. An "interpretation" of "Essentials" specified that "interpretation of the *kokutai*" meant that "the main aim is to secure the imperial line and carry out politics by the emperor. In the worse case scenario, however, the transfer of the throne to a successor might be unavoidable." Bix points out that Konoe "did not

dare to seek the emperor's approval of his attached 'Interpretation.' " Bix, "Japan's Delayed
Surrender," pp. 216–17 and nn. 61–62.

P. 229   "It is . . . hard to deny that the Japanese
authorities": SRH-086, p. 1.

P. 229   Sato's July 18 message: Magic Diplomatic Summary, No. 1212, 20 July 45.

P. 229   Togo's message of July 21: Ibid., No.
1214, 22 July 45; SRH-086, p. 2.

P. 230   Sato's July 20 message: Ibid. No. 1214,
22 July 45, Tab A; SRH-086, pp. 3–4.

P. 230   Sato's interview of July 25 and Togo's
response: Ibid. No. 1218, 26 July 45, Part II, and
No. 1219, 27 July 45, Part II; SRH-086, pp. 6–7.

P. 230   First two parts of Togo's message: Ibid.
No. 1218, 26 July 45, Part II; SRH-086, pp. 8–9.

P. 231   Impact of Zacharias's broadcasts: The
statement that the Zacharias broadcasts attracted
attention in the Foreign Ministry but had no impact on the Imperial Army is in *Daihon'ei Rikugun-Bu (10)*, pp. 409–10.

P. 231   Naval-intelligence analysis of July 27:
Magic Diplomatic Summary, No. 1219, 27 July
45, SRS-494.

P. 232   Sato's message of July 27: Ibid., No.
1221, 29 July 45, Part II.

P. 232   Potsdam Declaration: Papers of Harry
S. Truman, Naval Aide Files, Box 4, Folder:
Berlin Conference, Vol. 11, Japan, HSTL.

P. 233   Australian government reaction: Col.
Bowen to Capt. Vardaman, 29 Jul 45, White
House Map Room NR 281, containing a moni-
tored radio broadcast from Melbourne. Papers of
Harry S. Truman, Naval Aide Files, Subject File,
Box 10, Folder: Japan Surrender (Folder 1),
HSTL.

P. 233   Togo's reaction to the Potsdam Declaration: Statement of Shigenori Togo, Doc. No.
61340, pp. 6, 26–27, CMH; Statement of Hisatsune Sakomizu, 12 Dec 49, Doc. No. 62016, p. 2,
CMH; IMTFE Togo 35,785. According to Ikeda,
the cabinet in fact was strongly against accepting
the Potsdam Declaration, and Suzuki's later statement that he had favored acceptance but was
overborne by the strong opposition of the military
circles was not factual. Statement of Sumihisa
Ikeda, 16 Jun 50, Doc. No. 54479, p. 3, CMH.

P. 234   Publication of Potsdam Declaration:
Butow, *Japan's Decision to Surrender*, pp.
146–48; Sigal, *Fighting to a Finish*, pp. 148–51.

P. 234   Meaning of *mokusatsu* and reaction:
Butow, *Japan's Decision to Surrender*, pp.
145–49.

P. 234   Postwar theories on use of *mokusatsu:*
Ibid., p. 146 n. 12. A typical example of an attempt to shift the blame to the military for this
disaster is IMTFE Sakomizu 35,607–8, where
the chief cabinet secretary insists that the military demanded from the start that Suzuki effectively choose the *mokusatsu* response or its
equivalent. See also statement of Hiroshi Shimomura, 30 Mar 50, Doc. No. 57668, p. 2, CMH.

P. 234   Yonai's response to Takagi: Bix,
"Japan's Delayed Surrender," p. 206; Togo and
"wait and see": Statement of Shigenori Togo, 17
May 49, p. 29, CMH.

P. 235   Suzuki to Shimomura: Bix, "Japan's
Delayed Surrender," p. 208. In a postwar statement to American interviewers, Shimomura was
one of those attempting to depict Suzuki as committed from the outset to securing peace. Statement of Hiroshi Shimomura, 30 Mar 50, Doc.
No. 57668, p. 1, CMH. The chief of the Cabinet
Planning Bureau also recounts this episode and
insisted after the war that Suzuki's public rejection of the Potsdam Declaration accurately reflected his personal views. Statement of
Sumihisa Ikeda, 23 Dec 49, Doc. No. 54479, pp.
2–3, CMH.

P. 235   Emperor's reaction to *mokusatsu:
Showa Tenno Dokuhakuroku*, p. 139; Bix,
"Japan's Delayed Surrender," p. 206.

P. 235   Sato's message of July 29: Magic
Diplomatic Summary, No. 1222, 30 July 45, Part
II; SRH-088, pp. 2–3.

P. 235   Togo's message of July 28: Ibid. No.
1221, 29 July 45, Part II; SRH-088, p. 3.

P. 236   Sato's message of July 30: Ibid., No.
1224, 1 August 45, Part II; SRH-088, p. 4. From
Switzerland, Minister Kase sent a cable along
much the same lines as Sato's. He also noted that
no such softening was ever shown to Germany.
He found the silence about the Imperial household encouraging, as was the language discussing unconditional surrender in connection with
the army, not the people or the government. See
also Ibid., No. 1225, 2 Aug 45, Part II; SRH-088,
pp. 5–6.

P. 236   Sato's report of July 30 meeting: Ibid.,
No. 1223, 31 July 45, Part II; SRH-088, p. 6.

P. 236   Togo's message of August 2: Ibid., No.
1225, 2 Aug 45, No. 1226, Part II, 3 August 45,
Part II; SRH-088, pp. 7–8.

P. 237   Commentary on Sato's message: Ibid.,
No. 1226, 3 Aug 45, Part II.

P. 237   Sato's message of August 3: Ibid., No.
1228, 5 Aug 45, Part II; SRH-088, pp. 9–10.

P. 238 Sato's message of August 4: Ibid., No. 1228, 5 Aug 45, Part II; SRH-088, p. 11.

P. 238 Naval-intelligence analysis of August 6: Ibid., pp. 16–17.

P. 238 Togo's message of July 21: Ibid., 22 July 45, SRH-086, p. 2. It is conceivable that Togo's flat rejection reflected not his personal view but his assessment of the prospects of such a proposal were it presented to his colleagues on the Supreme Council for the Direction of the War. This is essentially a distinction without a practical difference as to ending the war.

P. 239 Exchanges between Sato and Togo: Sato's July 15 message: Ibid., No. 1208, 16 July 45; SRH-085, pp. 10–12; Togo's message of July 17: Ibid., No. 1209, 17 July 45; SRH-085, pp. 12–13.

15. Magic and Diplomacy with the Soviets

P. 240 Truman's trip to Potsdam: Truman left Washington at 11:00 P.M., July 6. He reached Europe on July 15 via the cruiser *Augusta* and reached Potsdam on July 17. He departed from Potsdam on August 2 at 8:00 P.M. and reached Washington at 10:50 P.M. August 8. Papers of Harry S. Truman, President's Secretary's Files, Memo to Mr. Lloyd from Kenneth Hechler, 5 Jan 53, HSTL.

P. 241 Map Room summaries: Naval Aide Files, Subject Files, Box 11, Folder: "Trips of the President May–September 16, 1945" (outgoing messages); Map Room Files, Boxes 5 and 6, Berlin Conference, Communications from Map Room, July 7 to Aug. 2, 1945 HSTL. The only glimmers of secret intelligence peek from a reference in the summary for August 1 to the existence of a "Black Book" (which is where Ultra was filed in the Map Room), with no mention of contents, and one raw message from the White House Map Room that noted a CINCPAC estimate of Japanese strength of 4,495 aircraft in the Japan-Korea area on July 29.

P. 241 Exchanges from White House Map Room to detachment with Truman: 13 July 45, Lt. Myers to Commander Tyree, Map Room Out No. 115, referring to Map Room Out No. 105. No. 115 notes Marshall and King "are being kept posted by their office." (Interestingly, in the Truman Library copy of the Map Room files, there is a record of receipt of Map Room Out 105, but no copy of the actual message.)

13 July 45, Cdr. Tyree to Lt. Myers, NR 43: "RE Mike Roger [MR] 115. If Admiral Edwards approves of information of this nature being passed to us, send it to us and address it quote for Leahy's eyes only unquote."

14 July 45, Transcript of [Teletype] Conference, in which Washington asks if Truman's Map Room operation in Potsdam has Map Room Out 105. The reply states that "105 is one of the messages that we get by locked pouch and cannot be transmitted here." An unnumbered message of 11 July (sent with Map Room Out 93) from the Map Room to Admiral Leahy contains a notation that a courier with a "pouch" was departing the White House Map Room at 2235 Greenwich Time, 10 July and could be expected at Potsdam at approximately 10:30, July 14.

17 July 45, Cdr. Tyree to Cdr. Pinney, Map Room In 73, which notes "Admiral Leahy is being kept informed by Frank McCarthy. . . . The Admiral informs the President as necessary. Present arrangements considered satisfactory." Naval Aide Files, Subject Files, Box 11, Folder: "Trips of the President May–September 16, 1945" (outgoing messages); Map Room Files, Boxes 5 and 6, Berlin Conference, Communications from Map Room, July 7 to Aug. 2, 1945, HSTL.

P. 241 McCarthy's status: Forrest C. Pogue, *George C. Marshall, Organizer of Victory, 1943–1945* (New York: Viking Press, 1973), p. 63.

P. 241 "These MAGIC reports were going directly to decision makers": Kreis, *Piercing the Fog,* pp. 103–4.

P. 242 Magic totals: The figure of 2,068 includes the number of pages listed on each summary, with the addition of a number of special reports attached to Magic summaries. Magic 1995 releases, RG 457, Boxes 15–18.

P. 242 Truman's familiarity with messages: *FRUS, 1945* 1:873. This refers specifically to Togo's cables of July 12 and July 25 (this contains the excerpt "In all likelihood the difficult point is the attitude of the enemy in insisting on the form of unconditional surrender. If America and England stick to this, the whole thing will break down on this one point"). Another aspect of this episode is that the editors of *FRUS* had copies of the cables, but not the actual Magic Diplomatic Summary, with its key editing and interpretive comments. Thus, they entirely missed the significance of the exchange in which Sato proposed that the best terms Japan could obtain were unconditional surrender with an exception for retention of the Imperial institution and the flat rejection of this proposal by Togo.

P. 242 "Fini Japs when that comes about": Truman, "Potsdam Diary," July 17, 1945, President's Secretary's Files, Box 322, Personal File,

Mr. and Mrs. Charles G. Ross, HSTL. This is also found more easily in Ferrell, *Off the Record,* p. 53.

P. 242 "Discussed Manhattan [Project]": Truman, "Potsdam Diary," July 18, 1945; Ferrell, *Off the Record,* pp. 53–54.

P. 242 Interpreting Truman's diary: Confirmation of the fact that Stalin was the source of the report of the "telegram from Jap Emperor asking for peace" is found in "Walter Brown's Book" (conventionally referred to as Walter Brown's Notes), James F. Byrnes Papers, Box 602, Clemson University Libraries, and in the Leahy diary, July 18.

P. 243 Truman's letter of July 18: Harry Truman to Bess Truman, July 18, 1945, in Robert H. Ferrell, ed., *Dear Bess* (New York: W. W. Norton, 1983), p. 519.

P. 243 "The terrible responsibilities": Churchill's cable is covered in Martin Gilbert, *Winston S. Churchill,* vol. 8, *"Never Despair," 1945–1965* (Boston: Houghton Mifflin, 1988), pp. 69–70.

P. 243 "At 10:15 I had Gen. Marshall": Truman, "Potsdam Diary," July 25, 1945; Ferrell, *Off the Record,* pp. 55–56.

P. 243 Truman requests Marshall's views: Stimson Diary, July 23–24, 1945.

P. 244 Mountbatten's personal diary: Philip Ziegler, *Personal Diary of Admiral the Lord Louis Mountbatten, Supreme Allied Commander, South-East Asia, 1943–1946* (London: Collins, 1988), pp. 228–32. Barton Bernstein pointed out to me that Mountbatten's published diary entry for July 25 shows he was purportedly recording unbelievably accurate projected dates for the first use of the atomic bomb and the date of the Japanese capitulation. While this is clear evidence of after-the-fact editing, I do not find that it warrants casting out the entire entry.

P. 244 Leahy's handling of Ultra in 1944: Bradley F. Smith, *The Ultra-Magic Deals* (Novato, Calif.: Presidio Press, 1992), p. 186.

P. 245 Memorandum from Marshall to President, July 25: Memorandum for the President ("Japanese Capitulation"), 25 July 1945, RG 165, Entry 422, Box 12, Executive #2, Item #11, NARA.

P. 245 Truman's recollection of Marshall's estimate: Letter from Truman to Cate, January 12, 1953, in Craven and Cates, *The Pacific,* between pp. 712 and 713.

P. 245 "Even if the Japs are savages": Truman, "Potsdam Diary," July 25, 1945.

P. 246 "A most important session": Ibid. An argument has been advanced that Truman's comment that he did not expect the Japanese to accept the Potsdam Declaration reveals that he knew the terms were too stiff. This argument is founded on the erroneous notion that the Japanese were susceptible to surrender if such an offer was made, however, the Magic evidence is clearly to the contrary.

P. 246 "The distribution of MAGIC material": George C. Marshall Papers, Box 74, Folder 20, Marshall Library.

P. 246 "President, Leahy, [Byrnes] [agreed]": Walter Brown's Notes.

P. 246 "a very important paper": Stimson Diary, July 16–25, August 9–10, 1945.

P. 247 "We have good reason to believe": Grew, *Turbulent Era,* pp. 2:1438–39.

P. 248 "First real evidence": Forrestal Diary, July 7, 13–30, 1945.

P. 249 Truman requests Marshall's views: Stimson Diary, July 23–24, 1945.

P. 249 Stimson sees bomb as tool: Ibid., February 15, 1945.

P. 249 Stimson and Truman see bomb as means to extract quid pro quo: Stimson Diary, June 6, 1945; Truman buttressed by news of successful test of atomic bomb: Ibid., July 21–22, 1945.

P. 250 Stimson sobered by direct dealings with Soviets: Ibid., July 19, 1945.

P. 250 Stalin's adherence to unconditional surrender: Hopkins to President, No. 5364, 300930 May 45, Incoming messages, Box 1, Folder: Incoming messages, exact translation (1945 April to May), File of Map Room, Papers of HST, HSTL; Walter Brown's Notes, July 18, 1945.

P. 250 "He was afraid it would be ditched": Forrestal Diary, July 6, 1945.

P. 250 American perception of Soviet ambitions: Stimson Diary, July 23, 1945.

P. 250 "Byrnes said he was most anxious": Forrestal Diary, July 28, 1945. Walter Brown's Notes, July 20 and 24, confirm the sentiment.

P. 250 Consensus of historians: J. Samuel Walker, "The Decision to Use the Bomb: A Historiography Update," *Diplomatic History* 14 (winter 1990): esp. 110–11. This consensus was forged before the disclosure by Ultra on the buildup on Kyushu, as well as before a great deal of the revelations from Japan about the actual stance of the Emperor.

P. 251   Stimson-Roosevelt meeting, December 31, 1944: Stimson Diary, December 31, 1944. Warren F. Kimball points out that no later than September 1943, Roosevelt knew of Soviet penetration of the Manhattan Project (*Forged in War* [New York: William Morrow and Co., 1997], p. 221). Kimball also confirms that FDR never shared the atomic-bomb secret with the Soviets and, in fact, that American authorities had not always been ready to share that information even with the British! Kimball admirably lays out our limited understanding of FDR's ultimate thinking about the bomb and plausibly suggests that the President evaded commitment to a definitive policy until the weapon had been tested (pp. 267, 279–81, 328–29). The fact remains, however, that whereas FDR pursued an overall policy of winning Soviet trust, he quite clearly and steadfastly refused to share the atomic secret with the Soviets. It is hard to believe that FDR could have maintained these contrasting policies without some intent to use the atomic bomb for its political implications.

16. Hiroshima

P. 252   "The bomb might well give": Barton Bernstein, "The Atomic Bombings Reconsidered," *Foreign Affairs* 74.1 (January–February 1995): 135–52, at p. 136. There are many accounts of the Manhattan Project. For an accurate, comprehensive, and relatively economical presentation, Vincent C. Jones, *Manhattan: The Army and the Atomic Bomb* (Washington, D.C.: Center of Military History, 1985), is unexcelled. Also excellent but somewhat dated is Richard Hewlett and Oscar E. Anderson, *A History of the United States Atomic Energy Commission*, vol. 1, *The New World, 1939–1946* (University Park, Pa.: Pennsylvania State University Press, 1962). More stylish but derivative and encumbered with political baggage is Richard Rhodes, *The Making of the Atomic Bomb* (New York: Simon and Schuster, 1986). For Roosevelt's views, see Barton Bernstein, "Roosevelt, Truman, and the Atomic Bomb, 1941–45: A Reinterpretation"; *Political Science Quarterly* 90 (spring 1975): 23–69, esp. 24–34; and Sherwin, *A World Destroyed*. Also well worth examining in this context is James Hershberg, *James B. Conant: Harvard to Hiroshima and the Making of the Nuclear Age* (New York: Alfred A. Knopf, 1993), pp. 190–91, 204–6, 226. One example of how the political implications of the bomb in relations with the Soviets were recognized is found in the Stimson Diary, February 15, 1945. There Stimson notes a proposal by Vannevar Bush on scientific exchanges and comments that the plan was "along the right lines but that it would be inadvisable to put it into full force until we have gotten all we could in Russia in the way of liberalization in exchange for S-1 [the atomic bomb]."

P. 252   Atomic-bomb program and General Groves: Jones, *Manhattan*, pp. 52, 72, 73, 82, 115–16, 272–74; Rhodes, *Making of the Atomic Bomb*, pp. 425–26, 447–48. Owing to a need for much-increased funding, three congressmen and four senators were secretly briefed on the program in 1944.

P. 252   German atomic-bomb program: Bernstein, "Atomic Bombings Reconsidered," p. 139; Jones, *Manhattan*, pp. 102–4, 287–91; Rhodes, *Making of the Atomic Bomb*, pp. 344–45. Thomas Powers argues that Werner Heisenberg, on moral grounds, deliberately sabotaged the German atomic-bomb program by overstating the critical mass. *Heisenberg's War* (Boston: Little, Brown, 1993), pp. 73–74, 447–52. To reach this conclusion, however, Powers has to explain away the simpler explanation, for which there is excellent evidence, that Heisenberg simply erred.

P. 253   Japanese atomic-bomb programs: *Hondo Boku Sakusen*, pp. 631–34; " 'NI' and 'F': Japan's Wartime Atomic Bomb Research," in Dower, *Japan in War and Peace*, pp. 55–100.

P. 253   Power of bombs: See Memorandum to the Chief of Staff, 7 August 1944, Subject: Atomic Fission Bombs—Present Status and Expected Progress; and Memorandum to the Chief of Staff, December 30, 1944, Subject: Atomic Fission Bombs. Copy kindly supplied to author by Barton Bernstein.

P. 253   Availability of bombs: Ibid., Memorandum of December 30, 1944.

P. 254   "I had set out as the governing factor": Leslie Groves, *Now It Can Be Told: The Story of the Manhattan Project* (New York: Harper and Brothers, 1962), p. 267.

P. 254   Strategy of shock and target criteria: Bernstein, "Atomic Bombings Reconsidered," pp. 139–41. For the strategy of shock, the key text is Henry L. Stimson, "The Decision to Use the Atomic Bomb," *Harper's*, February 1947, pp. 97–107. Marshall, in his own words, confirmed this view in Forrest C. Pogue, *George C. Marshall: Interviews and Reminiscences* (Lexington, Ky.: George C. Marshall Research Foundation, 1991), pp. 423–25. Hershberg notes that Conant and "others" on the Interim Committee likewise subscribed to the strategy of shock. Hershberg, *James B. Conant*, p. 227.

P. 254   May meeting: Bernstein, "Atomic Bombings Reconsidered," p. 141; Jones, *Manhattan*, p. 529.

P. 255 Power estimates: Rhodes, *Making of the Atomic Bomb,* pp. 630–31; Lawrence Freedman and Saki Dockrill, "Hiroshima: A Strategy of Shock," in Saki Dockrill, ed., *From Pearl Harbor to Hiroshima* (New York: St. Martin's Press, 1994), p. 198.

P. 255 "From the psychological point of view": Bernstein, "Atomic Bombings Reconsidered," pp. 140–42.

P. 256 Interim Committee and Marshall's targeting priorities: Bernstein, "Atomic Bombings Reconsidered," pp. 142–43; Memorandum of Conversation with General Marshall, May 29, 1945, Subject: Objectives towards Japan and methods of concluding war with minimum casualties, George C. Marshall Papers, Verifax 2798, Marshall Library. It was at this meeting that Marshall also broached the limited use of poison gas against fanatical and suicidal Japanese forces. The title of this memorandum evidences what drove policy making.

P. 256 May 31 meeting: Notes of the Interim Committee, May 31, 1945, reproduced as Appendix L, Sherwin, *A World Destroyed,* pp. 295–304. For the estimate of 20,000 Japanese deaths, see Bernstein, "Atomic Bombings Reconsidered," pp. 143–44.

The Interim Committee is one of the numerous flash points of the postwar debate on the use of atomic weapons. On the question of the military use of the bomb and the Interim Committee, see Bernstein, "Roosevelt, Truman, and the Atomic Bomb," pp. 36–37. Bernstein stresses that the committee was not explicitly charged to review military use, that its membership was imbued with the assumption that the bomb would be used, and that it actually entertained only relatively brief and cursory discussion over use. Alperovitz, *Decision to Use the Atomic Bomb,* pp. 163–65, if anything discounts the significance of the Interim Committee even more. Maddox comments that "most accounts exaggerate the importance of the [Interim Committee] meetings" (*Weapons for Victory,* p. 45). While all of Bernstein's points are valid, and the significance of the Interim Committee can be exaggerated, the committee did actually look, however briefly, at alternatives, and, compared with any other venue, this was probably the one clear instant when the momentum might have been checked, if Stimson and Marshall had chosen to question it. From what we know now about Ultra revelations on Olympic later in the summer, however, I believe that even if the use of atomic bombs had been reexamined in May–June, there is almost no chance they would not have been ultimately employed in August.

P. 257 "After much discussion": Notes of the Interim Committee, May 31, 1945.

P. 257 "The only reasonable conclusion": Maddox, *Weapons for Victory,* p. 108; Rhodes, *Making of the Atomic Bomb,* p. 651.

P. 257 Bernstein's analysis and Groves's quote: Bernstein, "Roosevelt, Truman, and the Atomic Bomb," pp. 34–35; Groves, *Now It Can Be Told,* p. 265.

P. 258 These men "all knew": Bernstein, "Atomic Bombings Reconsidered," p. 144.

P. 258 Stimson questions Arnold: Rhodes, *Making of the Atomic Bomb,* p. 650; Bernstein, "Atomic Bombings Reconsidered," pp. 146–47; "I have told": Truman, Potsdam Diary, July 25, 1945, President's Secretary's Files, Box 322, Personal File, Mr. and Mrs. Charles G. Ross, HSTL.

P. 258 Senior officials fail to grasp realities: Kimball, *Forged in War,* pp. 279–81. Kimball quotes James B. Conant for the propositions that Roosevelt had "only fleeting interest in the atom, and that the program never got very far past the threshold of his consciousness," and that FDR "really had no idea of the enormous importance of our [atomic] secrets."

P. 258 Bush and Conant positions: Hershberg, *James B. Conant,* pp. 218–19, 226–29; G. Pascal Zachary, *Endless Frontier: Vannevar Bush, Engineer of the American Century* (New York: Free Press, 1997), pp. 214–15, 283.

P. 258 Demonstration concept: Hewlett and Anderson, *New World,* p. 345.

P. 258 Bohr and Roosevelt: Bernstein, "Roosevelt, Truman, and the Atomic Bomb," pp. 28–29; Rhodes, *Making of the Atomic Bomb,* pp. 534–38, 561–62; Sherwin, *A World Destroyed,* pp. 105–14; David Holloway, *Stalin and the Bomb* (New Haven: Yale University Press, 1994), pp. 118–19.

P. 259 Leo Szilard: Maddox, *Weapons for Victory,* p. 65; Sherwin, *A World Destroyed,* p. 201. For Conant's complex views see Sherwin, p. 200, and especially Hershberg, *James B. Conant,* p. 229. The Byrnes-Szilard episode is easy to caricature in one of two ways: (a) Byrnes generally as a short sighted demon of anti-Soviet animus and Szilard a visionary saint; or (b) Byrnes as a hard-headed realist and Szilard as a quixotic and naive gadfly. Most notably, Szilard long after these events recalled Byrnes saying that the bomb "would make Russia more manageable in Europe." This has been repeatedly treated, very dubiously in my judgment, as a verbatim transcription.

P. 259 Szilard-Byrnes meeting: Maddox, *Weapons for Victory,* pp. 66–67; Sherwin, *A World Destroyed,* pp. 200–2.

P. 259 Franck Report: "The Political Implications of Atomic Weapons: Excerpts from the Franck Report, June 11, 1945," reproduced as Appendix S in Sherwin, *A World Destroyed,* pp. 323–33; Jones, *Manhattan,* pp. 532–33; Maddox, *Weapons for Victory,* pp. 61–62. Henry Wallace forwarded a memorandum from Szilard in September 1945 that read in part: "Three to six years from now, Russia is likely to have a stockpile of atomic bombs of her own. I do not believe that an armed peace in which the United States and Russia have large stockpiles of atomic bombs can be a durable peace." Wallace Memorandum with enclosure, September 27, 1945, President's Secretary's Files, Box 199, Subject File, NSC Atomic Bomb—Cabinet (Henry A. Wallace), HSTL.

P. 260 Panel report: "Science Panel: Recommendations on the Immediate Use of Nuclear Weapons, June 16, 1945," reproduced as Appendix M, in Sherwin, *A World Destroyed,* pp. 304–5.

P. 260 "As scientific men": Ibid. and pp. 213–17; Maddox, *Weapons for Victory,* pp. 63–64, 68–70, 85–87. Barton Bernstein pointed out to me that Bard denied meeting Truman in the August 15, 1960, edition of *U.S. News and World Report.* I have profound intuitive doubt about Bard's claim that he warned Truman of a million casualties, as opposed to simply serious casualties, but apart from a belief in the fickleness of human memory, I have no objective basis on which to prove or disprove this. If Bard did mention a million casualties, it would be further evidence that talk of such numbers floated widely in the Navy Department. Moreover, by at least August 10, Stimson was speaking in terms of such casualty totals.

P. 261 "The whole country was lighted": General Groves, Memorandum to the Secretary of War, 18 July 45, reproduced as Appendix P in Sherwin, *A World Destroyed,* pp. 308–14, also found in Papers of Lansing Lamont, HSTL; Jones, *Manhattan,* pp. 465, 478–81, 511–18; Rhodes, *Making of the Atomic Bomb,* pp. 651–78; Stimson Diary, July 21, 1945.

P. 261 Organization and movement of 509th: 20th AF Tactical Mission Report, 509th Group, 20 July–14 August, pp. 1–2; Jones, *Manhattan,* pp. 521–23; Paul W. Tibbets, Jr., *The Tibbets Story* (New York: Stein and Day, 1978), chaps. 12–16, 21. Tibbets indicates his original instructions were to ready units to drop atomic bombs in Europe and the Pacific (p. 179).

P. 261 Practice missions: 20th AF Tactical Mission Report, 509th Group, 20 July–14 August, pp. 1–3.

P. 262 Spaatz demands written orders; target-selection criteria; POW presence: General Thomas T. Handy to General Carl Spaatz, 25 July 1945, Spaatz Papers, Library of Congress, Box 21, Folder July; Headquarters Twentieth Air Force, Tactical Mission Report, Special Mission, 20 July–14 August 1945, pp. 3–5; Jones, *Manhattan,* pp. 528–30; Rhodes, *Making of the Atomic Bomb,* pp. 639–41, 647; Sherwin, *A World Destroyed,* p. 234; CINCPAC ADVANCE to COMINCH 030212 Aug 45, CINCPAC Command Summary, p. 3503. As to stories that Kyoto remained a target, a 1992 article distributed by the Associated Press contained the assertion by a Japanese researcher, Professor Morio Yoshida, that the practice missions flown in the vicinity of Kyoto signified that Kyoto was, in fact, on the list of prospective targets for atomic attack. Washington *Times,* December 6, 1992, p. 1. The documentary record that this was not so seems beyond reasonable dispute.

P. 262 "The entire northeast and eastern sides": Headquarters Twentieth Air Force, Tactical Mission Report, Special Mission, 20 July–14 August 1945, pp. 13–14.

P. 263 Troop presence in Hiroshima: Rhodes, *Making of the Atomic Bomb,* p. 713; SRH-203, 11/12 Aug, No. 120.

P. 264 Takeoff of August 6 mission: Headquarters Twentieth Air Force, Tactical Mission Report, Special Mission, 20 July–14 August 1945, p. 16; Jones, *Manhattan,* pp. 536–38. Little Boy was called a gun-type bomb because the two U-235 components were detonated by firing one of them (the "bullet") by a cordite charge down a gun barrel into the other (the "target").

P. 264 "Shimmering leaves, reflecting sunlight": Michihiko Hachiya, M.D., *Hiroshima Diary* (Chapel Hill: University of North Carolina Press, 1955), pp. 1–2, 34; time of alerts, *Daihon'ei Rikugun-Bu (10),* pp. 415; Adrian Weale, ed., *Eye Witness Hiroshima* (New York: Carroll and Graf, 1995), p. 149.

P. 264 "Dazzling gleam from its mighty flank": Weale, *Eye Witness Hiroshima,* p. 149; Rhodes, *Making of the Atomic Bomb,* p. 714.

P. 264 Story of P. Siomes: "Atomic Bombing of Hiroshima," Eyewitness Account of P. Siomes, Papers of Edmund J. Winslett, USAMHI; "Report of Army [Japanese] Medical Committee . . . 13 August 1945" (translation), RG 4, Box 1, Folder 2, MacArthur Archive. On the *pika-don,* see Hachiya, *Hiroshima Diary,* p. 37; Rhodes, *Making of the Atomic Bomb,* p. 717.

P. 265 Shadows: Col. A. E. Schanze Papers, "This Was the Army," USAMHI. Schanze was the assistant chief of staff, G-1, Eighth Army. There is a picture of the shadow of the man at the bank in *The Effects of the Atomic Bombs at Hiroshima and Nagasaki,* Report of the British Mission to Japan (London: His Majesty's Stationery Office, 1946) [hereafter "Report of the British Mission to Japan"], President's Secretary's Files, Box 199, Subject File: Atomic Bomb—Hiroshima and Nagasaki, HSTL. After ages two to four years, motor and sensory nerve conduction for normal humans ranges from forty to eighty meters per second; the value is lower in infants. Obviously, the speed of light is vastly faster than this. Raymond D. Adams, M.D., and Maurice Victor, M.D., *Principles of Neurology,* 2d ed. (New York: McGraw-Hill, 1981), p. 77.

P. 265 Light waves and primary burns: USSBS, no. 3, *Office of the Chairman, The Effects of Atomic Bombs on Hiroshima and Nagasaki,* p. 17; Rhodes, *Making of the Atomic Bomb,* p. 714; Cook and Cook, *Japan at War,* p. 396.

P. 265 Story of Michiko Yamaoka: Cook and Cook, *Japan at War,* pp. 384–86.

P. 266 Story of Shin Bok Su: Ibid., pp. 388–90.

P. 266 Initial reaction of Dr. Hachiya: Hachiya, *Hiroshima Diary,* pp. 1–2, 4.

P. 266 "Three high school girls": Rhodes, *Making of the Atomic Bomb,* p. 718.

P. 266 Dr. Hachiya and wife see bodies: Hachiya, *Hiroshima Diary,* p. 8.

P. 267 Hachiya and Katsutani quotes: Ibid., pp. 23, 15, 12, 19.

P. 267 Leveling of Hiroshima Castle: This is graphically illustrated by photographs in Goldstein, Dillon, and Wenger, *Rain of Ruin,* p. 61; evidence of the effect of bombs on Hata and staff of Second General Army is in Magic Far East Summary, 17 September 1945, SRS-539; "burnt sword was found": Fuller, *Shokan,* p. 91.

P. 267 Imperial Army medical report and British mission: "Report of Army [Japanese] Medical Committee . . . 13 August 1945" (translation), RG 4, Box 1, Folder 2, MacArthur Archive; "Report of the British Mission to Japan."

P. 267 Radiation deaths: Hachiya, *Hiroshima Diary,* pp. 21, 29, 36; Cook and Cook, *Japan at War,* pp. 390–91.

P. 268 "The gamma rays do not attack the cells": "Report of the British Mission to Japan."

P. 269 "As a result of the horrible catastrophes": SRS-505, 7 Aug 45.

P. 269 News reaches Tokyo: *Daihon'ei Rikugun-Bu (10),* p. 418; Freedman and Dockrill, "Hiroshima: A Strategy of Shock," p. 203; Statement of Lt. Gen. Torashiro Kawabe, 23 Aug 48, Doc. No. 61539, CMH; Butow, *Japan's Decision to Surrender,* pp. 150–51. Kawabe reported he was aware of the possibility of an atomic bomb from a briefing by Dr. Nishina or one of Nishina's associates.

P. 269 "We are now prepared to obliterate": Statement by the President of the United States (August 6, 1945), *FRUS, 1945,* 2:1376–78; Freedman and Dockrill, "Hiroshima: A Strategy of Shock," p. 204; Butow, *Japan's Decision to Surrender,* p. 151; Statement of Hiroshi Shimomura, 30 Mar 1050, Doc. No. 57668, p. 3, CMH; Statement of Hisatsune Sakomizu, 12 Dec 1949, Doc. No. 62016, p. 3, CMH; *Public Papers of the Presidents: Harry S. Truman, 1945* (Washington, D.C.: Government Printing Office, 1961), p. 149.

P. 270 "At a glance": Statements of Dr. Yoshio Nishina, 4 May 50, Doc. Nos. 60245–46, CMH; "Everything which is exposed gets burned": Statement of Lt. Gen. Seizo Arisue, Doc. No. 61411, CMH.

P. 270 Conflicting theories and conclusion of study: *Hondo Boku Sakusen,* pp. 634–42; see also Nishina's statement of May 4, 1950, in previous note.

P. 270 Effect of the atomic bomb on the royal family: Statement of Lt. Col. Masao Inaba, 13 Oct 49, Doc. No. 57692, p. 7, CMH.

P. 270 Reactions by senior officials to atomic bombing: Statement of Sumihisa Ikeda, 23 Dec 49, Doc. No. 54479, pp. 3–4, CMH (which indicates the Technical Board representative on the Atomic Bomb Countermeasures Committee "strongly insisted that the bomb was not an atomic bomb"); Statement of Admiral Soemu Toyoda, 29 Aug 49, Doc. No. 61340, p. 7, CMH; Statement by Foreign Minister Shigenori Togo, 17 May 49, p. 30, CMH. Toyoda observed that the scientific concept of an atomic bomb was "nothing novel," but his detailed understanding of the practical realities of making a bomb strongly suggests he gained the knowledge from Japan's nuclear program.

P. 271 Reaction of Kawabe to news of bomb: *Daihon'ei Rikugun-Bu (10),* p. 420. Kawabe, like Toyoda, understood the theoretical possibilities of an atomic bomb far better than his peers did due to a briefing by Dr. Nishina or one of his assistants. Statement of Lt. Gen. Torashiro Kawabe, 23 Aug 48, Doc. No. 61539, CMH.

P. 271 Togo searches for truth and Army response: Statement by Foreign Minister Shigenori Togo, 17 May 49, pp. 30–31, CMH; *Daihon'ei Rikugun-Bu (10),* pp. 421–22; see also Sadao Asada, "Shock of the Atomic Bomb." *Daihon'ei Rikugun-Bu (10)* notes that this meeting was variously reported as in the morning and in the afternoon.

P. 271 B-29 raid on August 7 and public announcement about atomic bomb: *Daihon'ei Rikugun-Bu (10),* pp. 421–22; 20th AF MR, No. 317. The only B-29 lost fell to flak, but the entire crew was saved.

P. 271 Reaction of Kido and Emperor: *Daihon'ei Rikugun-Bu (10),* p. 422; Asada, "Shock of the Atomic Bomb"; Statement of Koichi Kido, 17 May 49, Doc. No. 61541, p. 5, CMH. *Diary of Marquis Kido,* p. 443, records this exchange between Kido and the Emperor: "From 1:30 to 2:05 P.M. I was received by His Majesty in the imperial library. He was gravely concerned to save the situation, and asked me various questions."

P. 271 Togo's version of the interview: Asada, "Shock of the Atomic Bomb"; See also Butow, *Japan's Decision to Surrender,* pp. 152–53. Asada's source is Shigenori Togo, *Jidai No Ichiman: Taisen Gaikuo No Shuki* (An Aspect of the Showa Era: Memoirs of Wartime Diplomacy) (Tokyo, 1952), p. 341. In a postwar interview with American interrogators, Togo was recorded as stating: "The Emperor indicated clearly that the enemy's new weapon made it impossible to go on fighting" and agreed explicitly with Togo's view that Japan must "lose no time in ending the war" by accepting the Potsdam Declaration. Statement by Former Foreign Minister Shigenori Togo, 17 May 49, p. 31, CMH. *Daihon'ei Rikugun-Bu (10),* p. 426, however, observes that the Kido diary does not directly support Togo's account. The actual course of events, particularly during the afternoon of August 9, is also a challenge to Togo's account.

In a postwar statement, the Emperor's chief aide-de-camp claimed that the atomic bomb did not hasten the Emperor's decision to end the war immediately and that, being a scientist, Hirohito was "not so greatly perturbed." Statement by Shigeru Hasunuma, 31 Mar 50, Doc. No. 58225, p. 4, CMH. This statement may be discounted on the basis that it was given nearly five years after the event and that it is inconsistent with at least two contemporary sources, Kido's diary and the diary of another aide-de-camp. There is also the evidence of the Emperor's reference to the bomb at the Imperial conferences on August 9 and 14 and in his message announcing the surrender. Hasunuma's sense of the impact of the bomb

might be correct to the degree that through the afternoon of August 9, Kido, presumably representing the Emperor's views, appeared prepared to contemplate favorably a more generous peace proposal that clearly would have been unacceptable to the Allies. This subject is explored in the text below.

17. Manchuria and Nagasaki

P. 273 "The possible effect upon OLYMPIC operations": Joint War Plans Committee, JWPC 397 4 August 1945 (with attached copy of "Defensive Preparations in Japan," JIC), RG 218, NARA.

P. 274 Joint Staff Planners in July and August: Joint Staff Planners, Minutes of 210th Meeting, 4 Jul 45, 211th Meeting, 18 July 45, 212th Meeting, 1 (3) Aug 45, and 213th Meeting, 8 Aug 45, George C. Marshall Papers, Xerox 1540, part 9, Marshall Library.

P. 274 Joint Staff Planners on August 8: Joint Staff Planners, Minutes of 213th Meeting, 8 Aug 45, George C. Marshall Papers, Xerox 1540, part 9, Marshall Library.

P. 274 Marshall to MacArthur exchange: OPD (WAR) [Marshall] to MACARTHUR WAR 45369; CINCAFPAC [MacArthur] to WARCOS [Marshall] C 31897, CINCPAC Command Summary, Book Seven, pp. 3508–10. The exchange is also found in OPD Top Secret Incoming Msg Jul 28–Aug 17, 1945, RG 165, Box 39, NARA.

P. 275 "MacArthur consistently dismissed ULTRA evidence" and Luzon: Drea, *MacArthur's Ultra,* pp. 180–85, 229–30.

P. 276 "so prone to exaggerate": Stimson Diary, December 27, 1944. Along the same theme, in March, when Stimson contemplated MacArthur's fitness to command the final invasion of Japan, the Secretary of War noted that despite MacArthur's success, his "unpleasant" personality had affronted "all the men of the Army and the Navy with whom he has to work," and his staff, infected by his personality, was a "source of danger to harmony in what ought to be a most harmonious operation." Stimson Diary, March 30, 1945.

P. 276 King to Nimitz: COMINCH AND CNO TO CINCPAC ADV HQ 092205 Aug 45 (headed "KING TO NIMITZ EYES ONLY") and attached copies of CINCAFPAC to WARCOS C 31897 and OPD (WAR) to MACARTHUR WAR 45369, CINCPAC Command Summary, Book Seven, pp. 3508–10. This section of the Command Summary contains closely held or "EYES ONLY" traffic. The daily narrative in the Command Summary is silent on this exchange, and these messages are in scrambled order there, which may or may not reflect the sequence of transmission for security purposes. The conclusion that Nimitz never replied to King is based upon an exhaustive search of voluminous message files, including those dealing with secret flag-officer communications, with the invaluable assistance of the staff of the Naval History Center.

P. 277   Majestic substituted for Olympic: Joint Chiefs of Staff to Commander in Chief, Army Forces Pacific Command . . . [and Nimitz and Spaatz], 9 Aug 45, WARX 47190, 381 POA (6-10-43), Sec. 13, RG 218, NARA.

P. 277   August 8 raid: 20th AF MR, no. 319-20, pp. 1-18, Consolidated Statistical Summaries. The modest size of the strike force for Yawata was due to crashes that limited the 58th Wing to only thirty-five Superfortresses.

P. 277   Surprise Soviet attack: David M. Glantz, *August Storm: Soviet Tactical and Operational Combat in Manchuria, 1945,* Leavenworth Paper No. 8 (Fort Leavenworth, Kans.: Combat Studies Institute, U.S. Army Command and General Staff College, 1983), pp. 21-26, 28.

P. 277   "August Storm": David M. Glantz, *August Storm: The Soviet 1945 Strategic Offensive in Manchuria,* Leavenworth Paper No. 7 (Fort Leavenworth, Kans.: Combat Studies Institute, U.S. Army Command and General Staff College, 1983), pp. 5-7.

P. 277   Soviets plan for Manchuria offensive: Glantz, Ibid., pp. xvii, 1-2, 4; T. N. Depuy and Paul Martell, *Great Battles on the Eastern Front* (Indianapolis: Bobbs-Merrill, 1982), p. 241.

P. 278   Soviet organization: Glantz, *Soviet 1945 Strategic Offensive,* pp. 41-49, 52-56, 59; John Erickson, *The Road to Stalingrad* (New York: Harper and Row, 1975), pp. 122, 134, 280.

Based on data from Glantz, the Trans-Baikal Front spanned 2,300 kilometers and packed 41.4 percent of the total Soviet forces in the Far East with thirty rifle divisions, five cavalry divisions, two tank divisions, ten tank brigades, eight mechanized, motorized, or motorized armored brigades, and an array of support units.

The First Far Eastern Front was formed into thirty-one rifle divisions, one cavalry division, twelve tank brigades, two mechanized brigades, and support units. The importance of Meretskov's missions is illustrated by the fact that he had only seven hundred kilometers of frontage but 37.2 percent of the Soviet Far East forces.

The Second Far Eastern Front had 21.4 percent of Soviet Far East forces in twelve divisions

(including antiaircraft), seventeen brigades (including eight tank), thirty-five regiments, and five "Fortified Regions" (roughly the equivalent of regiments).

The basic operational unit on the front was the combined-arms army, roughly equivalent to a large Western corps. Its total strength numbered 80,000-100,000 men organized into seven to twelve rifle divisions divided among three rifle corps, two to three tank brigades, one or two gun artillery brigades, a tank-destroyer brigade, and supporting units. The standard tank corps (really a division by American, British, or German standards) comprised 11,788 men in three tank brigades and one motorized rifle brigade, which, with support units, fielded 228 tanks and 42 self-propelled guns. A mechanized corps numbered 16,314 men and reversed the organization of the tank corps with its three mechanized and one tank brigade. With support units, it fielded 183 tanks and 63 self-propelled guns. The authorized establishment of a rifle division in 1945 was 11,780 men, while a tank brigade of 1,354 men normally comprised 65 tanks with support units that incorporated a motorized rifle battalion.

P. 278   Soviet losses in Europe: David M. Glantz and Jonathan House, *When Titans Clashed* (Lawrence: University Press of Kansas, 1995), pp. 57, 285-86, 292 (Table A). The figures by Glantz and House show Red Army (which included aviation units) wartime losses as follows:

Killed in battle or died in evacuation	5,187,190
Died of wounds in hospital	1,100,327
Died of illness (nonbattle)	541,920
Subtotal (certain deaths)	6,829,437
Missing in action and captured	4,455,620
Total	11,285,057

Of the massive number of Soviet soldiers captured by the Germans, at least 3.3 million died in captivity. Thus, the total number of dead among Red Army members reached at least 10,129,437. The exact number of Soviet civilian losses during the war period remains controversial, though there is no doubt it was immense, at least equaling and far more likely exceeding the number of military deaths. Beyond the controversy over absolute numbers, there is a further question of whether the totals offered by Soviet officials incorporated deaths due to actions of the Soviet government, such as the mass deaths among some forcibly exiled nationalities.

P. 278   Soviet armored vehicles: Glantz, *Soviet 1945 Strategic Offensive,* pp. 44, 177.

P. 278 Strategic plans for "August Storm": Ibid., p. 73; David M. Glantz, "The Soviet Invasion of Japan," *Military History Quarterly* 7.3 (spring 1995): 96–97.

P. 278 Background of Kwantung Army: Glantz, *Soviet 1945 Strategic Offensive*, p. 25.

P. 278 Organization of Kwantung Army: Ibid., p. 29, table; Alvin D. Coox, "The Effectiveness of the Japanese Military Establishment in the Second World War," in Allan R. Millett and Williamson Murray, eds., *Military Effectiveness*, vol. 3, *The Second World War* (Boston: Allen and Unwin, 1988), p. 19; Fuller, *Shokan*, p. 231.

P. 280 Departure of units from Kwantung Army: *Daihon'ei Rikugun-Bu (10)*, p. 70; *Reports of General MacArthur, Japanese Operations in the Southwest Pacific Area*, p. 2:2:644 n. 112; Glantz, *Soviet 1945 Strategic Offensive*, pp. 26–33, 51; Coox, "Effectiveness of the Japanese Military Establishment," p. 19. The figure given by Glantz for Japanese aircraft strength is 1,800, but this is apparently derived from Soviet sources, and other information indicates that the total of fifty aircraft provided by Coox is far nearer the mark.

P. 280 Qualitative assessment of Kwantung Army: Glantz, *Soviet 1945 Strategic Offensive*, pp. 196–97.

P. 280 Revised strategic plans: Ibid., p. 34; *Daihon'ei Rikugun-Bu (10)*, pp. 68–71; failure to notify lower-level officers or civilians: Edward J. Drea, "Missing Intentions: Japanese Intelligence and the Soviet Invasion of Manchuria, 1945," *Military Affairs* (April 1984): 69.

P. 281 Observations by diplomatic couriers: Dip. No. 1159, 28 May 45, SRS-1681; see also Dip. No. 1150, 17 May 45, SRS-1672; Dip. No. 1175, 13 Jun 45, SRS-1697; Dip. No. 1185, 23 Jun 45, SRS-1707.

P. 281 Japanese intelligence assessment: Drea, "Missing Intentions," pp. 66–73.

P. 281 Japanese deployment: Glantz, *Soviet Tactical and Operational Combat*, pp. 12–14, 102; Glantz, *Soviet 1945 Strategic Offensive*, p. 120.

P. 281 Initial Soviet assault: Glantz, *Soviet Tactical and Operational Combat*, pp. 14–15, 17, 20, 29–35, 39–45, 49–51, 60–62, 66–73, 89–94; Glantz, *Soviet 1945 Strategic Offensive*, pp. 35, 136–37, 141–42.

P. 282 Geography of western Manchuria: Glantz, *Soviet 1945 Strategic Offensive*, pp. 8–9.

P. 282 Japanese strategic appreciation of western Manchuria: Glantz, *Soviet Tactical and Operational Combat*, p. 135.

P. 282 Soviet Thirty-sixth Army attack plans: Ibid., p. 166; Glantz, *Soviet 1945 Strategic Offensive*, p. 93.

P. 282 Japanese deployments around Hailar: Glantz, *Soviet Tactical and Operational Combat*, pp. 164–65.

P. 282 Initial attack of Soviet Thirty-sixth Army: Glantz, *Soviet Tactical and Operational Combat*, pp. 173–75; Glantz, *Soviet 1945 Strategic Offensive*, p. 93.

P. 282 Attack by Soviet Thirty-ninth Army: Glantz, *Soviet Tactical and Operational Combat*, pp. 139–43, 151–52; Glantz, *Soviet 1945 Strategic Offensive*, p. 88. Specifically, Lyudnikov detailed only the 124th Rifle Division to take on the main Japanese fortifications in the pass. Two other rifle divisions of the Ninety-fourth Rifle Corps were to swing north on a secondary attack toward Hailar. The Army's main punch comprised the tank division, both tank brigades, and the other six rifle divisions. It advanced south of the pass and aimed for Solun.

P. 282 Advances of Trans-Baikal front: Glantz, *Soviet 1945 Strategic Offensive*, pp. 2, 81–83, 96–99, 106–7, 136–37.

P. 283 Soviet Second Far Eastern Front mission: Glantz, *Soviet Tactical and Operational Combat*, p. 179.

P. 283 Purkayev's attack in northern Manchuria: Ibid., pp. 179–84; Glantz, *Soviet 1945 Strategic Offensive*, pp. 149–51, 153. Up to 150 kilometers to the west of Mamonov's effort, Lieutenant General Makar F. Terekhin's Second Red Banner Army of three rifle divisions and one mountain rifle regiment mounted a supporting attack from the Blagoveshchensk area to seize the Aihun and Sunwu Fortified Regions and penetrate south across the Lesser Khingan Mountains to Tsitsihar and Harbin. Over eighty marshy kilometers to the east of the Fifteenth Army, Major General I. Z. Pashkov's Fifth Separate Rifle Corps of two rifle divisions crossed the Ussuri to march south and link up with the Thirty-fifth Army of the First Far Eastern Front.

P. 283 Decision to speed up second bomb: Jones, *Manhattan*, pp. 538–40; Rhodes, *Making of the Atomic Bomb*, pp. 738–39.

P. 284 Mission planning for second bomb: 20th AF, Tactical Mission Report, Special Mission, 20 July to 14 August 1945, pp. 14, 16.

P. 284 Nagasaki as shipbuilding center: Parillo, *Japanese Merchant Marine in World War II*, pp. 153–55.

P. 284   Nagasaki as a target: 20th AF, Tactical Mission Report, Special Mission, 20 July to 14 August 1945, pp. 14–15.

P. 284   Nagasaki mission: Ibid., p. 16; Jones, *Manhattan,* pp. 540–41. The crew reported that the last twenty seconds of the run was made visually. Some critics have challenged this report, but in any event it appears that whatever visual opportunity was presented, it did not prevent an aiming error of the substantial magnitude common in radar-directed attacks.

P. 284   Mitsubishi   torpedo   factory   and Urakami Catholic Cathedral: Prange, *At Dawn We Slept,* pp. 321–23; Goldstein, Dillon, and Wenger, *Rain of Ruin,* pp. 102–4; Ian Buruma, "The War over the Bomb," *New York Review of Books* 42.14 (Sept. 21, 1995): 26–34.

P. 285   Power of the two bombs: Rhodes, *Making of the Atomic Bomb,* pp. 711, 740.

P. 285   Disruption of civil administration: USSBS, *Effects of Atomic Bombs on Hiroshima and Nagasaki,* p. 15; for figures on population, see *Daihon'ei Rikugun-Bu (10),* p. 417.

P. 285   November 1945 report: *Hondo Boku Sakusen,* p. 642.

P. 285   Japanese death figures: *Daihon'ei Rikugun-Bu (10),* p. 413.

P. 286   Tables of deaths and injuries: These are adopted from Jones, *Manhattan,* p. 547, with the addition of information from *Hondo Boku Sakusen,* Table 63.

P. 286   Massive postwar casualty numbers: The Committee for the Compilation of Materials on Damage Caused by the Atomic Bombs in Hiroshima and Nagasaki, *Hiroshima and Nagasaki: The Physical, Medical, and Social Effects of the Atomic Bombings,* trans. Eisei Ishikawa and David L. Swain (New York: Basic Books, 1981), pp. 363–69.

P. 287   Military casualties in Hiroshima and Nagasaki: Ibid. Another controversial topic is the number of Koreans killed by the bombs. Hiroshima undoubtedly held substantial numbers of Koreans who came as immigrants, as well as others conscripted in the war effort. Estimates range as high as over 80,000 in Hiroshima and its environs, with death totals as high as 30,000, but the more likely number is somewhere between 40,000 and 50,000, with deaths in the 5,000 to 8,000 range (pp. 468–71). The whole subject of Korean laborers is troublesome for Japanese accounts since their presence is linked to larger issues of Japan's empire and its treatment of other Asian peoples.

18. The Decisive Day

P. 288   "Day that [Japan's] future course was charted"; Statement by Former Foreign Minister Shigenori Togo, 17 May 1949, p. 36, CMH. The official history of the Army Division of Imperial Headquarters called it "the decisive day for the termination of the war," *Daihon'ei Rikugun-Bu (10),* p. 429; news of Soviet entry and reactions of Togo and Sakomizu, *Daihon'ei Rikugun-Bu (10),* p. 429.

P. 288   Suzuki's initial reaction: Statement of Sumihisa Ikeda, 23 Dec 49, Doc. No. 54479, p. 2, CMH. Suzuki's conduct over the next several days suggests Ikeda exaggerated or Suzuki, characteristically, vacillated (see below).

P. 289   Kawabe's reaction and martial-law plan: *Daihon'ei Rikugun-Bu (10),* pp. 430–31; Asada, "The Shock of the Atomic Bomb and Japan's Decision to Surrender: A Reconsideration," pp. 492–93, 504. *Daihon'ei Rikugun-Bu (10)* notes that a pair of staff officers in the Military Affairs Bureau of the Army Ministry drafted up a very similar program, with the declaration of martial law as its centerpiece. This illuminates the mindset at Imperial Headquarters. For explicit acknowledgment that martial law was targeted to stop the "peace faction," see Statement of Lt. Col. Masataka Ida, 23 May 1950, Doc. No. 62348, CMH. Ida was with the Military Affairs Section, Military Affairs Bureau. As to why martial law was not declared, Ida reported that he urged that the plan be carried out as soon as possible:

> but was told to remain quiet, for a day or two would make little difference so long as the entire army would unite in their determination to carry out the plan. I was convinced that everyone thought that at the last resort, military administration would be established through the enforcement of martial law [p. 2].

As to the low expectations of the General Staff for the Kwantung Army, see also Statement of Col. Sako Tanemura, 21 Aug 50, Doc. No. 61977, p. 9, CMH.

P. 289   Reactions of Umezu and Anami: *Daihon'ei Rikugun-Bu (10),* pp. 430, 440. "The inevitable has come": Statement of Col. Saburo Hayashi, 23 Dec 49, Doc. No. 54482, p. 3, CMH. On the Navy side, reactions varied sharply. Vice Admiral Zenshiro Hoshina found the mercurial vice chief of the Naval General Staff, Onishi, still insisting that Japan had "ample chances" for victory, while Navy Minister Yonai almost casually told the same interlocutor, "I have given up the war." Statement of Vice Admiral Zenshiro Hoshina, 9 Nov 49, Doc. No. 61978, p. 5, CMH.

P. 289 Japanese underestimate of Soviet attack: Glantz, *Soviet Tactical and Operational Combat*, p. 33. See also *Daihon'ei Rikugun-Bu (10)*, p. 432, which indicates the Kwantung Army initially estimated that the Soviets only intended some border incursions, but by 6:00 A.M. characterized the attack as an all-out one. The Kwantung Army, however, continued to drastically underestimate the scope of the Soviet effort.

P. 289 Togo's actions and Suzuki's attitude: *Daihon'ei Rikugun-Bu (10)*, p. 431. Note the characterization of Suzuki's response in comparison with that in Ikeda's postwar account. Asada reports that Sakomizu stated in 1973 that Suzuki actually told him on the night of August 8 that he intended to move to terminate the war. This would be significant as it shows Suzuki shifted his position prior to word of Soviet intervention. The problem, however, is that this is Sakomizu's recollection twenty-eight years after the event and conflicts with other statements. Asada, "The Shock of the Atomic Bomb and Japan's Decision to Surrender: A Reconsideration," p. 489.

P. 289 Kido's audience with the Emperor and instructions to Suzuki: *Daihon'ei Rikugun-Bu (10)*, pp. 431–32; IMTFE Kido 31,172–74 (here the IMTFE version is fuller and clearer than *Diary of Marquis Kido* variant). How Kido's diary phrases the Emperor's instruction is notable: "To have full talks with the Prime Minister about the peace plan or termination of the war, which it might be necessary to study and decide without loss of time, after pointing out that the Soviet Union declared war on Japan." Kido then records his meeting with Suzuki:

> At 10:10 A.M. Prime Minister Suzuki came to my room, when I conveyed Imperial wishes to him. I took occasion to stress the necessity for making peace, by taking advantage of the Potsdam Declaration. I also asked the Prime Minister to explain to the senior statesmen the situation in advance, reminding him that the Emperor wanted to seek their view of the importance of the matter.

P. 290 Murray Sayle renders this passage in the Kido diary as "now that the Soviets have entered the war with Japan, there is urgent need to resolve the problem of a cease fire." Murray Sayle, "Did the Bomb End the War?," Bird and Lifschultz, *Hiroshima's Shadow*, p. 40. This variant makes it appear that the Soviet entry was a or the major reason for the Emperor to press the government to end the war. The first problem with this reading is that neither the authoritative IMTFE translation nor the equally authoritative translation in *Diary of Marquis Kido* of this iden-

tical passage parse Kido's admittedly ambiguous entry the same way. The second is that, even assuming Sayle's variant was one way to read Kido's diary, the record shows that the Emperor repeatedly cited the atomic bomb and his lack of confidence in the ability of the Army to defend effectively against an invasion (as well as some less explicit references to his doubts about eroding national morale) as the reasons for his decision. As discussed further below in the text, the Emperor only mentioned the Soviet entry on August 14 to his senior military officers, and even then he coupled that to a reference to the atomic bomb.

P. 290 Meeting of Supreme Council and atmosphere: Asada, "The Shock of the Atomic Bomb and Japan's Decision to Surrender: A Reconsideration," pp. 490–91; Butow, *Japan's Decision to Surrender*, p. 160. *Daihon'ei Rikugun-Bu (10)*, p. 436, gives the time of the meeting as 10:30, based on contemporary notes. General Arisue reported he forwarded a rumor that Tokyo would be attacked on August 12. Statement of General Seizo Arisue, 16 Aug 49, CMH.

P. 290 Lieutenant McDilda's experience: William Craig, *The Fall of Japan* (New York: Dial Press, 1967), pp. 73–74. McDilda is not identified by name in the Japanese sources, but the date of capture, rank, and information given by the unnamed pilot in the Japanese sources match McDilda's circumstances and account. Furthermore, the Japanese communicated his stories by radio, and they were picked up and decoded as the accounts of "the P-51 pilot." See SRMD-007, 11 August.

P. 290 August 9 morning meeting: This and the subsequent account of the meeting is drawn from Statement by Former Foreign Minister Shigenori Togo, 17 May 49, pp. 32–33, CMH; Statement of Former Admiral Soemu Toyoda, 1 Dec 49, Doc. No. 57670, pp. 3–4, 6, CMH; Statement of Former Admiral Soemu Toyoda, 1 Dec 49, Doc. No. 61340, pp. 8–10, CMH; IMTFE Togo 35,787; Butow, *Japan's Decision to Surrender*, p. 161.

P. 290 Toyoda's assessment of meeting: Asada, "The Shock of the Atomic Bomb and Japan's Decision to Surrender: A Reconsideration," p. 491.

P. 290 News of the Nagasaki bomb and reaction: *Daihon'ei Rikugun-Bu (10)*, p. 442. This source says the report of the governor of Nagasaki prefecture was the "first report" and seems to clearly imply, but does not expressly state, that this report was precisely what was relayed to the Big Six meeting. The same source says the report reached Kawabe "around noon," and Kawabe's diary characterized the damage as "relatively small." I thus conclude that the report reaching the Big Six was identical or of very similar import. This might shed light on why the reaction to the news of the Nagasaki bombing was not strong on the surface. *Daihon'ei Rikugun-Bu (10)* does clearly offer the opinion that the Nagasaki bomb had relatively little effect.

During the Big Six meeting, the cabinet members' chief secretaries convened and concocted a proposal that the entire cabinet should resign over the failure to anticipate the Soviet entry. This action very probably would have greatly eased the way for the Army to abolish any civilian government. *Daihon'ei Rikugun-Bu (10)*, p. 437.

P. 291 Yonai's stance at the first meeting of the Big Six: Butow concluded that Yonai mentioned the four conditions, but supported Togo in this meeting (*Japan's Decision to Surrender,* p. 160). This conclusion is well supported by Toyoda, who related that, after putting the conditions forward for discussion, the navy minister stated he agreed with the foreign minister (1 Dec 49, Doc. No. 57670, pp. 3–4; 29 Aug 49, Doc. No. 61340, pp. 8–9, CMH). Togo also recollected Yonai's support. Statement by Former Foreign Minister Shigenori Togo, 17 May 49, p. 34, CMH. *Daihon'ei Rikugun-Bu (10)*, p. 438, however, notes Anami's contemporaneously recorded view that Yonai switched his position to join Togo and Suzuki later in the day. The Chief of the Cabinet Planning Bureau, Sumihisa Ikeda, also casts doubt on Yonai's position on the four conditions. In his postwar statement, Ikeda first said that Yonai "had not made up his mind on the four peace conditions and was uncertain on that point." Later in the same statement, Ikeda said that "Adm Yonai at first favored the conditions but later retracted." Statement of Sumihisa Ikeda, 23 Dec 49, Doc. No. 54479, pp. 2, 4, CMH. I believe the contemporaneous account reported by Anami raises profound questions about Yonai's initial stance. This interpretation is well fitted to Suzuki's presentation of the conclusion of the conference to Kido immediately after the meeting, as well as the description of the division of the Supreme Council at the Imperial Conference this same day. (These points are addressed in the text and notes below.)

P. 291 Kido, Konoye, Takamatsu, and Shigemitsu, 1:00 to 5:10: *Daihon'ei Rikugun-Bu (10)*, pp. 437–38, and IMTFE Togo 35,787, Kido 31,175–76 (the relevant segment of Kido's diary, except the quote of Shigemitsu's warning, which is the translation variant from *Diary of Marquis Kido,* p. 444). *Diary of Marquis Kido* fails to note his key meeting with the Emperor after the calls from Prince Takamatsu and Shigemitsu. For Kido's relationship with Shigemitsu, see *Showa*

Tenno Dokuhakuroku, p. 139. Significantly, *Daihon'ei Rikugun-Bu (10)* presents these events as occurring in this fashion exactly as reflected in Kido's original diary entry without equivocation. Bix, "Japan's Delayed Surrender," cites on these events the Japanese historian Nobummasa Tanaka:

> There was no evidence to show that the emperor and Kido initially sided with Togo and opposed the four conditions of the senior military leaders. The more likely inference is that they still sympathized with the military die-hards, who preferred to continue the suicidal war rather than surrender unconditionally [pp. 219–20].

On the contrary, instead of sympathy with the diehards, Kido and the Emperor more likely were motivated by fear that the military would not enforce compliance with an attempt to surrender.

This series of events is absent from Butow, *Japan's Decision to Surrender,* pp. 160–65, 169 n. 9. This omission is due to the fact that Butow accepted Kido's later assertion at the War Crimes Trials that his diary entry was in error (IMTFE Kido 31,175; Togo 35,787; and Sakomizu 35,609). Further support for the version that the vote on the four conditions was four to two at the morning meeting of the Big Six is contained in Memorandum of Vice Admiral Zenshiro Hoshina, Doc. No. 53437, p. 1, CMH (hereafter Hoshina, "Minutes"), and Statement of Sumihisa Ikeda, 27 Dec 49, Doc. No. 54483, CMH (hereafter Ikeda, "Minutes"), both prepared as a set of minutes for the Imperial Conference late on August 9, both of which show Suzuki presenting the four conditions as the "general agreement" of the Big Six that day. They are the principal authorities on the course of the meeting, if not all individual details.

P. 291 Kido's diary of August 9: IMTFE Kido 31,175, Togo 35,787, and Sakomizu 35,609, say no conclusion was reached.

P. 292 Afternoon meeting on August 9: *Daihon'ei Rikugun-Bu (10)*, pp. 439, 443; Statement by Former Foreign Minister Shigenori Togo, 17 May 1949, p. 33, CMH.

P. 292 Anami's report about the atomic bomb and B-29 raids: Freedman and Dockrill, "Hiroshima: A Strategy of Shock," p. 207, quoting the Ministry of Foreign Affairs, *Dai'niji Sekai Taisen Shusen Shiroku* (The Historical Record of the Termination of the Second World War), vol. 2 (Tokyo: Yamate, 1990), p. 778.

P. 292 Voting in cabinet meeting: Butow, *Japan's Decision to Surrender,* pp. 164–65.

P. 293 Suzuki and Togo report to Emperor: Ibid., p. 165.

P. 293 Supreme Council meeting, 11:50 P.M., August 9: This account is drawn from Statement by Former Foreign Minister Shigenori Togo, Doc. No. 50304, 17 May 49, pp. 32–33, CMH; Statement of Kiichiro Hiranuma, 16 Dec 49, Doc. No. 55127, pp. 10–15, CMH; Ikeda, "Minutes"; Hoshina, "Minutes"; Statement of Yoshizumi, Doc. No. 54484, CMH; IMTFE Sakomizu 35,608–9, Togo 35,788, Kido 31,177; *Daihon'ei Rikugun-Bu (10)*, p. 447 (account by Anami).

According to Ikeda, he recommended to Suzuki that Hiranuma should attend because the Privy Council would have to concur before any decision reached at the conference became final. Statement of Sumihisa Ikeda, 23 Dec 49, Doc. No. 54479, p. 4, CMH.

Sources materially differ on the presentation of options. The text starts with the contemporaneous account given by Anami, which indicated that Togo's proposition had been formalized in writing before the conference, whereas Anami's proposal was strictly oral. *Daihon'ei Rikugun-Bu (10)*, p. 447. Suzuki, however, is shown reporting the four conditions as the "general agreement" of the Big Six: Ikeda, "Minutes," p. 1; Hoshina, "Minutes," p. 1.

Suzuki's opening statement: Neither the Ikeda nor the Hoshina minutes show Suzuki declaring his intention at the outset to submit the matter to the Emperor. As Butow observes, sources differ as to whether the Prime Minister expressed his intention to do so at the beginning of the conference as well as at the end. The text follows Butow's conclusion and explanation of Suzuki's likely motives. Butow, *Japan's Decision to Surrender*, p. 169 n. 10.

P. 293 Togo's opening statement and Yonai's concurrence: Ikeda, "Minutes," p. 2; Hoshina, "Minutes," pp. 1–2.

P. 293 Presentations of Anami and Umezu: Ikeda, "Minutes," p. 2; Hoshina, "Minutes," pp. 2–3.

P. 293 Hiranuma's address: Hoshina, "Minutes," pp. 2–3; Ikeda, "Minutes," pp. 2–3.

P. 294 Hiranuma's exchanges and his analysis: Ikeda, "Minutes," pp. 3–5; Hoshina, "Minutes," pp. 3–5; Statement of Kiichiro Hiranuma, 16 Dec 49, Doc. No. 55127, p. 15, CMH. Hiranuma's ultimate vote on the proposals: Anami's uncertainty was reflected in the account he gave to an aide shortly thereafter and is duly recorded in *Daihon'ei Rikugun-Bu (10)*, p. 448. Moreover, a reading of the Ikeda minutes, pp. 3–5, and Hoshina minutes, pp. 3–5, shows how readily anyone could be confused about Hiranuma's ulti-

mate position. In *Showa Tenno Dokuhakuroku,* however, the Emperor stated that he counted Hiranuma as siding with the foreign minister (pp. 139–40).

P. 294 "The Japanese Government . . . was asking": Bix, "Japan's Delayed Surrender," p. 222. Bix cites Kisaburo Yokota, *Tennosei* [The Emperor System] (Tokyo: Rodo Bunkasha, 1949), pp. 183–84.

P. 295 Hiranuma addresses the Emperor: Ikeda, "Minutes," p. 5. Hiranuma alters Togo's language: Statement of Kiichiro Hiranuma, 16 Dec 49, Doc. No. 55127, pp. 13–14, CMH.

P. 295 Toyoda's presentation: Ikeda, "Minutes," pp. 3–5; Hoshina, "Minutes," pp. 3–5.

P. 295 Suzuki addresses the Emperor: Ikeda, "Minutes," p. 5.

P. 295 The Emperor's statement: No verbatim transcription of Hirohito's comments exists. The text here follows the re-creation by Butow, *Japan's Decision to Surrender,* pp. 175–76 (which is drawn primarily from Ikeda, "Minutes," pp. 5–6), and modified by material reported in *Daihon'ei Rikugun-Bu (10)*, p. 448, as part of the statement. Notably, this includes reference to the atomic bomb. There is a conflict in the record as to the sources of the Emperor's information on the status of the defenses outside Tokyo. The text follows the version in *Daihon'ei Rikugun-Bu (10)*. The Emperor's senior aide-de-camp, however, indicated that no such inspection took place and suggested the information came from Kido, at least partly based on the Lord Privy Seal's personal observations from his home in the region. Statement of Gen. Shigeru Hasunuma, 31 Mar 50, Doc. No. 58225, pp. 3–4, CMH. It is also notable that the Kido diary entry contains an abbreviated but still congruent account of what the Emperor stated as recorded immediately after the event, on the morning of August 10. The explicit documentation of this is in contrast to allegations about what the Emperor told Konoe on July 12 of his special envoy mission and what the Emperor allegedly stated to Togo on the morning of August 9 about the atomic bomb. IMTFE Kido 31,178–79.

P. 296 Anami and Suzuki exchange: *Daihon'ei Rikugun-Bu (10)*, p. 450. Action of Foreign Ministry officials: Butow, *Japan's Decision to Surrender,* pp. 177–78. In his diary, Kawabe sarcastically compared the sloth of the Foreign Ministry in furthering diplomatic efforts espoused by the Army with the alacrity with which it transmitted the surrender notification. *Daihon'ei Rikugun-Bu (10)*, p. 451.

P. 296 Complementary threats of revolt and assassination: Butow, *Japan's Decision to Surrender,* pp. 178–79.

P. 297 Anami briefs Kawabe: *Daihon'ei Rikugun-Bu (10),* pp. 452–53. Kawabe was also just as sure that the Army had squandered the confidence of the people at large, as well as the Emperor.

P. 297 "I do not know what excuse I can offer": Statement of Lt. Col. Masahiko Takeshita, 11 Jun 49, Doc. No. 50025-A, p. 3, CMH, as rendered in Butow, *Japan's Decision to Surrender,* p. 184; *Daihon'ei Rikugun-Bu (10),* pp. 453–54.

P. 297 Shock in Imperial Headquarters: *Daihon'ei Rikugun-Bu (10),* pp. 453, 456. Anami confounded by Suzuki's posture: Ibid., p. 454. About 11:00, Anami and Umezu also called together the senior available operational commanders: the First General Army and the Air General Army commanders. As reported by Kawabe, Umezu described the Emperor's decision as based on the loss of will of the government and the people to continue the war and His Majesty's loss of trust in the armed forces' plan for the decisive battle. While there was uncertainty as to whether the Allies would accept the condition, Kawabe believed it would be almost impossible for popular morale to be revived for battle once the offer became known (ibid., p. 456).

P. 297 August 10 strikes: Ibid., p. 460. FEAF strikes: Kit C. Carter and Robert Mueller, compilers, *U.S. Army Air Forces in World War II, Combat Chronology 1941–45* (Washington, D.C.: Center for Air Force History, 1991), p. 687.

P. 298 Japanese learn of Manchuria situation: *Daihon'ei Rikugun-Bu (10),* p. 457; Glantz, *Soviet 1945 Strategic Offensive,* pp. 95–98, 102.

P. 298 Senior statesmen meet: *Daihon'ei Rikugun-Bu (10),* pp. 450–51. The senior statesmen meeting was from 3:35 to 4:30.

P. 298 Announcement to public: Butow, *Japan's Decision to Surrender,* pp. 181–82.

P. 298 Rival public statements: Ibid., pp. 182–83; *Daihon'ei Rikugun-Bu (10),* p. 456.

P. 299 Conflict over Anami's statement: Butow, *Japan's Decision to Surrender,* p. 183; *Daihon'ei Rikugun-Bu (10),* pp. 456–57.

P. 299 Actions of Inaba and others: Statements of Lt. Col. Masao Inaba, 13 Oct 49 Doc. No. 57692, pp. 1–3, CMH; Masahibko Takeshita, 11 Jun 49 Doc. No. 50025-A, p. 4, CMH; Masao Yoshizumi, 6 Jun 49 Doc. No. 61338, p. 4, CMH; *Daihon'ei Rikugun-Bu (10),* p. 456, quoting Takeshita.

P. 299 Public broadcast statement: A copy of the Domei broadcast is in Naval Aide Files, Subject File, Box 10, Folder: Japan Surrender (Folder 1), HSTL; Butow, *Japan's Decision to Surrender,* pp. 186–87; Statement of Taihei Oshima, 18 Aug 49, Doc. No. 61059, CMH. The broadcast was timed as sent at 11:41, August 11, apparently Washington time.

P. 299 Plan for Emperor to broadcast announcement: *Daihon'ei Rikugun-Bu (10),* pp. 470–71; IMTFE Kido 31,180–82; Butow, *Japan's Decision to Surrender,* pp. 187–88. The Emperor approved the plan on August 11.

P. 300 Truman and conversion of economy: Bernstein, "The Struggle over History," p. 176. Economic issues, especially those relating to inflation and price controls, not the much-feared return of depression conditions, were the undoing of the Democratic party in the 1946 elections. Donovan, *Conflict and Crisis,* pp. 231–32, 235–37.

P. 300 Patterson-Harrison exchanges: Bernstein, "The Struggle over History," pp. 187–88.

P. 300 Forrestal letter to Truman: Forrestal Diary, August 8, 1945. A copy of the letter is enclosed. I found no direct evidence that Forrestal knew of King's message to Nimitz of August 9, thus it does not appear that these events were in any way related.

P. 300 Japanese surrender notice: Barton Bernstein, "The Perils and Politics of Surrender," *Pacific Historical Review* 46 (November 1977): 3, citing Stimson diary.

P. 300 Past policy on release of POW stories and draft warnings: See the series in ABC 383.6 Japan (17 Aug 42), RG 165, Box 393, NARA. These documents also show considerable uncertainty about the number of Americans held by Japan. An estimate on January 13, 1944, was that there were 12,725 U.S. POWs and 4,350 interned U.S. nationals. By May 15, 1945, the estimate was that Japan held 22,000 U.S. prisoners as well as 126,000 British (of whom 67,000 were Indian). The first reports confirming the horrifying conditions of American prisoners of war were brought out by escapees from the Philippines. They predicted that if circumstances did not improve, few prisoners would survive. They emphasized the vital importance of Red Cross supplies then being delivered by the relief ship *Gripsholm.* In September 1943, the Joint Chiefs of Staff recommended, and President Roosevelt approved, withholding these accounts from public distribution in order not to compromise future missions of the *Gripsholm.* They also feared that publication might actually increase the mistreatment and intended to review the policy after the *Gripsholm*'s cargo was distributed, a period estimated to take six months. By early 1944, however, Britain, Australia, and New Zealand prepared to release atrocity stories. This action, noted one officer, "changed the whole picture." The Joint Chiefs recommended on January 18, 1944, that the OWI be authorized to conduct a coordinated release of "verified Japanese atrocity stories." In April 1945, as the war drew near an end in Europe, Truman, Churchill, and Stalin issued a formal warning to Germany concerning the safety and welfare of Allied prisoners of war. Meanwhile, conditions of U.S. prisoners held by Japan continued to deteriorate, and by the spring of 1945 Swiss observers were being denied access to POW camps in Japan. Accordingly, a draft warning to Japan parallel to that issued to Germany was being worked on by the Joint Chiefs of Staff, parallel to Marshall's action.

P. 301   Draft Marshall message: Memorandum for the President, 10 August 1945, George C. Marshall Papers, Box 76, Folder 7, Marshall Library. POW estimate: JCS to MacArthur, Nimitz, Sultan, Wedemeyer, 132158 June 45, CINCPAC Command Summary, p. 2926. Truman's public statement: Statement by the President, June 1, 1945, Press Release File, 1945–53, Box 1, Folder: Truman Papers, May–June 1945, 2 of 2 June 45, HSTL; Memorandum for the President, August 10, 1945, Subject: Draft Warning . . . , State Department, White House Central Files, HSTL. Truman annotated this memorandum "Original approved & sent to Sec[retary of] St[ate]."

In another mark of how much difficulty Marshall expected before real peace was achieved, this same day, August 10, he signed a planning memorandum looking to provision an occupation force of 23⅔ divisions for Japan and Korea. This number reflected the expectation by MacArthur and Nimitz of "active post-surrender resistance of considerable proportions within Japan proper, particularly by suicidal elements of the armed forces who will take advantage of any weakness of our forces." Memorandum for Admiral Leahy from General Marshall, 10 Aug 45, George C. Marshall Papers, Marshall Library. See a similar fear of the high human cost of an occupation in Leahy Diary, June 18, 1945, Library of Congress.

P. 301   "In order to save us from a score of bloody Iwo Jimas and Okinawas": Stimson Diary, August 10, 1945. The figures are computed by multiplying twenty times the total of American combat deaths (8,586 at Iwo Jima and 12,520 at Okinawa) and total combat casualties (31,708 at Iwo Jima and 49,133 at Okinawa). Ca-

sualty numbers for Iwo Jima are from Garand and Strowbridge, *Western Pacific Operations*, Appendix H, and *The History of the Medical Department of the United States Navy in World War II: The Statistics of Diseases and Injuries*, Vol. 3, p. 173. The totals for Okinawa are from Appleman, Burns, Gugeler, and Stevens, *Okinawa: The Last Battle*, p. 473.

P. 301   Divisions within administration: Butow, *Japan's Decision to Surrender*, pp. 189–90.

P. 301   White House strategy session: Bernstein, "Perils and Politics of Surrender," p. 9; Butow, *Japan's Decision to Surrender*, p. 190; Henry H. Adams, *Witness to Power* (Annapolis: Naval Institute Press, 1985), p. 299.

P. 302   Byrnes's note: Quoted in ibid., p. 191, Appendix E; Bernstein, "Perils and Politics of Surrender," p. 6. John Dower has pointed out the vital benefits of the lack of guarantee in reordering Japan during the occupation. From the outset, occupation authorities insisted that Japan had surrendered unconditionally and "by initially keeping deliberately vague the future status of both the imperial institution and Emperor Hirohito personally, they were able to more effectively pressure the Japanese elites into actively cooperating with basic initial reform edicts." Dower, "Three Narrative of Our Humanity," n. 34.

P. 302   Securing Allied agreement: Bernstein, "Perils and Politics of Surrender," pp. 7–8; Butow, *Japan's Decision to Surrender*, pp. 191–92. The British advised deleting the requirement that the Emperor personally sign the surrender terms.

P. 302   Truman restricts military operations: Bernstein, "Perils and Politics of Surrender," pp. 9–10. Message on casualties in Hiroshima: SRS-507, Magic Far East Summary, 9 August 1945, p. 5.

P. 302   Shipment of third-bomb components halted: Groves, *Now It Can Be Told*, pp. 352–53. Contemporary documentation shows Marshall believed on August 13 that if Japan's leaders could be moved to surrender by atomic bombing at all, two bombs would be sufficient. Telephone conversation, General Hull and Col. "Seaman," 1325, 13 August 1945, George C. Marshall Papers, Verifax 2691, Marshall Library.

P. 303   Atomic-bomb target recommendation: COMAF 20 to CINCPAC, COMUSASTAF 090326 August 45, CINCPAC Command Summary, p. 3512 (copy also in Spaatz Papers, Library of Congress, Box 24). Twining recommendation: Twining, COMGEN AF 20 to COMGEN USASTAF, 140223Z Aug 45, Spaatz

Papers, Library of Congress, Box 24. On August 10, Spaatz sent a separate recommendation to Arnold for an attack on Tokyo: COMGEN USASTAF to COMGENAIR 10033 Aug 45, in ibid.

P. 304 Tribulations of conventional air attacks: Marshall to MacArthur, WAR 47899, 12 August 1945, RG 9, Box 156, Folder 1, MacArthur Archive. Problem with strategic attacks: Memorandum for the President, 11 August 1945, from the Chief of Staff, Papers of Harry S. Truman, President's Secretary's Files, Foreign Affairs File, Box 182, Folder: Japan, PSF Subject File, HSTL.

P. 304 Joint Target Group: This was formed in September 1944 to coordinate analysis of air targets in Japan. Although operating under the A-2 of the Army Air Forces, the group had representatives from the U.S. Navy and a special panel of consultants, some from the Committee of Operations Analysts. Kreis, *Piercing the Fog,* pp. 368–69.

P. 304 USSBS recommendations: Memorandum for the President from the Secretary of War, 2 July 1945, with attached Memorandum for the Secretary of War from Franklin D'Olivier, 11 June 45, President's Secretary's Files, Papers of Harry S. Truman, HSTL; David MacIsaac, *Strategic Bombing in World War Two: The Story of the United States Strategic Bombing Survey* (New York: Garland Publishing, 1976), pp. 98–102. Also pertinent to these considerations are "Report of USSBS and JTG Conferences" (from which the quotes are taken) and "Enclosure Directive to Commanding General, United States Army Strategic Air Forces," both in Spaatz Papers, Box 21, Folder July (1945), Library of Congress; see also Arnold to Spaatz, 041831 Aug 45, CINCPAC Command Summary, p. 3506. In addition to the work of the USSBS and the Joint Target Group, the staff of the Army Air Forces in Washington had been scrutinizing prospects for chemical attacks on Japanese food supplies, as well as a scheme to destroy schools of fish with medium bombers. Although the technical feasibility of the former plan appeared to be confirmed, it did not gain sanction, and the scheme to attack fish languished. Conrad C. Crane, *Bombs, Cities, and Civilians* (Lawrence: University Press of Kansas, 1993), p. 138. General Arnold, who was on a Pacific inspection tour when he learned of the impending June 18 meeting, radioed in an outline plan for "Bombing Japan into Submission." This scheme called for progressively increasing air attacks *after* the seizure of Kyushu to see if Japan could be conquered without "forceful occupation" of Honshu. These attacks would have reached a rate of 220,000 tons of bombs per month by March 1946. Arnold to Marshall for JCS, WD 1053, 17115 Jun 45, RG 4, Folder 4, Box 17, MacArthur Archive.

P. 304 USASTAF Operational Directive 11 August 1945: USAF HC File 703.302 29 Nov 45, Headquarters, United States Army Strategic Air Forces, Subject: Operation Directive. The Eighth Air Force list included eleven in Korea and two in Manchuria. Under this plan, responsibility for the mine campaign would be shifted from the Twentieth to the Eighth Air Force. Both air forces would incorporate fighter commands to provide escorts for daylight missions, destroy Japanese aircraft in the air and on the ground, and interdict transportation and communication lines. Both air forces also were to be ready to support "Olympic" during the interval X minus 8 to X-Day.

P. 305 Strength of Twentieth Air Force: USAF HC File 703.273, 1 Aug 45, USASAF Station List; File 760.01 1 Jul–2 Sep v. 23; File 760.01 Jul–2 Sep v. 14; File 760.01 v. 23 1 Jul–2 Sep. With the addition of a fourth squadron in three of the bomb wings, aircraft per wing would rise from 196 in August to 224 in November.

P. 305 Eighth Air Force deployment: USAF HC File 760.322, Memo: VHB Facilities on Okinawa, 18 June 1945; File 760.1623, Telecon Msg 17-5. The order of arrival of Eighth Air Force B-29 wings was 316th, 47th, 20th, 96th, and 13th.

P. 305 Projected aircraft strengths: USAF HC File 703.308 Jul & Aug 45, Headquarters, USASAF, Summary of Combat Operations.

P. 305 Bombing effectiveness: USAF HC File 760.01 1 Jul–2 Sep, v. 9, Twentieth AF Command Critique, 7 August; File 760-309-3, Bombing Activities Twentieth AF, p. 12; File 762.310A, XXI Bomber Command Evaluations, ltr. Griggs to Dr. Edward Bowles.

P. 306 Radar bombing aids: USAF HC File 760.235, Msg: HQ Twentieth Air Force to War Dept 29 Jul 45; File 760.302-1 Twentieth Air Force Weekly Activities report, week of 6–13 August; File 762.310A, XXI Bomber Command Evaluations, pp. 4–5, AFHC; for Shoran characteristics, see Freeman, *Mighty Eighth War Manual,* p. 240.

P. 306 Bomb tonnages: USAF HC File 760.309-3, Bombing Activities of Twentieth Air Force, Col. Montgomery; File 760.01 1 Jul–2 Sep 45, v.18.

P. 306 Planning factors for munitions: USAF HC File 760.01 1 Jul–2 Sep 45, v. 16.

P. 307 Aircrew and aircraft factors: USAF HC File 760.309-3, Bombing Activities, Twentieth AF Operations pp. 9, 11; File 760.113 Jul 45, Twentieth AF Monthly Activities Report. Arnold understood this factor and his message proposing an all-out air attack (post-Olympic) included the recommendation that three crews be provided for each unit's establishment aircraft. Arnold to Marshall for JCS, WD 1053, 17115 Jun 45, RG 4, Folder 4, Box 17, MacArthur Archive. In response to Arnold's message, General Ira Eaker in Washington responded that he was "making every effort to comply at early date and believe we can do it." Washington (COMGENAIR) to COMGENAFP (Eaker to Arnold) No. W18730, 19 Jun 45, RG 4, Folder 4, Box 17, MacArthur Archive.

P. 307 "Write [Assistant Secretary of War] Lovett": Spaatz Diary, 11 August 1945, Spaatz Papers, Box 21, Folder August, Library of Congress.

19. Surrender

P. 308 Orders to major commanders; Kawabe's diary entry: *Daihon'ei Rikugun-Bu (10)*, pp. 466–67. Kawabe's entry is remarkable. He confesses that at the end of fourteen years of war, the Army had failed to see or hear the misery of the people or their antagonism toward the Army. Further, he believed that the current leadership had squandered seventy years of labor since the Meiji Restoration to build Japan's prosperity. He peered darkly into a future where Japan's territory would contract to where it was three hundred or more years earlier, "the purity of the blood of the Japanese will be quickly contaminated," samurai ethics would be abolished (with suicide a crime), while Christianity and English would flourish.

P. 308 Receipt of Byrnes's note: Statement of Shunichi Matsumoto, 16 Nov 49, Doc. No. 61451, p. 1, CMH; Butow, *Japan's Decision to Surrender,* pp. 192–93; *Daihon'ei Rikugun-Bu (10)*, p. 484.

P. 308 Reaction in Army Ministry: *Daihon'ei Rikugun-Bu (10)*, pp. 476–78. As part of the immediate reaction to Byrnes's note, Toyoda and Umezu met with the Emperor to request that he reconsider his decision and "decisively reject" the note. According to his aide-de-camp, the Emperor viewed this effort as perfunctory. Statement of General Shigeru Hasunuma, 31 Mar 50, Doc. No. 58225, p. 3, CMH. As to the Army Ministry's draft proposal, apparently Umezu and Kawabe recognized the dim prospect of separating the Soviets from the other Allies.

P. 309 Motivations of Anami: Statement of Kawabe, 21 Nov 49, Doc. No. 52608, CMH ("A road to success will somehow be revealed to us if we carry on with strong determination"). One other factor governed Anami's behavior, and that is the unusually close and reciprocal personal affinity he harbored for the Emperor. On August 11, at a face-to-face meeting, the Emperor addressed him as "Anami," not by any official title or rank, a gesture that in the rigid protocol of Imperial politics marked an extraordinarily rare intimacy. Statement of Lt. Col. Takeshita, 11 Jun 49, Doc. No. 50025-A, p. 4; Statement of Lt. Col. Inaba, 13 Oct 49, Doc. No. 57592, p. 3, CMH.

P. 309 "Warfare, Anami insisted": Drea, *In Service of the Emperor,* p. 204.

P. 309 Meeting of the Imperial family: *Daihon'ei Rikugun-Bu (10)*, pp. 472, 483; IMTFE Kido 31,187; *Showa Tenno Dokuhakuroku*, pp. 141–42. In this last source, the Emperor detailed the past attitudes and quirks of the royal princes. Kido's diary speaks of "a very free and frank exchange of views," suggesting a rancorous meeting. The Emperor acknowledged that at least one prince asked him if he was prepared to continue the war if the national polity could not be preserved, and the Emperor replied in the affirmative. Following this session, Prince Mikasa confronted Anami with a lacerating lecture on the Army's history of violating the Emperor's wishes, which staggered the Army Minister. Statement of Lt. Col. Takeshita, 11 Jun 49, Doc. No. 50025-A, p. 3, CMH.

P. 309 "In any age the upper classes": Statement of Lt. Col. Masataka Ida, 23 May 50, Doc. No. 62238, p. 2, CMH.

P. 309 Suzuki switch and cabinet meeting: Butow, *Japan's Decision to Surrender,* pp. 194–95. According to Lt. Gen. Yoshizumi, Chief of the Military Affairs Bureau, during the break in these sessions, Anami reported that "the cabinet meeting is now taking a favorable turn" because of Suzuki's dissatisfaction with the Allied response. Statement of Lt. Gen. Masao Yoshizumi, 6 Jun 49, Doc. No. 61338, p. 4, CMH; for the general contents of this meeting, see *Daihon'ei Rikugun-Bu (10)*, pp. 484–85.

P. 309 Suzuki meets with Togo, Matsumoto, and Kido: *Daihon'ei Rikugun-Bu (10)*, p. 485; Statements of Lord Keeper of the Privy Seal Kido, 11 Aug 50, Doc. No. 61476, p. 13, and 14 Aug 50, Doc. No. 61541, p. 7, CMH; IMTFE Kido 31,184–86; Butow, *Japan's Decision to Surrender,* p. 196. Kido's diary in IMTFE mentions millions of innocents, while Butow cites hundreds of thousands. In a postwar statement, Minister Okamoto in Sweden confirmed that

Matsumoto had told him that his message stressing that adding terms would collapse talks proved vital to ending the war. Statement of Suemasa Okamoto, 29 Jul 50, Doc. No. 61477, pp. 4–5, CMH.

P. 310   Yonai to Emperor: Bix, "Japan's Delayed Surrender," pp. 217–18.

P. 310   Status of Soviet advance: *Daihon'ei Rikugun-Bu (10)*, pp. 485–86; Glantz, *Soviet 1945 Strategic Offensive*, p. 103. The bulk of the Sixth Guards Tank Army halted on August 12 and 13 to await fuel, and only reconnaissance and a few other units advanced.

P. 310   Threats to Kido: Statements of Lord Keeper of the Privy Seal Kido, 11 Aug 50, Doc. No. 61476, p. 13, and 14 Aug 50, Doc. No. 61541, p. 7, CMH; IMTFE Kido 31,187–88.

P. 310   Kido's exchange with Anami: IMTFE Kido 31,188–89; Statements of Lord Keeper of the Privy Seal Kido, 11 Aug 50, Doc. No. 61476, p. 13, and 14 Aug 50, Doc. No. 61541, p. 7, CMH; Butow, *Japan's Decision to Surrender*, pp. 199–200.

P. 310   Big Six meeting: Butow, *Japan's Decision to Surrender*, pp. 201–2; *Daihon'ei Rikugun-Bu (10)*, pp. 492–93. Perhaps strangely, Kido reported at the Tokyo War Crimes Trials that no meeting of the Big Six was held this day despite Suzuki's efforts. IMTFE Kido 31,189.

P. 311   Cabinet meeting: *Daihon'ei Rikugun-Bu (10)*, p. 494; see also Butow, *Japan's Decision to Surrender*, p. 202.

In one account, Anami is reported to have asked Suzuki after this meeting to postpone taking matters back to the Emperor for two more days. Suzuki reputedly refused and stated that they must act without delay. When Anami departed, an officer allegedly asked Suzuki why a two-day delay could not be granted, and Suzuki responded that such delay was impossible because the Russians would penetrate not only into Manchuria and Korea but also into northern Japan as well. Pacific War Research Society, *Japan's Longest Day* (Tokyo: Kodansha International, 1968), pp. 73–74. I do not find this story credible, because there is no source cited and it is inconsistent with contemporary documentation and Suzuki's postwar accounts.

P. 311   Manchuria on August 13: *Daihon'ei Rikugun-Bu (10)*, pp. 487–88, 508–9.

P. 311   Anami too busy to work with staff: *Daihon'ei Rikugun-Bu (10)*, p. 493. This refers to the observations of Kawabe.

P. 311   Need for stability: Butow, *Japan's Decision to Surrender*, pp. 203–4. In my view, though

not Butow's, this might also explain in part why Kawabe proposed and Anami approved declaring martial law and jettisoning any formalities of civil government upon Soviet entry into the war.

P. 311   Meeting of Togo, Anami, and Toyoda; Onishi's appearance: *Daihon'ei Rikugun-Bu (10)*, p. 495; Statement of Former Foreign Minister Shigenori Togo, 17 May 49, p. 41, CMH. On Onishi's well-recognized and "extremely strong" determination to continue the war, see Statement of Rear Admiral Sadatoshi Tamioka, 10 Feb 50, Doc. No. 60957, CMH.

P. 312   Togo confesses lack of Army and Navy agreement: SRH-090, pp. 9–10. Underscoring the uncertainty, when Togo urged his local representative to inform the Thai government that it could pursue its own settlement with the Allies, notwithstanding a December 1941 treaty binding the two governments not to seek a separate peace, the representative cabled back that he had not communicated with the Thai government because of his trepidations over the reaction of local Imperial Army officers; he requested Tokyo to "get the approval of the Army and Navy as quickly as possible in regard to these representations." August 11 message from Imperial General Headquarters: SRH-203, 12/13 Aug, No. 121.

P. 312   Bissell's estimate of August 12: Maj. Gen. Clayton Bissell, Memorandum for the Chief of Staff, Subject: Estimate of the Japanese Situation for the Next 30 Days, 12 August 1945, RG 165, Entry 422, Box 12, Executive No. 2, Item No. 11, NARA.

P. 312   Hull and Seeman conversation: 1325, 13 August 1945, George C. Marshall Papers, Verifax 2691, Marshall Library.

P. 313   Understanding of effects of bombs: Barton J. Bernstein, "Eclipsed by Hiroshima and Nagasaki: Early Thinking About Tactical Nuclear Weapons," *International Security* 15.4 (spring 1991): 149–73.

P. 313   Forrestal analyzes Japanese situation: Forrestal Diary, August 13, 1945.

P. 313   "The President directs": Marshall to General MacArthur and General Spaatz, WR 48689 131343 Aug 45, RG 9, Box 156, Folder 1, MacArthur Archive. Arnold directed Spaatz to attack Tokyo with the maximum number of aircraft "so as to impress Japanese officials that we mean business and are serious in getting them to accept our peace proposals without delay." Spaatz replied that Tokyo was no longer a good target "except for the atomic bomb" and dispatched his forces to other targets. Radio Teletype Conference, Aug. 14, 1945, Box 21, Spaatz Papers, Library of Congress. The use of additional air attacks on August 14 was criticized severely by Bernstein as "unnecessary in producing the surrender," as part of his larger critique of the whole affair of Byrnes's note. Bernstein, "Perils and Politics of Surrender," p. 17. I believe it reflects rather more the fact that to the very end American policy makers possessed only the dimmest outline of how their counterparts in Tokyo divided on the issue of surrender. As Bernstein acknowledges, it was entirely possible to read events as demonstrating that only toughness induced the Japanese to move to peace.

P. 313   Return of the B-29s: 20th AF MR, Nos. 325–30, pp. 1–14, 30–33, Consolidated Statistical Summaries; *Hondo Boku Sakusen,* Table 63.

P. 314   Kido reaction to leaflets: Statements of Kido, 11 Aug 50, Doc. No. 61476, pp. 5–6, and 14 Aug 50, Doc. No. 61541, pp. 5–6, CMH; IMTFE Kido 31,189–90; *Daihon'ei Rikugun-Bu (10),* pp. 502–3. *Daihon'ei Rikugun-Bu (10)* also indicates that the stirring of coup d'état plotters became known at the Imperial Palace and within the government and may have played a role in accelerating the time of the Imperial Conference (pp. 521–22). As to leaflets, see Arnold to Commanding General US Army Strategic Air Forces, WARX 48023, 11 Aug 45, Naval Aide Files, Subject File, Box 10, Folder: Japan Surrender (Folder 1), HSTL, and Butow, *Japan's Decision to Surrender,* pp. 205–6.

P. 314   Kido meets with Emperor, August 14: IMTFE Kido 31,189–91; Statement of Kido, 14 Aug 50, Doc. No. 61541, pp. 5–6; *Daihon'ei Rikugun-Bu (10),* pp. 502–3. Emperor sets time for the meeting: *Showa Tenno Dokuhakuroku,* p. 143.

P. 314   Meeting of Emperor and senior officers: *Daihon'ei Rikugun-Bu (10),* pp. 491–92, 504–5. As to Anami's expectations of Hata, see Statement of Lt. Col. Inaba, 13 Oct 49, Doc. No. 57592, p. 7, CMH. According to Inaba, Hata, prior to seeing the Emperor, said to Anami that the atomic bomb had hardly any effect on the ground one foot below the surface, and Anami urged him to relate this to the Emperor. Inaba emphasized that the atomic bomb appeared to staff officers at Imperial Headquarters to have "shaken extremely" the Imperial family. The account in *Daihon'ei Rikugun-Bu (10)* differs from the Emperor's recollection in *Showa Tenno Dokuhakuroku,* p. 143, where he says all three senior officers present urged him to continue the war. Both these sources are based on postwar evidence, and in this case I believe *Daihon'ei Rikugun-Bu (10)* is more accurate because Hata's subsequent behavior on August 14 fits far better with what he later reported he told the Emperor than with the Emperor's recollections.

P. 314   Imperial Conference: *Daihon'ei Rikugun-Bu (10),* pp. 506–7; Butow, *Japan's Decision to Surrender,* p. 207.

P. 315   Emperor's statement: No transcript exists; the text follows the reconstruction in Butow, *Japan's Decision to Surrender,* pp. 207–8.

P. 315   Cabinet meeting and transmission of notification: *Daihon'ei Rikugun-Bu (10),* p. 508; Butow, *Japan's Decision to Surrender,* pp. 208–9.

P. 316   Anami's conversation with Umezu: Statement of Sumihisa Ikeda, 16 Jun 50, Doc. No. 54479, p. 6, CMH. Ikeda reported he heard this direct from Umezu immediately after the conversation. Given Ikeda's long and close relationship with Umezu, the possibility that Ikeda fabricated this account to shed favorable light on Umezu has to be considered (see IMTFE Ikeda 36,942). But in view of Ikeda's severely critical description of Umezu's behavior in the decisive meetings ("Umezu was not a man of firm conviction"), it appears that Ikeda's report is trustworthy (Statement, p. 5). The exact sequence of Anami's conversations with Umezu, Hayashi, and Takeshita is not clear, but is most probably the order in the text.

P. 316   Anami's conversation with Hayashi: Statement of Col. Saburo Hayashi, 23 Dec. 49, Doc. No. 61436, p. 5, CMH.

P. 316   Anami meets with Takeshita: *Daihon'ei Rikugun-Bu (10),* p. 509. Given the reported exchange between Anami and Umezu just before Anami met with Takeshita, it appears doubtful that Umezu had been receptive to a coup. It is possible, however, that Umezu's sphinxlike conduct and comments could have led others—particularly parties anxious to extract such a meaning from any ambiguous remarks—to believe he entertained such thoughts.

P. 316   Anami briefs Army Ministry officers: Ibid., p. 512; Statement of Lt. Col. Masataka Ida, 23 May 50, Doc. No. 62348, pp. 4–5, CMH. Ida proposed the entire staff of the Army Ministry and General Staff kill themselves, but only 20 percent agreed. In a parallel performance, Umezu spoke to the Army Section of Imperial Headquarters a little before Anami made his statement at the Army Ministry (*Daihon'ei Rikugun-Bu [10],* p. 511). See also Statement of Lt. Col. Shiro Hara, 18 Feb 48, Doc. No. 56065, CMH, about the atmosphere of tremendous tension within the General Staff.

P. 316   Meeting of Kawabe, Wakamatsu, and senior commanders: Statement of Lt. Gen. Torashiro Kawabe, 3 Dec 1948, Doc. No. 50224, CMH; IMTFE Wakamatsu 36,937–40. Wakamatsu reported that when Kawabe broached the subject of securing agreement of the senior leaders of the army, he said this was also the intention of Umezu.

P. 317   Roles of Umezu, Kawabe, and Waka-matsu: This point was noted by Sumihisa Ikeda, who believed this trio "played a guiding role to prevent a coup d'état." Young officers contacted Anami while both sides ignored Chief of the Military Affairs Bureau Yoshizumi, who normally would have been expected to play a key role. On the other hand, of the critical senior officers in the Army, Ikeda suspected that Yoshizumi "vaguely hinted at" a coup d'état with comments such as "Please try to change the premier's decision, because acceptance of the Potsdam Declaration will invite serious action by the military circles." Statement of Sumihisa Ikeda, 16 Jun 50, Doc. No. 54479, p. 6, CMH. Lieutenant Colonel Ida believed that once Anami rejected a coup, there was no chance of success, but this assessment neglects the evidence that Anami wavered. Statement of Lt. Col. Masataka Ida, 23 May 50, Doc. No. 62348, p. 5, CMH.

P. 317   Plans of coup plotters: Statement of Lt. Col. Takeshita, 28 Feb 50, Doc. No. 56367, pp. 1–2, CMH, indicates that the conspirators did not think the Japanese race would be wiped out and foresaw that even in defeat in a decisive battle in the Homeland, Japanese forces would take to the mountains and continue the struggle. *Daihon'ei Rikugun-Bu (10)*, p. 497, is to the same effect using the same source.

P. 318   "Acting in compliance with the wishes": See Butow, *Japan's Decision to Surrender,* p. 210. Essentially, this represents a distillation of sentiments attributed to a Dr. Hiraizumi that were disseminated widely within military ranks through his lectures at the Military Academy and Army General Staff College and articulated in Statements of Col. Saburo Hayashi, 23 Dec 49, Doc. No. 61436, pp. 9–10, and Lt. Col. Takeshita, 11 Jun 49, Doc. No. 50025-A, p. 3, and 28 Feb 50, Doc. No. 56367, p. 1, both CMH. *Daihon'ei Rikugun-Bu (10)*, p. 498, points out that by no means all of Hiraizumi's disciples enlisted in the coup.

P. 318   Meeting of conspirators with Anami on August 12: Statements of Lt. Col. Takeshita, 11 Jun 49, Doc. No. 50025-A, p. 6, and 28 Feb 50, Doc. No. 56367, pp. 2–3, CMH; Statement of Lt. Col. Masao Inaba, 13 Oct 49, Doc. No. 57692, p. 4, CMH. After the June Diet meeting, there had been maneuvers by some to form an Anami cabinet and rumors floated about. But Anami's military secretary insisted that Anami was angered by this "very much" and warned Army Ministry of-

ficers against such schemes. Statement of Col. Saburo Hayashi, 23 Dec 49, Doc. No. 61436, p. 4, CMH.

P. 318   Meeting of conspirators with Anami on August 13: Statements of Col. Saburo Hayashi, 23 Dec 49, Doc. No. 61436, pp. 7–8, CMH; Statement of Lt. Col. Masao Inaba, 13 Oct 49, Doc. No. 57692, pp. 3–5, CMH; Statement of Lt. Col. Takeshita, 28 Feb 50, Doc. No. 56367, pp. 4–5, all CMH.

P. 318   Hayashi counsels Anami; Anami sees Arao: Statement of Col. Saburo Hayashi, 23 Dec 49, Doc. No. 61436, pp. 7–8, CMH. Hayashi specifically cited the fact that only 60 percent of war workers were reporting to factories.

P. 318   Drafting of forged order: *Daihon'ei Rikugun-Bu (10)*, p. 523; *Showa tenno dokuhakuroku*, pp. 143–44.

P. 319   General Tanaka restores order: Statements of Maj. Kiyoshi Tsukamoto, 6 Oct 50, Doc. No. 63041; Col. Hiroshi Fuwa, 1 Sep 50, Doc. No. 62238, pp. 1–2; Yoshihiro Tokugawa, 31 Oct 50, Doc. No. 63366, pp. 3–4, all CMH; *Daihon'ei Rikugun-Bu (10)*, pp. 524–25.

P. 319   Meeting of Hatanaka and Takeshita: Statement of Lt. Col. Takeshita, 28 Feb 50, Doc. No. 56367, CMH.

P. 319   Encounter between Takeshita and Anami: Statement of Lt. Col. Takeshita, 11 Jun 49, Doc. No. 50025A, p. 5, CMH.

P. 319   Death of Anami: Ibid.; Statement of Col. Saburo Hayashi, 23 Dec 49, Doc. No. 61436, pp. 6–7, 9–11, CMH. These sources differ over how Anami signed his wills. According to Hayashi, the statement referring to the "great crime" was prepared in Anami's capacity as Army Minister and was intended to encompass the coup attempt. It was also triggered by the deeply wounding remarks Prince Mikasa delivered to Anami on the day of the Imperial family conference. Hayashi believed the second statement was signed "Korechika," thus signifying that it was personal (p. 6), but Takeshita indicated it was signed "Army General Anami, Korechika."

P. 319   Anami's statement: This point was made originally in Butow, *Japan's Decision to Surrender,* pp. 219–20, but the Emperor's account raises further implications.

P. 320   Emperor's edict: Ibid., p. 248; Anami's editorial input: *Daihon'ei Rikugun-Bu (10)*, pp. 514–15.

P. 320   Radio commentary: *Daihon'ei Rikugun-Bu (10)*, p. 527.

P. 321 "Like others in the room": Hachiya, *Hiroshima Diary*, pp. 81–82.

P. 321 Imperial Army airmen curbed: Statement of Lt. Gen. Masao Yoshizumi, 6 Jun 49, Doc. No. 61338, p. 6, CMH; see also Butow, *Japan's Decision to Surrender*, pp. 222–23; Craig, *Fall of Japan*, p. 233.

P. 321 Incident at Atsugi: Craig, *Fall of Japan*, pp. 230–33, 255–56; Butow, *Japan's Decision to Surrender*, pp. 223–24.

P. 322 Battle in Mutanchiang on August 14–15: Glantz, *Soviet Tactical and Operational Combat*, pp. 96–102.

P. 322 Soviet offensive: Glantz, *Soviet 1945 Strategic Offensive*, pp. 149–62. The Soviets captured 17,061 Japanese at Sunwu and 4,520 at Aihun, the sites of determined resistance.

P. 322 Fighting around Hailar, Arshaan, and en route to Pokotu: Glantz, *Soviet Tactical and Operational Combat*, pp. 152–59, 176; Glantz, *Soviet 1945 Strategic Offensive*, pp. 102, 104, 110, 181.

P. 322 Advance of Trans-Baikal Front: Glantz, *Soviet 1945 Strategic Offensive*, pp. 82–83, 98–99, 103, 106–8.

P. 322 Kwantung Army orders cease-fire: *Record of Operations Against Soviet Russia, Eastern Front*, Japanese Monograph no. 154, Military History Section, Headquarters, U.S. Army Forces Far East, p. 22. The Kwantung Army had ordered units to cease active offensive operations on August 17.

P. 322 Hutou Fortified Region finally falls: Glantz, *Soviet Tactical and Operational Combat*, pp. 109–11, 113–14, 126–30.

P. 322 Stalin's ambitions: Glantz, "Soviet Invasion of Japan"; Glantz, *Soviet 1945 Strategic Offensive*, pp. 35, 136–37.

P. 322 The Soviet advance into Korea: Glantz, *Soviet 1945 Strategic Offensive*, pp. 143–46; J. Rohwer and G. Hummelchen, *Chronology of the War at Sea, 1939–1945*, rev. ed. (Annapolis: Naval Institute Press, 1992), p. 362.

P. 323 Soviet attacks on Sakhalin and Kurils: Glantz, "Soviet Invasion of Japan"; Rohwer and Hummelchen, *Chronology of the War at Sea*, pp. 362–63.

P. 323 Soviet plans to invade Hokkaido: Glantz, "Soviet Invasion of Japan," pp. 96–97.

P. 323 Truman and Stalin on Soviet forces in northern Hokkaido: President to Stalin No. 332, 15 Aug 45; Stalin to President 16 Aug 45; President to Stalin 18 Aug 45; Stalin to President 22 Aug 45, all in Naval Aide Files, Communications File, Box 9, Folder: Communications Stalin to Truman 1945, HSTL.

P. 324 Ishii and Japanese biological warfare: Sheldon H. Harris, *Factories of Death* (London: Routledge, 1994), pp. xvii, 18–21, 33, 66–67, 167. One of the major themes of Harris's work is that the Japanese biological-warfare program was on a much larger scale than earlier journalistic accounts reported, and that likewise the death toll was far higher. An example of a journalistic account is Peter Williams and David Wallace, *Unit 731* (New York: Free Press, 1989).

P. 324 Ping Fan: Harris, *Factories of Death*, pp. 21, 34–39.

P. 324 "The exquisite sarcastic 'humor' ": Ibid., p. 39.

P. 325 Experiments and disposition of *muratas*: Ibid., pp. 63–65, 69–71, 93–94. Experimentation went on at locations other than Ping Fan.

P. 325 Death toll at Ping Fan: Ibid., pp. 49–51. Harris explains that Ishii numbered his prisoners from 1 to 1,500 and then started over again. This makes it impossible to establish exactly how many human beings passed through Ping Fan. Harris regards the commonly given figure of 3,000 as far too low.

P. 325 Ultimate toll from biological warfare: Ibid., pp. 66–67, 72.

P. 325 Japanese losses in Manchuria: Glantz, *Soviet 1945 Strategic Offensive*, p. 229.

P. 325 Soviet casualties: Glantz and House, *When Titans Clashed*, Table B. In material, the Soviets lost only 78 tanks or self-propelled guns, 232 artillery pieces, and 62 aircraft.

P. 326 Deaths of Japanese nationals in Soviet hands: William F. Nimmo, *Behind a Curtain of Silence: Japanese in Soviet Custody, 1945–1956* (New York: Greenwood Press, 1998), chap. 7, esp. pp. 115–17. This is the only detailed study of which I am aware that covers this topic. Nimmo's figures are somewhat lower than two other sources. According to Dower, *War Without Mercy*, pp. 298–99 and nn., the postwar Japanese government calculated that 1.3 million Japanese nationals, both military and civilian, fell into Soviet hands. Of these, less than one million were repatriated to Japan after the war (877,015 by October 1948 and another 95,000 by November 1949). In the more recent *Embracing Defeat*, p. 50, Dower provides the figures for deaths in Manchuria in the first winter after the surrender. All total, the Japanese believed that no less than 374,041 Japanese, including approximately

60,000 civilians, were never accounted for after passing into Soviet control. Havens, *Valley of Darkness,* p. 172, provides somewhat different figures. He lists the missing and presumed dead in Soviet captivity as follows: 237,000 in Siberia, 79,000 in Karafuto and the Kurils, and 60,000 in Manchuria, making a grand total of 376,000. Havens is in close accord with *Record of Operations Against Soviet Russia,* Japanese Monograph no. 155, Appendix 4, Chart 2, Military History Section, Headquarters, U.S. Army Forces Far East. This monograph, however, cautions that its totals are based upon "incomplete data and unverified sources." There is no doubt that calculating the missing was difficult due to the circumstances of war, flight, and surrender. While the precise figure will probably never be known, it is clear that the number was huge.

P. 326 "Soviet commanders in Manchuria took great risks": Glantz, *Soviet 1945 Strategic Offensive,* p. 163.

P. 326 "A certain casualness": Ibid., pp. 164–66.

P. 326 Japanese resistance in specific Manchurian battles: Ibid., pp. 110–11.

P. 327 "The plans of the Southern Army": SRH-090, pp. 20–21.

P. 327 "Imperial Army and Navy shall": Ibid., p. 22.

P. 327 "Purpose of maintaining discipline": Ibid.

P. 327 "Firm determination to prosecute": Ibid., pp. 20–21.

P. 327 Truman's oscillating spirits: Truman displayed his optimism at the August 10 meeting when he remarked that he thought it would take about three days to complete "negotiations." Forrestal Diary, August 10, 1945. Comments as reported by Balfour: Bernstein, "Eclipsed by Hiroshima and Nagasaki," p. 167.

P. 327 Cease-fire orders: The Navy Ministry issued orders to cease fire, as well as a no-scuttle order, in a series of messages at 160230 and 161651 August (SRMD-007, 16, 17 August). The Imperial Army cease-fire order was issued at 160016 August (SRH-203, 17/18 Aug, No. 126).

P. 328 Request for advanced notification: SRH-090, pp. 16–19.

P. 328 Navy Minister explains role of Emperor in surrender: Ibid., pp. 22–23.

P. 328 "Since the outbreak of the conflict": Ibid., p. 24.

P. 328 "All papers relating to prisoners": Ibid., p. 34.

P. 328 "Such a disgrace": Ibid., pp. 24–25. General Kawabe indicated after the war that he had anticipated that the China Expeditionary Army would resist the surrender most strongly since it had a sense of mastery in China. Imperial Headquarters received with very great relief the message indicating Okamura would accept the surrender. Statement of Lt. Gen. Torashiro Kawabe, 23 Jun 48, Doc. No. 50226, p. 1, CMH.

P. 329 Army commanders protest surrender: SRMD-007, 18 August.

P. 329 Destruction of documents and code; reconnaissance continues: SRH-203, 17/18 Aug, No. 126.

P. 329 "A few minor exceptions": SRMD-007, 18 August.

P. 329 "Certain of Japan's leaders fail to grasp": SRH-090, p. 26.

P. 329 "To face all hardships": Ibid., pp. 26–27.

P. 329 August 15 cabinet decision: Ibid., pp. 27–28.

P. 329 Kase's warning: Ibid., p. 26.

P. 330 September 2 surrender: Butow, *Japan's Decision to Surrender,* p. 233.

P. 330 "It is incumbent": CINCPAC ADVANCE HQ to ALPAC, 150842 Aug 45, CINCPAC Command Summary, p. 3352.

P. 330 Truman preserves message: President's Secretary's Files, Subject Files, Japan, Box 182.

20. Assessing Realities

P. 331 Surrender treated as unconditional: One of the issues in the postwar debate has been whether or not Japan's surrender was, in fact, unconditional. In part, this echoes the question of whether "unconditional surrender" meant "no terms" (i.e., a blank check for the victors) or "no bargaining." Pearlman, *Unconditional Surrender,* pp. 3–5. The approach of the Potsdam Declaration was "no bargaining," with an implicit promise that the Imperial institution could be retained if that was the will of the Japanese people. Of course, the practical test of the Potsdam Declaration was in its application. John Dower has pointed out that U.S. occupation authorities "crisply informed" Japanese officials "that their capitulation was and always had been unconditional." *Embracing Defeat,* pp. 81–84. Moreover, by initially keeping deliberately vague the future status of both the Imperial institution and Emperor Hirohito personally, they were able to more effectively pressure the Japanese elites into actively cooperating with basic initial reform edicts.

P. 331 American leaders delivered from quandaries: Pearlman, *Unconditional Surrender,* p. 3. Looking back on this period, General Marshall later admitted that "political and economic institutions melted out from under us."

P. 331 American public support of atomic bombs: Bernstein, "The Struggle over History," p. 132.

P. 331 Attitudes of American servicemen: A classic statement of the veteran's position is provided in the self-explanatory title of Paul Fussell, *Thank God for the Atomic Bomb and Other Essays* (New York: Summit Books, 1988), pp. 19, 23, 27.

P. 331 "Patriotic orthodoxy": Michael S. Sherry, "Patriotic Orthodoxy and American Decline," in Linenthal and Engelhardt, *History Wars.*

P. 332 Postwar critical literature: This summary is drawn from Walker, "Decision to Use the Bomb," and Bernstein, "The Struggle over History."

P. 332 Shifting public opinions: Bernstein, "The Struggle over History," p. 202.

P. 332 Eisenhower and the atomic bomb: Barton J. Bernstein, "Ike and Hiroshima: Did He Oppose It?" *Journal of Strategic Studies* 10 (spring 1987): 377–89.

P. 333 Reduction of trade to blockade running: Johnson and Katcher, *Mines Against Japan,* pp. 129–31. This source also notes that one postwar study proclaimed: "As a result of the mining blockade of Japan, the end of effective military and civilian production became inevitable and the lack of food imports made starvation of a large part of the population a certainty."

P. 333 "The use of this barbarous weapon": William D. Leahy, *I Was There: The Personal Story of the Chief of Staff to Presidents Roosevelt and Truman, Based on His Notes and Diaries Made at the Time* (New York: Whittlesey House, 1950), p. 441.

P. 334 Destruction of housing stock: USSBS, *Effects of Strategic Bombing on Japanese Morale,* pp. 193–95, and *Japanese Wartime Standard of Living and Utilization of Manpower,* pp. 36, 41. Less than 0.5 percent of these totals were replaced. Refugees: D. Clayton James, *The Years of MacArthur: Triumph and Disaster, 1945–64* (Boston: Houghton Mifflin, 1985), p. 5. I follow James for refugees because his sources are firmer

than those used by the USSBS, which gives much lower numbers.

P. 334 USSBS figures: The figures of 333,000 dead and 472,000 wounded are in USSBS, no. 12, Medical Division, *The Effects of Bombing on Health and Medical Services in Japan,* pp. 5–6, 143, and USSBS, no. 1, Office of the Chairman, *Summary Report Pacific War,* p. 20. A figure of 268,157 dead is in USSBS, no. 11, Civil Defense Division, *Final Report Covering Air-Raid Protection and Allied Subjects in Japan,* p. 197.

The USSBS series also contains a much larger number in *Effects of Strategic Bombing on Japanese Morale,* pp. 193–95. The USSBS investigators were scathing about the accuracy of Japanese statistical teams, one of which, using a sampling technique, came up with a projection of 900,000 dead, and this huge number is now cited occasionally. The team admitted that the sample had an "unknown" error rate. The figure strains credulity, as it would indicate the Japanese were unable to count more than about a third of all fatalities. Further, such huge numbers would have required the bombing campaign against Japan to be vastly more efficient than that in Europe. The fact is that the disruption brought on by the attacks, self-evacuation by millions of civilians, and the postwar food situation (which discouraged people from returning to urban areas) made it impossible to secure a precise count. Although the 1949 figures might have been somewhat low, they are not off by an order of two or three.

P. 334 1949 Japanese figures: *Hiroshima and Nagasaki: The Physical, Medical, and Social Effects,* p. 367.

P. 334 Death count: All the totals are from *Hondo Boku Sakusen,* Table 63.

P. 334 Death estimate of 410,000: This number starts with the 330,000 figure used by the USSBS, to which the difference between my own estimate of up to 200,000 fatalities due to the atomic bombings and the 120,000 cited by the USSBS is added.

P. 335 "Standing in the ashes": Letter to President Truman, October 4, 1945, from Karl T. Compton, Papers of Harry S. Truman, President's Secretary's File, Box 182, Folder: PSF Subject File, HSTL. Compton added: "Incidentally, Bishop Spellman expressed considerable interest in these facts in connection with their bearing on the military justification for bombing the city." A Japanese reporter also explicitly acknowledged the damage inflicted on this system by incendiary attacks. Kato, *Lost War,* pp. 8–9.

P. 335 Critique of feeder system: Sherry, *Rise of American Air Power,* pp. 285–87. Sherry does not cite any specific contemporary intelligence showing the decline in the feeder system; rather, he cites indications of the loss of raw materials for factories and the dispersal of Japanese industries as implicating such a development.

P. 335   Lack of intelligence: Kreis, *Piercing the Fog*, pp. 51–52, 364–71. This account describes how Japanese secrecy long before the war severely limited the information available to American officials charged with planning an air assault on Japan. To a large extent, the planning of the air campaign against Japan was guided by European experience.

P. 335   "Much of LeMay's bombing": Sherry, *Rise of American Air Power*, p. 286.

P. 335   LeMay's decision to institute incendiary campaign: See Ibid., pp. 282–84. I concur with Kenneth P. Werrell that had LeMay not switched to urban-area fire attacks at about the time he did, he would likely have been replaced by Lauris Norstad, who was actively pushing for such attacks. Werrell, *Blankets of Fire*, p. 151.

P. 336   Race as factor in bombing: Sherry, *The Rise of American Air Power*, p. 284.

P. 336   Evolution of strategic bombing: Werrell argues that while the European strategic-bombing program "paved the way" for the Pacific effort, the two actually developed concurrently more than sequentially. Werrell, *Blankets of Fire*, p. 31. I disagree. The critical decisions in Europe to move to far less discriminate air attacks all occurred before the first mission of the Twentieth Air Force.

P. 336   FDR's failure to intervene: The principal works here are Schaffer, *Wings of Judgment;* Sherry, *Rise of American Air Power;* and Crane, *Bombs, Cities, and Civilians*. Schaffer argues that in signing the charter of what became the USSBS, which encompassed study of the physical and psychological effects of bombing on civilians, Roosevelt was signaling that "attacks aimed at terrorizing enemy civilians were acceptable" (p. 89). He goes on to credit the attitude of "the country's top civilian and military leaders," including explicitly Roosevelt, as the "most important factor moving the AAF toward Douhetian war [i.e., terror bombing]" (p. 106). Crane agrees that Roosevelt was not adverse to the terror bombing of enemy civilians, although he notes that the degree of control Roosevelt and Stimson exercised "over commanders in the field should not be overstated" (pp. 6, 31–33). Sherry also underscores the loose control of field commanders by Washington but maintains that, apart from a "forceful interest" in bombing Japanese cities from China, Roosevelt was "rarely involved in

the conduct of strategic air war, preferring to concentrate on prodding the mobilization of resources for it" (pp. 218–19).

P. 337   Stimson's concern: He expressed concern over the attack on Dresden (Stimson Diary, March 5, 1945), and he wrote to Truman on May 16 that he was holding the Air Force

> so far as possible, to the "precision" bombing which has done so well in Europe. I am told that it is possible and adequate. The reputation of the United States for fair play and humanitarianism is the world's biggest asset for peace in the coming decades. I believe the same rule of sparing the civilian population should be applied as far as possible to the use of any new weapons. [Stimson Diary, May 16, 1945]

He revisited the question again in June with Arnold. It is instructive that Stimson identified newspaper descriptions of late May raids on Tokyo, not operational reports, as the trigger of his concern. Arnold assured him that the AAF was trying to limit its attacks but that the feeder system of home workshops justified the tactics. The Secretary of War passed these assurances along to Truman and pressed no further (Stimson Diary, June 1, 6, 1945). Stimson's flickering interest is explained in large measure by his failing health, which rendered him incapable of full-time work, and his preoccupation with the atomic bomb, foreign-policy issues, and maintaining the Army's morale for the invasion.

P. 337   Roosevelt depicts Axis populations as led astray: Butow, *Japan's Decision to Surrender*, pp. 136–37. As Roosevelt phrased it in a February 1943 speech, "We mean no harm to the common people of the Axis nations," only to their leaders.

P. 337   Roosevelt sees Germans as "Prussianized": Warren F. Kimball, *The Juggler* (Princeton: Princeton University Press, 1991), pp. 76, 199. As Kimball phrases it, this was "one of Roosevelt's curious and most intensely held sociological assumptions," and it mandated a complete revamping of German society. As evidence for this, Kimball points out that after Tehran, Roosevelt stated, "We intend to rid [the German people] once and for all of Nazism and Prussian militarism and the fantastic and disastrous notion that they constitute the 'master race.' " In private, FDR even talked of literally emasculating Germans if they continued to breed an aggressive population.

The connection between unconditional surrender and the manner in which strategic bombing was conducted during World War II is important but seldom directly confronted. A. E. Campbell argued that Roosevelt saw no role for terror in the policy of unconditional surrender. Campbell further maintains that military leaders shaped the evolution of Anglo-American strategic bombing and that "it hardly occurred to anyone, and apparently not to Roosevelt, that [bombing] did not obviously suggest future leniency or an ability to distinguish between Germans and Nazis." A. E. Campbell, "Franklin Roosevelt and Unconditional Surrender," in Richard Langhorne, ed., *Diplomacy and Intelligence During the Second World War* (Cambridge: Cambridge University Press, 1985), pp. 219–315, at p. 236. I believe to the contrary that when one looks at how Roosevelt viewed the German people, his (admittedly few) explicit comments coupled with his generally permissive attitude toward the bombing campaign show that he saw the connection. The lack of intervention by Roosevelt must be viewed in the context of his willingness to guide war policy at other junctures. On FDR's willingness and ability to influence strategy and policy when he saw fit, see Kimball, *Juggler,* pp. 15–17.

P. 337   "It is of the utmost importance": Schaffer, *Wings of Judgment,* pp. 88–89. The quoted passage comes from an exchange between Roosevelt and Stimson in August 1944 on postwar policy in an occupied Germany; as Schaffer points out, its implications for bombing policy are obvious.

P. 338   Postwar casualty claims: Stimson, "Decision to Use the Atomic Bomb"; Truman: Letter, Truman to Cate, January 12, 1953, in Craven and Cate, *The Pacific,* between pp. 712 and 713; Truman, *Memoirs,* p. 1: 417; Alfred Steinberg, *The Man from Missouri* (New York: Putnam, 1962), p. 259. Churchill in his memoirs spoke of costs in an invasion of "a million American lives and half that number of British." Winston S. Churchill, *The Second World War,* vol. 6, *Triumph and Tragedy* (Boston: Houghton Mifflin, 1953), pp. 638–39. I leave the task of explaining where Churchill derived such numbers to British historians.

P. 338   Truman's figures: The correspondence and memorandums by Truman and his staff appear in the file "Atomic Bomb," Box 112, President's Secretary's File, HSTL. Much of this material has been collected and published in Robert H. Ferrell, ed., *Harry S. Truman and The Bomb: A Documentary History* (Worland, Wyo.: High Plains Publishing, 1996), pp. 97–107. One of Truman's defenders argues that the original draft also could be read as merely incomplete. Giangreco, "Casualty Projections for the U.S. Invasions of Japan," pp. 573–74.

P. 338   Truman's statements prior to 1953: Alperovitz, *Decision to Use the Atomic Bomb,* pp. 515–17.

P. 338   Attacks on casualty estimates: Examples, though by no means equal in weight, are Miles, "Hiroshima," and Bernstein, "A Postwar Myth," pp. 38–40. Bernstein, unlike Miles, uses his usual broad array of archival sources and does not connect it to any theory of "atomic diplomacy." See also Sherwin, *A World Destroyed,* Appendixes U–W, for the original array of documents concerning the June 18, 1945, meeting.

P. 339   April 1945 JCS paper: JCS 924/15, 25 April 1945; CCS 381 Pacific Ocean Operations (6-10-43), Sec. 11, RG 218, Box 686, NARA.

P. 339   Preparations for huge casualty totals: Palmer, Wiley, and Keast, *Procurement and Training of Ground Combat Troops,* pp. 219, 228–39; Giangreco, "Casualty Projections for the U.S. Invasions of Japan," pp. 565–66.

P. 340   Stimson's study: Palmer, Wiley, and Keast, *Procurement and Training of Ground Combat Troops,* pp. 234–37.

P. 340   Shockley's numbers: Shockley to Bowles, Subject: Proposals for Increasing the Scope of Casualty Studies, 21 July 1945, Edward L. Bowles Papers, Box 34, Folder 2, Library of Congress. This paper was discovered by Robert Newman (see *Truman and the Hiroshima Cult,* pp. 18–19). Shockley's larger purpose was to initiate a broad historical study "to determine to what extent the behavior of a nation in a war can be predicted from the behavior of her troops in individual battles." The figures quoted in the text were Shockley's projection on the assumption that the Japanese nation would fight on as fanatically as did her soldiers. Shockley's memorandum also confirmed the lack of correlation of information even within the War Department among the Surgeon General's Office, Army Ground Forces, G-1, and G-2 to project U.S. losses based on ratios of U.S. to Japanese casualties.

P. 341   Exchanges of Hull, Eaker, and Arnold: Gen. Arnold to Gen. Eaker 14 September 1945; Gen. Hull to Gen. Eaker 13 September 1945; Gen. Eaker to Gen. Hull 14 September 1945, OPD 704 (POT), Sect. 1, RG 165, Entry 418, Box 1687, NARA.

P. 341   Willoughby projection: Charles A. Willoughby, "Occupation of Japan and Japanese Reaction," *Military Review* (June 1946): 3–4. Of course, if Willoughby had possessed an exact accounting of the Japanese order of battle on Kyushu and before Tokyo, plus an appreciation for their reinforcement plans, his totals would have been significantly higher. For example, by the end of the war, the Twelfth Area Army (Eastern District Army), which defended Tokyo, fielded twenty divisions and twelve brigades—roughly the equivalent of twenty-four divisions; *War in Asia and the Pacific*, vol. 12, *Defense of the Homeland and End of the War* (New York: Garland Publishing, 1980), Appendix 7, pp. 239–46. Although some of the brigades might not have been able to participate in defense of the capital, this estimate excludes the divisions certain to have been transferred from other regions. It is interesting to note that MacArthur's original plan estimated that only fourteen divisions would defend Tokyo. DOWNFALL, Strategic Plans for Operations in the Japanese Archipelago, author's copy.

P. 342   Ennis memorandum: Memorandum for Chief, Strategic Policy Section, S & P Group, OPD, Subject: Use of Atomic Bomb on Japan, 30 April 1946; RG 165, Entry 421, ABC Decimal File, ABC 471.6 Atom (17 August 45), Sec. 7. The limited discussion of Japanese defensive preparation states correctly that by August 14, 1945, the Japanese had moved the maximum troop strength to Kyushu but claims erroneously that the Japanese planned no further reinforcement; plans existed to move four to five divisions to Kyushu. It does not mention that the total number of Japanese servicemen on Kyushu was 900,000 and depicts widespread shortages and lack of training to confront Olympic, whereas in reality these problems were confined to the most recently raised units of the Fortieth Army and one brigade in the Fifty-seventh Army. As to political developments, it departs from the conclusion that the Emperor decided to "terminate the war" on June 20, and as a result of this Premier Suzuki "decided to stop the war." This is flat wrong as to Suzuki's stance and neglects to examine what "terminate the war" meant in way of actual conditions. Ennis places Soviet intervention as the decisive event prompting surrender, claiming that "there was little mention of the use of the atomic bomb . . . in the discussions leading up to the 9 August decision." The reality is exactly the opposite.

P. 342   "Score of bloody Iwo Jimas and Okinawas": Stimson Diary, August 10, 1945. The total at Okinawa was 12,520 dead or missing and 36,613 wounded (Appleman, Burns, Gugeler, and Stevens, *Okinawa*, p. 473). So far, direct proof that Stimson saw the Shockley paper has not emerged, and it is possible to read Stimson's comments on August 10 as hyperbole. Stimson's postwar account, however, states that he "was informed" about huge casualty estimates. For a long time, critics challenged this on the basis that

they could locate *no* contemporary documentation that such numbers were vetted by any official within the War Department or Navy Department before Hiroshima. Since the Shockley memorandum (as well as JCS 924/15) provides such huge estimates, and since Stimson used large numbers on August 10, 1945, it is no longer possible, in my view, to argue that Stimson could only have invented these numbers after the fact. Further, Stimson ordered the study of the draft and replacement-training program that resulted in the Learned-Smith Report, which endorsed draft calls at over a million and a capacity to train over 720,000 infantry replacements per year. The supporting documentation for this, which presumably included projections for casualties, cannot now be located. Finally, anyone reading Stimson's diary or his submissions to Truman can see that he did not use language loosely, nor does the record show he was given to wild exaggeration. Thus, it is not easy to dismiss his comments on August 10 as mere hyperbole or his figures in 1947 as baseless.

P. 343   Total American battle casualties: The grand total was 1,080,465. *Army Battle Casualties and Nonbattle Deaths,* p. 5; *History of the Medical Department of the United States Navy,* pp. 3:84, 170. The overall ratio for all services is 3.7 wounded to each man killed, but this number is skewed by the fact that the Navy sustained a much lower ratio (nearly 1 to 1) than the other services.

P. 343   Lack of statements from Japanese principals: Proving a negative is, of course, impossible. The conclusion in the text is derived from a comprehensive review of the voluminous evidence provided by the Japanese and the conspicuous absence of any citation to such statements by critics. This question is separate from that of the relative importance of several events that combined to induce surrender, discussed further below.

P. 343   "When Hirohito and the peace faction": Drea, *In Service of the Emperor,* p. 205.

P. 344   Togo's acknowledgment that Japan sought mediation: Statement by Former Foreign Minister Shigenori Togo, 17 May 1949, pp. 24–27, CMH. Specifically, Togo advised Sato that Japan could surrender unconditionally without the Soviets but did not intend to do so. He added, "No one in Tokyo at that time agreed to unconditional surrender" (p. 27). This statement can be read as including the Emperor.

P. 344   Togo's message of July 21: Magic Diplomatic Summary, 22 July; SRH-086, p. 2. It is possible to read Togo's response as expressing not his personal views but his assessment of the acceptability of such terms to the other members of the Supreme Council for the Direction of the War. I suspect this is not so, but the significance of the message is the same in either case.

P. 345 Kido as Emperor's alter ego: In a revealing exchange with postwar American interviewers, Prince Konoe discussed how the advocates of peace would attempt to mobilize the Emperor as the counterweight to the army:

> The first thing was to work through or win over the Lord Keeper of the Privy Seal. If they could do that, that was all they would need. . . . Their only hope was appealing to the Emperor and the only way to the Emperor was through the Lord Keeper of the Privy Seal.

USSBS, Interrogation of Konoe, p. 17, M-1654, reel 5, RG 243, NARA. Butow describes Kido's role as the "eyes and ears of the Throne" and added: "If the Emperor asked the Privy Seal a question, it was Kido's job to supply the answer." *Japan's Decision to Surrender*, pp. 12–13.

P. 345 Internal situation as factor: Bix, "Japan's Delayed Surrender," pp. 211, 213–14, 217–18, n. 63. Though Butow concluded that Japanese public opinion had virtually no impact on Japanese decision makers (*Japan's Decision to Surrender*, p. 39), it has since become apparent that public opinion, or more precisely the fear of revolutionary civil disorder, was in fact a key consideration in the Emperor's decision to end the war and in Japanese citizens' compliance with that decision. The evidence of this begins with the Konoe Memorial to the Throne in February 1945, warning that an internal revolution posed more peril than military defeat. The danger of a fracture of public morale is then referenced in early June in both the paper titled "The Present State of National Power" for the June 8 Imperial Conference and in Kido's "Draft Plan for Controlling the Crisis Situation." Togo hinted of such fear of internal disorder in his July 11 message to Ambassador Sato (Magic Diplomatic Summary, No. 1204, 12 July 45). On August 9, Imperial General Headquarters received a report of the shattering effects of air raids on public morale in medium and smaller cities, with near panic in some locales. During that afternoon, even Anami conceded spreading defeatism, and at the Imperial Conference Hiranuma warned expressly that "continuation of the war will create greater domestic disturbances than would termination of the war," and this proposition was endorsed explicitly by Suzuki. The Emperor cited domestic considerations as a factor in his decision in the early hours of August 10, and Kawabe confessed in his diary that day that, once Japan's peace offer became known, it would not be possible to again rally public morale. Loss of public confidence was cited by Umezu to the General Staff on August 10 as a reason for surrender, and by Colonel Hayashi to Anami on August 13. Umezu again cited loss of public morale to Anami when the Army Minister toyed with the idea of continuing the war on August 14. The single clearest statement, however, was by Navy Minister Yonai on August 12 when he told his aide, Admiral Takagi, that his "anxiety over the domestic situation" was what really impelled him to end the war.

P. 345 Emperor's explanation: At the crucial meeting of the royal family on the afternoon of August 10, the Emperor identified his general loss of faith in the military as the basis for his decision. Meeting of royal family: *Daihon'ei Rikugun-Bu (10)*, pp. 472, 483.

P. 345 Meeting of Emperor and senior officers: Ibid., pp. 504–5.

P. 345 Imperial Conference, Suzuki's opening, and comments of Anami, Umezu, and Toyoda: *Daihon'ei Rikugun-Bu (10)*, pp. 506–7; Butow, *Japan's Decision to Surrender*, p. 207.

P. 346 Emperor describes reasons for his decision: Dower, *Embracing Defeat*, p. 290; *Showa Tenno Dokuhakuroku*, pp. 134–40.

P. 346 Defeat of Kwantung Army and Japanese surrender: Robert A. Pape, "Why Japan Surrendered," *International Security* 18.2 (fall 1993): 154–201, esp. pp. 178–79, argues it was decisive. Pape prepared his article without benefit of the Japanese source material used here and particularly without access to *Showa Tenno Dokuhakuroku*. Pape errs in describing the Kwantung Army as "Japan's premier fighting force"; he is unaware that Imperial Headquarters had written off Manchuria and stripped the Kwantung Army of both trained units and vital equipment. He also does not find significant Premier Suzuki's view that the atomic bomb undermined the fundamental premise that no amount of blockade or bombardment would force Japan to surrender. He also follows Butow in denying that civilian morale had any role in the surrender. As to the impact on the Emperor of Soviet intervention, Tsuneo Matsudaira, the Minister of the Imperial Household, remarked: "The Soviet Russian entry into the war had little influence on His Majesty's determination to bring about peace. It only served to strengthen his determination a little" (Statement of Matsudaira, 18 Jul 50, Doc. No. 60745, p. 5, CMH).

P. 347 Toyoda quotes: Toyoda Statement, 29 Aug 49, Doc. No. 61340, pp. 7–8, 12.

P. 347 "The Supreme War Council": Statement of Baron Suzuki, 26 Dec 45, Interrogation No. 531, p. 308, CMH. Less often quoted sections of the statements of Kawabe and Toyoda show they, too, agreed that the atomic bombs were important in securing compliance. Kawabe acknowledged that "the atomic bomb and the Russian declaration of war were shocks in quick succession, I cannot give a definite answer as to which of the two factors was more decisive in ending hostilities." Statement of Kawabe, 26 Nov 48, Doc. No. 52608, pp. 5–6, CMH. Even as Toyoda was assigning primacy to Soviet intervention, he acknowledged in the same statement that the atomic bomb's "very great effect upon public sentiment is indisputable. Various things are attributable to the relative calm that prevailed at the time of surrender. The fact that the atom bombing is among them cannot be contested." Statement of Toyoda, 29 Aug 49, Doc. No. 61340, p. 7, CMH.

P. 347 "If military leaders could convince themselves": Asada, "The Shock of the Atomic Bomb and Japan's Decision to Surrender: A Reconsideration," p. 507, citing *Diary of Marquis Kido*, p. 443.

P. 348 "In ending the war": Ibid. Another significant contemporary record of the relative impact of these two events comes from a senior official, Misao Oki, chief secretary of the House of Representatives, who wrote in his diary at the time, "Soviet entry into the war was of course anticipated." But, he added, "There is nothing we can do about the appearance of the atomic bomb. That nullifies everything. All our efforts until now have come to naught" (Ibid.)

21. Alternatives and Conclusions

P. 350 Distribution of Japan's population: *Hondo Boku Sakusen,* Table 62.

P. 350 Distribution of Japan's food sources: Army Service Forces Manual M 354-7, *Civil Affairs Handbook Japan,* Section 7; *Agriculture,* 1 April 1944, pp. 45–48, 70–72, 84, Folder MHDC, No. 698 (Folder 2), Papers of George L. McColm, HSTL. The handbook cites liberally from Japanese data supplied up to 1939. The handbook notes on p. 1 that the total land area of Japan is 147,416 square miles, almost exactly equal to Montana.

P. 350 Food deficit areas: *Civil Affairs Handbook Japan,* pp. 81–84; *Hondo Boku Sakusen,* Table 62. I did not locate comparable 1939 census figures, but overall population shifts during the war were generally toward the urbanized areas in south and west Honshu, thus increasing the concentration of the population in food-deficit areas until the bombing reversed this flow.

P. 350 Japanese wartime food production: "History of the Nonmilitary Activities of the Occupation of Japan," pp. 12:1–2. The proximate causes of the declining domestic production were the induction of farmworkers, the shift of rural population to urban centers, the allocation of farm animals to military work, and the diversion of chemicals from fertilizer to munitions, coupled with the actual destruction by air attack of eleven of sixteen chemical plants. Havens, *Valley of Darkness,* p. 115; USSBS, *Effects of Strategic Bombing on Japan's Economy,* p. 53; USSBS, *Japanese Wartime Standard of Living and Utilization of Manpower,* pp. 10–12; *Hondo Boku Sakusen,* pp. 582–83.

P. 350 Food deficit for 1945: Supreme Commander for the Allied Powers, Summation of Non-Military Activities in Japan and Korea, No. 2, November 1945, pp. 43–45; RG 5, Box 97, Folder 2, MacArthur Archive. Slightly higher figures for the 1945 and earlier harvests are found in USSBS, *Japanese Wartime Standard of Living and Utilization of Manpower,* p. 3, which reported that in 1945 the rice crop was "a disastrous failure," with a harvest of only 6.6 million metric tons, compared with 11.1 million in 1942 and 10.4 million in 1943.

P. 350 Decline of seafood catch: "History of the Nonmilitary Activities of the Occupation of Japan," pp. 12:1–2; USSBS, *Japanese Wartime Standard of Living and Utilization of Manpower,* pp. 14, 16.

P. 350 Role of food imports: "History of the Nonmilitary Activities of the Occupation of Japan," pp. 12:1–2; USSBS, *Japanese Wartime Standard of Living and Utilization of Manpower,* p. 2. There is some variance in the figures on the role of imports in the food supply. The USSBS figured that about 19 percent of Japan's food supply came across her docks, not from her fields.

P. 350 Collapse of food imports: Parillo, *Japanese Merchant Marine,* pp. 218–19; USSBS, *Effects of Strategic Bombing on Japan's Economy,* p. 54; USSBS, *War Against Japanese Transportation,* pp. 88, 92, 96. For the Korean situation, see Cohen, *Japan's Economy in War and Reconstruction,* p. 478.

P. 350 Government conservation measures: "History of the Nonmilitary Activities of the Occupation of Japan," p. 12:2. Japanese food-rationing system: USSBS, *Japanese Wartime Standard of Living and Utilization of Manpower,* p. 19.

P. 350 Collapse of ration system: "History of the Nonmilitary Activities of the Occupation of Japan," pp. 12:16, 50–57; USSBS, *Japanese*

Wartime Standard of Living and Utilization of Manpower, pp. 18–19, 28–29; James, *Years of MacArthur,* p. 5.

P. 350   Individual food ration: USSBS, *Effects of Strategic Bombing on Japan's Economy,* p. 53; USSBS, *Japanese Wartime Standard of Living and Utilization of Manpower,* p. 1.

P. 351   Weight loss: USSBS, *Japanese Wartime Standard of Living and Utilization of Manpower,* pp. 101–2.

P. 351   Early estimates of food availability: "History of the Nonmilitary Activities of the Occupation of Japan," p. 12:5; Supreme Commander for the Allied Powers, Summation of Non-Military Activities in Japan and Korea, No. 2, November 1945, pp. 43–45, RG 5, Box 97, Folder 2, MacArthur Archive.

P. 351   Breakdown of food collection: Summation of Non-Military Activities in Japan and Korea, No. 3, December 1945, Chart: "Food Supply in Major Japanese Cities," RG 5, Box 97, Folder 3, MacArthur Archive; "History of the Nonmilitary Activities of the Occupation of Japan," p. 12:16; Occupation Trends Japan and Korea 9 January 1946, RG 4, Box 37, Folder 1, MacArthur Archive.

P. 351   Countermeasures against the food deficit: "History of the Nonmilitary Activities of the Occupation of Japan," pp. 12:11, 13; Supreme Commander for the Allied Powers, Summation of Non-Military Activities in Japan and Korea, No. 2, November 1945, p. 44, RG 5, Box 97, Folder 2, MacArthur Archive.

P. 351   "Immediately after the defeat": Irokawa, *Age of Hirohito,* p. 37; Cohen, *Japan's Economy in War and Reconstruction,* p. 478.

P. 352   Mid-1946 food crisis: SCAP to WAR-COS 21 May 1946 C-61198 RG 9, Box 156, Folder "War Department Messages," February to 24 May 1946, MacArthur Archive; "History of the Nonmilitary Activities of the Occupation of Japan," pp. 12:14, 17–18; James, *Years of MacArthur,* p. 156; Mikiso Hane, *Eastern Phoenix: Japan Since 1945* (Boulder: Westview Press, 1996), pp. 10–11. The message comparing the American moral obligation with that of Japanese officers with American prisoners of war is in Political Adviser to Japan (Atcheson) to Secretary of State, Tokyo, April 26, 1946, in *Foreign Relations of the United States, 1946,* vol. 8, *The Far East* (Washington, D.C.: Government Printing Office, 1971), pp. 216–18 (see also pp. 149–50, 178–79). Atcheson's message was identified as sanctioned by MacArthur. A message of February 26, 1946, shows that the army estimated that by sometime in April, indigenous

food supplies for the nonfarm population would be largely exhausted.

P. 352   "It is quite clear": Cohen, *Japan's Economy in War and Reconstruction,* p. 478.

P. 352   "It was evident": "History of the Nonmilitary Activities of the Occupation of Japan," p. 12:14.

P. 352   Japan's reliance on merchant marine: USSBS, *War Against Japanese Transportation,* pp. 97–98. This report shows the aggregate merchant tonnage of vessels of over 400 tons was 1,818,071, but only 650,000 tons were within the Inner Zone (north of Shanghai). Moreover, about 13 percent of the tonnage was tankers, which were virtually useless for hauling other cargoes. An intercepted Japanese diplomatic message on September 9, 1945, indicated that the Japanese government calculated that it then possessed only 440,000 tons of seaworthy vessels. SRH-092, p. 18.

P. 352   Destruction of merchant marine: The table in chap. 10, p. 151, illustrates that Japanese shipping losses totaled 369,314 tons in June and 371,925 in July, the last two full months of the war. These figures do not include ships made unserviceable due to damage. Some of this loss was outside the Inner Zone, but raw losses do not reflect the effects of delays and disruption produced by mines and fears of air attack. Senior Japanese officers foresaw that the blockade would extinguish systematic communication within the Home Islands. Statement of Lt. Col. Michinori Ureshino, 20 Nov 48, Doc. No. 53013, CMH (he projected that by autumn there would be no sea transportation whatsoever); Statement of Captain Atsushi Oi, 15 Oct 49, Doc. No. 61341, CMH. Oi reported that the Combined Escort Force anticipated that small, powered sailing vessels would be Japan's only remaining shipping. Their shallow draft and diminutive size immunized them against the firing devices fitted to the American mines, but such light craft possessed very limited carrying capacity and were hopelessly vulnerable to strafing aircraft and thus could survive only in darkness. How such an armada could be hidden and protected by day he did not say.

P. 352   Japanese rail system: USSBS, *War Against Japanese Transportation,* pp. 1, 17–18, 27–28.

P. 352   Vulnerability of rail system: Ibid., pp. 1, 27.

P. 353   Inadequacy of roads: Ibid., p. 29; USSBS, *Effects of Strategic Bombing on Japan's Economy,* pp. 64–65. Of an approximate 300,000 kilometers of roads, only about 9,000 met the classification of major national highways, but even these were mostly unsurfaced. Such improved roads as existed adorned only the major industrial centers of Honshu and the northern rim of Kyushu. In 1940, the entire country possessed only 37,000 operational trucks. In 1945, the Imperial Army had only 8,900 trucks on the Home Islands, far too few to substitute for freight cars.

P. 353 "In view of the disrupted condition": Summation of Non-Military Activities in Japan and Korea, No. 2, November 1945, p. 89, RG 5, Box 97, Folder 2, MacArthur Archive.

P. 353 Vulnerability of rail system to air attack: USSBS, *War Against Japanese Transportation,* p. 10; Hansell, *Strategic Air War Against Japan,* p. 90. The USSBS calculated that just 650 B-29 sorties with 5,200 tons of general-purpose bombs or 1,740 carrier-plane sorties with 1,300 tons of bombs could have made the requisite railline cuts. A comparable or greater effort each month would have maintained the interdiction. In another detailed postwar analysis, General Hansell, a master planner whose forte was this type of calculation, indicated that 933 B-29 sorties in the initial month (no more than two days of full operations in August 1945) and another 3,732 sorties over the next four months would paralyze the Japanese rail system. This was easily within the capabilities of the B-29s in the Marianas alone. The USSBS also believed the Japanese rail system could have been destroyed with a mere hundred sorties with 800 tons of Azon bombs (which were partly steerable), which could have sealed off the Kanmon tunnel and erased vulnerable sections of line, while carrier planes dealt with the Hokkaido ferries. The Azon bomb–equipped B-29 units, however, were not due to deploy until after August.

P. 353 "There is very good reason": USSBS, *Effects of Strategic Bombing on Japan's Economy,* p. 64. On the Japanese side, Lieutenant Colonel Iwakeshi, a supply officer on the Imperial General Staff, testified that the bombing of factories rather than railroads surprised the General Staff, and that an attack on the railroads would have compelled an earlier surrender (n. 7).

P. 353 Reports on food situation: See Dip. No. 1086, 16 Mar 45, SRS-1608; Dip. No. 1102, 1 Apr 45, SRS-1624; Dip. No. 1115, 14 Apr 45, SRS-1637; Dip. No. 1121, 20 Apr 45, SRS-1643; Dip. No. 1137, 6 May 45, SRS-1659; Dip. No. 1152, 21 May 45, SRS-1674; Dip. No. 1162, 31 May 45, SRS-1684; Dip. No. 1191, 29 Jun 45, SRS-1713.

P. 353 Ambiguous intelligence on food situation: Johnson and Katcher, *Mines Against Japan,* p. 126; 18 Jun 45, SRS-455; 23 July 45, SRS-

490, pp. 3–4; SRMD-008, p. 183, 20 July p. 8. The CINCPAC summary leaned toward the view that the Japanese were stockpiling food to carry on a protracted struggle. SRMD-008, pp. 192–93, 27 Jul pp. 2–3.

P. 354 Faulty assessment of food situation: June 30 Enemy Situation Estimate: War Department, General Staff, Military Intelligence Service, G-2, Estimate of Enemy Situation 30 June 1945, COMINCH Strategic Plans Division, Box 176, NHC.

P. 354 Report on Japan's railroads: SRS-507, 8 Aug 45. See also Magic Far East Summary, 14 June 1945, p. A-9, SRS-451, which notes, "Full evidence is not available on either Japan's current food requirements and imports or her domestic foods stocks." This was by no means the first indication of the vulnerability of the Japanese rail system. As early as May 1945, a Magic Diplomatic Summary presented a message sent by German Military Attaché Kretschmer in Tokyo to Berlin underscoring the weakness of the Japanese railway system. He noted its "high vulnerability" to air attack due to its "countless bridges and tunnels." A note appended to the report commented that the line from Tokyo to Shimonoseki, known as the Tokaido-Sanyo line, passed over "about 150 bridges and through some 30 tunnels." Moreover, Kretschmer pointed out that the main lines "are not even approximately replaceable by less efficient secondary line." Dip. No. 1162, 31 May 45, SRS-1684.

P. 354 Consequences of rail bombing: USSBS, *Japanese Wartime Standard of Living and Utilization of Manpower,* p. 108. Unless Japan capitulated almost immediately after the rail-bombing campaign commenced, which is unlikely, the physical destruction of the rail lines and the lack of other transportation resources would have created a challenging situation for occupation authorities, even highly skilled and well-equipped American engineers. Meanwhile, the dislocation and migration of tens of millions of Japanese would have posed tremendous difficulties in feeding them.

P. 354 Fear of internal revolt: This is discussed above. See particularly Bix, "Japan's Delayed Surrender," pp. 211–14, 217–18 (including n. 63).

P. 355 "Based on a detailed investigation": USSBS, *Japan's Struggle to End the War,* p. 13.

P. 355 Statements of senior officers: There are many examples, cited extensively in virtually all the works critiquing the use of the atomic weapons. A comprehensive catalog of such after-the-event statements by naval, air, and military leaders is provided in Alperovitz, *Decision to Use the Atomic Bomb,* chaps. 26–29. This section commingles the question of modification of unconditional surrender, a topic on which there is contemporary record of military advice to the president favoring such action, and the question of whether any military leader actually advised the president before Hiroshima that the use of atomic weapons was unnecessary. On the latter point, there is not a scintilla of contemporary evidence. Admiral Leahy's outspoken condemnations of the use of atomic weapons because of their indiscriminate nature are quoted often, but to date no evidence whatsoever has emerged that Leahy spoke so to Truman prior to Hiroshima. As to the cost of alternative strategies, King's postwar memoir asserts his position that the naval blockade would have "starved the Japanese into submission through lack of oil, rice, medicines, and other essential materials." Ernest J. King and Walter Muir Whitehall, *Fleet Admiral King: A Naval Record* (New York: Norton, 1952), p. 621. Alperovitz (p. 327), among others, cites this but does not address what "starved" really means in noncombatant deaths.

P. 355   Invalidity of USSBS opinion: Newman, *Truman and the Cult of Hiroshima,* pp. 39–48, 51.

P. 356   Navy critique of atomic weapons: This is highlighted in Jeffrey G. Barlow, *Revolt of the Admirals: The Fight for Naval Aviation, 1945–50* (Washington, D.C.: Naval Historical Center, 1994), pp. 106, 110, 247–48, 261, and 360 n. 66.

P. 356   Deaths of Japanese nationals in Soviet hands: Nimmo, *Behind a Curtain of Silence,* chap. 7, esp. pp. 115–17; Dower, *War without Mercy,* pp. 298–99; Havens, *Valley of Darkness,* p. 172.

P. 357   Plan for attack on northern Honshu: Joint War Plans Committee, Plan for the Invasion of Northern Honshu, JWPC 398/1, 9 August 1945, Entry Geographic File 1942–45, CCS 381 Honshu (7-19-44), Box 90, RG 218. The attack on northern Honshu also suffered from the major deficiency that the 1,350 aircraft projected to be based in this area could only expect to attack the Kanto area visually at high level 15 percent of the time and visually at low level 25 to 30 percent of the time.

P. 357   Weather: Samuel Eliot Morison, *History of United States Naval Operations in World War II,* vol. 15, *Supplement and General Index* (Boston: Little, Brown, 1962), pp. 14–17; Memorandum for Chief, Strategic Policy Group, S&P Group, OPD, from R. F. Ennis, Subject: Use of Atomic Bomb on Japan, 30 April 1946, ABC Decimal File 1942–48, ABC 471.6 Atom (17 August 45), Sec. 7, RG 165, Entry 421, NARA. The Ennis memorandum concluded that the typhoon would not have had a major disruptive impact on air support or ground forces (which were being mounted from the Philippines) but would have disrupted the "slow tow" shipping of freighters, gasoline barges, and others that were slated for assembly at Okinawa. Vice Admiral Theodore Wilkinson monitored the storm carefully from his flagship in Tokyo Bay and with remarkable skill steered the echelons of amphibious vessels steaming toward Japan with occupation forces out of the path of the typhoon; whether assault convoys for a major invasion could have likewise been steered away is less clear.

P. 358   MacArthur's staff study for Coronet: General Headquarters, United States Army Forces, Pacific, Staff Study "CORONET" Operations in the Kanto Plain of Honshu, 15 Aug 45, RG 4, Box 39, Folder 2, MacArthur Archive. This staff study allowed for ultimate Japanese opposition of twenty-two infantry and two armored divisions.

P. 358   Contemporary JIC estimate: Joint War Plans Committee, JWPC 397 4 August 1945 (with attached copy of "Defensive Preparations in Japan," JIC), RG 218, NARA.

P. 358   Operation Zipper: For general discussions of Operation Zipper, see John Ehrman, *Grand Strategy,* vol. 6, *October 1944 to August 1945* (London: His Majesty's Stationery Office, 1956), pp. 248–49; H. P. Willmott, *Graveyard of a Dozen Schemes* (Annapolis: Naval Institute Press, 1996), Appendix D. For a specific argument that the atomic bombs avoided a bloodbath in Operation Zipper, see Stephen Harper, *Miracle of Deliverance: The Case for the Bombing of Hiroshima* (New York: Stein and Day, 1985).

Bibliographic Note

The end of the Pacific war is a vast topic, encompassing military and political issues in multiple nations. Magnifying the challenges presented by the sheer expanse of the area are language and secrecy barriers. No one individual can expect to examine all the primary sources that bear upon this subject. Moreover, many historians have contributed important work on critical issues from this period or on topics that are vital to place the events of 1945 in context. Thus, any historian approaching this area must make choices on where to focus primary-research efforts and where to rely upon others for background or context.

This work was conceived around the basic premise that the military realities and the perception of those realities by both sides are the keys to understanding how and why the war ended as it did. Research aimed at setting down those realities uncovered a story with many new and quite unanticipated dimensions. These revelations, in turn, redirected the focus of the primary research as well as the handling of material on background and context.

The primary source material that forms the foundation of this work came from the U.S. National Archives and Records Administration, the Naval Historical Center (Washington, D.C., Navy Yard), the Air Force Historical Research Agency (Maxwell Air Force Base), the Center for Air Force History (Bolling Air Force Base), the United States Army Military History Institute (Carlisle, Pennsylvania), the Center of Military History (Washington, D.C.), and the Library of Congress (Washington, D.C.). At the National Archives, Record Groups 38, 165, 218, and 457 yielded by far the most valuable documents. The massive holdings in RG 457 on both diplomatic and military radio intelligence forced reexamination of the strategic premises and the operational plans to end the war and the startling changes in American calculations in the summer of 1945. Army records in Groups 165 and 218 possess the inestimable virtues of good organization and relative completeness.

Records bearing upon the U.S. Navy are more problematic. Based on research for my previous book, I was cognizant of the importance of the Commander in Chief Pacific Fleet, Command Summary, at the Naval Historical Center. For 1942, the hundreds of pages of this source integrate radio intelligence with a daily narrative discussion of decisions and orders in a manner rarely found in World War II records. By 1945, however, the command summary extends to thousands of pages. Moreover, the jumbled organization and contents indicate that the number of individuals with access must have expanded significantly, and the commentary on key high-level thinking is much less extensive and candid. Even the invaluable attachments to the summary of the most important incoming and outgoing daily messages are arranged in a fashion that implies certain material was held in strict confidence for Fleet Admiral Chester W. Nimitz and a few of his staff officers. This section, not surprisingly, proved to have vital disclosures. Overall, however, there is no comparison between how the U.S. Army and the U.S. Navy organized and preserved their key records. The Navy's neglect has made the actual views of its leaders difficult to ferret out and also has assured that the Army's far more easily obtained viewpoint has enjoyed a major advantage in the historical literature.

The Air Force centers provided enough material for an operational and command history of the Twentieth Air Force, but most of this ultimately was not used due to the changed emphasis of this work. This research, however, yielded vital material describing Air Force plans and capabilities had the war continued. Broadly speaking, Air Force records are more accessible than those of the Navy, but they are not so well organized as those of the Army.

Beyond these primary centers, special mention must be made of the Center for Military History, the George C. Marshall Library, and the MacArthur Memorial Archive. These facilities are wonderfully staffed and enormously helpful. While much of their holdings are duplicated elsewhere, they are indexed and organized in ways that permit highly efficient research. The MacArthur Memorial Archive contained readily accessible material on the occupation period that was important to integrate with the new strategic-bombing directive of August 11, 1945.

My work at the Truman Library fortuitously came after the discoveries at the other centers pointed to areas of research that had not figured in my original concept. Although the Truman Library provided sources on many topics, of particular interest was the story of how Magic and Ultra messages were passed to Truman at the Potsdam Conference.

By deliberate choice, significant primary research was not attempted on two topics. There is a huge literature on the development and use of the atomic bombs. The great bulk of this scholarship takes the advent of nuclear weapons as the central focus for this period. Because this work aims to place Hiroshima and Nagasaki in context, it follows that secondary sources suffice for the scope and depth of coverage mounted here. Furthermore, I do not believe the superb work of David Glantz on the military aspects of Soviet intervention can be improved upon, and therefore no effort was made to conduct independent research.

Overall, the lack of coverage of the Japanese viewpoint in both depth and accuracy is the most consistent and grievous deficiency in English-language treatments of the end of the Pacific war. Anyone attempting to cover Japanese developments with Japanese source material, however, must be wary of the fact that a massive quantity of primary documents was destroyed to forestall announced Allied plans to conduct war-crimes trials. While certainly important material survived, every student must bear in mind that irretrievable damage to the historical record may have been perpetrated in 1945. This damage to the trove of written records was exacerbated by the fact that the key Japanese actors were themselves either individual targets or potential targets of war-crimes trials and thus wary and self-serving in the statements they provided soon after the war, when their memories of events were fresh. Many of these actors were likewise animated by a desire to preserve the Imperial institution. Finally, no really concerted effort was mounted by occupation authorities or by the International Military Tribunal for the Far East to set straight Emperor Hirohito's role.

During the occupation, a series of monographs and statements from Japanese officials were prepared that still remain useful. Also still valuable are the voluminous products of the United States Strategic Bombing Survey. For a far more coherent and accurate account of the Japanese military perspective, however, I turned to the official Japanese military history of the war, *Boeicho Boei Kenshujo Senshi Shitsu* (War History Office, Defense Agency) *Senshi Shosho* (War History Series). This huge enterprise generated over one hundred dense volumes on all aspects of the Pacific war. Translations from four volumes of the series prepared for my use form the bedrock of this narrative. The volume on policy making at Imperial General Headquarters proved to branch out into the political realm at considerable length. Translation of the statement prepared by Emperor Hirohito in March and April 1946 was also invaluable on Japanese political developments but demanded critical examination. This new information was combined with an array of secondary sources. Outstanding among these secondary sources are the works of Sadao Asada, John Dower, and Edward Drea, as well as those of Herbert Bix, with some reservations as to his interpretations. In a special category is the classic work of Robert Butow, *Japan's Decision to Surrender,* published in 1954 but still invaluable as a guide to sources and as an exemplar of scholarly analysis and supple prose. This narrative also profits enormously from the comprehensive use of what is now perhaps the most unquestionably authentic source material on Japanese political developments at the end of the Pacific war: declassified American radio-intelligence documents.

The following is a selected list of works cited:

Books and Monographs

Adams, Henry H., *Witness to Power,* Annapolis: Naval Institute Press, 1985.

Adams, Raymond D., M.D., and Maurice Victor, M.D., *Principles of Neurology,* 2d ed., New York: McGraw-Hill, 1981.

Alexander, Joseph H., *Utmost Savagery,* Annapolis: Naval Institute Press, 1995.

Alperovitz, Gar, *The Decision to Use the Atomic Bomb and the Architecture of an American Myth,* New York: Alfred A. Knopf, 1995.

Appleman, Roy E., James M. Burns, Russell A. Gugeler, and John Stevens, *Okinawa: The Last Battle,* Washington, D.C.: Government Printing Office, 1948.

Army Battle Casualties and Nonbattle Deaths in World War II, Final Report, 7 December 1941–31 December 1946, Washington, D.C.: Statistical and Accounting Branch, Office of the Adjutant General.

Army Service Forces Manual M 354-7, *Civil Affairs Handbook Japan,* April 1, 1944.

Baily, Charles M., *Faint Praise: American Tanks and Tank Destroyers During World War II,* Hamden, Conn.: Archon Books, 1983.

Barlow, Jeffrey G., *Revolt of the Admirals: The Fight for Naval Aviation, 1945–50,* Washington, D.C.: Naval Historical Center, 1994.

Bird, Kai, and Lawrence Lifschultz, *Hiroshima's Shadow,* Stony Creek, Conn.: Pamphleteer's Press, 1998.

Birdsall, Steve, *Flying Buccaneers,* Garden City, N.Y.: Doubleday, 1977.

Blair, Clay, *Silent Victory: The U.S. Submarine War Against Japan,* Philadelphia: J. B. Lippincott, 1975.

Boeicho Boei Kenshujo Senshi Shitsu (War History Office, Defense Agency) Senshi Shosho (War History Series), No. 19, Hondo Boku Sakusen (Home Air Defense Operations) (Tokyo).

———. No. 57, Hondo Kessen Junbi (2) Kyushu No Boei (Preparations for the Decisive Battle on the Homeland) (2) Defense of the Kyushu Area (Tokyo).

———. No. 82, Daihon'ei Rikugun-Bu (10) (Army Division, the Imperial General Head-quarters, vol. 10) (Tokyo, 1975).

Boyd, Carl, Hitler's Japanese Confidant, General Oshima Hiroshi and MAGIC Intelligence, 1941–45, Lawrence: University Press of Kansas, 1993.

Brown, David, Warship Losses of World War Two, London: Arms and Armor Press, 1990.

Butow, Robert J. C., Japan's Decision to Surrender, Stanford: Stanford University Press, 1954.

Caidin, Martin, A Torch to the Enemy, New York: Bantam Books, 1960.

Cannon, M. Hamlin, Leyte: The Return to the Philippines, Washington, D.C.: Government Printing Office, 1954.

Cantril, Hadley, ed., Public Opinion 1935–1946, Princeton: Princeton University Press, 1951.

Carter, Kit C., and Robert Mueller, compilers, U.S. Army Air Forces in World War II, Combat Chronology 1941–45, Washington, D.C.: Center for Air Force History, 1991.

Chamberlain, Peter, and Terry Gander, World War 2 Fact Files, Anti-Tank Weapons, New York: Arco, 1974.

Chappell, John D., Before the Bomb: How America Approached the End of the Pacific War, Lexington: University Press of Kentucky, 1996.

Churchill, Winston S., The Second World War, vol. 3, The Grand Alliance, London, 1950.

———. The Second World War, vol. 6, Triumph and Tragedy, Boston: Houghton Mifflin, 1953.

Coakley, Robert W., and Richard M. Leighton, Global Logistics and Strategy, 1943–1945, Washington, D.C.: Center of Military History, 1986.

Coffey, Thomas M., Iron Eagle, New York: Crown Publishers, 1986.

Cohen, Bernard M., and Maurice Z. Cooper, A Follow-up Study of World War II Prisoners of War, Washington, D.C.: Department of Medicine and Surgery, Veterans Administration, 1954.

Cohen, Jerome B., Japan's Economy in War and Reconstruction, Minneapolis: University of Minnesota Press, 1949.

Committee for the Compilation of Materials on Damage Caused by the Atomic Bombs in Hiroshima and Nagasaki, Hiroshima and Nagasaki: The Physical, Medical, and Social Effects of the Atomic Bombings, trans. Eisei Ishikawa and David L. Swain, New York: Basic Books, 1981.

Condon-Rall, Mary Ellen, and Albert E. Cowdrey, Medical Services in the War Against Japan, Washington, D.C.: Government Printing Office, 1998.

Conn, Stetson, Rose C. Engelman, and Byron Fairchild, Guarding the United States and Its Outposts, Washington, D.C.: Center of Military History, 1989.

Connaughton, Richard, John Pimlott, and Duncan Anderson, The Battle for Manila, Novato, Calif.: Presidio Press, 1995.

Cook, Haruko Taya, and Theodore Cook, Japan at War: An Oral History, New York: New Press, 1992.

Coox, Alvin, Japan: The Final Agony, Ballantine's Illustrated History of World War II, Campaign Book no. 9, New York: Ballantine Books, 1970.

Corum, James S., *The Luftwaffe: Creating the Operational Air War, 1918–1940,* Lawrence: University Press of Kansas, 1997.

Craig, William, *The Fall of Japan,* New York: Dial Press, 1967.

Crane, Conrad C., *Bombs, Cities, and Civilians,* Lawrence: University Press of Kansas, 1993.

Craven, W. F., and J. L. Cate, eds., *The Army Air Forces in World War II,* vol. 5, *The Pacific: Matterhorn to Nagasaki, June 1944 to August 1945,* Washington, D.C.: Office of Air Force History, 1953.

Crowl, Philip A., *The Campaign in the Marianas,* Washington, D.C.: Office of the Chief of Military History, 1960.

Crowl, Philip A., and Edmund G. Love, *Seizure of the Gilberts and Marshalls,* Washington, D.C.: Office of the Chief of Military History, 1955.

Dallek, Robert, *Franklin Roosevelt and American Foreign Policy, 1932–1945,* Oxford: Oxford University Press, 1979.

Davis, Richard G., *Carl A. Spaatz and the Air War in Europe,* Washington, D.C.: Center for Air Force History, 1993.

Daws, Gavan, *Prisoners of the Japanese,* New York: William Morrow and Co., 1994.

Depuy, T. N., and Paul Martell, *Great Battles on the Eastern Front,* Indianapolis: Bobbs-Merrill, 1982.

Diary of Marquis Kido, 1931–45: Selected Translations into English, Frederick, Md.: University Publications of America, 1984.

Donovan, Robert J., *Conflict and Crisis,* New York: W. W. Norton, 1977.

Dower, John, *Japan in War and Peace: Selected Essays,* New York: New Press, 1993.

Dower, John W., *Embracing Defeat: Japan in the Wake of World War II,* New York: W. W. Norton/New Press, 1999.

———. *War Without Mercy,* New York: Pantheon, 1986.

Drea, Edward J., *In Service of the Emperor: Essays on the Imperial Japanese Army,* Lincoln: University of Nebraska Press, 1998.

———. *MacArthur's Ultra: Codebreaking and the War Against Japan, 1942–1945,* Lawrence: University Press of Kansas, 1992.

Dyer, George C., *The Amphibians Came to Conquer,* Washington, D.C.: Government Printing Office, 1969.

Edoin, Hoito, *The Night Tokyo Burned,* New York: St. Martin's Press, 1987.

Effects of the Atomic Bombs at Hiroshima and Nagasaki, Report of the British Mission to Japan, London: His Majesty's Stationery Office, 1946.

Ehrman, John, *Grand Strategy,* vol. 6, *October 1944 to August 1945,* London: His Majesty's Stationery Office, 1956.

Entry of the Soviet Union into the War Against Japan, Washington, D.C.: Government Printing Office, 1955.

Erickson, John, *The Road to Stalingrad,* New York: Harper and Row, 1975.

Evans, David C., ed., *The Japanese Navy in World War II,* 2d ed., Annapolis: Naval Institute Press, 1986.

Evans, David C., and Mark R. Peattie, *Kaigun: Strategy, Tactics, and Technology in the Imperial Japanese Navy, 1887–1941,* Annapolis: Naval Institute Press, 1997.

Feifer, George, *Tennozan: The Battle of Okinawa and the Atomic Bomb,* New York: Ticknor and Fields, 1992.

Ferrell, Robert H., ed., *Dear Bess,* New York: W. W. Norton, 1983.

———. *Harry S. Truman and the Bomb: A Documentary History,* Worland, Wyo.: High Plains Publishing, 1996.

————. *Off the Record: The Private Papers of Harry S. Truman,* New York: Penguin, 1980.
Foreign Affairs Association of Japan, *The Japan Year Book 1943–44,* Tokyo: Republished
    by the Interdepartmental Committee for the Acquisition of Foreign Publications, n.d.
Foreign Relations of the United States, Diplomatic Papers: The Conference of Berlin 1945,
    vols. 1–2, Washington, D.C.: Government Printing Office, 1960.
Foreign Relations of the United States, Diplomatic Papers 1945, vol. 6, *The British Com-
    monwealth, the Far East,* Washington, D.C.: Government Printing Office, 1969.
Foreign Relations of the United States, 1946, vol. 8, *The Far East,* Washington, D.C.: Gov-
    ernment Printing Office, 1971.
Forrestal, James V., *The Forrestal Diaries,* ed. Walter Millis, New York: Viking Press, 1951.
Frank, Benis M., and Henry I. Shaw, *Victory and Occupation, History of U.S. Marine
    Corps Operations in World War II,* vol. 5, Washington, D.C.: Historical Branch, G-3
    Division, Headquarters, U.S. Marine Corps, 1968.
Frank, Richard B., *Guadalcanal: The Definitive Account of the Landmark Battle,* New
    York: Random House, 1990.
Freeman, Roger A., *The Mighty Eighth,* Garden City, N.Y.: Doubleday, 1970.
————. *Mighty Eighth War Diary,* London: Jane's, 1981.
————. *The Mighty Eighth War Manual,* London: Jane's, 1984.
Friedman, Norman, *U.S. Naval Weapons,* Annapolis: Naval Institute Press, 1985.
Fukui, Shizuo, *Japanese Naval Vessels at the End of World War II,* Annapolis: Naval Insti-
    tute Press, 1991.
Fuller, Richard, *Shokan: Hirohito's Samurai,* London: Arms and Armor Press, 1992.
Fussell, Paul, *Thank God for the Atomic Bomb and Other Essays,* New York: Summit
    Books, 1988.
Garand, George W., and Truman R. Strowbridge, *Western Pacific Operations, History of
    U.S. Marine Corps Operations in World War II,* vol. 4, Washington, D.C.: History Di-
    vision, Headquarters, U.S. Marine Corps, 1971.
Gilbert, Martin, *The First World War: A Complete History,* New York: Henry Holt, 1994.
————. *Winston S. Churchill,* vol. 6, *Finest Hour, 1939–1941,* Boston: Houghton Mifflin,
    1983.
————. *Winston S. Churchill,* vol. 7, *Road to Victory, 1941–1945,* Boston: Houghton Mif-
    flin, 1986.
————. *Winston S. Churchill,* vol. 8, *'Never Despair,' 1945–1965,* Boston: Houghton Mif-
    flin, 1988.
Gilmore, Allison B., *You Can't Fight Tanks with Bayonets: Psychological Warfare Against
    the Japanese Army in the Southwest Pacific,* Lincoln: University of Nebraska Press,
    1998.
Glantz, David M., *August Storm: The Soviet 1945 Strategic Offensive in Manchuria,* Leav-
    enworth Paper no. 7, Fort Leavenworth, Kans.: Combat Studies Institute, U.S. Army
    Command and General Staff College, 1983.
————. *August Storm: Soviet Tactical and Operational Combat in Manchuria, 1945,*
    Leavenworth Paper no. 8, Fort Leavenworth, Kans.: Combat Studies Institute, U.S.
    Army Command and General Staff College, 1983.
Glantz, David M., and Jonathan House, *When Titans Clashed,* Lawrence: University Press
    of Kansas, 1995.
Goldstein, Donald M., and Katherine V. Dillon, eds., *Fading Victory: The Diary of Admiral
    Matome Ugaki, 1941–1945,* trans. Masataka Chihaya, Pittsburgh: University of
    Pittsburgh Press, 1991.

Goldstein, Donald M., Katherine V. Dillon, and J. Michael Wenger, *Rain of Ruin: A Photographic History of Hiroshima and Nagasaki,* Washington, D.C.: Brassy's, 1995.

Green, William, and Gordon Swanborough, *Japanese Army Fighters,* pt. 2, *World War II Aircraft Fact Files,* New York: Arco Publishing, 1978.

Grew, Joseph C., *Turbulent Era: A Diplomatic Record of Forty Years,* vol. 2, Boston: Houghton Mifflin, 1952.

Groves, Leslie, *Now It Can Be Told: The Story of the Manhattan Project,* New York: Harper and Brothers, 1962.

Guillain, Robert, *I Saw Tokyo Burning: An Eyewitness Narrative from Pearl Harbor to Hiroshima,* Garden City, N.Y.: Doubleday, 1981.

Hachiya, Michihiko, M.D., *Hiroshima Diary,* Chapel Hill: University of North Carolina Press, 1955.

Hamby, Alonzo L., *Man of the People,* New York: Oxford University Press, 1995.

Hane, Mikiso, *Eastern Phoenix: Japan Since 1945,* Boulder: Westview Press, 1996.

Hansell, Haywood S., Jr., *Strategic Air War Against Japan,* Washington, D.C.: Government Printing Office, 1980.

Harper, Stephen, *Miracle of Deliverance: The Case for the Bombing of Hiroshima,* New York: Stein and Day, 1985.

Harries, Meirion, and Susie Harries, *Soldiers of the Sun: The Rise and Fall of the Imperial Japanese Army,* New York: Random House, 1991.

Harris, Sheldon H., *Factories of Death,* London: Routledge, 1994.

Hartmann, Gregory K., *Weapons That Wait: Mine Warfare in the U.S. Navy,* Annapolis: Naval Institute Press, 1979.

Hastings, Max, *Bomber Command,* New York: Dial Press/James Wade, 1979.

Havens, Thomas R., *Valley of Darkness: The Japanese People in World War Two,* Lanham, Md.: University Press of America, 1986.

Hayes, Grace Pearson, *The History of the Joint Chiefs of Staff in World War II: The War Against Japan,* Annapolis: Naval Institute Press, 1982.

Hershberg, James, *James B. Conant: Harvard to Hiroshima and the Making of the Nuclear Age,* New York: Alfred A. Knopf, 1993.

Hewlett, Richard, and Oscar E. Anderson, *A History of the United States Atomic Energy Commission,* vol. 1, *The New World, 1939–1946,* University Park, Pa.: Pennsylvania State University Press, 1962.

Hinsley, F. H., E. E. Thomas, C. A. G. Simkins, and C. F. G. Ransom, *British Intelligence in the Second World War,* vol. 3, pt. 2, New York: Cambridge University Press, 1988.

History of the Medical Department of the United States Navy in World War II; The Statistics of Diseases and Injuries, Division of Medical Statistics, Bureau of Medicine and Surgery, Navy Department, Navmed P-1318, vol. 3, Washington, D.C.: Government Printing Office, 1950.

Holloway, David, *Stalin and the Bomb,* New Haven: Yale University Press, 1994.

Hsiung, James C., and Steven I. Levine, eds., *China's Bitter Victory,* New York: M. E. Sharpe, 1992.

Huber, Thomas M., *Japan's Battle of Okinawa, April–June 1945,* Leavenworth Paper no. 18, Fort Leavenworth, Kans.: Combat Studies Institute, U.S. Army Command and General Staff College, 1990.

Huffman, Carl W., *Saipan,* Washington, D.C.: Historical Division, Headquarters, U.S. Marine Corps, 1950.

Hunnicutt, R. P., *Pershing: A History of the Medium Tank T20 Series,* Berkeley, Calif.: Feist
     Publications, 1971.
———. *Sherman: A History of the American Medium Tank,* Belmont, Calif.: Taurus En-
     terprises, 1978.
Inoguchi, Rikihei, and Tadashi Nakajima, with Roger Pineau, *The Divine Wind: Japan's
     Kamikaze Force in World War II,* Annapolis: Naval Institute Press, 1958.
Iriye, Akira, *Power and Culture: The Japanese American War, 1941–1945,* Cambridge,
     Mass.: Harvard University Press, 1981.
Irokawa, Daikichi, *The Age of Hirohito: In Search of Modern Japan,* New York: Free Press,
     1995.
James, D. Clayton, *The Years of MacArthur: Triumph and Disaster, 1945–64,* Boston:
     Houghton Mifflin, 1985.
Japanese Suicide Craft, S-02, U.S. Naval Technical Mission to Japan, January 1946.
Johnson, Ellis A., and David A. Katcher, *Mines Against Japan,* Washington, D.C.: Govern-
     ment Printing Office, 1973.
Joint Army Navy Assessment Committee, *Japanese Naval and Merchant Shipping Losses
     During World War II by All Causes,* February 1947.
Jones, Vincent C., *Manhattan: The Army and the Atomic Bomb,* Washington, D.C.: Center
     of Military History, 1985.
Kahn, David, *The Code Breakers,* New York: Macmillan, 1967.
Kato, Masuo, *The Lost War: A Japanese Reporter's Inside Story,* New York: Alfred A.
     Knopf, 1946.
Kerr, E. Bartlett, *Flames over Tokyo: The U.S. Army Air Forces' Incendiary Campaign
     Against Japan, 1944–1945,* New York: Donald I. Fine, 1991.
———. *Surrender and Survival,* New York: William Morrow and Co., 1985.
Kimball, Warren F., *Forged in War,* New York: William Morrow and Co., 1997.
———. *The Juggler,* Princeton: Princeton University Press, 1991.
King, Ernest J., and Walter Muir Whitehall, *Fleet Admiral King: A Naval Record,* New
     York: Norton, 1952.
Kreis, John F., *Piercing the Fog,* Washington, D.C.: Government Printing Office, 1996.
Krueger, Walter, *From Down Under to Nippon: The Story of Sixth Army in World War II,*
     Washington, D.C.: Combat Forces Press, 1953.
Kunhardt, Philip B., Jr., ed., *Life: World War II,* Boston: Little, Brown, 1990.
Leahy, William D., *I Was There: The Personal Story of the Chief of Staff to Presidents Roo-
     sevelt and Truman, Based on His Notes and Diaries Made at the Time,* New York:
     Whittlesey House, 1950.
Leary, William M., ed., *We Shall Return: MacArthur's Commanders and the Defeat of
     Japan,* Lexington: University Press of Kentucky, 1988.
LeMay, Curtis E., with MacKinlay Kantor, *Mission with LeMay,* Garden City, N.Y.: Dou-
     bleday, 1965.
MacIsaac, David, *Strategic Bombing in World War Two: The Story of the United States
     Strategic Bombing Survey,* New York: Garland Publishing, 1976.
Maddox, Robert James, *Weapons for Victory: The Hiroshima Decision Fifty Years Later,*
     Columbia: University of Missouri Press, 1995.
Masters, John, *The Road Past Mandalay,* New York: Harper and Brothers, 1961.
McCullough, David, *Truman,* New York: Simon and Schuster, 1992.
McFarland, Stephan L., *America's Pursuit of Precision Bombing, 1910–1945,* Washington,
     D.C.: Smithsonian Institution Press, 1995.

Middlebrook, Martin, *The Battle of Hamburg: Allied Forces Against a German City,* New York: Charles Scribner's Sons, 1980.

Middlebrook, Martin, and Chris Everitt, *The Bomber Command War Diaries,* New York: Penguin Books, 1990.

Mierzejewski, Alfred C., *The Collapse of the German War Economy, 1944–45: Allied Air Power and the German National Railway,* Chapel Hill: University of North Carolina Press, 1988.

Mikesh, Robert C., *Aichi M6A1 Seiran, Japan's Submarine Launched Panama Canal Bomber,* Monogram Close Up no. 13, Boylston: Monogram Aviation Publications, 1975.

Miller, Edward S., *War Plan Orange,* Annapolis: Naval Institute Press, 1991.

Miller, John D., *The United States Army in World War II, Organization and Role of the Army Service Forces,* Washington, D.C.: Center of Military History, 1954.

Morison, Samuel Eliot, *History of United States Naval Operations in World War II:* vol. 12: *Leyte, June 1944–January 1945,* Boston: Atlantic/Little, Brown, 1958.

———. vol. 13: *The Liberation of the Philippines, Luzon, Mindanao, the Visayas, 1944–45,* Boston: Little, Brown, 1959.

———. vol. 8: *New Guinea and the Marianas, March 1944 to August 1944,* Boston: Little, Brown, 1953.

———. vol. 3: *The Rising Sun in the Pacific, 1931 to April 1942,* Boston: Atlantic/Little, Brown, 1948.

———. vol. 15: *Supplement and General Index,* Boston: Little, Brown, 1962.

———. vol. 14: *Victory in the Pacific, 1945,* Boston: Little, Brown, 1960.

Morton, Louis, *The Fall of the Philippines,* Washington, D.C.: Government Printing Office, 1953.

———. *Strategy and Command: The First Two Years,* Washington, D.C.: Government Printing Office, 1962.

Murray, Williamson, *Luftwaffe,* Baltimore: Nautical and Aviation Publishing Company of America, 1985.

Naito, Hatsuho, *Thunder Gods: The Kamikaze Pilots Tell Their Story,* Tokyo: Kodansha International, 1989.

Newman, Robert P., *Truman and the Hiroshima Cult,* East Lansing: Michigan State University Press, 1995.

Nimmo, William F., *Behind a Curtain of Silence: Japanese in Soviet Custody, 1945–1956,* New York: Greenwood Press, 1998.

Office of the Chief of Military History, Department of the Army:

Japanese Monograph no. 17: Homeland Operations Record (n.d.).

Japanese Monograph no. 25: Air Defense of the Homeland, 1952.

Japanese Monograph no. 154: Record of Operations Against Soviet Russia, Eastern Front, 1954.

Japanese Monograph no. 155: Record of Operations Against Soviet Russia, 1954.

Office of the Surgeon General, Department of the Army, *Medical Statistics in World War II,* Washington, D.C.: Government Printing Office, 1975.

Operational Experience of Fast Battleships: World War II, Korea, Vietnam, Washington, D.C.: Naval Historical Center, 1989.

Overy, Richard, *Why the Allies Won,* New York: W. W. Norton, 1995.

Overy, R. J., *The Air War, 1939–45,* New York: Stein and Day, 1980.

Pacific War Research Society, *Japan's Longest Day,* Tokyo: Kodansha International, 1968.

Palmer, Robert R., Bell I. Wiley, and William R. Keast, *The Procurement and Training of Ground Combat Troops,* Washington, D.C.: Office of the Chief of Military History, Department of the Army, 1948.

Parillo, Mark P., *The Japanese Merchant Marine in World War II,* Annapolis: Naval Institute Press, 1993.

Pearlman, Michael D., *Unconditional Surrender, Demobilization, and the Atomic Bomb,* Fort Leavenworth, Kans.: Combat Studies Institute, U.S. Army Command and General Staff College, 1996.

Pogue, Forrest C., *George C. Marshall: Interviews and Reminiscences,* Lexington: George C. Marshall Research Foundation, 1991.

————. *George C. Marshall, Organizer of Victory, 1943–1945,* New York: Viking Press, 1973.

Powers, Thomas, *Heisenberg's War,* Boston: Little, Brown, 1993.

Prange, Gordon, *At Dawn We Slept,* New York: McGraw-Hill, 1981.

Public Papers of the Presidents: Harry S. Truman, 1945, Washington, D.C.: Government Printing Office, 1961.

Reilly, John C., Jr., *United States Navy Destroyers of World War II,* Poole, Dorset: Blandford Press, 1983.

Reports of General MacArthur, Japanese Operations in the Southwest Pacific Area, vol. 2, pt. 2, Washington, D.C.: Government Printing Office, 1966.

Rhodes, Richard, *The Making of the Atomic Bomb,* New York: Simon and Schuster, 1986.

Rohwer, J., and G. Hummelchen, *Chronology of the War at Sea, 1939–1945,* rev. ed., Annapolis: Naval Institute Press, 1992.

Rust, Ken, *Eighth Air Force Story,* Temple, Calif.: Historical Aviation Album, 1978.

————. *Twentieth Air Force Story,* Temple, Calif.: Historical Aviation Album, 1979.

————. *The Ninth Air Force in World War II,* Fallbrook, Calif.: Aero Publishers, 1970.

Schaffer, Ronald, *Wings of Judgment: American Bombing in World War II,* New York: Oxford University Press, 1985.

Selective Service and Victory: The Fourth Report of the Director of Selective Service, Washington, D.C.: Government Printing Office, 1948.

Sherry, Michael S., *The Rise of American Air Power: The Creation of Armageddon,* New Haven: Yale University Press, 1987.

Sherrod, Robert, *On to Westward,* New York: Duell, Sloan, and Pearce, 1945.

Sherwin, Martin, *A World Destroyed: Hiroshima and the Origins of the Arms Race,* New York: Vintage Books, 1987.

Sigal, Leon V., *Fighting to a Finish,* Ithaca: Cornell University Press, 1988.

Skates, John Ray, *The Invasion of Japan, Alternative to the Bomb,* Columbia: University of South Carolina Press, 1994.

Sledge, E. B., *With the Old Breed at Peleliu and Okinawa,* Novato, Calif.: Presidio Press, 1981.

Smith, Bradley F., *Sharing Secrets with Stalin,* Lawrence: University Press of Kansas, 1996.

————. *The Ultra-Magic Deals,* Novato, Calif.: Presidio Press, 1992.

Smith, Robert Ross, *The Approach to the Philippines,* Washington, D.C.: Government Printing Office, 1979.

————. *Triumph in the Philippines,* Washington, D.C.: Government Printing Office, 1963.

Special History of One Hundred Million Japanese During Showa Period, History of Japanese Warfare, no. 4, *Special Attack Forces,* Tokyo *Daily News,* Sept. 1, 1979.

Stanton, Shelby, *Order of Battle U.S. Army World War II,* Novato, Calif.: Presidio Press, 1984.

Steinberg, Alfred, *The Man from Missouri,* New York: Putnam, 1962.

Stimson, Henry L., and McGeorge Bundy, *On Active Service in Peace and War,* New York: Harper and Brothers, 1947.

Surlemont, Raymond, *Japanese Armor,* Milwaukee: Z and M Enterprises, 1976.

Terasaki, Hidenari, and Mariko Terasaki Miller, eds., *Showa Tenno Dokuhakuroku— Terasaki Hidenari Goyogakari Nikki* (The Showa Emperor's Monologue and the Diary of Hidenari Terasaki), *Bungei Shunjusha,* December 1990.

Terraine, John, *A Time for Courage,* New York: Macmillan, 1985.

Tibbets, Paul W., Jr., *The Tibbets Story,* New York: Stein and Day, 1978.

Tillman, Barrett, *Hellcat: The F6F in World War II,* Annapolis: Naval Institute Press, 1979.

Toland, John, *The Rising Sun: The Decline and Fall of the Japanese Empire, 1936–1945,* New York: Random House, 1970.

Truman, Harry S., *Memoirs,* vol. 1, *Year of Decisions,* Garden City, N.Y.: Doubleday, 1955.

Tuchman, Barbara W., *Stilwell and the American Experience in China, 1911–45,* New York: Macmillan, 1970.

United States Strategic Bombing Survey, Report no. 1, Office of the Chairman, *Summary Report Pacific War* (Washington, D.C.: Government Printing Office, 1946).

———. Report no. 2, Office of the Chairman, *Japan's Struggle to End the War* (Washington, D.C.: Government Printing Office, 1946).

———. Report no. 3, Office of the Chairman, *The Effects of Atomic Bombs on Hiroshima and Nagasaki* (Washington, D.C.: Government Printing Office, 1946).

———. Report no. 4, Civil Defense Division, *Field Report Covering Air Raid Protection and Allied Subjects Tokyo, Japan* (Washington, D.C.: U.S. Government, 1947).

———. Report no. 11, Civil Defense Division, *Final Report Covering Air-Raid Protection and Allied Subjects in Japan* (Washington, D.C.: U.S. Government, 1946).

———. Report no. 12, Medical Division, *The Effects of Bombing on Health and Medical Services in Japan* (Washington, D.C.: U.S. Government, 1947).

———. Report no. 14, Morale Division, *The Effects of Strategic Bombing on Japanese Morale* (Washington, D.C.: U.S. Government, 1947).

———. Report no. 15, Aircraft Division, *The Japanese Aircraft Industry* (Washington, D.C.: U.S. Government, 1947).

———. Report no. 42, Manpower, Food, and Civilian Supplies Division, *The Japanese Wartime Standard of Living and Utilization of Manpower* (Washington, D.C.: U.S. Government, 1947).

———. Report no. 53, Overall Economic Effects Division, *The Effects of Strategic Bombing on Japan's War Economy* (Washington, D.C.: U.S. Government, 1946).

———. Report no. 54, Transportation Division, *The War Against Japanese Transportation, 1941–1945* (Washington, D.C.: U.S. Government, 1947).

———. Report no. 55, Urban Areas Division, *The Effects of Air Attack on Japanese Urban Economy* (Washington, D.C.: U.S. Government, 1947).

———. Report no. 62, Military Analysis Division, *Japanese Air Power* (Washington, D.C.: U.S. Government, 1946).

———. Report no. 64, Military Analysis Division, *The Effects of Air Action on Japanese Ground Army Logistics* (Washington, D.C.: U.S. Government, 1947).

———. Report no. 78, Naval Analysis Division, *The Offensive Mine Laying Campaign Against Japan* (Washington, D.C.: U.S. Government, 1946).

Walch, Timothy, and Dwight M. Miller, *Herbert Hoover and Harry Truman: A Documentary History,* Worland, Wyo.: High Plains Publishing, 1992.

Walzer, Michael, *Just and Unjust Wars: A Moral Argument with Historical Illustrations,* 2d ed., Basic Books, 1977.

War in Asia and the Pacific, vol. 12, *Defense of the Homeland and End of the War,* New York: Garland Publishing, 1980.

Warner, Denis, Peggy Warner, and Sadao Seno, *The Sacred Warriors,* New York: Avon Books, 1982.

Warship XI, Annapolis: Naval Institute Press, n.d.

Waterford, Van, *Prisoners of the Japanese in World War II,* Jefferson, N.C.: McFarland and Co., 1994.

Watson, Mark S., *Chief of Staff: Prewar Plans and Preparations,* Washington, D.C.: Government Printing Office, 1950.

Weale, Adrian, ed., *Eye Witness Hiroshima,* New York: Carroll and Graf, 1995.

Weigley, Russell, *Eisenhower's Lieutenants,* Bloomington: Indiana University Press, 1981.

Weinberg, Gerhard L., *A World at Arms: A Global History of World War II,* Cambridge: Cambridge University Press, 1994.

Werrell, Kenneth P., *Blankets of Fire,* Washington, D.C.: Smithsonian Institution Press, 1996.

Williams, Peter, and David Wallace, *Unit 731,* New York: Free Press, 1989.

Willmott, H. P., *Empires in Balance: Japanese and Allied Pacific Strategies to April 1942,* Annapolis: Naval Institute Press, 1982.

———. *Graveyard of a Dozen Schemes,* Annapolis: Naval Institute Press, 1996.

———. *June 1944,* Poole, Dorset: Blandford Press, 1984.

Wohlstetter, Roberta, *Pearl Harbor: Warning and Decision,* Stanford: Stanford University Press, 1962.

Y'Blood, William T., *The Little Giants: U.S. Escort Carriers Against Japan,* Annapolis: Naval Institute Press, 1987.

Zachary, G. Pascal, *Endless Frontier: Vannevar Bush, Engineer of the American Century,* New York: Free Press, 1997.

Zaloga, Steven, and Victor Madej, *The Polish Campaign 1939,* New York: Hippocrene Books, Inc., 1985.

Ziegler, Philip, ed., *Personal Diary of Admiral the Lord Louis Mountbatten, Supreme Allied Commander, South-East Asia, 1943–1946,* London: Collins, 1988.

Articles

After the Battle 42 (1983).

Asada, Sadao, "The Shock of the Atomic Bomb and Japan's Decision to Surrender: A Reconsideration," *Pacific Historical Review* 64.4 (November 1998).

Bernstein, Barton, "The Atomic Bombings Reconsidered," *Foreign Affairs* 74.1 (January–February 1995).

———. "The Perils and Politics of Surrender," *Pacific Historical Review* 46 (November 1977).

———. "A Postwar Myth: 500,000 Lives Saved," *Bulletin of Atomic Scientists* (June–July 1986).

———. "Roosevelt, Truman, and the Atomic Bomb, 1941–45: A Reinterpretation," *Political Science Quarterly* 90 (spring 1975).

———. "The Struggle over History," in Philip Nobile, ed., *Judgment at the Smithsonian,* New York: Marlowe and Co., 1995.

Bernstein, Barton J., "Eclipsed by Hiroshima and Nagasaki: Early Thinking About Tactical Nuclear Weapons," *International Security* 15.4 (spring 1991).

———. "Ike and Hiroshima: Did He Oppose It?" *The Journal of Strategic Studies* 10 (spring 1987).

Bix, Herbert, "Japan's Delayed Surrender: A Reinterpretation," *Diplomatic History* 19.2 (spring 1995).

Bix, Herbert P., "The Showa Emperor's 'Monologue' and the Problem of War Responsibility," *Journal of Japanese Studies* 18:2 (1992)

Brower, Charles F., IV, "Sophisticated Strategist: General George A. Lincoln and the Defeat of Japan, 1944–45," *Diplomatic History* 15 (summer 1991).

Bruce, Roy W., "Done Blowed the Ship to Hell," *Naval History* 9.2 (March–April 1995).

Buruma, Ian, "The War over the Bomb," *New York Review of Books* 42.14 (September 21, 1995).

Campbell, A. E., "Franklin Roosevelt and Unconditional Surrender," in Richard Langhorne, ed., *Diplomacy and Intelligence During the Second World War,* Cambridge: Cambridge University Press, 1985.

Conquest, Robert, "The Evil This Time," *New York Review of Books* 40.15 (September 23, 1993).

Cook, Haruko Taya, "The Myth of the Saipan Suicides," *Military History Quarterly* 7.3 (spring 1995).

Coox, Alvin D., "The Effectiveness of the Japanese Military Establishment in the Second World War," in Allan R. Millett and Williamson Murray, eds., *Military Effectiveness,* vol. 3, *The Second World War,* Boston: Allen and Unwin, 1988.

Daniels, Gordon, "The Great Tokyo Air Raid, 9–10 March 1945," in W. G. Beasley, ed., *Modern Japan: Aspects of History, Literature, and Society,* London, Allen & Unwin, 1975.

Davies, Norman, "The Misunderstood Victory in Europe," *New York Review of Books* 42.9 (May 25, 1995).

"The Death Railway," *After the Battle* 26 (1979).

Dower, John W., "Three Narratives of Our Humanity," in Edward T. Linenthal and Tom Engelhardt, eds. *History Wars: The Enola Gay and Other Battles for the American Past,* New York: Metropolitan Books, 1996.

Drea, Edward J., "Missing Intentions: Japanese Intelligence and the Soviet Invasion of Manchuria, 1945," *Military Affairs* (April 1984).

Freedman, Lawrence, and Saki Dockrill, "Hiroshima: A Strategy of Shock," in Saki Dockrill, ed., *From Pearl Harbor to Hiroshima,* New York: St. Martin's Press, 1994.

Gauker, Eleanor D., and Christopher G. Blood, "Friendly Fire Incidents During World War II Naval Operations," *Naval War College Review* 48.1 (winter 1995).

Giangreco, D. M., "Casualty Projections for the U.S. Invasions of Japan, 1945–46: Planning and Policy Implications," *The Journal of Military History* 61 (July 1997).

———. "Operation Downfall: The Devil Was in the Details," *Joint Forces Quarterly* 9 (autumn 1995).

Glantz, David M., "The Soviet Invasion of Japan," *Military History Quarterly* 7.3 (spring 1995).

Hall, R. Cargill, "The Truth About the Overflights," *Military History Quarterly* 9.3 (spring 1997).

Huber, Thomas M., "Pastel: Deception in the Invasion of Japan," Fort Leavenworth, Kans.: Combat Studies Institute, U.S. Army Command and General Staff College, 1988.

Martin, Harold N., "Black Snow and Leaping Tigers," *Harper's* (February 1946).

Matsumoto, LTC Keisuke, Japanese Self-defense Forces Staff College, "Preparations for Decisive Battle in Southern Kyushu in Great East Asia War," October 1987, CMH.

McKelway, St. Clair, "A Reporter with the B-29s," *The New Yorker* (June 16, 1945, and June 23, 1945).

Miles, Rufus, "Hiroshima: The Strange Myth of Half a Million Lives Saved," *International Security* (fall 1985).

Miller, Edward S., "Savvy Planning," *Military History Quarterly* 7.3 (spring 1995).

Miller, Vernon J., "An Analysis of U.S. Submarine Losses During World War II," in *Warship XI*.

Nakayama, Takashi, "Strategic Concept at the End of the War and Defense of the Home Islands," U.S.-Japan History Exchange Conference, October 25, 1987, CMH.

Pape, Robert A., "Why Japan Surrendered," *International Security* 18.2 (fall 1993).

Sherry, Michael S., "Patriotic Orthodoxy and American Decline," in Edward T. Linenthal and Tom Engelhardt, eds., *History Wars,* New York: Metropolitan Books, 1996.

Sherwin, Martin, "Hiroshima and Modern Memory," *The Nation,* October 10, 1981.

Stimson, Henry L., "The Decision to Use the Atomic Bomb," *Harper's,* February 1947.

Tillitse, Lars, "When Bombs Rained on Us in Tokyo," *Saturday Evening Post,* January 12, 1946.

Walker, J. Samuel, "The Decision to Use the Bomb: A Historiography Update," *Diplomatic History* 14 (winter 1990).

Willoughby, Charles A., "Occupation of Japan and Japanese Reaction," *Military Review* (June 1946).

Statements of Japanese Officials

During the occupation, interviews with key Japanese civilian and military figures were conducted. This work is held in various archives under the title of Statements of Japanese Officials on World War II, General Headquarters, Far East Command, Military Intelligence Section, Historical Division. Many of these individuals provided more than one statement. Some statements are very long, others are very brief. Usually, though not always, the statement has a date and a document number. Generally, where the statement is lengthy, a page citation is provided and both the date and document number have been cited. For some of the very brief statements, no page citation was warranted. The material quoted in this work was located at the Center for Military History, Washington, D.C. Statements from the following Japanese officials are used in this work: Major General Masakasu Amano, Colonel Okikatsu Arao, Lieutenant General Seizo Arisue, Colonel Hiroshi Fuwa, Lieutenant Colonel Shiro Hara, Kiyoshi Hasegawa, Shigeru Hasunuma, Saburo Hayashi, Kiichiro Hiranuma, Vice Admiral Zenshiro Hoshina, Colonel Hiromu Hosoda, Lieutenant Colonel Masataka Ida, Sumihisa Ikeda, Lieutenant Colonel Masao Inaba, Lieutenant Colonel Shinroku Iwakoshi, Major Katsunori Kai, Lieutenant General Torashiro Kawabe, Koichi Kido, Major Yasuji Komuratani, Yasumasa Matsudaira, Shunichi Matsumoto, Major General Yatsuji Nagai, Admiral Nakamura, Dr. Yoshio Nishina, Lieutenant Colonel Kyoshi Ohta, Captain Atsushi Oi, Suemasa Okamoto, Taihei Oshima, Hisatsune Sakomizu, Seizo Sakonji, Major General Joichiro Sanada, Lieutenant Colonel Katsuo Sato, Mamoru Shigemitsu, Hiroshi Shimomura, Colonel Ichiji Sugita, Admiral Baron Kantaro Suzuki, Lieutenant

Colonel Mikize Takamura, Lieutenant Mikizo Takemura, Lieutenant Colonel Mosahibko Takeshita, Rear Admiral Sadatoshi Tamioka, Lieutenant Colonel Koji Tanaka, Colonel Sako Tanemura, Major General Kazuo Tanikawa, Shigenori Togo, Major Kinjiro Tokaji, Tokugawa, Admiral Soemu Toyoda, Major Kiyoshi Tsukamoto, Lieutenant Colonel Jiro Tsukushki, Lieutenant Colonel Michinori Ureshino, Lieutenant Colonel Yoshitaka Yoshinaga, Major General Yasumasa Yoshitake, Lieutenant General Masao Yoshizumi.

Testimony at the International Military Tribunal for the Far East

Various Japanese officials provided testimony at the International Military Tribunal for the Far East. Care has to be taken with this evidence, given the circumstances under which it was provided. This source is invaluable as it contains very extensive translations of the diary of Marquis Koichi Kido. Evidence from the following Japanese officials is used in this work: Sumihisa Ikeda, Koichi Kido, Yasumasa Matsudaira, Hisatsune Sakomizu, Admiral Baron Kantaro Suzuki, Shigenori Togo, Lieutenant General Tadaichi Wakamatsu.

Index

Page numbers in *italics* refer to maps.

ABOUT THE AUTHOR

RICHARD FRANK was born in Kansas in 1947. He graduated from the University of Missouri in 1969 and was commissioned that year in the United States Army. He served four years, including a tour in the Republic of Vietnam as an aerorifle platoon leader with the 101st Airborne Division. After graduating from Georgetown University Law Center in 1976, he began working with the Board of Veterans Appeals, where he is now a member of the Board. Random House published his first book, *Guadalcanal: The Definitive Account of the Landmark Battle,* in 1990; it was a main selection of the History Book Club and an alternate selection of the Book-of-the-Month Club. He lives with his wife, Janet, and their two children in Virginia.

ABOUT THE TYPE

This book was set in Times Roman, designed by Stanley Morison specifically for *The Times* of London. The typeface was introduced in the newspaper in 1932. Times Roman has had its greatest success in the United States as a book and commercial typeface, rather than one used in newspapers.